Quantitative Modules

Pearson

At Pearson, we have a simple mission: to help people make more of their lives through learning.

We combine innovative learning technology with trusted content and educational expertise to provide engaging and effective learning experience that serve people wherever and whenever they are learning.

We enable our customers to access a wide and expanding range of market-leading content from world-renowned authors and develop their own tailor-made book. From classroom to boardroom, our curriculum materials, digital learning tools and testing programmes help to educate millions of people worldwide — more than any other private enterprise.

Every day our work helps learning flourish, and wherever learning flourishes, so do people.

To learn more, please visit us at: www.pearson.com/uk

Quantitative Modules

Selected Chapters from:

Mathematics for Economics and Business
Ninth Edition
Ian Jacques

Statistics for Economics, Accounting and Business Studies
Seventh Edition
Michael Barrow

Statistics for Business and Economics
Eighth Edition
Paul Newbold, William L. Carlson and Betty M. Thorne

 Pearson

Harlow, England • London • New York • Boston • San Francisco • Toronto • Sydney • Dubai • Singapore • Hong Kong
Tokyo • Seoul • Taipei • New Dehli • Cape Town • São Paulo • Mexico City • Madrid • Amsterdam • Munich • Paris • Milan

Pearson
KAO Two
KAO Park
Harlow
Essex CM17 9NA

And associated companies throughout the world

Visit us on the World Wide Web at:
www.pearson.com/uk

© Pearson Education Limited 2018

Compiled from:

Mathematics for Economics and Business
Ninth Edition
Ian Jacques
ISBN 978-1-292-19166-9
© Pearson Education Limited 2013, 2015, 2018 (print and electronic)

Statistics for Economics, Accounting and Business Studies
Seventh Edition
Michael Barrow
ISBN 978-1-292-11870-3
© Pearson Education Limited 2001, 2006, 2009, 2013, 2017 (print and electronic)

Statistics for Business and Economics
Eighth Edition
Paul Newbold, William L. Carlson and Betty M. Thorne
ISBN 978-0-273-76706-0
© Pearson Education Limited 2013

ISBN 978-1-78726-767-1

Printed and bound in Great Britain by Ashford Colour Press Ltd.

CONTENTS

1.1.1 Negative numbers

In mathematics numbers are classified into one of three types: positive, negative or zero. At school you were probably introduced to the idea of a negative number via the temperature on a thermometer scale measured in degrees centigrade. A number such as -5 would then be interpreted as a temperature of 5 degrees below freezing. In personal finance a negative bank balance would indicate that an account is 'in the red' or 'in debit'. Similarly, a firm's profit of $-500\,000$ signifies a loss of half a million.

The rules for the multiplication of negative numbers are

$$\boxed{\text{negative}} \times \boxed{\text{negative}} = \boxed{\text{positive}}$$

$$\boxed{\text{negative}} \times \boxed{\text{positive}} = \boxed{\text{negative}}$$

It does not matter in which order two numbers are multiplied, so

$$\boxed{\text{positive}} \times \boxed{\text{negative}} = \boxed{\text{negative}}$$

These rules produce, respectively,

$(-2) \times (-3) = 6$

$(-4) \times 5 = -20$

$7 \times (-5) = -35$

Also, because division is the same sort of operation as multiplication (it just undoes the result of multiplication and takes you back to where you started), exactly the same rules apply when one number is divided by another. For example,

$(-15) \div (-3) = 5$

$(-16) \div 2 = -8$

$2 \div (-4) = -1/2$

In general, to multiply or divide lots of numbers it is probably simplest to ignore the signs to begin with and just to work the answer out. The final result is negative if the total number of minus signs is odd and positive if the total number is even.

Example

Evaluate

(a) $(-2) \times (-4) \times (-1) \times 2 \times (-1) \times (-3)$ (b) $\dfrac{5 \times (-4) \times (-1) \times (-3)}{(-6) \times 2}$

Solution

(a) Ignoring the signs gives

$2 \times 4 \times 1 \times 2 \times 1 \times 3 = 48$

There are an odd number of minus signs (in fact, five), so the answer is -48.

(b) Ignoring the signs gives

$\dfrac{5 \times 4 \times 1 \times 3}{6 \times 2} = \dfrac{60}{12} = 5$

There are an even number of minus signs (in fact, four), so the answer is 5.

> **Advice**
>
> Attempt the following problem yourself both with and without a calculator. On most machines a negative number such as -6 is entered by pressing the button labelled $(-)$ followed by 6.

Practice Problem

1. **(1)** Without using a calculator, evaluate

    (a) $5 \times (-6)$ **(b)** $(-1) \times (-2)$ **(c)** $(-50) \div 10$

    (d) $(-5) \div (-1)$ **(e)** $2 \times (-1) \times (-3) \times 6$ **(f)** $\dfrac{2 \times (-1) \times (-3) \times 6}{(-2) \times 3 \times 6}$

    (2) Confirm your answer to part (1) using a calculator.

To add or subtract negative numbers it helps to think in terms of a number line:

If b is a positive number, then

$$a - b$$

can be thought of as an instruction to start at a and to move b units to the left. For example,

$$1 - 3 = -2$$

because if you start at 1 and move 3 units to the left, you end up at -2:

Similarly,

$$-2 - 1 = -3$$

because 1 unit to the left of -2 is -3.

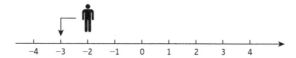

On the other hand,

$$a - (-b)$$

is taken to be $a + b$. This follows from the rule for multiplying two negative numbers, since

$$-(-b) = (-1) \times (-b) = b$$

Consequently, to evaluate

$$a - (-b)$$

you start at a and move b units to the right (that is, in the positive direction). For example,

$$-2 - (-5) = -2 + 5 = 3$$

because if you start at -2 and move 5 units to the right, you end up at 3.

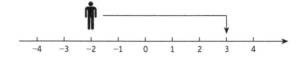

Practice Problem

2. **(1)** Without using a calculator, evaluate

   (a) $1 - 2$ **(b)** $-3 - 4$ **(c)** $1 - (-4)$

   (d) $-1 - (-1)$ **(e)** $-72 - 19$ **(f)** $-53 - (-48)$

   (2) Confirm your answer to part (1) using a calculator.

1.1.2 Expressions

In algebra, letters are used to represent numbers. In pure mathematics the most common letters used are x and y. However, in applications it is helpful to choose letters that are more meaningful, so we might use Q for quantity and I for investment. An algebraic expression is then simply a combination of these letters, brackets and other mathematical symbols such as $+$ or $-$. For example, the expression

$$P\left(1 + \frac{r}{100}\right)^n$$

can be used to work out how money in a savings account grows over a period of time. The letters P, r and n represent the original sum invested (called the principal – hence the use of the letter P), the rate of interest and the number of years, respectively. To work it all out, you not only need to replace these letters by actual numbers, but you also need to understand the various conventions that go with algebraic expressions such as this.

In algebra, when we multiply two numbers represented by letters, we usually suppress the multiplication sign between them. The product of a and b would simply be written as ab without bothering to put the multiplication sign between the symbols. Likewise, when a number represented by the letter Y is doubled, we write $2Y$. In this case we not only suppress the multiplication sign but adopt the convention of writing the number in front of the letter. Here are some further examples:

$P \times Q$ is written as PQ

$d \times 8$ is written as $8d$

$n \times 6 \times t$ is written as $6nt$

$z \times z$ is written as z^2 (using the index 2 to indicate squaring a number)

$1 \times t$ is written as t (since multiplying by 1 does not change a number)

In order to evaluate these expressions it is necessary to be given the numerical value of each letter. Once this has been done, you can work out the final value by performing the operations in the following order:

Brackets first	(B)
Indices second	(I)
Division and Multiplication third	(DM)
Addition and Subtraction fourth	(AS)

This is sometimes remembered using the acronym BIDMAS, and it is essential to use this ordering for working out all mathematical calculations. For example, suppose you wish to evaluate each of the following expressions when $n = 3$:

$2n^2$ and $(2n)^2$

Substituting $n = 3$ into the first expression gives

$2n^2 = 2 \times 3^2$ (the multiplication sign is revealed when we switch from algebra to numbers)

$\quad = 2 \times 9$ (according to BIDMAS, indices are worked out before multiplication)

$\quad = 18$

whereas in the second expression we get

$(2n)^2 = (2 \times 3)^2$ (again, the multiplication sign is revealed)

$\quad = 6^2$ (according to BIDMAS, we evaluate the inside of the brackets first)

$\quad = 36$

The two answers are not the same, so the order indicated by BIDMAS really does matter. Looking at the previous list, notice that there is a tie between multiplication and division for third place, and another tie between addition and subtraction for fourth place. These pairs of operations have equal priority, and under these circumstances you work from left to right when evaluating expressions. For example, substituting $x = 5$ and $y = 4$ in the expression, $x - y + 2$, gives

$x - y + 2 = 5 - 4 + 2$

$\quad = 1 + 2$ (reading from left to right, subtraction comes first)

$\quad = 3$

Example

(a) Find the value of $2x - 3y$ when $x = 9$ and $y = 4$.
(b) Find the value of $2Q^2 + 4Q + 150$ when $Q = 10$.
(c) Find the value of $5a - 2b + c$ when $a = 4$, $b = 6$ and $c = 1$.
(d) Find the value of $(12 - t) - (t - 1)$ when $t = 4$.

Solution

(a) $2x - 3y = 2 \times 9 - 3 \times 4$ (substituting numbers)

$\quad = 18 - 12$ (multiplication has priority over subtraction)

$\quad = 6$

(b) $2Q^2 + 4Q + 150 = 2 \times 10^2 + 4 \times 10 + 150$ (substituting numbers)

$\qquad\qquad\qquad\quad = 2 \times 100 + 4 \times 10 + 150$ (indices have priority over multiplication and addition)

$\qquad\qquad\qquad\quad = 200 + 40 + 150$ (multiplication has priority over addition)

$\qquad\qquad\qquad\quad = 390$

(c) $5a - 2b + c = 5 \times 4 - 2 \times 6 + 1$ (substituting numbers)

$\qquad\qquad\qquad = 20 - 12 + 1$ (multiplication has priority over addition and subtraction)

$\qquad\qquad\qquad = 8 + 1$ (addition and subtraction have equal priority, so work from left to right)

$\qquad\qquad\qquad = 9$

(d) $(12 - t) - (t - 1) = (12 - 4) - (4 - 1)$ (substituting numbers)

$\qquad\qquad\qquad\quad = 8 - 3$ (brackets first)

$\qquad\qquad\qquad\quad = 5$

Practice Problem

3. Evaluate each of the following by replacing the letters by the given numbers:

(a) $2Q + 5$ when $Q = 7$.

(b) $5x^2y$ when $x = 10$ and $y = 3$.

(c) $4d - 3f + 2g$ when $d = 7, f = 2$ and $g = 5$.

(d) $a(b + 2c)$ when $a = 5, b = 1$ and $c = 3$.

Like terms are multiples of the same letter (or letters). For example, $2P$, $-34P$ and $0.3P$ are all multiples of P and so are like terms. In the same way, xy, $4xy$ and $69xy$ are all multiples of xy and so are like terms. If an algebraic expression contains like terms which are added or subtracted together, then it can be simplified to produce an equivalent shorter expression.

Example

Simplify each of the following expressions (where possible):

(a) $2a + 5a - 3a$

(b) $4P - 2Q$

(c) $3w + 9w^2 + 2w$

(d) $3xy + 2y^2 + 9x + 4xy - 8x$

Solution

(a) All three are like terms since they are all multiples of a, so the expression can be simplified:

$\qquad 2a + 5a - 3a = 4a$

(b) The terms $4P$ and $2Q$ are unlike because one is a multiple of P and the other is a multiple of Q, so the expression cannot be simplified.

(c) The first and last are like terms since they are both multiples of w, so we can collect these together and write

$$3w + 9w^2 + 2w = 5w + 9w^2$$

This cannot be simpified any further because $5w$ and $9w^2$ are unlike terms.

(d) The terms $3xy$ and $4xy$ are like terms, and $9x$ and $8x$ are also like terms. These pairs can therefore be collected together to give

$$3xy + 2y^2 + 9x + 4xy - 8x = 7xy + 2y^2 + x$$

Notice that we write just x instead of $1x$ and also that no further simplication is possible since the final answer involves three unlike terms.

Practice Problem

4. Simplify each of the following expressions, where possible:

(a) $2x + 6y - x + 3y$ (b) $5x + 2y - 5x + 4z$ (c) $4Y^2 + 3Y - 43$

(d) $8r^2 + 4s - 6rs - 3s - 3s^2 + 7rs$ (e) $2e^2 + 5f - 2e^2 - 9f$ (f) $3w + 6W$

(g) $ab - ba$

1.1.3 Brackets

It is useful to be able to take an expression containing brackets and rewrite it as an equivalent expression without brackets, and vice versa. The process of removing brackets is called 'expanding brackets' or 'multiplying out brackets'. This is based on the **distributive law**, which states that for any three numbers a, b and c

$$a(b + c) = ab + ac$$

It is easy to verify this law in simple cases. For example, if $a = 2$, $b = 3$ and $c = 4$, then the left-hand side is

$$2(3 + 4) = 2 \times 7 = 14$$

However,

$$ab = 2 \times 3 = 6 \quad \text{and} \quad ac = 2 \times 4 = 8$$

and so the right-hand side is $6 + 8$, which is also 14.

This law can be used when there are any number of terms inside the brackets. We have

$$a(b + c + d) = ab + ac + ad$$
$$a(b + c + d + e) = ab + ac + ad + ae$$

and so on.

It does not matter in which order two numbers are multiplied, so we also have

$$(b + c)a = ba + ca$$
$$(b + c + d)a = ba + ca + da$$
$$(b + c + d + e)a = ba + ca + da + ea$$

Example

Multiply out the brackets in

(a) $x(x - 2)$

(b) $2(x + y - z) + 3(z + y)$

(c) $x + 3y - (2y + x)$

Solution

(a) The use of the distributive law to multiply out $x(x - 2)$ is straightforward. The x outside the bracket multiplies the x inside to give x^2. The x outside the bracket also multiplies the -2 inside to give $-2x$. Hence

$$x(x - 2) = x^2 - 2x$$

(b) To expand

$$2(x + y - z) + 3(z + y)$$

we need to apply the distributive law twice. We have

$$2(x + y - z) = 2x + 2y - 2z$$
$$3(z + y) = 3z + 3y$$

Adding together gives

$$2(x + y - z) + 3(z + y) = 2x + 2y - 2z + 3z + 3y$$
$$= 2x + 5y + z \quad \text{(collecting like terms)}$$

(c) It may not be immediately apparent how to expand

$$x + 3y - (2y + x)$$

However, note that

$$-(2y + x)$$

is the same as

$$(-1)(2y + x)$$

which expands to give

$$(-1)(2y) + (-1)x = -2y - x$$

Hence

$$x + 3y - (2y + x) = x + 3y - 2y - x = y$$

after collecting like terms.

Practice Problem

5. Multiply out the brackets, simplifying your answer as far as possible.

    (a) $(5 - 2z)z$ (b) $6(x - y) + 3(y - 2x)$ (c) $x - y + z - (x^2 + x - y)$

Mathematical formulae provide a precise way of representing calculations that need to be worked out in many business models. However, it is important to realise that these formulae may be valid only for a restricted range of values. Most large companies have a policy to reimburse employees for use of their cars for travel: for the first 50 miles they may be able to claim 90 cents a mile, but this could fall to 60 cents a mile thereafter. If the distance, x miles, is no more than 50 miles, then travel expenses, E (in dollars), could be worked out using the formula $E = 0.9x$. If x exceeds 50 miles, the employee can claim \$0.90 a mile for the first 50 miles but only \$0.60 a mile for the last $(x - 50)$ miles. The total amount is then

$$E = 0.9 \times 50 + 0.6(x - 50)$$
$$= 45 + 0.6x - 30$$
$$= 15 + 0.6x$$

Travel expenses can therefore be worked out using two separate formulae:

- $E = 0.9x$ when x is no more than 50 miles
- $E = 15 + 0.6x$ when x exceeds 50 miles.

Before we leave this topic, a word of warning is in order. Be careful when removing brackets from very simple expressions such as those considered in part (c) in the previous worked example and practice problem. A common mistake is to write

$$(a + b) - (c + d) = a + b - c + d \qquad \text{This is NOT true}$$

The distributive law tells us that the -1 multiplying the second bracket applies to the d as well as the c, so the correct answer has to be

$$(a + b) - (c + d) = a + b - c - d$$

In algebra, it is sometimes useful to reverse the procedure and put the brackets back in. This is called **factorisation**. Consider the expression $12a + 8b$. There are many numbers which divide into both 8 and 12. However, we always choose the biggest number, which is 4 in this case, so we attempt to take the factor of 4 outside the brackets:

$$12a + 8b = 4(? + ?)$$

where each ? indicates a mystery term inside the brackets. We would like 4 multiplied by the first term in the brackets to be $12a$, so we are missing $3a$. Likewise, if we are to generate an $8b$, the second term in the brackets will have to be $2b$.

Hence

$$12a + 8b = 4(3a + 2b)$$

As a check, notice that when you expand the brackets on the right-hand side, you really do get the expression on the left-hand side.

Example

Factorise

(a) $6L - 3L^2$

(b) $5a - 10b + 20c$

Solution

(a) Both terms have a common factor of 3. Also, because $L^2 = L \times L$, both $6L$ and $-3L^2$ have a factor of L. Hence we can take out a common factor of $3L$ altogether.

$$6L - 3L^2 = 3L(2) - 3L(L) = 3L(2 - L)$$

(b) All three terms have a common factor of 5, so we write

$$5a - 10b + 20c = 5(a) - 5(2b) + 5(4c) = 5(a - 2b + 4c)$$

Practice Problem

6. Factorise

   (a) $7d + 21$ (b) $16w - 20q$ (c) $6x - 3y + 9z$ (d) $5Q - 10Q^2$

We conclude our discussion of brackets by describing how to multiply two brackets together. In the expression $(a + b)(c + d)$ the two terms a and b must each multiply the single bracket $(c + d)$, so

$$(a + b)(c + d) = a(c + d) + b(c + d)$$

The first term $a(c + d)$ can itself be expanded as $ac + ad$. Likewise, $b(c + d) = bc + bd$. Hence

$$(a + b)(c + d) = ac + ad + bc + bd$$

This procedure then extends to brackets with more than two terms:

$$(a + b)(c + d + e) = a(c + d + e) + b(c + d + e) = ac + ad + ae + bc + bd + be$$

Example

Multiply out the brackets

(a) $(x + 1)(x + 2)$ **(b)** $(x + 5)(x - 5)$ **(c)** $(2x - y)(x + y - 6)$

simplifying your answer as far as possible.

Solution

(a) $(x + 1)(x + 2) = x(x + 2) + (1)(x + 2)$
$$= x^2 + 2x + x + 2$$
$$= x^2 + 3x + 2$$

(b) $(x + 5)(x - 5) = x(x - 5) + 5(x - 5)$
$$= x^2 - 5x + 5x - 25$$
$$= x^2 - 25 \quad \text{(the xs cancel)}$$

(c) $(2x - y)(x + y - 6) = 2x(x + y - 6) - y(x + y - 6)$
$$= 2x^2 + 2xy - 12x - yx - y^2 + 6y$$
$$= 2x^2 + xy - 12x - y^2 + 6y$$

Practice Problem

7. Multiply out the brackets.

    (a) $(x + 3)(x - 2)$
    (b) $(x + y)(x - y)$
    (c) $(x + y)(x + y)$
    (d) $(5x + 2y)(x - y + 1)$

Looking back at part (b) of the previous worked example, notice that

$$(x + 5)(x - 5) = x^2 - 25 = x^2 - 5^2$$

Quite generally

$$(a + b)(a - b) = a(a - b) + b(a - b)$$
$$= a^2 - ab + ba - b^2$$
$$= a^2 - b^2$$

The result

$$a^2 - b^2 = (a + b)(a - b)$$

is called the **difference of two squares** formula. It provides a quick way of factorising certain expressions.

Example

Factorise the following expressions:

(a) $x^2 - 16$ **(b)** $9x^2 - 100$

Solution

(a) Noting that

$$x^2 - 16 = x^2 - 4^2$$

we can use the difference of two squares formula to deduce that

$$x^2 - 16 = (x + 4)(x - 4)$$

(b) Noting that

$$9x^2 - 100 = (3x)^2 - (10)^2$$

$$(3x)^2 = 3x \times 3x = 9x^2$$

we can use the difference of two squares formula to deduce that

$$9x^2 - 100 = (3x + 10)(3x - 10)$$

Practice Problem

8. Factorise the following expressions:

   (a) $x^2 - 64$ **(b)** $4x^2 - 81$

Advice

This completes your first piece of mathematics. We hope that you have not found it quite as bad as you first thought. There now follow a few extra problems to give you more practice. Not only will they help to strengthen your mathematical skills, but also they should improve your overall confidence. Two alternative exercises are available. Exercise 1.1 is suitable for students whose mathematics may be rusty and who need to consolidate their understanding. Exercise 1.1* contains more challenging problems and so is more suitable for those students who have found this section very easy.

Key Terms

Difference of two squares   The algebraic result which states that $a^2 - b^2 = (a + b)(a - b)$.

Distributive law   The law of arithmetic which states that $a(b + c) = ab + ac$ for any numbers, a, b, c.

Factorisation   The process of writing an expression as a product of simpler expressions using brackets.

Like terms   Multiples of the same combination of algebraic symbols.

Exercise 1.1

1. Without using a calculator, evaluate

   (a) $10 \times (-2)$ (b) $(-1) \times (-3)$ (c) $(-8) \div 2$ (d) $(-5) \div (-5)$

   (e) $24 \div (-2)$ (f) $(-10) \times (-5)$ (g) $\dfrac{20}{-4}$ (h) $\dfrac{-27}{-9}$

   (i) $(-6) \times 5 \times (-1)$ (j) $\dfrac{2 \times (-6) \times 3}{(-9)}$

2. Without using a calculator, evaluate

   (a) $5 - 6$ (b) $-1 - 2$ (c) $6 - 17$ (d) $-7 + 23$

   (e) $-7 - (-6)$ (f) $-4 - 9$ (g) $7 - (-4)$ (h) $-9 - (-9)$

   (i) $12 - 43$ (j) $2 + 6 - 10$

3. Without using a calculator, evaluate

   (a) $5 \times 2 - 13$ (b) $\dfrac{-30 - 6}{-18}$ (c) $\dfrac{(-3) \times (-6) \times (-1)}{2 - 3}$ (d) $5 \times (1 - 4)$

   (e) $1 - 6 \times 7$ (f) $-5 + 6 \div 3$ (g) $2 \times (-3)^2$ (h) $-10 + 2^2$

   (i) $(-2)^2 - 5 \times 6 + 1$ (j) $\dfrac{(-4)^2 \times (-3) \times (-1)}{(-2)^3}$

4. Simplify each of the following algebraic expressions:

   (a) $2 \times P \times Q$ (b) $I \times 8$ (c) $3 \times x \times y$

   (d) $4 \times q \times w \times z$ (e) $b \times b$ (f) $k \times 3 \times k$

5. Simplify the following algebraic expressions by collecting like terms:

   (a) $6w - 3w + 12w + 4w$ (b) $6x + 5y - 2x - 12y$

   (c) $3a - 2b + 6a - c + 4b - c$ (d) $2x^2 + 4x - x^2 - 2x$

   (e) $2cd + 4c - 5dc$ (f) $5st + s^2 - 3ts + t^2 + 9$

6. Without using a calculator, find the value of the following:

   (a) $2x - y$ when $x = 7$ and $y = 4$.

   (b) $x^2 - 5x + 12$ when $x = 6$.

   (c) $2m^3$ when $m = 10$.

   (d) $5fg^2 + 2g$ when $f = 2$ and $g = 3$.

   (e) $2v + 4w - (4v - 7w)$ when $v = 20$ and $w = 10$.

7. If $x = 2$ and $y = -3$, evaluate

   (a) $2x + y$ (b) $x - y$ (c) $3x + 4y$

   (d) xy (e) $5xy$ (f) $4x - 6xy$

8. **(a)** Without using a calculator, work out the value of $(-4)^2$.

   (b) Press the following key sequence on your calculator:

   (−)   4 x^2

   Explain carefully why this does not give the same result as part (a) and give an alternative key sequence that *does* give the correct answer.

9. Without using a calculator, work out

   (a) $(5 - 2)^2$ **(b)** $5^2 - 2^2$

   Is it true in general that $(a - b)^2 = a^2 - b^2$?

10. Use your calculator to work out the following. Round your answer, if necessary, to two decimal places.

   (a) $5.31 \times 8.47 - 1.01^2$ **(b)** $(8.34 + 2.27)/9.41$

   (c) $9.53 - 3.21 + 4.02$ **(d)** $2.41 \times 0.09 - 1.67 \times 0.03$

   (e) $45.76 - (2.55 + 15.83)$ **(f)** $(3.45 - 5.38)^2$

   (g) $4.56(9.02 + 4.73)$ **(h)** $6.85/(2.59 + 0.28)$

11. Multiply out the brackets:

   (a) $7(x - y)$ **(b)** $3(5x - 2y)$ **(c)** $4(x + 3)$ **(d)** $7(3x - 1)$

   (e) $3(x + y + z)$ **(f)** $x(3x - 4)$ **(g)** $y + 2z - 2(x + 3y - z)$

12. Factorise

   (a) $25c + 30$ **(b)** $9x - 18$ **(c)** $x^2 + 2x$

   (d) $16x - 12y$ **(e)** $4x^2 - 6xy$ **(f)** $10d - 15e + 50$

13. Multiply out the brackets:

   (a) $(x + 2)(x + 5)$ **(b)** $(a + 4)(a - 1)$ **(c)** $(d + 3)(d - 8)$ **(d)** $(2s + 3)(3s + 7)$

   (e) $(2y + 3)(y + 1)$ **(f)** $(5t + 2)(2t - 7)$ **(g)** $(3n + 2)(3n - 2)$ **(h)** $(a - b)(a - b)$

14. Simplify the following expressions by collecting together like terms:

   (a) $2x + 3y + 4x - y$ **(b)** $2x^2 - 5x + 9x^2 + 2x - 3$

   (c) $5xy + 2x + 9yx$ **(d)** $7xyz + 3yx - 2zyx + yzx - xy$

   (e) $2(5a + b) - 4b$ **(f)** $5(x - 4y) + 6(2x + 7y)$

   (g) $5 - 3(p - 2)$ **(h)** $x(x - y + 7) + xy + 3x$

15. Use the formula for the difference of two squares to factorise

   (a) $x^2 - 4$ **(b)** $Q^2 - 49$ **(c)** $x^2 - y^2$ **(d)** $9x^2 - 100y^2$

16. Simplify the following algebraic expressions:

   (a) $3x - 4x^2 - 2 + 5x + 8x^2$ **(b)** $x(3x + 2) - 3x(x + 5)$

17. A law firm seeks to recruit top-quality experienced lawyers. The total package offered is the sum of three separate components: a basic salary which is 1.2 times the candidate's current salary together with an additional \$3000 for each year worked as a qualified lawyer and an extra \$1000 for every year that they are over the age of 21.

    Work out a formula that could be used to calculate the total salary, S, offered to someone who is A years of age, has E years of relevant experience and who currently earns \$N. Hence work out the salary offered to someone who is 30 years old with five years' experience and who currently earns \$150 000.

18. Write down a formula for each situation:

    (a) A plumber has a fixed call-out charge of \$80 and has an hourly rate of \$60. Work out the total charge, C, for a job that takes L hours in which the cost of materials and parts is \$K.

    (b) An airport currency exchange booth charges a fixed fee of \$10 on all transactions and offers an exchange rate of 1 dollar to 0.8 euros. Work out the total charge, C, (in \$) for buying x euros.

    (c) A firm provides 5 hours of in-house training for each of its semi-skilled workers and 10 hours of training for each of its skilled workers. Work out the total number of hours, H, if the firm employs a semi-skilled and b skilled workers.

    (d) A car hire company charges \$C a day together with an additional \$c per mile. Work out the total charge, \$X, for hiring a car for d days and travelling m miles during that time.

Exercise 1.1*

1. Without using a calculator, evaluate

   (a) $(12 - 8) - (6 - 5)$ (b) $12 - (8 - 6) - 5$ (c) $12 - 8 - 6 - 5$

2. Put a pair of brackets in the left-hand side of each of the following to give correct statements:

   (a) $2 - 7 - 9 + 3 = -17$ (b) $8 - 2 + 3 - 4 = -1$ (c) $7 - 2 - 6 + 10 = 1$

3. Without using a calculator, work out the value of each of the following expressions in the case when $a = 3$, $b = -4$ and $c = -2$:

   (a) $a(b - c)$ (b) $3c(a + b)$ (c) $a^2 + 2b + 3c$ (d) $2abc^2$

   (e) $\dfrac{c + b}{2a}$ (f) $\sqrt{2(b^2 - c)}$ (g) $\dfrac{b}{2c} - \dfrac{a}{3b}$ (h) $5a - b^3 - 4c^2$

4. Without using a calculator, evaluate each of the following expressions in the case when $x = -1$, $y = -2$ and $z = 3$:

   (a) $x^3 + y^2 + z$ (b) $\sqrt{\left(\dfrac{x^2 + y^2 + z}{x^2 + 2xy - z}\right)}$ (c) $\dfrac{xyz(x + z)(z - y)}{(x + y)(x - z)}$

5. Multiply out the brackets and simplify

   $(x - y)(x + y) - (x + 2)(x - y + 3)$

6. Simplify

    (a) $x - y - (y - x)$ **(b)** $(x - ((y - x) - y))$ **(c)** $x + y - (x - y) - (x - (y - x))$

7. Multiply out the brackets:

    (a) $(x + 4)(x - 6)$ **(b)** $(2x - 5)(3x - 7)$ **(c)** $2x(3x + y - 2)$

    (d) $(3 + g)(4 - 2g + h)$ **(e)** $(2x + y)(1 - x - y)$ **(f)** $(a + b + c)(a - b - c)$

8. Factorise

    (a) $9x - 12y$ **(b)** $x^2 - 6x$ **(c)** $10xy + 15x^2$

    (d) $3xy^2 - 6x^2y + 12xy$ **(e)** $x^3 - 2x^2$ **(f)** $60x^4y^6 - 15x^2y^4 + 20xy^3$

9. Use the formula for the difference of two squares to factorise

    (a) $p^2 - 25$ **(b)** $9c^2 - 64$ **(c)** $32v^2 - 50d^2$ **(d)** $16x^4 - y^4$

10. Evaluate the following without using a calculator:

    (a) $50\,563^2 - 49\,437^2$ **(b)** $90^2 - 89.99^2$

    (c) $759^2 - 541^2$ **(d)** $123\,456\,789^2 - 123\,456\,788^2$

11. A specialist paint manufacturer receives \$12 for each pot sold. The initial set-up cost for the production run is \$800 and the cost of making each tin of paint is \$3.

    (a) Write down a formula for the total profit, π, if the firm manufactures x pots of paint and sells y pots.

    (b) Use your formula to calculate the profit when $x = 1000$ and $y = 800$.

    (c) State any restrictions on the variables in the mathematical formula in part (a).

    (d) Simplify the formula in the case when the firm sells all that it manufactures.

12. Factorise

    (a) $2KL^2 + 4KL$ **(b)** $L^2 - 0.04K^2$ **(c)** $K^2 + 2LK + L^2$

SECTION 1.2
Further algebra

Objectives

At the end of this section you should be able to:

- Simplify fractions by cancelling common factors.
- Add, subtract, multiply and divide fractions.
- Solve equations by doing the same thing to both sides.
- Recognise the symbols $<$, $>$, $\leq$ and $\geq$.
- Solve linear inequalities.

This section is broken down into three manageable subsections:

- fractions;
- equations;
- inequalities.

The advice offered in Section 1.1 applies equally well here. Please try to study these topics on separate occasions and be prepared to work through the practice problems as they arise in the text.

1.2.1 Fractions

For a numerical fraction such as

$$\frac{7}{8}$$

the number 7, on the top, is called the **numerator** and the number 8, on the bottom, is called the **denominator**. In this text we are also interested in the case when the numerator and denominator involve letters as well as numbers. These are referred to as **algebraic fractions**. For example,

$$\frac{1}{x^2 - 2} \quad \text{and} \quad \frac{2x^2 - 1}{y + z}$$

are both algebraic fractions. The letters x, y and z are used to represent numbers, so the rules for the manipulation of algebraic fractions are the same as those for ordinary numerical fractions. It is therefore essential that you are happy manipulating numerical fractions without a calculator so that you can extend this skill to fractions with letters.

Two fractions are said to be **equivalent** if they represent the same numerical value. We know that 3/4 is equivalent to 6/8 since they are both equal to the decimal number 0.75. It is also intuitively obvious. Imagine breaking a bar of chocolate into four equal pieces and eating three

1.2.3 Inequalities

In Section 1.1.1 we made use of a number line:

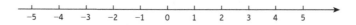

Although only whole numbers are marked on this diagram, it is implicitly assumed that it can also be used to indicate fractions and decimal numbers. Each point on the line corresponds to a particular number. Conversely, every number can be represented by a particular point on the line. For example, $-2^{1/2}$ lies exactly halfway between -3 and -2. Similarly, $4^{7/8}$ lies $^7/_8$ of the way between 4 and 5. In theory, we can even find a point on the line corresponding to a number such as $\sqrt{2}$, although it may be difficult to sketch such a point accurately in practice. My calculator gives the value of $\sqrt{2}$ to be 1.414 213 56 to eight decimal places. This number therefore lies just less than halfway between 1 and 2.

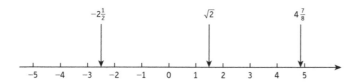

A number line can be used to decide whether or not one number is greater or less than another number. We say that a number a is greater than a number b if a lies to the right of b on the line, and we write this as

$a > b$

Likewise, we say that a is less than b if a lies to the left of b, and we write this as

$a < b$

From the diagram we see that

$-2 > -4$

because -2 lies to the right of -4. This is equivalent to the statement

$-4 < -2$

Similarly,

$0 > -1$ (or equivalently $-1 < 0$)

$2 > -2^{1/2}$ (or equivalently $-2^{1/2} < 2$)

$4^{7/8} > \sqrt{2}$ (or equivalently $\sqrt{2} < 4^{7/8}$)

There are occasions when we would like the letters a and b to stand for mathematical expressions rather than actual numbers. In this situation we sometimes use the symbols $\geq$ and $\leq$ to mean 'greater than or equal to' and 'less than or equal to', respectively.

We have already seen that we can manipulate equations in any way we like, provided that we do the same thing to both sides. An obvious question to ask is whether this rule extends to inequalities.

Consider the true statement

$$1 < 3 \qquad (*)$$

- Adding 4 to both sides gives $5 < 7$, which is true.
- Adding -5 to both sides gives $-4 < -2$, which is true.
- Multiplying both sides by 2 gives $2 < 6$, which is true.

However,

- Multiplying both sides by -6 gives $-6 < -18$, which is false. In fact, quite the reverse is true; -6 is actually greater than -18. This indicates that the rule needs modifying before we can extend it to inequalities and that we must be careful when manipulating inequalities.

Practice Problem

6. Starting with the true statement

$$6 > 3$$

decide which of the following are valid operations when performed on both sides:

(a) add 6   (b) multiply by 2   (c) subtract 3

(d) add -3 (e) divide by 3   (f) multiply by -4

(g) multiply by -1 (h) divide by -3 (i) add -10

These examples show that the usual rule does apply to inequalities with the important proviso that

> **if both sides are multiplied or divided by a negative number, then the sense of the inequality is reversed**

By this we mean that '>' changes to '<', '≤' changes to '≥' and so on.

To see how this works out in practice, consider the inequality

$$2x + 3 < 4x + 7$$

If we try to solve this like we did for equations, the first step would be to subtract $4x$ from both sides to get

$$-2x + 3 < 7$$

and then take 3 away from both sides to get

$$-2x < 4$$

Finally, we divide both sides by -2 to get

$$x > -2$$

Notice that the sense has been reversed at this stage because we have divided by a negative number.

Advice

You should check your answer using a couple of test values. Substituting $x = 1$ (which lies to the right of -2 and so should work) into both sides of the original inequality $2x + 3 < 4x + 7$ gives $5 < 11$, which is true. On the other hand, substituting $x = -3$ (which lies to the left of -2 and so should fail) gives $-3 < -5$, which is false. Of course, just checking a couple of numbers like this does not prove that the final inequality is correct, but it should protect you against gross blunders.

Practice Problem

7. Simplify the inequalities

(a) $2x < 3x + 7$ (b) $21x - 19 \geq 4x + 15$

Inequalities arise in business when there is a budgetary restriction on resource allocation. The following example shows how to set up and solve the relevant inequality.

Example

A firm's Human Resources department has a budget of \$25 000 to spend on training and laptops. Training courses cost \$700 and new laptops are \$1200.

(a) If the department trains E employees and buys L laptops, write down an inequality for E and L.

(b) If 12 employees attend courses, how many laptops could be bought?

Solution

(a) The cost of training E employees is $700E$ and the cost of buying L laptops is $1200L$. The total amount spent must not exceed \$25 000, so $700E + 1200L \leq 25\,000$.

(b) Substituting $E = 12$ into the inequality gives $8400 + 1200L \leq 25\,000$.

$$1200L \leq 16\,600 \quad \text{(subtract 8400 from both sides)}$$
$$L \leq 13\frac{5}{6} \quad \text{(divide both sides by 1200)}$$

so a maximum of 13 laptops could be bought.

Exercise 1.2

1. Reduce each of the following numerical fractions to their lowest terms:

   (a) $\dfrac{13}{26}$ (b) $\dfrac{9}{12}$ (c) $\dfrac{18}{30}$ (d) $\dfrac{24}{72}$ (e) $\dfrac{36}{27}$

2. In 2011 in the United States, 35 out of every 100 adults owned a smartphone. By 2013 this figure increased to 56 out of every 100.

   (a) Express both of these figures as fractions reduced to their lowest terms.

   (b) By what factor did smartphone ownership increase during this period? Give your answer as a mixed fraction in its lowest terms.

3. Reduce each of the following algebraic fractions to their lowest terms:

   (a) $\dfrac{6x}{9}$ (b) $\dfrac{x}{2x^2}$ (c) $\dfrac{b}{abc}$ (d) $\dfrac{4x}{6x^2y}$ (e) $\dfrac{15a^2b}{20ab^2}$

4. By factorising the numerators and/or denominators of each of the following fractions, reduce each to its lowest terms:

   (a) $\dfrac{2p}{4q + 6r}$ (b) $\dfrac{x}{x^2 - 4x}$ (c) $\dfrac{3ab}{6a^2 + 3a}$ (d) $\dfrac{14d}{21d - 7de}$ (e) $\dfrac{x + 2}{x^2 - 4}$

5. Which one of the following algebraic fractions can be simplified? Explain why the other two fractions cannot be simplified.

   $$\dfrac{x-1}{2x-2}, \quad \dfrac{x-2}{x+2}, \quad \dfrac{5t}{10t - s}$$

6. **(1)** Without using a calculator, work out the following, giving your answer in its lowest terms:

   (a) $\dfrac{1}{7} + \dfrac{2}{7}$ (b) $\dfrac{2}{9} - \dfrac{5}{9}$ (c) $\dfrac{1}{2} + \dfrac{1}{3}$ (d) $\dfrac{3}{4} - \dfrac{2}{5}$ (e) $\dfrac{1}{6} + \dfrac{2}{9}$ (f) $\dfrac{1}{6} + \dfrac{2}{3}$

   (g) $\dfrac{5}{6} \times \dfrac{3}{4}$ (h) $\dfrac{4}{15} \div \dfrac{2}{3}$ (i) $\dfrac{7}{8} \times \dfrac{2}{3}$ (j) $\dfrac{2}{75} \div \dfrac{4}{5}$ (k) $\dfrac{2}{9} \div 3$ (l) $3 \div \dfrac{2}{7}$

   (2) Use your calculator to check your answers to part (1).

7. It takes $1\frac{1}{4}$ hours to complete an annual service of a car. If a garage has $47\frac{1}{2}$ hours available, how many cars can it service?

8. Work out each of the following, simplifying your answer as far as possible:

   (a) $\dfrac{2}{3x} + \dfrac{1}{3x}$ (b) $\dfrac{2}{x} \times \dfrac{x}{5}$ (c) $\dfrac{3}{x} - \dfrac{2}{x^2}$ (d) $\dfrac{7}{x} + \dfrac{2}{y}$ (e) $\dfrac{a}{2} \div \dfrac{a}{6}$

   (f) $\dfrac{5c}{12} + \dfrac{5d}{18}$ (g) $\dfrac{x+2}{y-5} \times \dfrac{y-5}{x+3}$ (h) $\dfrac{4gh}{7} \div \dfrac{2g}{9h}$ (i) $\dfrac{t}{4} \div 5$ (j) $\dfrac{P}{Q} \times \dfrac{Q}{P}$

9. Solve each of the following equations. If necessary give your answer as a mixed fraction reduced to its lowest terms.

   (a) $x + 2 = 7$ (b) $3x = 18$ (c) $\dfrac{x}{9} = 2$ (d) $x - 4 = -2$

   (e) $2x - 3 = 17$ (f) $3x + 4 = 1$ (g) $\dfrac{x}{6} - 7 = 3$ (h) $3(x - 1) = 2$

   (i) $4 - x = 9$ (j) $6x + 2 = 5x - 1$ (k) $5(3x + 8) = 10$ (l) $2(x - 3) = 5(x + 1)$

   (m) $\dfrac{4x - 7}{3} = 2$ (n) $\dfrac{4}{x + 1} = 1$ (o) $5 - \dfrac{1}{x} = 1$

10. Which of the following inequalities are true?

    (a) $-2 < 1$ (b) $-6 > -4$ (c) $3 < 3$

    (d) $3 \leq 3$ (e) $-21 \geq -22$ (f) $4 < 25$

11. Simplify the following inequalities:

    (a) $2x > x + 1$ (b) $7x + 3 \leq 9 + 5x$ (c) $x - 5 > 4x + 4$ (d) $x - 1 < 2x - 3$

12. Simplify the following algebraic expression:

    $$\dfrac{4}{x^2 y} \div \dfrac{2x}{y}$$

13. **(a)** Solve the equation

    $$6(2 + x) = 5(1 - 4x)$$

    (b) Solve the inequality

    $$3x + 6 \geq 5x - 14$$

Exercise 1.2*

1. Simplify each of the following algebraic fractions:

    (a) $\dfrac{2x - 6}{4}$ (b) $\dfrac{9x}{6x^2 - 3x}$ (c) $\dfrac{4x + 16}{x + 4}$ (d) $\dfrac{x - 1}{1 - x}$

    (e) $\dfrac{x + 6}{x^2 - 36}$ (f) $\dfrac{(x + 3)(2x - 5)}{(2x - 5)(x + 4)}$ (g) $\dfrac{3x}{6x^3 - 15x^2 + 9x}$ (h) $\dfrac{4x^2 - 25y^2}{6x - 15y}$

2. (1) Without using your calculator, evaluate

    (a) $\dfrac{4}{5} \times \dfrac{25}{28}$ (b) $\dfrac{2}{7} \times \dfrac{14}{25} \times \dfrac{5}{8}$ (c) $\dfrac{9}{16} \div \dfrac{3}{8}$ (d) $\dfrac{2}{5} \times \dfrac{1}{12} \div \dfrac{8}{25}$

    (e) $\dfrac{10}{13} - \dfrac{12}{13}$ (f) $\dfrac{5}{9} + \dfrac{2}{3}$ (g) $2\dfrac{3}{5} + 1\dfrac{3}{7}$ (h) $5\dfrac{9}{10} - \dfrac{1}{2} + 1\dfrac{2}{5}$

    (i) $3\dfrac{3}{4} \times 1\dfrac{3}{5}$ (j) $\dfrac{3}{5} \times \left(2\dfrac{1}{3} + \dfrac{1}{2}\right)$ (k) $\dfrac{5}{6} \times \left(2\dfrac{1}{3} - 1\dfrac{2}{5}\right)$ (l) $\left(3\dfrac{1}{3} \div 2\dfrac{1}{6}\right) \div \dfrac{5}{13}$

    (2) Confirm your answer to part (1) using a calculator.

3. Find simplified expressions for the following fractions:

    (a) $\dfrac{x^2 + 6x}{x - 2} \times \dfrac{x - 2}{x}$ (b) $\dfrac{1}{x} \div \dfrac{1}{x + 1}$ (c) $\dfrac{2}{xy} + \dfrac{3}{xy}$ (d) $\dfrac{x}{2} + \dfrac{x + 1}{3}$

    (e) $\dfrac{3}{x} + \dfrac{4}{x + 1}$ (f) $\dfrac{3}{x} + \dfrac{5}{x^2}$ (g) $x - \dfrac{2}{x + 1}$ (h) $\dfrac{5}{x(x + 1)} - \dfrac{2}{x} + \dfrac{3}{x + 1}$

4. Solve the following equations:

    (a) $5(2x + 1) = 3(x - 2)$ (b) $5(x + 2) + 4(2x - 3) = 11$

    (c) $5(1 - x) = 4(10 + x)$ (d) $3(3 - 2x) - 7(1 - x) = 10$

    (e) $9 - 5(2x - 1) = 6$ (f) $\dfrac{3}{2x + 1} = 2$

    (g) $\dfrac{2}{x - 1} = \dfrac{3}{5x + 4}$ (h) $\dfrac{x}{2} + 3 = 7$

    (i) $5 - \dfrac{x}{3} = 2$ (j) $\dfrac{5(x - 3)}{2} = \dfrac{2(x - 1)}{5}$

    (k) $\sqrt{(2x - 5)} = 3$ (l) $(x + 3)(x - 1) = (x + 4)(x - 3)$

    (m) $(x + 2)^2 + (2x - 1)^2 = 5x(x + 1)$ (n) $\dfrac{2x + 7}{3} = \dfrac{x - 4}{6} + \dfrac{1}{2}$

    (o) $\sqrt{\dfrac{45}{2x - 1}} = 3$ (p) $\dfrac{4}{x} - \dfrac{3}{4} = \dfrac{1}{4x}$

5. Two-thirds of Ariadne's money together with five-sevenths of Brian's money is equal to three-fifths of Catriona's money. If Ariadne has \$2.40 and Catriona has \$11.25, write down an equation that you could use to work out how much Brian has. Solve this equation.

6. An amount P is placed in a savings account. The interest rate is $r\%$ compounded annually so that after n years the savings, S, will be

$$S = P\left(1 + \frac{r}{100}\right)^n$$

   (a) Find S when $P = 2000$, $n = 5$ and $r = 10$.

   (b) Find P when $S = 65\,563.62$, $n = 3$ and $r = 3$.

   (c) Find r when $S = 7320.50$, $P = 5000$ and $n = 4$.

7. Solve the following inequalities:

   (a) $2x - 19 > 7x + 24$ (b) $2(x - 1) < 5(3x + 2)$ (c) $\dfrac{2x - 1}{5} \geq \dfrac{x - 3}{2}$

   (d) $3 + \dfrac{x}{3} < 2(x + 4)$ (e) $x < 2x + 1 \leq 7$

8. The design costs of an advertisement in a glossy magazine are \$9000 and the cost per cm^2 of print is \$50.

   (a) Write down an expression for the total cost of publishing an advert which covers $x \text{ cm}^2$.

   (b) The advertising budget is between \$10\,800 and \$12\,500. Write down and solve an inequality to work out the minimum and maximum area that could be used.

9. List all the whole numbers that satisfy both of the following inequalities simultaneously:

   $-7 \leq 2x < 6$ and $4x + 1 \leq x + 2$

10. (a) Simplify

   $$\frac{31x - 8}{(2x - 1)(x + 2)} - \frac{14}{x + 2}$$

   (b) Solve the equation

   $$\frac{x + 1}{8} = \frac{x + 3}{4} - \frac{1}{2}$$

   (c) Simplify the inequality

   $$(2x + 1)(x - 5) \leq 2(x + 2)(x - 4)$$

11. Simplify

   $$\frac{x^2}{x + 1} \div \frac{2x}{x^2 - 1}$$

SECTION 1.3
Graphs of linear equations

Objectives

At the end of this section you should be able to:

- Plot points on graph paper given their coordinates.
- Sketch a line by finding the coordinates of two points on the line.
- Solve simultaneous linear equations graphically.
- Sketch a line by using its slope and intercept.

Consider the two straight lines shown in Figure 1.1. The horizontal line is referred to as the *x* axis and the vertical line is referred to as the *y* axis. The point where these lines intersect is known as the **origin** and is denoted by the letter O. These lines enable us to identify uniquely any point, P, in terms of its **coordinates** (x, y). The first number, x, denotes the horizontal distance along the x axis and the second number, y, denotes the vertical distance along the y axis. The arrows on the axes indicate the positive direction in each case.

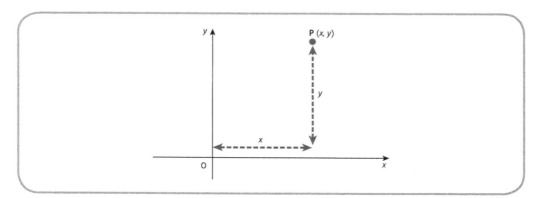

Figure 1.1

Figure 1.2 shows the five points A(2, 3), B(−1, 4), C(−3, −1), D(3, −2) and E(5, 0) plotted on coordinate axes. The point A with coordinates (2, 3) is obtained by starting at the origin, moving 2 units to the right and then moving 3 units vertically upwards. Similarly, the point B with coordinates (−1, 4) is located 1 unit to the left of O (because the x coordinate is negative) and 4 units up.

Note that the point C lies in the bottom left-hand quadrant since its x and y coordinates are both negative. It is also worth noticing that E actually lies on the x axis since its y coordinate is zero. Likewise, a point with coordinates of the form (0, y) for some number y would lie somewhere on the y axis. Of course, the point with coordinates (0, 0) is the origin, O.

The statement '0 = 5' is clearly nonsense and something has gone seriously wrong. To understand what is going on here, let us try to solve this problem graphically.

The line $x - 2y = 1$ passes through the points $(0, -1/2)$ and $(1, 0)$ (check this). The line $2x - 4y = -3$ passes through the points $(0, 3/4)$ and $(-3/2, 0)$ (check this). Figure 1.11 shows that these lines are parallel and so they do not intersect. It is therefore not surprising that we were unable to find a solution using algebra, because this system of equations does not have one. We could have deduced this before when subtracting the equations. The equation that only involves y in step 2 can be written as

$$0y = 5$$

and the problem is to find a value of y for which this equation is true. No such value exists, since

zero × any number = zero

and so the original system of equations does not have a solution.

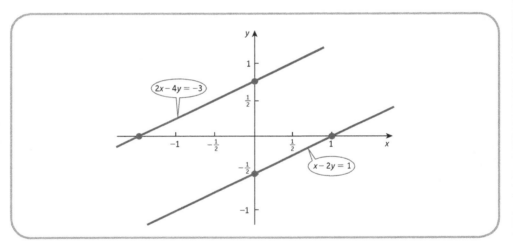

Figure 1.11

Example

Solve the equations

$$2x - 4y = 1$$
$$5x - 10y = 5/2$$

Solution

The variable x can be eliminated by multiplying the first equation by 5, multiplying the second equation by 2 and subtracting

$$10x - 20y = 5$$
$$10x - 20y = 5 -$$
$$\overline{\quad 0 = 0 \quad}$$

(everything cancels including the right-hand side!)

Again, it is easy to explain this using graphs. The line $2x - 4y = 1$ passes through $(0, -1/4)$ and $(1/2, 0)$. The line $5x - 10y = 5/2$ passes through $(0, -1/4)$ and $(1/2, 0)$. Consequently, both equations represent the same line. From Figure 1.12 the lines intersect along the whole of their length and any point on this line is a solution. This particular system of equations has infinitely many solutions. This can also be deduced algebraically. The equation involving y in step 2 is

$$0y = 0$$

which is true for any value of y.

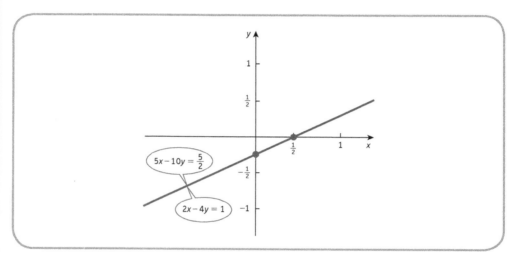

Figure 1.12

Practice Problem

2. Attempt to solve the following systems of equations:

(a) $3x - 6y = -2$ (b) $-5x + y = 4$
     $-4x + 8y = -1$ $10x - 2y = -8$

Comment on the nature of the solution in each case.

It is possible to identify when simultaneous equations fail to possess a unique solution by considering the general case:

$$ax + by = c$$
$$dx + ey = f$$

The variable y can be eliminated by multiplying the first equation by e, multiplying the second equation by b and subtracting:

$$aex + bey = ce$$
$$\underline{bdx + bey = bf} \quad -$$
$$(ae - bd)x = ce - bf$$

Advice

This does not depend on any subsequent sections, so you might like to read through this material now. Two techniques are suggested. A method based on inverse matrices is covered in Section 1.27 and an alternative using Cramer's rule can be found in Section 1.28.

Key Term

Elimination method   The method in which variables are removed from a system of simultaneous equations by adding (or subtracting) a multiple of one equation to (or from) a multiple of another.

Exercise 1.4

1. Use the elimination method to solve the following pairs of simultaneous linear equations:

    (a) $-2x + y = 2$ **(b)** $3x + 4y = 12$ **(c)** $2x + y = 4$ **(d)** $x + y = 1$
    $\quad\ \ 2x + y = -6$ $\quad\ \ x + 4y = 8$ $\quad\ \ 4x - 3y = 3$ $\quad\ \ 6x + 5y = 15$

2. The total annual sales of a book in either paper or electronic form are 3500. Each paper copy of the book costs \$30 and each e-book costs \$25. The total cost is \$97 500.

    (a) If x and y denote the number of copies in paper and electronic form, write down a pair of simultaneous equations.

    (b) Solve the equations to find the number of e-books sold.

3. Sketch the following lines on the same diagram:

    $$2x - 3y = 6, \quad 4x - 6y = 18, \quad x - \frac{3}{2}y = 3$$

    Hence comment on the nature of the solutions of the following systems of equations:

    (a) $2x - 3y = 6$ **(b)** $4x - 6y = 18$
    $\quad\ \ x - \dfrac{3}{2}y = 3$ $\quad\ \ x - \dfrac{3}{2}y = 3$

4. Use the elimination method to attempt to solve the following systems of equations. Comment on the nature of the solution in each case.

    (a) $-3x + 5y = 4$ **(b)** $6x - 2y = 3$
    $\quad\ \ 9x - 15y = -12$ $\quad\ \ 15x - 5y = 4$

5. If the following system of linear equations has infinitely many solutions, find the value of k.

    $$6x - 4y = 2$$
    $$-3x + 2y = k$$

Exercise 1.4*

1. Solve the following pairs of simultaneous equations:

   (a) $y = 3x - 1$ **(b)** $2x + y = 6$ **(c)** $2x + 3y = 5$ **(d)** $3x + 4y = -12$

   $\quad\ y = 2x + 1$ $x - y = -3$ $5x - 2y = -16$ $-2x + 3y = 25$

2. Write down a possible set of values of the numbers a and b for which the simultaneous equations:

   (a) $2x + 3y = 4$ have infinitely many solutions

   $\quad\ ax + 6y = b$

   (b) $4x - 6y = 1$ have no solutions

   $\quad\ 2x + ay = b$

3. By eliminating x from the system

   $$ax + by = c$$
   $$dx + ey = f$$

   show that

   $$y = \frac{af - cd}{ae - bd}$$

4. Solve the following systems of equations:

   (a) $x - 3y + 4z = 5$ (1)   **(b)** $3x + 2y - 2z = -5$ (1)

   $\quad\ 2x + y + z = 3$ (2) $4x + 3y + 3z = 17$ (2)

   $\quad\ 4x + 3y + 5z = 1$ (3) $2x - y + z = -1$ (3)

5. Attempt to solve the following systems of equations. Comment on the nature of the solution in each case.

   (a) $x - 2y + z = -2$ (1)   **(b)** $2x + 3y - z = 13$ (1)

   $\quad\ x + y - 2z = 4$ (2) $x - 2y + 2z = -3$ (2)

   $\quad\ -2x + y + z = 12$ (3) $3x + y + z = 10$ (3)

6. If the following system of equations has infinitely many solutions, find the value of the constant, k.

   $$x + 2y - 5z = 1$$
   $$2x - y + 3z = 4$$
   $$4x + 3y - 7z = k$$

   What can you say about the nature of the solution for other values of k?

7. A distribution centre sends three different types of parcels. One consignment has 6 small, 8 medium and 9 large parcels which cost \$173.20 to post. Another consignment has 7 small, 13 medium and 17 large parcels with total postage \$291.05. A large parcel costs twice as much to post as a small one. Work out the total cost of posting 3 small parcels, 9 medium parcels and 2 large parcels.

SECTION 1.5
Transposition of formulae

Objectives

At the end of this section you should be able to:

- Manipulate formulae.
- Draw a flow chart representing a formula.
- Use a reverse flow chart to transpose a formula.
- Change the subject of a formula involving several letters.

Mathematical modelling involves the use of formulae to represent the relationship between economic variables. In microeconomics we have already seen how useful supply and demand formulae are. These provide a precise relationship between price and quantity. For example, the connection between price, P, and quantity, Q, might be modelled by

$$P = -4Q + 100$$

Given any value of Q it is trivial to deduce the corresponding value of P by merely replacing the symbol Q by a number. A value of $Q = 2$, say, gives

$$P = -4 \times 2 + 100$$
$$= -8 + 100$$
$$= 92$$

On the other hand, given P, it is necessary to solve an equation to deduce Q. For example, when $P = 40$, the equation is

$$-4Q + 100 = 40$$

which can be solved as follows:

$$-4Q = -60 \quad \text{(subtract 100 from both sides)}$$
$$Q = 15 \quad \text{(divide both sides by } -4\text{)}$$

This approach is reasonable when only one or two values of P are given. However, if we are given many values of P, it is clearly tedious and inefficient for us to solve the equation each time to find Q. The preferred approach is to **transpose** the formula for P. In other words, we rearrange the formula

$$P = \text{an expression involving } Q$$

into

$$Q = \text{an expression involving } P$$

Written this way round, the formula enables us to find Q by replacing P by a number. For the specific formula

$$-4Q + 100 = P$$

the steps are

$$-4Q = P - 100 \qquad \text{(subtract 100 from both sides)}$$

$$Q = \frac{P - 100}{-4} \qquad \text{(divide both sides by } -4\text{)}$$

Notice that

$$\frac{P - 100}{-4} = \frac{P}{-4} - \frac{100}{-4}$$

$$= -\tfrac{1}{4}P + 25$$

so the rearranged formula simplifies to

$$Q = -\tfrac{1}{4}P + 25$$

If we now wish to find Q when $P = 40$, we immediately get

$$Q = -\tfrac{1}{4} \times 40 + 25$$

$$= -10 + 25$$

$$= 15$$

The important thing to notice about the algebra is that the individual steps are identical to those used previously for solving the equation

$$-4Q + 100 = 40$$

i.e. the operations are again

'subtract 100 from both sides'

followed by

'divide both sides by -4'

Practice Problem

1. **(a)** Solve the equation

    $$\tfrac{1}{2}Q + 13 = 17$$

    State clearly exactly what operation you have performed to both sides at each stage of your solution.

    (b) By performing the same operations as part (a), rearrange the formula

    $$\tfrac{1}{2}Q + 13 = P$$

    into the form

    $$Q = \text{an expression involving } P$$

    (c) By substituting $P = 17$ into the formula derived in part (b), check that this agrees with your answer to part (a).

In general, there are two issues concerning formula transposition. First, we need to decide what to do to both sides of the given formula and the order in which they should be performed. Secondly, we need to carry out these steps accurately. The first of these is often the more difficult. However, there is a logical strategy that can be used to help. To illustrate this, consider the task of making Q the subject of

$$P = \tfrac{1}{3}Q + 5$$

that is, of rearranging this formula into the form

$$Q = \text{an expression involving } P$$

Imagine starting with a value of Q and using a calculator to work out P from

$$P = \tfrac{1}{3}Q + 5$$

The diagram that follows shows that two operations are required and indicates the order in which they must be done. This diagram is called a **flow chart**.

To go backwards from P to Q we need to undo these operations. Now the reverse of 'divide by 3' is 'multiply by 3' and the reverse of 'add 5' is 'subtract 5', so the operations needed to transpose the formula are as follows:

This diagram is called a **reverse flow chart**. The process is similar to that of unwrapping a parcel (or peeling an onion); you start by unwrapping the outer layer first and work inwards. If we now actually perform these steps in the order specified by the reverse flow chart, we get

$$
\begin{aligned}
\tfrac{1}{3}Q + 5 &= P \\
\tfrac{1}{3}Q &= P - 5 &\text{(subtract 5 from both sides)} \\
Q &= 3(P - 5) &\text{(multiply both sides by 3)}
\end{aligned}
$$

The rearranged formula can be simplified by multiplying out the brackets to give

$$Q = 3P - 15$$

Incidentally, if you prefer, you can actually use the reverse flow chart itself to perform the algebra for you. All you have to do is to pass the letter P through the reverse flow chart. Working from right to left gives

Notice that taking P as the input to the box 'subtract 5' gives the output $P - 5$, and if the whole of this is taken as the input to the box 'multiply by 3', the final output is the answer, $3(P - 5)$. Hence

$$Q = 3(P - 5)$$

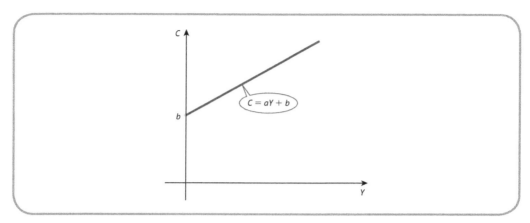

Figure 1.13

The relation

$$Y = C + S$$

enables the precise form of the savings function to be determined from any given consumption function.

To be specific, suppose that the consumption function is given by

$$C = 0.6Y + 10$$

The graph is sketched in Figure 1.14 using the fact that it passes through (0, 10) and (40, 34).

To find the savings function we use the relation

$$Y = C + S$$

which gives

$$
\begin{aligned}
S &= Y - C. && \text{(subtract C from both sides)} \\
&= Y - (0.6Y + 10) && \text{(substitute C)} \\
&= Y - 0.6Y - 10 && \text{(multiply out the brackets)} \\
&= 0.4Y - 10 && \text{(collect terms)}
\end{aligned}
$$

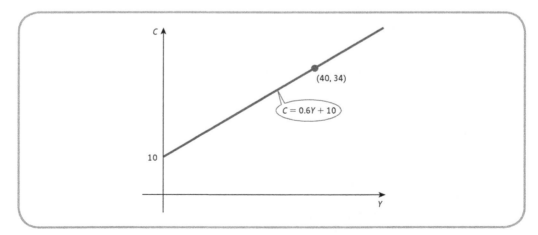

Figure 1.14

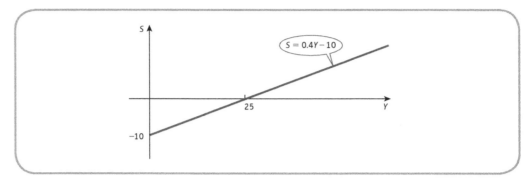

Figure 1.15

The savings function is also linear. Its graph has intercept -10 and slope 0.4. This is sketched in Figure 1.15 using the fact that it passes through $(0, -10)$ and $(25, 0)$.

Practice Problem

1. Determine the savings function that corresponds to the consumption function

   $$C = 0.8Y + 25$$

For the general consumption function

$$C = aY + b$$

we have

$$
\begin{aligned}
S &= Y - C \\
&= Y - (aY + b) \quad \text{(substitute } C) \\
&= Y - aY - b \quad \text{(multiply out the brackets)} \\
&= (1 - a)Y - b \quad \text{(take out a common factor of } Y)
\end{aligned}
$$

The slope of the savings function is called the **marginal propensity to save** (MPS) and is given by $1 - a$: that is,

$$\text{MPS} = 1 - a = 1 - \text{MPC}$$

Moreover, since $a < 1$, we see that the slope, $1 - a$, is positive. Figure 1.16 shows the graph of this savings function. One interesting feature, which contrasts with other economic functions considered so far, is that it is allowed to take negative values. In particular, note that **autonomous savings** (that is, the value of S when $Y = 0$) are equal to $-b$, which is negative because $b > 0$. This is to be expected because whenever consumption exceeds income, households must finance the excess expenditure by withdrawing savings.

Advice

The result, MPC + MPS = 1, is always true, even if the consumption function is non-linear. A proof of this generalisation can be found in Section 1.19.3.

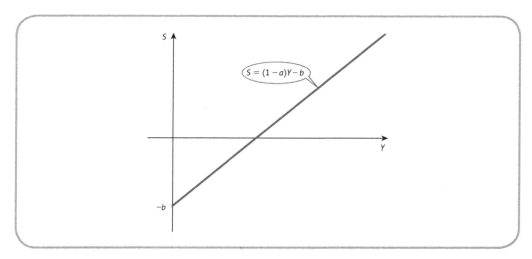

Figure 1.16

The simplest model of the national economy is illustrated in Figure 1.17, which shows the circular flow of income and expenditure. This is fairly crude, since it fails to take into account government activity or foreign trade. In this diagram, **investment**, I, is an injection into the circular flow in the form of spending on capital goods.

Let us examine this more closely and represent the diagrammatic information in symbols. Consider first the box labelled 'Households'. The flow of money entering this box is Y and the flow leaving it is $C + S$. Hence we have the familiar relation

$$Y = C + S$$

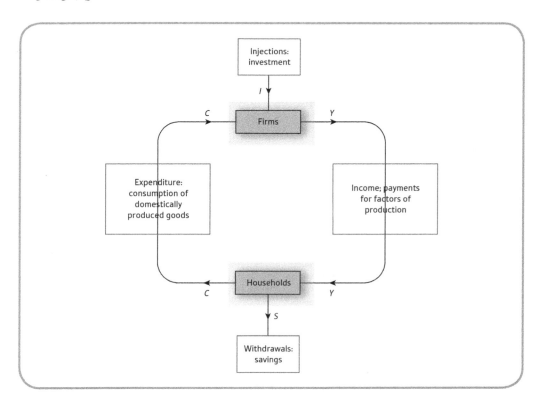

Figure 1.17

For the box labelled 'Firms' the flow entering it is $C + I$ and the flow leaving it is Y, so

$Y = C + I$

Suppose that the level of investment that firms plan to inject into the economy is known to be some fixed value, I^*. If the economy is in equilibrium, the flow of income and expenditure balance so that

$Y = C + I^*$

From the assumption that the consumption function is

$C = aY + b$

for given values of a and b, these two equations represent a pair of simultaneous equations for the two unknowns Y and C. In these circumstances C and Y can be regarded as endogenous variables, since their precise values are determined within the model, whereas I^* is fixed outside the model and is exogenous.

Example

Find the equilibrium level of income and consumption if the consumption function is

$C = 0.6Y + 10$

and planned investment $I = 12$.

Solution

We know that

$Y = C + I$	(from theory)
$C = 0.6Y + 10$	(given in problem)
$I = 12$	(given in problem)

If the value of I is substituted into the first equation, then

$Y = C + 12$

The expression for C can also be substituted to give

$Y = 0.6Y + 10 + 12$

$Y = 0.6Y + 22$

$0.4Y = 22$ (subtract $0.6Y$ from both sides)

$Y = 55$ (divide both sides by 0.4)

The corresponding value of C can be deduced by putting this level of income into the consumption function to get

$C = 0.6(55) + 10 = 43$

The equilibrium income can also be found graphically by plotting expenditure against income. In this example the aggregate expenditure, $C + I$, is given by $0.6Y + 22$. This is sketched in Figure 1.18 using the fact that it passes through $(0, 22)$ and $(80, 70)$. Also sketched is the '45° line', so called because it makes an angle of 45° with the horizontal. This line passes through the points $(0, 0)$, $(1, 1)$, . . . , $(50, 50)$ and so on. In other words, at any point on this line expenditure and income are in balance. The equilibrium income can therefore be found by inspecting the point of intersection of this line and the aggregate expenditure line, $C + I$. From Figure 1.18 this occurs when $Y = 55$, which is in agreement with the calculated value.

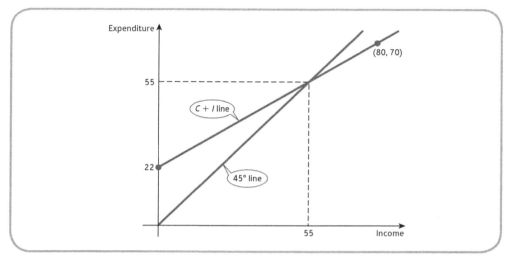

Figure 1.18

Practice Problem

2. Find the equilibrium level of income if the consumption function is

$$C = 0.8Y + 25$$

and planned investment $I = 17$. Calculate the new equilibrium income if planned investment rises by 1 unit.

To make the model more realistic, let us now include **government expenditure**, G, and **taxation**, T, in the model. The injections box in Figure 1.17 now includes government expenditure in addition to investment, so

$$Y = C + I + G$$

We assume that planned government expenditure and planned investment are autonomous with fixed values G^* and I^*, respectively, so that in equilibrium

$$Y = C + I^* + G^*$$

The withdrawals box in Figure 1.17 now includes taxation. This means that the income that households have to spend on consumer goods is no longer Y but rather $Y - T$ (income less tax), which is called **disposable income**, Y_d. Hence

$$C = aY_d + b$$

with

$$Y_d = Y - T$$

In practice, the tax will either be autonomous ($T = T^*$ for some lump sum T^*) or be a proportion of national income ($T = tY$ for some proportion t), or a combination of both ($T = tY + T^*$).

Example

Given that

$$G = 20$$
$$I = 35$$
$$C = 0.9Y_d + 70$$
$$T = 0.2Y + 25$$

calculate the equilibrium level of national income.

Solution

At first sight this problem looks rather forbidding, particularly since there are so many variables. However, all we have to do is to write down the relevant equations and to substitute systematically one equation into another until only Y is left.

We know that

$Y = C + I + G$	(from theory)	(1)
$G = 20$	(given in problem)	(2)
$I = 35$	(given in problem)	(3)
$C = 0.9Y_d + 70$	(given in problem)	(4)
$T = 0.2Y + 25$	(given in problem)	(5)
$Y_d = Y - T$	(from theory)	(6)

This represents a system of six equations in six unknowns. The obvious thing to do is to put the fixed values of G and I into equation (1) to get

$$Y = C + 35 + 20 = C + 55 \qquad (7)$$

This has at least removed G and I, so there are only three more variables (C, Y_d and T) left to eliminate. We can remove T by substituting equation (5) into (6) to get

$$Y_d = Y - (0.2Y + 25)$$
$$= Y - 0.2Y - 25$$
$$= 0.8Y - 25 \qquad (8)$$

and then remove Y_d by substituting equation (8) into (4) to get

$$C = 0.9(0.8Y - 25) + 70$$
$$= 0.72Y - 22.5 + 70$$
$$= 0.72Y + 47.5 \qquad (9)$$

We can eliminate C by substituting equation (9) into (7) to get

$Y = C + 55$

$\quad = 0.72Y + 47.5 + 55$

$\quad = 0.72Y + 102.5$

Finally, solving for Y gives

$0.28Y = 102.5$ (subtract $0.72Y$ from both sides)

$\quad\quad Y = 366$ (divide both sides by 0.28)

Practice Problem

3. Given that

$G = 40$

$I = 55$

$C = 0.8Y_d + 25$

$T = 0.1Y + 10$

calculate the equilibrium level of national income.

To conclude this section we return to the simple two-sector model:

$Y = C + I$

$C = aY + b$

Previously, the investment, I, was taken to be constant. It is more realistic to assume that planned investment depends on the rate of interest, r. As the interest rate rises, so investment falls and we have a relationship

$I = cr + d$

where $c < 0$ and $d > 0$. Unfortunately, this model consists of three equations in the four unknowns Y, C, I and r, so we cannot expect it to determine national income uniquely. The best we can do is to eliminate C and I, say, and to set up an equation relating Y and r. This is most easily understood by an example. Suppose that

$C = 0.8Y + 100$

$I = -20r + 1000$

We know that the commodity market is in equilibrium when

$Y = C + I$

Substitution of the given expressions for C and I into this equation gives

$Y = (0.8Y + 100) + (-20r + 1000)$

$\quad = 0.8Y - 20r + 1100$

which rearranges as

$$0.2Y + 20r = 1100$$

This equation, relating national income, Y, and interest rate, r, is called the IS schedule.

We obviously need some additional information before we can pin down the values of Y and r. This can be done by investigating the equilibrium of the money market. The money market is said to be in equilibrium when the supply of money, M_S, matches the demand for money, M_D: that is, when

$$M_S = M_D$$

There are many ways of measuring the money supply. In simple terms it can be thought of as consisting of the notes and coins in circulation, together with money held in bank deposits. The level of M_S is assumed to be controlled by the central bank and is taken to be autonomous, so that

$$M_S = M_S^*$$

for some fixed value M_S^*.

The demand for money comes from three sources: transactions, precautions and speculations. The transactions demand is used for the daily exchange of goods and services, whereas the precautionary demand is used to fund any emergencies requiring unforeseen expenditure. Both are assumed to be proportional to national income. Consequently, we lump these together and write

$$L_1 = k_1 Y$$

where L_1 denotes the aggregate transaction–precautionary demand and k_1 is a positive constant. The speculative demand for money is used as a reserve fund in case individuals or firms decide to invest in alternative assets such as government bonds. As interest rates rise, speculative demand falls. We model this by writing

$$L_2 = k_2 r + k_3$$

where L_2 denotes speculative demand, k_2 is a negative constant and k_3 is a positive constant. The total demand, M_D, is the sum of the transaction–precautionary demand and speculative demand: that is,

$$M_D = L_1 + L_2$$
$$= k_1 Y + k_2 r + k_3$$

If the money market is in equilibrium, then

$$M_S = M_D$$

that is,

$$M_S^* = k_1 Y + k_2 r + k_3$$

This equation, relating national income, Y, and interest rate, r, is called the LM schedule. If we assume that equilibrium exists in both the commodity and money markets, then the IS and LM schedules provide a system of two equations in two unknowns, Y and r. These can easily be solved either by elimination or by graphical methods.

(a) autonomous consumption;

(b) marginal propensity to consume.

Transpose this formula to express Y in terms of C and hence find the value of Y when $C = 110$.

4. Write down expressions for the savings function given that the consumption function is

    (a) $C = 0.9Y + 72$ **(b)** $C = 0.8Y + 100$

5. For a closed economy with no government intervention, the consumption function is

    $$C = 0.6Y + 30$$

    and planned investment is

    $$I = 100$$

    Calculate the equilibrium level of

    (a) national income;

    (b) consumption;

    (c) savings.

6. A consumption function is given by $C = aY + b$.
    It is known that when $Y = 10$, the value of C is 28, and that when $Y = 30$, the value of C is 44.
    By solving a pair of simultaneous equations, find the values of a and b, and deduce that the corresponding savings function is given by

    $$S = 0.2Y - 20$$

    Determine the equilibrium level of income when planned investment $I = 13$.

7. Given that

    $$G = 50$$
    $$I = 40$$
    $$C = 0.75Y_d + 45$$
    $$T = 0.2Y + 80$$

    calculate the equilibrium level of national income.

Exercise 1.6*

1. Write down an expression for the savings function, simplified as far as possible, given that the consumption function is

    (a) $C = 0.7Y + 30$ **(b)** $C = \dfrac{Y^2 + 500}{Y + 10}$

2. If

$$C = aY + b$$
$$Y = C + I$$
$$I = I^*$$

show that

$$Y = \frac{b + I^*}{1 - a}$$

and obtain a similar expression for C in terms of a, b and I^*.

3. Transpose the formula

$$Y = \frac{b + I^*}{1 - a}$$

to express a in terms of Y, b and I^*.

4. An open economy is in equilibrium when

$$Y = C + I + G + X - M$$

where

Y = national income
C = consumption
I = investment
G = government expenditure
X = exports
M = imports

Determine the equilibrium level of income given that

$C = 0.8Y + 80$
$I = 70$
$G = 130$
$X = 100$
$M = 0.2Y + 50$

5. Given that

consumption,	$C = 0.8Y + 60$
investment,	$I = -30r + 740$
money supply,	$M_S = 4000$
transaction–precautionary demand for money,	$L_1 = 0.15Y$
speculative demand for money,	$L_2 = -20r + 3825$

determine the values of national income, Y, and interest rate, r, on the assumption that both the commodity and the money markets are in equilibrium.

6. Consider the national income model

$$Y = C + I$$
$$C = aY_d + 50$$
$$I = 24$$
$$Y_d = Y - T$$
$$T = 20$$

Show that the equilibrium level of national income is given by

$$Y = \frac{74 - 20a}{1 - a}$$

Transpose this equation to express a in terms of Y.

Hence, or otherwise, find the value of a for which $Y = 155$ and find the value of C.

7. Consider the national income model

$$Y = C + I^* + G^*$$
$$C = a(Y - T), \quad 0 < a < 1$$
$$T = tY, \quad 0 < t < 1$$

Show that

$$Y = \frac{I^* + G^*}{1 + a(t - 1)}$$

and hence state what happens to Y when

(a) G^* increases   **(b)** t increases

SECTION 1.7
Quadratic functions

Objectives

At the end of this section you should be able to:

- Solve a quadratic equation using 'the formula'.
- Solve a quadratic equation given its factorisation.
- Sketch the graph of a quadratic function using a table of function values.
- Sketch the graph of a quadratic function by finding the coordinates of the intercepts.
- Solve quadratic inequalities using graphs.
- Solve inequalities using sign diagrams.
- Determine equilibrium price and quantity given a pair of quadratic demand and supply functions.

Section 1.1 considered the topic of linear mathematics. In particular, we described how to sketch the graph of a linear function and how to solve a linear equation (or system of simultaneous linear equations). It was also pointed out that not all economic functions are of this simple form. In assuming that the demand and supply graphs are straight lines, we are certainly making the mathematical analysis easy, but we may well be sacrificing realism. It may be that the demand and supply graphs are curved and, in these circumstances, it is essential to model them using more complicated functions. The simplest non-linear function is known as a **quadratic function** and takes the form

$$f(x) = ax^2 + bx + c$$

for some parameters a, b and c. (In fact, even if the demand function is linear, functions derived from it, such as total revenue and profit, turn out to be quadratic. We investigate these functions in the next section.) For the moment we concentrate on the mathematics of quadratics and show how to sketch graphs of quadratic functions and how to solve quadratic equations.

Consider the elementary equation

$$x^2 - 9 = 0 \qquad \text{(x^2 is an abbreviation for $x \times x$)}$$

It is easy to see that the expression on the left-hand side is a special case of the above with $a = 1$, $b = 0$ and $c = -9$. To solve this equation, we add 9 to both sides to get

$$x^2 = 9$$

so we need to find a number, x, which when multiplied by itself produces the value 9. A moment's thought should convince you that there are exactly two numbers that work, namely 3 and -3, because

$$3 \times 3 = 9 \quad \text{and} \quad (-3) \times (-3) = 9$$

These two solutions are called the **square roots** of 9. The symbol $\sqrt{}$ is reserved for the positive square root, so in this notation the solutions are $\sqrt{9}$ and $-\sqrt{9}$. These are usually combined and written as $\pm\sqrt{9}$. The equation

$$x^2 - 9 = 0$$

is trivial to solve because the number 9 has obvious square roots. In general, it is necessary to use a calculator to evaluate square roots. For example, the equation

$$x^2 - 2 = 0$$

can be written as

$$x^2 = 2$$

and so has solutions $x = \pm\sqrt{2}$. My calculator gives 1.414 213 56 (correct to eight decimal places) for the square root of 2, so the above equation has solutions

1.414 213 56   and $-1.414\ 213\ 56$

Example

Solve the following quadratic equations:

(a) $5x^2 - 80 = 0$ **(b)** $x^2 + 64 = 0$ **(c)** $(x + 4)^2 = 81$

Solution

(a) $5x^2 - 80 = 0$

$$5x^2 = 80 \quad \text{(add 80 to both sides)}$$

$$x^2 = 16 \quad \text{(divide both sides by 5)}$$

$$x = \pm 4 \quad \text{(square root both sides)}$$

(b) $x^2 + 64 = 0$

$$x^2 = -64 \quad \text{(subtract 64 from both sides)}$$

This equation does not have a solution because you cannot square a real number and get a negative answer.

(c) $(x + 4)^2 = 81$

$$x + 4 = \pm 9 \quad \text{(square root both sides)}$$

The two solutions are obtained by taking the $+$ and $-$ signs separately. Taking the $+$ sign,

$$x + 4 = 9 \quad \text{so} \quad x = 9 - 4 = 5$$

Taking the $-$ sign,

$$x + 4 = -9 \quad \text{so} \quad x = -9 - 4 = -13$$

The two solutions are 5 and -13.

Solution

The graph of the function $f(x) = -x^2 + 8x - 12$ has already been sketched in Figure 1.23.
The parabola lies above the x axis (that is, the line $y = 0$) between 2 and 6 and is below the x axis outside these values.

(a) The quadratic function takes positive values when the graph is above the x axis, so the inequality has the solution $2 < x < 6$. The values of 2 and 6 must be excluded from the solution since we require the quadratic to be strictly greater than zero.

(b) The graph is on or below the x axis at or to the left of 2, and at or to the right of 6, so the complete solution is $x \leq 2$ and $x \geq 6$.

Practice Problem

5. Use your answers to Practice Problem 4 to write down the solution to each of the following quadratic inequalities:

(a) $2x^2 - 11x - 6 \leq 0$ **(b)** $x^2 - 6x + 9 > 0$

If the quadratic is in factorised form, an alternative method can be used to solve the associated inequality. This is based on a sign diagram. It avoids the need to draw a graph and the method has the added advantage that it can be used to solve other inequalities. We illustrate the technique in the following example.

Example

Use a sign diagram to solve the following inequalities:

(a) $(x - 2)(x + 3) \geq 0$ **(b)** $\dfrac{x}{x + 2} < 0$

Solution

(a) We know that the factor $x - 2$ is zero at $x = 2$. If x is smaller than 2, the factor is negative (for example, when $x = 1$, the factor takes the value $-1 < 0$), and when x is bigger than 2, the factor is positive (for example, when $x = 4$, the factor takes the value $2 > 0$). These results are illustrated on the number line:

The second factor, $x + 3$, takes the value zero at $x = -3$, is negative to the left of -3 and is positive to the right of -3. This is illustrated in the number line diagram:

The expression $(x - 2)(x + 3)$ is the product of the two factors. To the left of -3 the number lines show that both factors are negative, so their product is positive. Between -3 and 2 one factor is negative and the other positive, so their product is negative. Of course, if one factor is zero, the product is automatically zero, irrespective of the sign of the second factor. The complete sign diagram for the product is shown below.

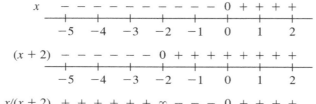

$(x - 2)(x + 3)$ + + + + 0 – – – – – – – – – 0 + + + +
-5 -4 -3 -2 -1 0 1 2 3 4

The diagram shows immediately that the inequality $(x - 2)(x + 3) \geq 0$ is satisfied by $x \leq -3, x \geq 2$.

(b) The factor $(x + 2)$ is zero at $x = -2$, negative to the left of $x = -2$, and positive to the right of this. The factor x is obviously zero at $x = 0$, negative to the left of $x = 0$, and positive to the right of this. The complete sign diagram is shown below:

x – – – – – – – – – – – 0 + + + +
-5 -4 -3 -2 -1 0 1 2

$(x + 2)$ – – – – – – – 0 + + + + + + + +
-5 -4 -3 -2 -1 0 1 2

$x/(x + 2)$ + + + + + + ∞ – – – 0 + + + +
-5 -4 -3 -2 -1 0 1 2

The rules for dividing negative numbers are the same as those for multiplying, so the diagram is completed in the same way as before. The only exception occurs at $x = -2$ because we cannot divide by zero. This is indicated on the diagram by putting the symbol ∞ (infinity) at this position on the line. This diagram shows that the inequality

$$\frac{x}{x + 2} < 0 \text{ is satisfied by } -2 < x < 0.$$

Practice Problem

6. Use a sign diagram to solve the following inequalities:

(a) $(x - 1)(x - 4) \leq 0$ (b) $\dfrac{x - 1}{x + 2} \geq 0$

We conclude this section by solving a particular problem in microeconomics. In Section 1.5 the concept of market equilibrium was introduced, and in each of the problems the supply and demand functions were always given to be linear. The following example shows this to be an unnecessary restriction and indicates that it is almost as easy to manipulate quadratic supply and demand functions.

Example

Given the supply and demand functions

$$P = Q_S^2 + 14Q_S + 22$$
$$P = -Q_D^2 - 10Q_D + 150$$

calculate the equilibrium price and quantity.

Solution

In equilibrium, $Q_S = Q_D$, so if we denote this equilibrium quantity by Q, the supply and demand functions become

$$P = Q^2 + 14Q + 22$$
$$P = -Q^2 - 10Q + 150$$

Hence

$$Q^2 + 14Q + 22 = -Q^2 - 10Q + 150$$

since both sides are equal to P. Collecting like terms gives

$$2Q^2 + 24Q - 128 = 0$$

which is just a quadratic equation in the variable Q. Before using the formula to solve this it is a good idea to divide both sides by 2 to avoid large numbers. This gives

$$Q^2 + 12Q - 64 = 0$$

and so

$$Q = \frac{-12 \pm \sqrt{((12^2) - 4(1)(-64))}}{2(1)}$$
$$= \frac{-12 \pm \sqrt{(400)}}{2}$$
$$= \frac{-12 \pm 20}{2}$$

The quadratic equation has solutions $Q = -16$ and $Q = 4$. Now, the solution $Q = -16$ can obviously be ignored because a negative quantity does not make sense. The equilibrium quantity is therefore 4. The equilibrium price can be calculated by substituting this value into either the original supply or demand equation.

From the supply equation,

$$P = 4^2 + 14(4) + 22 = 94$$

As a check, the demand equation gives

$$P = -(4)^2 - 10(4) + 150 = 94 \quad ✓$$

You might be puzzled by the fact that we actually obtain two possible solutions, one of which does not make economic sense. The supply and demand curves are sketched in Figure 1.24. This shows that there are indeed two points of intersection, confirming the mathematical solution. However, in economics the quantity and price are both positive, so the functions are defined only in the top right-hand (that is, positive) quadrant. In this region there is just one point of intersection, at (4, 94).

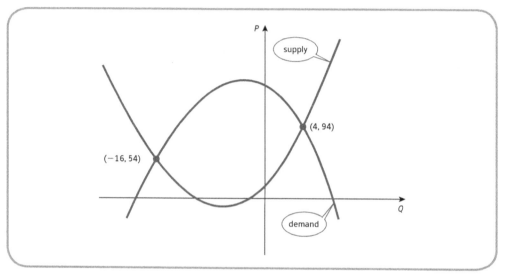

Figure 1.24

Practice Problem

7. Given the supply and demand functions

$$P = 2Q_S^2 + 10Q_S + 10$$
$$P = -Q_D^2 - 5Q_D + 52$$

calculate the equilibrium price and quantity.

Key Terms

Discriminant   The number $b^2 - 4ac$, which is used to indicate the number of solutions of the quadratic equation $ax^2 + bx + c = 0$.

Parabola   The shape of the graph of a quadratic function.

Quadratic function   A function of the form $f(x) = ax^2 + bx + c$ where $a \neq 0$.

Square root   A number that when multiplied by itself equals a given number; the solutions of the equation $x^2 = c$ which are written $\pm\sqrt{c}$.

U-shaped curve   A term used by economists to describe a curve, such as a parabola, which bends upwards, like the letter U.

Exercise 1.7

1. Solve the following quadratic equations:

   (a) $x^2 = 81$ **(b)** $x^2 = 36$ **(c)** $2x^2 = 8$

   (d) $(x - 1)^2 = 9$ **(e)** $(x + 5)^2 = 16$

2. Write down the solutions of the following equations:

   (a) $(x - 1)(x + 3) = 0$ **(b)** $(2x - 1)(x + 10) = 0$ **(c)** $x(x + 5) = 0$

   (d) $(3x + 5)(4x - 9) = 0$ **(e)** $(5 - 4x)(x - 5) = 0$

3. Use 'the formula' to solve the following quadratic equations. (Round your answers to two decimal places.)

   (a) $x^2 - 5x + 2 = 0$ **(b)** $2x^2 + 5x + 1 = 0$ **(c)** $-3x^2 + 7x + 2 = 0$

   (d) $x^2 - 3x - 1 = 0$ **(e)** $2x^2 + 8x + 8 = 0$ **(f)** $x^2 - 6x + 10 = 0$

4. Solve the equation $f(x) = 0$ for each of the following quadratic functions:

   (a) $f(x) = x^2 - 16$ **(b)** $f(x) = x(100 - x)$ **(c)** $f(x) = -x^2 + 22x - 85$

   (d) $f(x) = x^2 - 18x + 81$ **(e)** $f(x) = 2x^2 + 4x + 3$

5. Sketch the graphs of the quadratic functions given in Question 4.

6. Use the results of Question 5 to solve each of the following inequalities:

   (a) $x^2 - 16 \geq 0$ **(b)** $x(100 - x) > 0$ **(c)** $-x^2 + 22x - 85 \geq 0$

   (d) $x^2 - 18x + 81 \leq 0$ **(e)** $2x^2 + 4x + 3 > 0$

7. The production levels of coffee in Mexico, Q (in suitable units) depends on the average summer temperature, T (in °C).

   A statistical model of recent data shows that $Q = -0.046T^2 + 2.3T + 27.6$.

   (a) Complete the table of values and draw a graph of Q against T in the range, $23 \leq T \leq 30$.

T	23	24	25	26	27	28	29	30
Q								

   (b) Average summer temperatures over the last few decades have been about 25°C. However, some climate change models predict that this could rise by several degrees over the next 50 years. Use your graph to comment on the likely impact that this may have on coffee growers in Mexico.

8. Use a sign diagram to solve the following inequalities:

   (a) $x(x - 3) > 0$ **(b)** $(x - 1)(x + 1) \geq 0$ **(c)** $\dfrac{x + 4}{x - 2} < 0$

9. Given the quadratic supply and demand functions

   $$P = Q_S^2 + 2Q_S + 12$$
   $$P = -Q_D^2 - 4Q_D + 68$$

   determine the equilibrium price and quantity.

10. Given the supply and demand functions

$$P = Q_S^2 + 2Q_S + 7$$
$$P = -Q_D + 25$$

   determine the equilibrium price and quantity.

11. A clothing supplier sells T-shirts to retailers for $7 each. If a store agrees to buy more than 30, the supplier is willing to reduce the unit price by 3 cents for each shirt bought above 30, with a maximum single order of 100 shirts.

   (a) How much does an order of 40 shirts cost?

   (b) If the total cost of an order is $504.25, how many T-shirts did the store buy altogether?

Exercise 1.7*

1. Solve the following quadratic equations:

   (a) $x^2 = 169$ (b) $(x - 5)^2 = 64$ (c) $(2x - 7)^2 = 121$

2. Find the solutions (in terms of d) of the quadratic equation

   $$x^2 + 6dx - 7d^2 = 0$$

3. Write down the solutions of the following equations:

   (a) $(x - 3)(x + 8) = 0$ (b) $(3x - 2)(2x + 9) = 0$ (c) $x(4x - 3) = 0$
   (d) $(6x - 1)^2 = 0$ (e) $(x - 2)(x + 1)(4 - x) = 0$

4. Solve the following quadratic equations, rounding your answers to two decimal places, if necessary:

   (a) $x^2 - 15x + 56 = 0$ (b) $2x^2 - 5x + 1 = 0$ (c) $4x^2 - 36 = 0$
   (d) $x^2 - 14x + 49 = 0$ (e) $3x^2 + 4x + 7 = 0$ (f) $x^2 - 13x + 200 = 16x + 10$

5. Solve the following inequalities:

   (a) $x^2 \geq 64$ (b) $x^2 - 10x + 9 \leq 0$ (c) $2x^2 + 15x + 7 < 0$
   (d) $-3x^2 + 2x + 5 \geq 0$ (e) $x^2 + 2x + 1 \leq 0$

6. One solution of the quadratic equation

   $$x^2 - 8x + c = 0$$

   is known to be $x = 2$. Find the second solution.

7. Find the value of k so that the equation

   $$x^2 - 10x + 2k = 8x - k$$

   has exactly one root.

8. Use a sign diagram to solve the following inequalities:

   (a) $(x + 3)(x - 4) \geq 0$ **(b)** $(2 - x)(x + 1) > 0$ **(c)** $(x - 1)(x - 2)(x - 3) \leq 0$

   (d) $\dfrac{(x - 2)}{(x - 3)(x - 5)} \geq 0$

9. A firm's monthly cost for paying cleaners' wages is \$47 250. Under a new pay deal each cleaner earns \$375 more each month. If the new pay deal goes through, the firm realises that it will need to reduce the number of cleaners by 3 if it is to cover its costs within the existing budget. What is the monthly salary of a cleaner before the pay rise?

10. Given the supply and demand functions

    $$P = Q_S^2 + 10Q_S + 30$$
    $$P = -Q_D^2 - 8Q_D + 200$$

    calculate the equilibrium price, correct to two decimal places.

11. A pottery can make B bowls and P plates in a week according to the relation

    $$2B^2 + 5B + 25P = 525$$

    (a) If it makes five bowls, how many plates can it make in a week?

    (b) What is the maximum number of bowls that it can produce in a week?

12. A city centre tour guide currently charges \$34 for a full day's tour. The average number of customers is 48. Market research suggests that for every \$1 increase in tour price, the guide can expect to lose two customers per tour.

    (a) Show that if the price increase is \$$x$, then the expected revenue from each tour is

    $$-2x^2 - 20x + 1632$$

    (b) The guide needs to ensure that the expected revenue is at least \$1440. By solving a quadratic inequality, find the range of prices that need to be charged.

    (c) What price should be charged to maximise expected revenue?

13. Given the supply and demand functions

    $$Q_S = (P + 8)\sqrt{P + 20}$$
    $$Q_D = \frac{460 - 12P - 3P^2}{\sqrt{P + 20}}$$

    calculate the equilibrium price and quantity.

SECTION 1.8
Indices and logarithms

Objectives

At the end of this section you should be able to:

- Evaluate b^n in the case when n is positive, negative, a whole number or a fraction.
- Simplify algebraic expressions using the rules of indices.
- Investigate the returns to scale of a production function.
- Evaluate logarithms in simple cases.
- Use the rules of logarithms to solve equations in which the unknown occurs as a power.

Advice

This section is quite long, with some important ideas. If you are comfortable using the rules of indices and already know what a logarithm is, you should be able to read through the material in one sitting, concentrating on the applications. However, if your current understanding is hazy (or non-existent), you should consider studying this topic on separate occasions. To help with this, the material in this section has been split into the following convenient sub-sections:

- index notation;
- rules of indices;
- logarithms;
- summary.

1.8.1 Index notation

We have already used b^2 as an abbreviation for $b \times b$. In this section we extend the notation to b^n for any value of n, positive, negative, whole number or fraction. In general, if

$$M = b^n$$

we say that b^n is the **exponential form** of M to base b. The number n is then referred to as the **index, power** or **exponent**. An obvious way of extending

$$b^2 = b \times b$$

to other positive whole number powers, n, is to define

$$b^3 = b \times b \times b$$
$$b^4 = b \times b \times b \times b$$

and, in general,

$$b^n = b \times b \times b \times b \times \ldots \times b$$

a total of n bs multiplied together

To include the case of negative powers, consider the following table of values of 2^n:

2^{-3}	2^{-2}	2^{-1}	2^0	2^1	2^2	2^3	2^4
?	?	?	?	2	4	8	16

To work from left to right along the completed part of the table, all you have to do is to multiply each number by 2. Equivalently, if you work from right to left, you simply divide by 2. It makes sense to continue this pattern beyond $2^1 = 2$. Dividing this by 2 gives

$$2^0 = 2 \div 2 = 1$$

and dividing again by 2 gives

$$2^{-1} = 1 \div 2 = \tfrac{1}{2}$$

and so on. The completed table is then

2^{-3}	2^{-2}	2^{-1}	2^0	2^1	2^2	2^3	2^4
$\frac{1}{8}$	$\frac{1}{4}$	$\frac{1}{2}$	1	2	4	8	16

Notice that

$$2^{-1} = \frac{1}{2} = \frac{1}{2^1}$$

$$2^{-2} = \frac{1}{4} = \frac{1}{2^2}$$

$$2^{-3} = \frac{1}{8} = \frac{1}{2^3}$$

In other words, negative powers are evaluated by taking the reciprocal of the corresponding positive power. Motivated by this particular example, we define

$$b^0 = 1$$

and

$$b^{-n} = \frac{1}{b^n}$$

where n is any positive whole number.

Example

Evaluate

(a) 3^2 (b) 4^3 (c) 7^0 (d) 5^1 (e) 5^{-1}

(f) $(-2)^6$ (g) 3^{-4} (h) $(-2)^{-3}$ (i) $(1.723)^0$

Solution

Using the definitions

$$b^n = b \times b \times b \times \ldots \times b$$

$$b^0 = 1$$

$$b^{-n} = \frac{1}{b^n}$$

(b) To solve

$$5^x = 2(3)^x$$

we take logarithms of both sides to get

$$\log(5^x) = \log(2 \times 3^x)$$

The right-hand side is the logarithm of a product and, according to rule 1, can be written as the sum of the logarithms, so the equation becomes

$$\log(5^x) = \log(2) + \log(3^x)$$

As in part (a), the key step is to use rule 3 to 'bring down the powers'. If rule 3 is applied to both $\log(5^x)$ and $\log(3^x)$, then the equation becomes

$$x \log(5) = \log(2) + x \log(3)$$

This is now the type of equation that we know how to solve. We collect xs on the left-hand side to get

$$x \log(5) - x \log(3) = \log(2)$$

and then pull out a common factor of x to get

$$x[\log(5) - \log(3)] = \log(2)$$

Now, by rule 2, the difference of two logarithms is the same as the logarithm of their quotient, so

$$\log(5) - \log(3) = \log(5 \div 3)$$

Hence the equation becomes

$$x \log\left(\frac{5}{3}\right) = \log(2)$$

so

$$x = \frac{\log(2)}{\log(5/3)}$$

Finally, taking logarithms to base 10 using a calculator gives

$$x = \frac{0.301\ 029\ 996}{0.221\ 848\ 750} = 1.36$$

to two decimal places.

As a check, the original equation

$$5^x = 2(3)^x$$

becomes

$$5^{1.36} = 2(3)^{1.36}$$

that is,

$$8.92 = 8.91 \quad \checkmark$$

Again, the slight discrepancy is due to rounding errors in the value of x.

Practice Problem

7. Solve the following equations for x:

(a) $3^x = 7$ (b) $5(2)^x = 10^x$

Advice

In this section we have met a large number of definitions and rules concerning indices and logarithms. For convenience, we have collected these together in the form of a summary. The facts relating to indices are particularly important, and you should make every effort to memorise these before proceeding with the rest of this text.

1.8.4 Summary

Indices

If n is a positive whole number, then

$$b^n = b \times b \times \ldots \times b$$
$$b^0 = 1$$
$$b^{-n} = 1/b^n$$
$$b^{1/n} = n\text{th root of } b$$

Also, if p and q are whole numbers with $q > 0$, then

$$b^{p/q} = (b^p)^{1/q} = (b^{1/q})^p$$

The four rules of indices are:

Rule 1 $b^m \times b^n = b^{m+n}$

Rule 2 $b^m \div b^n = b^{m-n}$

Rule 3 $(b^m)^n = b^{mn}$

Rule 4 $(ab)^n = a^n b^n$

Logarithms

If $M = b^n$, then $n = \log_b M$. The three rules of logarithms are:

Rule 1 $\log_b(x \times y) = \log_b x + \log_b y$

Rule 2 $\log_b(x \div y) = \log_b x - \log_b y$

Rule 3 $\log_b x^m = m \log_b x$

Exercise 1.8

1. **(1)** Without using your calculator, evaluate

   (a) 8^2 **(b)** 2^1 **(c)** 3^{-1} **(d)** 17^0 **(e)** $1^{1/5}$ **(f)** $36^{1/2}$ **(g)** $8^{2/3}$ **(h)** $49^{-3/2}$

   (2) Confirm your answer to part (1) using a calculator.

2. Use the rules of indices to simplify

   (a) $a^3 \times a^8$ **(b)** $\dfrac{b^7}{b^2}$ **(c)** $(c^2)^3$ **(d)** $\dfrac{x^4 y^5}{x^2 y^3}$ **(e)** $(xy^2)^3$

   (f) $y^3 \div y^7$ **(g)** $(x^{1/2})^8$ **(h)** $f^2 \times f^4 \times f$ **(i)** $\sqrt{(y^6)}$ **(j)** $\dfrac{x^3}{x^{-2}}$

3. Write the following expressions using index notation:

   (a) $\sqrt{x}$ **(b)** $\dfrac{1}{x^2}$ **(c)** $\sqrt[3]{x}$ **(d)** $\dfrac{1}{x}$ **(e)** $\dfrac{1}{\sqrt{x}}$ **(f)** $x\sqrt{x}$

4. For the production function, $Q = 200K^{1/4}L^{2/3}$, find the output when

   (a) $K = 16, L = 27$ **(b)** $K = 10\,000, L = 1000$

5. Which of the following production functions are homogeneous? For those functions which are homogeneous, write down their degrees of homogeneity and comment on their returns to scale.

(a) $Q = 500K^{1/3}L^{1/4}$

(b) $Q = 3LK + L^2$

(c) $Q = L + 5L^2K^3$

6. Write down the values of x which satisfy each of the following equations:

   (a) $5^x = 25$ (b) $3^x = \dfrac{1}{3}$ (c) $2^x = \dfrac{1}{8}$

   (d) $2^x = 64$ (e) $100^x = 10$ (f) $8^x = 1$

7. Write down the value of

   (a) $\log_b b^2$ (b) $\log_b b$ (c) $\log_b 1$ (d) $\log_b \sqrt{b}$ (e) $\log_b(1/b)$

8. Use the rules of logs to express each of the following as a single log:

   (a) $\log_b x + \log_b z$

   (b) $3\log_b x - 2\log_b y$

   (c) $\log_b y - 3\log_b z$

9. Express the following in terms of $\log_b x$ and $\log_b y$:

   (a) $\log_b x^2 y$

   (b) $\log_b \left(\dfrac{x}{y^2} \right)$

   (c) $\log_b x^2 y^7$

10. Solve the following equations for x. Give your answers to two decimal places.

    (a) $5^x = 8$ (b) $10^x = 50$ (c) $1.2^x = 3$ (d) $1000 \times 1.05^x = 1500$

11. (1) State the values of

    (a) $\log_2 32$ (b) $\log_9\left(\dfrac{1}{3}\right)$

    (2) Use the rules of logs to express

    $2\log_b x - 4\log_b y$

    as a single logarithm.

    (3) Use logs to solve the equation

    $10(1.05)^x = 300$

    Give your answer correct to one decimal place.

12. (1) State the values of x that satisfy the following equations:

    (a) $81 = 3^x$ (b) $\dfrac{1}{25} = 5^x$ (c) $16^{1/2} = 2^x$

    (2) Use the rules of indices to simplify:

    (a) $\dfrac{x^6 y^9}{x^3 y^8}$ (b) $(x^3 y)^5$ (c) $\sqrt{\dfrac{x^9 y^4}{x^5}}$

13. The number of complaints, N, received by a small company each month can be modelled by

$$N = 80\log_{10}(7 + 10t)$$

where t denotes the number of months since the company's launch.

(a) Estimate the number of complaints received by the company each month for the first six months of trading.

(b) Plot a graph of N against t and hence comment on how N varies with t.

14. If two firms A and B use the same labour input, L, their output in the short term is given by $Q_A = 108\sqrt{L}$ and $Q_B = 4L^2$, respectively. Find the non-zero value of L which produces the same level of output for these two firms.

Exercise 1.8*

1. **(1)** Evaluate the following without using a calculator:

   (a) $32^{3/5}$ (b) $64^{-5/6}$ (c) $\left(\dfrac{1}{125}\right)^{-4/3}$ (d) $\left(3\dfrac{3}{8}\right)^{2/3}$ (e) $\left(2\dfrac{1}{4}\right)^{-1/2}$

   (2) Confirm your answer to part (1) using a calculator.

2. Use the rules of indices to simplify

   (a) $y^{3/2} \times y^{1/2}$ (b) $\dfrac{x^2 y}{xy^{-1}}$ (c) $(xy^{1/2})^4$

   (d) $(p^2)^{1/3} \div (p^{1/3})^2$ (e) $(24q)^{1/3} \div (3q)^{1/3}$ (f) $(25p^2q^4)^{1/2}$

3. Write the following expressions using index notation:

   (a) $\dfrac{1}{x^7}$ (b) $\sqrt[4]{x}$ (c) $\dfrac{1}{x\sqrt{x}}$ (d) $2x^5\sqrt{x}$ (e) $\dfrac{8}{x(\sqrt[3]{x})}$

4. If $a = \dfrac{2\sqrt{x}}{y^3}$ and $b = 3x^4 y$, simplify $\dfrac{4b}{a^2}$.

5. Show that the production function

   $$Q = A[bK^\alpha + (1 - b)L^\alpha]^{1/\alpha}$$

   is homogeneous and displays constant returns to scale.

6. Solve the following equations:

   (a) $2^{3x} = 4$ (b) $4 \times 2^x = 32$ (c) $8^x = 2 \times \left(\dfrac{1}{2}\right)^x$

7. Use the rules of logs to express each of the following as a single log:

   (a) $\log_b(xy) - \log_b x - \log_b y$

   (b) $3\log_b x - 2\log_b y$

   (c) $\log_b y + 5\log_b x - 2\log_b z$

   (d) $2 + 3\log_b x$

8. Express the following in terms of $\log_b x$, $\log_b y$ and $\log_b z$:

(a) $\log_b(x^2 y^3 z^4)$ (b) $\log_b\left(\dfrac{x^4}{y^2 z^5}\right)$ (c) $\log_b\left(\dfrac{x}{\sqrt{yz}}\right)$

9. If $\log_b 2 = p$, $\log_b 3 = q$ and $\log_b 10 = r$, express the following in terms of p, q and r:

(a) $\log_b\left(\dfrac{1}{3}\right)$ (b) $\log_b 12$ (c) $\log_b 0.000\,3$ (d) $\log_b 600$

10. Solve the following equations. Round your answers to two decimal places.

(a) $10(1.07)^x = 2000$ (b) $10^{x-1} = 3$ (c) $5^{x-2} = 5$ (d) $2(7)^{-x} = 3^x$

11. Solve the inequalities giving the bounds to three decimal places:

(a) $3^{2x+1} \le 7$ (b) $0.8^x < 0.04$

12. Solve the equation

$$\log_{10}(x+2) + \log_{10} x - 1 = \log_{10}\left(\frac{3}{2}\right)$$

13. (1) Define the term *homogeneous* when used to describe a production function $f(K, L)$.

(2) If the production function

$$f(K, L) = 4K^m L^{1/3} + 3K$$

is homogeneous, state the value of m.
Does the function display decreasing, constant or increasing returns to scale?

14. (1) State the values of x that satisfy the following equations:

(a) $4 = 8^x$ (b) $5 = \left(\dfrac{1}{25}\right)^x$

(2) Express y in terms of x:

$$2\log_a x = \log_a 7 + \log_a y$$

15. Show that $2\log_{10} x - \dfrac{1}{2}\log_{10} y - \dfrac{1}{3}\log_{10} 1000$ can be simplified to

$$\log_{10}\left(\sqrt{\frac{x^4}{y}}\right) - 1$$

16. Transpose each of the following production functions for L:

(a) $Q = AK^\alpha L^\beta$ (b) $Q = A[bK^\alpha + (1-b)L^\alpha]^{1/\alpha}$

17. Show that each of these functions is homogeneous and state the degree of homogeneity:

(a) $f(K,L) = \dfrac{K^2 + L^2}{K + L}$

(b) $f(K,L) = KL\log\left(\dfrac{K^2 + L^2}{KL}\right)$

(c) $f(K,L) = A[aK^m + bL^m]^{n/m}$

(d) $f(K,L) = KL^2 g(L/K)$ where g is a general function.

SECTION 1.9

The exponential and natural logarithm functions

Objectives

At the end of this section you should be able to:

- Sketch graphs of general exponential functions.
- Understand how the number e is defined.
- Use the exponential function to model growth and decay.
- Use log graphs to find unknown parameters in simple models.
- Use the natural logarithm function to solve equations.

In the previous section we described how to define numbers of the form b^x, and we discussed the idea of a logarithm, $\log_b x$. It turns out that there is one base (the number e = 2.718 281 . . .) that is particularly important in mathematics. The purpose of this section is to introduce you to this strange number and to consider a few simple applications.

We begin by investigating the graphs of the functions,

$$f(x) = 2^x \quad \text{and} \quad g(x) = 2^{-x}$$

As we pointed out in Section 1.8, a number such as 2^x is said to be in exponential form. The number 2 is called the base and x is called the exponent. Values of this function are easily found either by pressing the power key $\boxed{x^y}$ on a calculator or by using the definition of b^n given in Section 1.8. A selection of these is given in the following table:

x	-3	-2	-1	0	1	2	3	4	5
2^x	0.125	0.25	0.5	1	2	4	8	16	32

A graph of $f(x)$ based on this table is sketched in Figure 1.25. Notice that the graph approaches the x axis for large negative values of x, and it rises rapidly as x increases.

A graph of the negative exponential, $g(x) = 2^{-x}$, shown in Figure 1.26, is based on the following table of values:

x	-5	-4	-3	-2	-1	0	1	2	3
2^{-x}	32	16	8	4	2	1	0.5	0.25	0.125

This function is sketched in Figure 1.26. It is worth noticing that the numbers appearing in the table of 2^{-x} are the same as those of 2^x but arranged in reverse order. Hence the graph of 2^{-x} is obtained by reflecting the graph of 2^x in the y axis.

Figure 1.25 displays the graph of a particular exponential function, 2^x. Quite generally, the graph of any exponential function

$$f(x) = b^x$$

Practice Problem

6. Immediately after the launch of a new product, the monthly sales figures (in thousands) are as follows:

t (months)	1	3	6	12
s (sales)	1.8	2.7	5.0	16.5

(1) Complete the following table of values of ln s:

t	1	3	6	12
ln s	0.59		1.61	

(2) Plot these points on graph paper with the values of ln s on the vertical axis and t on the horizontal axis. Draw a straight line passing close to these points. Write down the value of the vertical intercept and calculate the slope.

(3) Use your answers to part (2) to estimate the values of A and B in the relation $s = Be^{At}$.

(4) Use the exponential model derived in part (3) to estimate the sales when

(a) $t = 9$ **(b)** $t = 60$

Which of these estimates would you expect to be the more reliable? Give a reason for your answer.

Key Terms

Exponential function   The function $f(x) = e^x$; an exponential function in which the base is the number e = 2.718 281. . . .

Limited growth   Used to describe an economic variable which increases over time but which tends to a fixed quantity.

Natural logarithm   A logarithm to base e; if $M = e^n$ then n is the natural logarithm of M and we write, $n = \ln M$.

Unlimited growth   Used to describe an economic variable which increases without bound.

Exercise 1.9

1. The number of items, N, produced each day by an assembly-line worker, t days after an initial training period, is modelled by

$$N = 100 - 100e^{-0.4t}$$

(1) Calculate the number of items produced daily

(a) 1 day after the training period;

(b) 2 days after the training period;

(c) 10 days after the training period.

(2) What is the worker's daily production in the long run?

(3) Sketch a graph of N against t and explain why the general shape might have been expected.

2. Use the rules of logs to expand each of the following:

(a) $\ln xy$ (b) $\ln xy^4$ (c) $\ln (xy)^2$

(d) $\ln \dfrac{x^5}{y^7}$ (e) $\ln \sqrt{\dfrac{x}{y}}$ (f) $\ln \sqrt{\dfrac{xy^3}{z}}$

3. Use the rules of logs to express each of the following as a single logarithm:

(a) $\ln x + 2 \ln x$ (b) $4 \ln x - 3 \ln y + 5 \ln z$

4. Solve each of the following equations. (Round your answer to two decimal places.)

(a) $e^x = 5.9$ (b) $e^x = 0.45$ (c) $e^x = -2$

(d) $e^{3x} = 13.68$ (e) $e^{-5x} = 0.34$ (f) $4e^{2x} = 7.98$

5. The value of a second-hand car reduces exponentially with age, so that its value y after t years can be modelled by the formula

$$y = Ae^{-ax}$$

If the car was worth $50 000 when new and $38 000 after two years, find the values of A and a, correct to three decimal places.

Use this model to predict the value of the car

(a) when the car is five years old;

(b) in the long run.

6. Solve the following equations:

(a) $\ln x = 5$ (b) $\ln x = 0$

7. Future sales of two products A and B are given by $S_A = 5e^{0.01t}$ and $S_B = 2e^{0.02t}$. Find the time, t, when sales of the two products are the same.

8. Show that the following production function is homogeneous and state whether it displays decreasing, increasing or constant returns to scale.

$$f(K,L) = (K^2 + L^2)e^{K/L}$$

Exercise 1.9*

1. The value (in cents) of shares, t years after their flotation on the stock market, is modelled by

$$V = 6e^{0.8t}$$

Find the increase in the value of these shares, four years and two months later. Give your answer to the nearest cent.

2. Solve each of the following equations, correct to two decimal places:

(a) $6e^{-2x} = 0.62$ (b) $5 \ln(4x) = 9.84$ (c) $3 \ln(5x) - 2 \ln(x) = 7$

3. A team of financial advisers guiding the launch of a national newspaper has modelled the future circulation of the newspaper by the equation

    $$N = c(1 - e^{-kt})$$

    where N is the daily circulation after t days of publication, and c and k are positive constants. Transpose this formula to show that

    $$t = \frac{1}{k} \ln\left(\frac{c}{c - N}\right)$$

    When the paper is launched, audits show that

    $$c = 700\,000 \quad \text{and} \quad k = \frac{1}{30} \ln 2$$

    (a) Calculate the daily circulation after 30 days of publication.

    (b) After how many days will the daily circulation first reach 525 000?

    (c) What advice can you give the newspaper proprietor if it is known that the paper will break even only if the daily circulation exceeds 750 000?

4. A Cobb–Douglas production function is given by

    $$Q = 3L^{1/2}K^{1/3}$$

    Find an expression for $\ln Q$ in terms of $\ln L$ and $\ln K$.
      If a graph were to be sketched of $\ln Q$ against $\ln K$ (for varying values of Q and K but with L fixed), explain briefly why the graph will be a straight line and state its slope and vertical intercept.

5. The following table gives data relating a firm's output, Q, and labour, L:

L	1	2	3	4	5
Q	0.50	0.63	0.72	0.80	0.85

    The firm's short-run production function is believed to be of the form

    $$Q = AL^n$$

    (a) Show that

    $$\ln Q = n \ln L + \ln A$$

    (b) Using the data supplied, copy and complete the following table:

$\ln L$		0.69		1.39	
$\ln Q$	−0.69		−0.33		−0.16

    Plot these points with $\ln L$ on the horizontal axis and $\ln Q$ on the vertical axis. Draw a straight line passing as close as possible to all five points.

    (c) By finding the slope and vertical intercept of the line sketched in part (b), estimate the values of the parameters n and A.

6. (a) Multiply out the brackets

    $$(3y - 2)(y + 5)$$

(b) Solve the equation

$$3e^{2x} + 13e^x = 10$$

Give your answer correct to three decimal places.

7. **(a)** Make y the subject of the equation

$$x = ae^{by}$$

(b) Make x the subject of the equation

$$y = \ln(3 + e^{2x})$$

8. Solve the following equations for x:

(a) $\ln(x - 5) = 0$ **(b)** $\ln(x^2 - x - 1) = 0$ **(c)** $x \ln(\sqrt{x} - 4) = 0$

(d) $e^{5x+1} = 10$ **(e)** $e^{-x^2/2} = 0.25$

9. The demand and supply functions of a good are given by

$$Q_D = Ae^{-k_1 P} \quad \text{and} \quad Q_S = Be^{k_2 P} \text{ respectively}$$

where A, B, k_1 and k_2 are positive constants.

Find the equilibrium price and show that the equilibrium quantity is given by $(A^{k_2}B^{k_1})^{\frac{1}{k_2+k_1}}$.

SECTION 1.10
The derivative of a function

Objectives

At the end of this section you should be able to:

- Find the slope of a straight line given any two points on the line.
- Detect whether a line is uphill, downhill or horizontal using the sign of the slope.
- Recognise the notation $f'(x)$ and dy/dx for the derivative of a function.
- Estimate the derivative of a function by measuring the slope of a tangent.
- Differentiate power functions.

This introductory section is designed to get you started with differential calculus in a fairly painless way. There are really only three things that we are going to do. We discuss the basic idea of something called a derived function, give you two equivalent pieces of notation to describe it, and finally show you how to write down a formula for the derived function in simple cases.

The slope of a straight line was defined to be the change in the value of y brought about by a 1-unit increase in x. In fact, it is not necessary to restrict the change in x to a 1-unit increase. More generally, the **slope**, or **gradient**, of a line is taken to be the change in y divided by the corresponding change in x as you move between any two points on the line. It is customary to denote the change in y by Δy, where Δ is the Greek letter 'delta'. Likewise, the change in x is written Δx. In this notation we have

$$\text{slope} = \frac{\Delta y}{\Delta x}$$

Example

Find the slope of the straight line passing through

(a) A (1, 2) and B (3, 4)   **(b)** A (1, 2) and C (4, 1)   **(c)** A (1, 2) and D (5, 2)

Solution

(a) Points A and B are sketched in Figure 1.30. As we move from A to B, the y coordinate changes from 2 to 4, which is an increase of 2 units, and the x coordinate changes from 1 to 3, which is also an increase of 2 units. Hence

$$\text{slope} = \frac{\Delta y}{\Delta x} = \frac{4 - 2}{3 - 1} = \frac{2}{2} = 1$$

Exercise 1.10*

1. Verify that the points $(0, b)$ and $(1, a + b)$ lie on the line

    $$y = ax + b$$

    Hence show that this line has slope a.

2. Differentiate each of the following functions, expressing your answer in a similar form:

    (a) x^{15} **(b)** $x^4\sqrt{x}$ **(c)** $\sqrt[3]{x}$ **(d)** $\dfrac{1}{\sqrt[4]{x}}$ **(e)** $\dfrac{\sqrt{x}}{x^7}$

3. For each of the graphs

    (a) $y = \sqrt{x}$ **(b)** $y = x\sqrt{x}$ **(c)** $y = \dfrac{1}{\sqrt{x}}$

    A is the point where $x = 4$, and B is the point where $x = 4.1$. In each case find

    (i)   the y coordinates of A and B;

    (ii) the gradient of the chord AB;

    (iii) the value of $\dfrac{dy}{dx}$ at A.

    Compare your answers to parts (ii) and (iii).

4. Find the coordinates of the point(s) at which the curve has the specified gradient.

    (a) $y = x^{2/3}$ gradient $= \dfrac{1}{3}$ **(b)** $y = x^5$, gradient $= 405$

    (c) $y = \dfrac{1}{x^2}$, gradient $= 16$ **(d)** $y = \dfrac{1}{x\sqrt{x}}$, gradient $= -\dfrac{3}{64}$

SECTION 1.11
Rules of differentiation

Objectives

At the end of this section you should be able to:

- Use the constant rule to differentiate a function of the form $cf(x)$.
- Use the sum rule to differentiate a function of the form $f(x) + g(x)$.
- Use the difference rule to differentiate a function of the form $f(x) - g(x)$.
- Evaluate and interpret second-order derivatives.

Advice

In this section we consider three elementary rules of differentiation. Subsequent sections of this chapter describe various applications to economics. However, before you can tackle these successfully, you must have a thorough grasp of the basic techniques involved. The problems in this section are repetitive in nature. This is deliberate. Although the rules themselves are straightforward, it is necessary for you to practise them over and over again before you can become proficient in using them. In fact, mastering the rules of this section is essential for you to proceed further with the rest of the text.

Rule 1 The constant rule

$$\text{If } h(x) = cf(x) \quad \text{then} \quad h'(x) = cf'(x)$$

for any constant c.

This rule tells you how to find the derivative of a constant multiple of a function:

> **differentiate the function and multiply by the constant**

Example

Differentiate

(a) $y = 2x^4$ **(b)** $y = 10x$

Solution

(a) To differentiate $2x^4$ we first differentiate x^4 to get $4x^3$ and then multiply by 2. Hence

$$\text{if } y = 2x^4 \quad \text{then} \quad \frac{dy}{dx} = 2(4x^3) = 8x^3$$

(b) To differentiate $10x$ we first differentiate x to get 1 and then multiply by 10. Hence

$$\text{if } y = 10x \quad \text{then} \quad \frac{dy}{dx} = 10(1) = 10$$

Practice Problem

1. Differentiate

    (a) $y = 4x^3$ **(b)** $y = 2/x$

The constant rule can be used to show that

> constants differentiate to zero

To see this, note that the equation

$y = c$

is the same as

$y = cx^0$

because $x^0 = 1$. By the constant rule we first differentiate x^0 to get $0x^{-1}$ and then multiply by c. Hence

$$\text{if } y = c \quad \text{then} \quad \frac{dy}{dx} = c(0x^{-1}) = 0$$

This result is also apparent from the graph of $y = c$, sketched in Figure 1.39, which is a horizontal line c units away from the x axis. It is an important result and explains why lone constants lurking in mathematical expressions disappear when differentiated.

Rule 2 The sum rule

If $h(x) = f(x) + g(x)$ then $h'(x) = f'(x) + g'(x)$

This rule tells you how to find the derivative of the sum of two functions:

> differentiate each function separately and add

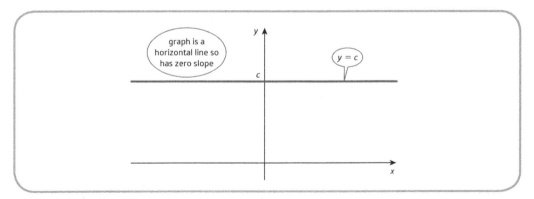

Figure 1.39

Example

Differentiate

(a) $y = x^2 + x^{50}$ **(b)** $y = x^3 + 3$

Solution

(a) To differentiate $x^2 + x^{50}$ we need to differentiate x^2 and x^{50} separately and add. Now

x^2 differentiates to $2x$

and

x^{50} differentiates to $50x^{49}$

so

if $y = x^2 + x^{50}$ then $\dfrac{dy}{dx} = 2x + 50x^{49}$

(b) To differentiate $x^3 + 3$ we need to differentiate x^3 and 3 separately and add. Now

x^3 differentiates to $3x^2$

and

3 differentiates to 0   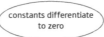 constants differentiate to zero

so

if $y = x^3 + 3$ then $\dfrac{dy}{dx} = 3x^2 + 0 = 3x^2$

Practice Problem

2. Differentiate

(a) $y = x^5 + x$ **(b)** $y = x^2 + 5$

Rule 3 The difference rule

If $h(x) = f(x) - g(x)$ then $h'(x) = f'(x) - g'(x)$

This rule tells you how to find the derivative of the difference of two functions:

differentiate each function separately and subtract

Example

Differentiate

(a) $y = x^5 - x^2$ **(b)** $y = x - \dfrac{1}{x^2}$

Solution

(a) To differentiate $x^5 - x^2$ we need to differentiate x^5 and x^2 separately and subtract. Now

x^5 differentiates to $5x^4$

and

x^2 differentiates to $2x$

so

if $y = x^5 - x^2$ then $\dfrac{dy}{dx} = 5x^4 - 2x$

(b) To differentiate $x - \dfrac{1}{x^2}$ we need to differentiate x and $\dfrac{1}{x^2}$ separately and subtract. Now

x differentiates to 1

and

$\dfrac{1}{x^2}$ differentiates to $-\dfrac{2}{x^3}$ x^{-2} differentiates to $-2x^{-3}$

so

if $y = x - \dfrac{1}{x^2}$ then $\dfrac{dy}{dx} = 1 - \left(-\dfrac{2}{x^3}\right) = 1 + \dfrac{2}{x^3}$

Practice Problem

3. Differentiate

(a) $y = x^2 - x^3$ **(b)** $y = 50 - \dfrac{1}{x^3}$

It is possible to combine these three rules and so to find the derivative of more involved functions, as the following example demonstrates.

Example

Differentiate

(a) $y = 3x^5 + 2x^3$ (b) $y = x^3 + 7x^2 - 2x + 10$ (c) $y = 2\sqrt{x} + \dfrac{3}{x}$

Solution

(a) The sum rule shows that to differentiate $3x^5 + 2x^3$, we need to differentiate $3x^5$ and $2x^3$ separately and add. By the constant rule

$3x^5$ differentiates to $3(5x^4) = 15x^4$

and

$2x^3$ differentiates to $2(3x^2) = 6x^2$

so

if $y = 3x^5 + 2x^3$ then $\dfrac{dy}{dx} = 15x^4 + 6x^2$

With practice you will soon find that you can just write the derivative down in a single line of working by differentiating term by term. For the function

$y = 3x^5 + 2x^3$

we could just write

$$\frac{dy}{dx} = 3(5x^4) + 2(3x^2) = 15x^4 + 6x^2$$

(b) So far we have only considered expressions comprising at most two terms. However, the sum and difference rules still apply to lengthier expressions, so we can differentiate term by term as before. For the function

$y = x^3 + 7x^2 - 2x + 10$

we get

$$\frac{dy}{dx} = 3x^2 + 7(2x) - 2(1) + 0 = 3x^2 + 14x - 2$$

(c) To differentiate

$$y = 2\sqrt{x} + \frac{3}{x}$$

we first rewrite it using the notation of indices as

$y = 2x^{1/2} + 3x^{-1}$

Differentiating term by term then gives

$$\frac{dy}{dx} = 2\left(\frac{1}{2}\right)x^{-1/2} + 3(-1)x^{-2} = x^{-1/2} - 3x^{-2}$$

which can be written in the more familiar form

$$\frac{1}{\sqrt{x}} - \frac{3}{x^2}$$

Practice Problem

4. Differentiate

(a) $y = 9x^5 + 2x^2$

(b) $y = 5x^8 - \dfrac{3}{x}$

(c) $y = x^2 + 6x + 3$

(d) $y = 2x^4 + 12x^3 - 4x^2 + 7x - 400$

Whenever a function is differentiated, the thing that you end up with is itself a function. This suggests the possibility of differentiating a second time to get the 'slope of the slope function'. This is written as

$f''(x)$ ⟨ read '*f* double dashed of *x*' ⟩

or

$\dfrac{d^2y}{dx^2}$ ⟨ read 'dee two *y* by dee *x* squared' ⟩

For example, if

$f(x) = 5x^2 - 7x + 12$

then differentiating once gives

$f'(x) = 10x - 7$

and if we now differentiate $f'(x)$ we get

$f''(x) = 10$

The function $f'(x)$ is called the **first-order derivative** and $f''(x)$ is called the **second-order derivative**.

Example

Evaluate $f''(1)$ where

$$f(x) = x^7 + \frac{1}{x}$$

Solution

To find $f''(1)$ we need to differentiate

$f(x) = x^7 + x^{-1}$

twice and put $x = 1$ into the end result. Differentiating once gives

$f'(x) = 7x^6 + (-1)x^{-2} = 7x^6 - x^{-2}$

and differentiating a second time gives

$f''(x) = 7(6x^5) - (-2)x^{-3} = 42x^5 + 2x^{-3}$

Finally, substituting $x = 1$ into

$$f''(x) = 42x^5 + \frac{2}{x^3}$$

gives

$f''(1) = 42 + 2 = 44$

Practice Problem

5. Evaluate $f''(6)$ where

$$f(x) = 4x^3 - 5x^2$$

It is possible to give a graphical interpretation of the sign of the second-order derivative. Remember that the first-order derivative, $f'(x)$, measures the gradient of a curve. If the derivative of $f'(x)$ is positive (that is, if $f''(x) > 0$) then $f'(x)$ is increasing, so the graph gets steeper as you move from left to right. The curve bends upwards and the function is said to be **convex**. On the other hand, if $f''(x) < 0$, the gradient $f'(x)$ must be decreasing, so the curve bends downwards. The function is said to be **concave**. It is perfectly possible for a curve to be convex for a certain range of values of x and concave for others. This is illustrated in Figure 1.40. For this function, $f''(x) < 0$ to the left of $x = a$, and $f''(x) > 0$ to the right of $x = a$. At $x = a$ itself, the curve changes from bending downwards to bending upwards, and at this point, $f''(a) = 0$.

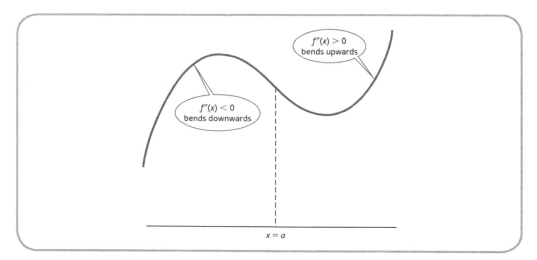

Figure 1.40

The second-order derivative can be used to confirm the convexity of the general quadratic function

$$f(x) = ax^2 + bx + c$$

The first- and second-order derivatives are $f'(x) = 2ax + b$ and $f''(x) = 2a$.

- If $a > 0$, then $f''(x) > 0$, so the parabola is convex.
- If $a < 0$, then $f''(x) < 0$, so the parabola is concave.

Of course, if $a = 0$, then $f(x) = bx + c$, which is the equation of a straight line, so the graph bends neither upwards nor downwards.

Throughout this section the functions have all been of the form $y = f(x)$, where the letters x and y denote the variables involved. In economic functions, different symbols are used. It should be obvious, however, that we can still differentiate such functions by applying the rules of this section. For example, if a supply function is given by

$$Q = P^2 + 3P + 1$$

and we need to find the derivative of Q with respect to P, then we can apply the sum and difference rules to obtain

$$\frac{dQ}{dP} = 2P + 3$$

Key Terms

Concave   Graph bends downwards when $f''(x) < 0$.

Convex   Graph bends upwards when $f''(x) > 0$.

First-order derivative   The rate of change of a function with respect to its independent variable. It is the same as the 'derivative' of a function, $y = f(x)$, and is written as $f'(x)$ or dy/dx.

Second-order derivative   The derivative of the first-order derivative. The expression obtained when the original function, $y = f(x)$, is differentiated twice in succession and is written as $f''(x)$ or d^2y/dx^2.

Exercise 1.11

1. Differentiate

    (a) $y = 5x^2$

    (b) $y = \dfrac{3}{x}$

    (c) $y = 2x + 3$

    (d) $y = x^2 + x + 1$

    (e) $y = x^2 - 3x + 2$

    (f) $y = 3x - \dfrac{7}{x}$

    (g) $y = 2x^3 - 6x^2 + 49x - 54$

    (h) $y = ax + b$

    (i) $y = ax^2 + bx + c$

    (j) $y = 4x - \dfrac{3}{x} + \dfrac{7}{x^2}$

2. Evaluate $f'(x)$ for each of the following functions at the given point:

    (a) $f(x) = 3x^9$ at $x = 1$

    (b) $f(x) = x^2 - 2x$ at $x = 3$

    (c) $f(x) = x^3 - 4x^2 + 2x - 8$ at $x = 0$

    (d) $f(x) = 5x^4 - \dfrac{4}{x^4}$ at $x = -1$

    (e) $f(x) = \sqrt{x} - \dfrac{2}{x}$ at $x = 4$

3. By writing $x^2\left(x^2 + 2x - \dfrac{5}{x^2}\right) = x^4 + 2x^3 - 5$, differentiate $x^2\left(x^2 + 2x - \dfrac{5}{x^2}\right)$.

Use a similar approach to differentiate

(a) $x^2(3x - 4)$

(b) $x(3x^3 - 2x^2 + 6x - 7)$

(c) $(x + 1)(x - 6)$

(d) $\dfrac{x^2 - 3}{x}$

(e) $\dfrac{x - 4x^2}{x^3}$

(f) $\dfrac{x^2 - 3x + 5}{x^2}$

4. Find expressions for d^2y/dx^2 in the case when

(a) $y = 7x^2 - x$

(b) $y = \dfrac{1}{x^2}$

(c) $y = ax + b$

5. Evaluate $f''(2)$ for the function

$$f(x) = x^3 - 4x^2 + 10x - 7$$

6. If $f(x) = x^2 - 6x + 8$, evaluate $f'(3)$. What information does this provide about the graph of $y = f(x)$ at $x = 3$?

7. By writing $\sqrt{4x} = \sqrt{4} \times \sqrt{x} = 2\sqrt{x}$, differentiate $\sqrt{4x}$.

Use a similar approach to differentiate

(a) $\sqrt{25x}$ (b) $\sqrt[3]{27x}$ (c) $\sqrt[4]{16x^3}$ (d) $\sqrt{\dfrac{25}{x}}$

8. Find expressions for

(a) $\dfrac{dQ}{dP}$ for the supply function $Q = P^2 + P + 1$

(b) $\dfrac{d(TR)}{dQ}$ for the total revenue function $TR = 50Q - 3Q^2$

(c) $\dfrac{d(AC)}{dQ}$ for the average cost function $AC = \dfrac{30}{Q} + 10$

(d) $\dfrac{dC}{dY}$ for the consumption function $C = 3Y + 7$

(e) $\dfrac{dQ}{dL}$ for the production function $Q = 10\sqrt{L}$

(f) $\dfrac{d\pi}{dQ}$ for the profit function $\pi = -2Q^3 + 15Q^2 - 24Q - 3$

Exercise 1.11*

1. Find the value of the first-order derivative of the function

$$y = 3\sqrt{x} - \frac{81}{x} + 13$$

when $x = 9$.

2. Find expressions for

   (a) $\dfrac{dQ}{dP}$ for the supply function $Q = 2P^2 + P + 1$

   (b) $\dfrac{d(TR)}{dQ}$ for the total revenue function $TR = 40Q - 3Q\sqrt{Q}$

   (c) $\dfrac{d(AC)}{dQ}$ for the average cost function $AC = \dfrac{20}{Q} + 7Q + 25$

   (d) $\dfrac{dC}{dY}$ for the consumption function $C = Y(2Y + 3) + 10$

   (e) $\dfrac{dC}{dL}$ for the production function $Q = 200L - 4\sqrt[4]{L}$

   (f) $\dfrac{d\pi}{dQ}$ for the profit function $\pi = -Q^3 + 20Q^2 - 7Q - 1$

3. Find the value of the second-order derivative of the following function at the point $x = 4$:

   $$f(x) = -2x^3 + 4x^2 + x - 3$$

   What information does this provide about the shape of the graph of $f(x)$ at this point?

4. Consider the graph of the function

   $$f(x) = 2x^5 - 3x^4 + 2x^2 - 17x + 31$$

   at $x = -1$.

   Giving reasons for your answers,

   (a) state whether the tangent slopes uphill, slopes downhill or is horizontal;

   (b) state whether the graph is concave or convex at this point.

5. Use the second-order derivative to show that the graph of the cubic,

   $$f(x) = ax^3 + bx^2 + cx + d \ (a > 0)$$

   is convex when $x > -b/3a$ and concave when $x < -b/3a$.

6. Find the equation of the tangent to the curve

   $$y = 4x^3 - 5x^2 + x - 3$$

   at the point where it crosses the y axis.

7. A Pareto income distribution function is given by

$$f(x) = \frac{A}{x^a}, \quad x \geq 1$$

where A and a are positive constants and x is measured in $100 000s.

(a) Find an expression for $f'(x)$ and hence comment on the slope of this function.

(b) Find an expression for $f''(x)$ and hence comment on the convexity of this function.

(c) Sketch a graph of $f(x)$.

(d) The area under the graph between $x = b$ and $x = c$ measures the proportion of people whose income is in the range, $b \leq x \leq c$. What does this graph indicate about the distributions of income above a threshold of $100 000?

8. A utility function, $U(x)$, measures the amount of satisfaction gained by an individual who buys x units of a product or service. The Arrow–Pratt coefficient of relative risk aversion is defined by

$$r = -\frac{xU''(x)}{U'(x)}$$

Show that the coefficient of relative risk aversion is constant for the utility function

$$U(x) = \frac{x^{1-\gamma}}{1-\gamma}$$

SECTION 1.12

Further rules of differentiation

Objectives

At the end of this section you should be able to:

- Use the chain rule to differentiate a function of a function.
- Use the product rule to differentiate the product of two functions.
- Use the quotient rule to differentiate the quotient of two functions.
- Differentiate complicated functions using a combination of rules.

Section 1.11 introduced you to the basic rules of differentiation. Unfortunately, not all functions can be differentiated using these rules alone. For example, we are unable to differentiate the functions

$$x\sqrt{(2x - 3)} \quad \text{and} \quad \frac{x}{x^2 + 1}$$

using just the constant, sum or difference rules. The aim of the present section is to describe three further rules which allow you to find the derivative of more complicated expressions. Indeed, the totality of all six rules will enable you to differentiate any mathematical function. Although you may find that the rules described in this section take you slightly longer to grasp than before, they are vital to any understanding of economic theory.

The first rule that we investigate is called the chain rule, and it can be used to differentiate functions such as

$$y = (2x + 3)^{10} \quad \text{and} \quad y = \sqrt{(1 + x^2)}$$

The distinguishing feature of these expressions is that they represent a 'function of a function'. To understand what we mean by this, consider how you might evaluate

$$y = (2x + 3)^{10}$$

on a calculator. You would first work out an intermediate number u, say, given by

$$u = 2x + 3$$

and then raise it to the power of 10 to get

$$y = u^{10}$$

This process is illustrated using the flow chart in Figure 1.41. Note how the incoming number x is first processed by the inner function, 'double and add 3'. The output u from this is then passed on to the outer function, 'raise to the power of 10', to produce the final outgoing number y.

The function

$$y = \sqrt{(1 + x^2)}$$

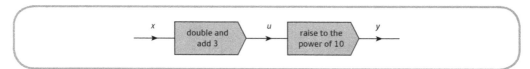

Figure 1.41

can be viewed in the same way. To calculate y you perform the inner function, 'square and add 1', followed by the outer function, 'take square roots'.

The chain rule for differentiating a function of a function may now be stated.

Rule 4 The chain rule

If y is a function of u, which is itself a function of x, then

$$\frac{dy}{dx} = \frac{dy}{du} \times \frac{du}{dx}$$

> differentiate the outer function and multiply by the derivative of the inner function

To illustrate this rule, let us return to the function

$$y = (2x + 3)^{10}$$

in which

$$y = u^{10} \quad \text{and} \quad u = 2x + 3$$

Now

$$\frac{dy}{du} = 10u^9 = 10(2x + 3)^9$$

$$\frac{du}{dx} = 2$$

The chain rule then gives

$$\frac{dy}{dx} = \frac{dy}{du} \times \frac{du}{dx} = 10(2x + 3)^9(2) = 20(2x + 3)^9$$

With practice it is possible to perform the differentiation without explicitly introducing the variable u. To differentiate

$$y = (2x + 3)^{10}$$

we first differentiate the outer power function to get

$$10(2x + 3)^9$$

and then multiply by the derivative of the inner function, $2x + 3$, which is 2, so

$$\frac{dy}{dx} = 20(2x + 3)^9$$

Example

Differentiate

(a) $y = (3x^2 - 5x + 2)^4$

(b) $y = \dfrac{1}{3x + 7}$

(c) $y = \sqrt{(1 + x^2)}$

Solution

(a) The chain rule shows that to differentiate $(3x^2 - 5x + 2)^4$ we first differentiate the outer power function to get

$$4(3x^2 - 5x + 2)^3$$

and then multiply by the derivative of the inner function, $3x^2 - 5x + 2$, which is $6x - 5$. Hence if

$$y = (3x^2 - 5x + 2)^4 \quad \text{then} \quad \frac{dy}{dx} = 4(3x^2 - 5x + 2)^3(6x - 5)$$

(b) To use the chain rule to differentiate

$$y = \frac{1}{3x + 7}$$

recall that reciprocals are denoted by negative powers, so that

$$y = (3x + 7)^{-1}$$

The outer power function differentiates to get

$$-(3x + 7)^{-2}$$

and the inner function, $3x + 7$, differentiates to get 3. By the chain rule we just multiply these together to deduce that

$$\text{if } y = \frac{1}{3x + 7} \quad \text{then} \quad \frac{dy}{dx} = -(3x + 7)^{-2}(3) = \frac{-3}{(3x + 7)^2}$$

(c) To use the chain rule to differentiate

$$y = \sqrt{(1 + x^2)}$$

recall that roots are denoted by fractional powers, so that

$$y = (1 + x^2)^{1/2}$$

The outer power function differentiates to get

$$\frac{1}{2}(1 + x^2)^{-1/2}$$

and the inner function, $1 + x^2$, differentiates to get $2x$. By the chain rule we just multiply these together to deduce that

$$\text{if } y = \sqrt{(1 + x^2)} \quad \text{then} \quad \frac{dy}{dx} = \frac{1}{2}(1 + x^2)^{-1/2}(2x) = \frac{x}{\sqrt{(1 + x^2)}}$$

The derivative of the exponential and natural logarithm functions

In this section we investigate the derived functions associated with the exponential and natural logarithm functions, e^x and $\ln x$. The approach that we adopt is similar to that used in Section 1.10. The derivative of a function determines the slope of the graph of a function. Consequently, to discover how to differentiate an unfamiliar function, we first produce an accurate sketch and then measure the slopes of the tangents at selected points.

Figure 1.42 shows a sketch of the exponential function, e^x, based on the table of values:

x	−2.0	−1.5	−1.0	−0.5	0.0	0.5	1.0	1.5
$f(x)$	0.14	0.22	0.37	0.61	1.00	1.65	2.72	4.48

From the graph we see that the slopes of the tangents at $x = -1$, $x = 0$ and $x = 1$ are

$$f'(-1) = \frac{0.20}{0.50} = 0.4$$

$$f'(0) = \frac{0.50}{0.50} = 1.0$$

$$f'(1) = \frac{1.35}{0.50} = 2.7$$

These results are obtained by measurement and so are quoted to only one decimal place. We cannot really expect to achieve any greater accuracy using this approach.

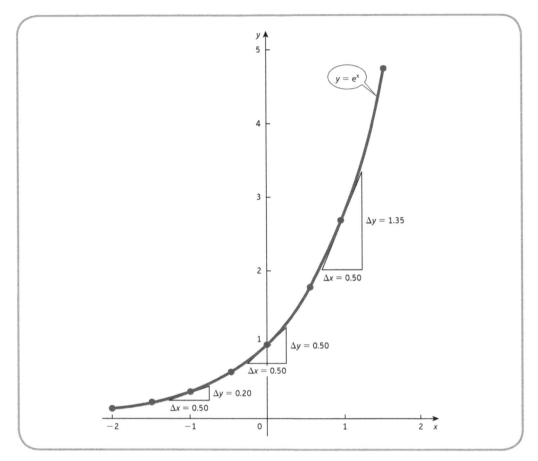

Figure 1.42

The values of x, $f(x)$ and $f'(x)$ are summarised in the following table. The values of $f(x)$ are rounded to one decimal place in order to compare with the graphical estimates of $f'(x)$.

x	-1	0	1
$f(x)$	0.4	1.0	2.7
$f'(x)$	0.4	1.0	2.7

Notice that the values of $f(x)$ and $f'(x)$ are identical to within the accuracy quoted.

These results suggest that the slope of the graph at each point is the same as the function value at that point: that is, e^x differentiates to itself. Symbolically,

> if $f(x) = e^x$ then $f'(x) = e^x$

or, equivalently,

> if $y = e^x$ then $\dfrac{dy}{dx} = e^x$

Practice Problem

1. Use your calculator to complete the following table of function values and hence sketch an accurate graph of $f(x) = \ln x$:

x	0.50	1.00	1.50	2.00	2.50	3.00	3.50	4.00
$f(x)$			0.41				1.25	

Draw the tangents to the graph at $x = 1$, 2 and 3. Hence estimate the values of $f'(1)$, $f'(2)$ and $f'(3)$. Suggest a general formula for the derived function $f'(x)$.

[Hint: for the last part you may find it helpful to rewrite your estimates of $f'(x)$ as simple fractions.]

In fact, it is possible to prove that, for any value of the constant m,

$$\text{if } y = e^{mx} \text{ then } \frac{dy}{dx} = me^{mx}$$

and

$$\text{if } y = \ln mx \text{ then } \frac{dy}{dx} = \frac{1}{x}$$

In particular, we see by setting $m = 1$ that

e^x differentiates to e^x

and that

$\ln x$ differentiates to $\dfrac{1}{x}$

which agree with our practical investigations.

Example

Differentiate

(a) $y = e^{2x}$

(b) $y = e^{-7x}$

(c) $y = \ln 5x \; (x > 0)$

(d) $y = \ln 559x \; (x > 0)$

Solution

(a) Setting $m = 2$ in the general formula shows that

$$\text{if } y = e^{2x} \text{ then } \frac{dy}{dx} = 2e^{2x}$$

Notice that when exponential functions are differentiated, the power itself does not change. All that happens is that the coefficient of x comes down to the front.

(b) Setting $m = -7$ in the general formula shows that

$$\text{if} \quad y = e^{-7x} \quad \text{then} \quad \frac{dy}{dx} = -7e^{-7x}$$

(c) Setting $m = 5$ in the general formula shows that

$$\text{if} \quad y = \ln 5x \quad \text{then} \quad \frac{dy}{dx} = \frac{1}{x}$$

Notice the restriction $x > 0$ stated in the question. This is needed to ensure that we do not attempt to take the logarithm of a negative number, which is impossible.

(d) Setting $m = 559$ in the general formula shows that

$$\text{if} \quad y = \ln 559x \quad \text{then} \quad \frac{dy}{dx} = \frac{1}{x}$$

Notice that we get the same answer as part (c). The derivative of the natural logarithm function does not depend on the coefficient of x. This fact may seem rather strange, but it is easily accounted for. The first rule of logarithms shows that $\ln 559x$ is the same as

$$\ln 559 + \ln x$$

The first term is merely a constant and so differentiates to zero, and the second term differentiates to $1/x$.

Practice Problem

2. Differentiate

    (a) $y = e^{3x}$ **(b)** $y = e^{-x}$ **(c)** $y = \ln 3x \ (x > 0)$ **(d)** $y = \ln 51\ 234x \ (x > 0)$

The chain rule can be used to explain what happens to the m when differentiating e^{mx}. The outer function is the exponential, which differentiates to itself, and the inner function is mx, which differentiates to m. Hence, by the chain rule,

$$\text{if} \quad y = e^{mx} \quad \text{then} \quad \frac{dy}{dx} = e^{mx} \times m = me^{mx}$$

Similarly, noting that the natural logarithm function differentiates to the reciprocal function,

$$\text{if} \quad y = \ln mx \quad \text{then} \quad \frac{dy}{dx} = \frac{1}{mx} \times m = \frac{1}{x}$$

The chain, product and quotient rules can be used to differentiate more complicated functions involving e^x and $\ln x$.

Example

Differentiate

(a) $y = x^3 e^{2x}$ (b) $y = \ln(x^2 + 2x + 1)$ (c) $y = \dfrac{e^{3x}}{x^2 + 2}$

Solution

(a) The function $x^3 e^{2x}$ involves the product of two simpler functions, x^3 and e^{2x}, so we need to use the product rule to differentiate it. Putting

$$u = x^3 \quad \text{and} \quad v = e^{2x}$$

gives

$$\frac{du}{dx} = 3x^2 \quad \text{and} \quad \frac{dv}{dx} = 2e^{2x}$$

By the product rule,

$$\frac{dy}{dx} = u\frac{dv}{dx} + v\frac{du}{dx} = x^3\left[2e^{2x}\right] + e^{2x}\left[3x^2\right] = 2x^3 e^{2x} + 3x^2 e^{2x}$$

There is a common factor of $x^2 e^{2x}$, which goes into the first term $2x$ times and into the second term 3 times. Hence

$$\frac{dy}{dx} = x^2 e^{2x}(2x + 3)$$

(b) The expression $\ln(x^2 + 2x + 1)$ can be regarded as a function of a function, so we can use the chain rule to differentiate it. We first differentiate the outer log function to get

$$\frac{1}{x^2 + 2x + 1}$$

and then multiply by the derivative of the inner function, $x^2 + 2x + 1$, which is $2x + 2$. Hence

$$\frac{dy}{dx} = \frac{2x + 2}{x^2 + 2x + 1}$$

(c) The function

$$\frac{e^{3x}}{x^2 + 2}$$

is the quotient of the simpler functions

$$u = e^{3x} \quad \text{and} \quad v = x^2 + 2$$

for which

$$\frac{du}{dx} = 3e^{3x} \quad \text{and} \quad \frac{dv}{dx} = 2x$$

By the quotient rule,

$$\frac{dy}{dx} = \frac{v\dfrac{du}{dx} - u\dfrac{dv}{dx}}{v^2} = \frac{(x^2 + 2)(3e^{3x}) - e^{3x}(2x)}{(x^2 + 2)^2} = \frac{e^{3x}[3(x^2 + 2) - 2x]}{(x^2 + 2)^2} = \frac{e^{3x}(3x^2 - 2x + 6)}{(x^2 + 2)^2}$$

Practice Problem

3. Differentiate

(a) $y = x^4 \ln x$ **(b)** $y = e^{x^2}$ **(c)** $y = \dfrac{\ln x}{x + 2}$

Notice the effect that the chain rule has on the derivative of an exponential function such as $y = e^{x^2}$ which you differentiated in part (b) of Practice Problem 3. In general:

If $y = e^{u(x)}$ then $\dfrac{dy}{dx} = e^{u(x)} \times u'(x)$

All you have to do is to write down the original function and then multiply by the derivative of the exponent. To differentiate $y = e^{x^2}$, first write down e^{x^2} and then multiply it by $\dfrac{d}{dx}(x^2) = 2x$ to get $2xe^{x^2}$.

Advice

If you ever need to differentiate a function of the form:

ln (an inner function involving products, quotients or powers of *x*)

then it is usually quicker to use the rules of logs to expand the expression before you begin. The three rules are

Rule 1 $\ln(x \times y) = \ln x + \ln y$

Rule 2 $\ln(x \div y) = \ln x - \ln y$

Rule 3 $\ln x^m = m \ln x$

The following example shows how to apply this 'trick' in practice.

Example

Differentiate

(a) $y = \ln(x(x + 1)^4)$ **(b)** $y = \ln\left(\dfrac{x}{\sqrt{(x + 5)}}\right)$

Solution

(a) From rule 1

$\ln(x(x + 1)^4) = \ln x + \ln(x + 1)^4$

which can be simplified further using rule 3 to give

$y = \ln x + 4 \ln(x + 1)$

Differentiation of this new expression is simple. We see immediately that

$\dfrac{dy}{dx} = \dfrac{1}{x} + \dfrac{4}{x + 1}$

If desired, the final answer can be put over a common denominator

$$\frac{1}{x} + \frac{4}{x+1} = \frac{(x+1)+4x}{x(x+1)} = \frac{5x+1}{x(x+1)}$$

(b) The quickest way to differentiate

$$y = \ln\left(\frac{x}{\sqrt{(x+5)}}\right)$$

is to expand first to get

$$y = \ln x - \ln(x+5)^{1/2} \quad \text{(rule 2)}$$

$$= \ln x - \frac{1}{2}\ln(x+5) \quad \text{(rule 3)}$$

Again this expression is easy to differentiate:

$$\frac{dy}{dx} = \frac{1}{x} - \frac{1}{2(x+5)}$$

If desired, this can be written as a single fraction:

$$\frac{1}{x} - \frac{1}{2(x+5)} = \frac{2(x+5)-x}{2x(x+5)} = \frac{x+10}{2x(x+5)}$$

Practice Problem

4. Differentiate the following functions by first expanding each expression using the rules of logs:

(a) $y = \ln(x^3(x+2)^4)$ **(b)** $y = \ln\left(\frac{x^2}{2x+3}\right)$

Exponential and natural logarithm functions provide good mathematical models in many areas of economics, and we conclude this chapter with some illustrative examples.

Example

A firm's short-run production function is given by

$$Q = L^2 e^{-0.01L}$$

Find the value of L that maximises the average product of labour.

Solution

The average product of labour is given by

$$AP_L = \frac{Q}{L} = \frac{L^2 e^{-0.01L}}{L} = Le^{-0.01L}$$

To maximise this function we adopt the strategy described in Section 1.14.

Step 1

At a stationary point

$$\frac{d(AP_L)}{dL} = 0$$

To differentiate $Le^{-0.01L}$, we use the product rule. If

$$u = L \quad \text{and} \quad v = e^{-0.01L}$$

then

$$\frac{du}{dL} = 1 \quad \text{and} \quad \frac{dv}{dL} = -0.01e^{-0.01L}$$

 e^{mx} differentiates to me^{mx}

By the product rule,

$$\frac{d(AP_L)}{dL} = u\frac{dv}{dL} + v\frac{du}{dL} = L(-0.01e^{-0.01L}) + e^{-0.01L} = (1 - 0.01L)e^{-0.01L}$$

We know that a negative exponential is never equal to zero. (Although $e^{-0.01L}$ gets ever closer to zero as L increases, it never actually reaches it for finite values of L.) Hence the only way that

$$(1 - 0.01L)e^{-0.01L}$$

can equal zero is when

$$1 - 0.01L = 0$$

which has the solution $L = 100$.

Step 2

To show that this is a maximum we need to differentiate a second time. To do this we apply the product rule to

$$(1 - 0.01L)e^{-0.01L}$$

taking

$$u = 1 - 0.01L \quad \text{and} \quad v = e^{-0.01L}$$

for which

$$\frac{du}{dL} = -0.01 \quad \text{and} \quad \frac{dv}{dL} = -0.01e^{-0.01L}$$

Hence

$$\frac{d^2(AP_L)}{dL^2} = u\frac{dv}{dL} + v\frac{du}{dL} = (1 - 0.01L)(-0.01e^{-0.01L}) + e^{-0.01L}(-0.01) = (-0.02 + 0.0001L)e^{-0.01L}$$

Finally, putting $L = 100$ into this gives

$$\frac{d^2(AP_L)}{dL^2} = -0.0037$$

The fact that this is negative shows that the stationary point, $L = 100$, is indeed a maximum.

Practice Problem

5. The demand function of a good is given by

    $Q = 1000e^{-0.2P}$

    If fixed costs are 100 and the variable costs are 2 per unit, show that the profit function is given by

    $\pi = 1000Pe^{-0.2P} - 2000e^{-0.2P} - 100$

    Find the price needed to maximise profit.

Example

A firm estimates that the total revenue received from the sale of Q goods is given by

$TR = \ln(1 + 1000Q^2)$

Calculate the marginal revenue when $Q = 10$.

Solution

The marginal revenue function is obtained by differentiating the total revenue function. To differentiate $\ln(1 + 1000Q^2)$, we use the chain rule. We first differentiate the outer log function to get

$$\frac{1}{1 + 1000Q^2}$$ natural logs differentiate to reciprocals

and then multiply by the derivative of the inner function, $1 + 1000Q^2$, to get $2000Q$. Hence

$$MR = \frac{d(TR)}{dQ} = \frac{2000Q}{1 + 1000Q^2}$$

At $Q = 10$,

$$MR = \frac{2000(10)}{1 + 1000(10)^2} = 0.2$$

Practice Problem

6. If the demand equation is

    $P = 200 - 40\ln(Q + 1)$

    calculate the price elasticity of demand when $Q = 20$.

Exercise 1.13

1. Write down the derivative of

    (a) $y = e^{6x}$ (b) $y = e^{-342x}$ (c) $y = 2e^{-x} + 4e^x$ (d) $y = 10e^{4x} - 2x^2 + 7$

2. If \$4000 is saved in an account offering a return of 4% compounded continuously, the future value, S, after t years is given by

    $$S = 4000e^{0.04t}$$

    (1) Calculate the value of S when

     (a) $t = 5$ (b) $t = 5.01$

     and hence estimate the rate of growth at $t = 5$. Round your answers to two decimal places.

    (2) Write down an expression for $\dfrac{dS}{dt}$ and hence find the exact value of the rate of growth after five years.

3. Write down the derivative of

    (a) $y = \ln(3x)$ $(x > 0)$ (b) $y = \ln(-13x)$ $(x < 0)$

4. Use the chain rule to differentiate

    (a) $y = e^{x^3}$ (b) $y = \ln(x^4 + 3x^2)$

5. Use the product rule to differentiate

    (a) $y = x^4 e^{2x}$ (b) $y = x \ln x$

6. Use the quotient rule to differentiate

    (a) $y = \dfrac{e^{4x}}{x^2 + 2}$ (b) $y = \dfrac{e^x}{\ln x}$

7. Find and classify the stationary points of

    (a) $y = xe^{-x}$ (b) $y = \ln x - x$

    Hence sketch their graphs.

8. Since the beginning of the year, weekly sales of a luxury good are found to have decreased exponentially. After t weeks, sales can be modelled by $3000e^{-0.02t}$.

    (a) Work out the weekly sales when $t = 12$ and $t = 13$ and hence find the decrease in sales during this time.

    (b) Use differentiation to work out the rate of decrease in sales after 12 weeks and compare this with your answer to part (a).

9. Find the output needed to maximise profit given that the total cost and total revenue functions are

    $$TC = 2Q \text{ and } TR = 100 \ln(Q + 1)$$

    respectively.

10. If a firm's production function is given by

    $$Q = 700Le^{-0.02L}$$

    find the value of L that maximises output.

11. The demand function of a good is given by

$$P = 100e^{-0.1Q}$$

Show that demand is unit elastic when $Q = 10$.

Exercise 1.13*

1. Differentiate:

   (a) $y = e^{2x} - 3e^{-4x}$ (b) xe^{4x} (c) $\dfrac{e^{-x}}{x^2}$ (d) $x^m \ln x$ (e) $x(\ln x - 1)$

   (f) $\dfrac{x^n}{\ln x}$ (g) $\dfrac{e^{mx}}{(ax + b)^n}$ (h) $\dfrac{e^{ax}}{(\ln bx)^n}$ (i) $\dfrac{e^x - 1}{e^x + 1}$

2. Use the rules of logarithms to expand each of the following functions. Hence find their derivatives.

   (a) $y = \ln\left(\dfrac{x}{x+1}\right)$ (b) $y = \ln(x\sqrt{(3x-1)})$ (c) $y = \ln\sqrt{\dfrac{x+1}{x-1}}$

3. The growth rate of an economic variable, y, is defined to be $\dfrac{dy}{dt} \div y$.

   (a) Use this definition to find the growth rate of the variable, $y = Ae^{kt}$.

   (b) The gross domestic product, GDP, and the size of the population, N, of a country grow exponentially, so that after t years, $GDP = Ae^{at}$ and $N = Be^{bt}$.

   (i) State the growth rates for GDP and N.

   (ii) Show that the GDP per capita also grows exponentially and write down its growth rate.

4. Differentiate the following functions with respect to x, simplifying your answers as far as possible:

   (a) $y = x^4 e^{-2x^2}$ (b) $y = \ln\left(\dfrac{x}{(x+1)^2}\right)$

5. Find and classify the stationary points of

   (a) $y = xe^{ax}$ (b) $y = \ln(ax^2 + bx)$

   where $a < 0$.

6. (a) Use the quotient rule to show that the derivative of the function

   $$y = \dfrac{2x + 1}{\sqrt{4x + 3}}$$

   is given by

   $$\dfrac{4(x + 1)}{(4x + 3)\sqrt{4x + 3}}$$

(b) Use the chain rule to differentiate the function

$$y = \ln\left(\frac{2x + 1}{\sqrt{4x + 3}}\right)$$

(c) Confirm that your answer to part (b) is correct by first expanding

$$\ln\left(\frac{2x + 1}{\sqrt{4x + 3}}\right)$$

using the rules of logs and then differentiating.

7. A firm's short-run production function is given by

$$Q = L^3 e^{-0.02L}$$

Find the value of L that maximises the average product of labour.

8. Find an expression for the price elasticity of demand for the demand curve

$$P = 500 - 75 \ln(2Q + 1)$$

9. Find an expression for the marginal revenue for each of the following demand curves:

(a) $P = \dfrac{e^{Q^2}}{Q^2}$ **(b)** $P = \ln\left(\dfrac{2Q}{3Q + 1}\right)$

10. The demand function of a good is given by $Q = 4000e^{-0.01P}$

(a) Find an expression, in terms of P, for the elasticity of demand and hence determine the range of values of P when the demand is inelastic.

(b) Find the price which maximises total revenue.

11. If the total cost function is given by $TC = 20\sqrt{Q}e^{Q/4}$, find the value of Q which minimises average cost.

12. The logistic model of growth takes the general form,

$$y = \frac{k}{1 + be^{-at}}$$

where k, a and b are positive constants.

(a) Find an expression for dy/dt and deduce that the gradient is positive.

(b) Find an expression for d^2y/dt^2 and deduce that the graph is convex when $t < (\ln b)/a$ and concave when $t > (\ln b)/a$.

(c) State the coordinates of the point where the graph intercepts the y axis, and describe the behaviour of the graph as $t \to \infty$.

(d) Sketch a graph of this logistic function.

13. An art collector owns a painting which is currently valued at \$2 million. After t years it is expected that the painting will be worth V million dollars where $V = 2e^{\sqrt{t}}$.

(a) If the interest rate is 10% compounded continuously, show that after t years the present value of the painting is given by $PV = 2e^{\sqrt{t}-0.1t}$.

(b) The collector decides to sell the painting after T years where T is chosen to maximise PV. Work out the value of T.

SECTION 1.14
Optimisation of economic functions

Objectives

At the end of this section you should be able to:

- Use the first-order derivative to find the stationary points of a function.
- Use the second-order derivative to classify the stationary points of a function.
- Find the maximum and minimum points of an economic function.
- Use stationary points to sketch graphs of economic functions.

In Section 1.7 a simple three-step strategy was described for sketching graphs of quadratic functions of the form

$$f(x) = ax^2 + bx + c$$

The basic idea is to solve the corresponding equation

$$ax^2 + bx + c = 0$$

to find where the graph crosses the x axis. Provided that the quadratic equation has at least one solution, it is then possible to deduce the coordinates of the maximum or minimum point of the parabola. For example, if there are two solutions, then by symmetry the graph turns round at the point exactly halfway between these solutions. Unfortunately, if the quadratic equation has no solution, then only a limited sketch can be obtained using this approach.

In this section we show how the techniques of calculus can be used to find the coordinates of the turning point of a parabola. The beauty of this approach is that it can be used to locate the maximum and minimum points of any economic function, not just those represented by quadratics. Look at the graph in Figure 1.43. Points B, C, D, E, F and G are referred to as the **stationary points** (sometimes called **critical points**, **turning points** or **extrema**) of the function. At a stationary point the tangent to the graph is horizontal, and so has zero slope.

Consequently, at a stationary point of a function $f(x)$,

$$f'(x) = 0$$

The reason for using the word 'stationary' is historical. Calculus was originally used by astronomers to predict planetary motion. If a graph of the distance travelled by an object is sketched against time, then the speed of the object is given by the slope, since this represents the rate of change of distance with respect to time. It follows that if the graph is horizontal at some point, then the speed is zero and the object is instantaneously at rest: that is, stationary.

Stationary points are classified into one of three types: local maxima, local minima and stationary points of inflection.

At a **local maximum** (sometimes called a relative maximum), the graph falls away on both sides. Points B and E are the local maxima for the function sketched in Figure 1.43.

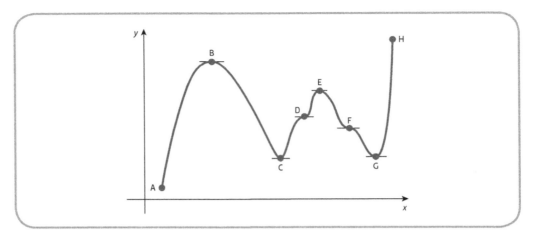

Figure 1.43

The word 'local' is used to highlight the fact that, although these are the maximum points relative to their locality or neighbourhood, they may not be the overall or global maximum. In Figure 1.43 the highest point on the graph actually occurs at the right-hand end, H, which is not a stationary point, since the slope is not zero at H.

At a **local minimum** (sometimes called a relative minimum), the graph rises on both sides. Points C and G are the local minima in Figure 1.43. Again, it is not necessary for the global minimum to be one of the local minima. In Figure 1.43 the lowest point on the graph occurs at the left-hand end, A, which is not a stationary point.

At a **stationary point of inflection**, the graph rises on one side and falls on the other. The stationary points of inflection in Figure 1.43 are labelled D and F. These points are of little value in economics, although they do sometimes assist in sketching graphs of economic functions. Maxima and minima, on the other hand, are important. The calculation of the maximum points of the revenue and profit functions is clearly worthwhile. Likewise, it is useful to be able to find the minimum points of average cost functions.

For most examples in economics, the local maximum and minimum points coincide with the global maximum and minimum. For this reason we shall drop the word 'local' when describing stationary points. However, always bear in mind that the global maximum and minimum could actually be attained at an end point and this possibility may need to be checked. This can be done by comparing the function values at the end points with those of the stationary points and then deciding which of them gives rise to the largest or smallest values.

Two obvious questions remain. How do we find the stationary points of any given function, and how do we classify them? The first question is easily answered. As we mentioned earlier, stationary points satisfy the equation

$$f'(x) = 0$$

so all we need is to differentiate the function, to equate to zero and to solve the resulting algebraic equation. The classification is equally straightforward. It can be shown that if a function has a stationary point at $x = a$, then

- if $f''(a) > 0$, then $f(x)$ has a minimum at $x = a$;
- if $f''(a) < 0$, then $f(x)$ has a maximum at $x = a$.

Therefore, we need only to differentiate the function a second time and to evaluate this second-order derivative at each point. A point is a minimum if this value is positive and a maximum if this value is negative. These facts are consistent with our interpretation of the second-order derivative in Section 1.11. If $f''(a) > 0$, the graph bends upwards at $x = a$ (points C and G in Figure 1.43). If $f''(a) < 0$, the graph bends downwards at $x = a$ (points B and E in Figure 1.43). There is, of course, a third possibility, namely $f''(a) = 0$. Sadly, when this happens, it provides no information whatsoever about the stationary point. The point $x = a$ could be a maximum, minimum or inflection. This situation is illustrated in Question 2 in Exercise 1.14* at the end of this section.

Advice

If you are unlucky enough to encounter this case, you can always classify the point by tabulating the function values in the vicinity and use these to produce a local sketch.

To summarise, the method for finding and classifying stationary points of a function, $f(x)$, is as follows:

Step 1

Solve the equation $f'(x) = 0$ to find the stationary points, $x = a$.

Step 2

If

- $f''(a) > 0$, then the function has a minimum at $x = a$.
- $f''(a) < 0$, then the function has a maximum at $x = a$.
- $f''(a) = 0$, then the point cannot be classified using the available information.

Example

Find and classify the stationary points of the following functions. Hence sketch their graphs.

(a) $f(x) = x^2 - 4x + 5$ (b) $f(x) = 2x^3 + 3x^2 - 12x + 4$

Solution

(a) In order to use steps 1 and 2 we need to find the first- and second-order derivatives of the function

$$f(x) = x^2 - 4x + 5$$

Differentiating once gives

$$f'(x) = 2x - 4$$

and differentiating a second time gives

$$f''(x) = 2$$

Step 1

The stationary points are the solutions of the equation

$$f'(x) = 0$$

so we need to solve

$$2x - 4 = 0$$

This is a linear equation so has just one solution. Adding 4 to both sides gives

$$2x = 4$$

and dividing through by 2 shows that the stationary point occurs at

$$x = 2$$

Step 2

To classify this point we need to evaluate

$$f''(2)$$

In this case

$$f''(x) = 2$$

for all values of x, so in particular

$$f''(2) = 2$$

This number is positive, so the function has a minimum at $x = 2$.

We have shown that the minimum point occurs at $x = 2$. The corresponding value of y is easily found by substituting this number into the function to get

$$y = (2)^2 - 4(2) + 5 = 1$$

so the minimum point has coordinates $(2, 1)$. A graph of $f(x)$ is shown in Figure 1.44.

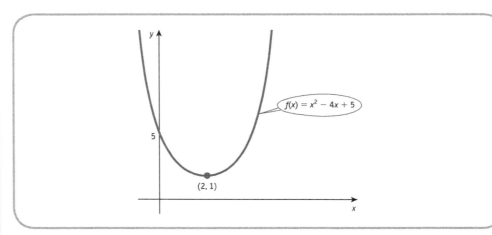

Figure 1.44

(b) In order to use steps 1 and 2 we need to find the first- and second-order derivatives of the function

$$f(x) = 2x^3 + 3x^2 - 12x + 4$$

Differentiating once gives

$$f'(x) = 6x^2 + 6x - 12$$

and differentiating a second time gives

$$f''(x) = 12x + 6$$

Step 1

The stationary points are the solutions of the equation

$$f'(x) = 0$$

so we need to solve

$$6x^2 + 6x - 12 = 0$$

This is a quadratic equation and so can be solved using 'the formula'. However, before doing so, it is a good idea to divide both sides by 6 to avoid large numbers. The resulting equation

$$x^2 + x - 2 = 0$$

has solution

$$x = \frac{-1 \pm \sqrt{(1^2 - 4(1)(-2))}}{2(1)} = \frac{-1 \pm \sqrt{9}}{2} = \frac{-1 \pm 3}{2} = -2, 1$$

In general, whenever $f(x)$ is a cubic function, the stationary points are the solutions of a quadratic equation, $f'(x) = 0$. Moreover, we know from Section 1.7 that such an equation can have two, one or no solutions. It follows that a cubic equation can have two, one or no stationary points. In this particular example we have seen that there are two stationary points, at $x = -2$ and $x = 1$.

Step 2

To classify these points we need to evaluate $f''(-2)$ and $f''(1)$. Now,

$$f''(-2) = 12(-2) + 6 = -18$$

This is negative, so there is a maximum at $x = -2$. When $x = -2$,

$$y = 2(-2)^3 + 3(-2)^2 - 12(-2) + 4 = 24$$

so the maximum point has coordinates $(-2, 24)$. Now

$$f''(1) = 12(1) + 6 = 18$$

This is positive, so there is a minimum at $x = 1$. When $x = 1$,

$$y = 2(1)^3 + 3(1)^2 - 12(1) + 4 = -3$$

so the minimum point has coordinates $(1, -3)$.

This information enables a partial sketch to be drawn as shown in Figure 1.45. Before we can be confident about the complete picture, it is useful to plot a few more points such as those below:

x	−10	0	10
y	−1816	4	2184

This table indicates that when x is positive, the graph falls steeply downwards from a great height. Similarly, when x is negative, the graph quickly disappears off the bottom of the page. The curve cannot wiggle and turn round except at the two stationary points already plotted (otherwise it would have more stationary points, which we know is not the case). We now have enough information to join up the pieces and so sketch a complete picture as shown in Figure 1.46.

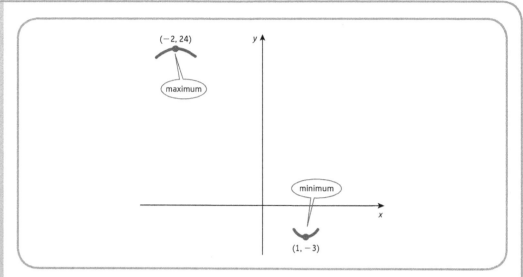

Figure 1.45

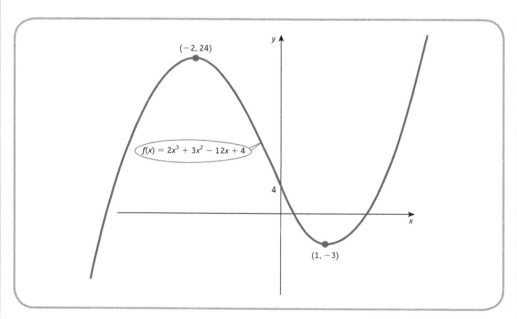

Figure 1.46

In an ideal world it would be nice to calculate the three points at which the graph crosses the x axis. These are the solutions of

$$2x^3 + 3x^2 - 12x + 4 = 0$$

There is a formula for solving cubic equations, just as there is for quadratic equations, but it is extremely complicated and is beyond the scope of this text.

Practice Problem

1. Find and classify the stationary points of the following functions. Hence sketch their graphs.

   (a) $y = 3x^2 + 12x - 35$ (b) $y = -2x^3 + 15x^2 - 36x + 27$

The task of finding the maximum and minimum values of a function is referred to as optimisation. This is an important topic in mathematical economics. It provides a rich source of examination questions, and we devote the remaining part of this section and the whole of the next to applications of it. In this section we demonstrate the use of stationary points by working through four 'examination-type' problems in detail. These problems involve the optimisation of specific revenue, cost, profit and production functions. They are not intended to exhaust all possibilities, although they are fairly typical. The next section describes how the mathematics of optimisation can be used to derive general theoretical results.

Example

A firm's short-run production function is given by

$$Q = 6L^2 - 0.2L^3$$

where L denotes the number of workers.

(a) Find the size of the workforce that maximises output and hence sketch a graph of this production function.

(b) Find the size of the workforce that maximises the average product of labour. Calculate MP_L and AP_L at this value of L. What do you observe?

Solution

(a) In the first part of this example we want to find the value of L, which maximises

$$Q = 6L^2 - 0.2L^3$$

Step 1

At a stationary point

$$\frac{dQ}{dL} = 12L - 0.6L^2 = 0$$

This is a quadratic equation and so we could use 'the formula' to find L. However, this is not really necessary in this case because both terms have a common factor of L, and the equation may be written as

$$L(12 - 0.6L) = 0$$

It follows that either

$$L = 0 \text{ or } 12 - 0.6L = 0$$

that is, the equation has solutions

$$L = 0 \text{ and } L = 12/0.6 = 20$$

Step 2

It is obvious on economic grounds that $L = 0$ is a minimum and presumably $L = 20$ is the maximum. We can, of course, check this by differentiating a second time to get

$$\frac{\mathrm{d}^2 Q}{\mathrm{d}L^2} = 12 - 1.2L$$

When $L = 0$,

$$\frac{\mathrm{d}^2 Q}{\mathrm{d}L^2} = 12 > 0$$

which confirms that $L = 0$ is a minimum. The corresponding output is given by

$$Q = 6(0)^2 - 0.2(0)^3 = 0$$

as expected. When $L = 20$,

$$\frac{\mathrm{d}^2 Q}{\mathrm{d}L^2} = -12 < 0$$

which confirms that $L = 20$ is a maximum.

The firm should therefore employ 20 workers to achieve a maximum output

$$Q = 6(20)^2 - 0.2(20)^3 = 800$$

We have shown that the minimum point on the graph has coordinates (0, 0) and the maximum point has coordinates (20, 800). There are no further turning points, so the graph of the production function has the shape sketched in Figure 1.47.

It is possible to find the precise values of L at which the graph crosses the horizontal axis. The production function is given by

$$Q = 6L^2 - 0.2L^3$$

so we need to solve

$$6L^2 - 0.2L^3 = 0$$

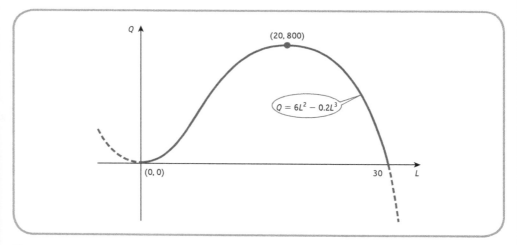

Figure 1.47

We can take out a factor of L^2 to get

$$L^2(6 - 0.2L) = 0$$

Hence, either

$$L^2 = 0 \text{ or } 6 - 0.2L = 0$$

The first of these merely confirms the fact that the curve passes through the origin, whereas the second shows that the curve intersects the L axis at $L = 6/0.2 = 30$.

(b) In the second part of this example we want to find the value of L which maximises the average product of labour. This is a concept that we have not met before in this text, although it is not difficult to guess how it might be defined.

The **average product of labour**, AP_L, is taken to be total output divided by labour, so that in symbols

$$\mathrm{AP}_L = \frac{Q}{L}$$

This is sometimes called **labour productivity**, since it measures the average output per worker.

In this example,

$$\mathrm{AP}_L = \frac{6L^2 - 0.2L^3}{L} = 6L - 0.2L^2$$

Step 1

At a stationary point

$$\frac{\mathrm{d}(\mathrm{AP}_L)}{\mathrm{d}L} = 0$$

so

$$6 - 0.4L = 0$$

which has solution $L = 6/0.4 = 15$.

Step 2

To classify this stationary point we differentiate a second time to get

$$\frac{\mathrm{d}(\mathrm{AP}_L)}{\mathrm{d}L} = -0.4 < 0$$

which shows that it is a maximum.

The labour productivity is therefore greatest when the firm employs 15 workers. In fact, the corresponding labour productivity, AP_L, is

$$6(15) - 0.2(15)^2 = 45$$

In other words, the largest number of goods produced per worker is 45.

Finally, we are invited to calculate the value of MP_L at this point. To find an expression for MP_L we need to differentiate Q with respect to L to get

$$\mathrm{MP}_L = 12L - 0.6L^2$$

When $L = 15$,

$$\mathrm{MP}_L = 12(15) - 0.6(15)^2 = 45$$

We observe that at $L = 15$ the values of MP_L and AP_L are equal.

In this particular example we discovered that at the point of maximum average product of labour

marginal product of labour = average product of labour

There is nothing special about this example, and in the next section we show that this result holds for any production function.

Practice Problem

2. A firm's short-run production function is given by

$$Q = 300L^2 - L^4$$

where L denotes the number of workers. Find the size of the workforce that maximises the average product of labour and verify that at this value of L

$$MP_L = AP_L$$

Example

The demand equation of a good is

$$P + Q = 30$$

and the total cost function is

$$TC = \frac{1}{2}Q^2 + 6Q + 7$$

(a) Find the level of output that maximises total revenue.

(b) Find the level of output that maximises profit. Calculate MR and MC at this value of Q. What do you observe?

Solution

(a) In the first part of this example we want to find the value of Q which maximises total revenue. To do this we use the given demand equation to find an expression for TR and then apply the theory of stationary points in the usual way.

The total revenue is defined by

$$TR = PQ$$

We seek the value of Q which maximises TR, so we express TR in terms of the variable Q only. The demand equation

$$P + Q = 30$$

can be rearranged to get

$$P = 30 - Q$$

Hence

$$TR = (30 - Q)Q$$
$$= 30Q - Q^2$$

Step 1

At a stationary point

$$\frac{d(TR)}{dQ} = 0$$

so

$$30 - 2Q = 0$$

which has the solution $Q = 30/2 = 15$.

Step 2

To classify this point we differentiate a second time to get

$$\frac{d^2(TR)}{dQ^2} = -2$$

This is negative, so TR has a maximum at $Q = 15$.

(b) In the second part of this example we want to find the value of Q which maximises profit. To do this we begin by determining an expression for profit in terms of Q. Once this has been done, it is then a simple matter to work out the first- and second-order derivatives and so to find and classify the stationary points of the profit function.

   The profit function is defined by

$$\pi = TR - TC$$

From part (a)

$$TR = 30Q - Q^2$$

We are given the total cost function

$$TC = \tfrac{1}{2}Q^2 + 6Q + 7$$

Hence

$$\begin{aligned}\pi &= (30Q - Q^2) - (\tfrac{1}{2}Q^2 + 6Q + 7) \\ &= 30Q - Q^2 - \tfrac{1}{2}Q^2 - 6Q - 7 \\ &= -\tfrac{3}{2}Q^2 + 24Q - 7\end{aligned}$$

Step 1

At a stationary point

$$\frac{d\pi}{dQ} = 0$$

so

$$-3Q + 24 = 0$$

which has solution $Q = 24/3 = 8$.

Step 2

To classify this point we differentiate a second time to get

$$\frac{d^2\pi}{dQ^2} = -3$$

This is negative, so π has a maximum at $Q = 8$. In fact, the corresponding maximum profit is

$$\pi = -{}^3/_2(8)^2 + 24(8) - 7 = 89$$

Finally, we are invited to calculate the marginal revenue and marginal cost at this particular value of Q. To find expressions for MR and MC we need only differentiate TR and TC, respectively. If

$$\text{TR} = 30Q - Q^2$$

then

$$\text{MR} = \frac{d(\text{TR})}{dQ}$$
$$= 30 - 2Q$$

so when $Q = 8$

$$\text{MR} = 30 - 2(8) = 14$$

If

$$\text{TC} = {}^1/_2Q^2 + 6Q + 7$$

then

$$\text{MC} = \frac{d(\text{TC})}{dQ}$$
$$= Q + 6$$

so when $Q = 8$

$$\text{MC} = 8 + 6 = 14$$

We observe that at $Q = 8$, the values of MR and MC are equal.

In this particular example we discovered that at the point of maximum profit,

marginal revenue = marginal cost

There is nothing special about this example, and in the next section we show that this result holds for any profit function.

Practice Problem

3. The demand equation of a good is given by

$$P + 2Q = 20$$

and the total cost function is

$$Q^3 - 8Q^2 + 20Q + 2$$

(a) Find the level of output that maximises total revenue.

(b) Find the maximum profit and the value of Q at which it is achieved. Verify that, at this value of Q, MR = MC.

Example

The cost of building an office block, x floors high, is made up of three components:

(1) $10 million for the land;

(2) $\$^{1}/_{4}$ million per floor;

(3) specialised costs of $10 000$x$ per floor.

How many floors should the block contain if the average cost per floor is to be minimised?

Solution

The $10 million for the land is a fixed cost because it is independent of the number of floors. Each floor costs $\$^{1}/_{4}$ million, so if the building has x floors altogether, then the cost will be 250 000x.

In addition there are specialised costs of 10 000x per floor, so if there are x floors, this will be

$$(10\ 000x)x = 10\ 000x^2$$

Notice the square term here, which means that the specialised costs rise dramatically with increasing x. This is to be expected, since a tall building requires a more complicated design. It may also be necessary to use more expensive materials.

The total cost, TC, is the sum of the three components: that is,

$$TC = 10\ 000\ 000 + 250\ 000x + 10\ 000x^2$$

The average cost per floor, AC, is found by dividing the total cost by the number of floors: that is,

$$AC = \frac{TC}{x} = \frac{10\ 000\ 000 + 250\ 000x + 10\ 000x^2}{x}$$

$$= \frac{10\ 000\ 000}{x} + 250\ 000 + 10\ 000x$$

$$= 10\ 000\ 000x^{-1} + 250\ 000 + 10\ 000x$$

Step 1

At a stationary point

$$\frac{d(AC)}{dx} = 0$$

In this case

$$\frac{d(AC)}{dx} = -10\ 000\ 000x^{-2} + 10\ 000 = \frac{-10\ 000\ 000}{x^2} + 10\ 000$$

so we need to solve

$$10\ 000 = \frac{10\ 000\ 000}{x^2} \text{ or equivalently, } 10\ 000x^2 = 10\ 000\ 000$$

Hence

$$x^2 = \frac{10\ 000\ 000}{10\ 000} = 1000$$

This has the solution

$$x = \pm\sqrt{1000} = \pm 31.6$$

We can obviously ignore the negative value because it does not make sense to build an office block with a negative number of floors, so we can deduce that $x = 31.6$.

Step 2

To confirm that this is a minimum we need to differentiate a second time. Now

$$\frac{d(AC)}{dx} = -10\,000\,000x^{-2} + 10\,000$$

so

$$\frac{d^2(AC)}{dx^2} = -2(-10\,000\,000)x^{-3} = \frac{20\,000\,000}{x^3}$$

When $x = 31.6$, we see that

$$\frac{d^2(AC)}{dx^2} = \frac{20\,000\,000}{(31.6)^3} = 633.8$$

It follows that $x = 31.6$ is indeed a minimum because the second-order derivative is a positive number.

At this stage it is tempting to state that the answer is 31.6. This is mathematically correct but is a physical impossibility since x must be a whole number. To decide whether to take x to be 31 or 32, we simply evaluate AC for these two values of x and choose the one that produces the lower average cost.

When $x = 31$,

$$AC = \frac{10\,000\,000}{31} + 250\,000 + 10\,000(31) = \$882\,581$$

When $x = 32$,

$$AC = \frac{10\,000\,000}{32} + 250\,000 + 10\,000(32) = \$882\,500$$

Therefore, an office block 32 floors high produces the lowest average cost per floor.

Practice Problem

4. The total cost function of a good is given by

$$TC = Q^2 + 3Q + 36$$

Calculate the level of output that minimises average cost. Find AC and MC at this value of Q. What do you observe?

Example

The supply and demand equations of a good are given by

$$P = Q_S + 8$$

and

$$P = -3Q_D + 80$$

respectively.

The government decides to impose a tax, t, per unit. Find the value of t which maximises the government's total tax revenue on the assumption that equilibrium conditions prevail in the market.

Solution

In this example t is unknown. All we need to do is to carry the letter t through the usual calculations and then to choose t at the end so as to maximise the total tax revenue.

To take account of the tax we replace P by $P - t$ in the supply equation. This is because the price that the supplier actually receives is the price, P, that the consumer pays less the tax, t, deducted by the government. The new supply equation is then

$$P - t = Q_S + 8$$

so that

$$P = Q_S + 8 + t$$

In equilibrium

$$Q_S = Q_D$$

If this common value is denoted by Q, then the supply and demand equations become

$$P = Q + 8 + t$$
$$P = -3Q + 80$$

Hence

$$Q + 8 + t = -3Q + 80$$

since both sides are equal to P. This can be rearranged to give

$$Q = -3Q + 72 - t \quad \text{(subtract } 8 + t \text{ from both sides)}$$
$$4Q = 72 - t \quad \text{(add } 3Q \text{ to both sides)}$$
$$Q = 18 - \tfrac{1}{4}t \quad \text{(divide both sides by 4)}$$

Now, if the number of goods sold is Q and the government raises t per good, then the total tax revenue, T, is given by

$$T = tQ$$
$$= t(18 - \tfrac{1}{4}t)$$
$$= 18t - \tfrac{1}{4}t^2$$

This, then, is the expression that we wish to maximise.

Step 1

At a stationary point

$$\frac{\mathrm{d}T}{\mathrm{d}t} = 0$$

so

$$18 - \frac{1}{2}t = 0$$

which has solution

$$t = 36$$

Step 2

To classify this point we differentiate a second time to get

$$\frac{\mathrm{d}^2 T}{\mathrm{d}t^2} = -\frac{1}{2} < 0$$

which confirms that it is a maximum.

Hence the government should impose a tax of \$36 on each good.

Practice Problem

5. The supply and demand equations of a good are given by

$$P = \tfrac{1}{2}Q_S + 25$$

and

$$P = -2Q_D + 50$$

respectively.

The government decides to impose a tax, t, per unit. Find the value of t which maximises the government's total tax revenue on the assumption that equilibrium conditions prevail in the market.

In theory a spreadsheet such as Excel could be used to solve optimisation problems, although it cannot handle the associated mathematics. The preferred method is to use a symbolic computation system such as Maple, Matlab, Mathcad or Derive which can not only sketch the graphs of functions but also differentiate and solve equations. Consequently, it is possible to obtain the exact solution using one of these packages.

Key Terms

Average product of labour (labour productivity)   Output per worker: $AP_L = Q/L$.

Maximum (local) point   A point on a curve which has the highest function value in comparison with other values in its neighbourhood; at such a point the first-order derivative is zero and the second-order derivative is either zero or negative.

Minimum (local) point   A point on a curve which has the lowest function value in comparison with other values in its neighbourhood; at such a point the first-order derivative is zero and the second-order derivative is either zero or positive.

Optimisation   The determination of the optimal (usually stationary) points of a function.

Stationary point of inflection   A stationary point that is neither a maximum nor a minimum; at such a point both the first- and second-order derivatives are zero.

Stationary points (critical points, turning points, extrema)   Points on a graph at which the tangent is horizontal; at a stationary point the first-order derivative is zero.

Exercise 1.14

1. Find and classify the stationary points of the following functions. Hence give a rough sketch of their graphs.

    (a) $y = -x^2 + x + 1$ **(b)** $y = x^2 - 4x + 4$ **(c)** $y = x^2 - 20x + 105$ **(d)** $y = -x^3 + 3x$

2. If the demand equation of a good is

    $$P = 40 - 2Q$$

    find the level of output that maximises total revenue.

3. A firm's short-run production function is given by

    $$Q = 30L^2 - 0.5L^3$$

    Find the value of L which maximises AP_L and verify that $MP_L = AP_L$ at this point.

4. If the fixed costs are 13 and the variable costs are $Q + 2$ per unit, show that the average cost function is

    $$AC = \frac{13}{Q} + Q + 2$$

    (a) Calculate the values of AC when $Q = 1, 2, 3, \ldots, 6$. Plot these points on graph paper and hence produce an accurate graph of AC against Q.

    (b) Use your graph to estimate the minimum average cost.

    (c) Use differentiation to confirm your estimate obtained in part (b).

5. The demand and total cost functions of a good are

    $$4P + Q - 16 = 0$$

    and

    $$TC = 4 + 2Q - \frac{3Q^2}{10} + \frac{Q^3}{20}$$

    respectively.

(a) Find expressions for TR, π, MR and MC in terms of Q.

(b) Solve the equation

$$\frac{d\pi}{dQ} = 0$$

and hence determine the value of Q which maximises profit.

(c) Verify that, at the point of maximum profit, MR = MC.

6. The supply and demand equations of a good are given by

$$3P - Q_s = 3$$

and

$$2P + Q_D = 14$$

respectively.

   The government decides to impose a tax, t, per unit. Find the value of t which maximises the government's total tax revenue on the assumption that equilibrium conditions prevail in the market.

7. A manufacturer has fixed costs of $200 each week, and the variable costs per unit can be expressed by the function, $VC = 2Q - 36$.

   (a) Find an expression for the total cost function and deduce that the average cost function is given by

   $$AC = \frac{200}{Q} + 2Q - 36$$

   (b) Find the stationary point of this function and show that this is a minimum.

   (c) Verify that, at this stationary point, average cost is the same as marginal cost.

8. A firm's short-run production function is given by

   $$Q = 3\sqrt{L}$$

   where L is the number of units of labour.

   If the price per unit sold is $50 and the price per unit of labour is $10, find the value of L needed to maximise profits. You may assume that the firm sells all that it produces, and you can ignore all other costs.

9. The average cost per person of hiring a tour guide on a week's river cruise for a maximum party size of 30 people is given by

   $$AC = 3Q^2 - 192Q + 3500 \qquad (0 < Q \le 30)$$

   Find the minimum average cost for the trip.

10. An electronic components firm launches a new product on 1 January. During the following year a rough estimate of the number of orders, S, received t days after the launch is given by

    $$S = t^2 - 0.002t^3$$

    What is the maximum number of orders received on any one day of the year?

Exercise 1.14*

1. A firm's demand function is

    $P = 60 - 0.5Q$

   If fixed costs are 10 and variable costs are $Q + 3$ per unit, find the maximum profit.

2. Show that all of the following functions have a stationary point at $x = 0$. Verify in each case that $f''(0) = 0$. Classify these points by producing a rough sketch of each function.

   (a) $f(x) = x^3$ **(b)** $f(x) = x^4$ **(c)** $f(x) = -x^6$

3. If fixed costs are 15 and the variable costs are $2Q$ per unit, write down expressions for TC, AC and MC. Find the value of Q which minimises AC and verify that AC = MC at this point.

4. Daily sales, S, of a new product for the first two weeks after the launch is modelled by

    $S = t^3 - 24t^2 + 180t + 60$ $(0 \leq t \leq 13)$

   where t is the number of days.

   (a) Find and classify the stationary points of this function.

   (b) Sketch a graph of S against t on the interval $0 \leq t \leq 13$.

   (c) Find the maximum and minimum daily sales during the period between $t = 5$ and $t = 9$.

5. If the demand function of a good is

    $P = \sqrt{(1000 - 4Q)}$

   find the value of Q which maximises total revenue.

6. A firm's total cost and demand functions are given by

    $TC = Q^2 + 50Q + 10$ and $P = 200 - 4Q$

   respectively.

   (a) Find the level of output needed to maximise the firm's profit.

   (b) The government imposes a tax of $\$t$ per good. If the firm adds this tax to its costs and continues to maximise profit, show that the price of the good increases by two-fifths of the tax, irrespective of the value of t.

7. Given that the cubic function $f(x) = x^3 + ax^2 + bx + c$ has a stationary point at $(2, 5)$ and that it passes through $(1, 3)$, find the values of a, b and c.

8. The total revenue function of a good is given by:

    $TR = 0.2Q^3$ on $0 \leq Q \leq 5$

    $TR = -4Q^2 + 55Q - 150$ on $5 \leq Q \leq 10$

   (a) Sketch a graph of TR against Q on the interval $0 \leq Q \leq 10$.

   (b) Find the maximum revenue and the value of Q at which it is achieved.

   (c) For what value of Q is the marginal revenue a maximum?

SECTION 1.15

Indefinite integration

Objectives

At the end of this section you should be able to:

- Recognise the notation for indefinite integration.
- Write down the integrals of simple power and exponential functions.
- Integrate functions of the form $af(x) + bg(x)$.
- Find the total cost function given any marginal cost function.
- Find the total revenue function given any marginal revenue function.
- Find the consumption and savings functions given either the marginal propensity to consume or the marginal propensity to save.
- Use the method of inspection to integrate more complicated functions.

Throughout mathematics there are many pairs of operations which cancel each other out and take you back to where you started. Perhaps the most obvious pair is multiplication and division. If you multiply a number by a non-zero constant, k, and then divide by k, you end up with the number you first thought of. This situation is described by saying that the two operations are **inverses** of each other. In calculus, the inverse of differentiation is called **integration**.

Suppose that you are required to find a function, $F(x)$, which differentiates to

$$f(x) = 3x^2$$

Can you guess what $F(x)$ is in this case? Given such a simple function, it is straightforward to write down the answer by inspection. It is

$$F(x) = x^3$$

because

$$F'(x) = 3x^2 = f(x) \quad ✓$$

as required.

As a second example, consider

$$f(x) = x^7$$

Can you think of a function, $F(x)$, which differentiates to this? Recall that when power functions are differentiated, the power decreases by 1, so it makes sense to do the opposite here and to try

$$F(x) = x^8$$

Unfortunately, this does not quite work out, because it differentiates to

$$8x^7$$

which is eight times too big. This suggests that we try

$$F(x) = \tfrac{1}{8}x^8$$

which does work because

$$F'(x) = {}^8/_8 x^7 = x^7 = f(x) \quad \checkmark$$

In general, if $F'(x) = f(x)$, then $F(x)$, is said to be the **integral** (sometimes called the **anti-derivative** or **primitive**) of $f(x)$ and is written

$$F(x) = \int f(x)dx$$

> read 'integral of f
> of x dee x'

In this notation

$$\int 3x^2 dx = x^3$$

and

$$\int x^7 dx = {}^1/_8 x^8$$

Here is a problem for you to try. Do not let the notation

$$\int dx$$

put you off. It is merely an instruction for you to think of a function that differentiates to whatever is squashed between the integral sign '$\int$' and dx. If you get stuck, try adding 1 on to the power. Differentiate your guess, and if it does not quite work out, then go back and try again, adjusting the coefficient accordingly.

Practice Problem

1. Find

(a) $\int 2x dx$ (b) $\int 4x^3 dx$ (c) $\int 100x^{99} dx$ (d) $\int x^3 dx$ (e) $\int x^{18} dx$

In Practice Problem 1(a) you probably wrote

$$\int 2x dx = x^2$$

However, there are other possibilities. For example, both of the functions

$$x^2 + 6 \text{ and } x^2 - 59$$

differentiate to $2x$, because constants differentiate to zero. In fact, we can add any constant, c, to x^2 to obtain a function that differentiates to $2x$. Hence

$$\int 2x dx = x^2 + c$$

which differentiates to give

$$F'(x) = -2\left(1 + 4x^2\right)^{-3} \times 8x = \frac{-16x}{\left(1 + 4x^2\right)^3}$$

This is -16 times too big, so

$$\int \frac{x}{\left(1 + 4x^2\right)^3}dx = \frac{-1}{16\left(1 + 4x^2\right)^2} + c$$

(c) For the integral,

$$\int \frac{x^9}{1 + x^{10}}dx$$

we notice that the top of the fraction is basically the derivative of the bottom. Reciprocal functions like this integrate to natural logarithms, so our first guess at the answer is

$$F(x) = \ln(1 + x^{10})$$

The chain rule automatically gives us the extra x^9 that we need. Differentiating our guess gives

$$F'(x) = \frac{1}{1 + x^{10}} \times 10x^9 = \frac{10x^9}{1 + x^{10}}$$

This is 10 times too big, so

$$\int \frac{x^9}{1 + x^{10}}dx = \frac{1}{10}\ln(1 + x^{10}) + c$$

Practice Problem

5. Find

(a) $\displaystyle\int (5x + 1)^3 dx$ (b) $\displaystyle\int x(1 + x^2)^7 dx$ (c) $\displaystyle\int \frac{4x^3}{2 + x^4}dx$ (d) $\displaystyle\int e^x(1 + e^x)^3 dx$

Key Terms

Anti-derivative   A function whose derivative is a given function.

Constant of integration   The arbitrary constant that appears in an expression when finding an indefinite integral.

Definite integration   The process of finding the area under a graph by subtracting the values obtained when the limits are substituted into the anti-derivative.

Indefinite integration   The process of obtaining an anti-derivative.

Integral   The number $\int_a^b f(x)dx$ (definite integral) or the function $\int f(x)dx$ (indefinite integral).

Integration   The generic name for the evaluation of definite or indefinite integrals.

Inverse (operation)   The operation that reverses the effect of a given operation and takes you back to the original. For example, the inverse of halving is doubling.

Primitive   An alternative word for an anti-derivative.

Exercise 1.15

1. Find

(a) $\int 6x^5 dx$ 　　　 **(b)** $\int x^4 dx$ 　　　 **(c)** $\int 10e^{10x} dx$

(d) $\int \frac{1}{x} dx$ 　　　 **(e)** $\int x^{3/2} dx$ 　　　 **(f)** $\int (2x^3 - 6x) dx$

(g) $\int (x^2 - 8x + 3) dx$ 　 **(h)** $\int (ax + b) dx$ 　 **(i)** $\int \left(7x^3 + 4e^{-2x} - \frac{3}{x^2}\right) dx$

2. **(a)** Find the total cost if the marginal cost is

$$MC = Q + 5$$

and fixed costs are 20.

(b) Find the total cost if the marginal cost is

$$MC = 3e^{0.5Q}$$

and fixed costs are 10.

3. The marginal cost function is given by

$$MC = 2Q + 6$$

If the total cost is 212 when $Q = 8$, find the total cost when $Q = 14$.

4. Find the total revenue and demand functions corresponding to each of the following marginal revenue functions:

(a) $MR = 20 - 2Q$ 　　　 **(b)** $MR = \dfrac{6}{\sqrt{Q}}$

5. Find the consumption function if the marginal propensity to consume is 0.6 and consumption is 10 when income is 5. Deduce the corresponding savings function.

6. Find the short-run production functions corresponding to each of the following marginal product of labour functions:

(a) $1000 - 3L^2$ 　　　 **(b)** $\dfrac{6}{\sqrt{L}} - 0.01$

7. A firm's marginal revenue and marginal cost functions are given by

$$MR = 10 - 4Q \text{ and } MC = 1$$

If fixed costs are 4, find the profit when $Q = 2$.

8. **(1)** Differentiate

$$F(x) = (2x + 1)^5$$

Hence find

$$\int (2x + 1)^4 dx$$

(2) Use the approach suggested in part (1) to find

(a) $\displaystyle\int (3x-2)^7 dx$ (b) $\displaystyle\int (2-4x)^9 dx$ (c) $\displaystyle\int \sqrt{2x+1}\,dx$ (d) $\displaystyle\int \frac{1}{7x+3}dx$

Exercise 1.15*

1. Find

(a) $\displaystyle\int x(x^5-2)dx$ (b) $\displaystyle\int x^{10}-3\sqrt{x}+e^{-x}dx$ (c) $\displaystyle\int x^3 - \frac{5}{x^6} + \frac{2}{x} - 4e^{-4x}dx$

2. (a) Find the consumption function given that

$$MPC = 20 + \frac{10}{Y^{3/4}}$$

and that consumption is 420 when $Y = 16$.

(b) If the marginal cost is

$$MC = 15 + 3Q^2$$

find an expression for the variable cost per unit.

3. Find the total cost function, TC, when the fixed costs are C and the marginal cost is

(a) $aQ + b$ (b) ae^{bQ}

4. Use integration by inspection to write down the indefinite integral of:

(a) $(4x-7)^5$ (b) $\dfrac{1}{3x+1}$ (c) $\dfrac{1}{\sqrt{2x+3}}$ (d) $x(1+x^2)^4$

(e) $\dfrac{x^3}{(1+x^4)^2}$ (f) xe^{-x^2} (g) $\dfrac{(1+\ln x)^2}{x}$ (h) $\dfrac{x^2}{\sqrt{x^3+5}}$

5. (a) Show that

$$\sqrt{x}(\sqrt{x}+x^2) = x + x^{5/2}$$

Hence find

$$\int \sqrt{x}(\sqrt{x}+x^2)dx$$

(b) Use the approach suggested in part (a) to integrate each of the following functions:

$$x^4\left(x^6 + \frac{1}{x^2}\right), \quad e^{2x}(e^{3x}+e^{-x}+3), \quad x^{3/2}\left(\sqrt{x}-\frac{1}{\sqrt{x}}\right)$$

6. (a) Show that

$$\frac{x^4 - x^2 + \sqrt{x}}{x} = x^3 - x + x^{-1/2}$$

Hence find

$$\int \frac{x^4 - x^2 + \sqrt{x}}{x}\, dx$$

(b) Use the approach suggested in part (a) to integrate each of the following functions:

$$\frac{x^2 - x}{x^3}, \quad \frac{e^x - e^{-x}}{e^{2x}}, \quad \frac{\sqrt{x} - x\sqrt{x} + x^2}{x\sqrt{x}}$$

7. Find an expression for the savings function when

$$\text{MPC} = 0.4 + \frac{0.4}{\sqrt{Y}} \quad \text{and} \quad C = 50 \quad \text{when} \quad Y = 100$$

8. Find $f(x)$ when $f''(x) = 6x$, $f(0) = 2$ and $f'(0) = -4$.

9. (a) Differentiate the function, $x \ln x$.

(b) Use the result of part (a) to find $\int \ln x\, dx$.

10. The number of units, N, produced each hour by a new employee after t hours on the job satisfies

$$\frac{dN}{dt} = 10e^{-0.1t}$$

Assuming that she is unable to produce any goods at the beginning of her shift, calculate how many she can produce per hour after eight hours. How many units per hour will she be able to produce in the long run?

11. The rate of growth in the number of shops, n, in a chain of local grocery stores after t months satisfies

$$\frac{dn}{dt} = \frac{3}{\sqrt{t}}$$

Initially there are two stores.
    Estimate the number of shops in the chain after 9 months.

12. A firm's marginal revenue and marginal cost functions are given by

$$\text{MR} = 240 - 0.6Q^2 \quad \text{and} \quad \text{MC} = 150 + 0.3Q^2$$

If fixed costs are 50, determine the maximum profit.

13. Use integration by inspection to find:

(a) $\displaystyle\int (ax + b)^n dx \quad (n \neq -1)$ (b) $\displaystyle\int e^{ax+b}\, dx$ (c) $\displaystyle\int \frac{1}{ax + b}\, dx$

14. Use differentiation to show that

(a) $\displaystyle\int \frac{4x}{(2x + 3)^2}\, dx = \ln(2x + 3) + \frac{3}{2x + 3} + c$

(b) $\displaystyle\int x^2 e^x\, dx = e^x(x^2 - 2x + 2) + c$

SECTION 1.16
Definite integration

Objectives

At the end of this section you should be able to:

- Recognise the notation for definite integration.
- Evaluate definite integrals in simple cases.
- Calculate the consumer's surplus.
- Calculate the producer's surplus.
- Calculate the capital stock formation.
- Calculate the present value of a continuous revenue stream.

One rather tedious task that you may remember from school is that of finding areas. Sketched in Figure 1.48 is a region bounded by the curve $y = x^2$, the lines $x = 1$ and $x = 2$, and the x axis. At school you may well have been asked to find the area of this region by 'counting' squares on graph paper. A much quicker and more accurate way of calculating this area is to use integration. We begin by integrating the function

$$f(x) = x^2$$

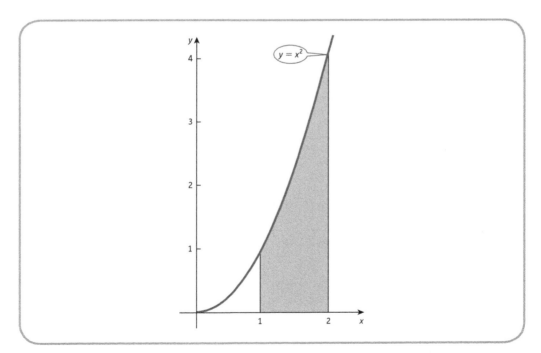

Figure 1.48

to get

$$F(x) = \frac{1}{3}x^3$$

In our case we want to find the area under the curve between $x = 1$ and $x = 2$, so we evaluate

$$F(1) = \frac{1}{3}(1)^3 = \frac{1}{3}$$

$$F(2) = \frac{1}{3}(2)^3 = \frac{8}{3}$$

Finally, we subtract $F(1)$ from $F(2)$ to get

$$F(2) - F(1) = \frac{8}{3} - \frac{1}{3} = \frac{7}{3}$$

This number is the exact value of the area of the region sketched in Figure 1.48. Given the connection with integration, we write this area as

$$\int_1^2 x^2 dx$$

In general, the **definite integral**

$$\int_a^b f(x)dx$$

denotes the area under the graph of $f(x)$ between $x = a$ and $x = b$ as shown in Figure 1.49. The numbers a and b are called the **limits of integration**, and it is assumed throughout this section that $a < b$ and that $f(x) \geq 0$ as indicated in Figure 1.49.

The technique of evaluating definite integrals is as follows. A function $F(x)$ is found which differentiates to $f(x)$. Methods of obtaining $F(x)$ have already been described in Section 1.15. The new function, $F(x)$, is then evaluated at the limits $x = a$ and $x = b$ to get $F(a)$ and $F(b)$. Finally, the second number is subtracted from the first to get the answer

$$F(b) - F(a)$$

In symbols,

$$\int_a^b f(x)dx = F(b) - F(a)$$

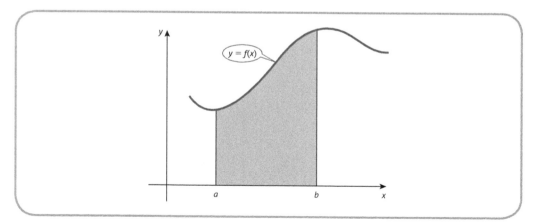

Figure 1.49

The process of evaluating a function at two distinct values of x and subtracting one from the other occurs sufficiently frequently in mathematics to warrant a special notation. We write

$$[F(x)]_a^b$$

as an abbreviation for $F(b) - F(a)$, so that definite integrals are evaluated as

$$\int_a^b f(x)\mathrm{d}x = [F(x)]_a^b = F(b) - F(a)$$

where $F(x)$ is the indefinite integral of $f(x)$. Using this notation, the evaluation of

$$\int_1^2 x^2\mathrm{d}x$$

would be written as

$$\int_1^2 x^2\mathrm{d}x = \left[\frac{1}{3}x^3\right]_1^2 = \frac{1}{3}(2)^3 - \frac{1}{3}(1)^3 = \frac{7}{3}$$

Note that it is not necessary to include the constant of integration, because it cancels out when we subtract $F(a)$ from $F(b)$.

Example

Evaluate the definite integrals

(a) $\displaystyle\int_2^6 3\mathrm{d}x$ **(b)** $\displaystyle\int_0^2 (x + 1)\mathrm{d}x$

Solution

(a) $\displaystyle\int_2^6 3\mathrm{d}x = [3x]_2^6 = 3(6) - 3(2) = 12$

This value can be confirmed graphically. Figure 1.50 shows the region under the graph of $y = 3$ between $x = 2$ and $x = 6$. This is a rectangle, so its area can be found from the formula

    area = base × height

which gives

    area = 4 × 3 = 12   ✓

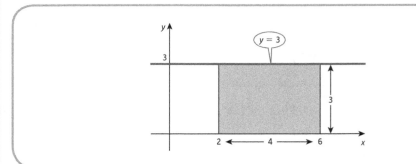

Figure 1.50

Key Terms

Consumer's surplus   The excess cost that a person would have been prepared to pay for goods over and above what is actually paid.

Definite integral   The number $\int_a^b f(x)dx$ which represents the area under the graph of $f(x)$ between $x = a$ and $x = b$.

Limits of integration   The numbers a and b which appear in the definite integral, $\int_a^b f(x)dx$.

Net investment   Rate of change of capital stock over time: $I = dK/dt$.

Producer's surplus   The excess revenue that a producer has actually received over and above the lower revenue that it was prepared to accept for the supply of its goods.

Exercise 1.16

1. Evaluate each of the following integrals:

   (a) $\int_1^3 4x^2dx$ (b) $\int_2^3 \frac{2}{x^3}dx$ (c) $\int_1^4 \frac{6}{\sqrt{x}}dx$ (d) $\int_1^2 4x^3 - 3x^2 + 4x + 2\,dx$

2. Find the exact areas under each of the following curves:

   (a) $y = 2x^2 + x + 3$ between $x = 1$ and $x = 5$
   (b) $y = (x - 2)^2$ between $x = 2$ and $x = 3$
   (c) $y = 3\sqrt{x}$ between $x = 4$ and $x = 25$
   (d) $y = e^x$ between $x = 0$ and $x = 1$
   (e) $y = \frac{1}{x}$ between $x = 1$ and $x = e$

3. Evaluate each of the following definite integrals:

   (a) $\int_0^2 x^3dx$ (b) $\int_{-2}^2 x^3dx$

   By sketching a rough graph of the cube function between and $x = -2$ and 2, suggest a reason for your answer to part (b). What is the actual area between the x axis and the graph of $y = x^3$, over this range?

4. Find the consumer's surplus at $P = 5$ for the following demand functions:

   (a) $P = 25 - 2Q$ (b) $P = \frac{10}{\sqrt{Q}}$

5. Find the producer's surplus at $Q = 9$ for the following supply functions:

   (a) $P = 12 + 2Q$ (b) $P = 20\sqrt{Q} + 15$

6. Find the consumer's surplus for the demand function

   $P = 50 - 2Q - 0.01Q^2$

   when

   (a) $Q = 10$ (b) $Q = 11$

7. Given the demand function

    $$P = -Q_D^2 - 4Q_D + 68$$

    and the supply function

    $$P = Q_S^2 + 2Q_S + 12$$

    Find

    (a) the consumer's surplus

    (b) the producer's surplus

    assuming pure competition.

8. If the investment flow is

    $$I(t) = 5000t^{1/4}$$

    calculate the capital formation from the end of the second year to halfway through the fifth year. Give your answer to the nearest whole number.

9. Given the investment flow

    $$I(t) = 2400\sqrt{t}$$

    (a) Calculate the total capital formation during the first four years.

    (b) Find an expression for the annual capital formation during the Nth year and hence find the first year in which the annual capital formation exceeds $4000.

10. Calculate the present value of a revenue stream for eight years at a constant rate of $12 000 per year if the discount rate is 7.5%.

11. A company begins its extraction of oil from a newly discovered oil field at $t = 0$. The rate of extraction, measured in thousands of barrels per year, is given by

    $$\frac{dN}{dt} = 30t^2 - 4t^3$$

    Calculate the number of barrels extracted during the first four years of operation.

Exercise 1.16*

1. Evaluate

    (a) $\displaystyle\int_{-1}^{2} 5x^2 - 4x + 6\,dx$ **(b)** $\displaystyle\int_{2}^{10} \frac{1}{(2x + 5)\sqrt{(2x + 5)}}\,dx$

2. **(a)** Find the consumer's surplus at $Q = 8$ for the demand function

    $$P = 50 - 4Q$$

    (b) The producer's surplus at $Q = a$ for the supply function

    $$P = 6 + 8Q$$

    is known to be 400. Find the value of a.

3. The demand function is given by

$$P = 74 - Q_D^2$$

and the supply function is

$$P = (Q_S + 2)^2$$

Calculate the consumer's and producer's surplus under pure competition.

4. If the supply and demand functions are given by $P = Q + 50$ and $P = \dfrac{4000}{Q + 20}$, respectively, find the equilibrium price and quantity, and calculate the consumer's and producer's surplus.

5. If the supply and demand functions are given by $P = 20e^{0.4Q}$ and $P = 100e^{-0.2Q}$, respectively, find the equilibrium price and quantity, and calculate the consumer's and producer's surplus.

6. If the net investment function is given by

$$I(t) = 100e^{0.1t}$$

calculate

   (a) the capital formation from the end of the second year to the end of the fifth year;

   (b) the number of years required before the capital stock exceeds $100 000.

7. Find the expression for capital formation between $t = 0$ and $t = T$ for the following net investment functions:

   (a) $I(t) = At^\alpha$ **(b)** $I(t) = Ae^{\alpha t}$

   where A and α are positive constants.

8. Calculate the present value of a continuous revenue stream of $1000 per year if the discount rate is 5% and the money is paid

   (a) for 3 years   **(b)** for 10 years   **(c)** for 100 years   **(d)** in perpetuity

9. The present value of a continuous revenue stream of $5000 per year with a discount rate of 10% over n years is $25 000. Find the value of n correct to one decimal place.

10. Write down an expression for $g'(x)$ when

$$g(x) = \int_2^x (5t^2 - 2t)\,dt$$

11. Write down an expression for the present value of a continuous revenue stream for n years at a constant rate of S per year if the discount rate is $r\%$.

12. If a firm's profit function is $\pi = f(Q)$ and the level of output, Q, varies between a and b units, then the firm's average profit is given by

$$\frac{1}{b - a} \int_a^b f(Q)\,dQ$$

Calculate a firm's average profit when $TR = 100(1 - e^{-0.1Q})$, $TC = 0.1Q^2 + 2Q + 1$ and output varies from 3 to 8 units.

13. A newly elected government decides to reduce pollution in major cities by investing in a green spaces project. The subsequent investment flow is given by

$$I(t) = 0.6t^2 + 10$$

where t is measured in years from the start of the government term and I is measured in millions of dollars per year. Five years later, as a result of a change of administration, planned investment is dramatically reduced so that for the following five years, investment flow $J(t)$ is given by

$$J(t) = 25e^{0.4(5-t)} \text{ for } 5 \leq t \leq 10$$

(a) Verify that $I(5) = J(5)$ and sketch a graph of the investment flow for the complete 10-year period.

(b) After how many years does the total capital spent on this project first exceed $110 million? Give your answer to one decimal place.

14. The demand function of a good is given by $P = 80 - 6\sqrt{Q}$

(a) Find the change in consumer's surplus due to a decrease in price from $P = 62$ to $P = 56$.

(b) Sketch a graph of the demand function and shade the area which corresponds to the change in consumer's surplus calculated in part (a).

SECTION 1.17
Supply and demand analysis

Objectives

At the end of this section you should be able to:

- Use the function notation, $y = f(x)$.
- Identify the endogenous and exogenous variables in an economic model.
- Identify and sketch a linear demand function.
- Identify and sketch a linear supply function.
- Determine the equilibrium price and quantity for a single-commodity market both graphically and algebraically.
- Determine the equilibrium price and quantity for a multicommodity market by solving simultaneous linear equations.

Microeconomics is concerned with the analysis of the economic theory and policy of individual firms and markets. In this section we focus on one particular aspect known as market equilibrium, in which the supply and demand balance. We describe how the mathematics introduced in the previous two sections can be used to calculate the equilibrium price and quantity. However, before we do this it is useful to explain the concept of a function. This idea is central to nearly all applications of mathematics in economics.

A **function**, f, is a rule which assigns to each incoming number, x, a uniquely defined outgoing number, y. A function may be thought of as a 'black box' that performs a dedicated arithmetic calculation. As an example, consider the rule 'double and add 3'. The effect of this rule on two specific incoming numbers, 5 and -17, is illustrated in Figure 1.54.

Unfortunately, such a representation is rather cumbersome. There are, however, two alternative ways of expressing this rule which are more concise. We can write either

$$y = 2x + 3 \text{ or } f(x) = 2x + 3$$

The first of these is familiar to you from our previous work; corresponding to any incoming number, x, the right-hand side tells you what to do with x to generate the outgoing number, y.

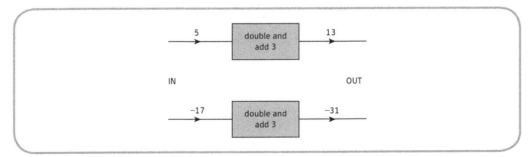

Figure 1.54

Practice Problem

3. The demand and supply functions of a good are given by

$$P = -4Q_D + 120$$
$$P = \tfrac{1}{3}Q_S + 29$$

where P, Q_D and Q_S denote the price, quantity demanded and quantity supplied, respectively.

(a) Calculate the equilibrium price and quantity.

(b) Calculate the new equilibrium price and quantity after the imposition of a fixed tax of $13 per good. Who pays the tax?

We conclude this section by considering a more realistic model of supply and demand, taking into account substitutable and complementary goods. Let us suppose that there are two goods in related markets, which we call good 1 and good 2. The demand for either good depends on the prices of both good 1 and good 2. If the corresponding demand functions are linear, then

$$Q_{D_1} = a_1 + b_1P_1 + c_1P_2$$
$$Q_{D_2} = a_2 + b_2P_1 + c_2P_2$$

where P_i and Q_{D_i} denote the price and demand for the ith good and a_i, b_i and c_i are parameters. For the first equation, $a_1 > 0$ because there is a positive demand when the prices of both goods are zero. Also, $b_1 < 0$ because the demand of a good falls as its price rises. The sign of c_1 depends on the nature of the goods. If the goods are substitutable, then an increase in the price of good 2 would mean that consumers would switch from good 2 to good 1, causing Q_{D_1} to increase. Substitutable goods are therefore characterised by a positive value of c_1. On the other hand, if the goods are complementary, then a rise in the price of either good would see the demand fall, so c_1 is negative. Similar results apply to the signs of a_2, b_2 and c_2. The calculation of the equilibrium price and quantity in a two-commodity market model is demonstrated in the following example.

Example

The demand and supply functions for two interdependent commodities are given by

$$Q_{D_1} = 10 - 2P_1 + P_2$$
$$Q_{D_2} = 5 + 2P_1 - 2P_2$$
$$Q_{S_1} = -3 + 2P_1$$
$$Q_{S_2} = -2 + 3P_2$$

where Q_{D_i}, Q_{S_i} and P_i denote the quantity demanded, quantity supplied and price of good i, respectively. Determine the equilibrium price and quantity for this two-commodity model.

Solution

In equilibrium, we know that the quantity supplied is equal to the quantity demanded for each good, so that

$$Q_{D_1} = Q_{S_1} \quad \text{and} \quad Q_{D_2} = Q_{S_2}$$

Let us write these respective common values as Q_1 and Q_2. The demand and supply equations for good 1 then become

$$Q_1 = 10 - 2P_1 + P_2$$
$$Q_1 = -3 + 2P_1$$

Hence

$$10 - 2P_1 + P_2 = -3 + 2P_1$$

since both sides are equal to Q_1. It makes sense to tidy this equation up a bit by collecting all of the unknowns on the left-hand side and putting the constant terms on to the right-hand side:

$$10 - 4P_1 + P_2 = -3 \quad \text{(subtract } 2P_1 \text{ from both sides)}$$
$$-4P_1 + P_2 = -13 \quad \text{(subtract 10 from both sides)}$$

We can perform a similar process for good 2. The demand and supply equations become

$$Q_2 = 5 + 2P_1 - 2P_2$$
$$Q_2 = -2 + 3P_2$$

because $Q_{D_2} = Q_{S_2} = Q_2$ in equilibrium. Hence

$$5 + 2P_1 - 2P_2 = -2 + 3P_2$$
$$5 + 2P_1 - 5P_2 = -2 \quad \text{(subtract } 3P_2 \text{ from both sides)}$$
$$2P_1 - 5P_2 = -7 \quad \text{(subtract 5 from both sides)}$$

We have therefore shown that the equilibrium prices, P_1 and P_2, satisfy the simultaneous linear equations

$$-4P_1 + P_2 = -13 \tag{1}$$
$$2P_1 - 5P_2 = -7 \tag{2}$$

which can be solved by elimination. Following the steps described in Section 1.4, we proceed as follows.

Step 1

Double equation (2) and add to equation (1) to get

$$-4P_1 + \quad P_2 = -13$$
$$\underline{\quad 4P_1 - 10P_2 = -14} + \tag{3}$$
$$-9P_2 = -27$$

Step 2

Divide both sides of equation (3) by -9 to get $P_2 = 3$.

Step 3

If this is substituted into equation (1), then

$$-4P_1 + 3 = -13$$
$$-4P_1 = -16 \quad \text{(subtract 3 from both sides)}$$
$$P_1 = 4 \quad \text{(divide both sides by } -4)$$

Step 4

As a check, equation (2) gives

$$2(4) - 5(3) = -7 \quad ✓$$

Hence $P_1 = 4$ and $P_2 = 3$.

Finally, the equilibrium quantities can be deduced by substituting these values back into the original supply equations. For good 1,

$$Q_1 = -3 + 2P_1 = -3 + 2(4) = 5$$

For good 2,

$$Q_2 = -2 + 3P_2 = -2 + 3(3) = 7$$

As a check, the demand equations also give

$$Q_1 = 10 - 2P_1 + P_2 = 10 - 2(4) + 3 = 5 \quad ✓$$
$$Q_2 = 5 + 2P_1 - 2P_2 = 5 + 2(4) - 2(3) = 7 \quad ✓$$

Practice Problem

4. The demand and supply functions for two interdependent commodities are given by

$$Q_{D_1} = 40 - 5P_1 - P_2$$
$$Q_{D_2} = 50 - 2P_1 - 4P_2$$
$$Q_{S_1} = -3 + 4P_1$$
$$Q_{S_2} = -7 + 3P_2$$

where Q_{D_i}, Q_{S_i} and P_i denote the quantity demanded, quantity supplied and price of good i, respectively. Determine the equilibrium price and quantity for this two-commodity model. Are these goods substitutable or complementary?

For a two-commodity market the equilibrium prices and quantities can be found by solving a system of two simultaneous equations. Exactly the same procedure can be applied to a three-commodity market, which requires the solution of a system of three simultaneous equations.

Advice

An example of a three-commodity model can be found in Question 6 of Exercise 1.17. In general, with n goods it is necessary to solve n equations in n unknowns and, as pointed out in Section 1.4, this is best done using a computer package whenever n is large.

Key Terms

Complementary goods   A pair of goods consumed together. As the price of either goes up, the demand for both goods goes down.

Decreasing function   A function, $y = f(x)$, in which y decreases as x increases.

Demand function   A relationship between the quantity demanded and various factors that affect demand, including price.

Dependent variable   A variable whose value is determined by that taken by the independent variables; in $y = f(x)$, the dependent variable is y.

Endogenous variable   A variable whose value is determined within a model.

Equilibrium (market)   This state occurs when quantity supplied and quantity demanded are equal.

Exogenous variable   A variable whose value is determined outside a model.

Function   A rule that assigns to each incoming number, x, a uniquely defined outgoing number, y.

Increasing function   A function, $y = f(x)$, in which y increases as x increases.

Independent variable   A variable whose value determines that of the dependent variable; in $y = f(x)$, the independent variable is x.

Inferior good   A good whose demand decreases as income increases.

Inverse function   A function, written f^{-1}, which reverses the effect of a given function, f, so that $x = f^{-1}(y)$ when $y = f(x)$.

Modelling   The creation of a piece of mathematical theory which represents (a simplification of) some aspect of practical economics.

Normal good   A good whose demand increases as income increases.

Parameter   A constant whose value affects the specific values but not the general form of a mathematical expression, such as the constants a, b and c in $ax^2 + bx + c$.

Substitutable goods   A pair of goods that are alternatives to each other. As the price of one good goes up, the demand for the other rises.

Supply function   A relationship between the quantity supplied and various factors that affect supply, including price.

Exercise 1.17

1. If $f(x) = 3x + 15$ and $g(x) = \frac{1}{3}x - 5$, evaluate

   (a) $f(2)$ (b) $f(10)$ (c) $f(0)$ (d) $g(21)$ (e) $g(45)$ (f) $g(15)$

   What word describes the relationship between f and g?

2. Sketch a graph of the supply function

   $$P = \frac{1}{3}Q + 7$$

   Hence, or otherwise, determine the value of

   (a) P when $Q = 12$
   (b) Q when $P = 10$
   (c) Q when $P = 4$

3. The demand function of a good is

    $Q = 100 - P + 2Y + \frac{1}{2}A$

    where Q, P, Y and A denote quantity demanded, price, income and advertising expenditure, respectively.

    (a) Calculate the demand when $P = 10$, $Y = 40$ and $A = 6$. Assuming that price and income are fixed, calculate the additional advertising expenditure needed to raise demand to 179 units.

    (b) Is this good inferior or normal?

4. The demand, Q, for a certain good depends on its own price, P, and the price of an alternative good, P_A, according to

    $Q = 30 - 3P + P_A$

    (a) Find Q if $P = 4$ and $P_A = 5$.

    (b) Is the alternative good substitutable or complementary? Give a reason for your answer.

    (c) Determine the value of P if $Q = 23$ and $P_A = 11$.

5. The demand for a good priced at $50 is 420 units, and when the price is $80, demand is 240 units. Assuming that the demand function takes the form $Q = aP + b$, find the values of a and b.

6. (a) Copy and complete the following table of values for the supply function

    $P = \frac{1}{2}Q + 20$

Q	0		50
P		25	

    Hence, or otherwise, draw an accurate sketch of this function using axes with values of Q and P between 0 and 50.

    (b) On the same axes draw the graph of the demand function

    $P = 50 - Q$

    and hence find the equilibrium quantity and price.

    (c) The good under consideration is normal. Describe the effect on the equilibrium quantity and price when income rises.

7. The demand and supply functions of a good are given by

    $P = -3Q_D + 48$

    $P = \frac{1}{2}Q_S + 23$

    Find the equilibrium quantity if the government imposes a fixed tax of $4 on each good.

8. The demand and supply functions for two interdependent commodities are given by

    $Q_{D_1} = 100 - 2P_1 + P_2$

    $Q_{D_2} = 5 + 2P_1 - 3P_2$

    $Q_{S_1} = -10 + P_1$

    $Q_{S_2} = -5 + 6P_2$

where Q_D, Q_S and P_i denote the quantity demanded, quantity supplied and price of good i, respectively. Determine the equilibrium price and quantity for this two-commodity model.

9. A demand function of a certain good is given by

$$Q = -20P + 0.04Y + 4T + 3P_r$$

where Q and P denote the quantity and price of the good, Y is income, T is taste and P_r is the price of a related good.

(a) Calculate Q when $P = 8$, $Y = 1000$, $T = 15$ and $P_r = 30$.

(b) Is the related good substitutable or complementary? Give a reason for your answer.

(c) Find the value of P when $Q = 235$, $Y = 8000$, $T = 30$ and $P_r = 25$.

(d) The exogenous variables are now fixed at $Y = 2000$, $T = 10$ and $P_r = 5$. State the values of the slope and vertical intercept when the demand function is sketched with

(i) P on the horizontal axis and Q on the vertical axis;

(ii) Q on the horizontal axis and P on the vertical axis.

Exercise 1.17*

1. Describe the effect on the demand curve due to an increase in

(a) the price of substitutable goods;

(b) the price of complementary goods;

(c) advertising expenditure.

2. If the line, $P = -\frac{2}{3}Q + 6$, is sketched with P on the horizontal axis and Q on the vertical axis, find the gradient, m, and the vertical intercept, c.

3. If the demand function of a good is

$$2P + 3Q_D = 60$$

where P and Q_D denote price and quantity demanded, respectively, find the largest and smallest values of P for which this function is economically meaningful.

4. The demand and supply functions of a good are given by

$$P = -5Q_D + 80$$
$$P = 2Q_S + 10$$

where P, Q_D and Q_S denote price, quantity demanded and quantity supplied, respectively.

(1) Find the equilibrium price and quantity

(a) graphically;

(b) algebraically.

(2) If the government deducts, as tax, 15% of the market price of each good, determine the new equilibrium price and quantity.

5. The supply and demand functions of a good are given by

    $P = Q_S + 8$

    $P = -3Q_D + 80$

    where P, Q_S and Q_D denote price, quantity supplied and quantity demanded, respectively.

    (a) Find the equilibrium price and quantity if the government imposes a fixed tax of $36 on each good.

    (b) Find the corresponding value of the government's tax revenue.

6. The demand and supply functions for three interdependent commodities are

    $Q_{D_1} = 15 - P_1 + 2P_2 + P_3$

    $Q_{D_2} = 9 + P_1 - P_2 - P_3$

    $Q_{D_3} = 8 + 2P_1 - P_2 - 4P_3$

    $Q_{S_1} = -7 + P_1$

    $Q_{S_2} = -4 + 4P_2$

    $Q_{S_3} = -5 + 2P_3$

    where Q_{D_i}, Q_{S_i} and P_i denote the quantity demanded, quantity supplied and price of good i, respectively. Determine the equilibrium price and quantity for this three-commodity model.

7. The demand and supply functions of a good are given by

    $P = -3Q_D + 60$

    $P = 2Q_S + 40$

    respectively. If the government decides to impose a tax of $$t$ per good, show that the equilibrium quantity is given by

    $Q = 4 - \frac{1}{5}t$

    and write down a similar expression for the equilibrium price.

    (a) If it is known that the equilibrium quantity is 3, work out the value of t. How much of this tax is paid by the firm?

    (b) If, instead of imposing a tax, the government provides a subsidy of $5 per good, find the new equilibrium price and quantity.

8. The linear supply and demand functions for a good are given by

    $P = aQ + b$ and $P = cQ + d$

    (a) State whether each of the values of the parameters a, b, c and d are positive or negative.

    (b) Find expressions, simplified as far as possible, for equilibrium price and quantity.

SECTION 1.18

Revenue, cost and profit

Objectives

At the end of this section you should be able to:

- Sketch the graphs of the total revenue, total cost, average cost and profit functions.
- Find the level of output that maximises total revenue.
- Find the level of output that maximises profit.
- Find the break-even levels of output.

The main aim of this section is to investigate one particular function in economics, namely profit. By making reasonable simplifying assumptions, the profit function is shown to be quadratic and so the methods developed in Section 1.7 can be used to analyse its properties. We describe how to find the levels of output required for a firm to break even and to maximise profit. The **profit** function is denoted by the Greek letter π (pi, pronounced 'pie') and is defined to be the difference between total revenue, TR, and total cost, TC: that is,

$$\pi = TR - TC$$

This definition is entirely sensible because TR is the amount of money received by the firm from the sale of its goods, and TC is the amount of money that the firm has to spend to produce these goods. We begin by considering the total revenue and total cost functions in turn.

The **total revenue** received from the sale of Q goods at price P is given by

$$TR = PQ$$

For example, if the price of each good is \$70 and the firm sells 300, then the revenue is

$$\$70 \times 300 = \$21\ 000$$

Given any particular demand function, expressing P in terms of Q, it is a simple matter to obtain a formula for TR solely in terms of Q. A graph of TR against Q can then be sketched.

Example

Given the demand function

$$P = 100 - 2Q$$

express TR as a function of Q and hence sketch its graph.

(a) For what values of Q is TR zero?

(b) What is the maximum value of TR?

Solution

Total revenue is defined by

$$TR = PQ$$

SECTION 1.19
Marginal functions

Objectives

At the end of this section you should be able to:

● Calculate marginal revenue and marginal cost.

● Derive the relationship between marginal and average revenue for both a monopoly and perfect competition.

● Calculate marginal product of labour.

● State the law of diminishing marginal productivity using the notation of calculus.

● Calculate marginal propensity to consume and marginal propensity to save.

At this stage you may be wondering what on earth differentiation has to do with economics. In fact, we cannot get very far with economic theory without making use of calculus. In this section we concentrate on three main areas that illustrate its applicability:

● revenue and cost;

● production;

● consumption and savings.

We consider each of these in turn.

1.19.1 Revenue and cost

In Section 1.18 we investigated the basic properties of the revenue function, TR. It is defined to be PQ, where P denotes the price of a good and Q denotes the quantity demanded. In practice, we usually know the demand function, which provides a relationship between P and Q. This enables a formula for TR to be written down solely in terms of Q. For example, if

$$P = 100 - 2Q$$

then

$$TR = PQ = (100 - 2Q)Q = 100Q - 2Q^2$$

The formula can be used to calculate the value of TR corresponding to any value of Q. Not content with this, we are also interested in the effect on TR of a change in the value of Q from some existing level. To do this we introduce the concept of marginal revenue. The **marginal revenue**, MR, of a good is defined by

$$MR = \frac{d(TR)}{dQ}$$

> marginal revenue is the derivative of total revenue with respect to demand

For example, the marginal revenue function corresponding to

$$TR = 100Q - 2Q^2$$

is given by

$$\frac{d(TR)}{dQ} = 100 - 4Q$$

If the current demand is 15, say, then

$$MR = 100 - 4(15) = 40$$

You may be familiar with an alternative definition often quoted in elementary economics textbooks. Marginal revenue is sometimes taken to be the change in TR brought about by a 1 unit increase in Q. It is easy to check that this gives an acceptable approximation to MR, although it is not quite the same as the exact value obtained by differentiation. For example, substituting $Q = 15$ into the total revenue function considered previously gives

$$TR = 100(15) - 2(15)^2 = 1050$$

An increase of 1 unit in the value of Q produces a total revenue

$$TR = 100(16) - 2(16)^2 = 1088$$

This is an increase of 38, which, according to the non-calculus definition, is the value of MR when Q is 15. This compares with the exact value of 40 obtained by differentiation.

It is instructive to give a graphical interpretation of these two approaches. In Figure 1.69 the point A lies on the TR curve corresponding to a quantity Q_0. The exact value of MR at this point is equal to the derivative

$$\frac{d(TR)}{dQ}$$

and so is given by the slope of the tangent at A. The point B also lies on the curve but corresponds to a 1-unit increase in Q. The vertical distance from A to B therefore equals the change in TR when Q increases by 1 unit. The slope of the line joining A and B (known as a **chord**) is

$$\frac{\Delta(TR)}{\Delta Q} = \frac{\Delta(TR)}{1} = \Delta(TR)$$

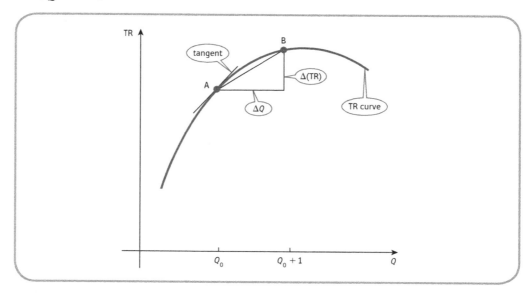

Figure 1.69

In other words, the slope of the chord is equal to the value of MR obtained from the non-calculus definition. Inspection of the diagram reveals that the slope of the tangent is approximately the same as that of the chord joining A and B. In this case the slope of the tangent is slightly the larger of the two, but there is not much in it. We therefore see that the 1-unit-increase approach produces a reasonable approximation to the exact value of MR given by

$$\frac{\text{d(TR)}}{\text{d}Q}$$

Practice Problem

1. If the demand function is

$$P = 60 - Q$$

find an expression for TR in terms of Q.

(1) Differentiate TR with respect to Q to find a general expression for MR in terms of Q. Hence write down the exact value of MR at $Q = 50$.

(2) Calculate the value of TR when

(a) $Q = 50$ **(b)** $Q = 51$

and hence confirm that the 1-unit-increase approach gives a reasonable approximation to the exact value of MR obtained in part (1).

The approximation indicated by Figure 1.69 holds for any value of ΔQ. The slope of the tangent at A is the marginal revenue, MR. The slope of the chord joining A and B is $\Delta(\text{TR})/\Delta Q$. It follows that

$$\text{MR} \cong \frac{\Delta(\text{TR})}{\Delta Q}$$

This equation can be transposed to give

$$\Delta(\text{TR}) \cong MR \times \Delta Q \qquad$$ multiply both sides by ΔQ

that is,

change in total revenue $\cong$ marginal revenue $\times$ change in demand

Moreover, Figure 1.69 shows that the smaller the value of ΔQ, the better the approximation becomes.

Example

If the total revenue function of a good is given by

$$100Q - Q^2$$

write down an expression for the marginal revenue function. If the current demand is 60, estimate the change in the value of TR due to a 2-unit increase in Q.

Solution

If

$$TR = 100Q - Q^2$$

then

$$MR = \frac{d(TR)}{dQ}$$
$$= 100 - 2Q$$

When $Q = 60$

$$MR = 100 - 2(60) = -20$$

If Q increases by 2 units, $\Delta Q = 2$ and the formula

$$\Delta(TR) \cong MR \times \Delta Q$$

shows that the change in total revenue is approximately

$$(-20) \times 2 = -40$$

A 2-unit increase in Q therefore leads to a decrease in TR of about 40.

Practice Problem

2. If the total revenue function of a good is given by

    $$1000Q - 4Q^2$$

    write down an expression for the marginal revenue function. If the current demand is 30, find the approximate change in the value of TR due to a

    (a) 3-unit increase in Q;

    (b) 2-unit decrease in Q.

The simple model of demand, originally introduced in Section 1.5, assumed that price, P, and quantity, Q, are linearly related according to an equation,

$$P = aQ + b$$

where the slope, a, is negative and the intercept, b, is positive. A downward-sloping demand curve such as this corresponds to the case of a monopolist. A single firm, or possibly a group

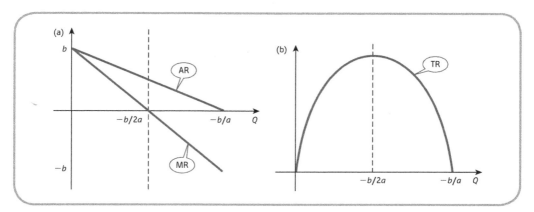

Figure 1.70

of firms forming a cartel, is assumed to be the only supplier of a particular product and so has control over the market price. As the firm raises the price, so demand falls. The associated total revenue function is given by

$$\text{TR} = PQ$$
$$= (aQ + b)Q$$
$$= aQ^2 + bQ$$

An expression for marginal revenue is obtained by differentiating TR with respect to Q to get

$$\text{MR} = 2aQ + b$$

It is interesting to notice that, on the assumption of a linear demand equation, the marginal revenue is also linear with the same intercept, b, but with slope $2a$. The marginal revenue curve slopes downhill exactly twice as fast as the demand curve. This is illustrated in Figure 1.70(a).

The **average revenue**, AR, is defined by

$$\text{AR} = \frac{\text{TR}}{Q}$$

and, since $\text{TR} = PQ$, we have

$$\text{AR} = \frac{PQ}{Q} = P$$

For this reason the demand curve is labelled average revenue in Figure 1.70(a). The above derivation of the result $\text{AR} = P$ is independent of the particular demand function. Consequently, the terms 'average revenue curve' and 'demand curve' are synonymous.

Figure 1.70(a) shows that the marginal revenue takes both positive and negative values. This is to be expected. The total revenue function is a quadratic, and its graph has the familiar parabolic shape indicated in Figure 1.70(b). To the left of $-b/2a$ the graph is uphill, corresponding to a positive value of marginal revenue, whereas to the right of this point it is downhill, giving a negative value of marginal revenue. More significantly, at the maximum point of the TR curve, the tangent is horizontal with zero slope, and so MR is zero.

At the other extreme from a monopolist is the case of **perfect competition**. For this model we assume that there are a large number of firms all selling an identical product and that

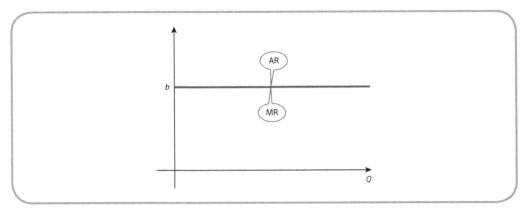

Figure 1.71

there are no barriers to entry into the industry. Since any individual firm produces a tiny proportion of the total output, it has no control over price. The firm can sell only at the prevailing market price and, because the firm is relatively small, it can sell any number of goods at this price. If the fixed price is denoted by b, then the demand function is

$$P = b$$

and the associated total revenue function is

$$TR = PQ = bQ$$

An expression for marginal revenue is obtained by differentiating TR with respect to Q and, since b is just a constant, we see that

$$MR = b$$

In the case of perfect competition, the average and marginal revenue curves are the same. They are horizontal straight lines, b units above the Q axis, as shown in Figure 1.71.

So far we have concentrated on the total revenue function. Exactly the same principle can be used for other economic functions. For instance, we define the marginal cost, MC, by

$$MC = \frac{d(TC)}{dQ}$$

> marginal cost is the derivative of total cost with respect to output

Again, using a simple geometrical argument, it is easy to see that if Q changes by a small amount ΔQ, then the corresponding change in TC is given by

$$\Delta(TC) \cong MC \times \Delta Q$$

> change in total cost $\cong$ marginal cost $\times$ change in output

In particular, putting $\Delta Q = 1$ gives

$$\Delta(TC) \cong MC$$

so that MC gives the approximate change in TC when Q increases by 1 unit.

Example

If the average cost function of a good is

$$AC = 2Q + 6 + \frac{13}{Q}$$

find an expression for MC. If the current output is 15, estimate the effect on TC of a 3-unit decrease in Q.

Solution

We first need to find an expression for TC using the given formula for AC. Now we know that the average cost is just the total cost divided by Q: that is,

$$AC = \frac{TC}{Q}$$

Hence

$$TC = (AC)Q$$
$$= \left(2Q + 6 + \frac{13}{Q}\right)Q$$

and, after multiplying out the brackets, we get

$$TC = 2Q^2 + 6Q + 13$$

In this formula the last term, 13, is independent of Q and so must denote the fixed costs. The remaining part, $2Q^2 + 6Q$, depends on Q and so represents the total variable costs. Differentiating gives

$$MC = \frac{d(TC)}{dQ}$$
$$= 4Q + 6$$

Notice that because the fixed costs are constant, they differentiate to zero and so have no effect on the marginal cost. When $Q = 15$,

$$MC = 4(15) + 6 = 66$$

Also, if Q decreases by 2 units, then $\Delta Q = -2$. Hence the change in TC is given by

$$\Delta(TC) \cong MC \times \Delta Q = 66 \times (-2) = -132$$

so TC decreases by 132 units approximately.

Practice Problem

3. Find the marginal cost given the average cost function

$$AC = \frac{100}{Q} + 2$$

Deduce that a 1-unit increase in Q will always result in a 2-unit increase in TC, irrespective of the current level of output.

1.19.2 Production

Production functions were introduced in Section 1.8. In the simplest case output, Q is assumed to be a function of labour, L, and capital, K. Moreover, in the short run the input K can be assumed to be fixed, so Q is then only a function of one input L. (This is not a valid assumption in the long run, and in general, Q must be regarded as a function of at least two inputs.) The variable L is usually measured in terms of the number of workers or possibly in terms of the number of worker hours. Motivated by our previous work, we define the **marginal product of labour**, MP_L, by

$$MP_L = \frac{dQ}{dL}$$

> marginal product of labour is the derivative of output with respect to labour

As before, this gives the approximate change in Q that results from using 1 more unit of L.

It is instructive to work out numerical values of MP_L for the particular production function

$$Q = 300L^{1/2} - 4L$$

where L denotes the actual size of the workforce.

Differentiating Q with respect to L gives

$$\begin{aligned}
MP_L &= \frac{dQ}{dL} \\
&= 300(\tfrac{1}{2} L^{-1/2}) - 4 \\
&= 150L^{-1/2} - 4 \\
&= \frac{150}{\sqrt{L}} - 4
\end{aligned}$$

Substituting $L = 1, 9, 100$ and 2500 in turn into the formula for MP_L gives:

(a) When $L = 1$

$$MP_L = \frac{150}{\sqrt{9}} - 4 = 146$$

(b) When $L = 9$

$$MP_L = \frac{150}{\sqrt{1}} - 4 = 46$$

(c) When $L = 100$

$$MP_L = \frac{150}{\sqrt{100}} - 4 = 11$$

(d) When $L = 2500$

$$MP_L = \frac{150}{\sqrt{2500}} - 4 = -1$$

Notice that the values of MP_L decline with increasing L. Part (a) shows that if the workforce consists of only one person then to employ two people would increase output by approximately 146. In part (b) we see that to increase the number of workers from 9 to 10 would result in about 46 additional units of output. In part (c) we see that a 1-unit increase in labour from a level of 100 increases output by only 11. In part (d) the situation is even worse. This indicates that to increase staff actually reduces output! The latter is a rather surprising result, but it is borne out by what occurs in real production processes. This may be due to problems of overcrowding on the shopfloor or to the need to create an elaborate administration to organise the larger workforce.

This production function illustrates the **law of diminishing marginal productivity** (sometimes called the **law of diminishing returns**). It states that the increase in output due to a 1-unit increase in labour will eventually decline. In other words, once the size of the workforce has reached a certain threshold level, the marginal product of labour will get smaller. For the production function

$$Q = 300L^{1/2} - 4L$$

the value of MP_L continually goes down with rising L. This is not always so. It is possible for the marginal product of labour to remain constant or to go up to begin with for small values of L. However, if it is to satisfy the law of diminishing marginal productivity, then there must be some value of L above which MP_L decreases.

A typical product curve is sketched in Figure 1.72, which has slope

$$\frac{dQ}{dL} = MP_L$$

Between 0 and L_0 the curve bends upwards, becoming progressively steeper, and so the slope function, MP_L, increases. Mathematically, this means that the slope of MP_L is positive: that is,

$$\frac{d(MP_L)}{dQ} > 0$$

Now MP_L is itself the derivative of Q with respect to L, so we can use the notation for the second-order derivative and write this as

$$\frac{d^2Q}{dL^2} > 0$$

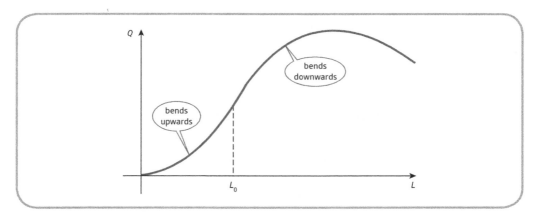

Figure 1.72

Similarly, if L exceeds the threshold value of L_0, then Figure 1.72 shows that the product curve bends downwards and the slope decreases. In this region, the slope of the slope function is negative, so that

$$\frac{d^2Q}{dL^2} < 0$$

The law of diminishing returns states that this must happen eventually: that is,

$$\frac{d^2Q}{dL^2} < 0$$

for sufficiently large L.

Practice Problem

4. A Cobb–Douglas production function is given by

$$Q = 5L^{1/2}K^{1/2}$$

Assuming that capital, K, is fixed at 100, write down a formula for Q in terms of L only. Calculate the marginal product of labour when

(a) $L = 1$ (b) $L = 9$ (c) $L = 10\ 000$

Verify that the law of diminishing marginal productivity holds in this case.

1.19.3 Consumption and savings

In Section 1.1 the relationship between consumption, C, savings, S, and national income, Y, was investigated. If we assume that national income is only used up in consumption and savings then

$$Y = C + S$$

Of particular interest is the effect on C and S due to variations in Y. Expressed simply, if national income rises by a certain amount, are people more likely to go out and spend their extra income on consumer goods, or will they save it? To analyse this behaviour we use the concepts **marginal propensity to consume**, MPC, and **marginal propensity to save**, MPS, which are defined by

$$\text{MPC} = \frac{dC}{dY} \quad \text{and} \quad \text{MPS} = \frac{dS}{dY}$$

> marginal propensity to consume is the derivative of consumption with respect to income

> marginal propensity to save is the derivative of savings with respect to income

These definitions are consistent with those given in Section 1.6, where MPC and MPS were taken to be the slopes of the linear consumption and savings curves, respectively. At first sight it appears that, in general, we need to work out two derivatives in order to evaluate MPC and

MPS. However, this is not strictly necessary. Recall that we can do whatever we like to an equation provided we do the same thing to both sides. Consequently, we can differentiate both sides of the equation

$$Y = C + S$$

with respect to Y to deduce that

$$\frac{dY}{dY} = \frac{dC}{dY} + \frac{dS}{dY} = MPC + MPS$$

Now we are already familiar with the result that when we differentiate x with respect to x, the answer is 1. In this case Y plays the role of x, so

$$\frac{dY}{dY} = 1$$

Hence

$$1 = MPC + MPS$$

This formula is identical to the result given in Section 1.6 for simple linear functions. In practice, it means that we need only work out one of the derivatives. The remaining derivative can then be calculated directly from this equation.

Example

If the consumption function is

$$C = 0.01Y^2 + 0.2Y + 50$$

calculate MPC and MPS when $Y = 30$.

Solution

In this example the consumption function is given, so we begin by finding MPC. To do this we differentiate C with respect to Y. If

$$C = 0.01Y^2 + 0.2Y + 50$$

then

$$\frac{dC}{dY} = 0.02Y + 0.2$$

so, when $Y = 30$,

$$MPC = 0.02(30) + 0.2 = 0.8$$

To find the corresponding value of MPS we use the formula

$$MPC + MPS = 1$$

which gives

$$MPS = 1 - MPC = 1 - 0.8 = 0.2$$

This indicates that when national income increases by 1 unit (from its current level of 30), consumption rises by approximately 0.8 units, whereas savings rise by only about 0.2 units. At this level of income the nation has a greater propensity to consume than it has to save.

Practice Problem

5. If the savings function is given by

$$S = 0.02Y^2 - Y + 100$$

calculate the values of MPS and MPC when $Y = 40$. Give a brief interpretation of these results.

Key Terms

Average revenue   Total revenue per unit of output: $AR = TR/Q = P$.

Chord   A straight line joining two points on a curve.

Law of diminishing marginal productivity (law of diminishing returns)   Once the size of the workforce exceeds a particular value, the increase in output due to a 1-unit increase in labour will decline: $d^2Q/dL^2 < 0$ for sufficiently large L.

Marginal cost   The cost of producing 1 more unit of output: $MC = d(TC)/dQ$.

Marginal product of labour   The extra output produced by 1 more unit of labour: $MP_L = dQ/dL$.

Marginal propensity to consume   The fraction of a rise in national income which goes into consumption: $MPC = dC/dY$.

Marginal propensity to save   The fraction of a rise in national income which goes into savings: $MPS = dS/dY$.

Marginal revenue   The extra revenue gained by selling 1 more unit of a good: $MR = d(TR)/dQ$.

Monopolist   The only firm in the industry.

Perfect competition   A situation in which there are no barriers to entry in an industry where there are many firms selling an identical product at the market price.

Exercise 1.19

1. If the demand function is

   $$P = 100 - 4Q$$

   find expressions for TR and MR in terms of Q. Hence estimate the change in TR brought about by a 0.3-unit increase in output from a current level of 12 units.

2. If the demand function is

   $$P = 80 - 3Q$$

   show that

   $$MR = 2P - 80$$

3. A monopolist's demand function is given by

   $$P + Q = 100$$

   Write down expressions for TR and MR in terms of Q and sketch their graphs. Find the value of Q which gives a marginal revenue of zero and comment on the significance of this value.

4. If the average cost function of a good is

$$AC = \frac{15}{Q} + 2Q + 9$$

find an expression for TC. What are the fixed costs in this case? Write down an expression for the marginal cost function.

5. A firm's production function is

$$Q = 50L - 0.01L^2$$

where L denotes the size of the workforce. Find the value of MP_L in the case when

(a) $L = 1$ (b) $L = 10$ (c) $L = 100$ (d) $L = 1000$

Does the law of diminishing marginal productivity apply to this particular function?

6. If the consumption function is

$$C = 50 + 2\sqrt{Y}$$

calculate MPC and MPS when $Y = 36$ and give an interpretation of these results.

7. If the consumption function is

$$C = 0.02Y^2 + 0.1Y + 25$$

find the value of Y when MPS = 0.38.

8. The price of a company's shares, P, recorded in dollars at midday is a function of time, t, measured in days since the beginning of the year. Give an interpretation of the statement:

$$\frac{dP}{dt} = 0.25$$

when $t = 6$.

9. If the demand function is

$$P = 3000 - 2\sqrt{Q}$$

find expressions for TR and MR. Calculate the marginal revenue when $Q = 9$ and give an interpretation of this result.

Exercise 1.19*

1. A firm's demand function is given by

$$P = 100 - 4\sqrt{Q} - 3Q$$

(a) Write down an expression for total revenue, TR, in terms of Q.

(b) Find an expression for the marginal revenue, MR, and find the value of MR when $Q = 9$.

(c) Use the result of part (b) to *estimate* the change in TR when Q increases by 0.25 units from its current level of 9 units and compare this with the exact change in TR.

2. The consumption function is

$$C = 0.01Y^2 + 0.8Y + 100$$

(a) Calculate the values of MPC and MPS when $Y = 8$.

(b) Use the fact that $C + S = Y$ to obtain a formula for S in terms of Y. By differentiating this expression, find the value of MPS at $Y = 8$ and verify that this agrees with your answer to part (a).

3. The fixed costs of producing a good are 100 and the variable costs are $2 + Q/10$ per unit.

(a) Find expressions for TC and MC.

(b) Evaluate MC at $Q = 30$ and hence estimate the change in TC brought about by a 2-unit increase in output from a current level of 30 units.

(c) At what level of output does MC = 22?

4. Show that the law of diminishing marginal productivity holds for the production function

$$Q = 6L^2 - 0.2L^3$$

5. A firm's production function is given by

$$Q = 5\sqrt{L} - 0.1L$$

(a) Find an expression for the marginal product of labour, MP_L.

(b) Solve the equation $MP_L = 0$ and briefly explain the significance of this value of L.

(c) Show that the law of diminishing marginal productivity holds for this function.

6. A firm's average cost function takes the form

$$AC = 4Q + a + \frac{6}{Q}$$

and it is known that MC = 35 when $Q = 3$. Find the value of AC when $Q = 6$.

7. The total cost of producing a good is given by

$$TC = 250 + 20Q$$

The marginal revenue is 18 at $Q = 219$. If production is increased from its current level of 219, would you expect profit to increase, decrease or stay the same? Give reasons for your answer.

8. Given the demand and total cost functions

$$P = 150 - 2Q \quad \text{and} \quad TC = 40 + 0.5Q^2$$

find the marginal profit when $Q = 25$ and give an interpretation of this result.

9. If the total cost function is given by $TC = aQ^2 + bQ + c$, show that

$$\frac{d(AC)}{dQ} = \frac{MC - AC}{Q}$$

SECTION 1.20
Elasticity

Objectives

At the end of this section you should be able to:

- Calculate price elasticity averaged along an arc.
- Calculate price elasticity evaluated at a point.
- Decide whether supply and demand are inelastic, unit elastic or elastic.
- Understand the relationship between price elasticity of demand and revenue.
- Determine the price elasticity for general linear demand functions.

One important problem in business is to determine the effect on revenue of a change in the price of a good. Let us suppose that a firm's demand curve is downward-sloping. If the firm lowers the price, then it will receive less for each item, but the number of items sold increases. The formula for total revenue, TR, is

$$\text{TR} = PQ$$

and it is not immediately obvious what the net effect on TR will be as P decreases and Q increases. The crucial factor here is not the absolute changes in P and Q but rather the proportional or percentage changes. Intuitively, we expect that if the percentage rise in Q is greater than the percentage fall in P, then the firm experiences an increase in revenue. Under these circumstances we say that demand is **elastic**, since the demand is relatively sensitive to changes in price. Similarly, demand is said to be **inelastic** if demand is relatively insensitive to price changes. In this case, the percentage change in quantity is less than the percentage change in price. A firm can then increase revenue by raising the price of the good. Although demand falls as a result, the increase in price more than compensates for the reduced volume of sales and revenue rises. Of course, it could happen that the percentage changes in price and quantity are equal, leaving revenue unchanged. We use the term **unit elastic** to describe this situation.

We quantify the responsiveness of demand to price change by defining the **price elasticity of demand** to be

$$E = \frac{\text{percentage change in demand}}{\text{percentage change in price}}$$

Notice that because the demand curve slopes downwards, a positive change in price leads to a negative change in quantity and vice versa. Consequently, the value of E is always negative. It is usual for economists to ignore the negative sign and consider just the magnitude of elasticity. If this positive value is denoted by $|E|$, then the previous classification of demand functions can be restated more succinctly as:

As usual, we denote the changes in P and Q by ΔP and ΔQ respectively, and seek a formula for E in terms of these symbols. To motivate this, suppose that the price of a good is \$12 and that it rises to \$18. A moment's thought should convince you that the percentage change in price is then 50%. You can probably work this out in your head without thinking too hard. However, it is worthwhile identifying the mathematical process involved. To obtain this figure we first express the change

$$18 - 12 = 6$$

as a fraction of the original to get

$$\frac{6}{12} = 0.5$$

and then multiply by 100 to express it as a percentage. This simple example gives us a clue as to how we might find a formula for E. In general, the percentage change in price is

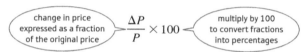

$$\underbrace{\text{change in price expressed as a fraction of the original price}}\quad \frac{\Delta P}{P} \times 100 \quad \underbrace{\text{multiply by 100 to convert fractions into percentages}}$$

Similarly, the percentage change in quantity is

$$\frac{\Delta Q}{Q} \times 100$$

Hence

$$E = \left(\frac{\Delta Q}{Q} \times 100 \right) \div \left(\frac{\Delta P}{P} \times 100 \right)$$

Now, when we divide two fractions, we turn the denominator upside down and multiply, so

$$E = \left(\frac{\Delta Q}{Q} \times \cancel{100} \right) \times \left(\frac{P}{\cancel{100} \times \Delta P} \right)$$
$$= \frac{P}{Q} \times \frac{\Delta Q}{\Delta P}$$

A typical demand curve is illustrated in Figure 1.73, in which a price fall from P_1 to P_2 causes an increase in demand from Q_1 to Q_2.

To be specific, let us suppose that the demand function is given by

$$P = 200 - Q^2$$

with $P_1 = 136$ and $P_2 = 119$.

The corresponding values of Q_1 and Q_2 are obtained from the demand equation

$$P = 200 - Q^2$$

by substituting $P = 136$ and 119, respectively, and solving for Q. For example, if $P = 136$, then

$$136 = 200 - Q^2$$

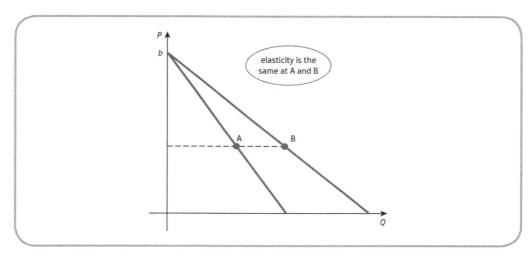

Figure 1.74

Another interesting feature of the result

$$E = \frac{P}{P - b}$$

is the fact that b occurs in the denominator of this fraction, so that corresponding to any price, P, the larger the value of the intercept, b, the smaller the magnitude of the elasticity. In Figure 1.75, the magnitude of the elasticity at C is smaller than that at D because C lies on the curve with the larger intercept.

The dependence of E on P is also worthy of note. It shows that elasticity varies along a linear demand curve. This is illustrated in Figure 1.76. At the left-hand end, $P = b$, so

$$E = \frac{b}{b - b} = \frac{b}{0} = \infty \quad \text{(read 'infinity')}$$

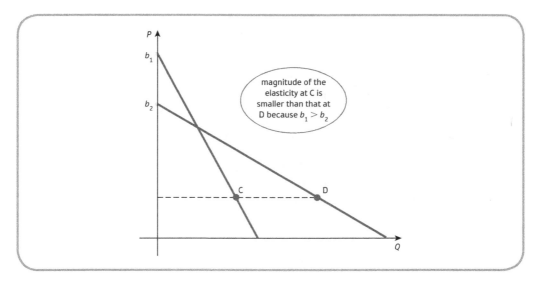

Figure 1.75

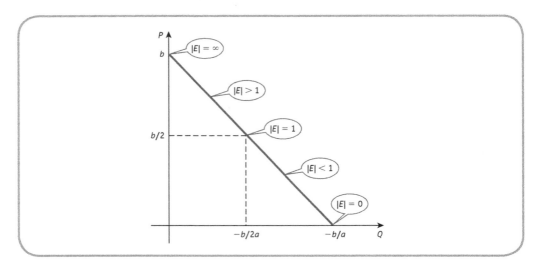

Figure 1.76

At the right-hand end, $P = 0$, so

$$E = \frac{0}{0 - b} = \frac{0}{-b} = 0$$

As you move down the demand curve, the magnitude of elasticity decreases from ∞ to 0, taking all possible values. Demand is unit elastic when $E = -1$ and the price at which this occurs can be found by solving

$$\frac{P}{P - b} = -1 \quad \text{for} \quad P$$

$$P = b - P \quad \text{(multiply both sides by } P - b)$$

$$2P = b \quad \text{(add } P \text{ to both sides)}$$

$$P = \frac{b}{2} \quad \text{(divide both sides by 2)}$$

The corresponding quantity can be found by substituting $P = b/2$ into the transposed demand equation to get

$$Q = \frac{1}{a}\left(\frac{b}{2} - b\right) = -\frac{b}{2a}$$

Demand is unit elastic exactly halfway along the demand curve. To the left of this point, $|E| > 1$ and demand is elastic, whereas to the right, $|E| < 1$ and demand is inelastic.

In our discussion of general demand functions, we have concentrated on those which are represented by straight lines since these are commonly used in simple economic models. There are other possibilities, and Question 4 in Exercise 1.20* investigates a class of functions that have constant elasticity.

Key Terms

Arc elasticity   Elasticity measured between two points on a curve.

Elastic demand   Where the percentage change in demand is more than the corresponding percentage change in price: $|E| > 1$.

Inelastic demand   Where the percentage change in demand is less than the corresponding percentage change in price: $|E| < 1$.

Point elasticity   Elasticity measured at a particular point on a curve: $E = \dfrac{P}{Q} \times \dfrac{dQ}{dP}$.

Price elasticity of demand   A measure of the responsiveness of the change in demand due to a change in price: (percentage change in demand) ÷ (percentage change in price).

Price elasticity of supply   A measure of the responsiveness of the change in supply due to a change in price: (percentage change in supply) ÷ (percentage change in price).

Unit elasticity of demand   Where the percentage change in demand is the same as the percentage change in price: $|E| = 1$.

Exercise 1.20

1. Given the demand function

    $$P = 500 - 4Q^2$$

    calculate the price elasticity of demand averaged along an arc joining $Q = 8$ and $Q = 10$.

2. Find the price elasticity of demand at the point $Q = 9$ for the demand function

    $$P = 500 - 4Q^2$$

    and compare your answer with that of Question 1.

3. Find the price elasticity of demand at $P = 6$ for each of the following demand functions:

    (a) $P = 30 - 2Q$

    (b) $P = 30 - 12Q$

    (c) $P = \sqrt{(100 - 2Q)}$

4. (a) If an airline increases prices for business class flights by 8%, demand falls by about 2.5%. Estimate the elasticity of demand. Is demand elastic, inelastic or unit elastic?

    (b) Explain whether you would expect a similar result to hold for economy class flights.

5. The demand function of a good is given by

    $$Q = \frac{1000}{P^2}$$

    (a) Calculate the price elasticity of demand at $P = 5$ and hence estimate the percentage change in demand when P increases by 2%.

    (b) Comment on the accuracy of your estimate in part (a) by calculating the exact percentage change in demand when P increases from 5 to 5.1.

6. (a) Find the elasticity of demand in terms of Q for the demand function, $P = 20 - 0.05Q$.

   (b) For what value of Q is demand unit elastic?

   (c) Find an expression for MR and verify that MR = 0 when demand is unit elastic.

7. Consider the supply equation

   $$Q = 4 + 0.1P^2$$

   (a) Write down an expression for dQ/dP.

   (b) Show that the supply equation can be rearranged as

   $$P = \sqrt{(10Q - 40)}$$

   Differentiate this to find an expression for dP/dQ.

   (c) Use your answers to parts (a) and (b) to verify that

   $$\frac{dQ}{dP} = \frac{1}{dP/dQ}$$

   (d) Calculate the elasticity of supply at the point $Q = 14$.

8. If the supply equation is

   $$Q = 7 + 0.1P + 0.004P^2$$

   find the price elasticity of supply if the current price is 80.

   (a) Is supply elastic, inelastic or unit elastic at this price?

   (b) Estimate the percentage change in supply if the price rises by 5%.

Exercise 1.20*

1. Find the elasticity for the demand function

   $$Q = 80 - 2P - 0.5P^2$$

   averaged along an arc joining $Q = 32$ to $Q = 50$. Give your answer to 2 decimal places.

2. Consider the supply equation

   $$P = 7 + 2Q^2$$

   By evaluating the price elasticity of supply at the point $P = 105$, estimate the percentage increase in supply when the price rises by 7%.

3. If the demand equation is

   $$Q + 4P = 60$$

   find a general expression for the price elasticity of demand in terms of P. For what value of P is demand unit elastic?

4. Show that the price elasticity of demand is constant for the demand functions

   $$P = \frac{A}{Q^n}$$

   where A and n are positive constants.

5. Find a general expression for the point elasticity of supply for the function

$$Q = aP + b \ (a > 0)$$

Deduce that the supply function is

(a) unit elastic when $b = 0$;

(b) elastic when $b < 0$.

Give a brief geometrical interpretation of these results.

6. A supply function is given by

$$Q = 40 + 0.1P^2$$

(1) Find the price elasticity of supply averaged along an arc between $P = 11$ and $P = 13$. Give your answer correct to three decimal places.

(2) Find an expression for price elasticity of supply at a general point, P.

Hence:

(a) Estimate the percentage change in supply when the price increases by 5% from its current level of 17. Give your answer correct to one decimal place.

(b) Find the price at which supply is unit elastic.

7. (a) Show that the elasticity of the supply function

$$P = aQ + b$$

is given by

$$E = \frac{P}{P - b}$$

(b) Consider the two supply functions

$$P = 2Q + 5 \text{ and } P = aQ + b$$

The quantity supplied is the same for both functions when $P = 10$, and at this point, the price elasticity of supply for the second function is five times larger than that for the first function. Find the values of a and b.

8. (a) If E denotes the elasticity of a general supply function, $Q = f(P)$, show that the elasticity of:

(i) $Q = [f(P)]^n$ is nE (ii) $Q = \lambda f(P)$ is E (iii) $Q = \lambda + f(P)$ is $\dfrac{f(P)E}{\lambda + f(P)}$

where n and λ are positive constants.

(b) Show that the elasticity of the supply function $Q = P$ is 1 and use the results of part (a) to write down the elasticity of

(i) $Q = P^3$ (ii) $Q = 10P\sqrt{P}$ (iii) $Q = 5\sqrt{P} - 2$

SECTION 1.21
Further optimisation of economic functions

Objectives

At the end of this section you should be able to:

- Show that, at the point of maximum profit, marginal revenue equals marginal cost.
- Show that, at the point of maximum profit, the slope of the marginal revenue curve is less than that of marginal cost.
- Maximise profits of a firm with and without price discrimination in different markets.
- Show that, at the point of maximum average product of labour, average product of labour equals marginal product of labour.
- Derive a formula for the economic order quantity in stock control.

The previous section demonstrated how mathematics can be used to optimise particular economic functions. Those examples suggested two important results:

1. If a firm maximises profit, then MR = MC.

2. If a firm maximises average product of labour, then $AP_L = MP_L$.

Although these results were found to hold for all of the examples considered in Section 1.14, it does not necessarily follow that the results are always true. The aim of this section is to prove these assertions without reference to specific functions and hence to demonstrate their generality.

Advice

You may prefer to skip these proofs at a first reading and just concentrate on the worked example (as well as Practice Problem 2 and Question 3 in Exercise 1.21*) on price discrimination.

Justification of the first result turns out to be really quite easy. Profit, π, is defined to be the difference between total revenue, TR, and total cost, TC: that is,

$$\pi = \text{TR} - \text{TC}$$

To find the stationary points of π we differentiate with respect to Q and equate to zero: that is,

$$\frac{d\pi}{dQ} = \frac{d(\text{TR})}{dQ} - \frac{d(\text{TC})}{dQ} = 0$$

where we have used the difference rule to differentiate the right-hand side. In Section 1.19 we defined

$$\text{MR} = \frac{d(\text{TR})}{dQ} \text{ and } \text{MC} = \frac{d(\text{TC})}{dQ}$$

so the previous equation is equivalent to

$$\text{MR} - \text{MC} = 0$$

and so MR = MC as required.

The stationary points of the profit function can therefore be found by sketching the MR and MC curves on the same diagram and inspecting the points of intersection. Figure 1.77 shows typical marginal revenue and marginal cost curves. The result

$$\text{MR} = \text{MC}$$

holds for any stationary point. Consequently, if this equation has more than one solution, then we need some further information before we can decide on the profit-maximising level of output. In Figure 1.77 there are two points of intersection, Q_1 and Q_2, and it turns out (as you discovered in Practice Problem 3 and Question 5 of Exercise 1.14 in the previous section) that one of these is a maximum while the other is a minimum. Obviously, in any actual example, we can classify these points by evaluating second-order derivatives. However, it would be nice to make this decision just by inspecting the graphs of marginal revenue and marginal cost. To see how this can be done, let us return to the equation

$$\frac{d\pi}{dQ} = \text{MR} - \text{MC}$$

and differentiate again with respect to Q to get

$$\frac{d^2\pi}{dQ^2} = \frac{d(\text{MR})}{dQ} - \frac{d(\text{MC})}{dQ}$$

Now, if $d^2\pi/dQ^2 < 0$, then the profit is a maximum. This will be so when

$$\frac{d(\text{MR})}{dQ} < \frac{d(\text{MC})}{dQ}$$

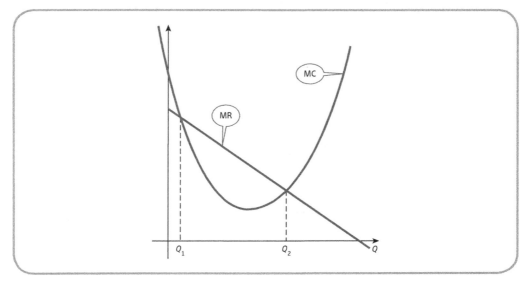

Figure 1.77

Key Term

Economic order quantity   The quantity of a product that should be ordered so as to minimise the total cost that includes ordering costs and holding costs.

Exercise 1.21*

1. A firm's demand function is

$$P = aQ + b \ (a < 0, b > 0)$$

Fixed costs are c and variable costs per unit are d.

(a) Write down general expressions for TR and TC.

(b) By differentiating the expressions in part (a), deduce MR and MC.

(c) Use your answers to (b) to show that profit, π, is maximised when

$$Q = \frac{d - b}{2a}$$

2. (a) In Section 1.20 the following relationship between marginal revenue, MR, and price elasticity of demand, E, was derived:

$$MR = P\left(1 + \frac{1}{E}\right)$$

Use this result to show that at the point of maximum total revenue, $E = -1$.

(b) Verify the result of part (a) for the demand function

$$2P + 3Q = 60$$

3. The demand functions for a firm's domestic and foreign markets are

$$P_1 = 50 - 5Q_1$$
$$P_2 = 30 - 4Q_2$$

and the total cost function is

$$TC = 10 + 10Q$$

where $Q = Q_1 + Q_2$. Determine the prices needed to maximise profit

(a) with price discrimination;

(b) without price discrimination.

Compare the profits obtained in parts (a) and (b).

4. Show that if the marginal cost curve cuts the marginal revenue curve from above, then profit is a minimum.

5. (a) Find an expression for the second-order derivative, d^2C/dQ^2, of the cost function

$$C = \frac{DR}{Q} + \frac{HQ}{2}$$

and hence show that the economic order quantity, $Q = \sqrt{\frac{2DR}{H}}$, is a minimum point.

(b) Obtain a simplified expression for the minimum cost.

6. (a) The annual demand of a good is 2000 units, the fixed cost of placing an order is $40 and the annual cost of storing an item is $100. Assuming that the same order is placed at regular intervals throughout the year, and that the firm waits for stock levels to reduce to zero before ordering new stock, work out how many items should be ordered each time to minimise total costs. What is the minimum total cost?

    (b) Repeat part (a) if the annual cost of storage costs falls to $64.

    (c) Repeat part (a) if the fixed cost of placing an order rises to $160.

    (d) What effect do changes in order costs and holding costs have on the minimum total cost?

7. If the total cost function $TC = aQ^2 + bQ + c$, write down an expression for the average cost function, AC. Show that AC is a minimum when $Q = \sqrt{\dfrac{c}{a}}$ and find the corresponding value of AC.

8. (a) Show that, at a stationary point of an average cost function, average cost equals marginal cost.

    (b) Show that if the marginal cost curve cuts the average cost curve from below, then average cost is a minimum.

9. In a competitive market the equilibrium price, P, and quantity, Q, are found by setting $Q_S = Q_D = Q$ in the supply and demand equations

    $$P = aQ_S + b \ (a > 0, b > 0)$$
    $$P = -cQ_D + d \ (c > 0, d > 0)$$

    If the government levies an excise tax, t, per unit, show that

    $$Q = \frac{d - b - t}{a + c}$$

    Deduce that the government's tax revenue, $T = tQ$, is maximised by taking

    $$t = \frac{d - b}{2}$$

SECTION 1.22
Functions of several variables

Objectives

At the end of this section you should be able to:

- Use the function notation, $z = f(x, y)$.
- Determine the first-order partial derivatives, f_x and f_y.
- Determine the second-order partial derivatives, f_{xx}, f_{xy}, f_{yx} and f_{yy}.
- Appreciate that, for most functions, $f_{xy} = f_{yx}$.
- Use the small increments formula.
- Perform implicit differentiation.

Most relationships in economics involve more than two variables. The demand for a good depends not only on its own price but also on the price of substitutable and complementary goods, incomes of consumers, advertising expenditure and so on. Likewise, the output from a production process depends on a variety of inputs, including land, capital and labour. To analyse general economic behaviour, we must extend the concept of a function, and particularly the differential calculus, to functions of several variables.

A **function, f, of two variables** is a rule that assigns to each incoming pair of numbers, (x, y), a uniquely defined outgoing number, z. This is illustrated in Figure 1.81. The 'black box' f performs some arithmetic operation on x and y to produce z. For example, the rule might be 'multiply the two numbers together and add twice the second number'. In symbols we write this either as

$$f(x, y) = xy + 2y$$

or as

$$z = xy + 2y$$

In order to be able to evaluate the function, we have to specify the numerical values of both x and y.

For example, substituting $x = 3$ and $y = 4$ gives

$$f(3,4) = 3 \times 4 + 2 \times 4 = 20$$

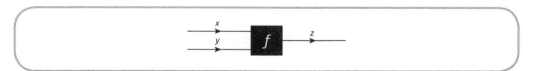

Figure 1.81

and substituting $x = 4$ and $y = 3$ gives

$$f(4,3) = 4 \times 3 + 2 \times 3 = 18$$

Notice that, for this function, $f(3,4)$ is not the same as $f(4,3)$, so in general we must be careful to write down the correct ordering of the variables.

We have used the labels x and y for the two incoming numbers (called the **independent variables**) and z for the outgoing number (called the **dependent variable**). We could equally well have written the above function as

$$y = x_1x_2 + 2x_2$$

say, using x_1 and x_2 to denote the independent variables and using y this time to denote the dependent variable. The use of subscripts may seem rather cumbersome, but it provides an obvious extension to functions of more than two variables. In general, a function of n variables can be written

$$y = f(x_1, x_2, \ldots, x_n)$$

Practice Problem

1. If

$$f(x, y) = 5x + xy^2 - 10$$

and

$$g(x_1, x_2, x_3) = x_1 + x_2 + x_3$$

evaluate

(a) $f(0, 0)$ (b) $f(1, 2)$ (c) $f(2, 1)$ (d) $g(5, 6, 10)$ (e) $g(0, 0, 0)$ (f) $g(10, 5, 6)$

A function of one variable can be given a pictorial description using graphs, which help to give an intuitive feel for its behaviour. Figure 1.82 shows the graph of a typical function

$$y = f(x)$$

in which the horizontal axis determines the incoming number, x, and the vertical axis determines the corresponding outgoing number, y. The height of the curve directly above any point on the x axis represents the value of the function at this point.

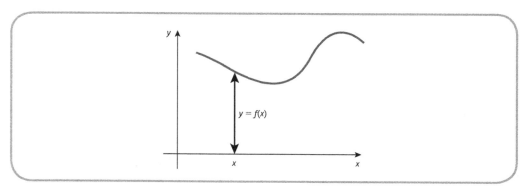

Figure 1.82

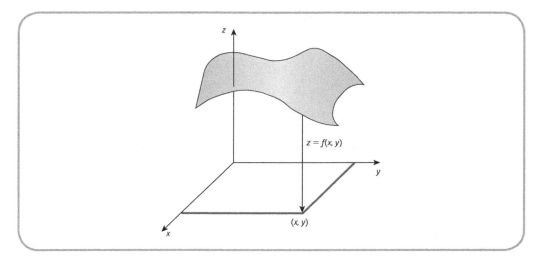

Figure 1.83

An obvious question to ask is whether there is a pictorial representation of functions of several variables. The answer is yes in the case of functions of two variables, although it is not particularly easy to construct. A function

$z = f(x, y)$

can be thought of as a surface, rather like a mountain range, in three-dimensional space as shown in Figure 1.83. If you visualise the incoming point with coordinates (x, y) as lying in a horizontal plane, then the height of the surface, z, directly above it represents the value of the function at this point. As you can probably imagine, it is not an easy task to sketch the surface by hand from an equation such as

$f(x, y) = xy^3 + 4x$

although three-dimensional graphics packages are available for most computers which can produce such a plot.

It is impossible to provide any sort of graphical interpretation for functions of more than two variables. For example, a function of, say, four variables would require five dimensions, one for each of the incoming variables and a further one for the outgoing variable! In spite of this setback we can still perform the task of differentiating functions of several variables and, such derivatives play a vital role in analysing economic behaviour.

Given a function of two variables,

$z = f(x, y)$

we can determine two first-order derivatives. The **partial derivative** of f with respect to x is written as

$$\frac{\partial z}{\partial x} \quad \text{or} \quad \frac{\partial f}{\partial x} \quad \text{or} \quad f_x$$

and is found by differentiating f with respect to x, with y held constant. Similarly, the **partial derivative** of f with respect to y is written as

$$\frac{\partial z}{\partial y} \quad \text{or} \quad \frac{\partial f}{\partial y} \quad \text{or} \quad f_y$$

7. **(a)** If

$$f(x, y) = y - x^3 + 2x$$

write down expressions for f_x and f_y. Hence use implicit differentiation to find dy/dx given that

$$y - x^3 + 2x = 1$$

(b) Confirm your answer to part (a) by rearranging the equation

$$y - x^3 + 2x = 1$$

to give y explicitly in terms of x and using ordinary differentiation.

8. Find the first-order partial derivatives, $\dfrac{\partial z}{\partial u}, \dfrac{\partial z}{\partial v}, \dfrac{\partial z}{\partial w}$, for each of the following functions:

   (a) $z = u + v^2 - 5w^3 + 2uv$ **(b)** $z = 6u^{1/2}v^{1/3}w^{1/6}$

9. **(a)** Use the small increments formula to estimate the change in

$$z = x^3 - 2xy$$

when x increases from 5 to 5.5 and y increases from 8 to 8.8.

   (b) By evaluating z at $(5, 8)$ and $(5.5, 8.8)$, work out the exact change in z, and hence calculate the percentage error in using the small increments formula.

Exercise 1.22*

1. If

$$f(x, y) = 2xy + 3x$$

verify that $f(5, 7) \neq f(7, 5)$. Find all pairs of numbers, (x, y) for which $f(x, y) = f(y, x)$.

2. If

$$f(w, x, y) = 5w^{0.34}x^{0.25}y^{0.41}$$

show that $f(kw, kx, ky) = kf(w, x, y)$

3. Find expressions for all first- and second-order partial derivatives of the following functions. In each case verify that

$$\frac{\partial^2 z}{\partial y \partial x} = \frac{\partial^2 z}{\partial x \partial y}$$

   (a) $z = xy$ **(b)** $z = e^x y$ **(c)** $z = x^2 + 2x + y$ **(d)** $z = 16x^{1/4}y^{3/4}$ **(e)** $z = \dfrac{y}{x^2} + \dfrac{x}{y}$

4. If

$$z = x^2y^3 - 10xy + y^2$$

evaluate $\partial z/\partial x$ and $\partial z/\partial y$ at the point $(2, 3)$. Hence estimate the change in z as x increases by 0.2 and y decreases by 0.1.

5. Find the first-order derivatives, $\dfrac{\partial z}{\partial u}, \dfrac{\partial z}{\partial v}, \dfrac{\partial z}{\partial w}$, for each of the following functions

   (a) $z = (6u + vw^3)^4$ (b) $z = u\sqrt{w}e^{-vw}$

6. If $f(x,y) = x^3e^{-2y}$ evaluate all first- and second-order derivatives at $(e, 1)$.

7. Verify that $x = 1$, $y = -1$ satisfy the equation $x^2 - 2y^3 = 3$. Use implicit differentiation to find the value of dy/dx at this point.

8. A function of three variables is given by

$$f(x_1, x_2, x_3) = \frac{x_1x_3^2}{x_2} + \ln(x_2x_3)$$

   Find all of the first- and second-order derivatives of this function and verify that

$$f_{12} = f_{21}, \quad f_{13} = f_{31} \quad \text{and} \quad f_{23} = f_{32}$$

9. Write down an expression for a function, $f(x, y)$, with first-order partial derivatives,

$$\frac{\partial f}{\partial x} = 3xy(xy + 2) \qquad \frac{\partial f}{\partial y} = x^2(2xy + 3)$$

10. Evaluate the second-order partial derivative, f_{23}, of the function

$$f(x_1, x_2 x_3) = \frac{x_3x_2^3}{x_1} + x_2e^{x_3}$$

    at the point, $(3, 2, 0)$.

11. Find the value of $\dfrac{dy}{dx}$ at the point $(-2, 1)$ for the function which is defined implicitly by

$$x^2y - \frac{x}{y} = 6$$

12. Use implicit differentiation to find expressions, in terms of x and y, for $\dfrac{dy}{dx}$ for each of the following:

   (a) $x^3y + 4xy^2 = 6$ (b) $12x^{1/3}y^{1/4} + x = 8$ (c) $ye^{xy} = 10$ (d) $\dfrac{x^2 + y^2}{x + y} = 5$

SECTION 1.23
Partial elasticity and marginal functions

Objectives

At the end of this section you should be able to:

- Calculate partial elasticities.
- Calculate marginal utilities.
- Calculate the marginal rate of commodity substitution along an indifference curve.
- Calculate marginal products.
- Calculate the marginal rate of technical substitution along an isoquant.
- State Euler's theorem for homogeneous production functions.

Section 1.22 described the technique of partial differentiation. Hopefully, you have discovered that partial differentiation is no more difficult than ordinary differentiation. The only difference is that for functions of several variables you have to be clear at the outset which letter in a mathematical expression is to be the variable, and to bear in mind that all remaining letters are then just constants in disguise! Once you have done this, the actual differentiation itself obeys the usual rules. In Sections 1.19 and 1.20 we considered various microeconomic applications. Given the intimate relationship between ordinary and partial differentiation, you should not be too surprised to learn that we can extend these applications to functions of several variables. We concentrate on three main areas:

- elasticity of demand;
- utility;
- production.

We consider each of these in turn.

1.23.1 Elasticity of demand

Suppose that the demand, Q, for a certain good depends on its price, P, the price of an alternative good, P_A, and the income of consumers, Y, so that

$$Q = f(P, P_A, Y)$$

for some demand function, f.

Of particular interest is the responsiveness of demand to changes in any one of these three variables. This can be measured quantitatively using elasticity. The (own) **price elasticity of demand** is defined to be

$$E_P = \frac{\text{percentage change in } Q}{\text{percentage change in } P}$$

with P_A and Y held constant. This definition is identical to the one given in Section 1.20, so following the same mathematical argument presented there, we deduce that

$$E_P = \frac{P}{Q} \times \frac{\partial Q}{\partial P}$$

The partial derivative notation is used here because Q is now a function of several variables, and P_A and Y are held constant.

In an analogous way we can measure the responsiveness of demand to changes in the price of the alternative good. The **cross-price elasticity of demand** is defined to be

$$E_{P_A} = \frac{\text{percentage change in } Q}{\text{percentage change in } P_A}$$

with P and Y held constant. Again, the usual mathematical argument shows that

$$E_{P_A} = \frac{P_A}{Q} \times \frac{\partial Q}{\partial P_A}$$

The sign of E_{P_A} could turn out to be positive or negative depending on the nature of the alternative good. If the alternative good is substitutable, then Q increases as P_A rises, because consumers buy more of the given good as it becomes relatively less expensive. Consequently,

$$\frac{\partial Q}{\partial P_A} > 0$$

and so $E_{P_A} > 0$. If the alternative good is complementary, then Q decreases as P_A rises, because the bundle of goods as a whole becomes more expensive. Consequently,

$$\frac{\partial Q}{\partial P_A} < 0$$

and so $E_{P_A} < 0$.

Finally, the **income elasticity of demand** is defined to be

$$E_Y = \frac{\text{percentage change in } Q}{\text{percentage change in } Y}$$

and can be found from

$$E_Y = \frac{Y}{Q} \times \frac{\partial Q}{\partial Y}$$

Again, E_Y can be positive or negative. If a good is inferior, then demand falls as income rises and E_Y is negative. Canned vegetables, a supermarket's own-brand white bread and bus transportation are examples of inferior goods. If a good is normal, then demand rises as income rises and E_Y is positive. Sometimes the value of E_Y of a normal good might even exceed 1. These goods are called **superior**. For these goods the percentage rise in consumption is greater than the percentage increase in income. If income elasticity of demand is 1.25, a rise of 40% in income leads to a 50% increase in consumption. Examples of superior goods include sports cars, caviar and quality wine.

Example

Given the demand function

$$Q = 100 - 2P + P_A + 0.1Y$$

where $P = 10$, $P_A = 12$ and $Y = 1000$, find the

(a) price elasticity of demand;

(b) cross-price elasticity of demand;

(c) income elasticity of demand.

Is the alternative good substitutable or complementary?

Solution

We begin by calculating the value of Q when $P = 10$, $P_A = 12$ and $Y = 1000$. The demand function gives

$$Q = 100 - 2(10) + 12 + 0.1(1000) = 192$$

(a) To find the price elasticity of demand we partially differentiate

$$Q = 100 - 2P + P_A + 0.1Y$$

with respect to P to get

$$\frac{\partial Q}{\partial P} = -2$$

Hence

$$E_P = \frac{P}{Q} \times \frac{\partial Q}{\partial P} = \frac{10}{192} \times (-2) = -0.10$$

(b) To find the cross-price elasticity of demand we partially differentiate

$$Q = 100 - 2P + P_A + 0.1Y$$

with respect to P_A to get

$$\frac{\partial Q}{\partial P_A} = 1$$

Hence

$$E_{P_A} = \frac{P_A}{Q} \times \frac{\partial Q}{\partial P_A} = \frac{12}{192} \times 1 = 0.06$$

The fact that this is positive shows that the two goods are substitutable.

(c) To find the income elasticity of demand we partially differentiate

$$Q = 100 - 2P + P_A + 0.1Y$$

with respect to Y to get

$$\frac{\partial Q}{\partial Y} = 0.1$$

Hence

$$E_Y = \frac{Y}{Q} \times \frac{\partial Q}{\partial Y} = \frac{1000}{192} \times 0.1 = 0.52$$

Marginal product of labour   The additional output produced by a 1-unit increase in labour: $MP_L = \partial Q/\partial L$.

Marginal rate of commodity substitution (MRCS)   The amount by which one input needs to increase to maintain a constant value of utility when the other input decreases by 1 unit: $MRCS = \partial U/\partial x_1 \div \partial U/\partial x_2$.

Marginal rate of technical substitution (MRTS)   The amount by which capital needs to rise to maintain a constant level of output when labour decreases by 1 unit: $MRTS = MP_L/MP_K$.

Marginal utility   The extra satisfaction gained by consuming 1 extra unit of a good: $\partial U/\partial x_i$.

Price elasticity of demand   A measure of the responsiveness of the change in demand due to a change in price: (percentage change in demand) ÷ (percentage change in price).

Superior good   A normal good for which the percentage rise in consumption exceeds the percentage increase in income.

Utility   The satisfaction gained from the consumption of a good.

Exercise 1.23

1. Given the demand function

   $$Q = 1000 - 5P - P_A^2 + 0.005Y^3$$

   where $P = 15$, $P_A = 20$ and $Y = 100$, find the income elasticity of demand and explain why this is a superior good.

   Give your answer correct to two decimal places.

2. Given the demand function

   $$Q = 200 - 2P - P_A + 0.1Y^2$$

   where $P = 10$, $P_A = 15$ and $Y = 100$, find

   (a) the price elasticity of demand;

   (b) the cross-price elasticity of demand;

   (c) the income elasticity of demand.

   Estimate the percentage change in demand if P_A rises by 3%. Is the alternative good substitutable or complementary?

3. A utility function is given by $U = 2x^2 + y^2$.

   (a) State the equation of the indifference curve which passes through (4, 2).

   (b) Calculate the marginal utilities at (4, 2) and hence work out the gradient of the curve at this point.

4. The satisfaction gained by consuming x units of good 1 and y units of good 2 is measured by the utility function

   $$U = 2x^2 + 5y^3$$

   Currently an individual consumes 20 units of good 1 and 8 units of good 2.

   (a) Find the marginal utility of good 1 and hence estimate the increase in satisfaction gained from consuming one more unit of good 1.

   (b) Find the marginal utility of good 2 and hence estimate the increase in satisfaction gained from consuming one more unit of good 2.

5. Given the demand function

$$Q = \frac{P_A Y}{P^2}$$

find the income elasticity of demand.

6. Given the utility function

$$U = x_1^{1/2} x_2^{1/3}$$

determine the value of the marginal utilities

$$\frac{\partial U}{\partial x_1} \quad \text{and} \quad \frac{\partial U}{\partial x_2}$$

at the point (25, 8). Hence

(a) estimate the change in utility when x_1 and x_2 both increase by 1 unit;

(b) find the marginal rate of commodity substitution at this point.

7. Evaluate MP_K and MP_L for the production function

$$Q = 2LK + \sqrt{L}$$

given that the current levels of K and L are 7 and 4, respectively. Hence

(a) write down the value of MRTS;

(b) estimate the increase in capital needed to maintain the current level of output given a 1-unit decrease in labour.

8. If $Q = 2K^3 + 3L^2 K$, show that $K(MP_K) + L(MP_L) = 3Q$.

9. The demand functions for two commodities, A and B, are given by

$$Q_A = AP^{-0.5}Y^{0.5} \text{ and } Q_B = BP^{-1.5}Y^{1.5} \quad \text{where } A \text{ and } B \text{ are positive constants}$$

(a) Find the price elasticity of demand for each good and hence comment on the relative sensitivity of demand due to changes in price.

(b) Find the income elasticity of demand for each good. Which good is normal and which is superior? Give a reason for your answer.

10. A firm's production function is given by $Q = 18K^{1/6}L^{5/6}$.

(a) Show that this function displays constant returns to scale.

(b) Find expressions for the marginal products of capital and labour.

(c) State what happens to the marginal product of labour when

(i) labour increases with capital held constant;

(ii) capital increases with labour held constant.

Exercise 1.23*

1. The demand function of a good is given by

    $$Q = 500 - 4P + 0.02Y$$

    Price and income are known to be $P = 20$ and $Y = 14\,000$, respectively.

    (a) Find the income elasticity of demand.

    (b) Estimate the percentage change in demand when income rises by 8%, and comment on the growth potential of this good in an expanding economy.

2. Find the value of the marginal rate of technical substitution for the production function,

    $$Q = 300K^{2/3}L^{1/2}$$

    when $K = 40$, $L = 60$.

3. A utility function is given by

    $$U = x_1^{2/3}x_2^{1/2}$$

    Find the value of x_2 if the points $(64, 256)$ and $(512, x_2)$ lie on the same indifference curve.

4. Show that the Cobb–Douglas production function $Q = AK^{\alpha}L^{\beta}$ is homogeneous of degree $\alpha + \beta$ and that

    (a) $K\dfrac{\partial Q}{\partial K} + L\dfrac{\partial Q}{\partial L} = (\alpha + \beta)Q$

    (b) $K^2\dfrac{\partial^2 Q}{\partial K^2} + 2KL\dfrac{\partial^2 Q}{\partial K\partial L} + L^2\dfrac{\partial^2 Q}{\partial L^2} = (\alpha + \beta)(\alpha + \beta - 1)Q$

5. An individual's utility function is given by

    $$U = Ax_1^{0.7}x_2^{0.5}$$

    where x_1 and x_2 denote the number of units consumed of goods 1 and 2.

    (a) Show that the marginal utility of x_1 is positive and give an interpretation of this result.

    (b) Show that the second-order derivative $\dfrac{\partial^2 U}{\partial x_1 \partial x_2}$ is positive and give an interpretation of this result.

    (c) Show that the second-order derivative $\dfrac{\partial^2 U}{\partial x_1^2}$ is negative and give an interpretation of this result.

6. If a firm's production function is given by

    $$Q = 5L + 7K$$

    sketch the isoquant corresponding to an output level, $Q = 700$. Use your graph to find the value of MRTS and confirm this using partial differentiation.

7. A firm's production function is given by

    $$Q = 10\sqrt{(KL)} + 3L$$

    with $K = 90$ and $L = 40$.

    (a) Find the values of the marginal products, MP_K and MP_L.

    (b) Use the results of part (a) to estimate the overall effect on Q when K increases by 3 units and L decreases by 2 units.

    (c) State the value of the marginal rate of technical substitution and give an interpretation of this value.

8. A firm's production function is

   $$Q = A[bK^\alpha + (1 - b)L^\alpha]^{1/\alpha}$$

   (a) Show that the marginal rate of technical substitution is given by

   $$\text{MRTS} = \frac{1 - b}{b}\left(\frac{K}{L}\right)^{1-\alpha}$$

   (b) Show that the marginal products satisfy the relation

   $$K\frac{\partial Q}{\partial K} + L\frac{\partial Q}{\partial L} = Q$$

9. The demand function of a good is given by

   $$Q = a - bP - cP_A + dY$$

   where P is the price of the good, P_A is the price of an alternative good, Y is income and the coefficients a, b, c and d are all positive. It is known that $P = 50$, $P_A = 30$, $Y = 1000$ and $Q = 5000$.

   (a) Is the alternative good substitutable or complementary? Give a reason for your answer.

   (b) Find expressions, in terms of b, c and d, for the

      (i)   price elasticity of demand;

      (ii) cross-price elasticity of demand;

      (iii) income elasticity of demand.

   (c) The cross-price elasticity is -0.012. The income elasticity is four times the magnitude of the price elasticity. When income increases by 10%, the demand increases by 2%. Determine the values of a, b, c and d.

10. The demand function of a good is given by

    $$Q = kP^{-a}P_A^b Y^c$$

    where P is the own price, P_A is the price of an alternative good and Y is income. The letters k, a, b and c are positive constants.

    (a) Explain why the alternative good is substitutable.

    (b) Show that own price elasticity, cross-price elasticity and income elasticity are $-a$, b and c, respectively.

    (c) Explain briefly why the proportion of income spent on this good is given by PQ/Y and deduce that for this demand function, this proportion is

    $$kP^{1-a}P_A^b Y^{c-1}$$

    Hence show that when $c > 1$, the proportion of income spent on this good rises with income.

11. Find the marginal rate of commodity substitution for each of these utility functions and hence state whether the indifference map consists of convex curves, concave curves or straight lines.

    (a) $U = (2x_1 + 3x_2)^3$ **(b)** $U = 5x_1^3 x_2$ **(c)** $U = 2\sqrt{x_1} + 6\sqrt{x_2}$

SECTION 1.24
Unconstrained optimisation

Objectives

At the end of this section you should be able to:

- Use the first-order partial derivatives to find the stationary points of a function of two variables.
- Use the second-order partial derivatives to classify the stationary points of a function of two variables.
- Find the maximum profit of a firm that produces two goods.
- Find the maximum profit of a firm that sells a single good in different markets with price discrimination.

As you might expect, methods for finding the maximum and minimum points of a function of two variables are similar to those used for functions of one variable. However, the nature of economic functions of several variables forces us to subdivide optimisation problems into two types, unconstrained and constrained. To understand the distinction, consider the utility function

$$U(x_1, x_2) = x_1^{1/4} x_2^{3/4}$$

The value of U measures the satisfaction gained from buying x_1 items of a good G1 and x_2 items of a good G2. The natural thing to do here is to try to pick x_1 and x_2 to make U as large as possible, thereby maximising utility. However, a moment's thought should convince you that, as it stands, this problem does not have a finite solution. The factor $x_1^{1/4}$ can be made as large as we please by taking ever-increasing values of x_1 and likewise for the factor $x_2^{3/4}$. In other words, utility increases without bound as more and more items of goods G1 and G2 are bought. In practice, of course, this does not occur, since there is a limit to the amount of money that an individual has to spend on these goods. For example, suppose that the cost of each item of G1 and G2 is $2 and $3, respectively, and that we allocate $100 for the purchase of these goods. The total cost of buying x_1 items of G1 and x_2 items of G2 is

$$2x_1 + 3x_2$$

so we require

$$2x_1 + 3x_2 = 100$$

The problem now is to maximise the utility function

$$U = x_1^{1/4} x_2^{3/4}$$

subject to the budgetary constraint

$$2x_1 + 3x_2 = 100$$

The constraint prevents us from taking ever-increasing values of x_1 and x_2 and leads to a finite solution.

7. A monopolist sells its product in two isolated markets with demand functions

    $$P_1 = 32 - Q_1 \quad \text{and} \quad P_2 = 40 - 2Q_2$$

    The total cost function is $TC = 4(Q_1 + Q_2)$.

    (a) Show that the profit function is given by

    $$\pi = 28Q_1 + 36Q_2 - Q_1^2 - 2Q_2^2$$

    (b) Find the values of Q_1 and Q_2 which maximise profit and calculate the value of the maximum profit. Verify that the second-order conditions for a maximum are satisfied.

8. **(a)** If the monopolist in Question 7 is no longer allowed to discriminate between the two markets and must charge the same price, P, show that the total demand, $Q = Q_1 + Q_2$, is given by

    $$Q = 52 - \frac{3}{2}P$$

    and deduce that the profit function is $\pi = \frac{1}{3}(92Q - 2Q^2)$.

    (b) Find the maximum profit in part (a) and hence work out how much profit is lost by the firm when it can no longer discriminate between the two markets.

Exercise 1.24*

1. Find and classify the stationary points of the each of the following functions:

    (a) $f(x, y) = x^3 + x^2 - xy + y^2 + 10$
    (b) $f(x, y) = (2xy + y^2)e^x$
    (c) $f(x, y) = x^2 - y^2 - 4xy - y^3$

2. A firm's production function is given by

    $$Q = 2L^{1/2} + 3K^{1/2}$$

    where Q, L and K denote the number of units of output, labour and capital. Labour costs are \$2 per unit, capital costs are \$1 per unit and output sells at \$8 per unit. Show that the profit function is

    $$\pi = 16L^{1/2} + 24K^{1/2} - 2L - K$$

    and hence find the maximum profit and the values of L and K at which it is achieved.

3. A firm sells a good to both UK and EU customers. The demand function is the same for both markets and is given by

    $$20P_i + Q_i = 5000$$

    where the subscript, i, takes the values 1 and 2 corresponding to the UK and EU, respectively.

    Although the variable and fixed costs are the same for each market, the EU now charges a fixed tariff of \$50 per unit, so the joint total cost function is

    $$TC = 40Q_1 + 90Q_2 + 2000$$

    Find the maximum total profit.

4. The demand functions for a firm's domestic and foreign markets are

$$P_1 = 50 - 5Q_1$$

$$P_2 = 30 - 4Q_2$$

and the total cost function is

$$TC = 10 + 10Q$$

where $Q = Q_1 + Q_2$. Determine the prices needed to maximise profit with price discrimination and calculate the value of the maximum profit.

[You have already solved this particular example in Question 3(a) in Exercise 1.21*.]

5. A firm is able to sell its product in two different markets. The corresponding demand functions are

$$P_1 + 2Q_1 = 100$$

$$2P_2 + Q_2 = 2a$$

and the total cost function is

$$TC = 500 + 10Q$$

where $Q = Q_1 + Q_2$ and a is a positive constant.

Determine, in terms of a, the prices needed to maximise profit

(a) with price discrimination;

(b) without price discrimination.

Show that the profit with price discrimination is always greater than the profit without discrimination, irrespective of the value of a.

6. (a) A firm's production function is given by $Q = f(K, L)$. The fixed prices of each unit of output, capital and labour are p, r and w, respectively. Explain briefly why the profit function is given by

$$\pi(K, L) = pf(K, L) - rK - wL$$

Show that at a stationary point

$$\frac{\partial f}{\partial K} = \frac{r}{p} \quad \text{and} \quad \frac{\partial f}{\partial L} = \frac{w}{p}$$

Give an economic interpretation of these results.

(b) Use the result of part (a), or otherwise, to find the values of K and L which maximise profit when the production function is $Q = K^{1/2}L^{1/3}$, $p = 24$, $r = 1.5$ and $w = 8$. Verify that the second-order conditions for a maximum are satisfied in this case.

7. A firm manufactures two goods labelled 1 and 2. It sells Q_i items of good i for a fixed price per unit of p_i. The total cost of producing good i is $c_iQ_i^2$.

Explain briefly why the profit function is given by

$$\pi(Q_1, Q_2) = p_1Q_1 + p_2Q_2 - c_1Q_1^2 - c_2Q_2^2$$

Find the values of Q_1 and Q_2 which maximise π and verify that the second-order conditions for a maximum are satisfied. Find an expression for the maximum profit.

8. The unit prices of two goods A and B are p and q. The total cost of producing x items of type A and y items of type B is

$$TC = 4x^2 + 2y^2 + 2xy + 100$$

Find the values of x and y that maximise profit.

SECTION 1.25
Constrained optimisation

Objectives

At the end of this section you should be able to:

- Give a graphical interpretation of constrained optimisation.

- Show that when a firm maximises output subject to a cost constraint, the ratio of marginal product to price is the same for all inputs.

- Show that when a consumer maximises utility subject to a budgetary constraint, the ratio of marginal utility to price is the same for all goods.

- Use the method of substitution to solve constrained optimisation problems in economics.

Advice

In this section we begin by proving some theoretical results before describing the method of substitution. You might prefer to skip the theory at a first reading and begin with the examples.

In Section 1.24 we described how to find the optimum (that is, maximum or minimum) of a function of two variables

$$z = f(x, y)$$

where the variables x and y are free to take any values. As we pointed out at the beginning of that section, this assumption is unrealistic in many economic situations. An individual wishing to maximise utility is subject to an income constraint, and a firm wishing to maximise output is subject to a cost constraint.

In general, we want to optimise a function,

$$z = f(x, y)$$

called the **objective function** subject to a constraint

$$\varphi(x, y) = M$$

Here φ, the Greek letter phi, is a known function of two variables and M is a known constant. The problem is to pick the pair of numbers (x, y) which maximises or minimises $f(x, y)$ as before. This time, however, we limit the choice of pairs to those which satisfy

$$\varphi(x, y) = M$$

A graphical interpretation should make this clear. To be specific, let us suppose that a firm wants to maximise output and that the production function is of the form

$$Q = f(K, L)$$

Let the costs of each unit of capital and labour be P_K and P_L, respectively. The cost to the firm of using as input K units of capital and L units of labour is

$$P_K K + P_L L$$

so if the firm has a fixed amount, M, to spend on these inputs, then

$$P_K K + P_L L = M$$

The problem is one of trying to maximise the objective function

$$Q = f(K, L)$$

subject to the cost constraint

$$P_K K + P_L L = M$$

Sketched in Figure 1.88 is a typical isoquant map. As usual, points on any one isoquant yield the same level of output, and as output rises, the isoquants themselves move further away from the origin. Also sketched in Figure 1.88 is the cost constraint. This is called an **isocost curve** because it gives all combinations of K and L which can be bought for a fixed cost, M.

The fact that

$$P_K K + P_L L = M$$

is represented by a straight line should come as no surprise to you by now. We can even rewrite it in the more familiar '$y = ax + b$' form and so identify its slope and intercept. In Figure 1.88, L is plotted on the horizontal axis and K is plotted on the vertical axis, so we need to rearrange

$$P_K K + P_L L = M$$

to express K in terms of L. Subtracting $P_L L$ from both sides and dividing through by P_K gives

$$K = \left(-\frac{P_L}{P_K}\right) L + \frac{M}{P_K}$$

The isocost curve is therefore a straight line with slope $-P_L/P_K$ and intercept M/P_K. Graphically, our constrained problem is to choose that point on the isocost line which maximises output. This is given by the point labelled A in Figure 1.88. Point A certainly lies on the isocost line

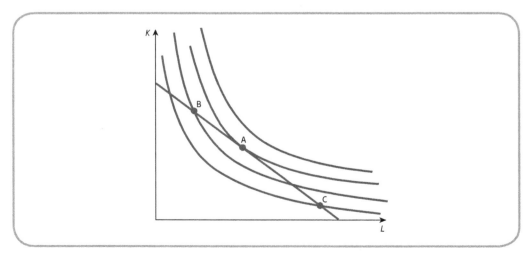

Figure 1.88

and it maximises output because it also lies on the highest isoquant. Other points, such as B and C, also satisfy the constraint, but they lie on lower isoquants and so yield smaller levels of output than A. Point A is characterised by the fact that the isocost line is tangential to an isoquant. In other words, the slope of the isocost line is the same as that of the isoquant at A.

Now we have already shown that the isocost line has slope $-P_L/P_K$. In Section 1.23 we defined the marginal rate of technical substitution, MRTS, to be minus the slope of an isoquant, so at point A we must have

$$\frac{P_L}{P_K} = \text{MRTS}$$

We also showed that

$$\text{MRTS} = \frac{\text{MP}_L}{\text{MP}_K}$$

so

$$\frac{P_L}{P_K} = \frac{\text{MP}_L}{\text{MP}_K}$$

> the ratio of the input prices is equal to the ratio of their marginal products

This relationship can be rearranged as

$$\frac{\text{MP}_L}{P_L} = \frac{\text{MP}_K}{P_K}$$

so when output is maximised subject to a cost constraint

> the ratio of marginal product to price is the same for all inputs

The marginal product determines the change in output due to a 1-unit increase in input. This optimisation condition therefore states that the last dollar spent on labour yields the same addition to output as the last dollar spent on capital.

The above discussion has concentrated on production functions. An analogous situation arises when we maximise utility functions

$$U = U(x_1, x_2)$$

where x_1, x_2 denote the number of items of goods G1, G2 that an individual buys. If the prices of these goods are denoted by P_1 and P_2 and the individual has a fixed budget, M, to spend on these goods then, the corresponding constraint is

$$P_1 x_1 + P_2 x_2 = M$$

This budgetary constraint plays the role of the cost constraint, and indifference curves are analogous to isoquants. Consequently, we analyse the problem by superimposing the budget line on an indifference map. The corresponding diagram is virtually indistinguishable from that of Figure 1.88. The only change is that the axes would be labelled x_1 and x_2 rather than L and K. Once again, the maximum point of the constrained problem occurs at the point of tangency, so that at this point the slope of the budget line is that of an indifference curve. Hence

$$\frac{P_1}{P_2} = \text{MRCS}$$

Exercise 1.25

1. (a) Make y the subject of the formula $9x + 3y = 2$.

    (b) The function,

    $$z = 3xy$$

    is subject to the constraint

    $$9x + 3y = 2$$

    Use your answer to part (a) to show that

    $$z = 2x - 9x^2$$

    Hence find the maximum value of z and the corresponding values of x and y.

2. Find the maximum value of

    $$z = 6x - 3x^2 + 2y$$

    subject to the constraint

    $$y - x^2 = 2$$

3. Find the maximum value of

    $$z = 80x - 0.1x^2 + 100y - 0.2y^2$$

    subject to the constraint

    $$x + y = 500$$

4. A firm's production function is given by

    $$Q = 50KL$$

    Unit capital and labour costs are \$2 and \$3, respectively. Find the values of K and L which minimise total input costs if the production quota is 1200.

5. The total cost of producing x items of product A and y items of product B is

    $$TC = 22x^2 + 8y^2 - 5xy$$

    If the firm is committed to producing 20 items in total, write down the constraint connecting x and y. Hence find the number of each type that should be produced to minimise costs.

6. Find the maximum value of the utility function, $U = x_1 x_2$, subject to the budgetary constraint, $x_1 + 4x_2 = 360$.

7. A firm produces two goods A and B. The weekly cost of producing x items of A and y items of B is

    $$TC = 0.2x^2 + 0.05y^2 + 0.1xy + 2x + 5y + 1000$$

    (a) State the minimum value of TC in the case when there are no constraints.

    (b) Find the minimum value of TC when the firm is committed to producing 500 goods of either type in total.

8. A firm's production function is given by $Q = AKL$ where A is a positive constant.

Unit costs of capital and labour are $2 and $1, respectively. The firm spends a total of $1000 on these inputs.

(a) Write down the cost constraint.

(b) Write down expressions for the marginal products of capital and labour.

(c) Use the fact that at the maximum output, the ratio of the input prices is equal to the ratio of their marginal products to show that $L = 2K$.

(d) Use your answers to parts (a) and (c) to find the values of K and L which maximise output.

Exercise 1.25*

1. (a) Find the minimum value of the objective function

$$z = 9x^2 + 2y^2 - 3xy$$

subject to the constraint

$$x + y = 40.$$

(b) Find the maximum value of the objective function

$$-16x^2 - 2y^2 + 4x + 9y + 2xy$$

subject to the constraint

$$y = 4x$$

2. A firm's production function is given by

$$Q = 10K^{1/2}L^{1/4}$$

Unit capital and labour costs are $4 and $5, respectively, and the firm spends a total of $60 on these inputs. Find the values of K and L which maximise output.

3. A firm's production function is given by

$$Q = 2L^{1/2} + 3K^{1/2}$$

where Q, L and K denote the number of units of output, labour and capital, respectively. Labour costs are $2 per unit, capital costs are $1 per unit and output sells at $8 per unit. If the firm is prepared to spend $99 on input costs, find the maximum profit and the values of K and L at which it is achieved.

[You might like to compare your answer with the corresponding unconstrained problem that you solved in Question 2 of Exercise 1.24*.]

4. A consumer's utility function is

$$U = \ln x_1 + 2 \ln x_2$$

Find the values of x_1 and x_2 which maximise U subject to the budgetary constraint

$$2x_1 + 3x_2 = 18$$

5. An individual's utility function is given by

$$U = x_1\sqrt{x_2}$$

where x_1 and x_2 denote the monthly consumption of two goods. Unit prices of these goods are \$2 and \$4, respectively, and the total monthly expenditure on these goods is \$300.

(a) Write down the budgetary constraint.

(b) Show that if the budgetary constraint is satisfied, the maximum value of U is 500, and write down the corresponding values of x_1 and x_2. Verify that the stationary point is a maximum.

(c) Draw the three indifference curves, $x_1\sqrt{x_2} = 400$, $x_1\sqrt{x_2} = 500$ and $x_1\sqrt{x_2} = 600$, on the same diagram. Hence show that the maximum point of the constrained problem occurs at a point where the budgetary constraint is a tangent to an indifference curve.

6. A firm wishes to maximise output, $Q = K^2L$, subject to a budgetary constraint

$$3K + 2L = 900$$

(a) Find the values of K and L which maximise output.

(b) Draw a graph to illustrate the fact that at this maximum output the budget line is a tangent to a particular isoquant.

7. A utility function, $U(x_1, x_2) = \sqrt{x_1} + x_2$, is subject to a budgetary constraint, $x_2 = b - ax_1$ where a and b are positive constants.

(a) Show that the maximum value of U is $U^* = \dfrac{4ab + 1}{4a}$.

(b) By considering the signs of $\dfrac{\partial U^*}{\partial a}$ and $\dfrac{\partial U^*}{\partial b}$, state what happens to the value of the optimal utility due to changes in a or b.

SECTION 1.26
Basic matrix operations

Objectives

At the end of this section you should be able to:

- Understand the notation and terminology of matrix algebra.
- Find the transpose of a matrix.
- Add and subtract matrices.
- Multiply a matrix by a scalar.
- Multiply matrices together.
- Represent a system of linear equations in matrix notation.

Suppose that a firm produces three types of good, G1, G2 and G3, which it sells to two customers, C1 and C2. The monthly sales for these goods are given in Table 1.2.

During the month the firm sells 3 items of G2 to customer C1, 6 items of G3 to customer C2, and so on. It may well be obvious from the context exactly what these numbers represent. Under these circumstances it makes sense to ignore the table headings and to write this information more concisely as

$$A = \begin{bmatrix} 7 & 3 & 4 \\ 1 & 5 & 6 \end{bmatrix}$$

which is an example of a matrix. Quite generally, any rectangular array of numbers surrounded by a pair of brackets is called a **matrix** (plural **matrices**), and the individual numbers constituting the array are called **entries** or **elements**. In this text we use square brackets, although it is equally correct to use parentheses (that is, round brackets) instead. It helps to think of a matrix as being made up of rows and columns. The matrix A has two rows and three columns and is said to have order 2×3. In general, a matrix of **order** $m \times n$ has m rows and n columns.

We denote matrices by capital letters in bold type (that is, A, B, C, . . .) and their elements by the corresponding lower-case letter in ordinary type. In fact, we use a rather clever double subscript notation so that a_{ij} stands for the element of A which occurs in row i and column j. Referring to the matrix A above, we see that

$a_{12} = 3$ (row 1 and column 2 of A)

and $a_{23} = 6$ (row 2 and column 3 of A)

Table 1.2

		Monthly sales for goods		
		G1	G2	G3
Sold to	C1	7	3	4
customer	C2	1	5	6

A general matrix **D** of order 3×2 would be written

$$\begin{bmatrix} d_{11} & d_{12} \\ d_{21} & d_{22} \\ d_{31} & d_{32} \end{bmatrix}$$

Similarly, a 3×3 matrix labelled **E** would be written

$$\begin{bmatrix} e_{11} & e_{12} & e_{13} \\ e_{21} & e_{22} & e_{23} \\ e_{31} & e_{32} & e_{33} \end{bmatrix}$$

Practice Problem

1. Let

$$\mathbf{A} = \begin{bmatrix} 1 & 2 \\ 3 & 4 \end{bmatrix} \quad \mathbf{B} = [1 \quad -1 \quad 0 \quad 6 \quad 2] \quad \mathbf{C} = \begin{bmatrix} 1 & 0 & 2 & 3 & 1 \\ 5 & 7 & 9 & 0 & 2 \\ 3 & 4 & 6 & 7 & 8 \end{bmatrix} \quad \mathbf{D} = [6]$$

(a) State the orders of the matrices **A**, **B**, **C** and **D**.

(b) Write down (if possible) the values of

$a_{11}, \; a_{22}, \; b_{14}, \; c_{25}, \; c_{33}, \; c_{43}, \; d_{11}$

All we have done so far is to explain what matrices are and to provide some notation for handling them. A matrix certainly gives us a convenient shorthand to describe information presented in a table. However, we would like to go further than this and to use matrices to solve problems in economics. To do this we describe several mathematical operations that can be performed on matrices, namely:

● transposition;
● addition and subtraction;
● scalar multiplication;
● matrix multiplication.

One obvious omission from the list is matrix division. Strictly speaking, it is impossible to divide one matrix by another, although we can get fairly close to the idea of division by defining something called an inverse, which we consider in Section 1.27.

Advice

If you have not met matrices before, you might like to split this section into two separate parts. You are advised to work through the material as far as 7.1.4 now, leaving matrix multiplication for another session.

The number c_{12} lies in the first row and second column, so to find its value we multiply the first row of **A** into the second column of **B** to get

$$\begin{bmatrix} \boxed{2} & \boxed{1} & \boxed{0} \\ 1 & 0 & 4 \end{bmatrix} \begin{bmatrix} 3 & \boxed{1} & 2 & 1 \\ 1 & \boxed{0} & 1 & 2 \\ 5 & \boxed{4} & 1 & 1 \end{bmatrix} \begin{bmatrix} 7 & \boxed{2} & c_{13} & c_{14} \\ c_{21} & c_{22} & c_{23} & c_{24} \end{bmatrix}$$

because $2(1) + 1(0) + 0(4) = 2$.

The values of c_{13} and c_{14} are then found in a similar way by multiplying the first row of **A** into the third and fourth columns of **B**, respectively, to get

$$\begin{bmatrix} \boxed{2} & \boxed{1} & \boxed{0} \\ 1 & 0 & 4 \end{bmatrix} \begin{bmatrix} 3 & 1 & \boxed{2} & \boxed{1} \\ 1 & 0 & \boxed{1} & \boxed{2} \\ 5 & 4 & \boxed{1} & \boxed{1} \end{bmatrix} \begin{bmatrix} 7 & 2 & \boxed{5} & \boxed{4} \\ c_{21} & c_{22} & c_{23} & c_{24} \end{bmatrix}$$

because $2(2) + 1(1) + 0(1) = 5$ and $2(1) + 1(2) + 0(1) = 4$.

Finally, we repeat the whole procedure along the second row of **C**. The elements c_{21}, c_{22}, c_{23} and c_{24} are calculated by multiplying the second row of **A** into the four columns of **B** in succession to get

$$\begin{bmatrix} 2 & 1 & 0 \\ \boxed{1} & \boxed{0} & \boxed{4} \end{bmatrix} \begin{bmatrix} \boxed{3} & \boxed{1} & \boxed{2} & \boxed{1} \\ \boxed{1} & \boxed{0} & \boxed{1} & \boxed{2} \\ \boxed{5} & \boxed{4} & \boxed{1} & \boxed{1} \end{bmatrix} \begin{bmatrix} 7 & 2 & 5 & 4 \\ \boxed{23} & \boxed{17} & \boxed{6} & \boxed{5} \end{bmatrix}$$

because

$1(3) + 0(1) + 4(5) = 23$

$1(1) + 0(0) + 4(4) = 17$

$1(2) + 0(1) + 4(1) = 6$

$1(1) + 0(2) + 4(1) = 5$

In this example we have indicated how to build up the matrix **C** in a step-by-step manner and have used highlights to show you how the calculations are performed. This approach has been adopted merely as a teaching device. There is no need for you to set your calculations out in this way, and you are encouraged to write down your answer in a single line of working.

Advice

Take the trouble to check before you begin that it is possible to form the matrix product and to anticipate the order of the end result. This can be done by jotting down the orders of the original matrices side by side. The product exists if the inner numbers are the same and the order of the answer is given by the outer numbers: that is,

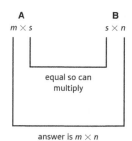

For example, if **A**, **B** and **C** have orders 3 × 5, 5 × 2 and 3 × 4 respectively, then **AB** exists and has order 3 × 2 because

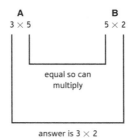

but it is impossible to form **AC** because

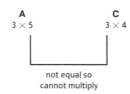

Practice Problem

6. Write down the order of the matrices

$$A = \begin{bmatrix} 1 & 2 \\ 0 & 1 \\ 3 & 1 \end{bmatrix} \quad \text{and} \quad B = \begin{bmatrix} 1 & 2 \\ 3 & 4 \end{bmatrix}$$

Hence verify that it is possible to form the matrix product

$$C = AB$$

and write down the order of **C**. Calculate all of the elements of **C**.

We have already noted that matrix operations have similar properties to those of ordinary arithmetic. Some particular rules of arithmetic are:

$a(b + c) = ab + ac$ (distributive law)

$(a + b)c = ac + bc$ (distributive law)

$a(bc) = (ab)c$ (associative law)

$ab = ba$ (commutative law)

An obvious question to ask is whether they have a counterpart in matrix algebra. It turns out that provided the matrices **A**, **B** and **C** have the correct orders for the appropriate sums and products to exist, then

$A(B + C) = AB + AC$

$(A + B)C = AC + BC$

$A(BC) = (AB)C$

However, although it is true that

$$ab = ba$$

for numbers, this result does **not** extend to matrices. Even if **AB** and **BA** both exist, it is not necessarily true that

AB = BA

This is illustrated in the following example.

Example

If

$$\mathbf{A} = \begin{bmatrix} 1 & -1 \\ 2 & 1 \end{bmatrix} \quad \text{and} \quad \mathbf{B} = \begin{bmatrix} 1 & 3 \\ 1 & 2 \end{bmatrix}$$

evaluate **AB** and **BA**.

Solution

It is easy to check that it is possible to form both products **AB** and **BA** and that they both have order 2×2. In fact

$$\mathbf{AB} = \begin{bmatrix} 1 & -1 \\ 2 & 1 \end{bmatrix}\begin{bmatrix} 1 & 3 \\ 1 & 2 \end{bmatrix} = \begin{bmatrix} 0 & 1 \\ 3 & 8 \end{bmatrix}$$

$$\mathbf{BA} = \begin{bmatrix} 1 & 3 \\ 1 & 2 \end{bmatrix}\begin{bmatrix} 1 & -1 \\ 2 & 1 \end{bmatrix} = \begin{bmatrix} 7 & 2 \\ 5 & 1 \end{bmatrix}$$

so **AB ≠ BA**.

There are certain pairs of matrices which do commute (that is, for which **AB = BA**) and we shall investigate some of these in the next section. However, these are very much the exception. We therefore have the 'non-property' that, in general,

AB ≠ BA

Practice Problems

7. Let

$$\mathbf{A} = \begin{bmatrix} 2 & 1 & 1 \\ 5 & 1 & 0 \\ -1 & 1 & 4 \end{bmatrix}, \quad \mathbf{B} = \begin{bmatrix} 1 \\ 2 \\ 1 \end{bmatrix}, \quad \mathbf{C} = \begin{bmatrix} 1 & 2 \\ 3 & 1 \end{bmatrix}, \quad \mathbf{D} = \begin{bmatrix} 1 & 1 \\ -1 & 1 \\ 2 & 1 \end{bmatrix} \quad \text{and} \quad \mathbf{E} = \begin{bmatrix} 1 & 2 & 3 \\ 4 & 5 & 6 \end{bmatrix}$$

Find (where possible)

(a) AB   (b) BA   (c) CD   (d) DC

(e) AE   (f) EA   (g) DE   (h) ED

8. Evaluate the matrix product **Ax**, where

$$A = \begin{bmatrix} 1 & 4 & 7 \\ 2 & 6 & 5 \\ 8 & 9 & 5 \end{bmatrix} \quad \text{and} \quad \mathbf{x} = \begin{bmatrix} x \\ y \\ z \end{bmatrix}$$

Hence show that the system of linear equations

$$x + 4y + 7z = -3$$
$$2x + 6y + 5z = 10$$
$$8x + 9y + 5z = 1$$

can be written as **Ax = b** where

$$\mathbf{b} = \begin{bmatrix} -3 \\ 10 \\ 1 \end{bmatrix}$$

We conclude this section by showing you how to express a familiar problem in matrix notation. Section 1.4 described the method of elimination for solving systems of simultaneous linear equations. For example, we might want to find values of x and y which satisfy

$$2x - 5y = 6$$
$$7x + 8y = -1$$

Motivated by the result of Practice Problem 8, we write this as

Ax = b

where

$$A = \begin{bmatrix} 2 & -5 \\ 7 & 8 \end{bmatrix} \quad \mathbf{x} = \begin{bmatrix} x \\ y \end{bmatrix} \quad \mathbf{b} = \begin{bmatrix} 6 \\ -1 \end{bmatrix}$$

It is easy to check that this is correct simply by multiplying out **Ax** to get

$$\begin{bmatrix} 2 & -5 \\ 7 & 8 \end{bmatrix}\begin{bmatrix} x \\ y \end{bmatrix} = \begin{bmatrix} 2x - 5y \\ 7x + 8y \end{bmatrix}$$

and so the matrix equation **Ax = b** reads

$$\begin{bmatrix} 2x - 5y \\ 7x + 8y \end{bmatrix} = \begin{bmatrix} 6 \\ -1 \end{bmatrix}$$

that is,

$$2x - 5y = 6$$
$$7x + 8y = -1$$

Quite generally, any system of n linear equations in n unknowns can be written as

Ax = b

where $\mathbf{A}$, $\mathbf{x}$ and $\mathbf{b}$ are $n \times n$, $n \times 1$ and $n \times 1$ matrices, respectively. The matrix $\mathbf{A}$ consists of the coefficients, the vector $\mathbf{x}$ consists of the unknowns and the vector $\mathbf{b}$ consists of the right-hand sides. The definition of matrix multiplication allows us to write a linear system in terms of matrices, although it is not immediately obvious that there is any advantage in doing so. In the next section we introduce the concept of a matrix inverse and show you how to use this to solve systems of equations expressed in matrix form.

Throughout this section we have noted various properties that matrices satisfy. For convenience these are summarised in the next sub-section.

1.26.5 Summary

Provided that the indicated sums and products make sense,

$$\mathbf{A} + \mathbf{B} = \mathbf{B} + \mathbf{A}$$
$$\mathbf{A} - \mathbf{A} = \mathbf{0}$$
$$\mathbf{A} + \mathbf{0} = \mathbf{A}$$
$$k(\mathbf{A} + \mathbf{B}) = k\mathbf{A} + k\mathbf{B}$$
$$k(l\mathbf{A}) = (kl)\mathbf{A}$$
$$\mathbf{A}(\mathbf{B} + \mathbf{C}) = \mathbf{AB} + \mathbf{AC}$$
$$(\mathbf{A} + \mathbf{B})\mathbf{C} = \mathbf{AC} + \mathbf{BC}$$
$$\mathbf{A}(\mathbf{BC}) = (\mathbf{AB})\mathbf{C}$$

We also have the non-property that, in general,

$$\mathbf{AB} \neq \mathbf{BA}$$

Key Terms

Column vector   A matrix with one column.

Elements   The individual numbers inside a matrix. (Also called **entries**.)

Matrix   A rectangular array of numbers, set out in rows and columns, surrounded by a pair of brackets. (Plural **matrices**.)

Order (of a matrix)   The dimensions of a matrix. A matrix with m rows and n columns has order $m \times n$.

Row vector   A matrix with one row.

Transpose (of a matrix)   The matrix obtained from a given matrix by interchanging rows and columns. The transpose of a matrix $\mathbf{A}$ is written $\mathbf{A}^\mathsf{T}$.

Zero matrix   A matrix in which every element is zero.

Exercise 1.26

1. The monthly sales (in thousands) of burgers (B1) and bites (B2) in three fast-food restaurants (R1, R2, R3) are as follows:

	R1	R2	R3
B1	35	27	13
B2	42	39	24

January

	R1	R2	R3
B1	31	17	3
B2	25	29	16

February

(a) Write down two 2×3 matrices **J** and **F**, representing sales in January and February, respectively.

(b) By finding $\mathbf{J} + \mathbf{F}$, write down the matrix for the total sales over the two months.

(c) By finding $\mathbf{J} - \mathbf{F}$, write down the matrix for the difference in sales for the two months.

2. If

$$\mathbf{A} = \begin{bmatrix} 2 & 3 & 1 & 9 \\ 1 & 0 & 5 & 0 \\ 6 & 7 & 8 & 4 \end{bmatrix} \quad \mathbf{B} = \begin{bmatrix} 1 & 7 & 9 & 6 \\ 2 & 1 & 0 & 5 \\ 6 & 4 & 5 & 3 \end{bmatrix}$$

work out

(a) $2\mathbf{A}$ (b) $2\mathbf{B}$ (c) $2\mathbf{A} + 2\mathbf{B}$ (d) $2(\mathbf{A} + \mathbf{B})$

Do you notice any connection between your answers to parts (c) and (d)?

3. If **A**, **B** and **C** are matrices with orders, 3×3, 2×3 and 4×2, respectively, which of the following matrix calculations are possible? If the calculation *is* possible, state the order of the resulting matrix

    $4\mathbf{B}, \quad \mathbf{A} + \mathbf{B}, \quad 3\mathbf{B}^{\mathrm{T}} + \mathbf{C}, \quad \mathbf{AB}, \quad \mathbf{B}^{\mathrm{T}}\mathbf{A}, \quad (\mathbf{CB})^{\mathrm{T}}, \quad \mathbf{CBA}$

4. A firm manufactures three products, P1, P2 and P3, which it sells to two customers, C1 and C2. The number of items of each product that are sold to these customers is given by

$$\mathbf{A} = \begin{array}{c} \text{C1} \\ \text{C2} \end{array} \begin{bmatrix} 6 & 7 & 9 \\ 2 & 1 & 2 \end{bmatrix} \begin{array}{c} \text{P1 P2 P3} \end{array}$$

The firm charges both customers the same price for each product according to

$$\begin{array}{ccc} \text{P1} & \text{P2} & \text{P3} \end{array}$$
$$\mathbf{B} = [100 \quad 500 \quad 200]^{\mathrm{T}}$$

To make each item of type P1, P2 and P3, the firm uses four raw materials, R1, R2, R3 and R4. The number of tonnes required per item is given by

$$\mathbf{C} = \begin{array}{c} \text{P1} \\ \text{P2} \\ \text{P3} \end{array} \begin{bmatrix} 1 & 0 & 0 & 1 \\ 1 & 1 & 2 & 1 \\ 0 & 0 & 1 & 1 \end{bmatrix} \begin{array}{cccc} \text{R1} & \text{R2} & \text{R3} & \text{R4} \end{array}$$

The cost per tonne of raw materials is

$$\begin{array}{cccc} R1 & R2 & R3 & R4 \end{array}$$
$$D = [20 \quad 10 \quad 15 \quad 15]^{T}$$

In addition, let

$$E = [1 \quad 1]$$

Find the following matrix products and give an interpretation of each one.

(a) AB   (b) AC   (c) CD   (d) ACD   (e) EAB

(f) EACD   (g) EAB – EACD

5. A firm orders 12, 30 and 25 items of goods G1, G2 and G3. The cost of each item of G1, G2 and G3 is $8, $30 and $15, respectively.

(a) Write down suitable price and quantity vectors, and use matrix multiplication to work out the total cost of the order.

(b) Write down the new price vector when the cost of G1 rises by 20%, the cost of G2 falls by 10% and the cost of G3 is unaltered. Use matrix multiplication to work out the new cost of the order and hence find the overall percentage change in total cost.

6. (1) Let

$$A = \begin{bmatrix} 1 & 2 \\ 3 & 4 \\ 5 & 6 \end{bmatrix} \quad \text{and} \quad B = \begin{bmatrix} 1 & -1 \\ 2 & 1 \\ -3 & 4 \end{bmatrix}$$

Find

(a) A^{T} (b) B^{T} (c) $A + B$ (d) $(A + B)^{T}$

Do you notice any connection between $(A + B)^{T}$, A^{T} and B^{T}?

(2) Let

$$C = \begin{bmatrix} 1 & 4 \\ 5 & 9 \end{bmatrix} \quad \text{and} \quad D = \begin{bmatrix} 2 & 1 & 0 \\ -1 & 0 & 1 \end{bmatrix}$$

Find

(a) C^{T} (b) D^{T} (c) CD   (d) $(CD)^{T}$

Do you notice any connection between $(CD)^{T}$, C^{T} and D^{T}?

7. Verify the equations

(a) $A(B + C) = AB + AC$ (b) $(AB)C = A(BC)$

in the case when

$$A = \begin{bmatrix} 5 & -3 \\ 2 & 1 \end{bmatrix}, \quad B = \begin{bmatrix} 1 & 5 \\ 4 & 0 \end{bmatrix} \quad \text{and} \quad C = \begin{bmatrix} -1 & 1 \\ 1 & 2 \end{bmatrix}$$

8. If

$$A = [1 \quad 2 \quad -4 \quad 3] \quad \text{and} \quad B = \begin{bmatrix} 1 \\ 7 \\ 3 \\ 2 \end{bmatrix}$$

find AB and BA.

9. **(a)** Evaluate the matrix product **Ax**, where

$$\mathbf{A} = \begin{bmatrix} 7 & 5 \\ 1 & 3 \end{bmatrix} \quad \text{and} \quad \mathbf{x} = \begin{bmatrix} x \\ y \end{bmatrix}$$

Hence show that the system of linear equations

$$7x + 5y = 3$$
$$x + 3y = 2$$

can be written as **Ax** = **b** where $\mathbf{b} = \begin{bmatrix} 3 \\ 2 \end{bmatrix}$.

(b) The system of equations

$$2x + 3y - 2z = 6$$
$$x - y + 2z = 3$$
$$4x + 2y + 5z = 1$$

can be expressed in the form **Ax** = **b**. Write down the matrices **A**, **x** and **b**.

Exercise 1.26*

1. Matrices **A**, **B**, **C** and **D** have orders 3×5, 5×2, 5×5 and 3×5, respectively. State whether it is possible to perform the following matrix operations.

   If it *is* possible, state the order of the resulting matrix.

   (a) 7**B**   **(b)** $(\mathbf{A} + \mathbf{C})^{\mathrm{T}}$ **(c)** **A** − 2**D**   **(d)** **BC**

   (e) $\mathbf{CB}^{\mathrm{T}}$ **(f)** $\mathbf{D}^{\mathrm{T}}\mathbf{A}$ **(g)** $\mathbf{A}^{\mathrm{T}} + \mathbf{B}^{\mathrm{T}}$

2. Two matrices **A** and **B** are given by

$$\mathbf{A} = \begin{bmatrix} a-1 & b \\ a+b & 3c-b \end{bmatrix} \quad \text{and} \quad \mathbf{B} = \begin{bmatrix} 1 & 3a \\ 2c & d+1 \end{bmatrix}$$

   If **A** = **B**, find the values of a, b, c and d.

3. Consider the matrices

$$\mathbf{A} = \begin{bmatrix} a & b & c \\ d & e & f \end{bmatrix} \quad \text{and} \quad \mathbf{B} = \begin{bmatrix} g & h \\ i & j \\ k & l \end{bmatrix}$$

   (a) Write down the matrices $\mathbf{A}^{\mathrm{T}}$ and $\mathbf{B}^{\mathrm{T}}$.

   (b) Work out the matrix products **AB** and $\mathbf{B}^{\mathrm{T}}\mathbf{A}^{\mathrm{T}}$.

   (c) State the relationship between **AB** and $\mathbf{B}^{\mathrm{T}}\mathbf{A}^{\mathrm{T}}$, and use this result to simplify $(\mathbf{A}^{\mathrm{T}}\mathbf{B}^{\mathrm{T}}\mathbf{C}^{\mathrm{T}})^{\mathrm{T}}$.

4. A chain of sports shops, A, B and C, sells T-shirts, trainers and tennis racquets. The weekly sales and profit per item are shown in the tables below:

Sales per week	Shop A	Shop B	Shop C
T-shirts	60	40	25
Trainers	80	123	90
Tennis racquets	10	0	25

Profit per item	Shop A ($)	Shop B ($)	Shop C ($)
T-shirts	1	1	1.50
Trainers	5	8	6
Tennis racquets	20	25	30

The 3×3 matrices formed from the sales and profit tables are denoted by **S** and **P**, respectively.

(a) If $\mathbf{SP}^{\mathrm{T}}$ is denoted by **A**, find the element a_{11} and give a brief interpretation of this number.

(b) If $\mathbf{S}^{\mathrm{T}}\mathbf{P}$ is denoted by **B**, find the element b_{33} and give a brief interpretation of this number.

5. On a small island there are supermarkets A, L, S and W. In the current year, 30% of customers buy groceries from A, 20% from L, 40% from S and 10% from W. However, each year,

A retains 80% of its customers but loses 10% to L, 5% to S and 5% to W.
L retains 90% of its customers but loses 5% to A and 5% to S.
S retains 75% of its customers but loses 10% to A, 10% to L and 5% to W.
W retains 85% of its customers losing 5% to A, 5% to L and 5% to S.

(a) If the original market share is represented by the column vector

$$\mathbf{x} = \begin{bmatrix} 0.3 \\ 0.2 \\ 0.4 \\ 0.1 \end{bmatrix}$$

and the matrix representing the transition in supermarket loyalty is

$$\mathbf{T} = \begin{bmatrix} 0.8 & 0.05 & 0.1 & 0.05 \\ 0.1 & 0.9 & 0.1 & 0.05 \\ 0.05 & 0.05 & 0.75 & 0.05 \\ 0.05 & 0 & 0.05 & 0.85 \end{bmatrix}$$

work out the matrix product, **Tx**, and give an interpretation of the elements of the resulting vector.

(b) Assuming that the same transition matrix applies in subsequent years, work out the percentage of customers who buy groceries in supermarket L after

(i) two years   (ii) three years

6. If $\mathbf{A} = \begin{bmatrix} 3 & -1 & 4 \\ 0 & 2 & 1 \end{bmatrix}$ and $\mathbf{B} = \begin{bmatrix} 4 & 0 & 7 \\ 2 & 5 & 1 \end{bmatrix}$ find the matrix **X** which satisfies the matrix equation: $2\mathbf{A} + \mathbf{X}^{\mathrm{T}} = 3\mathbf{B}$.

7. Matrices, **A**, **B** and **C** are given by

$$A = \begin{bmatrix} 3 & -2 & 4 \\ 6 & 1 & 0 \\ -5 & 9 & 5 \end{bmatrix}, \quad B = \begin{bmatrix} 1 & 5 & 0 \\ 4 & 4 & 7 \\ 2 & 3 & -9 \end{bmatrix} \quad \text{and} \quad C = \begin{bmatrix} 3 & -2 & -7 \\ -4 & 5 & 1 \\ 3 & 0 & 6 \end{bmatrix}$$

If $D = A(2B + 3C)$, find d_{23}.

8. Let

$$A = \begin{bmatrix} a & b \\ c & d \end{bmatrix}, \quad A^{-1} = \frac{1}{ad - bc} \begin{bmatrix} d & -b \\ -c & a \end{bmatrix} \qquad (ad - bc \neq 0)$$

$$I = \begin{bmatrix} 1 & 0 \\ 0 & 1 \end{bmatrix} \quad \text{and} \quad x = \begin{bmatrix} x \\ y \end{bmatrix}$$

Show that

(a) $AI = A$ and $IA = A$ **(b)** $A^{-1}A = I$ and $AA^{-1} = I$ **(c)** $Ix = x$

9. For the commodity market:

$$C = aY + b \quad \text{and} \quad I = cr + d$$

For the money market:

$$M_S = M_S^* \quad \text{and} \quad M_D = k_1Y + k_2r + k_3$$

If both markets are in equilibrium, find the matrix, **A**, such that $Ax = b$, where $x = \begin{bmatrix} r \\ Y \end{bmatrix}$

and $b = \begin{bmatrix} M_s^* - k_3 \\ b + d \end{bmatrix}$.

Example

Find the determinants of the following matrices:

$$\mathbf{A} = \begin{bmatrix} 2 & 4 & 1 \\ 4 & 3 & 7 \\ 2 & 1 & 3 \end{bmatrix} \quad \text{and} \quad \mathbf{B} = \begin{bmatrix} 10 & 7 & 5 \\ 0 & 2 & 0 \\ 2 & 7 & 3 \end{bmatrix}$$

Solution

We have already calculated all nine cofactors of the matrix

$$\mathbf{A} = \begin{bmatrix} 2 & 4 & 1 \\ 4 & 3 & 7 \\ 2 & 1 & 3 \end{bmatrix}$$

in the previous example. It is immaterial which row or column we use. Let us choose the second row. The cofactors corresponding to the three elements 4, 3, 7 in the second row were found to be −11, 4, 6, respectively. Consequently, if we expand along this row, we get

$$\begin{vmatrix} 2 & 4 & 1 \\ 4 & 3 & 7 \\ 2 & 1 & 3 \end{vmatrix} = 4(-11) + 3(4) + 7(6) = 10$$

As a check, let us also expand down the third column. The elements in this column are 1, 7, 3 with cofactors −2, 6, −10, respectively. Hence, if we multiply each element by its cofactor and add, we get

$$1(-2) + 7(6) + 3(-10) = 10$$

which is the same as before. If you are interested, you might like to confirm for yourself that the value of 10 is also obtained when expanding along rows 1 and 3, and down columns 1 and 2.

The matrix

$$\mathbf{B} = \begin{bmatrix} 10 & 7 & 5 \\ 0 & 2 & 0 \\ 2 & 7 & 3 \end{bmatrix}$$

is entirely new to us, so we have no prior knowledge about its cofactors. In general, we need to evaluate all three cofactors in any one row or column to find the determinant of a 3×3 matrix. In this case, however, we can be much lazier. Observe that all but one of the elements in the second row are zero, so when we expand along this row, we get

$$\begin{aligned} \det(\mathbf{B}) &= b_{21}B_{21} + b_{22}B_{22} + b_{23}B_{23} \\ &= 0B_{21} + 2B_{22} + 0B_{23} \\ &= 2B_{22} \end{aligned}$$

Hence B_{22} is the only cofactor that we need to find. This corresponds to the element in the second row and second column, so we delete this row and column to produce the 2×2 matrix

$$\begin{bmatrix} 10 & 5 \\ 2 & 3 \end{bmatrix}$$

The element b_{22} is in a plus position, so

$$B_{22} = + \begin{vmatrix} 10 & 5 \\ 2 & 3 \end{vmatrix} = 20$$

Hence,

$$\det(B) = 2B_{22} = 2 \times 20 = 40$$

Practice Problem

5. Find the determinants of

$$A = \begin{bmatrix} 1 & 3 & 3 \\ 1 & 4 & 3 \\ 1 & 3 & 4 \end{bmatrix} \quad \text{and} \quad B = \begin{bmatrix} 270 & -372 & 0 \\ 552 & 201 & 0 \\ 999 & 413 & 0 \end{bmatrix}$$

[Hint: you might find your answer to Practice Problem 4 useful when calculating the determinant of **A**.]

The inverse of the 3×3 matrix

$$A = \begin{bmatrix} a_{11} & a_{12} & a_{13} \\ a_{21} & a_{22} & a_{23} \\ a_{31} & a_{32} & a_{33} \end{bmatrix}$$

is given by

$$A^{-1} = \frac{1}{|A|} \begin{bmatrix} A_{11} & A_{21} & A_{31} \\ A_{12} & A_{22} & A_{32} \\ A_{13} & A_{23} & A_{33} \end{bmatrix}$$

Once the cofactors of **A** have been found, it is easy to construct $\mathbf{A}^{-1}$. We first stack the cofactors in their natural positions

$$\begin{bmatrix} A_{11} & A_{12} & A_{13} \\ A_{21} & A_{22} & A_{23} \\ A_{31} & A_{32} & A_{33} \end{bmatrix}$$

called the adjugate matrix

Secondly, we take the transpose to get

$$\begin{bmatrix} A_{11} & A_{21} & A_{31} \\ A_{12} & A_{22} & A_{32} \\ A_{13} & A_{23} & A_{33} \end{bmatrix}$$

called the adjoint matrix

Finally, we multiply by the scalar

$$\frac{1}{|A|}$$

to get

$$\mathbf{A}^{-1} = \frac{1}{|\mathbf{A}|} \begin{bmatrix} A_{11} & A_{21} & A_{31} \\ A_{12} & A_{22} & A_{32} \\ A_{13} & A_{23} & A_{33} \end{bmatrix}$$

divide each element by the determinant

The last step is impossible if

$$|\mathbf{A}| = 0$$

because we cannot divide by zero. Under these circumstances, the inverse does not exist and the matrix is singular.

Advice

It is a good idea to check that no mistakes have been made by verifying that

$$\mathbf{A}^{-1}\mathbf{A} = \mathbf{I} \quad \text{and} \quad \mathbf{A}\mathbf{A}^{-1} = \mathbf{I}$$

Example

Find the inverse of

$$\mathbf{A} = \begin{bmatrix} 2 & 4 & 1 \\ 4 & 3 & 7 \\ 2 & 1 & 3 \end{bmatrix}$$

Solution

The cofactors of this particular matrix have already been calculated as

$$A_{11} = 2, \quad A_{12} = 2, \quad A_{13} = -2$$
$$A_{21} = -11, \quad A_{22} = 4, \quad A_{23} = 6$$
$$A_{31} = 25, \quad A_{32} = -10, \quad A_{33} = -10$$

Stacking these numbers in their natural positions gives the adjugate matrix

$$\begin{bmatrix} 2 & 2 & -2 \\ -11 & 4 & 6 \\ 25 & -10 & -10 \end{bmatrix}$$

The adjoint matrix is found by transposing this to get

$$\begin{bmatrix} 2 & -11 & -25 \\ 2 & 4 & -10 \\ -2 & 6 & -10 \end{bmatrix}$$

In the previous example the determinant was found to be 10, so

$$\mathbf{A}^{-1} = \frac{1}{10} \begin{bmatrix} 2 & -11 & 25 \\ 2 & 4 & -10 \\ -2 & 6 & -10 \end{bmatrix} = \begin{bmatrix} 1/5 & -11/10 & 5/2 \\ 1/5 & 2/5 & -1 \\ -1/5 & 3/5 & -1 \end{bmatrix}$$

As a check:

$$\mathbf{A}^{-1}\mathbf{A} = \begin{bmatrix} 1/5 & -11/10 & 5/2 \\ 1/5 & 2/5 & -1 \\ -1/5 & 3/5 & -1 \end{bmatrix} \begin{bmatrix} 2 & 4 & 1 \\ 4 & 3 & 7 \\ 2 & 1 & 3 \end{bmatrix} = \begin{bmatrix} 1 & 0 & 0 \\ 0 & 1 & 0 \\ 0 & 0 & 1 \end{bmatrix} = \mathbf{I} \; \checkmark$$

$$\mathbf{A}\mathbf{A}^{-1} = \begin{bmatrix} 2 & 4 & 1 \\ 4 & 3 & 7 \\ 2 & 1 & 3 \end{bmatrix} \begin{bmatrix} 1/5 & -11/10 & 5/2 \\ 1/5 & 2/5 & -1 \\ -1/5 & 3/5 & -1 \end{bmatrix} = \begin{bmatrix} 1 & 0 & 0 \\ 0 & 1 & 0 \\ 0 & 0 & 1 \end{bmatrix} = \mathbf{I} \; \checkmark$$

Practice Problem

6. Find (where possible) the inverses of

$$\mathbf{A} = \begin{bmatrix} 1 & 3 & 3 \\ 1 & 4 & 3 \\ 1 & 3 & 4 \end{bmatrix} \quad \text{and} \quad \mathbf{B} = \begin{bmatrix} 270 & -372 & 0 \\ 552 & 201 & 0 \\ 999 & 413 & 0 \end{bmatrix}$$

[Hint: you might find your answers to Practice Problems 4 and 5 useful.]

Inverses of 3×3 matrices can be used to solve systems of three linear equations in three unknowns. The general system

$$a_{11}x + a_{12}y + a_{13}z = b_1$$
$$a_{21}x + a_{22}y + a_{23}z = b_2$$
$$a_{31}x + a_{32}y + a_{33}z = b_3$$

can be written as

$$\mathbf{A}\mathbf{x} = \mathbf{b}$$

where

$$\mathbf{A} = \begin{bmatrix} a_{11} & a_{12} & a_{13} \\ a_{21} & a_{22} & a_{23} \\ a_{31} & a_{32} & a_{33} \end{bmatrix} \quad \mathbf{x} = \begin{bmatrix} x \\ y \\ z \end{bmatrix} \quad \mathbf{b} = \begin{bmatrix} b_1 \\ b_2 \\ b_3 \end{bmatrix}$$

The vector of unknowns, $\mathbf{x}$, can be found by inverting the coefficient matrix, $\mathbf{A}$, and multiplying by the right-hand-side vector, $\mathbf{b}$, to get

$$\mathbf{x} = \mathbf{A}^{-1}\mathbf{b}$$

Example

Determine the equilibrium prices of three interdependent commodities that satisfy

$$2P_1 + 4P_2 + P_3 = 77$$
$$4P_1 + 3P_2 + 7P_3 = 114$$
$$2P_1 + P_2 + 3P_3 = 48$$

Solution

In matrix notation this system of equations can be written as

$$\mathbf{Ax} = \mathbf{b}$$

where

$$A = \begin{bmatrix} 2 & 4 & 1 \\ 4 & 3 & 7 \\ 2 & 1 & 3 \end{bmatrix} \quad x = \begin{bmatrix} P_1 \\ P_2 \\ P_3 \end{bmatrix} \quad b = \begin{bmatrix} 77 \\ 114 \\ 48 \end{bmatrix}$$

The inverse of the coefficient matrix has already been found in the previous example and is

$$A^{-1} = \begin{bmatrix} 1/5 & -11/10 & 5/2 \\ 1/5 & 2/5 & -1 \\ -1/5 & 3/5 & -1 \end{bmatrix}$$

so

$$\begin{bmatrix} P_1 \\ P_2 \\ P_3 \end{bmatrix} = \begin{bmatrix} 1/5 & -11/10 & 5/2 \\ 1/5 & 2/5 & -1 \\ -1/5 & 3/5 & -1 \end{bmatrix} \begin{bmatrix} 77 \\ 114 \\ 48 \end{bmatrix} = \begin{bmatrix} 10 \\ 13 \\ 5 \end{bmatrix}$$

The equilibrium prices are therefore given by

$$P_1 = 10, \quad P_2 = 13, \quad P_3 = 5$$

Practice Problem

7. Determine the equilibrium prices of three interdependent commodities that satisfy

$$P_1 + 3P_2 + 3P_3 = 32$$
$$P_1 + 4P_2 + 3P_3 = 37$$
$$P_1 + 3P_2 + 4P_3 = 35$$

[Hint: you might find your answer to Practice Problem 6 useful.]

Throughout this section, we have concentrated on 2×2 and 3×3 matrices. The method described can be extended to larger matrices of order $n \times n$. The cofactor A_{ij} would be the determinant of the $(n-1) \times (n-1)$ matrix left when row i and column j are deleted prefixed by $(-1)^{i+j}$. However, the cofactor approach is very inefficient. The amount of working rises dramatically as n increases, making this method inappropriate for large matrices. The preferred method for solving simultaneous equations is based on the elimination idea that we described in Section 1.4. This is easily programmed, and a computer can solve large systems of equations in a matter of seconds.

Key Terms

Cofactor   The cofactor of the element, a_{ij}, is the determinant of the matrix left when row i and column j are deleted, multiplied by $+1$ or -1, depending on whether $i + j$ is even or odd, respectively.

Determinant   A determinant can be expanded as the sum of the products of the elements in any one row or column and their respective cofactors.

Identity matrix   An $n \times n$ matrix, **I**, in which every element on the main diagonal is 1 and the other elements are all 0. If **A** is any $n \times n$ matrix, then **AI** = **A** = **IA**.

Inverse matrix   A matrix, $\mathbf{A}^{-1}$, with the property that $\mathbf{A}^{-1}\mathbf{A} = \mathbf{I} = \mathbf{AA}^{-1}$.

Minor   The name given to the cofactor before the '$\pm$' pattern is imposed.

Non-singular matrix   A square matrix with a non-zero determinant.

Singular matrix   A square matrix with a zero determinant. A singular matrix fails to possess an inverse.

Square matrix   A matrix with the same number of rows as columns.

Exercise 1.27

1. (a) Find the determinant of

$$\text{(i)} \begin{bmatrix} 2 & 7 \\ 1 & 4 \end{bmatrix} \quad \text{(ii)} \begin{bmatrix} 5 & 6 \\ 3 & 4 \end{bmatrix} \quad \text{(iii)} \begin{bmatrix} -2 & -10 \\ 1 & 4 \end{bmatrix} \quad \text{(iv)} \begin{bmatrix} -6 & -4 \\ -8 & -7 \end{bmatrix}$$

(b) Find the inverse of each matrix in part (a).

2. Let

$$\mathbf{A} = \begin{bmatrix} 2 & 1 \\ 5 & 1 \end{bmatrix} \quad \text{and} \quad \mathbf{B} = \begin{bmatrix} 1 & 0 \\ 2 & 4 \end{bmatrix}$$

(1) Find

(a) $|\mathbf{A}|$ (b) $|\mathbf{B}|$ (c) $|\mathbf{AB}|$

Do you notice any connection between $|\mathbf{A}|$, $|\mathbf{B}|$ and $|\mathbf{AB}|$?

(2) Find

(a) $\mathbf{A}^{-1}$ (b) $\mathbf{B}^{-1}$ (c) $(\mathbf{AB})^{-1}$

Do you notice any connection between $\mathbf{A}^{-1}$, $\mathbf{B}^{-1}$ and $(\mathbf{AB})^{-1}$?

3. If the matrices

$$\begin{bmatrix} 2 & -1 \\ 3 & a \end{bmatrix} \quad \text{and} \quad \begin{bmatrix} 2 & b \\ 3 & -4 \end{bmatrix}$$

are singular, find the values of a and b.

4. Evaluate the matrix product, $\begin{bmatrix} 5 & -3 \\ -10 & 8 \end{bmatrix}\begin{bmatrix} 8 & 3 \\ 10 & 5 \end{bmatrix}$.

Hence, or otherwise, write down the inverse of $\begin{bmatrix} 8 & 3 \\ 10 & 5 \end{bmatrix}$.

5. Use matrices to solve the following pairs of simultaneous equations:

   (a) $3x + 4y = -1$ **(b)** $x + 3y = 8$

        $5x - y = 6$ $4x - y = 6$

6. The demand and supply functions for two interdependent goods are given by

$$Q_{D_1} = 50 - 2P_1 + P_2$$
$$Q_{D_2} = 10 + P_1 - 4P_2$$
$$Q_{S_1} = -20 + P_1$$
$$Q_{S_2} = -10 + 5P_2$$

   (a) Show that the equilibrium prices satisfy

$$\begin{bmatrix} 3 & -1 \\ -1 & 9 \end{bmatrix} \begin{bmatrix} P_1 \\ P_2 \end{bmatrix} = \begin{bmatrix} 70 \\ 20 \end{bmatrix}$$

   (b) Find the inverse of the 2×2 matrix in part (a) and hence find the equilibrium prices.

7. If a, b and k are non-zero, show that

   (a) each of these 2×2 matrices is singular:

   (i) $\begin{bmatrix} a & 0 \\ b & 0 \end{bmatrix}$ **(ii)** $\begin{bmatrix} a & b \\ ka & kb \end{bmatrix}$ **(iii)** $\begin{bmatrix} a & b \\ \dfrac{1}{b} & \dfrac{1}{a} \end{bmatrix}$

   (b) each of these 2×2 matrices is non-singular:

   (i) $\begin{bmatrix} a & b \\ 0 & k \end{bmatrix}$ **(ii)** $\begin{bmatrix} 0 & a \\ -a & 0 \end{bmatrix}$ **(iii)** $\begin{bmatrix} a & b \\ -b & a \end{bmatrix}$

Exercise 1.27*

1. If the matrices

$$A = \begin{bmatrix} 1 & 2 \\ a & b \end{bmatrix} \quad \text{and} \quad B = \begin{bmatrix} a & 4 \\ 2 & b \end{bmatrix}$$

   are both singular, determine all possible values of a and b.

2. **(a)** If

$$A = \begin{bmatrix} a & b \\ c & d \end{bmatrix} \quad \text{and} \quad B = \begin{bmatrix} e & f \\ g & h \end{bmatrix}$$

   work out the matrix product, **AB**.

   (b) Hence, show that $\det(\mathbf{AB}) = \det(\mathbf{A}) \times \det(\mathbf{B})$

(c) If **A** is singular and **B** is non-singular, what, if anything, can be deduced about **AB**? Give a brief reason for your answer.

3. Which one of the following matrices has an inverse which is not listed?

$$\mathbf{A} = \begin{bmatrix} 1 & 1 \\ 1 & 0 \end{bmatrix}, \quad \mathbf{B} = \begin{bmatrix} 1 & 0 \\ 0 & 1 \end{bmatrix}, \quad \mathbf{C} = \begin{bmatrix} 0 & 1 \\ 1 & -1 \end{bmatrix}, \quad \mathbf{D} = \begin{bmatrix} 1 & -1 \\ -1 & 0 \end{bmatrix}, \quad \mathbf{E} = \begin{bmatrix} -1 & 0 \\ 0 & 1 \end{bmatrix}$$

4. Find the determinant of the matrix

$$\begin{bmatrix} 5 & -2 & 3 \\ 4 & -1 & -5 \\ 6 & 7 & 9 \end{bmatrix}$$

5. Find the cofactor, A_{23}, of the matrix

$$\mathbf{A} = \begin{bmatrix} 5 & -2 & 7 \\ 6 & 1 & -9 \\ 4 & -3 & 8 \end{bmatrix}$$

6. Find (where possible) the inverse of the matrices

$$\mathbf{A} = \begin{bmatrix} 2 & 1 & -1 \\ 1 & 3 & 2 \\ -1 & 2 & 1 \end{bmatrix} \quad \text{and} \quad \mathbf{B} = \begin{bmatrix} 1 & 4 & 5 \\ 2 & 1 & 3 \\ -1 & 3 & 2 \end{bmatrix}$$

Are these matrices singular or non-singular?

7. For the commodity market

$$C = aY + b \quad (0\ a < 1, b > 0)$$
$$I = cr + d \quad (c < 0, d > 0)$$

For the money market

$$M_S = M_S^*$$
$$M_D = k_1 Y + k_2 r + k_3 \ (k_1, k_3 > 0, k_2 < 0)$$

Show that when the commodity and money markets are both in equilibrium, the income, Y, and interest rate, r, satisfy the matrix equation

$$\begin{bmatrix} 1 - a & -c \\ k_1 & k_2 \end{bmatrix} \begin{bmatrix} Y \\ r \end{bmatrix} = \begin{bmatrix} b + d \\ M_s^* - k_3 \end{bmatrix}$$

and solve this system for Y and r. Write down the multiplier for r due to changes in M_S^* and deduce that interest rates fall as the money supply grows.

8. Find the determinant of the matrix

$$\mathbf{A} = \begin{bmatrix} 2 & 1 & 3 \\ 1 & 0 & a \\ 3 & 1 & 4 \end{bmatrix}$$

in terms of a. Deduce that this matrix is non-singular provided $a \neq 1$ and find $\mathbf{A}^{-1}$ in this case.

9. Find the inverse of

$$\begin{bmatrix} -2 & 2 & 1 \\ 1 & -5 & -1 \\ 2 & -1 & -6 \end{bmatrix}$$

Hence find the equilibrium prices of the three-commodity market model given in Question 6 of Exercise 1.17*.

10. Find the inverse of the matrix

$$\mathbf{A} = \begin{bmatrix} 6 & 3 & a \\ 5 & 4 & 2 \\ 7 & 2 & 3 \end{bmatrix}$$

in terms of a.

For what value of a will simultaneous equations of the form

$$6x + 3y + az = b$$
$$5x + 4y + 2z = c$$
$$7x + 2y + 3z = d$$

fail to possess a unique solution?

11. **(a)** Multiply out the brackets in the expression $(a - b)(a - c)(c - b)$.

(b) Show that the determinant of the matrix

$$\mathbf{A} = \begin{bmatrix} 1 & 1 & 1 \\ a & b & c \\ a^2 & b^2 & c^2 \end{bmatrix}$$

is $(a - b)(a - c)(c - b)$ and deduce that the simultaneous equations

$$x + y + z = l$$
$$ax + by + cz = m$$
$$a^2x + b^2y + c^2z = n$$

have a unique solution provided, a, b, and c are distinct.

SECTION 1.28

Cramer's rule

Objectives

At the end of this section you should be able to:

- Appreciate the limitations of using inverses to solve systems of linear equations.
- Use Cramer's rule to solve systems of linear equations.
- Apply Cramer's rule to analyse static macroeconomic models.
- Apply Cramer's rule to solve two-country trading models.

In Section 1.27 we described the mechanics of calculating the determinant and inverse of 2×2 and 3×3 matrices. These concepts can be extended to larger systems in an obvious way, although the amount of effort needed rises dramatically as the size of the matrix increases. For example, consider the work involved in solving the system

$$\begin{bmatrix} 1 & 0 & 2 & 3 \\ -1 & 5 & 4 & 1 \\ 0 & 7 & -3 & 6 \\ 2 & 4 & 5 & 1 \end{bmatrix} \begin{bmatrix} x_1 \\ x_2 \\ x_3 \\ x_4 \end{bmatrix} = \begin{bmatrix} -1 \\ 1 \\ -24 \\ 15 \end{bmatrix}$$

using the method of matrix inversion. In this case the coefficient matrix has order 4×4 and so has 16 elements. Corresponding to each of these elements is a cofactor. This is defined to be the 3×3 determinant obtained by deleting the row and column containing the element, prefixed by a '+' or '−' according to the following pattern:

$$\begin{bmatrix} + & - & + & - \\ - & + & - & + \\ + & - & + & - \\ - & + & - & - \end{bmatrix}$$

Determinants are found by expanding along any one row or column, and inverses are found by stacking cofactors as before. However, given that there are 16 cofactors to be calculated, even the most enthusiastic student is likely to view the prospect with some trepidation. To make matters worse, it frequently happens in economics that only a few of the variables x_i are actually needed. For instance, it could be that the variable x_3 is the only one of interest. Under these circumstances, it is clearly wasteful expending a large amount of effort calculating the inverse matrix, particularly since the values of the remaining variables, x_1, x_2 and x_4, are not required.

In this section we describe an alternative method that finds the value of one variable at a time. This new method requires less effort if only a selection of the variables is required. It is known as Cramer's rule and makes use of matrix determinants. **Cramer's rule** for solving any $n \times n$ system, $\mathbf{Ax} = \mathbf{b}$, states that the ith variable, x_i, can be found from

$$x_i = \frac{\det(\mathbf{A}_i)}{\det(\mathbf{A})}$$

where $\mathbf{A}_i$ is the $n \times n$ matrix found by replacing the ith column of $\mathbf{A}$ by the right-hand-side vector $\mathbf{b}$. To understand this, consider the simple 2×2 system

$$\begin{bmatrix} 7 & 2 \\ 4 & 5 \end{bmatrix} \begin{bmatrix} x_1 \\ x_2 \end{bmatrix} = \begin{bmatrix} -6 \\ 12 \end{bmatrix}$$

and suppose that we need to find the value of the second variable, x_2, say. According to Cramer's rule, this is given by

$$x_2 = \frac{\det(\mathbf{A}_2)}{\det(\mathbf{A})}$$

where

$$\mathbf{A} = \begin{bmatrix} 7 & 2 \\ 4 & 5 \end{bmatrix} \quad \text{and} \quad \mathbf{A}_2 = \begin{bmatrix} 7 & -6 \\ 4 & 12 \end{bmatrix}$$

Notice that x_2 is given by the quotient of two determinants. The one on the bottom is that of the original coefficient matrix $\mathbf{A}$. The one on the top is that of the matrix found from $\mathbf{A}$ by replacing the second column (since we are trying to find the second variable) by the right-hand-side vector

$$\begin{bmatrix} -6 \\ 12 \end{bmatrix}$$

In this case the determinants are easily worked out to get

$$\det(\mathbf{A}_2) = \begin{vmatrix} 7 & -6 \\ 4 & 12 \end{vmatrix} = 7(12) - (-6)(4) = 108$$

$$\det(\mathbf{A}) = \begin{vmatrix} 7 & 2 \\ 4 & 5 \end{vmatrix} = 7(5) - 2(4) = 27$$

Hence

$$x_2 = \frac{108}{27} = 4$$

Example

Solve the system of equations

$$\begin{bmatrix} 1 & 2 & 3 \\ -4 & 1 & 6 \\ 2 & 7 & 5 \end{bmatrix} \begin{bmatrix} x_1 \\ x_2 \\ x_3 \end{bmatrix} = \begin{bmatrix} 9 \\ -9 \\ 13 \end{bmatrix}$$

using Cramer's rule to find x_1.

5. Consider the macroeconomic model defined by

national income: $Y = C + I + G^*$ $(G^* > 0)$

consumption: $C = aY + b$ $(0 < a < 1, b > 0)$

investment: $I = cr + d$ $(c < 0, d > 0)$

money supply: $M_S^* = k_1 Y + k_2 r$ $(k_1 > 0, k_2 < 0, M_S^* > 0)$

Show that this system can be written as $\mathbf{Ax} = \mathbf{b}$, where

$$\mathbf{A} = \begin{bmatrix} 1 & -1 & -1 & 0 \\ -a & 1 & 0 & 0 \\ 0 & 0 & 1 & -c \\ k_1 & 0 & 0 & k_2 \end{bmatrix} \quad \mathbf{x} = \begin{bmatrix} Y \\ C \\ I \\ r \end{bmatrix} \quad \mathbf{b} = \begin{bmatrix} G^* \\ b \\ d \\ M_s^* \end{bmatrix}$$

Use Cramer's rule to show that

$$r = \frac{M^*(1-a) - k_1(b + d + G^*)}{k_2(1-a) + ck_1}$$

Write down the government expenditure multiplier for r and deduce that the interest rate, r, increases as government expenditure, G^*, increases.

6. The equations defining a model of two trading nations are given by

$Y_1 = C_1 + I_1^* + X_1 - M_1$ $Y_2 = C_2 + I_2^* + X_2 - M_2$

$C_1 = 0.6Y_1 + 50$ $C_2 = 0.8Y_2 + 80$

$M_1 = 0.2Y_1$ $M_2 = 0.1Y_2$

If $I_2^* = 70$, find the value of I_1^* if the balance of payments is zero.

[Hint: construct a system of three equations for the three unknowns, Y_1, Y_2 and I_1^*.]

7. The equations defining a general model of two trading countries are given by

$Y_1 = C_1 + I_1^* + X_1 - M_1$ $Y_2 = C_2 + I_2^* + X_2 - M_2$

$C_1 = a_1 Y_1 + b_1$ $C_2 = a_2 Y_2 + b_2$

$M_1 = m_1 Y_1$ $M_2 = m_2 Y_2$

where $0 < a_i < 1$, $b_i > 0$ and $0 < m_i < 1$ $(i = 1, 2)$. Express this system in matrix form and use Cramer's rule to solve this system for Y_1. Write down the multiplier for Y_1 due to changes in I_2^* and hence give a general description of the effect on the national income of one country due to a change in investment in the other.

SECTION 1.29
Lagrange multipliers

Objectives

At the end of this section you should be able to:

- Use the method of Lagrange multipliers to solve constrained optimisation problems.
- Give an economic interpretation of Lagrange multipliers.
- Use Lagrange multipliers to maximise a Cobb–Douglas production function subject to a cost constraint.
- Use Lagrange multipliers to show that when a firm maximises output subject to a cost constraint, the ratio of marginal product to price is the same for all inputs.

We now describe the method of Lagrange multipliers for solving constrained optimisation problems. This is the preferred method, since it handles non-linear constraints and problems involving more than two variables with ease. It also provides some additional information that is useful when solving economic problems.

To optimise an objective function

$$f(x, y)$$

subject to a constraint

$$\varphi(x, y) = M$$

we work as follows.

Step 1

Define a new function

$$g(x, y, \lambda) = f(x, y) + \lambda[M - \varphi(x, y)]$$

Step 2

Solve the simultaneous equations

$$\frac{\partial g}{\partial x} = 0$$

$$\frac{\partial g}{\partial y} = 0$$

$$\frac{\partial g}{\partial \lambda} = 0$$

for the three unknowns, x, y and λ.

The basic steps of the method are straightforward. In step 1 we combine the objective function and constraint into a single function. To do this we first consider

$$M - \varphi(x, y)$$

and multiply by the scalar (i.e. number) λ (the Greek letter 'lambda'). This scalar is called the **Lagrange multiplier**. Finally, we add on the objective function to produce the new function

$$g(x, y, \lambda) = f(x, y) + \lambda[M - \varphi(x, y)]$$

This is called the **Lagrangian** function. The right-hand side involves the three letters x, y and λ, so g is a function of three variables.

In step 2 we work out the three first-order partial derivatives

$$\frac{\partial g}{\partial x}, \frac{\partial g}{\partial y}, \frac{\partial g}{\partial \lambda}$$

and equate these to zero to produce a system of three simultaneous equations for the three unknowns x, y and λ. The point (x, y) is then the optimal solution of the constrained problem. The number λ can also be given a meaning, and we consider this later.

To illustrate the new method consider trying to optimise the value of

$$x^2 - 3xy + 12x$$

subject to the constraint

$$2x + 3y = 6$$

Step 1

In this case

$$f(x, y) = x^2 - 3xy + 12x$$

$$\varphi(x, y) = 2x + 3y$$

$$M = 6$$

so the Lagrangian function is given by

$$g(x, y, \lambda) = x^2 - 3xy + 12x + \lambda(6 - 2x - 3y)$$

Step 2

Working out the three partial derivatives of g gives

$$\frac{\partial g}{\partial x} = 2x - 3y + 12 - 2\lambda$$

$$\frac{\partial g}{\partial y} = -3x - 3\lambda$$

$$\frac{\partial g}{\partial \lambda} = 6 - 2x - 3y$$

so we need to solve the simultaneous equations

$$2x - 3y + 12 - 2\lambda = 0$$

$$-3x - 3\lambda = 0$$

$$6 - 2x - 3y = 0$$

that is,

$$2x - 3y - 2\lambda = -12 \tag{1}$$

$$-3x - 3\lambda = 0 \tag{2}$$

$$2x + 3y = 6 \tag{3}$$

We can eliminate x from equation (2) by multiplying equation (1) by 3, multiplying equation (2) by 2 and adding. Similarly, x can be eliminated from equation (3) by subtracting equation (3) from (1). These operations give

$$-9y - 12\lambda = -36 \tag{4}$$

$$-6y - 2\lambda = -18 \tag{5}$$

The variable y can be eliminated by multiplying equation (4) by 6 and equation (5) by 9, and subtracting to get

$$-54\lambda = -54 \tag{6}$$

so $\lambda = 1$. Substituting this into equations (5) and (2) gives $y = 8/3$ and $x = -1$, respectively.

The optimal solution is therefore $(-1, 8/3)$, and the corresponding value of the objective function

$$x^2 - 3xy + 12x$$

is

$$(-1)^2 - 3(-1)(^8/_3) + 12(-1) = -3$$

Practice Problem

1. Use Lagrange multipliers to optimise

$$2x^2 - xy$$

subject to

$$x + y = 12$$

Looking back at your own solution to Practice Problem 1, notice that the third equation in step 2 is just a restatement of the original constraint. It is easy to see that this is always the case because if

$$g(x, y, \lambda) = f(x, y) + \lambda[M - \varphi(x, y)]$$

then

$$\frac{\partial g}{\partial \lambda} = M - \varphi(x, y)$$

The equation

$$\frac{\partial g}{\partial \lambda} = 0$$

then implies the constraint

$$\varphi(x, y) = M$$

Example

A monopolistic producer of two goods, G1 and G2, has a joint total cost function

$$TC = 10Q_1 + Q_1Q_2 + 10Q_2$$

where Q_1 and Q_2 denote the quantities of G1 and G2 respectively. If P_1 and P_2 denote the corresponding prices then the demand equations are

$$P_1 = 50 - Q_1 + Q_2$$

$$P_2 = 30 + 2Q_1 - Q_2$$

Find the maximum profit if the firm is contracted to produce a total of 15 goods of either type. Estimate the new optimal profit if the production quota rises by 1 unit.

Solution

The first thing that we need to do is to write down expressions for the objective function and constraint. The objective function is profit and is given by

$$\pi = TR - TC$$

The total cost function is given to be

$$TC = 10Q_1 + Q_1Q_2 + 10Q_2$$

However, we need to use the demand equations to obtain an expression for TR. Total revenue from the sale of G1 is

$$TR_1 = P_1Q_1 = (50 - Q_1 + Q_2)Q_1 = 50Q_1 - Q_1^2 + Q_2Q_1$$

and total revenue from the sale of G2 is

$$TR_2 = P_2Q_2 = (30 + 2Q_1 - Q_2)Q_2 = 30Q_2 + 2Q_1Q_2 - Q_2^2$$

so

$$\begin{aligned} TR &= TR_1 + TR_2 \\ &= 50Q_1 - Q_1^2 + Q_2Q_1 + 30Q_2 + 2Q_1Q_2 - Q_2^2 \\ &= 50Q_1 - Q_1^2 + 3Q_1Q_2 + 30Q_2 - Q_2^2 \end{aligned}$$

Hence

$$\begin{aligned} \pi &= TR - TC \\ &= (50Q_1 - Q_1^2 + 3Q_1Q_2 + 30Q_2 - Q_2^2) - (10Q_1 + Q_1Q_2 + 10Q_2) \\ &= 40Q_1 - Q_1^2 + 2Q_1Q_2 + 20Q_2 - Q_2^2 \end{aligned}$$

The constraint is more easily determined. We are told that the firm produces 15 goods in total, so

$$Q_1 + Q_2 = 15$$

The mathematical problem is to maximise the objective function

$$\pi = 40Q_1 - Q_1^2 + 2Q_1Q_2 + 20Q_2 - Q_2^2$$

subject to the constraint

$$Q_1 + Q_2 = 15$$

5. Find the maximum value of

$$Q = 10\sqrt{(KL)}$$

subject to the cost constraint

$$K + 4L = 16$$

Estimate the change in the optimal value of Q if the cost constraint is changed to

$$K + 4L = 17$$

6. A consumer's utility function is given by

$$U = \alpha \ln x_1 + \beta \ln x_2$$

Find the values of x_1 and x_2 which maximise U subject to the budgetary constraint

$$P_1 x_1 + P_2 x_2 = M$$

7. An advertising agency spends \$$x$ on a newspaper campaign and a further \$$y$ promoting its client's products on local radio. It receives 15% commission on all sales that the client receives. The agency has \$10 000 to spend in total, and the client earns \$$M$ from its sales, where

$$M = \frac{100\,000x}{50 + x} + \frac{40\,000y}{30 + y}$$

Use the method of Lagrange multipliers to determine how much should be spent on advertising in newspapers and on radio to maximise the agency's net income. Give your answers correct to two decimal places.

8. A firm produces three goods, A, B and C. The number of items of each are x, y and z, respectively. The firm is committed to producing a total number of 30 items of types A and B. The firm's associated profit function is

$$\pi = 8x + 12y + 4z - 0.5x^2 - 0.5y^2 - z^2$$

How many goods of each type must be produced to maximise profit subject to the constraint?

9. A firm decides to invest x units of capital in project A and y units in project B. The expected return for 1 unit of investment is \$400 in project A and \$800 in project B. However, in order to meet the expectations of the firm's ethical and environmental policy, the values of x and y must satisfy the constraint

$$x^2 + y^2 - 4x - 6y = 67$$

How many units of each type should the firm buy in order to maximise total return?

10. Use the method of Lagrange multipliers to show that when a utility function, $U = U(x_1, x_2)$, is optimised subject to a budgetary constraint, $P_1 x_1 + P_2 x_2 = M$, the ratio of marginal utility to price is the same for both goods.

11. A function, $z = ax + by$, is to be optimised subject to the constraint, $x^2 + y^2 = 1$ where a and b are positive constants. Use Lagrange multipliers to show that this problem has only one solution in the positive quadrant (i.e. in the region $x > 0$, $y > 0$) and that the optimal value of z is $\sqrt{a^2 + b^2}$.

APPENDIX 1
Hessians

In this appendix we describe what a Hessian is, and how it can be used to classify the stationary points of an unconstrained optimization problem. In Section 1.24 (page 344) the conditions for a function $f(x, y)$ to have a minimum were stated as:

$$f_{xx} > 0, f_{yy} > 0 \quad \text{and} \quad f_{xx} - f_{xy}^2 > 0$$

where all of the partial derivatives are evaluated at a stationary point, (a, b).

It turns out that the second condition, $f_{yy} > 0$, is actually redundant. If the first and third conditions are met then the second one is automatically true. To see this notice that

$$f_{xx}f_{yy} - f_{xy}^2 > 0$$

is the same as $f_{xx}f_{yy} > f_{xy}^2$. The right-hand side is non-negative (being a square term) and so

$$f_{xx}f_{yy} > 0$$

The only way that the product of two numbers is positive is when they are either both positive or both negative. Consequently, when $f_{xx} > 0$, say, the other factor f_{yy} will also be positive.

Similarly, for a maximum point $f_{xx} < 0$, which forces the condition $f_{yy} < 0$.

The two conditions for a minimum point, $f_{xx} > 0$ and $f_{xx}f_{yy} - f_{xy}^2 > 0$ can be expressed more succinctly in matrix notation.

The 2×2 matrix, $H = \begin{bmatrix} f_{xx} & f_{xy} \\ f_{yx} & f_{yy} \end{bmatrix}$ (where $f_{xy} = f_{yx}$) made from second-order partial derivatives is called a **Hessian matrix** and has determinant

$$\begin{vmatrix} f_{xx} & f_{xy} \\ f_{yx} & f_{yy} \end{vmatrix} = f_{xx}f_{yy} - f_{xy}^2$$

so the conditions for a minimum are:

(1) the number in the top left-hand corner of H (called the **first principal minor**) is positive

(2) the determinant of H (called the **second principal minor**) is positive.

For a maximum, the first principal minor is negative and the second principal minor is positive.

Example

Use Hessians to classify the stationary point of the function

$$\pi = 50Q_1 - 2Q_1^2 + 95Q_2 - 4Q_2^2 - 3Q_1Q_2$$

Solution

This profit function, considered in Practice Problem 2 in Section 1.24 (page 340), has a stationary point at $Q_1 = 5$, $Q_2 = 10$. The second-order partial derivatives are

$$\frac{\partial^2 \pi}{\partial Q_1^2} = -4, \frac{\partial^2 \pi}{\partial Q_2^2} = -8 \quad \text{and} \quad \frac{\partial^2 \pi}{\partial Q_1 \partial Q_2} = -3$$

so the Hessian matrix is

$$\mathbf{H} = \begin{bmatrix} -4 & -3 \\ -3 & -8 \end{bmatrix}$$

The first principal minor $-4 < 0$.

The second principal minor $(-4)(-8) - (-3)^2 = 23 > 0$.

Hence the stationary point is a maximum.

Practice Problems

1. The function

   $$z = x^2 + y^2 - 2x - 4y + 15$$

   has a stationary point at $(1, 2)$. Write down the associated Hessian matrix and hence determine the nature of this point.

   [This surface was previously sketched using Maple in Question 6(a) in Exercise 1.24 on page 346.]

2. The profit function

   $$\pi = 1000Q_1 + 800Q_2 - 2Q_1^2 - 2Q_1Q_2 - Q_2^2$$

   has a stationary point at $Q_1 = 100$, $Q_2 = 300$.

   Use Hessians to show that this is a maximum.

   [This is the worked example on page 338 of Section 1.24.]

3. The profit function

   $$\pi = 16L^{1/2} + 24K^{1/2} - 2L - K$$

   has a stationary point at $L = 16$, $K = 144$.

   Write down a general expression for the Hessian matrix in terms of L and K, and hence show that the stationary point is a maximum.

   [This is Question 2 in Exercise 1.24* on page 345.]

Matrices can also be used to classify the maximum and minimum points of constrained optimization problems. In Section 1.29 the Lagrangian function was defined as

$$g(x, y, \lambda) = f(x, y) + \lambda(M - \phi(x, y))$$

Optimum points are found by applying the three first-order conditions:

$$g_x = 0, \quad g_y = 0 \quad \text{and} \quad g_\lambda = 0$$

To classify as a maximum or minimum we consider the determinant of the 3×3 matrix of second-order derivatives:

$$\bar{H} = \begin{bmatrix} g_{xx} & g_{xy} & g_{x\lambda} \\ g_{xy} & g_{yy} & g_{y\lambda} \\ g_{x\lambda} & g_{y\lambda} & g_{\lambda\lambda} \end{bmatrix}$$

If $|\bar{H}| > 0$ the optimum point is a maximum, whereas if $|\bar{H}| < 0$, the optimum point is a minimum. Note that

$$\frac{\partial g}{\partial \lambda} = M - \phi(x, y)$$

so that

$$\frac{\partial^2 g}{\partial x \partial \lambda} = -\phi_x, \frac{\partial^2 g}{\partial y \partial \lambda} = -\phi_y \quad \text{and} \quad \frac{\partial^2 g}{\partial \lambda^2} = 0$$

so $\bar{H}$ is given by

$$\begin{bmatrix} g_{xx} & g_{xy} & -\phi_x \\ g_{xy} & g_{yy} & -\phi_y \\ -\phi_x & -\phi_y & 0 \end{bmatrix}$$

This is called a **bordered Hessian** because it consists of the usual 2×2 Hessian

$$\begin{bmatrix} g_{xx} & g_{xy} \\ g_{xy} & g_{yy} \end{bmatrix}$$

'bordered' by a row and column of first-order derivatives, $-\phi_x, -\phi_y$ and 0.

Example

Use the bordered Hessian to classify the optimal point when the objective function

$$U = x_1^{1/2} + x_2^{1/2}$$

is subject to the budgetary constraint

$$P_1 x_1 + P_2 x_2 = M$$

Solution

The optimal point has already been found in Practice Problem 3 of Section 1.29 (page 419). The first-order conditions

$$\frac{\partial g}{\partial x_1} = \tfrac{1}{2}x_1^{-1/2} - \lambda P_1 = 0, \quad \frac{\partial g}{\partial x_2} = \tfrac{1}{2}x_2^{-1/2} - \lambda P_2 = 0, \quad \frac{\partial g}{\partial \lambda} = M - P_1 x_1 - P_2 x_2 = 0$$

were seen to have solution

$$x_1 = \frac{P_2 M}{P_1(P_1 + P_2)} \quad \text{and} \quad x_2 = \frac{P_1 M}{P_2(P_1 + P_2)}$$

The bordered Hessian is

$$\bar{H} = \begin{bmatrix} -\dfrac{1}{4} x_1^{-3/2} & 0 & -P_1 \\ 0 & -\dfrac{1}{4} x_2^{-3/2} & -P_2 \\ -P_1 & -P_2 & 0 \end{bmatrix}$$

Expanding along the third row gives

$$|\bar{H}| = -P_1 \begin{vmatrix} 0 & -P_1 \\ -\dfrac{1}{4} x_2^{-3/2} & -P_2 \end{vmatrix} - (-P_2) \begin{vmatrix} -\dfrac{1}{4} x_1^{-3/2} & -P_1 \\ 0 & -P_2 \end{vmatrix} = \tfrac{1}{4} P_1^2 x_2^{-3/2} + \tfrac{1}{4} P_2^2 x_2^{-3/2}$$

This is positive so the point is a maximum.

Practice Problems

4. Use the bordered Hessian to show that the optimal value of the Lagrangian function

$$g(Q_1, Q_2, \lambda) = 40Q_1 - Q_1^2 + 2Q_1Q_2 + 20Q_2 - Q_2^2 + \lambda(15 - Q_1 - Q_2)$$

is a maximum.

[This is the worked example on page 415 of Section 1.29.]

5. Use the bordered Hessian to classify the optimal value of the Lagrangian function

$$g(x, y, \lambda) = 2x^2 - xy + \lambda(12 - x - y)$$

[This is Practice Problem 1 on page 414 of Section 1.29.]

Key Terms

Bordered Hessian matrix   A Hessian matrix augmented by an extra row and column containing partial derivatives formed from the constraint in the method of Lagrange multipliers.

First principal minor   The 1×1 determinant in the top left-hand corner of a matrix; the element a_{11} of a matrix A.

Hessian matrix   A matrix whose elements are the second-order partial derivatives of a given function.

Second principal minor   The 2×2 determinant in the top left-hand corner of a matrix.

Key Terms

Complementary function of a difference equation   The solution of the difference equation $Y_t = bY_{t-1} + c$ when the constant c is replaced by zero.

Difference equation   An equation that relates consecutive terms of a sequence of numbers.

Dynamics   Analysis of how equilibrium values vary over time.

Equilibrium value of a difference equation   A solution of a difference equation that does not vary over time; it is the limiting value of Y_n as n tends to infinity.

General solution of a difference equation   The solution of a difference equation that contains an arbitrary constant. It is the sum of the complementary function and a particular solution.

Initial condition   The value of Y_0 that needs to be specified to obtain a unique solution of a difference equation.

Particular solution of a difference equation   Any one solution of a difference equation such as $Y_t = bY_{t-1} + c$.

Recurrence relation   An alternative term for a difference equation. It is an expression for Y_n in terms of Y_{n-1} (and possibly Y_{n-2}, Y_{n-3}, etc.).

Stable (unstable) equilibrium   An economic model in which the solution of the associated difference equation converges (diverges).

Uniformly convergent sequence   A sequence of numbers which progressively increases (or decreases) to a finite limit.

Uniformly divergent sequence   A sequence of numbers which progressively increases (or decreases) without a finite limit.

Exercise 1.30

1. Calculate the first four terms of the sequences defined by the following difference equations. Hence write down a formula for Y_t in terms of t. Comment on the qualitative behaviour of the solution in each case.

   (a) $Y_t = Y_{t-1} + 2; Y_0 = 0$ (b) $Y_t = -Y_{t-1} + 6; Y_0 = 4$ (c) $Y_t = 0Y_{t-1} + 3; Y_0 = 3$

2. Solve the following difference equations with the specified initial conditions:

   (a) $Y_t = \frac{1}{4}Y_{t-1} + 6; Y_0 = 1$ (b) $Y_t = -4Y_{t-1} + 5; Y_0 = 2$

   Comment on the qualitative behaviour of the solution as t increases.

3. Consider the two-sector model:

   $$Y_t = C_t + I_t$$
   $$C_t = 0.7Y_{t-1} + 400$$
   $$I_t = 0.1Y_{t-1} + 100$$

   Given that $Y_0 = 3000$, find an expression for Y_t. Is this system stable or unstable?

4. Consider the supply and demand equations

   $$Q_{S_t} = 0.4P_{t-1} - 12$$
   $$Q_{D_t} = -0.8P_t + 60$$

Assuming that equilibrium conditions prevail, find an expression for P_t when $P_0 = 70$. Is the system stable or unstable?

5. Consider the two-sector model:

$$Y_t = C_t + I_t$$
$$C_t = 0.75Y_{t-1} + 400$$
$$I_t = 200$$

Find the value of C_2, given that, $Y_0 = 400$.

6. The Harrod–Domar model of the growth of an economy is based on three assumptions.

   (1) Savings, S_t, in any time period are proportional to income, Y_t, in that period, so that

   $$S_t = \alpha Y_t \qquad (\alpha > 0)$$

   (2) Investment, I_t, in any time period is proportional to the change in income from the previous period to the current period so that

   $$I_t = \beta(Y_t - Y_{t-1}) \quad (\beta > 0)$$

   (3) Investment and savings are equal in any period so that

   $$I_t = S_t$$

   Use these assumptions to show that

   $$Y_1 = \left(\frac{\beta}{\beta - \alpha}\right)Y_{t-1}$$

   and hence write down a formula for Y_t in terms of Y_0. Comment on the stability of the system in the case when $\alpha = 0.1$ and $\beta = 1.4$.

Exercise 1.30*

1. Describe the qualitative behaviour of the sequence of numbers which satisfy

$$Y_t = -\frac{1}{2}Y_{t-1}^2$$

with initial condition $Y_0 = -1$.

2. (a) Write down the next four terms of the sequence defined by

   $$Y_t = \frac{1}{1 - Y_{t-1}}; Y_0 = 2$$

   Deduce the value of Y_{200}.

   (b) Write down the next four terms of the sequence defined by

   $$Y_t = Y_{t-1} + 4; Y_0 = 3$$

   Write down a formula for Y_t in terms of t.

3. Find the solution of the difference equation

$$Y_t = bY_{t-1} + c$$

with initial condition, $Y_0 = a$.

4. Consider the two-sector model:

$$Y_t = C_t + I_t$$
$$C_t = 0.85Y_{t-1} + 300$$
$$I_t = 0.15Y_{t-1} + 100$$

Given that $Y_0 = 4000$, find an expression for Y_t. Is this system stable or unstable?

5. Consider the supply and demand equations

$$Q_{S_t} = aP_{t-1} - b$$
$$Q_{D_t} = -cP_t + d$$

where the constants a, b, c and d are all positive.

(a) Assuming that the market is in equilibrium, show that

$$P_t = \left(-\frac{a}{c}\right)P_{t-1} + \frac{b+d}{c}$$

(b) Show that $\dfrac{b+d}{a+c}$ is a particular solution of the difference equation in part (a), and write down an expression for the general solution.

(c) State the conditions under which the solution in part (a) is guaranteed to converge, and state the equilibrium price and quantity. Simplify your answers.

6. Find the reduced form connecting P_t and P_{t-1} for the market model:

$$Q_{S_t} = aP_t - b$$
$$Q_{D_t} = -cP_t + d$$
$$P_t = P_{t-1} - e(Q_{S_{t-1}} - Q_{D_{t-1}})$$

7. A bank offers an individual a loan of \$A$ at a rate of interest of $r\%$ compounded monthly. The individual pays off the loan by monthly instalments of \$a$. If u_t denotes outstanding balance after t months, explain why

$$u_t = \left(1 + \frac{r}{1200}\right)u_{t-1} - a$$

and show that

$$u_t = \left(A - \frac{1200a}{r}\right)\left(1 + \frac{r}{1200}\right)^t + \frac{1200a}{r}$$

Hence write down an expression for the monthly repayment if the loan is paid off after N months.

8. Consider the difference equation

$$Y_t = 0.1Y_{t-1} + 5(0.6)^t$$

(a) Write down the complementary function.

(b) By substituting $Y_t = D(0.6)^t$ into this equation, find a particular solution.

(c) Use your answers to parts (a) and (b) to write down the general solution and hence find the specific solution that satisfies the initial condition, $Y_0 = 9$.

(d) Is the solution in part (c) stable or unstable?

9. Consider the difference equation

$$Y_t = 0.2Y_{t-1} + 0.8t + 5$$

(a) Write down the complementary function.

(b) By substituting $Y_t = Dt + E$ into this equation, find a particular solution.

(c) Use your answers to parts (a) and (b) to write down the general solution and hence find the specific solution that satisfies the initial condition, $Y_0 = 10$.

(d) Is the solution in part (c) stable or unstable?

Statistics

Introduction

Statistics is a subject which can be (and is) applied to every aspect of our lives. The printed publication *Guide to Official Statistics* is, sadly, no longer produced but the UK Office for National Statistics website[1] categorises data by 'themes', including education, unemployment, social cohesion, maternities and more. Many other agencies, both public and private, national and international, add to this ever-growing volume of data. It seems clear that whatever subject you wish to investigate, there are data available to illuminate your study. However, it is a sad fact that many people do not understand the use of statistics, do not know how to draw proper inferences (conclusions) from them, or misrepresent them. Even (especially?) politicians are not immune from this. As I write the UK referendum campaign on continued EU membership is in full swing, with statistics being used for support rather than illumination. For example, the 'Leave' campaign claims the United Kingdom is more important to the European Union than the EU is to the UK, since the EU exports more to the UK than vice versa. But the correct statistic to use is the *proportion* of exports (relative to GDP). About 45% of UK exports go to the EU but only about 8% of EU exports come to the UK, so the UK is actually the more dependent one. Both sets of figures are factually correct but one side draws the wrong conclusion from them.

People's intuition is often not very good when it comes to statistics – we did not need this ability to evolve, so it is not innate. A majority of people will still believe crime is on the increase even when statistics show unequivocally that it is decreasing. We often take more notice of the single, shocking story than of statistics which count all such events (and find them rare). People also have great difficulty with probability, which is the basis for statistical inference, and hence make erroneous judgements (e.g. how much it is worth investing to improve safety). Once you have studied statistics, you should be less prone to this kind of error.

Two types of statistics

The subject of statistics can usefully be divided into two parts: descriptive statistics and inferential statistics, which are based upon the theory of probability. Descriptive statistics are used to summarise information which would otherwise be too complex to take in, by means of techniques such as averages and graphs. The graph shown in Figure 2.1 is an example, summarising drinking habits in the United Kingdom.

The graph reveals, for instance, that about 43% of men and 57% of women drink between 1 and 10 units of alcohol per week (a unit is roughly equivalent to one glass of wine or half a pint of beer). The graph also shows that men tend to

---

[1] https://www.ons.gov.uk/

It is now clear how economic status differs according to education and the result is quite dramatic. In particular:

- The proportion of people unemployed or inactive increases rapidly with lower educational attainment.
- The biggest difference is between the no qualifications category and the other three, which have relatively smaller differences between them. In particular, A levels and other qualifications show a similar pattern.

Thus we have looked at the data in different ways, drawing different charts and seeing what they can tell us. You need to consider which type of chart is most suitable for the data you have and the questions you want to ask. There is no one graph which is ideal for all circumstances.

Can we safely conclude therefore that the probability of your being unemployed is significantly reduced by education? Could we go further and argue that the route to lower unemployment generally is via investment in education? The answer *may* be 'yes' to both questions, but we have not proved it. Two important considerations are as follows:

- Innate ability has been ignored. Those with higher ability are more likely to be employed *and* are more likely to receive more education. Ideally we would like to compare individuals of similar ability but with different amounts of education.
- Even if additional education does reduce a person's probability of becoming unemployed, this may be at the expense of someone else, who loses their job to the more educated individual. In other words, additional education does not reduce total unemployment but only shifts it around amongst the labour force. Of course, it is still rational for individuals to invest in education if they do not take account of this externality.

Producing charts using Microsoft Excel

You can draw charts by hand on graph paper, and this is still a very useful way of really learning about graphs. Nowadays, however, most charts are produced by computer software, notably Excel. Most of the charts in this text were produced using Excel's charting facility. You should aim for a similar, uncluttered look. Some tips you might find useful are:

- Make the grid lines dashed in a light grey colour (they are not actually part of the chart, and hence should be discrete) or eliminate them altogether.
- Get rid of any background fill (grey by default; alter to 'No fill'). It will look much better when printed.
- On the *x*-axis, make the labels horizontal or vertical, not slanted – it is difficult to see which point they refer to.
- On the *y*-axis, make the axis title horizontal and place it at the top of the axis. It is much easier for the reader to see.
- Colour charts look great on-screen but unclear if printed in black and white. Change the style of the lines or markers (e.g. make some of them dashed) to distinguish them on paper.
- Both axes start at zero by default. If all your observations are large numbers, then this may result in the data points being crowded into one corner of the graph. Alter the scale on the axes to fix this – set the minimum value on the axis to be slightly less than the minimum observation. Note, however, that this distorts the relative heights of the bars and could mislead. Use with caution.

Figure 2.7
Educational qualifications
of those in work

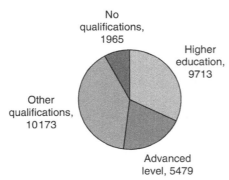

Note: If you have to draw a pie chart by hand, the angle of each slice can be calculated as follows:

$$angle = \frac{frequency}{total\,frequency} \times 360.$$

The angle of the first slice, for example, is

$$\frac{9713}{27330} \times 360 = 127.9°.$$

The pie chart

Another common way of presenting information graphically is the pie chart, which is a good way to describe how a variable is distributed between different categories. For example, from Table 2.1 we have the distribution of educational qualifications for those in work (the first row of the table). This can alternatively be shown as a pie chart, as in Figure 2.7.

The area (and angle) of each slice is proportional to the respective frequency, and the pie chart is an alternative means of presentation to the bar chart shown in Figure 2.3. The numbers falling into each education category have been added around the chart, but this is not essential. For presentational purposes, it is best not to have too many slices in the chart: beyond about six the chart tends to look crowded. It might be worth amalgamating less important categories to make such a chart look clearer.

The chart reveals, as did the original bar chart, that 'higher education' and 'other qualifications' are the two biggest categories. However, it is more difficult to compare them accurately; it is more difficult to compare angles than it is to compare heights. The results may be contrasted with Figure 2.8 which shows a similar

Figure 2.8
Educational qualifications
of the unemployed

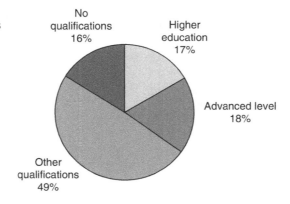

pie chart for the unemployed (the second row of Table 2.1). This time, we have put the proportion in each category in the labels (Excel has an option which allows this), rather than the absolute number.

The 'other qualifications' category is now substantially larger and the 'no qualifications' group now accounts for 16% of the unemployed, a bigger proportion than for those employed. Further, the proportion with a degree approximately halves from 35% to 17%.

Notice that we would need three pie charts (another for the 'inactive' group) to convey the same information as the multiple bar chart in Figure 2.4. It is harder to look at the three pie charts than it is to look at one bar chart, so in this case the bar chart is the better method of presenting the data.

Exercise 2.1

The following table shows the total numbers (in millions) of tourists visiting each country and the numbers of English tourists visiting each country:

	France	Germany	Italy	Spain
All tourists	12.4	3.2	7.5	9.8
English tourists	2.7	0.2	1.0	3.6

Adapted from data from the Office for National Statistics licensed under the Open Government Licence v.3.0.
Source: Office for National Statistics.

(a) Draw a bar chart showing the total numbers visiting each country.

(b) Draw a stacked bar chart which shows English and non-English tourists making up the total visitors to each country.

(c) Draw a pie chart showing the distribution of all tourists between the four destination countries. Do the same for English tourists and compare results.

Experiment with the presentation of each graph to see which works best. Try a horizontal (rather than vertical) bar chart, try different colours, make all text horizontal (including the title of the vertical axis and the labels on the horizontal axis), place the legend in different places, etc.

Looking at cross-section data: wealth in the United Kingdom in 2005

Frequency tables and charts

We now move on to examine data in a different form. The data on employment and education consisted simply of frequencies, where a characteristic (such as higher education) was either present or absent for a particular individual. We now look at the distribution of wealth, a variable which can be measured on a ratio scale so that a different value is associated with each individual. For example, one person might have £1000 of wealth, and another might have £1 million. Different presentational techniques will be used to analyse this type of data. We use these techniques to investigate questions such as how much wealth does the average person have and whether wealth is evenly distributed or not.

The data are given in Table 2.3 which shows the distribution of wealth in the United Kingdom for the year 2005 (the latest available at the time of writing), available at http://webarchive.nationalarchives.gov.uk/+/http://www.hmrc.gov.uk/stats/personal_wealth/archive.htm. This is an example of a frequency table. Wealth

Table 2.3 **The distribution of wealth, United Kingdom, 2005**

Class interval (£)	Numbers (thousands)
0–9999	1 668
10 000–24 999	1 318
25 000–39 999	1 174
40 000–49 999	662
50 000–59 999	627
60 000–79 999	1 095
80 000–99 999	1 195
100 000–149 999	3 267
150 000–199 999	2 392
200 000–299 999	2 885
300 000–499 999	1 480
500 000–999 999	628
1 000 000–1 999 999	198
2 000 000 or more	88
Total	18 667

Note: It would be impossible to show the wealth of all 18 million individuals, so it has been summarised in this frequency table.
Source: Adapted from HM Revenue and Customs Statistics, 2005, contains public sector information licensed under the Open Government Licence (OGL) v3.0. http://www.nationalarchives.gov.uk/doc/open-government-licence/open-government

is difficult to define and to measure; the data shown here refer to *marketable* wealth (i.e. items such as the right to a pension, which cannot be sold, are excluded) and are estimates for the population (of adults) as a whole based on taxation data.

Wealth is divided into 14 class intervals: £0 up to (but not including) £10 000; £10 000 up to £24 999, etc., and the number (or frequency) of individuals within each class interval is shown. Note that the widths of the intervals (the class widths) vary up the wealth scale: the first is £10 000, the second £15 000 (= 25 000 − 10 000), the third £15 000 also and so on. This will prove an important factor when it comes to graphical presentation of the data.

This table has been constructed from the original 18 667 000 observations on individuals' wealth, so it is already a summary of the original data (note that all the frequencies have been expressed in thousands in the table) and much of the original information is unavailable. The first decision to make if one had to draw up such a frequency table from the raw data is how many class intervals to have and how wide they should be. It simplifies matters if they are all of the same width, but in this case it is not feasible: if 10 000 were chosen as the standard width for each class, there would be many intervals between 500 000 and 1 000 000 (50 of them in fact), most of which would have a zero or very low frequency. If 100 000 were the standard width, there would be only a few intervals and the first of them (0 − 100 000) would contain 7739 observations (41% of all observations), so almost all the interesting detail would be lost. A compromise between these extremes has to be found.

A useful rule of thumb is that the number of class intervals should equal the square root of the total frequency, subject to a maximum of about 12 intervals. Thus, for example, a total of 25 observations should be allocated to 5 intervals; 100 observations should be grouped into 10 intervals and 18 667 should be grouped into about 12 (14 are used here). The class widths should be equal insofar as this is feasible but should increase when the frequencies become very small.

Figure 2.9
Bar chart of the distribution of wealth in the United Kingdom, 2005

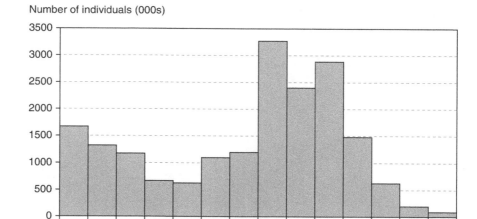

To present these data graphically one could draw a bar chart, as in the case of education above, and this is presented in Figure 2.9. Note that although the original data are on a ratio scale, we have transformed them so that we are now counting individuals in each category. Hence we can make use of the bar chart again, although note that the *x*-axis has categories differentiated by the value of wealth rather than some characteristic such as education. Before reading on, spend some time looking at the figure and ask yourself what is wrong with it.

The answer is that the figure gives a completely misleading picture of the data. (Incidentally, this is the picture that you will get using a spreadsheet program. All the standard packages appear to do this, so beware. One wonders how many decisions have been influenced by data presented in this incorrect manner.)

Why is the figure wrong? Consider the following argument. The diagram appears to show that there are few individuals around £40000 to £50000 (the frequency is approximately 660 thousand) but many around £150000. But this is just the result of the difference in the class width at these points (10000 at £40000 and 50000 at £150000). Suppose that we divide up the £150000-to-£200000 class into two: £150000 to £175000 and £175000 to £200000. We divide the frequency of 2392 equally between the two classes (this is an arbitrary decision but illustrates the point). The graph now looks like Figure 2.10.

Comparing Figures 2.9 and 2.10 reveals a difference: the hump around £150000 has now gained a substantial crater. But this is disturbing: it means that the shape of the distribution can be altered simply by altering the class widths. The underlying data are exactly the same. So how can we rely upon visual inspection of the distribution? What does the 'real' distribution look like? A better method would make the shape of the distribution independent of how the class intervals are arranged. This can be done by drawing a histogram.

The histogram

A histogram is similar to a bar chart except that it corrects for differences in class widths. If all the class widths are identical, then there is no difference between a bar chart and a histogram. The calculations required to produce the histogram are shown in Table 2.4.

Figure 2.10
The wealth distribution
with alternative class
intervals

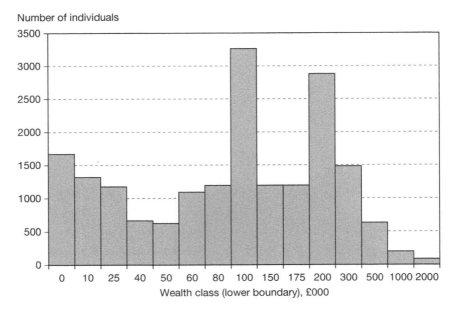

The new column in the table shows the **frequency density**, which measures the frequency *per unit of class width*. Hence it allows a direct comparison of different class intervals, i.e. accounting for the difference in class widths.

The frequency density is defined as follows:

$$frequency\ density = \frac{frequency}{class\ width} \tag{1.1}$$

Using this formula corrects the figures for differing class widths. Thus

$$0.1668 = \frac{1668}{10\,000} \text{ is the first frequency density,}$$

$$0.0789 = \frac{1318}{15\,000} \text{ is the second, etc.}$$

Table 2.4 Calculation of frequency densities

Range	Frequency	Class width	Frequency density
0–	1668	10 000	0.1668
10 000–	1318	15 000	0.0879
25 000–	1174	15 000	0.0783
40 000–	662	10 000	0.0662
50 000–	627	10 000	0.0627
60 000–	1095	20 000	0.0548
80 000–	1195	20 000	0.0598
100 000–	3267	50 000	0.0653
150 000–	2392	50 000	0.0478
200 000–	5279	3 800 000	0.0014

Note: As an alternative to the frequency density, one could calculate the frequency per 'standard' class width, with the standard width chosen to be 10 000 (the narrowest class). The values in column 4 would then be 1668; 879(= 1318 ÷ 1.5); 783, etc. This would lead to the same shape of histogram as using the frequency density.

Above £200 000, the class widths are very large and the frequencies small (too small to be visible on a histogram), so these classes have been combined.

The width of the final interval is unknown, so it has to be estimated in order to calculate the frequency density. It is likely to be extremely wide since the wealthiest person may well have assets valued at several £m (or even £bn); the value we assume will affect the calculation of the frequency density and therefore of the shape of the histogram. Fortunately, it is in the tail of the distribution and only affects a small number of observations. Here we assume (arbitrarily) a width of £3.8m to be a 'reasonable' figure, giving an upper class boundary of £4m.

The frequency density, not the frequency, is then plotted on the vertical axis against wealth on the horizontal axis to give the histogram. One further point needs to be made: for clarity, the scale on the horizontal wealth axis should be linear as far as possible, e.g. £50 000 should be twice as far from the origin as £25 000. However, it is difficult to fit all the values onto the horizontal axis without squeezing the graph excessively at lower levels of wealth, where most observations are located. Therefore, the classes above £100 000 have been squeezed, and the reader's attention is drawn to this. The result is shown in Figure 2.11.

The effect of taking frequency densities is to make the *area* of each block in the histogram represent the frequency, rather than the height, which now shows the density. This has the effect of giving an accurate picture of the shape of the distribution. Note that it is very different from the preceding graph.

Now that all this has been done, what does the histogram show?

- The histogram is heavily skewed to the right (i.e. the long tail is to the right).
- The modal class interval is £0 to £10 000 (i.e. has the greatest density: no other £10 000 interval has more individuals in it).

Figure 2.11
Histogram of the distribution of wealth in the United Kingdom, 2005

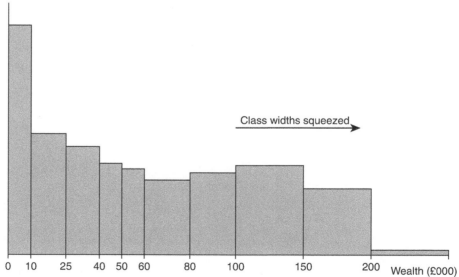

Note: A frequency polygon would be the result if, instead of drawing blocks for the histogram, one drew lines connecting the centres of the top of each block. The diagram is better drawn with blocks, in general.

- Looking at the graph, it appears that more than half of all people have wealth of less than £100 000. However, this is misleading as the graph is squeezed beyond £100 000. In fact, about 41% have wealth below this figure.

The figure shows quite a high degree of inequality in the wealth distribution. Whether this is acceptable or even desirable is a value judgement. It should be noted that part of the inequality is due to differences in age: younger people have not yet had enough time to acquire much wealth and therefore appear worse off, although in lifetime terms this may not be the case. To get a better picture of the distribution of wealth would require some analysis of the acquisition of wealth over the life-cycle (or comparison of individuals of a similar age). In fact, correcting for age differences does not make a big difference to the pattern of wealth distribution. On this point and on inequality in wealth in general, see Atkinson (1983).

Relative frequency and cumulative frequency distributions

An alternative way of illustrating the wealth distribution uses the relative and cumulative frequencies of the data. The relative frequencies show the *proportion* of observations that fall into each class interval, so, for example, 3.5% of individuals have wealth holdings between £40 000 and £50 000 (662 000 out of 18 677 000 individuals). Relative frequencies are shown in the third column of Table 2.5, calculated using the following formula:

$$Relative\,frequency = \frac{frequency}{sum\,of\,frequencies} = \frac{f}{\sum f} \qquad (1.2)$$

Note: If you are unfamiliar with the Σ notation, then read Appendix 2A to this chapter before continuing.

Table 2.5 Calculation of relative and cumulative frequencies

Range	Frequency, f	Relative frequency (%)	Cumulative frequency, F
0–	1 668	8.9	1 668
10 000–	1 318	7.1	2 986
25 000–	1 174	6.3	4 160
40 000–	662	3.5	4 822
50 000–	627	3.4	5 449
60 000–	1 095	5.9	6 544
80 000–	1 195	6.4	7 739
100 000–	3 267	17.5	11 006
150 000–	2 392	12.8	13 398
200 000–	2 885	15.4	16 283
300 000–	1 480	7.9	17 763
500 000–	628	3.4	18 391
1 000 000–	198	1.1	18 589
2 000 000–	88	0.5	18 677
Total	18 677	100.0	

Note: Relative frequencies are calculated in the same way as the column percentages in Table 2.2. Thus for example, 8.9% is 1668 divided by 18 667. Cumulative frequencies are obtained by cumulating, or successively adding, the frequencies. For example, 2986 is 1668 + 1318, 4160 is 2986 + 1174, etc.

The AIDS epidemic

To illustrate how descriptive statistics can be helpful in presenting information we show below the 'population pyramid' for Botswana (one of the countries most seriously affected by AIDS), projected for the year 2020. This is essentially two bar charts (one for men, one for women) laid on their sides, showing the frequencies in each age category (rather than wealth categories). The inner pyramid (in the darker colour) shows the projected population given the existence of AIDS; the outer pyramid assumes no deaths from AIDS.

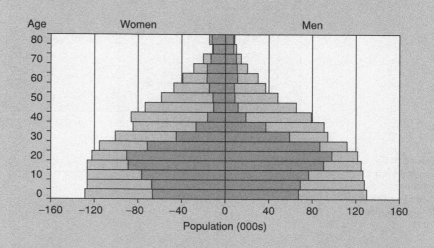

One can immediately see the huge effect of AIDS, especially on the 40 to 60 age group (currently aged 30–50), for both men and women. These people would normally be in the most productive phase of their lives but, with AIDS, the country will suffer enormously with many old and young people dependent on a small working population.

Original source of data: US Census Bureau, *World Population Profile 2000*. Graph adapted from the UNAIDS website at http://www.unaids.org/epidemic_update/report/Epi_report.htm#thepopulation.

The sum of the relative frequencies has to be 100%, and this acts as a check on the calculations.

The cumulative frequencies, shown in the fourth column, are obtained by cumulating (successively adding) the frequencies. The cumulative frequencies show the total number of individuals with wealth *up to* a given amount; for example, about 7.7 million people have less than £100000 of wealth.

Both relative and cumulative frequency distributions can be drawn, in a similar way to the histogram. In fact, the relative frequency distribution has exactly the same shape as the frequency distribution. This is shown in Figure 2.12. This time we have written the relative frequencies above the appropriate column, although this is not essential.

The cumulative frequency distribution is shown in Figure 2.13, where the blocks increase in height as wealth increases. The simplest way to draw this is to cumulate the frequency densities (shown in the final column of Table 2.4) and to use these values as the *y*-axis coordinates.

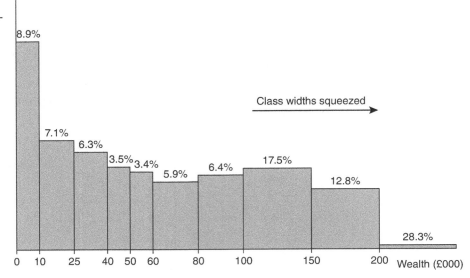

Figure 2.12
The relative frequency distribution of wealth in the United Kingdom, 2005

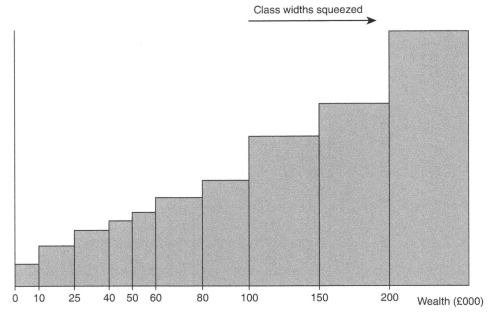

Figure 2.13
The cumulative frequency distribution of wealth in the United Kingdom, 2005

Note: The *y*-axis coordinates are obtained by cumulating the frequency densities in Table 2.4. For example, the first two *y* coordinates are 0.1668, 0.2547.

Worked example 2.1

There is a mass of detail in the sections above, so this worked example is intended to focus on the essential calculations required to produce the summary graphs. Simple artificial data are deliberately used to avoid the distraction of a lengthy interpretation of the results and their meaning. The data on the variable X and its frequencies f are shown in the following table, with the calculations required:

X	Frequency, f	Relative frequency	Cumulative frequency, F
10	6	0.17	6
11	8	0.23	14
12	15	0.43	29
13	5	0.14	34
14	1	0.03	35
Total	35	1.00	

Notes:

The X values are unique but could be considered the mid-point of a range, as earlier.

The relative frequencies are calculated as $0.17 = 6/35$, $0.23 = 8/35$, etc. Note that these are expressed as decimals rather than percentages; either form is acceptable.

The cumulative frequencies are calculated as $14 = 6 + 8$, $29 = 6 + 8 + 15$, etc.

The symbol F usually denotes the cumulative frequency in statistical work.

The resulting bar chart and cumulative frequency distribution are:

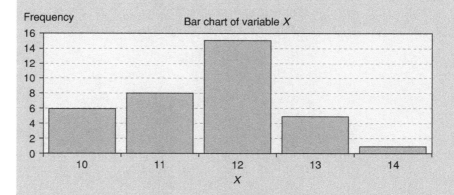

and

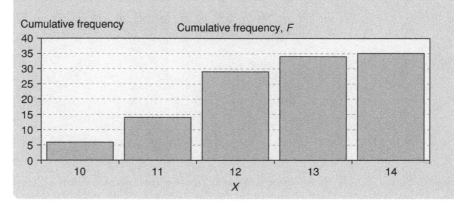

Exercise 2.2

Given the following data:

Range	Frequency
0–10	20
11–30	40
31–60	30
61–100	20

(a) Draw both a bar chart and a histogram of the data and compare them.

(b) Calculate cumulative frequencies and draw a cumulative frequency diagram.

Improving the presentation of graphs — an example

Today we are assailed with information presented in the form of graphs, sometimes done well but often badly. We give an example below of how presentation might be improved for one particular graph, showing employers' perceptions of economics graduates' skills. One can learn a lot from looking at examples of graphs in reports and academic papers and thinking how they might be improved. The original graph[1] is not actually a bad one, but it could be better.

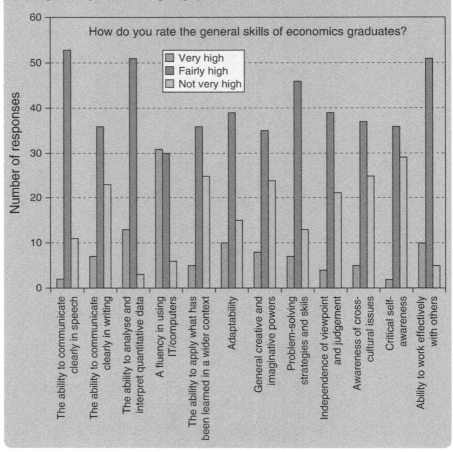

[1]See the original at http://www.economicsnetwork.ac.uk/projects/surveys/employers14-15. This is the author's rendition, which tries to mimic the original as accurately as possible.

Problems with this graph include:

1. The category labels are difficult to read, being small and wrap-around text.
2. The vertical axis title is sideways, so difficult to read.
3. It is difficult to compare across categories. For example, which skill has the most 'very high' or 'fairly high' responses?
4. A subjective judgement, but the colours are not particularly harmonious.

The version below takes the same data but presents it slightly differently:

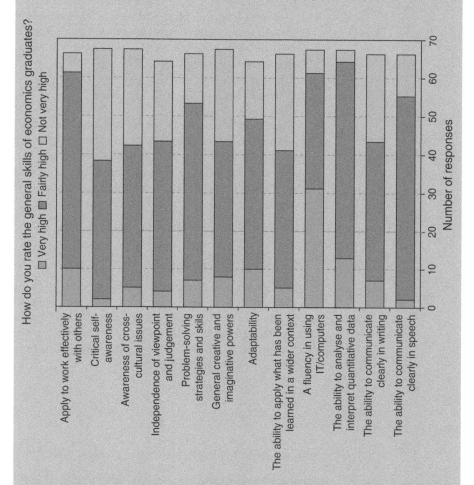

Turning the graph on its side makes the labels much easier to read, as is the horizontal axis label. Using a stacked bar saves space and makes it look less cluttered. It is fairly easy to see that 'interpreting quantitative data' scores the most 'very high' or 'fairly high' responses – hopefully this text makes some contribution towards that. Using different shades of the same colour makes for a better appearance (and probably works better if printed in greyscale too).

You might have noticed that the categories are now in a different order. This is a quirk of Excel; the same data table was used for both charts. Fortunately, the ordering does not matter. We shall give similar examples of good practice at other places in this text.

Summarising data using numerical techniques

Graphical methods are an excellent means of obtaining a quick overview of the data, but they are not particularly precise, nor do they lend themselves to further analysis. For this, we must turn to numerical measures such as the average. There are a number of different ways in which we may describe a distribution such as that for wealth. If we think of trying to describe the histogram, it is useful to have:

- A measure of location giving an idea of whether people own a lot of wealth or a little. An example is the average, which gives some idea of where the distribution is located along the x-axis. In fact, we will encounter three different measures of the 'average':
  - ○ The mean
  - ○ The median
  - ○ The mode
- A measure of dispersion showing how wealth is dispersed around the average, whether it is concentrated close to the average or is generally far away from it. An example here is the standard deviation.
- A measure of skewness showing how symmetric the distribution is, i.e. whether the left half of the distribution is a mirror image of the right half. This is obviously not the case for the wealth distribution.

We consider each type of measure in turn.

Measures of location: the mean

The arithmetic mean, commonly called the average, is the most familiar measure of location and is obtained simply by adding all the wealth observations and dividing by the number of observations. If we denote the wealth of the ith household by x_i (so that the index i runs from 1 to N, where N is the number of observations; as an example, x_3 would be the wealth of the third household), then the mean is given by the following formula:

$$\mu = \frac{\sum_{i=1}^{i=N} x_i}{N} \tag{1.3}$$

where μ (the Greek letter mu, pronounced 'myu'[2]) denotes the mean and $\sum_{i=1}^{i=N} x_i$ (read 'sigma $x i$, from $i = 1$ to N', Σ being the Greek capital letter sigma) means the sum of the x values. We may simplify this to

$$\mu = \frac{\sum x}{N} \tag{1.4}$$

when it is obvious which x values are being summed (usually all the available observations). This latter form is more easily readable, and we will generally use this.

---

[2]Mathematicians pronounce it like this, but modern Greeks do not. For them, it is 'mi'.

Worked example 2.2

We will find the mean of the values 17, 25, 28, 20, 35. The total of these five numbers is 125, so we have $N = 5$ and $\Sigma x = 125$. Therefore the mean is

$$\mu = \frac{\Sigma x}{N} = \frac{125}{5} = 25$$

Formula 1.3 can only be used when all the individual x values are known. The frequency table for wealth does not show all 18 million observations, however, but only the range of values for each class interval and the associated frequency. In the case of such grouped data the following equivalent formula may be used:

$$\mu = \frac{\sum_{i=1}^{i=C} f_i x_i}{\sum_{i=1}^{i=C} f_i} \tag{1.5}$$

or, more simply,

$$\mu = \frac{\Sigma fx}{\Sigma f} \tag{1.6}$$

In this formula:

- x denotes the mid-point of each class interval, since the individual x values are unknown. The mid-point is used as the representative x value for each class. In the first class interval, for example, we do not know precisely where each of the 1668 observations lies. Hence we *assume* they all lie at the mid-point, £5000. This will cause a slight inaccuracy – because the distribution is so skewed, there are likely more households below the mid-point than above it in every class interval except, perhaps, the first. We ignore this problem here, and it is less of a problem for most distributions which are less skewed than this one.
- The summation runs from 1 to C, the number of class intervals, or mid-point x values. f times x gives the total wealth in each class interval. If we sum over the 14 class intervals, we get the total wealth of all individuals.
- $\Sigma f_i = N$ gives the total number of observations, the sum of the individual frequencies.

The calculation of the mean, μ, for the wealth data is shown in Table 2.6. From this we obtain:

$$\mu = \frac{3\,490\,260}{18\,677} = 186.875$$

Note that the x values are expressed in £000, so we must remember that the mean will also be in £000; the average wealth holding is therefore £186 875. Note that the frequencies have also been divided by 1000, but this has no effect upon the calculation of the mean since f appears in both numerator and denominator of the formula for the mean.

The mean tells us that if the total wealth were divided up equally between all individuals, each would have £186 875. This value may seem surprising, since the

Table 2.6 The calculation of average wealth

Range	x	f	fx
0–	5.0	1 668	8 340
10 000–	17.5	1 318	23 065
25 000–	32.5	1 174	38 155
40 000–	45.0	662	29 790
50 000–	55.0	627	34 485
60 000–	70.0	1 095	76 650
80 000–	90.0	1 195	107 550
100 000–	125.0	3 267	408 375
150 000–	175.0	2 392	418 600
200 000–	250.0	2 885	721 250
300 000–	400.0	1 480	592 000
500 000–	750.0	628	471 000
1 000 000–	1 500.0	198	297 000
2 000 000–	3 000.0	88	264 000
Total		18 677	3 490 260

Note: The *fx* column gives the product of the values in the *f* and *x* columns (so, for example, 5.0 × 1668 = 8340, which is the total wealth held by those in the first class interval). The sum of the *fx* values gives total wealth.

histogram clearly shows most people have wealth below this point (approximately two-thirds of individuals are below the mean, in fact). The mean does not seem to be typical of the wealth that most people have. The reason the mean has such a high value is that there are some individuals whose wealth is way above the figure of £186 875 – up into the £millions, in fact. The mean is the 'balancing point' of the distribution – if the histogram were a physical model, it would balance on a fulcrum placed at 186 875. The few very high wealth levels exert a lot of leverage and counterbalance the more numerous individuals below the mean.

Worked example 2.3

Suppose we have 10 families with a single television in their homes, 12 families with two televisions each and three families with three. You can probably work out in your head that there are 43 televisions in total (10 + 24 + 9) owned by the 25 families (10 + 12 + 3). The average number of televisions per family is therefore 43/25 = 1.72.

Setting this out formally, we have (as for the wealth distribution, but simpler):

x	f	fx
1	10	10
2	12	24
3	3	9
Totals	25	43

This gives our resulting mean as 1.72. The data are discrete values in this case and we have the actual values, not a broad class interval. Note that no single family could actually have 1.72 television sets; it is the average over all families.

The mean as the expected value

We also refer to the mean as the expected value of x and write:

$$E(x) = \mu = 186\,875 \tag{1.7}$$

$E(x)$ is read 'E of x' or 'the expected value of x'. The mean is the expected value in the sense that if we selected a household at random from the population, we would 'expect' its wealth to be £186 875. It is important to note that this is a *statistical* expectation, rather than the everyday use of the term. Most of the random individuals we encounter have wealth substantially below this value. Most people might therefore 'expect' a lower value because that is their everyday experience; but statisticians are different; they refer to the mean as the expected value.

The expected value notation is particularly useful in keeping track of the effects upon the mean of certain data transformations (e.g. dividing wealth by 1000 also divides the mean by 1000); Appendix 2B provides a detailed explanation. Use is also made of the E operator in inferential statistics, to describe the properties of estimators.

The sample mean and the population mean

Very often we have only a sample of data (as in worked example 2.3), and it is important to distinguish this case from the one where we have all the possible observations. For this reason, the sample mean is given by:

$$\bar{x} = \frac{\sum x}{n} \quad \text{or} \quad \bar{x} = \frac{\sum fx}{\sum f} \quad \text{for grouped data} \tag{1.8}$$

Note the distinctions between μ (the population mean) and $\bar{x}$ (the sample mean), and between N (the size of the population) and n (the sample size). Otherwise, the calculations are identical. It is a convention to use Greek letters, such as μ, to refer to the population and Roman letters, such as $\bar{x}$, to refer to a sample.

The weighted average

Sometimes observations have to be given different weightings in calculating the average, as in the following example. Consider the problem of calculating the average spending per pupil by an education authority. Some figures for spending on primary (ages 5–11), secondary (11–16) and post-16 pupils are given in Table 2.7.

Clearly, significantly more is spent on secondary and post-16 pupils (a general pattern throughout England and most other countries) and the overall average should lie somewhere between 1750 and 3820. However, taking a simple average of these three values would give the wrong answer, because there are different numbers of children in the three age ranges. The numbers and proportions of children in each age group are given in Table 2.8.

Table 2.7 Cost per pupil in different types of school (£ p.a.)

	Primary	Secondary	Post-16
Unit cost	1750	3100	3820

Table 2.8 Numbers and proportions of pupils in each age range

	Primary	Secondary	Post-16	Total
Numbers	8000	7000	3000	18 000
Proportion	44.4%	38.9%	16.7%	

Since there are relatively more primary schoolchildren than secondary, and relatively fewer post-16 pupils, the primary unit cost should be given greatest weight in the averaging process and the post-16 unit cost the least. The **weighted average** is obtained by multiplying each unit cost figure by the proportion of children in each category and summing. The weighted average is therefore

$$0.444 \times 1750 + 0.389 \times 3100 + 0.167 \times 3820 = 2620.8 \qquad (1.9)$$

The weighted average gives an answer closer to the primary unit cost than does the simple average of the three figures (2890 in this case), which would be misleading. The formula for the weighted average is

$$\bar{x}_w = \sum_i w_i x_i \qquad (1.10)$$

where w represents the weights, *which must sum to one*, i.e.

$$\sum_i w_i = 1 \qquad (1.11)$$

and x represents the unit cost figures.

Notice that what we have done is equivalent to multiplying each unit cost by its frequency (8000, etc.) and then dividing the sum by the grand total of 18 000. This is the same as the procedure we used for the wealth calculation. The difference with weights is that we first divide 8000 by 18 000 (and 7000 by 18 000, etc.) to get the weights, which must then sum to one, and use these weights in formula (1.10).

Calculating your degree result

If you are a university student your final degree result will probably be calculated as a weighted average of your marks on the individual courses. The weights may be based on the credits associated with each course or on some other factors. For example, in my university the average mark for a year is a weighted average of the marks on each course, the weights being the credit values of each course.

The grand mean G, on which classification is based, is then a weighted average of the averages for the different years, as follows:

$$G = \frac{0 \times Year\,1 + 40 \times Year\,2 + 60 \times Year\,3}{100}$$

i.e. the year 3 mark has a weight of 60%, year 2 is weighted 40% and the first year is not counted at all.

For students taking a year abroad the formula is slightly different:

$$G = \frac{0 \times Year\,1 + 40 \times Year\,2 + 25 \times Yabroad + 60 \times Year\,3}{125}$$

Note that, to accommodate the year abroad mark, the weights on years 2 and 3 are effectively reduced (to $40/125 = 32\%$ and $60/125 = 48\%$, respectively).

 The median

Returning to the study of wealth, the unrepresentative result for the mean suggests that we may prefer a measure of location which is not so strongly affected by outliers (extreme observations) and skewness.

The median is a measure of location which is more robust to such extreme values; it may be defined by the following procedure. Imagine everyone in a line from poorest to wealthiest. Go to the individual located halfway along the line. Ask her what her wealth is. Her answer is the median. The median is clearly unaffected by extreme values, unlike the mean: if the wealth of the richest person were doubled (with no reduction in anyone else's wealth), there would be no effect upon the median. The calculation of the median is not so straightforward as for the mean, especially for grouped data. The following worked example first shows how to calculate the median for ungrouped data.

Worked example 2.4 The median

Calculate the median of the following values: 45, 12, 33, 80, 77.

First we put them into ascending order: 12, 33, 45, 77, 80.

It is then easy to see that the middle value is 45. This is the median. Note that if the value of the largest observation changes to, say, 150, the value of the median is unchanged. This is not the case for the mean, which would change from 49.4 to 63.4.

If there is an even number of observations, then there is no middle observation. The solution is to take the average of the two middle observations. For example:

Find the median of 12, 33, 45, 63, 77, 80.

Note the new observation, 63, making six observations. The median value is halfway between the third and fourth observations, i.e. $(45 + 63)/2 = 54$.

For grouped data there are two stages to the calculation: first we must identify the class interval which contains the median person, and then we must calculate where in the interval that person lies.

(1) To find the appropriate class interval: since there are 18 677 000 observations, we need the wealth of the person who is 9 338 500 in rank order. The table of cumulative frequencies (see Table 2.5) is the most suitable for this. There are

7 739 000 individuals with wealth of less than £100 000 and 11 006 000 with wealth of less than £150 000. The middle person therefore falls into the £100 000–150 000 class. Furthermore, given that 9 338 500 falls roughly half-way between 7 739 000 and 11 006 000, it follows that the median should be close to the middle of the class interval. We now go on to make this statement more precise.

(2) To find the position in the class interval, we can now use formula (1.12):

$$median = x_L + (x_U - x_L)\frac{\left\{\dfrac{N+1}{2} - F\right\}}{f} \tag{1.12}$$

where:

x_L = the lower limit of the class interval containing the median
x_U = the upper limit of this class interval
N = the number of observations (using $N + 1$ rather than N in the formula is only important when N is relatively small)
F = the cumulative frequency of the class intervals up to (but not including) the one containing the median
f = the frequency for the class interval containing the median.

For the wealth distribution we have:

$$median = 100\,000 + (150\,000 - 100\,000)\left\{\frac{\dfrac{18\,677\,000}{2} - 7\,739\,000}{3\,267\,000}\right\}$$

$$= £124\,480$$

This alternative measure of location gives a very different impression: it is around two-thirds of the mean. Nevertheless, it is an equally valid statistic, despite having a different meaning. It demonstrates that the person 'in the middle' has wealth of £124 480 and in this sense is typical of the UK population. Before going on to compare these measures further we examine a third, the mode.

Generalising the median – quantiles

The idea of the median as the middle of the distribution can be extended: quartiles divide the distribution into 4 equal parts, quintiles into 4, deciles into 10, and finally percentiles divide the distribution into 100 equal parts. Generically they are known as quantiles. We shall illustrate the idea by examining deciles (quartiles are covered below).

The first decile occurs one-tenth of the way along the line of people ranked from poorest to wealthiest. This means we require the wealth of the person ranked 1 867 700 ($= N/10$) in the distribution. From the table of cumulative frequencies, this person lies in the second class interval. Adapting formula (1.12), we obtain:

$$first\ decile = 10\,000 + (25\,000 - 10\,000) \times \left\{\frac{1\,867\,700 - 1\,668\,000}{1\,318\,000}\right\} = £12\,273$$

Thus we estimate that any household with less than £12 273 of wealth falls into the bottom 10% of the wealth distribution. In a similar fashion, the ninth decile can be found by calculating the wealth of the household ranked 16 809 300 ($= N \times 9/10$) in the distribution.

The mode

The mode is defined as that level of wealth which occurs with the greatest frequency, in other words the value that occurs most often. It is most useful and easiest to calculate when one has all the data and there are relatively few distinct observations. This is the case in the simple example below.

Suppose we have the following data on sales of dresses by a shop, according to size:

Size	Sales
8	7
10	25
12	36
14	11
16	3
18	1

The modal size is 12. There are more women buying dresses of this size than any other. This may be the most useful form of average as far as the shop is concerned. Although it needs to stock a range of sizes, it knows it needs to order more dresses in size 12 than any other size. The mean would not be so helpful in this case (it is $\bar{x} = 11.7$), as it is not an actual dress size.

In the case of grouped data, matters are more complicated. The modal class interval is required, once the intervals have been corrected for width (otherwise a wider class interval is unfairly compared with a narrower one). For this, we can again make use of the frequency densities. From Table 2.4 it can be seen that it is the first interval, from £0 to £10 000, which has the highest frequency density. It is 'typical' of the distribution because it is the one which occurs most often (using the frequency densities, *not* frequencies). The wealth distribution is most concentrated at this level, and more people are like this in terms of wealth than anything else. Once again, it is notable how different the mode is from both the median and the mean.

The three measures of location give different messages because of the skewness of the distribution: if it were symmetric, then they would all give approximately the same answer. Here we have a rather extreme case of skewness, but it serves to illustrate how the different measures of location compare. When the distribution is skewed to the right, as here, they will be in the order mode, median, mean; if skewed to the left, the order is reversed. If the distribution has more than one peak, then this rule for orderings may not apply.

Which of the measures is 'correct' or most useful? In this particular case the mean is not very useful: it is heavily influenced by extreme values. The median is therefore often used when discussing wealth (and income) distributions. Where inequality is even more pronounced, as in some less developed countries, the mean is even less informative. The mode is also quite useful in telling us about a large section of the population, although it can be sensitive to how the class intervals are arranged. If the data were arranged such that there was a class interval of £5000 to £15 000, then this might well be the modal class, conveying a slightly different impression.

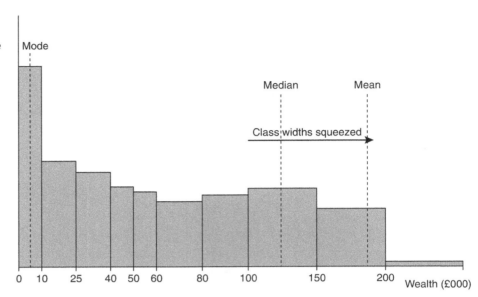

Figure 2.14
The histogram with the mean, median and mode marked

The three different measures of location are marked on the histogram in Figure 2.14. This brings out the substantial difference between the measures for a skewed distribution, such as for wealth.

Exercise 2.3

(a) For the data in Exercise 2.2, calculate the mean, median and mode of the data.

(b) Mark these values on the histogram you drew for Exercise 2.2.

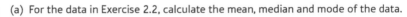 Measures of dispersion

Two different distributions (e.g. wealth in two different countries) might have the same mean yet look very different, as shown in Figure 2.15 (the distributions have

Figure 2.15
Two distributions with different degrees of dispersion

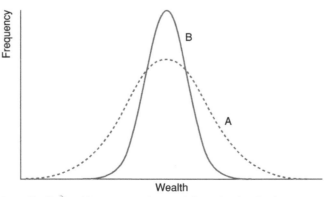

Note: Distribution A has a greater degree of dispersion than B, where everyone has similar levels of wealth.

been drawn using smooth curves rather than bars to improve clarity). In one country, everyone might have a similar level of wealth (curve B). In another, although the average is the same, there might be extremes of great wealth and poverty (curve A). A measure of dispersion is a number which allows us to distinguish between these two situations.

The simplest measure of dispersion is the range, which is the difference between the smallest and largest observations. It is impossible to calculate accurately from the table of wealth holdings since the largest observation is not available. In any case, it is not a very useful figure since it relies on two extreme values and ignores the rest of the distribution. In simpler cases, it might be more informative. For example, in an exam the marks may range from a low of 28% to a high of 74%. In this case the range is $74 - 28 = 46$ and this tells us something useful.

An improvement is the inter-quartile range, which is the difference between the first and third quartiles. It therefore defines the limits of wealth of the middle half of the distribution and ignores the very extremes of the distribution. To calculate the first quartile (which we label Q_1) we have to go one-quarter of the way along the line of wealth holders (ranked from poorest to wealthiest) and ask the person in that position what their wealth is. Their answer is the first quartile. The calculation is as follows:

- one-quarter of 18 677 observations is 4669.25;
- the person ranked 4669.25 is in the £40 000–50 000 class;
- adapting formula (1.12):

$$Q_1 = 40\,000 + (50\,000 - 40\,000)\left\{\frac{4669.25 - 4160}{662}\right\} = 47\,692.6 \qquad (1.13)$$

The third quartile is calculated in similar fashion:

- three-quarters of 18 677 is 14 007.75;
- the person ranked 14 007.75 is in the £200 000 to 300 000 class;
- again using (1.12):

$$Q_3 = 200\,000 + (300\,000 - 200\,000)\left\{\frac{14\,007.75 - 13\,398}{2885}\right\} = 221\,135.1$$

and therefore the inter-quartile range is $Q_3 - Q_1 = 221\,135 - 47\,693 = 173\,442$. This might be reasonably rounded to £175 000 given the approximations in our calculation, and is a much more memorable figure. Thus, the 50% of people in the middle of the distribution have wealth between £48 000 and £221 000 of wealth, approximately.

This gives one summary measure of the dispersion of the distribution: the higher the value the more spread out is the distribution. Therefore, two different wealth distributions might be compared according to their inter-quartile ranges, with the country having the larger figure exhibiting greater inequality. Note that the figures would have to be expressed in a common unit of currency for this comparison to be valid.

Worked example 2.5 The range and inter-quartile range

Suppose 110 children take a test, with the following results:

Mark, X	Frequency, f	Cumulative frequency, F
13	5	5
14	13	18
15	29	47
16	33	80
17	17	97
18	8	105
19	4	109
20	1	110
Total	110	

The range is simply $20 - 13 = 7$. The inter-quartile range requires calculation of the quartiles. Q_1 is given by the value of the 27.5th observation ($= 110/4$), which is 15. Q_3 is the value of the 82.5th observation ($= 110 \times 0.75$) which is 17. The IQR is therefore $17 - 15 = 2$ marks.

Notice that a slight change in the data (three more students getting 16 rather than 17 marks) would alter the IQR to 1 mark ($16 - 15$). The result should therefore be treated with some caution. This is a common problem when there are few distinct values of the variable (eight in this example). It is often worth considering whether a few small changes to the data could alter a calculation considerably. In such a case, the original result might not be very robust.

The variance

A more useful measure of dispersion is the **variance**, which makes use of all of the information available, rather than just trimming the extremes of the distribution. The variance is denoted by the symbol σ^2. σ is the Greek lower-case letter sigma, so σ^2 is read 'sigma squared'. It has a completely different meaning from Σ (capital sigma) used before. Its formula is:

$$\sigma^2 = \frac{\sum (x - \mu)^2}{N} \tag{1.14}$$

In this formula, $x - \mu$ measures the distance from each observation to the mean. Squaring these makes all the deviations positive, whether above or below the mean. We then take the average of all the squared deviations from the mean. A more dispersed distribution (such as A in Figure 2.15) will tend to have larger deviations from the mean and hence a larger variance. In comparing two distributions with similar means, therefore, we could examine their variances to see which of the two has the greater degree of dispersion. With grouped data the formula becomes:

$$\sigma^2 = \frac{\sum f(x - \mu)^2}{\sum f} \tag{1.15}$$

The calculation of the variance of wealth is shown in Table 2.9, and from this we obtain:

$$\sigma^2 = \frac{1\,499\,890\,455.1}{18\,677} = 80\,306.8$$

This calculated value is before translating back into the original units of measurement, as was done for the mean by multiplying by 1000. In the case of the variance, however, we must multiply by 1 000 000, which is the *square* of 1000. The variance of the original data is therefore 80 306 800 000. Multiplying by the square of 1000 is a consequence of using squared deviations in the variance formula (see Appendix 2B on E and V operators for more details of this).

One thus needs to be a little careful about the units of measurement. If the mean is reported at 186.875, then it is appropriate to report the variance as 80 306.8. If the mean is reported as 186 875, then the variance should be reported as 80 306 800 000. Note that it is only the presentation which changes; the underlying facts are the same.

The standard deviation

In what units is the variance measured? Since we have used a squaring procedure in the calculation we end up with something like 'squared' £s, which is not very convenient, nor does it make much sense. Because of this, it is useful to define the

Table 2.9 The calculation of the variance of wealth

Range	Mid-point x (£000)	Frequency, f	Deviation $(x - \mu)$	$(x - \mu)^2$	$f(x - \mu)^2$
0–	5.0	1 668	−181.9	33 078.4	55 174 821.9
10 000–	17.5	1 318	−169.4	28 687.8	37 810 535.3
25 000–	32.5	1 174	−154.4	23 831.6	27 978 261.2
40 000–	45.0	662	−141.9	20 128.4	13 325 033.3
50 000–	55.0	627	−131.9	17 391.0	10 904 128.1
60 000–	70.0	1 095	−116.9	13 659.7	14 957 383.4
80 000–	90.0	1 195	−96.9	9 384.7	11 214 740.7
100 000–	125.0	3 267	−61.9	3 828.5	12 507 665.8
150 000–	175.0	2 392	−11.9	141.0	337 296.1
200 000–	250.0	2 885	63.1	3 984.8	11 496 134.1
300 000–	400.0	1 480	213.1	45 422.4	67 225 100.9
500 000–	750.0	628	563.1	317 110.0	199 145 098.5
1 000 000–	1 500.0	198	1 313.1	1 724 297.9	341 410 980.4
2 000 000–	3 000.0	88	2 813.1	7 913 673.6	696 403 275.4
Totals		18 677			1 499 890 455.1

standard deviation as the square root of the variance, which is therefore back in £s. The standard deviation is therefore given by:

$$\sigma = \sqrt{\frac{\sum(x - \mu)^2}{N}} \tag{1.16}$$

or, for grouped data:

$$\sigma = \sqrt{\frac{\sum f(x - \mu)^2}{N}} \tag{1.17}$$

These are simply the square roots of (1.14) and (1.15). The standard deviation of wealth is therefore $\sqrt{80\,306.8} = 283.385$. This is in £000, so the standard deviation is actually £283 385 (note that this is the square root of 80 306 800 000, as it should be). On its own the standard deviation (and the variance) is not easy to interpret since it is not something we have an intuitive feel for, unlike the mean. It is more useful when used in a comparative setting. This will be illustrated later on.

The variance and standard deviation of a sample

As with the mean, a different symbol is used to distinguish a variance calculated from the population and one calculated from a sample. In addition, the sample variance is calculated using a slightly different formula from the one for the population variance. The sample variance is denoted by s^2 and its formula is given by equations (1.18) and (1.19) below:

$$s^2 = \frac{\sum(x - \bar{x})^2}{n - 1} \tag{1.18}$$

and, for grouped data:

$$s^2 = \frac{\sum f(x - \bar{x})^2}{n - 1} \tag{1.19}$$

where n is the sample size. The reason $n - 1$ is used in the denominator rather than n (as one might expect) is the following. Our real interest is in the population variance, and the sample variance is an estimate of it. The former is measured by the dispersion around μ and the sample variance should ideally be measured around μ also. However, μ is unknown, so $\bar{x}$ is used in the formula instead. But the variation of the sample observations around $\bar{x}$ tends to be smaller than that around μ. Using $n - 1$ rather than n in the formula compensates for this and the result is an unbiased[3] (i.e. correct on average) estimate of the population variance.

Using the correct formula is more important the smaller is the sample size, as the proportionate difference between $n - 1$ and n increases. For example, if $n = 10$, the adjustment amounts to 10% of the variance; when $n = 100$, the adjustment is only 1%.

The sample standard deviation is given by the square root of equation (1.18) or (1.19).

---

[3]The concept of *bias* is treated in more detail in Chapter 7.

> **Worked example 2.6 The variance and standard deviation**
>
> We continue with the previous worked example, relating to students' marks. The variance and standard deviation can be calculated as:
>
> | X | f | fx | $x - \mu$ | $(x - \mu)^2$ | $f(x - \mu)^2$ |
> |---|---|---|---|---|---|
> | 13 | 5 | 65 | −2.81 | 7.89 | 39.45 |
> | 14 | 13 | 182 | −1.81 | 3.27 | 42.55 |
> | 15 | 29 | 435 | −0.81 | 0.65 | 18.98 |
> | 16 | 33 | 528 | 0.19 | 0.04 | 1.20 |
> | 17 | 17 | 289 | 1.19 | 1.42 | 24.11 |
> | 18 | 8 | 144 | 2.19 | 4.80 | 38.40 |
> | 19 | 4 | 76 | 3.19 | 10.18 | 40.73 |
> | 20 | 1 | 20 | 4.19 | 17.56 | 17.56 |
> | Totals | 110 | 1739 | | | 222.99 |
>
> The mean is calculated as $1739/110 = 15.81$ and from this the deviations column $(x - \mu)$ is calculated (so $-2.81 = 13 - 15.81$, etc.).
>
> The variance is calculated as $\sum f(x - \mu)^2/(n - 1) = 222.99/109 = 2.05$. The standard deviation is therefore 1.43, the square root of 2.05. (Calculations are shown to 2 decimal places but have been calculated using exact values.)
>
> For distributions which are approximately symmetric and bell-shaped (i.e. the observations are clustered around the mean), there is an approximate relationship between the standard deviation and the inter-quartile range. This rule of thumb is that the IQR is 1.3 times the standard deviation. In this case, $1.3 \times 1.43 = 1.86$, close to the value calculated earlier, 2.

Alternative formulae for calculating the variance and standard deviation

The following formulae give the same answers as equations (1.14) to (1.17) but are simpler to calculate, either by hand or using a spreadsheet. For the population variance one can use

$$\sigma^2 = \frac{\sum x^2}{N} - \mu^2 \tag{1.20}$$

or, for grouped data,

$$\sigma^2 = \frac{\sum fx^2}{\sum f} - \mu^2 \tag{1.21}$$

The calculation of the variance using equation (1.21) is shown in Figure 2.16.

The sample variance can be calculated using

$$s^2 = \frac{\sum x^2 - n\bar{x}^2}{n - 1} \tag{1.22}$$

Figure 2.16
**Descriptive statistics
calculated using Excel**

	A	B	C	D	E	F	G	H	I
				WEALTH DATA 2005					
1				WEALTH DATA 2005					
2									
3	Wealth	Mid-point	Frequency						
4	Range	x	f	fx	fx squared		Summary statistics		
5	0	5.0	1,668	8,340	41,700				
6	10,000	17.5	1,318	23,065	403,638		Mean	186.875	
7	25,000	32.5	1,174	38,155	1,240,038		Variance	80306.8	
8	40,000	45.0	662	29,790	1,340,550		Std devn	283.385	
9	50,000	55.0	627	34,485	1,896,675		Coef varn.	1.516	
10	60,000	70.0	1,095	76,650	5,365,500				
11	80,000	90.0	1,195	107,550	9,679,500				
12	100,000	125.0	3,267	408,375	51,046,875				
13	150,000	175.0	2,392	418,600	73,255,000				
14	200,000	250.0	2,885	721,250	180,312,500				
15	300,000	400.0	1,480	592,000	236,800,000				
16	500,000	750.0	628	471,000	353,250,000				
17	1,000,000	1 500.0	198	297,000	445,500,000				
18	2,000,000	3 000.0	88	264,000	792,000,000				
19									
20	Totals		18,677	3,490,260	2,152,131,975				
21									

(H7 cell formula: =E20/C20-H6^2)

or, for grouped data,

$$s^2 = \frac{\sum fx^2 - n\bar{x}^2}{n-1} \qquad\qquad (1.23)$$

The standard deviation may of course be obtained as the square root of these formulae.

Using a calculator or computer for calculation

Electronic calculators and (particularly) computers have simplified the calculation of the mean, etc. Figure 2.16 shows how to set out the above calculations in Microsoft Excel, including some of the appropriate cell formulae.

The variance in this case is calculated using the formula $\sigma^2 = \dfrac{\sum fx^2}{\sum f} - \mu^2$ which is the formula given in equation (1.21). Note that it gives the same result as that calculated in the text.

The following formulae are contained in the cells:

D5:	= C5*B5	to calculate f times x
E5:	= D5*B5	to calculate f times x^2
C20:	= SUM(C5:C18)	to sum the frequencies, Σf
H6:	= D20/C20	calculates $\Sigma fx / \Sigma f$
H7:	= E20/C20 − H6^2	calculates $\Sigma fx^2 / \Sigma f - \mu^2$
H8:	= SQRT(H7)	calculates Σ
H9:	= H8/H6	calculates σ / μ

The coefficient of variation

The measures of dispersion examined so far are all measures of absolute dispersion and, in particular, their values depend upon the units in which the variable is measured. It is therefore difficult to compare the degrees of dispersion of two variables which are measured in different units. For example, one could not compare wealth in the United Kingdom with that in Germany if the former uses £s and the latter euros for measurement. Nor could one compare the wealth distribution in one country between two points in time because inflation alters the value of the currency over time. The solution is to use a measure of relative dispersion, which is independent of the units of measurement. One such measure is the coefficient of variation, defined as:

$$\text{Coefficient of variation} = \frac{\sigma}{\mu} \tag{1.24}$$

i.e. the standard deviation divided by the mean. Whenever the units of measurement are changed, the effect upon the mean and the standard deviation is the same; hence the coefficient of variation is unchanged. For the wealth distribution its value is $283.385/186.875 = 1.516$, i.e. the standard deviation is 152% of the mean. This may be compared directly with the coefficient of variation of a different wealth distribution to see which exhibits a greater relative degree of dispersion.

Independence of units of measurement

It is worth devoting a little attention to this idea, that some summary measures are independent of the units of measurement and some are not, as it occurs quite often in statistics and is not often appreciated at first. A statistic which is independent of the units of measurement is one which is unchanged, even when the units of measurement are changed. It is therefore more useful in general than a statistic which is not independent, since one can use it to make comparisons, or judgements, without worrying too much about how it was measured.

The mean is not independent of the units of measurement. If we are told the average income in the United Kingdom is 30 000, for example, we need to know whether it is measured in pounds sterling, euros or even dollars. The underlying level of income is the same, of course, but it is measured differently. By contrast, the rate of growth (described in detail shortly) is independent of the units of measurement. If we are told it is 3% p.a., it would be the same whether the calculation was based on pound, euro or dollar figures. If told that the rate of growth in the United States is 2% p.a., we can immediately conclude that the United Kingdom is growing faster, and no further information is needed.

Most measures we have encountered so far, such as the mean and variance, do depend on units of measurement. The coefficient of variation is one that does not. We now go on to describe another means of measuring dispersion that avoids the units of measurement problem.

The standard deviation of the logarithm

Another solution to the problem of different units of measurement is to use the logarithm[4] of wealth rather than the actual value. The reason why this works can best be illustrated by an example. Suppose that between 1997 and 2005 each individual's wealth doubled, so that

$$X_i^{2005} = 2X_i^{1997}$$

where X_i^t indicates the wealth of individual i in year t. It follows that the standard deviation of wealth in 2005 is exactly twice that of 1997 (and hence the coefficient of variation is unchanged). Taking logs, we have $\ln X_i^{2005} = \ln 2 + \ln X_i^{1997}$, so it follows that the distribution of $\ln X^{2005}$ is the same as that of $\ln X^{1997}$ except that it is shifted to the right by $\ln 2$ units. The variances (and hence standard deviations) of the two logarithmic distributions must therefore be the same, indicating no change in the *relative* dispersion of the two wealth distributions.

The use of logarithms in data analysis is very common, so it is worth making sure you understand the principles and mechanics of using them.

The standard deviation of the logarithm of wealth is calculated from the data in Table 2.10. The variance turns out to be:

$$\sigma^2 = \frac{\sum fx^2}{\sum f} - \mu^2 = \frac{417\,772.5}{18\,677} - \left(\frac{848\,40.9}{18\,677}\right)^2 = 1.734$$

and the standard deviation $\sigma = 1.317$. The larger this figure is, the greater the dispersion. On its own the number is difficult to interpret; it is only really useful when compared to another such figure.

Table 2.10 The calculation of the standard deviation of the logarithm of wealth

Range	Mid-point, x	ln (x)	Frequency, f	fx	fx squared
0–	5.0	1.609	1 668	2 684.5	4 320.6
10 000–	17.5	2.862	1 318	3 772.4	10 797.3
25 000–	32.5	3.481	1 174	4 087.0	14 227.7
40 000–	45.0	3.807	662	2 520.0	9 592.8
50 000–	55.0	4.007	627	2 512.6	10 068.8
60 000–	70.0	4.248	1 095	4 652.1	19 764.4
80 000–	90.0	4.500	1 195	5 377.3	24 196.7
100 000–	125.0	4.828	3 267	15 774.1	76 162.3
150 000–	175.0	5.165	2 392	12 354.2	63 806.6
200 000–	250.0	5.521	2 885	15 929.4	87 953.6
300 000–	400.0	5.991	1 480	8 867.4	53 128.5
500 000–	750.0	6.620	628	4 157.4	27 522.3
1 000 000–	1 500.0	7.313	198	1 448.0	10 589.7
2 000 000–	3 000.0	8.006	88	704.6	5 641.0
Totals			18 677	84 840.9	417 772.5

Notes: Use the 'ln' key on your calculator or the = LN() function in a spreadsheet to obtain natural logarithms of the data. You should obtain ln 5 = 1.609, ln 17.5 = 2.862, etc.
The column headed 'fx' is the product of the f and ln(x) columns.

---

[4]See Appendix 2C if you are unfamiliar with logarithms. Note that we use the natural logarithm here, but the effect would be the same using logs to base 10.

For comparison, the standard deviation of log wealth in 1979 (discussed in more detail later on) is 1.310, so there appears to have been little change in relative dispersion over this time period. Thus we have found two different ways of measuring relative dispersion. In a later chapter we will meet a third, the Gini coefficient.

Measuring deviations from the mean: z scores

Imagine the following problem. A man and a woman are arguing over their career records. The man says he earns more than she does, so he is more successful. The woman replies that women are discriminated against and that, relative to other women, she is doing better than the man is, relative to other men. Can the argument be resolved?

Suppose the data are as follows: the average male salary is £19 500 and the average female salary £16 800. The standard deviation of male salaries is £4750 and for women it is £3800. The man's salary is £31 375, while the woman's is £26 800. The man is therefore £11 875 above the mean, and the woman is £10 000 above. However, women's salaries are less dispersed than men's, so the woman has done well to get to £26 800.

One way to resolve the problem is to calculate the **z score**, which gives the salary in terms of the *number of standard deviations from the mean*. Thus for the man, the z score is

$$z = \frac{X - \mu}{\sigma} = \frac{31\,375 - 19\,500}{4750} = 2.50 \tag{1.25}$$

Thus the man is 2.5 standard deviations above the male mean salary, i.e. $31\,375 = 19\,500 + 2.5 \times 4\,750$. For the woman the calculation is

$$z = \frac{268\,00 - 16\,800}{3800} = 2.632 \tag{1.26}$$

The woman is 2.632 standard deviations above her mean and therefore wins the argument – she is nearer the top of her distribution than is the man and so is more of an outlier. Actually, this probably won't end the argument, but is the best the statistician can do. The z score is an important concept which will be used again when we cover hypothesis testing.

Chebyshev's inequality

Use of the z score leads on naturally to **Chebyshev's inequality**, which tells us about the proportion of observations that fall into the tails of any distribution, regardless of its shape. The theorem is expressed as follows:

At least $(1 - 1/k^2)$ of the observation in any distribution
lie within k standard deviations of the mean $\tag{1.27}$

If we take the female wage distribution given above, we can ask what proportion of women lie beyond 2.632 standard deviations from the mean (in both tails of the distribution). Setting $k = 2.632$, then

$$\left(1 - \frac{1}{k^2}\right) = \left(1 - \frac{1}{2.632^2}\right) = 0.8556.$$

So at least 85% of women have salaries within $\pm$ 2.632 standard deviations of the mean, i.e. between £6800 and £26 800 (16 800 $\pm$ 2.632 × 3800). Fifteen percent of women therefore lie outside this range.

Chebyshev's inequality is a very conservative rule since it applies to *any* distribution; if we know more about the shape of a particular distribution (for example, men's heights follow a Normal distribution), then we can make a more precise statement. In the case of the Normal distribution, over 99% of men are within 2.632 standard deviations of the average height because there is a concentration of observations near the centre of the distribution.

We can also use Chebyshev's inequality to investigate the inter-quartile range. The formula (1.27) implies that 50% of observations lie within $\sqrt{2}$ = 1.41 standard deviations of the mean, a more conservative value than our previous 1.3.

Exercise 2.4

(a) For the data in Exercise 2.2, calculate the inter-quartile range, the variance and the standard deviation.

(b) Calculate the coefficient of variation.

(c) Check if the relationship between the IQR and the standard deviation stated in the text (worked example 2.6) is approximately true for this distribution.

(d) Approximately how much of the distribution lies within one standard deviation either side of the mean? How does this compare with the prediction from Chebyshev's inequality?

Measuring skewness

The skewness of a distribution is the third characteristic that was mentioned earlier, in addition to location and dispersion. The wealth distribution is heavily skewed to the right, or positively skewed; it has its long tail in the right-hand end of the distribution. A measure of skewness gives a numerical indication of how asymmetric is the distribution.

One measure of skewness, known as the coefficient of skewness, is

$$\frac{\sum f(x - \mu)^3}{N\sigma^3} \tag{1.28}$$

and it is based upon *cubed* deviations from the mean. The result of applying formula (1.28) is positive for a right-skewed distribution (such as wealth), zero for a symmetric one, and negative for a left-skewed one. Table 2.11 shows the calculation for the wealth data (some rows are omitted for brevity).

Table 2.11 Calculation of the skewness of the wealth data

Range	Mid-point x	Frequency f	$x - \mu$	$(x - \mu)^3$	$f(x - \mu)^3$
0–	5.0	1668	−181.9	−6 016 132	−10 034 907 815
10 000–	17.5	1318	−169.4	−4 858 991	−6 404 150 553
:	:	:	:	:	:
1 000 000–	1 500.0	198	1 313.1	2 264 219 059	448 315 373 613
2 000 000–	3 000.0	88	2 813.1	22 262 154 853	1 959 069 627 104
Total		18 677	3 898.8	24 692 431 323	2 506 882 551 023

From this we obtain:

$$\frac{\sum f(x-\mu)^3}{N} = \frac{2\,506\,882\,551\,023}{18\,677} = 134\,222\,977.5$$

and dividing by Σ^3 gives $\dfrac{134\,222\,977.5}{22\,757\,714} = 5.898$ which is positive, as expected.

The measure of skewness is much less useful in practical work than measures of location and dispersion, and even knowing the value of the coefficient does not always give much idea of the shape of the distribution: two quite different distributions can share the same coefficient. In descriptive work, it is probably better to draw the histogram itself.

Comparison of the 2005 and 1979 distributions of wealth

Some useful lessons may be learned about these measures by comparing the 2005 distribution with its counterpart from 1979. This covers the period of Conservative government starting with Mrs Thatcher in 1979 and much of the following Labour administration. This shows how useful the various summary statistics are when it comes to comparing two different distributions. The wealth data for 1979 are given in Problem 2.1.5, where you are asked to confirm the following calculations.

Average wealth in 1979 was £16 399, about one-eleventh of its 2005 value. The average increased substantially therefore (at about 10% p.a., on average), but some of this was due to inflation rather than a real increase in the quantity of assets held. In fact, between 1979 and 2005 the retail price index rose from 52.0 to 217.9, i.e. it increased approximately four times. Thus the nominal[5] increase (i.e. in cash terms, before any adjustment for rising prices) in wealth is made up of two parts: (a) an inflationary part which more than quadrupled measured wealth and (b) a real part, consisting of a 2.75-fold increase (thus $4 \times 2.75 = 11$, approximately). It is likely that the extent of the real increase in wealth is overstated here due to the use of the retail price index rather than an index of asset prices. A substantial part of the increase in asset values over the period is probably due to the very rapid rise in house prices (houses form a significant part of the wealth of many households).

The standard deviation is similarly affected by inflation. The 1979 value is 25 552 compared to 2005's 283 385, which is about 11 times larger (as was the mean). The spread of the distribution appears to be about the same therefore (even if we take account of the general price effect). Looking at the coefficient of variation reveals a similar finding: the value has changed from 1.56 to 1.52, which is a modest difference. The spread of the distribution *relative to its mean* has not changed by much. This is confirmed by calculating the standard deviation of the logarithm: for 1979 this gives a figure of 1.310, almost identical to the 2005 figure (1.317).

The measure of skewness for the 1979 data comes out as 5.723, only slightly smaller than the 2005 figure (5.898). This suggests that the 1979 distribution is similarly skewed to the 2005 one. Again, these two figures can be directly com-

---

[5]This is a different meaning of the term 'nominal' from that used earlier to denote data measured on a nominal scale, i.e. data grouped into categories without an obvious ordering. Unfortunately, both meanings of the word are in common (statistical) usage, though it should be obvious from the context which use is meant.

pared because they do not depend upon the units in which wealth is measured. However, the relatively small difference is difficult to interpret in terms of how the shape of the distribution has changed.

The box and whiskers diagram

Having calculated these various summary statistics, we can now return to a useful graphical method of presentation. This is the box and whiskers diagram (sometimes called a box plot) which shows the median, quartiles and other aspects of a distribution on a single diagram. Figure 2.17 shows the box plot for the wealth data.

Wealth is measured on the vertical axis. The rectangular box stretches (vertically) from the first to third quartile and therefore encompasses the middle half of the distribution. The horizontal line through it is at the median and lies slightly less than halfway up the box. This tells us that there is a degree of skewness even within the central half of the distribution, though it does not appear very severe. The two 'whiskers' extend above and below the box as far as the highest and lowest observations, *excluding outliers*. An outlier is defined to be any observation which is more than 1.5 times the inter-quartile range (which is the same as the height of the box) above or below the box. Earlier we found the IQR to be 173 443 and the upper quartile to be 221 135, so an (upper) outlier lies beyond $221\,135 + 1.5 \times 173\,443 = 481\,300$. There are no outliers below the box as wealth cannot fall below zero. The top whisker is thus substantially longer than the bottom one, and indicates the extent of dispersion towards the tails of the distribution. The crosses indicate the outliers and in reality extend far beyond those shown in the diagram.

A simple diagram thus reveals a lot of information about the distribution.

Figure 2.17
Box plot of the wealth distribution

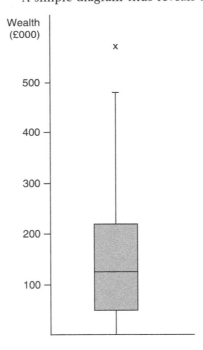

Other boxes and whiskers could be placed alongside in the same diagram (perhaps representing other countries), making comparisons straightforward. Some statistical software packages, such as SPSS and STATA, can generate box plots from the original data, without the need for the user to calculate the median, etc. However, spreadsheet packages do not yet have this useful facility.

Time-series data: investment expenditures 1977–2009

The data on the wealth distribution give a snapshot of the situation at particular points in time, and comparisons can be made between the 1979 and 2005 snapshots. Often, however, we wish to focus on the time-path of a variable and therefore we use **time-series data**. The techniques of presentation and summarising are slightly different than for cross-section data. As an example, we use data on investment in the United Kingdom for the period 1977–2009. These data are available from the Office of National Statistics (ONS) website. However, even after its recent redesign, it is almost impossible to find the data that you want. To save a lot of frustration, use the Econstats website (http://www.econstats.com/uk/index.htm), a U.S. site which aggregates economic data from around the world. The data series used is total gross fixed capital formation (series NPQX), which is measured in current prices (i.e. not adjusted for inflation). We will refer to this series simply as 'investment'.

Investment expenditure is important to the economy because it is one of the primary determinants of growth. Until recent years, the UK economy's growth record had been poor by international standards and lack of investment may have been a cause. The variable studied here is total gross (i.e. before depreciation is deducted) domestic fixed capital formation, measured in £m. The data are shown in Table 2.12.

It should be remembered that the data are in current prices so that the figures reflect price increases as well as changes in the volume of physical investment. The series in Table 2.12 thus shows the actual amount of cash that was spent each year on investment. The techniques used below for summarising the investment

Table 2.12 UK investment, 1977–2009 (£m)

Year	Investment	Year	Investment	Year	Investment
1977	28 351	1988	97 956	1999	161 722
1978	32 387	1989	113 478	2000	167 172
1979	38 548	1990	117 027	2001	171 782
1980	43 612	1991	107 838	2002	180 551
1981	43 746	1992	103 913	2003	186 700
1982	47 935	1993	103 997	2004	200 415
1983	52 099	1994	111 623	2005	209 758
1984	59 278	1995	121 364	2006	227 234
1985	65 181	1996	130 346	2007	249 517
1986	69 581	1997	138 307	2008	240 361
1987	80 344	1998	155 997	2009	204 270

Note: Time-series data consist of observations on one or more variables over several time periods. The observations can be daily, weekly, monthly, quarterly or, as here, annually.

Source: Data adapted from the Office for National Statistics licensed under the Open Government Licence(OGL) v.3.0. http://www.nationalarchives.gov.uk/doc/open-government-licence/open-government

Figure 2.18
Time-series graph of
investment in the United
Kingdom, 1977–2009

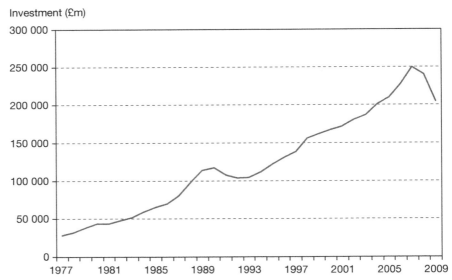

Note: The *X, Y* coordinates are the values {year, investment}; the first data point has the coordinates {1977, 28 351}, for example.

data could equally well be applied to a series showing the volume of investment.

First of all, we can use graphical techniques to gain an insight into the characteristics of investment. Figure 2.18 shows a **time-series graph** of investment. The graph plots the time periods on the horizontal axis and the investment variable on the vertical.

Plotting the data in this way brings out clearly some key features of the series:

● The **trend** in investment is upwards, with only a few years in which there was either no increase or a decrease.

● There is a 'hump' in the data in the late 1980s/early 1990s, before the series returns to its trend. Something unusual must have happened around that time. If we want to know what factors determine investment (or the effect of investment upon other economic magnitudes), we should get some useful insights from this period of the data.

● The trend is slightly **non-linear** – it follows an increasingly steep curve over time. This is essentially because investment grows by a *percentage* or *proportionate* amount each year. As we shall see shortly, it grows by about 6.2% each year. Therefore, as the level of investment increases each year, so does the increase in the level, giving a non-linear graph.

● The years 2008 and 2009 show a significant fall in investment, reflecting the financial crisis that occurred in 2008. Not only is investment below its 2007 level, it is substantially below what we might have expected, if the long-term trend had continued. Again, because of unusual movements in the data, we are likely to learn something about the causes and consequences of investment from what happened in these years.

● Successive values of the investment variable are similar in magnitude, i.e. the value in year *t* is similar to that in *t* − 1. Investment does not change from £40bn in one year to £10bn the next, and then back to £50bn, for instance. In fact, the value in one year appears to be based on the value in the previous year,

Table 2.13 The change in investment

Year	Δ Investment	Year	Δ Investment	Year	Δ Investment
1977	2 711	1988	17 612	1999	5 725
1978	4 036	1989	15 522	2000	5 450
1979	6 161	1990	3 549	2001	4 610
1980	5 064	1991	−9 189	2002	8 769
1981	134	1992	−3 925	2003	6 149
1982	4 189	1993	84	2004	13 715
1983	4 164	1994	7 626	2005	9 343
1984	7 179	1995	9 741	2006	17 476
1985	5 903	1996	8 982	2007	22 283
1986	4 400	1997	7 961	2008	−9 156
1987	10 763	1998	17 690	2009	−36 091

Note: The change in investment is obtained by taking the difference between successive observations. For example, 4036 is the difference between 32 387 and 28 351. The first figure of 2711 is obtained using the investment level for 1976 of 25 640 (not shown in Table 2.12).

plus (in general) 6.2% or so. We refer to this phenomenon of an observation being related to its previous value as serial correlation, and it is one of the aspects of the data that we might wish to investigate. The *ordering* of the data matters, unlike the case with cross-section data where the ordering is usually irrelevant. In deciding how to model investment behaviour, we might focus on *changes* in investment from year to year.

● The series seems 'smoother' in some periods than others. There appear to be two particular periods of volatility, where investment varies more widely around its trend, (i.e. has a greater variance around the trend). This is known as heteroscedasticity; a constant variance is termed homoscedasticity.

We may gain further insight into how investment evolves over time by focusing on the *change* in investment from year to year. If we denote investment in year t by I_t then the change in investment[6], ΔI_t is given by $I_t - I_{t-1}$. Table 2.13 shows the changes in investment each year, and Figure 2.19 provides a time-series graph.

Figure 2.19
Time-series graph of the change in investment

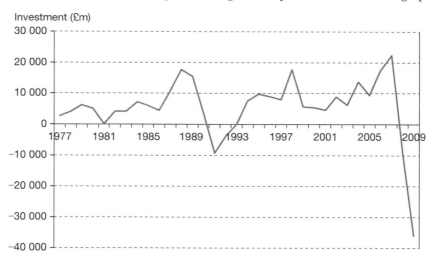

Investment (£m)

6The delta symbol, Δ, is often used to indicate the change in a variable.

This series is made up mainly of positive values, indicating that investment increases over time. It also shows that the increase tends to grow each year, although this may simply be a reflection of inflation rather than a genuine increase. The periods of volatility around 1990 and 2008 stand out as exceptions to this account, and both suggest large increases in investment before rapid and deep declines in the series.

Outliers

Graphing data also allows you to see outliers (unusual observations). Outliers might be due to an error in inputting the data (e.g. typing 97 instead of 970) or because something unusual happened (e.g. the investment figure for 2008). Either of these should be apparent from an appropriate graph. For example, the graph of the change in investment highlights the 2008 and 2009 figures. In the case of a straightforward error you should obviously correct it. If you are satisfied that the outlier is not simply a typo, you might want to think about the possible reasons for its existence and whether it distorts the descriptive picture you are trying to paint.

Another useful way of examining the data is to look at the logarithm of investment. This transformation has the effect of straightening out the non-linear investment series. Table 2.14 shows the transformed values, and Figure 2.20 graphs the series. In this case, we use the natural (base e) logarithm.

This new series is much smoother than the original one (as is usually the case when taking logs) and is helpful in showing the long-run trend, although it tends to mask some of the volatility of investment. Even the sharp fall in 2008–9 appears as a gentle downturn in this graph. The slope of this graph gives an approximation to the average rate of growth of investment over the period (expressed as a decimal). This is calculated as follows:

$$\text{slope} = \frac{\text{change in (ln) investment}}{\text{number of years}} = \frac{12.227 - 10.252}{32} = 0.062 \qquad (1.29)$$

i.e. 6.2% p.a. Note that although there are 33 observations, there are only 32 years of growth. Note also that this calculation uses the two end-points of the graph; hence it

Table 2.14 The logarithm of investment and the change in the logarithm

Year	ln Investment	Δ ln Investment	Year	ln Investment	Δ ln Investment	Year	ln Investment	Δ ln Investment
1977	10.252	0.101	1988	11.492	0.198	1999	11.994	0.036
1978	10.386	0.133	1989	11.639	0.147	2000	12.027	0.033
1979	10.560	0.174	1990	11.670	0.031	2001	12.054	0.027
1980	10.683	0.123	1991	11.588	−0.082	2002	12.104	0.050
1981	10.686	0.003	1992	11.551	−0.037	2003	12.137	0.033
1982	10.778	0.091	1993	11.552	0.001	2004	12.208	0.071
1983	10.861	0.083	1994	11.623	0.071	2005	12.254	0.046
1984	10.990	0.129	1995	11.707	0.084	2006	12.334	0.080
1985	11.085	0.095	1996	11.778	0.071	2007	12.427	0.094
1986	11.150	0.065	1997	11.837	0.059	2008	12.390	−0.037
1987	11.294	0.144	1998	11.958	0.120	2009	12.227	−0.163

Note: For 1977, 10.252 is the natural logarithm of 28 351, i.e. ln 28 351 = 10.252. The table also shows the changes in ln investment, calculated as the difference between successive values of the logarithm of investment.

Figure 2.20
Time-series graph of the logarithm of investment expenditures

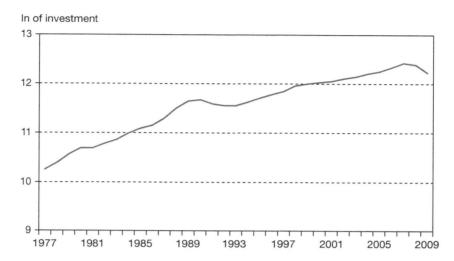

is sensitive to changes in these two observations. For example, if we measure the average growth rate from 1977 to 2007, we get 7.25% p.a. A further word of warning: you must use natural (base *e*) logarithms, not logarithms to the base 10, for this calculation to work. Remember also that the growth of the *volume* of investment will be less than 6.2% p.a. because part of it is due to price increases.

The logarithmic presentation is useful when comparing two different data series: when graphed in logs it is easy to see which is growing faster – just notice which series has the steeper slope.

A corollary of equation (1.29) is that the change in the natural logarithm of investment from one year to the next represents the *percentage* change in the data over that year. For example, the natural logarithm of investment in 1977 is 10.252, while in 1978 it is 10.386. The difference is 0.134, so the rate of growth is 13.4%.

Finally, we can graph the difference of the logarithm, as we graphed the difference of the level. This is shown in Figure 2.21 (the calculations are in Table 2.14) and presents the changes in *proportionate* terms.

Figure 2.21
Time-series graph of the difference of the logarithmic series

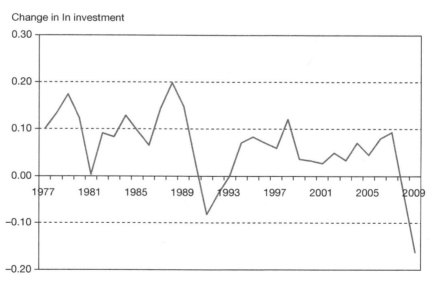

Figure 2.22
A multiple time-series
graph of investment

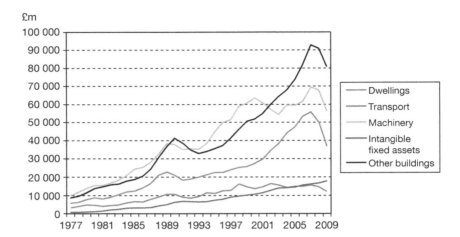

This is quite revealing. It shows the series fluctuating about the value of approximately 0.06 (the average calculated in equation (1.29)), with a slight downward trend (i.e. the growth of investment is slowing down). From the graph it is easy to read off that investment in 2009 fell by roughly 15% from its level in 2008, which was itself about 5% below the figure for 2007.

Graphing multiple series

Investment is made up of different categories: the table in Problem 2.1.14 presents investment data under five different headings: dwellings, transport, machinery, intangible fixed assets and other buildings. Together they make up total investment. It is often useful to show all of the series together on one graph. Figure 2.22 shows a **multiple time-series graph** of these investment data.

Construction of this type of graph is straightforward; it is just an extension of the technique for presenting a single series. The chart shows that all investment categories have increased over time in a fairly similar way, including the rise then fall in 2008, apart from the 'intangible fixed assets' category. This series includes items such as the value of patents held by a company, which is hard to measure, and the estimated values are likely not to vary much from year to year.

Other noticeable features of the graph are the particularly steep decline in investment in dwellings in 2008–9 and the fall in machinery investment around 2000 while other categories, particularly dwellings, continued to increase. It is difficult from the graph to tell which categories have increased most rapidly over time: the 1977 values are relatively small and hard to distinguish. In fact, it is the 'intangible fixed assets' category (the smallest one) which has increased fastest in proportionate terms. This is easier to observe with a few numerical calculations rather than trying to read a cramped graph.

Reading too much into a graph

It is possible to draw too many conclusions from a graph. Humans seem programmed to look for patterns and to find them, even when they are not there. In 1998, there was a small blip in investment in transport (see Figure 2.22). So what caused it? The answer is probably 'nothing'; it is just a random movement in the data. It is difficult to separate random movements from causal effects, and the temptation is often to favour the latter.

My belief, based on practical experience, is that you rarely get more than two or three genuine findings from a graph and they will be pretty obvious to see. If you have a list of 10, you have probably imagined most of them. For the investment graphs, the findings are (i) the general upward trend, (ii) the hump around 1990 and (iii) the steep decline in 2008. To find more subtle effects in the data you need to use more sophisticated methods, many of which are covered in later chapters.

One could also produce a multiple series graph of the logarithms of the variables and also of the change, as was done for the total investment series. Since the log transformation tends to squeeze the values (on the y-axis) closer together (compare Figures 2.18 and 2.20), it might be easier to see the relative rates of growth of the series using this method. This is left as an exercise for the reader.

Another complication arises when the series are of different orders of magnitude and it is difficult to make all the series visible on the chart. Some lie along the very bottom of the chart, others at the top. In this case you can chart some of the series against a second vertical scale, on the right-hand axis. An example is shown in Figure 2.23, plotting the (total) investment data with the interest rate, which has much smaller numerical values. If the same axis were used for both series, the interest rate would appear as a horizontal line coinciding with the x-axis. This would reveal no useful information to the viewer.

It would usually be inappropriate to use this technique on data such as the investment categories graphed in Figure 2.22. Those are directly comparable to each other and to magnify one of the series by plotting it on a separate axis risks distorting the message for the reader. However, investment and interest rates are measured in inherently different ways and one cannot directly compare their sizes; hence it is acceptable to use separate axes. The graph allows one to observe the *movements* of the series together and hence perhaps infer something about the relationship between them. The rising investment and falling interest rate suggest an inverse relationship between them.

Figure 2.23
Time-series graph using two vertical scales: investment (LH scale) and the interest rate (RH scale), 1985–2005

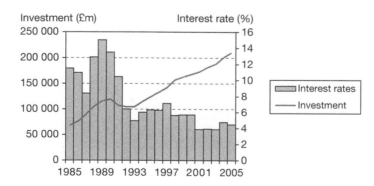

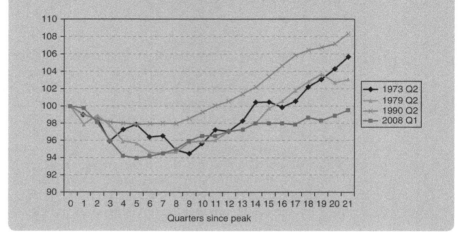

Overlapping the ranges of the data series

The graph below provides a nice example of how to compare different time periods on a single chart. The aim is to compare the recessions starting in 1973Q2, 1979Q2, 1990Q2 and 2008Q1 and the subsequent recoveries of real gross domestic product (GDP). Instead of plotting time on the horizontal axis, the number of quarters since the start of each recession is used, so that the series overlap. To aid comparison, all the series have been set to a value of 100 in the initial quarter. From this, one can see that the most recent recession, starting in 2008, was deeper and longer lasting than the earlier ones.

The investment categories may also be illustrated by means of an area graph, which plots the four series stacked one on top of the other, as illustrated in Figure 2.24.

This shows, for example, the 'dwellings' and 'machinery' categories each take up about one quarter of total investment. This is easier to see from the area graph than from the multiple series graph in Figure 2.22.

Figure 2.24
Area graph of investment categories, 1977–2009

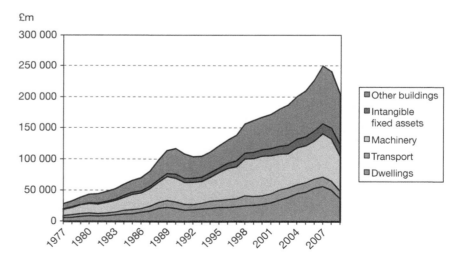

'Chart junk'

With modern computer software it is easy to get carried away and produce a chart that actually hides more than it reveals. There is a great temptation to add some 3-D effects, liven it up with a bit of colour, rotate and tilt the viewpoint, etc. This sort of stuff is generally known as 'chart junk'. As an example, look at Figure 2.25 which is an alternative to the area graph in Figure 2.24. It was fun to create, but it doesn't get the message across at all. Taste is, of course, personal, but moderation is usually an essential part of it.

Figure 2.25
Over-the-top graph of investment

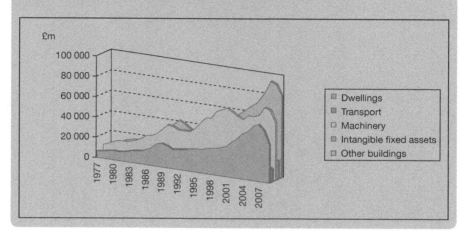

Exercise 2.5

Given the following data:

	1990	1991	1992	1993	1994	1995	1996	1997	1998	1999
Profit	50	60	25	−10	10	45	60	50	20	40
Sales	300	290	280	255	260	285	300	310	300	330

(a) Draw a multiple time-series graph of the two variables. Label both axes appropriately and provide a title for the graph.

(b) Adjust the graph by using the right-hand axis to measure profits, the left hand axis sales. What difference does this make?

Improving the presentation of graphs – example 2: time series

Earlier we showed how a bar chart might be improved. Here we look at a slightly curious presentation of time-series data, taken from the Office for National Statistics[7] and relating to the importance of the EU to UK trade. This chart shows the GDP of various

[7] See http://www.ons.gov.uk/ons/rel/international-transactions/outward-foreign-affiliates-statistics/how-important-is-the-european-union-to-uk-trade-and-investment-/sty-eu.html. This is the author's rendition, so the colours do not quite match the more vivid original.

countries or groups of countries, separated into EU and non-EU territories, from 1993 to 2013.

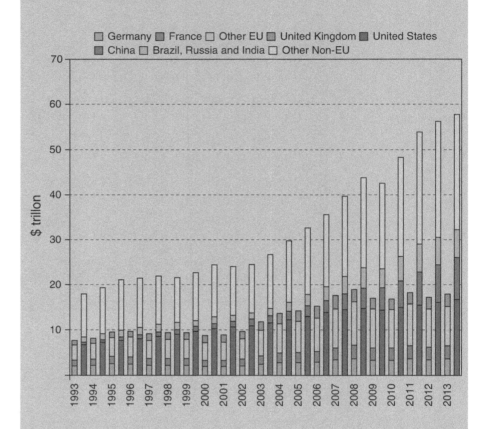

It actually takes a while to interpret this graph; it is not at all intuitive. Among the reasons are:

1. A bar chart is used to present time-series data.
2. There are actually two time series presented, summarised in the two sets of bars, one for EU countries, one for the rest.
3. The colours give information about individual countries, but it is difficult to go from the colour to the legend, and then back again to see the pattern. The author seems to have just used the Excel defaults for this type of graph.

How could this be improved? It presents a lot of information, so the answer is not immediately obvious. It helps to focus on what messages are being conveyed. From the text of the ONS document these are:

1. EU combined GDP is larger than that of any individual country, surpassing the USA in 2003, and
2. EU growth has been slower than non-EU growth.

We therefore do not need all of the information in the original graph; for example, nothing is said about individual EU economies. Hence, a better version of the chart would be as follows:

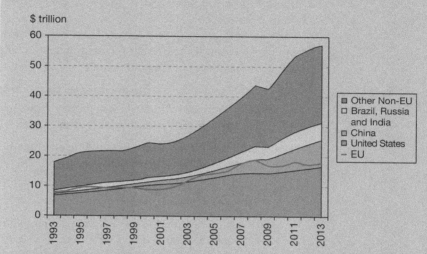

Now it is much easier to see the relevant features. The EU (blue line) overtakes the United States in 2003 (though it was also bigger pre-1999, hard to see from the original chart) and EU growth is slower than all non-EU territories, principally since 2008. One can also see the rapid growth of China, again difficult to see in the initial chart. The legend is put on the right-hand side, and it is very easy to match up the colours to the associated country or region.

This revised chart is what Excel calls a 'combo' chart, which shows two different types of chart in the same picture. The non-EU territories make up an area graph (hence filled with colour), while the EU is a line chart.

Numerical summary statistics

The graphs have revealed quite a lot about the data already, but we can also calculate numerical descriptive statistics as we did for the cross-section data. First, we consider the mean, and then the variance and standard deviation.

The mean of a time series

We could calculate the mean of investment itself, but this would not be very informative. Because the series is trended over time, it passes through the mean at some point between 1977 and 2005 but never returns to it. The mean of the series is actually £123.1bn, achieved in 1995–6, but this is not very informative since it tells nothing about its value today, for instance. The problem is that the variable is trended, so that the mean is not typical of the series. The annual increase in investment is also trended (though much less so), so it is subject to similar criticism (see Figure 2.19).

It is better in this case to calculate the average growth rate, since this is less likely to have a trend and hence more likely to be representative of the whole time period. The average growth rate of investment spending was calculated in equation (1.29) as 6.2% p.a. by measuring the slope of the graph of the log investment series, but this is only one way of measuring the growth rate. Furthermore, different methods give slightly different answers, although this is rarely important in practice.

The growth rate may be calculated based upon annual compounding or continuous compounding principles. The former is probably the more common and simpler method, so we explain this first.

Calculating the growth rate based upon annual compounding

This method likens growth to the way money grows in a savings account as interest is added annually. We can calculate the growth rate in the following way:

(1) Calculate the overall **growth factor** of the series, i.e. x_T/x_1 where x_T is the final observation and x_1 is the initial observation. This is:

$$\frac{x_T}{x_1} = \frac{204\,270}{28\,351} = 7.2050,$$

i.e. investment expenditure is 7.2 times larger in 2009 than in 1977.

(2) To get the annual figure, take the $T-1$ root of the growth factor, where T is the number of observations. Since $T = 33$ we calculate $\sqrt[32]{7.205} = 1.0637$ (This can be performed on a scientific calculator by raising 7.205 to the power $7.205^{(1/32)} = 1.0637$.)

(3) Subtract 1 from the result in the previous step, giving the growth rate as a decimal. In this case we have $1.0637 - 1 = 0.0637$.

Thus the average growth rate of investment is 6.4% p.a., slightly different from the 6.2% calculated earlier (which, as we will see, is based on continuous compounding). The difference is small in practical terms, and neither is definitively the right answer. Both are estimates of the true growth rate. To emphasise this issue, note that since the calculated growth rate is based only upon the initial and final observations, it could be unreliable if either of these two values is an outlier (as in this case, the 2009 value). For example, if the growth rate is measured from 1977 to 2007, then the answer is 7.0%. With a sufficient span of time, however, such outliers are unlikely to be a serious problem.

The power of compound growth

The *Economist* provided some amusing and interesting examples of how a $1 investment can grow over time. They assumed that an investor (they named her Felicity Foresight, for reasons that become obvious) started with $1 in 1900 and had the foresight or luck to invest, each year, in the best performing asset of the year. Sometimes she invested in equities, some years in gold and so on. By the end of the century she had amassed $9.6 quintillion ($9.6 \times 10^{18}$, more than world GDP, so impossible in practice). This is equivalent to an average annual growth rate of 55%. In contrast, Henry Hindsight did the same, but invested in the *previous year's* best asset. This might be thought more realistic. Unfortunately, his $1 turned into only $783, a still respectable annual growth rate of 6.9%. This, however, is beaten by the strategy of investing in the previous year's *worst* performing asset (what goes down must come up . . .). This turned $1 into $1730, a return of 7.7%. Food for thought!

Source: Based on *The Economist*, 12 February 2000, p. 111.

The geometric mean

In calculating the average growth rate of investment we have implicitly calculated the geometric mean of a series. If we have a series of n values, then their geometric mean is calculated as the nth root of the *product* of the values, i.e.

$$\textit{geometric mean} = \sqrt[n]{\prod_{i=1}^{n} x_i} \qquad (1.30)$$

The x values in this case are the growth factors in each year, as in Table 2.15 (the values in intermediate years are omitted). The '$\prod$' symbol is similar to the use of Σ, but means 'multiply together' rather than 'add up'.

The product of the 32 growth factors is 7.205 (the same as is obtained by dividing the final observation by the initial one – why?) and the 32nd root of this is 1.0637. This latter figure, 1.0637, is the geometric mean of the growth factors, and from it we can derive the growth rate of 6.37% p.a. by subtracting 1.

Whenever one is dealing with growth data (or any series that is based on a multiplicative process), one should ideally use the geometric mean rather than the arithmetic mean to get the answer. However, using the arithmetic mean in this case generally gives a similar answer, as long as the growth rate is reasonably small. If we take the arithmetic mean of the growth factors, we obtain:

$$\frac{1.142 + 1.190 + \cdots + 0.963 + 0.850}{32} = 1.0664$$

giving an estimate of the growth rate of $1.0664 - 1 = 0.0664 = 6.64\%$ p.a. – close to the correct value. Equivalently, one could take the average of the annual growth rates (0.142, 0.190, etc.), giving 0.0664, to get the same result. Use of the arithmetic mean is justified in this context if one needs only an approximation to the right answer and annual growth rates are reasonably small. It is usually quicker and easier to calculate the arithmetic rather than geometric mean, especially if one does not use a computer.

Table 2.15 Calculation of the geometric mean – annual growth factors

	Investment	Growth factors	
1977	28351		
1978	32387	1.142	(= 32387/28351)
1979	38548	1.190	(= 38548/32387)
1980	43612	1.131	etc.
2006	227234	1.083	
2007	249517	1.098	
2008	240361	0.963	
2009	204270	0.850	

Note: Each growth factor simply shows the ratio of that year's investment to the previous year's.

Calculating the growth rate based upon continuous compounding

This method is based upon the idea that growth is a continuous process, according to an equation such as

$$x_T = x_1 e^{g(T-1)}$$

Obtaining the growth rate g as the subject of this equation requires a little mathematics. Taking natural logs:

$$\ln x_T - \ln x_1 \times g(T-1)$$

and hence

$$g = \frac{\ln x_T - \ln x_1}{T-1}$$

This is what was calculated earlier (equation 1.29) when we found the slope of the graph of the logarithm of investment. That calculation gave a result of 6.2% p.a. The continuous method will always provide a slightly smaller estimate of the growth rate than the annual compounding method.

To conclude this section we note that the two methods' results are related and that one can be derived from the other. If we start with the continuous method estimate of 0.062 we can obtain:

$$e^{0.062} - 1 = 0.064$$

which gives the result calculated by the annual compounding method.

Compound interest

The calculations we have performed relating to growth rates are analogous to computing compound interest. If we invest £100 at a rate of interest of 10% p.a., then the investment will grow at 10% p.a. (assuming all the interest is reinvested). Thus after one year the total will have grown to £100 $\times$ 1.1(£110), after two years to £100 $\times$ 1.1^2(£121) and after t years to £100 $\times$ 1.1^t. The general formula for the terminal value S_t of a sum S_0 invested for t years at a rate of interest r is

$$S_t = S_0(1+r)^t \tag{1.31}$$

where r is expressed as a decimal. Rearranging (1.31) to make r the subject yields

$$r = \sqrt[t]{S_t/S_0} - 1 \tag{1.32}$$

which is precisely the formula for the average growth rate. To give a further example: suppose an investment fund turns an initial deposit of £8000 into £13 500 over 12 years. What is the average rate of return on the investment? Setting $S_0 = 8$, $S_t = 13.5$, $t = 12$ and using (1.32), we obtain

$$r = \sqrt[12]{13.5/8} - 1 = 0.045$$

or 4.5% p.a.

Formula (1.32) can also be used to calculate the depreciation rate and the amount of annual depreciation on a firm's assets. In this case, S_0 represents the initial value of the asset, S_t represents the final or scrap value and the annual rate of depreciation (as a negative number) is given by r from equation (1.32).

The variance of a time series

How should we interpret the variance of a time series? For cross-section data (wealth), the variance measured the spread of the distribution, comparing richer with poorer. But the spread of investment values is conceptually different. The variance of the investment data can be calculated, but it would be uninformative in the same way as the mean. Since the series is trended, and this is likely to continue in the longer run, the variance is in principle equal to infinity. The calculated variance would be closely tied to the sample size: the larger it is, the larger the variance.

We can use the variance, however, to measure the volatility of a time series, how much it varies from year to year around the (growing) mean value. For this, it makes sense to calculate the variance of the growth rate, which has little trend in the long run.

This variance can be calculated from the formula:

$$s^2 = \frac{\sum (x - \bar{x})^2}{n - 1} = \frac{\sum x^2 - n\bar{x}^2}{n - 1} \tag{1.33}$$

Where x is the rate of growth and $\bar{x}$ is its average value. The calculation is set out in Table 2.16 using the right-hand formula in (1.33).

The variance is therefore

$$s^2 = \frac{0.3230 - 32 \times 0.0664^2}{31} = 0.0059$$

and the standard deviation is 0.0766, the square root of the variance. The coefficient of variation is

$$cv = \frac{0.0766}{0.0664} = 1.15$$

i.e. the standard deviation of the growth rate is about 115% of the mean.

Note three things about this calculation: first, we have used the arithmetic mean (using the geometric mean makes very little difference); second, we have used the formula for the sample variance since the period 1977 to 2005 constitutes a sample of all the possible data we could collect and third, we could have equally used the growth factors for the calculation of the variance (why?).

Table 2.16 Calculation of the variance of the growth rate

Year	Investment	Growth rate, x	x^2
1978	32 387	0.142	0.020
1979	38 548	0.190	0.036
1980	43 612	0.131	0.017
:	:	:	:
2006	227 234	0.083	0.007
2007	249 517	0.098	0.010
2008	240 361	−0.037	0.001
2009	204 270	−0.150	0.023
Totals		2.1253	0.3230

Worked example 2.7

Given the following data:

Year	1999	2000	2001	2002	2003
Price of a laptop PC	1100	900	800	750	700

we can work out the average rate of price growth p.a. as follows. The overall growth factor is $\frac{700}{1100} = 0.6363$. The fact that this number is less than one simply reflects the fact that the price has fallen over time. It has fallen to 64% of its original value. To find the annual rate, we take the fourth root of 0.6363 (four years of growth). Hence, we get $\sqrt[4]{0.6363} = 0.893$, i.e. each year the price falls to 89% of its value the previous year. This implies price is falling at $0.893 - 1 = -0.107$, or approximately an 11% fall each year.

We can see if the fall is more or less the same by calculating each year's growth factor. These are:

Year	1999	2000	2001	2002	2003
Laptop price	1100	900	800	750	700
Growth factor		0.818	0.889	0.9375	0.933
Price fall		−19	−11	−6	−7

The price fall was larger in the earlier years, in percentage as well as in absolute terms. Calculating the standard deviation of the values in the final row provides a measure of the variability from year to year. The variance is given by

$$s^2 = \frac{(19 - 11)^2 + (11 - 11)^2 + (6 - 11)^2 + (7 - 11)^2}{3} = 30.7.$$

The standard deviation is then 5.54%. (The calculations are shown rounded, but the answer is accurate.)

Exercise 2.6

(a) Using the data in Exercise 2.5, calculate the average level of profit over the time period and the average growth rate of profit over the time period. Which appears more useful?

(b) Calculate the variance of profit and compare it to the variance of sales.

Graphing bivariate data: the scatter diagram

The analysis of investment is an example of the use of univariate methods: only a single variable is involved. However, we often wish to examine the relationship between two (or sometimes more) variables and have to use bivariate (or multivariate) methods. To illustrate the methods involved we shall examine the relationship between investment expenditures and gross domestic product

Table 2.17 GDP data (£m)

Year	GDP	Year	GDP	Year	GDP
1977	146 973	1988	478 510	1999	928 730
1978	169 344	1989	525 274	2000	976 533
1979	199 220	1990	570 283	2001	1 021 828
1980	233 184	1991	598 664	2002	1 075 564
1981	256 279	1992	622 080	2003	1 139 746
1982	281 024	1993	654 196	2004	1 202 956
1983	307 207	1994	692 987	2005	1 254 058
1984	329 913	1995	733 266	2006	1 328 363
1985	361 758	1996	781 726	2007	1 404 845
1986	389 149	1997	830 094	2008	1 445 580
1987	428 665	1998	879 102	2009	1 394 989

(GDP). Economics tells us to expect a positive relationship between these variables; higher GDP is usually associated with higher investment. Table 2.17 provides data on GDP for the United Kingdom.

A scatter diagram (also called an *XY* chart) plots one variable (in this case investment) on the *y*-axis, the other (GDP) on the *x*-axis, and therefore shows the relationship between them. For example, one can see whether high values of one variable tend to be associated with high values of the other. Figure 2.26 shows the relationship for investment and GDP.

The chart shows a strong linear relationship between the two variables, apart from a dip in the middle. This reflects the sharp fall in investment after 1990 which is *not* matched by a fall in GDP (if it were, the *XY* chart would show a linear relationship without the dip). It is important to recognise the difference between the time-series plot and the *XY* chart. The sharp fall in investment in 2008 which we noted earlier is matched by a similar fall in GDP; hence the *XY* chart does not reveal this.

Figure 2.26
Scatter diagram of investment (vertical axis) against GDP (horizontal axis) (nominal values)

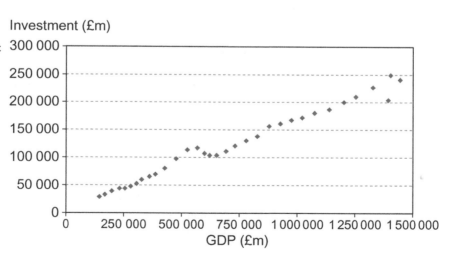

Note: The (*x*, *y*) coordinates of each point are given by the values of investment and GDP, respectively. Thus the first (1977) data point is drawn 28 351 units above the horizontal axis and 146 973 units from the vertical one.

Figure 2.27
The relationship
between real
investment and
real output

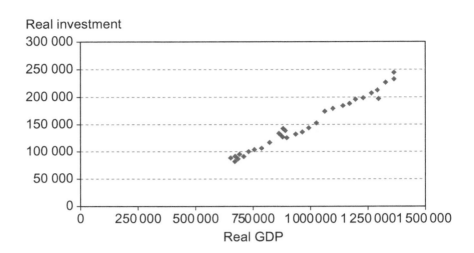

Because of inflation and growth, later observations tend to be towards the top right of the *XY* chart (both investment and GDP are increasing over time) but this does not *have* to happen; if both variables fluctuated up and down, later observations could be at the bottom left (or centre, or anywhere). By contrast, in a time-series plot, later observations are always further to the right.

Note that both variables are in nominal terms, i.e. they make no correction for inflation over the time period. This may be seen algebraically: investment expenditure is made up of the *volume* of investment (I) times its *price* (P_I). Similarly, nominal GDP is real GDP (Y) times its price (P_Y). Thus the scatter diagram actually charts $P_I \times I$ against $P_Y \times Y$. It is likely that the two prices follow a similar trend over time and that this might dominate the movements in real investment and GDP. The chart then shows the relationship between a mixture of prices and quantities, when the more interesting relationship is between the quantities of investment and output.

Figure 2.27 shows the relationship between the quantities of investment and output, i.e. after the strongly trending price effects have been removed. It is not so straightforward as the nominal graph. There is now a 'knot' of points in the centre where perhaps both (real) investment and GDP fluctuated up and down. Overall, it is clear that something 'interesting' happened around 1990 that merits additional investigation.

Exercise 2.7

(a) Once again using the data from Exercise 2.5, draw an *XY* chart with profits on the vertical axis and sales on the horizontal axis. Choose the scale of the axes appropriately.

(b) If using Excel to produce graphs, right click on the graph, choose 'Add trendline' and choose a linear trend. This gives the 'line of best fit'. What does this appear to show?

Improving graphs – scatter plot example

Our third example of how to improve a graph starts with the following picture. You might want to look at it for a few moments and think how you might better present the data before reading on. The picture looks at life satisfaction and GDP across some OECD countries.

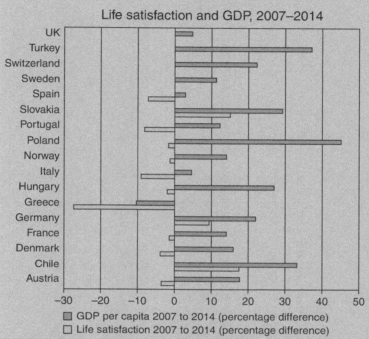

Source: adapted from http://www.ons.gov.uk/ons/dcp171766_406995.pdf, Figure 2.

The chart presents two data series, for life satisfaction and for GDP, and one can try to draw conclusions from it. GDP has grown in most countries (exception: Greece), but life satisfaction more often goes down rather than up. It is difficult to see if or how growth of GDP relates to increased satisfaction. Sometimes the bars are in the same direction (for a country), sometimes opposed. The *Guardian* turned this into an interactive info-graphic[8] which allowed you to see *either* GDP *or* satisfaction but not both together. This is terrible.

Since there are two variables, this really cries out for a scatter plot, as shown here.

_____
[8]http://www.theguardian.com/news/datablog/2015/jul/01/greece-life-satisfaction-rating-oecd-countries

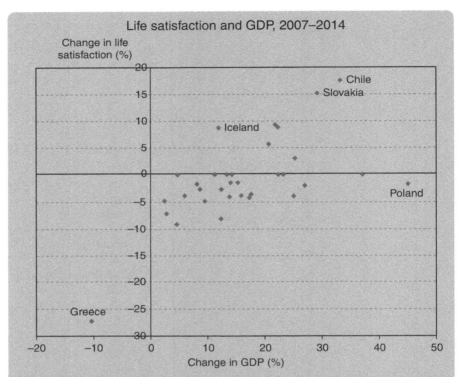

Now one can see a lot more, more clearly (and the scatter plot actually shows more countries). There seems to be a positive relation between the variables, and below about 20% growth (over seven years, so 2.6% p.a.) satisfaction generally falls. The exception to this is Iceland, recovering from its severe banking crisis. Chile and Slovakia show the greatest increase in life satisfaction and contrast with Poland which has even higher GDP growth, yet a fall in satisfaction.

One piece of information that is missing from the improved version is the country names, apart from a selected few. However, the aim is to show the general relationship so these are not all needed. One can add individual labels (as shown) if one wants to comment upon a particular country.

Data transformations

In analysing employment and investment data in the examples above, we have often changed the variables in some way in order to bring out the important characteristics. In statistics, one usually works with data that have been transformed in some way rather than using the original numbers. It is therefore worth summarising the main data transformations available, providing justifications for their use and exploring the implications of such adjustments to the original data. We briefly deal with the following transformations:

- rounding
- grouping
- dividing or multiplying by a constant

- differencing
- taking logarithms
- taking the reciprocal
- deflating.

Rounding

Rounding improves readability. Too much detail can confuse the message, so rounding the answer makes it more memorable. To give an example, the average wealth holding calculated earlier in this chapter is actually £186 875.766 (to three decimal places). It would be absurd to present it in this form, however. We do not know for certain that this figure is accurate (in fact, it almost certainly is not). There is a spurious degree of precision which might mislead the reader. How much should this be rounded for presentational purposes? Remember that the figures have already been effectively rounded by allocation to classes of width 10 000 or more (all observations have been rounded to the mid-point of the interval). However, much of this rounding is offsetting, i.e. numbers rounded up offset those rounded down, so the class mean is reasonably accurate. Rounding to £187 000 makes the figure much easier to remember, and is only a change of 0.07% (187 000/186 874.766 = 1.00067), so is a reasonable compromise. In a report, it might be best to use the figure of £187 000 therefore. In the text above, the answer was not rounded to such an extent since the purpose was to highlight the methods of calculation.

Inflation in Zimbabwe

'Zimbabwe's rate of inflation surged to 3731.9%, driven by higher energy and food costs, and amplified by a drop in its currency, official figures show.'
BBC news online, 17 May 2007.

Whether official or not, it is impossible that the rate of inflation is known with such accuracy (to one decimal place), especially when prices are rising so fast. It would be more reasonable to report a figure of 3700% in this case. Sad to say, inflation rose even further in subsequent months.

Rounding is a 'trapdoor' function: you cannot obtain the original value from the transformed (rounded) value. Therefore, if you are going to need the original value in further calculations, you should not round your answer. Furthermore, small rounding errors can cumulate, leading to a large error in the final answer. Therefore, you should *never* round an intermediate answer, only the final one. Even if you only round the intermediate answer by a small amount, the final answer could be grossly inaccurate. Try the following: calculate $60.29 \times 30.37 - 1831$ both before and after rounding the first two numbers to integers. In the first case you get 0.0073, and in the second −31.

Grouping

When there is too much data to present easily, grouping solves the problem, although at the cost of hiding some of the information. The examples relating to education and unemployment and to wealth used grouped data. Using the raw data would have given us far too much information, so grouping is a first stage in data analysis. Grouping is another trapdoor transformation: once it's done you cannot recover the original information (unless you have access to the raw data, of course).

Dividing/multiplying by a constant

This transformation is carried out to make numbers more readable or to make calculation simpler by removing trailing zeros. The data on wealth were divided by 1000 to ease calculation; otherwise the fx^2 column would have contained extremely large values. Some summary statistics (e.g. the mean) will be affected by the transformation, but not all (e.g. the coefficient of variation). Try to remember which are affected. E and V operators (see Appendix 2B) can help. The transformation is easy to reverse.

Differencing

In time-series data there may be a trend, and it is better to describe the features of the data relative to the trend. The result may also be more economically meaningful, e.g. governments are often more concerned about the growth of output than about its level. Differencing is one way of eliminating the trend. Differencing was used for the investment data for both of these reasons. One of the implications of differencing is that information about the *level* of the variable is lost.

Taking logarithms

Taking logarithms is used to linearise a non-linear series, in particular one that is growing at a fairly constant rate. It is often easier to see the important features of such a series if the logarithm is graphed rather than the raw data. The logarithmic transformation is also useful in regression because it yields estimates of **elasticities** (e.g. of demand). Taking the logarithm of the investment data linearised the series and tended to smooth it. The inverses of the logarithmic transformations are 10^x (for common logarithms) and e^x (for natural logarithms) so one can recover the original data.

Taking the reciprocal

The reciprocal of a variable might have a useful interpretation and provide a more intuitive explanation of a phenomenon. The reciprocal transformation will also turn a linear series into a non-linear one. The reciprocal of turnover in the labour market (i.e. the number leaving unemployment divided by the number unemployed) gives an idea of the duration of unemployment. If one-half of those unemployed find work each year (turnover = 0.5), then the average duration of unemployment is two years (=1/0.5). If a graph of turnover shows a linear decline over time, then the average duration of unemployment will be rising, at a faster and faster rate. Repeating the reciprocal transformation recovers the original data.

Deflating

Deflating turns a nominal series into a real one, i.e. one that reflects changes in quantities without the contamination of price changes. It is often more meaningful in economic terms to talk about a real variable than a nominal one. Consumers are more concerned about their real income than about their money income, for example.

Confusing real and nominal variables is dangerous. For example, someone's nominal (money) income may be rising yet their real income falling (if prices are rising faster than money income). It is important to know which series you are dealing with (this is a common failing among students new to statistics). An income series that is growing at 2 to 3 p.a. is probably a real series; one that is growing at 10% p.a. or more is likely to be nominal.

The information and data explosion

Recent developments in technology, especially those relating to the web, have led to a huge increase in data availability. Data files can now have tags allowing other websites to query the data, provide 'mashups' and exhibit the data in new ways. This is leading to a democratisation of data – anyone can now obtain them, draw graphs, interpret them and so on. Most of the data manipulation is done behind the scenes; the user does not need to have any understanding of the formulae nor of the calculations involved. This has some implications for those producing and using statistics, which we consider here.

First, however, we take a look at some examples of such 'data visualisation'. One of the most striking is Gapminder (www.gapminder.org), a site which allows you to construct interactive graphs of many variables. It is innovative in that it provides an enormous amount of information in each graph. Figure 2.28 shows a graph of CO_2 emissions against real GDP (an XY chart) for countries around the world in 1950.

As well as the two main variables, note the additional features:

- The data points are coloured bubbles. The colour represents the region and the size of the bubble represents the total emissions of the country (the variable on the y-axis is emissions *per capita*). Hence, we actually have four variables represented on the chart.
- Much of the graph can be customised. The axes can be linear or log scale (note that Gapminder has chosen a linear scale for emissions graphed against the log of income). The size of the bubble can be changed to represent alternative variables, e.g. an index of urbanisation.
- By hovering the cursor over a bubble, the country name is revealed (here, the United States) and the values for that observation are shown on the axes.
- By 'playing' the graph or using the slider, one can go forward through time to see the changes in a most vivid way. Unfortunately, this cannot be replicated in this text, but Figure 2.29 is the same graph for 2008.

The new graph shows how total emissions have grown (note China in particular) over the time period. A good feature of Gapminder is that the underlying data can be downloaded so that you can carry out your own further analysis if you wish to.

Figure 2.28
CO$_2$ emissions versus real
GDP in 1950

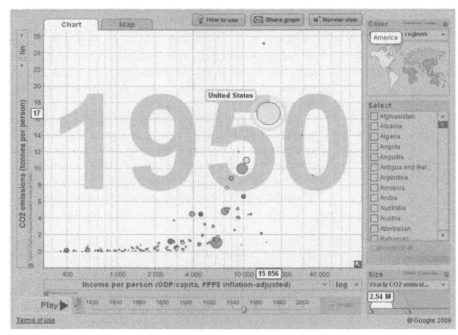

Source: From www.gapminder.org, Visualization formGapminder World, powered by Trendalyzer from www.gapminder.org.

Figure 2.29
CO$_2$ emissions versus real
GDP in 2008

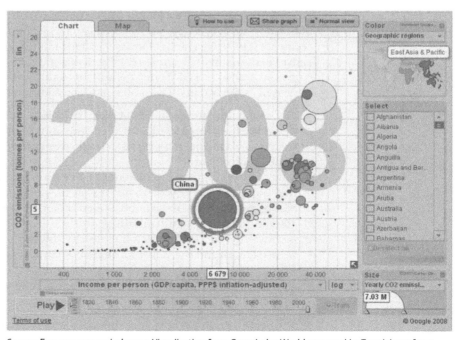

Source: From www.gapminder.org, Visualization from Gapminder World, powered by Trendalyzer from www.gapminder.org.

Google (of course) is another company developing such tools, such as Trends, Correlate and Fusion Tables. Some of these are still in beta, so will no doubt have developed by the time you read this. To locate them, use Google.

Another interesting example is the Mayor of London's Datastore (data.london. gov.uk/) which aims to open up London's data to the public, for free. It contains a multitude of data, some of it from other sites, and unlike Gapminder it only provides the data, with the idea being that other companies will create websites, mobile apps, and so forth that will interpret the data for you.

Sites such as Yahoo Finance (http://uk.finance.yahoo.com/) or Google Finance (http://www.google.co.uk/finance) allow you to examine a large amount of financial data and draw graphs of the data simply by selecting from a few menus.

Another development is 'data mining', which uses artificial intelligence techniques to 'mine' large databases of information, looking for trends and other features. For example, it is used by supermarkets to analyse their sales data with a view to spotting spending patterns and exploit them. Not only does one not need to perform calculations on the data, one does not even need to know what questions to ask of it.

Do these developments mean that there is less need to study statistics? Obviously, I am unlikely to answer 'yes' to this! The interpretation of the results still requires human judgement, aided by statistical tests to ensure one is not just observing random variations. Furthermore, the use of pictures (which many of such sites rely on) can be highly informative but it is difficult to convey that to another person without the picture. One can look at a graph of CO_2 emissions, but to convey the trend it is easier to pass on the average growth rate of those emissions. Looking at the Gapminder graphs above, how would you convey to another person (without showing them the graphs) how fast US emissions have risen? (The answer is only 0.2% p.a., somewhat surprisingly. China's have risen by 6.4% p.a.)

Easy access to such data also means it will be used indiscriminately by those unaware of its shortcomings, unsure how to correctly interpret them and eager to use them for support rather than illumination. It is all the more important, therefore, that more people are trained to understand and not be misled by statistics.

Writing statistical reports

This text presents most of the results of statistical analyses in a fairly formal way, since the aim is exposition and explanation of the methods. However, more often you might be writing or reading a short statistical report which requires a punchier and more concise presentation. This will attract attention, but it is important to maintain the accuracy of what is said.

Here is some advice on writing such a report, organised in sections on writing, graphs and tables. I have drawn on two excellent documents of the UN Economic Commission for Europe[9] on 'making data meaningful', and I recommend that you go to those sources.

---

[9]UNECE, *Making Data Meaningful*, parts 1 and 2, available at http://www.unece.org/stats/documents/writing/.

Writing

In a report, you should put the most important facts first, less important and supporting material afterwards. This is known as the 'inverted pyramid'. The opening paragraph should be concise and tell the story, making little use of numbers if possible.

Each paragraph should focus on one or two main points, explained using short sentences. Aim to avoid jargon, so-called elevator statistics (". . . this went up, that went down . . ."), acronyms and making the reader refer to tables in order to understand the point. The text should provide interpretation and context rather than repeating values which are in tables.

Break up the text with sub-headings, which should include a verb (to encourage you to make a point with the heading). For example, "More Britons finding work" is better than "Employment trends in Britain". Once you have completed the story, write the headline with the aim of catching the reader's attention.

As an example, consider the discussion earlier on the comparison of 1979 and 2005 wealth distributions in the United Kingdom. That was written in textbook style for the purpose of learning, but in a report might be better presented as follows.

Britons becoming wealthier but inequality persists

In 2005 the average Briton had wealth of around £187,000, about 11 times greater than in 1979. Adjusting for inflation, wealth has grown by nearly three times, or an average of 4% p.a. Despite this, the gap between rich and poor has remained much the same, with someone in the top 10% of the distribution owning 25 times more wealth than someone in the bottom 10%.

Tables

Tables in a report should be simple, sometimes called presentation tables, in contrast to reference tables which are best kept to an appendix. Many of the tables in this text are reference tables, such as the table calculating average wealth, Table 2.6. These are generally too complex to put into the text of a report and would have to be simplified in some way, according to the point that is being made.

Tables should be comprehensible in themselves, without the reader needing to look for further information. One way to ensure this is to ask if the table could be cut and pasted into another document and still make sense. Hence the table needs at least an informative title.

Another useful tip is to order the categories in a table according to frequency where this is appropriate. Consider the table used in Exercise 2.1(b) earlier, on tourist destinations. There is no natural ordering of the four countries, so why not order the countries by the number of tourists, as follows?

Tourists (millions) visiting European countries, 2013

	France	Spain	Italy	Germany
All tourists	12.4	9.8	7.5	3.2
English tourists	2.7	3.6	1.0	0.2
Non-English tourists	9.7	6.2	6.5	3.0

Note the difference in presentation from the exercise and how this makes it easier to read the table. In presentation tables it is important to keep decimal places as small as possible (also aligning the numbers properly) to aid readability. In this text, we often use more decimal places so that you can follow calculation of various statistics. This is not necessary for presentation tables.

Graphs

Much advice has already been given about drawing graphs already, but there are some additional points relevant to a report. Make sure that each graph tells a simple story with not more than one or two elements. An informative title helps with this, as shown below illustrating the tourism data.

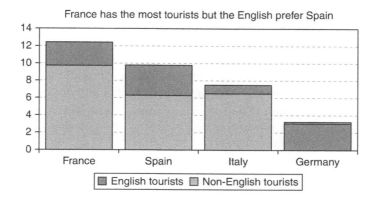

Compare this chart with the answer to Exercise 2.1, where the countries are not ordered by frequency. This one is easier to read, and the title spells out the essential messages.

Guidance to the student: how to measure your progress

Now you have reached the end of the chapter your work is not yet over. It is very unlikely that you have fully understood everything after one reading. What you should do now is:

- Check back over the learning outcomes at the start of the chapter. Do you feel you have achieved them? For example, can you list the various different data types you should be able to recognise (the first learning outcome)?
- Read the chapter summary below to help put things in context. You should recognise each topic and be aware of the main issues, techniques, etc., within them. There should be no surprises or gaps.
- Read the list of key terms. You should be able to give a brief and precise definition or description of each one. Do not worry if you cannot remember all the formulae (though you should try to memorise simple ones, such as that for the mean).
- Try out the problems (most important!). Answers to odd-numbered problems are at the back of the text, so you can check your answers. There is more detail for some of the answers on the text's website.

From all of this, you should be able to work out whether you have really mastered the chapter. Do not be surprised if you have not – it will take more than one reading. Go back over those parts where you feel unsure of your knowledge. Use these same learning techniques for each chapter.

Summary

- Descriptive statistics are useful for summarising large amounts of information, highlighting the main features but omitting the detail.
- Different techniques are suited to different types of data, e.g. bar charts for cross-section data and rates of growth for time series.
- Graphical methods, such as the bar chart, provide a picture of the data. These give an informal summary, but they are unsuitable as a basis for further analysis.
- Important graphical techniques include the bar chart, frequency distribution, relative and cumulative frequency distributions, histogram and pie chart. For time-series data, a time-series chart of the data is informative.
- Numerical techniques are more precise as summaries. Measures of location (such as the mean), of dispersion (the variance) and of skewness form the basis of these techniques.
- Important numerical summary statistics include the mean, median and mode; variance, standard deviation and coefficient of variation; coefficient of skewness.
- For bivariate data, the scatter diagram (or *XY* graph) is a useful way of illustrating the data.
- Data are often transformed in some way before analysis, e.g. by taking logs. Transformations often make it easier to see key features of the data in graphs and sometimes make summary statistics easier to interpret. For example, with time-series data the average rate of growth may be more appropriate than the mean of the series.

Key terms and concepts

absolute dispersion	compound interest
area graph	cross-section data
arithmetic mean	cross-tabulation
average growth rate	data transformation
bar chart	decile
bivariate method	depreciation rate
box and whiskers plot	elasticity
Chebyshev's inequality	expected value
class interval	frequency
class width	frequency density
coefficient of skewness	frequency table
coefficient of variation	geometric mean
compound growth	growth factor

→

heteroscedasticity	quantile solidus quantiles
histogram	quartile
homoscedasticity	quintile
inter-quartile range	range
logarithm	ratio scale
mean	reference tables
measure of dispersion	relative and cumulative frequencies
measure of location	relative dispersion
measure of skewness	scatter diagram (*XY* chart)
median	serial correlation
mid-point	skewness
mode	stacked bar chart
multiple bar chart	standard deviation
multiple time-series graph	standard width
multivariate method	time-series data
nominal scale	time-series graph
non-linear trend	transformed data
ordinal scale	trend
outliers	unbiased
percentile	univariate method
pie chart	variance
positively skewed	weighted average
presentation tables	*z* score

Reference   Atkinson, A. B., *The Economics of Inequality*, 2nd edn, Oxford University Press, 1983.

Formulae used in this chapter

Formula	Description	Notes
$\mu = \dfrac{\sum x}{N}$	Mean of a population	Use when all individual observations are available. N is the population size.
$\mu = \dfrac{\sum fx}{\sum f}$	Mean of a population	Use with grouped data. f represents the class or group frequencies, x represents the mid-point of the class interval
$\bar{x} = \dfrac{\sum x}{n}$	Mean of a sample	n is the number of observations in the sample
$\bar{x} = \dfrac{\sum fx}{\sum f}$	Mean of a sample	Use with grouped data
$m = x_L + (x_U - x_L)\left\{\dfrac{\frac{N+1}{2} - F}{f}\right\}$	Median (where data are grouped)	x_L and x_U represent the lower and upper limits of the interval containing the median. F represents the cumulative frequency up to (but excluding) the interval
$\sigma^2 = \dfrac{\sum (x - \mu)^2}{N}$	Variance of a population	N is the population size.
$\sigma^2 = \dfrac{\sum f(x - \mu)^2}{\sum f}$	Population variance (grouped data)	
$s^2 = \dfrac{\sum (x - \bar{x})^2}{n-1}$	Sample variance	
$s^2 = \dfrac{\sum f(x - \bar{x})^2}{n-1}$	Sample variance (grouped data)	
$c.v = \dfrac{\sigma}{\mu}$	Coefficient of variation	The ratio of the standard deviation to the mean. A measure of dispersion.
$z = \dfrac{x - \mu}{\sigma}$	z score	Measures the distance from observation x to the mean μ measured in standard deviations
$\dfrac{\sum f(x - \mu)^3}{N\sigma^3}$	Coefficient of skewness	A positive value means the distribution is skewed to the right (long tail to the right).
$g = \sqrt[t-1]{\dfrac{x_T}{x_1}} - 1$	Rate of growth	Measures the average annual rate of growth between years 1 and T
$\sqrt[n]{\Pi x}$	Geometric mean (of n observations on x)	
$1 - \dfrac{1}{k^2}$	Chebyshev's inequality	Minimum proportion of observations lying within k standard deviations of the mean of any distribution

Problems

Some of the more challenging problems are indicated by highlighting the problem number in colour.

2.1.1 The following data show the education and employment status of women aged 20–29:

	Higher education	A levels	Other qualification	No qualification	Total
In work	209	182	577	92	1060
Unemployed	12	9	68	32	121
Inactive	17	34	235	136	422
Sample	238	225	880	260	1603

(a) Draw a bar chart of the numbers in work in each education category (the first line of the table). Can this be easily compared with the similar diagram in the text, for both males and females (Figure 2.3)?

(b) Draw a stacked bar chart using all the employment states, similar to Figure 2.5. Comment upon any similarities and differences from the diagram in the text.

(c) Convert the table into (column) percentages and produce a stacked bar chart similar to Figure 2.6. Comment upon any similarities and differences.

(d) Draw a pie chart showing the distribution of educational qualifications of those in work and compare it to Figure 2.7 in the text.

2.1.2 The data below show the average hourly earnings (in £s) of those in full-time employment, by category of education (NVQ levels. NVQ 4 corresponds to a university degree).

	NVQ 4	NVQ 3	NVQ 2	Below NVQ 2	No qualification
Males	17.69	12.23	11.47	10.41	8.75
Females	14.83	9.57	9.40	9.24	7.43

(a) In what fundamental way do the data in this table differ from those in Problem 2.1.1?

(b) Construct a bar chart showing male and female earnings by education category. What does it show?

(c) Why would it be inappropriate to construct a stacked bar chart of the data? How should one graphically present the combined data for males and females? What extra information is necessary for you to do this?

2.1.3 Using the data from Problem 2.1.1:

(a) Which education category has the highest proportion of women in work? What is the proportion?

(b) Which category of employment status has the highest proportion of women with a degree? What is the proportion?

2.1.4   Using the data from Problem 2.1.2:

(a) What is the premium, in terms of average earnings, of a degree over A levels (NVQ 3)? Does this differ between men and women?

(b) Would you expect *median* earnings to show a similar picture? What differences, if any, might you expect?

2.1.5   The distribution of marketable wealth in 1979 in the United Kingdom is shown in the table below (adapted from *Inland Revenue Statistics, 1981*, contains public sector information licensed under the Open Government Licence (OGL) v3.0, http://www.nationalarchives.gov.uk/doc/open-government-licence/open-government:

Range	Number 000s	Amount £m
0–	1 606	148
1 000–	2 927	5 985
3 000–	2 562	10 090
5 000–	3 483	25 464
10 000–	2 876	35 656
15 000–	1 916	33 134
20 000–	3 425	104 829
50 000–	621	46 483
100 000–	170	25 763
200 000–	59	30 581

Draw a bar chart and histogram of the data (assume the final class interval has a width of 200 000). Comment on the differences between the two types of chart. Comment on any differences between this histogram and the latest one for 2005 given in the text of this chapter.

2.1.6   The data below show the number of enterprises in the United Kingdom in 2010, arranged according to employment:

Number of employees	Number of firms
1–	1 740 685
5–	388 990
10–	215 370
20–	141 920
50–	49 505
100–	25 945
250–	7 700
500–	2 795
1 000–	1 320

Draw a bar chart and histogram of the data (assume the mid-point of the last class interval is 2000). What are the major features apparent in each and what are the differences?

2.1.7   Using the data from Problem 2.1.5:

(a) Calculate the mean, median and mode of the distribution. Why do they differ?

(b) Calculate the inter-quartile range, variance, standard deviation and coefficient of variation of the data.

(c) Calculate the skewness of the distribution.

(d) From what you have calculated, and the data in the chapter, can you draw any conclusions about the degree of inequality in wealth holdings, and how this has changed?

(e) What would be the effect upon the mean of assuming the final class width to be £10m? What would be the effects upon the median and mode?

2.1.8 Using the data from Problem 2.1.6:

(a) Calculate the mean, median and mode of the distribution. Why do they differ?

(b) Calculate the inter-quartile range, variance, standard deviation and coefficient of variation of the data.

(c) Calculate the coefficient of skewness of the distribution.

2.1.9 A motorist keeps a record of petrol purchases on a long journey, as follows:

Petrol station	1	2	3
Litres purchased	33	40	25
Price per litre (pence)	134	139	137

Calculate the average petrol price for the journey.

2.1.10 Demonstrate that the weighted average calculation given in equation (1.9) is equivalent to finding the total expenditure on education divided by the total number of pupils.

2.1.11 On a test taken by 100 students, the average mark is 65, with variance 144. Student A scores 83; student B scores 47.

(a) Calculate the z scores for these two students.

(b) What is the maximum number of students with a score either better than A's or worse than B's?

(c) What is the maximum number of students with a score better than A's?

2.1.12 The average income of a group of people is £8000, and 80% of the group have incomes within the range £6000–10 000. What is the minimum value of the standard deviation of the distribution?

2.1.13 The following data show car registrations in the United Kingdom for 1987–2010:

Year	Registrations	Year	Registrations	Year	Registrations
1987	2212.6	1995	2024.0	2003	2820.7
1988	2437.0	1996	2093.3	2004	2784.7
1989	2535.2	1997	2244.3	2005	2603.6
1990	2179.9	1998	2367.0	2006	2499.1
1991	1708.5	1999	2342.0	2007	2539.3
1992	1694.4	2000	2430.0	2008	2188.3
1993	1853.4	2001	2710.0	2009	1959.1
1994	1991.7	2002	2816.0	2010	1994.6

(a) Draw a time-series graph of car registrations. Comment upon the main features of the series. (It looks daunting, but it will take you less than 10 minutes to type in these data.)

(b) Draw time-series graphs of the change in registrations, the (natural) log of registrations and the change in the ln. Comment upon the results.

2.1.14 The table below shows the different categories of investment in the United Kingdom over a series of years:

Year	Dwellings	Transport	Machinery	Intangible fixed assets	Other buildings
1977	5699	3248	9950	797	8657
1978	6325	4112	11709	760	9481
1979	7649	4758	13832	964	11289
1980	8674	4707	15301	1216	13680
1981	8138	4011	15454	1513	14603
1982	8920	4489	16734	2040	15730
1983	10447	4756	18377	2337	16157
1984	11932	5963	20782	2918	17708
1985	12219	6676	24349	3239	18648
1986	14140	6527	25218	3219	20477
1987	16548	7871	28226	3430	24269
1988	21097	9228	32615	4305	30713
1989	22771	10625	38419	4977	36689
1990	21048	10572	37776	6298	41334
1991	18339	9051	35094	6722	38632
1992	18826	8420	35426	6584	34657
1993	19886	9315	35316	6492	32988
1994	21155	11395	38426	6702	33945
1995	22448	11036	45012	7272	35596
1996	22516	12519	50102	7889	37320
1997	23928	12580	51465	8936	41398
1998	25222	16113	58915	9461	46286
1999	25700	14683	60670	10023	50646
2000	27394	13577	63535	10670	51996
2001	29806	14656	60929	11326	55065
2002	34499	16314	57152	12614	59972
2003	38462	15592	54441	13850	64355
2004	44298	14339	59632	14164	67982
2005	47489	14763	59486	14386	73634
2006	53331	14855	61497	15531	82020
2007	55767	15482	69411	16049	92808
2008	50292	14570	67837	16726	90936
2009	37044	12127	56411	17710	80978

Use appropriate graphical techniques to analyse the properties of any one of the investment series. Comment upon the results. (Although this seems a lot of data, it shouldn't take long to type in, even less time if two people collaborate and share their results.)

2.1.15 Using the data from Problem 2.1.13:

(a) Calculate the average rate of growth of the series.

(b) Calculate the standard deviation around the average growth rate.

(c) Does the series appear to be more or less volatile than the investment figures used in the chapter? Suggest reasons.

2.1.16 Using the data from Problem 2.1.14:

(a) Calculate the average rate of growth of the series for dwellings.

(b) Calculate the standard deviation around the average growth rate.

(c) Does the series appear to be more or less volatile than the investment figures used in the chapter? Suggest reasons.

2.1.17 How would you expect the following time-series variables to look when graphed? (e.g. Trended? Linear trend? Trended up or down? Stationary? Homoscedastic? Autocorrelated? Cyclical? Anything else?)

(a) Nominal national income.

(b) Real national income.

(c) The nominal interest rate.

2.1.18 How would you expect the following time-series variables to look when graphed?

(a) The price level.

(b) The inflation rate.

(c) The £/$ exchange rate.

2.1.19 (a) A government bond is issued, promising to pay the bearer £1000 in five years' time. The prevailing market rate of interest is 7%. What price would you expect to pay now for the bond? What would its price be after two years? If, after two years, the market interest rate jumped to 10%, what would the price of the bond be?

(b) A bond is issued which promises to pay £200 p.a. over the next five years. If the prevailing market interest rate is 7%, how much would you be prepared to pay for the bond? Why does the answer differ from the previous question? (Assume interest is paid at the end of each year.)

2.1.20 A firm purchases for £30 000 a machine which is expected to last for 10 years, after which it will be sold for its scrap value of £3000. Calculate the average rate of depreciation p.a., and calculate the written-down value of the machine after one, two and five years.

2.1.21 Depreciation of BMW and Mercedes cars is given in the following table of new and used car prices:

Age	BMW 525i	Mercedes 200E
Current	22 275	21 900
1 year	18 600	19 700
2 years	15 200	16 625
3 years	12 600	13 950
4 years	9 750	11 600
5 years	8 300	10 300

(a) Calculate the average rate of depreciation of each type of car.

(b) Use the calculated depreciation rates to estimate the value of the car after 1, 2, etc., years of age. How does this match the actual values?

(c) Graph the values and estimated values for each car.

2.1.22 A bond is issued which promises to pay £400 p.a. in perpetuity. How much is the bond worth now, if the interest rate is 5%? (Hint: the sum of an infinite series of the form

$$\frac{1}{1+r} + \frac{1}{(1+r)^2} + \frac{1}{(1+r)^3} + \cdots$$

is $1/r$, as long as $r > 0$.)

significance level. These observed associations could well have arisen by chance so the evidence is much less convincing.

Are significant results important?

We might ask if a certain value of the correlation coefficient is economically important as well as significant. We saw earlier that 'significant' results need not be important. The difficulty in this case is that we have little intuitive understanding of the correlation coefficient. Is $\rho = 0.5$ important, for example? Would it make much difference if it were only 0.4?

Our understanding may be helped if we look at some graphs of variables with different correlation coefficients (these data were generated artificially to illustrate the point). Three are shown in Figure 2.32. Panel (a) of the figure graphs two variables with a correlation coefficient of 0.2. Visually there seems little association between the variables, yet the correlation coefficient is (just) significant: $t = 2.06$ ($n = 100$ and the Prob-value is 0.046). This is a significant result which does not impress much.

Figure 2.32
Variables with different degrees of correlation

(a)

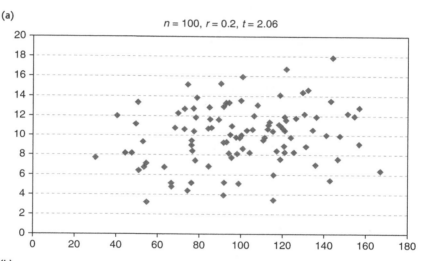

(b)

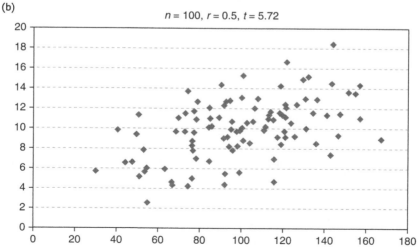

Figure 2.32
(*cont'd*)

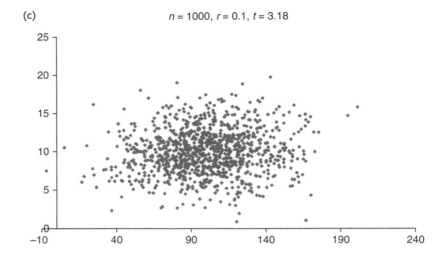

(c) $n = 1000, r = 0.1, t = 3.18$

In panel (b) the correlation coefficient is 0.5 and the association seems a little stronger visually, although there is still a substantial scatter of the observations around a straight line. Yet the t statistic in this case is 5.72, highly significant (Prob-value 0.000).

Finally, panel (c) shows an example where $n = 1000$. To the eye this looks much like a random scatter, with no discernible pattern. Yet the correlation coefficient is 0.1 and the t statistic is 3.18, again highly significant (Prob-value = 0.002).

The lessons from this seem fairly clear. What looks like a random scatter on a chart may in fact reveal a relationship between variables which is statistically significant, especially if there are a large number of observations. On the other hand, a high t statistic and correlation coefficient can still indicate a lot of variation in the data, revealed by the chart. Panel (b) suggests, for example, that we are unlikely to get a very reliable prediction of the value of y, even if we know the value of x.

Exercise 2.9

(a) Test the hypothesis that there is no association between the birth rate and the income ratio.

(b) Look up the Prob-value associated with the test statistic and confirm that it does not reject the null hypothesis.

Correlation and causality

It is important to test the significance of any result because almost every pair of variables will have a non-zero correlation coefficient, even if they are totally unconnected (the chance of the sample correlation coefficient being *exactly* zero is very, very small). Therefore, it is important to distinguish between correlation coefficients which are significant and those which are not, using the t test just outlined. But even when the result is significant one should beware of the danger of 'spurious' correlation. Many variables which clearly cannot be related turn out to be 'significantly' correlated with each other. One now famous example is between the price level and cumulative rainfall. Since they both rise year after year, it is easy to see why they are correlated, yet it is hard to think of a plausible reason why they should be causally related to each other.

Apart from spurious correlation, there are four possible reasons for a non-zero value of r:

(1) X influences Y.
(2) Y influences X.
(3) X and Y jointly influence each other.
(4) Another variable, Z, influences both X and Y.

Correlation alone does not allow us to distinguish between these alternatives. For example, wages (X) and prices (Y) are highly correlated. Some people believe this is due to cost–push inflation, i.e. that wage rises lead to price rises. This is case (1) above. Others believe that wages rise to keep up with the cost of living (i.e. rising prices), which is (2). Perhaps a more convincing explanation is (3), a wage–price spiral where each feeds upon the other. Others would suggest that it is the growth of the money supply, Z, which allows both wages and prices to rise. To distinguish between these alternatives is important for the control of inflation, but correlation alone does not allow that distinction to be made.

Correlation is best used therefore as a suggestive and descriptive piece of analysis, rather than a technique which gives definitive answers. It is often a preparatory piece of analysis, which gives some clues to what the data might yield, to be followed by more sophisticated techniques such as regression.

The coefficient of rank correlation

On occasion it is inappropriate or impossible to calculate the correlation coefficient as described above and an alternative approach is helpful. Sometimes the original data are unavailable but the ranks are. For example, schools may be ranked in terms of their exam results, but the actual pass rates are not available. Similarly, they may be ranked in terms of spending per pupil, with actual spending levels unavailable. Although the original data are missing, one can still test for an association between spending and exam success by calculating the correlation between the ranks. If extra spending improves exam performance, schools ranked higher on spending should also be ranked higher on exam success, leading to a positive correlation.

Second, even if the raw data are available, they may be highly skewed and hence the correlation coefficient may be influenced heavily by a few outliers. In this case the hypothesis test for correlation may be misleading as it is based on the assumption of underlying Normal distributions for the data. In this case we could transform the values to ranks, and calculate the correlation of the ranks. In a similar manner to the median, this can effectively deal with heavily skewed distributions.

Note the difference between the two cases. In the first, we would prefer to have the actual school pass rates and expenditures because our analysis would be better. We could actually see how much extra we have to spend in order to get better results. In the second case we actually prefer to use the ranks because the original data might mislead us, through the presence of outliers for example. **Non-parametric statistics** are those which are robust to the distribution of the data, such as the calculation of the median, rather than the mean which is a parametric measure. We do not cover many examples of the former in this text, but the **rank correlation coefficient** is one of them.

Spearman's coefficient of rank correlation is a measure that is robust to the underlying distribution of the data. It does not matter, for example, if the data are skewed. (The 'standard' correlation coefficient described above is more fully known as **Pearson's product-moment correlation coefficient**, to distinguish it.) The formula to be applied is the same as before, although there are a few tricks to be learned about constructing the ranks, and also the hypothesis test is conducted in a different manner.

Using the ranks is generally less efficient than using the original data, because one is effectively throwing away some of the information (e.g. by *how much* do countries' growth rates differ?). However, there is a trade-off: the rank correlation coefficient is more robust, i.e. it is less influenced by outliers or highly skewed distributions. If one suspects this is a risk, it may be better to use the ranks. This is similar to the situation where the median can prove superior to the mean as a measure of central tendency.

We will calculate the rank correlation coefficient for the data on birth and growth rates, to provide a comparison with the ordinary correlation coefficient calculated earlier. It is unlikely that the distributions of birth or of growth rates are particularly skewed (and we have too few observations to reliably tell), so the Pearson measure might generally be preferred, but we calculate the Spearman coefficient for comparison. Table 2.20 presents the data for birth and growth rates in the form of ranks. Calculating the ranks is fairly straightforward, although there are a couple of points to note.

The country with the highest birth rate has the rank of 1, the next highest 2, and so on. Similarly, the country with the highest growth rate ranks 1, etc. One could reverse a ranking, so the lowest birth rate ranks 1, for example; the direction of ranking is somewhat arbitrary. This would leave the rank correlation coefficient unchanged in value, but the sign would change, e.g. -0.691 would become $+0.691$. This could be confusing as we would now have a 'positive' correlation rather than a negative one (though the birth rate variable would now have to be redefined). It is better to use the 'natural' order of ranking for each variable, i.e. rank *both* variables in ascending order or *both* in descending order.

Table 2.20 Calculation of Spearman's rank correlation coefficient

Country	Birth rate Y	Growth rate X	Rank Y R_Y	Rank X R_X	R_Y^2	R_X^2	$R_X R_Y$
Brazil	30	5.1	7	3	49	9	21
Colombia	29	3.2	9	6	81	36	54
Costa Rica	30	3.0	7	7	49	49	49
India	35	1.4	4	10	16	100	40
Mexico	36	3.8	2.5	5	6.25	25	12.5
Peru	36	1.0	2.5	11	6.25	121	27.5
Philippines	34	2.8	5	8	25	64	40
Senegal	48	−0.3	1	12	1	144	12
South Korea	24	6.9	11	1	121	1	11
Sri Lanka	27	2.5	10	9	100	81	90
Taiwan	21	6.2	12	2	144	4	24
Thailand	30	4.6	7	4	49	16	28
Totals			78	78	647.5	650	409

Note: The country with the highest growth rate (South Korea) is ranked 1 for variable *X*; Taiwan, the next fastest growth nation, is ranked 2, etc. For the birth rate, Senegal is ranked 1, having the highest birth rate, 48. Taiwan has the lowest birth rate and so is ranked 12 for variable *Y*.

Confusion will usually follow if you rank one variable in ascending order, the other descending.

Where two or more observations are the same, as are the birth rates of Mexico and Peru, then they are given the same rank, which is the average of the relevant ranking values. For example, both countries are given the rank of 2.5, which is the average of 2 and 3. Similarly, Brazil, Costa Rica and Thailand are all given the rank of 7, which is the average of 6, 7 and 8. The next country, Colombia, is then given the rank of 9.

Excel warning

Microsoft Excel has a *rank.avg( )* function built in, which takes a variable and calculates a new variable consisting of the ranks, similar to the above table. This can obviously save a bit of work. A word of warning, however: the *rank( )* and *rank.eq( )* functions, also in *Excel*, will give incorrect answers if there are ties in the data. The *rank.avg( )* function is new from Excel 2010 onwards, earlier versions of Excel only have the unreliable functions.

We now apply formula (2.1) to the ranked data, giving:

$$r_s = \frac{n\sum XY - \sum X\sum Y}{\sqrt{(n\sum X^2 - (\sum X)^2)(n\sum Y^2 - (\sum Y)^2)}}$$

$$= \frac{12 \times 409 - 78 \times 78}{\sqrt{(12 \times 650 - 78^2)(12 \times 647.5 - 78^2)}} = -0.691$$

This indicates a negative rank correlation between the two variables, as with the standard correlation coefficient ($r = -0.824$), but with a slightly smaller absolute value.

To test the significance of the result a hypothesis test can be performed on the value of ρ_s, the corresponding population parameter:

$H_0: \rho_s = 0$
$H_1: \rho_s \neq 0$

This time the t distribution cannot be used (because we are no longer relying on the parent distribution being Normal), but prepared tables of the critical values for ρ_s itself may be consulted; these are given in Table 2.21.

The critical value at the 5% significance level, for $n = 12$, is 0.591. Hence the null hypothesis is rejected if the rank correlation coefficient falls outside the range

Table 2.21 Critical values of the rank correlation coefficient

n	10%	5%	2%	1%
5	0.900			
6	0.829	0.886	0.943	
⋮	⋮	⋮	⋮	⋮
11	0.523	0.623	0.763	0.794
12	0.497	0.591	0.703	0.780
13	0.475	0.566	0.673	0.746

Note: The critical value is given at the intersection of the shaded row and column.

[−0.591, 0.591], which it does in this case. Thus the null can be rejected with 95% confidence; the data do support the hypothesis of a relationship between the birth rate and growth. This critical value shown in the table is for a two-tail test. For a one-tail test, the significance level given in the top row of the table should be halved, so we could reject the null at the 2.5% significance level or 97.5% confidence level in this case.

Exercise 2.10

(a) Rank the observations for the income ratio across countries (highest $= 1$) and calculate the coefficient of rank correlation with the birth rate.

(b) Test the hypothesis that $\rho_s = 0$.

(c) Reverse the rankings for both variables and confirm that this does not affect the calculated test statistic.

(d) Reverse the rankings of just the income ratio variable. How would you expect this to affect the value of the rank correlation coefficient?

Worked example 2.8

To illustrate all the calculations and bring them together without distracting explanation, we work through a simple example with the following data on X and Y:

Y	17	18	19	20	27	18
X	3	4	7	6	8	5

An XY graph of the data reveals the following picture, which suggests positive correlation:

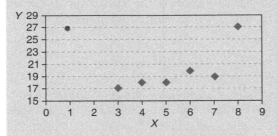

Note that one point appears to be something of an outlier. All the calculations for correlations may be based on the following table:

Obs	Y	X	Y^2	X^2	XY	Rank Y R_Y	Rank X R_X	R_Y^2	R_X^2	$R_X R_Y$
1	17	3	289	9	51	6	6	36	36	36
2	18	4	324	16	72	4.5	5	20.25	25	22.5
3	19	7	361	49	133	3	2	9	4	6
4	20	6	400	36	120	2	3	4	9	6
5	27	8	729	64	216	1	1	1	1	1
6	18	5	324	25	90	4.5	4	20.25	16	18
Totals	119	33	2427	199	682	21	21	90.5	91	89.5

The (Pearson) correlation coefficient r is therefore:

$$r = \frac{n\sum XY - \sum X \sum Y}{\sqrt{(n\sum X^2 - (\sum X)^2)(n\sum Y^2 - (\sum Y)^2)}}$$

$$= \frac{6 \times 682 - 33 \times 119}{\sqrt{(6 \times 199 - 33^2)(6 \times 2427 - 119^2)}} = 0.804$$

The hypothesis $H_0: \rho = 0$ versus $H_1: \rho \neq 0$ can be tested using the t test statistic:

$$t = \frac{r\sqrt{n-2}}{\sqrt{1-r^2}} = \frac{0.804 \times \sqrt{6-2}}{\sqrt{1-0.804^2}} = 2.7$$

which is compared to a critical value of 2.776, so the null hypothesis is not rejected, narrowly. This is largely due to the small number of observations, and anyway, it may be unwise to use the t distribution on such a small sample. The rank correlation coefficient is calculated as (using the R_X, R_Y etc., values)

$$r = \frac{n\sum XY - \sum X \sum Y}{\sqrt{(n\sum X^2 - (\sum X)^2)(n\sum Y^2 - (\sum Y)^2)}}$$

$$= \frac{6 \times 89.5 - 21 \times 21}{\sqrt{(6 \times 91 - 21^2)(6 \times 90.5 - 21^2)}} = 0.928$$

The critical value at the 5% significance level is 0.886, so the rank correlation coefficient *is* significant, in contrast to the previous result. Not too much should be read into this, however; with few observations the ranking process can easily alter the result substantially.

Regression analysis

Regression analysis is a more sophisticated way of examining the relationship between two (or more) variables than is correlation. The major differences between correlation and regression are the following:

- Regression can investigate the relationships between two *or more* variables.
- A *direction* of causality is asserted, from the explanatory variable (or variables) to the dependent variable.
- The *influence* of each explanatory variable upon the dependent variable is measured.
- The *significance* of each explanatory variable's influence can be ascertained.

Thus regression permits answers to such questions as:

- Does the growth rate influence a country's birth rate?
- If the growth rate increases, by how much might a country's birth rate be expected to fall?
- Are other variables important in determining the birth rate?

Figure 2.33
The line of best fit

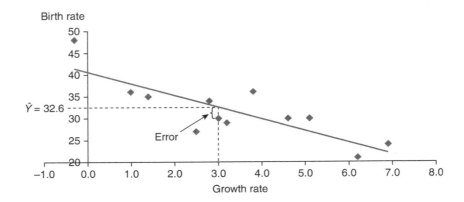

In this example we assert that the direction of causality is from the growth rate (X) to the birth rate (Y) and not vice versa. The growth rate is therefore the explanatory variable (also referred to as the independent or exogenous variable) and the birth rate is the dependent variable (also called the explained or endogenous variable).

Regression analysis describes this causal relationship by fitting a straight line drawn through the data, which best summarises them. It is sometimes called 'the line of best fit' for this reason. This is illustrated in Figure 2.33 for the birth rate and growth rate data. Note that (by convention) the explanatory variable is placed on the horizontal axis, the explained on the vertical axis. This regression line is downward sloping (its derivation will be explained shortly) for the same reason that the correlation coefficient is negative, i.e. high values of Y are generally associated with low values of X and vice versa.

Since the regression line summarises knowledge of the relationship between X and Y, it can be used to predict the value of Y given any particular value of X. In Figure 2.33 the value of $X = 3$ (the observation for Costa Rica) is related via the regression line to a value of Y (denoted[2] by $\hat{Y}$) of 32.6. This predicted value is close (but not identical) to the actual birth rate of 30. The difference reflects the absence of perfect correlation between the two variables.

The difference between the actual value, Y, and the predicted value, $\hat{Y}$, is called the error term or residual. It is labelled 'Error', e, in Figure 2.33[3]. Why should such errors occur? The relationship is never going to be an exact one for a variety of reasons. There are bound to be other factors besides growth which might affect the birth rate (e.g. the education of women) and these effects are all subsumed into the error term. There might additionally be simple measurement error (of Y) and, of course, people do act in a somewhat random fashion rather than follow rigid rules of behaviour.

All of these factors fall into the error term, and this means that the observations lie around the regression line rather than on it. If there are many of these factors, none of which is predominant, and they are independent of each other, then these errors may be assumed to be Normally distributed about the regression line.

---

[2] A 'hat' (^) over a symbol is often used to indicate the estimate of that variable.

[3] The italic e denoting the error term should not be confused with the use of the same letter as the base for natural logarithms. The correct interpretation should be clear from the context.

Why not include these factors explicitly? On the face of it this would seem to be an improvement, making the model more realistic. However, the costs of doing this are that the model becomes more complex, calculation becomes more difficult (not so important now with computers) and it is generally more difficult for the reader (or researcher) to interpret what is going on. If these other factors have only small effects upon the dependent variable, then it might be better to ignore them, adopt a simple model and focus upon the main relationship of interest. There is a virtue in simplicity, as long as the simplified model still gives an undistorted view of the relationship.

Calculation of the regression line

The equation of the sample regression line may be written

$$\hat{Y}_i = a + bX_i \tag{2.6}$$

where $\hat{Y}_i$ is the predicted value of Y for observation (country) i, X_i is the value of the explanatory variable for observation i, and a and b are fixed coefficients to be estimated; a measures the intercept of the regression line on the Y-axis, b measures its slope. This is illustrated in Figure 2.34.

The first task of regression analysis is to find the values of a and b so that the regression line may be drawn. To do this we proceed as follows. The difference between the actual value, Y_i, and its predicted value, $\hat{Y}_i$, is e_i, the error. Thus

$$Y_i = \hat{Y}_i + e_i \tag{2.7}$$

Substituting equation (2.6) into equation (2.7), the regression equation can be written as

$$Y_i = a + bX_i + e_i \tag{2.8}$$

Equation (2.8) shows that observed birth rates are made up of two components:

(1) that part explained by the growth rate, $a + bX_i$, and
(2) an error component, e_i.

In a good model, part (1) should be large relative to part (2) and the regression line is based upon this principle. The line of best fit is therefore found by finding

Figure 2.34
Intercept and slope of the regression line

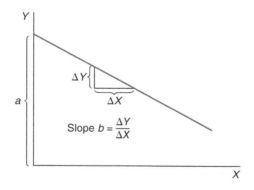

the values of a and b which *minimise the sum of squared errors* $(\sum e_i^2)$ from the regression line. For this reason, this method is known as 'the method of least squares' or simply 'ordinary least squares' (OLS). The use of this criterion will be justified later on, but it can be said in passing that the sum of the errors is not minimised because that would not lead to a unique answer for the values a and b. In fact, there is an infinite number of possible lines through the data which all yield a sum of errors equal to zero. Minimising the sum of *squared* errors does yield a unique answer.

The task is therefore to

$$\text{minimise } \sum e_i^2 \tag{2.9}$$

by choice of a and b.

Rearranging equation (2.8), the error is given by

$$e_i = Y_i - a - bX_i \tag{2.10}$$

so equation (7.9) becomes

$$\text{minimise } \sum(Y_i - a - bX_i)^2 \tag{2.11}$$

by choice of a and b.

Finding the solution to (2.11) requires the use of differential calculus, and is not presented here. The resulting formulae for a and b are

$$b = \frac{n\sum XY - \sum X \sum Y}{n\sum X^2 - (\sum X)^2} \tag{2.12}$$

and

$$a = \overline{Y} - b\overline{X} \tag{2.13}$$

where $\overline{X}$ and $\overline{Y}$ are the mean values of X and Y, respectively. The values necessary to evaluate equations (2.12) and (2.13) can be obtained from Table 2.19 which was used to calculate the correlation coefficient. These values are repeated for convenience:

$$\sum Y = 380 \qquad \sum Y^2 = 12\,564$$
$$\sum X = 40.2 \qquad \sum X^2 = 184.04$$
$$\sum XY = 1139.70 \qquad n = 12$$

Using these values, we obtain

$$b = \frac{12 \times 1139.70 - 40.2 \times 380}{12 \times 184.04 - 40.2^2} = -2.700$$

and

$$a = \frac{380}{12} - (-2.700) \times \frac{40.2}{12} = 40.711$$

Thus the regression equation can be written, to two decimal places for clarity, as

$$Y_i = 40.71 - 2.70X_i + e_i$$

Interpretation of the slope and intercept

The most important part of the result is the slope coefficient $b = -0.27$ since it measures the effect of X upon Y. This result implies that a unit increase in the growth rate (e.g. from 2% to 3% p.a.) would lower the birth rate by 2.7, e.g. from 30 births per 1000 population to 27.3. Given that the growth data refer to a 20-year period (1961–81), this increase in the growth rate might need to be sustained over such a time, not an easy task. It is unlikely that an increase in the growth rate in one year would have such an immediate effect on the birth rate. How big is the effect upon the birth rate? The average birth rate in the sample is 31.67, so a reduction of 2.7 for an average country would be a fall of 8.5% ($2.7/31.67 \times 100$). This is reasonably substantial (though not enough to bring the birth rate down to developed country levels) but would need a considerable, sustained increase in the growth rate to bring it about.

The value of a, the **intercept**, may be interpreted as the predicted birth rate of a country with zero growth (since $\hat{Y}_i = a$ at $X = 0$). This value of 40.71 is fairly close to that of Senegal, which actually had negative growth over the period and whose birth rate was 48, a little higher than the intercept value. Although a has a sensible interpretation in this case, this is not always so. For example, in a regression of the demand for a good on its price, a would represent demand at zero price, which is unlikely ever to be observed.

Exercise 2.11

(a) Calculate the regression line relating the birth rate to the income ratio.

(b) Interpret the coefficients of this equation.

Measuring the goodness of fit of the regression line

Having calculated the regression line, we now ask whether it provides a good fit for the data, i.e. do the observations tend to lie close to, or far away from, the line? Even though we have fitted a regression line, by itself this tells us nothing about the closeness of the fit. If the fit is poor, perhaps the effect of X upon Y is not so strong after all. Note that even if X has *no* true effect upon Y, we can still calculate a regression line and its slope coefficient b. Although b is likely to be small, it is unlikely to be exactly zero. Measuring the goodness of fit of the data to the line helps us to distinguish between good and bad regressions.

We proceed by comparing the three competing models explaining the birth rate. Which of them fits the data best? Using the income ratio and the GNP variable gives the following regressions (calculations not shown) to compare with our original model:

for the income ratio (IR): $B = 26.44 + 1.045 \times IR + e$
for GNP: $B = 34.72 - 0.003 \times GNP + e$
for growth: $B = 40.71 - 2.70 \times GROWTH + e$

How can we decide which of these three is 'best' on the basis of the regression equations alone? From Figure 2.30 it is evident that some relationships appear stronger than others, yet this is not revealed by examining the regression equation alone. More information is needed. (You cannot choose the best equation simply by looking at the size of the coefficients. Consider why that is so.)

The goodness of fit is calculated by comparing two lines: the regression line and the 'mean line' (i.e. a horizontal line drawn at the mean value of Y). The regression line *must* fit the data better (if the mean line were the best fit, that is

Figure 2.35
The calculation of R^2

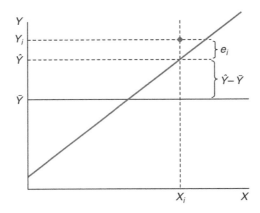

Figure 2.35
The calculation of R^2

also where the regression line would be) but the question is how much better? This is illustrated in Figure 2.35, which demonstrates the principle behind the calculation of the **coefficient of determination**, denoted by R^2 and usually more simply referred to as 'R squared'.

The figure shows the mean value of Y, the calculated sample regression line and an arbitrarily chosen sample observation (X_i, Y_i). The difference between Y_i and $\overline{Y}$ (length $Y_i - \overline{Y}$) can be divided up into:

(1) That part 'explained' by the regression line, $\hat{Y}_i - \overline{Y}$ (i.e. explained by the value of X_i).
(2) The error term $e_i = Y_i - \hat{Y}_i$.

In algebraic terms,

$$Y_i - \overline{Y} = (Y - \hat{Y}_i) + (\hat{Y}_i - \overline{Y}) \tag{2.14}$$

A good regression model should 'explain' a large part of the differences between the Y_i values and $\overline{Y}$, i.e. the length $(\hat{Y}_i - \overline{Y})$ should be large relative to $Y_i - \overline{Y}$. A measure of fit could therefore be $(\hat{Y}_i - \overline{Y})/(Y_i - \overline{Y})$. We need to apply this to all observations rather than just a single one; hence we could sum this expression over all the sample observations. A problem with this is that some of the terms would take a negative value and offset the positive terms. To measure the goodness of fit, we do not want the positive and negative terms to cancel each other out. Hence, to get round this problem, we square each of the terms in equation (2.14) to make them all positive, and then sum over the observations. This gives

$\sum (Y_i - \overline{Y})^2$, known as the **total sum of squares** (TSS)
$\sum (\hat{Y}_i - \overline{Y})^2$, the **regression sum of squares** (RSS), and
$\sum (Y_i - \hat{Y}_i)^2$, the **error sum of squares** (ESS)

The measure of goodness of fit, R^2, is then defined as the ratio of the regression sum of squares to the total sum of squares, i.e.

$$R^2 = \frac{\text{RSS}}{\text{TSS}} \tag{2.15}$$

The better the divergences between Y_i and $\overline{Y}$ are explained by the regression line, the better the goodness of fit, and the higher the calculated value of R^2. Further, it is true that

$$\text{TSS} = \text{RSS} + \text{ESS} \tag{2.16}$$

From equations (2.15) and (2.16) we can then see that R^2 must lie between 0 and 1 (note that since each term in equation (2.16) is a sum of squares, none of them can be negative). Thus

$$0 \leq R^2 \leq 1$$

A value of $R^2 = 1$ (and hence ESS = 0) indicates that all the sample observations lie exactly on the regression line (equivalent to perfect correlation). If $R^2 = 0$, then the regression line is of no use at all $-X$ does not influence Y (linearly) at all, and to try to predict a value of Y one might as well use the mean $\overline{Y}$ rather than the value X_i inserted into the sample regression equation.

To calculate R^2, alternative formulae to those above make the task easier. Instead we use:

$$\text{TSS} = \Sigma(Y_i - \overline{Y})^2 = \Sigma Y_i^2 - n\overline{Y}^2 = 12564 - 12 \times 31.67^2 = 530.667 \tag{2.17a}$$

$$\text{ESS} = \Sigma(Y_i - \hat{Y})^2 = \Sigma Y_i^2 - a\Sigma Y_i - b\Sigma X_i Y_i$$
$$= 12564 - 40.711 \times 380 - (-2.7) \times 1139.70 = 170.754 \tag{2.17b}$$

$$\text{RSS} = \text{TSS} - \text{ESS} = 530.667 - 170.754 = 359.913 \tag{2.17c}$$

This gives the result

$$R^2 = \frac{\text{RSS}}{\text{TSS}} = \frac{359.913}{530.667} = 0.678$$

This is interpreted as follows. Countries' birth rates vary around the overall mean value of 31.67 and 67.8% of this variation is explained by variation in countries' growth rates. This is quite a respectable figure to obtain, leaving only 32.8% of the variation in Y left to be explained by other factors (or pure random variation). The regression seems to make a worthwhile contribution to explaining why birth rates differ. However, it does not explain the *mechanism* by which higher growth leads to a lower birth rate.

It turns out that in simple regression (i.e. where there is only one explanatory variable), R^2 is simply the square of the correlation coefficient between X and Y. Thus, for the income ratio and for GNP, we have:

for IR: $R^2 = 0.35^2 = 0.13$
for GNP: $R^2 = -0.26^2 = 0.07$

This shows, once again, that these other variables are not terribly useful in explaining why birth rates differ. Each of them explains only a small proportion of the variation in Y.

It should be emphasised at this point that R^2 is not the only criterion (or even an adequate one in all cases) for judging the quality of a regression equation and that other statistical measures, set out below, are also helpful.

Exercise 2.12

(a) Calculate the R^2 value for the regression of the birth rate on the income ratio, calculated in Exercise 2.11.

(b) Confirm that this result is the same as the square of the correlation coefficient between these two variables, calculated in Exercise 2.8.

Summary

- Correlation refers to the extent of association between two variables. The (sample) correlation coefficient is a measure of this association, extending from $r = -1$ to $r = +1$.

- Positive correlation ($r > 0$) exists when high values of X tend to be associated with high values of Y and low X values with low Y values.

- Negative correlation ($r < 0$) exists when high values of X tend to be associated with low values of Y and vice versa.

- Values of r around 0 indicate an absence of correlation.

- As the sample correlation coefficient is a random variable, we can test for its significance, i.e. test whether the true value is zero or not. This test is based upon the t distribution.

- The existence of correlation (even if 'significant') does not necessarily imply causality. There can be other reasons for the observed association.

- Regression analysis extends correlation by asserting a causality from X to Y and then measuring the relationship between the variables via the regression line, the 'line of best fit'.

- The regression line $Y = a + bX$ is defined by the intercept a and slope coefficient b. Their values are found by minimising the sum of squared errors around the regression line.

- The slope coefficient b measures the responsiveness of Y to changes in X.

- A measure of how well the regression line fits the data is given by the coefficient of determination, R^2, varying between 0 (very poor fit) and 1 (perfect fit).

- The coefficients a and b are unbiased point estimates of the true values of the parameters. Confidence interval estimates can be obtained, based on the t distribution. Hypothesis tests on the parameters can also be carried out using the t distribution.

- A test of the hypothesis $R^2 = 0$ (implying the regression is no better at predicting Y than simply using the mean of Y) can be carried out using the F distribution.

- The regression line may be used to predict Y for any value of X by assuming the residual to be zero for that observation.

- The measured response of Y to X (given by b) depends upon the units of measurement of X and Y. A better measure is often the elasticity, which is the proportionate response of Y to a proportionate change in X.

- Data are often transformed prior to regression (e.g. by taking logs) for a variety of reasons (e.g. to fit a curve to the original data).

Key terms and concepts

autocorrelation	Pearson's product-moment correlation
coefficient of determination (R^2)	coefficient
correlation coefficient	positive correlation
dependent (endogenous) variable	prediction
elasticity	prediction interval
error sum of squares	rank correlation coefficient
error term (or residual)	regression line or equation
estimated variance of the error term	regression sum of squares
explained (endogenous) variable	slope
explanatory variable	Spearman's coefficient of rank correlation
independent (exogenous) variable	standard error
intercept	t distribution
negative correlation	total sum of squares
non-parametric statistics	zero correlation

References

Maddala, G.S., and K. Lahiri, *Introduction to Econometrics*, 4th edn, Wiley, 2009.
Todaro, M.P., *Economic Development in the Third World*, 3rd edn, Longman, 1985.

Formulae used in this chapter

Formula	Description	Notes
$r = \dfrac{n\sum XY - \sum X \sum Y}{\sqrt{(n\sum X^2 - (\sum X)^2)(n\sum Y^2 - (\sum Y)^2)}}$	Correlation coefficient	$-1 \le r \le 1$
$t = \dfrac{r\sqrt{n-2}}{\sqrt{1-r^2}}$	Test statistic for H_0: $\rho = 0$	$\nu = n - 2$
$r_s = 1 - \dfrac{6\sum d^2}{n(n^2-1)}$	Spearman's rank correlation coefficient	$-1 \le r_s \le 1$. d is the difference in ranks between the two variables. Only works if there are no tied ranks. Otherwise use standard correlation formula.
$b = \dfrac{n\sum XY - \sum X \sum Y}{n\sum X^2 - (\sum X)^2}$	Slope of the regression line (simple regression)	
$a = \bar{Y} - b\bar{X}$	Intercept (simple regression)	
$TSS = \sum Y^2 - n\bar{Y}^2$	Total sum of squares	
$ESS = \sum Y^2 - a\sum Y - b\sum XY$	Error sum of squares	
$RSS = TSS - ESS$	Regression sum of squares	
$R^2 = \dfrac{RSS}{TSS}$	Coefficient of determination	

$$s_e^2 = \frac{ESS}{n-2}$$

Variance of the error term in regression

Replace $n-2$ by $n-k-1$ in multiple regression

$$s_b^2 = \frac{s_e^2}{\sum (X - \bar{X})^2}$$

Variance of the slope coefficient in simple regression

$$s_a^2 = s_e^2 = \sqrt{\frac{1}{n} + \frac{\bar{X}^2}{\sum (X - \bar{X})^2}}$$

Variance of the intercept in simple regression

$$b \pm t_\nu \times s_b$$

Confidence interval estimate for b in simple regression

t_ν is the critical value of the t distribution with $\nu = n - 2$ degrees of freedom

$$t = \frac{b - \beta}{s_b}$$

Test statistic for $H_0: \beta = 0$

$\nu = n - 2$ in simple regression, $n - k - 1$ in multiple regression

$$F = \frac{RSS/1}{ESS/(n-2)}$$

Test statistic for $H_0: R^2 = 0$

$\nu = k, n - k - 1$ in multiple regression

$$\hat{Y} \pm t_\nu \times s_e \sqrt{\frac{1}{n} + \frac{(X_P - \bar{X})^2}{\sum (X - \bar{X})^2}}$$

Confidence interval for a prediction (simple regression) at $X = X_P$

$\nu = n - 2$

$$\hat{Y} \pm t_\nu \times s_e \sqrt{1 + \frac{1}{n} + \frac{(X_P - \bar{X})^2}{\sum (X - \bar{X})^2}}$$

Confidence interval for an observation on Y at $X = X_P$

$\nu = n - 2$

Problems

Some of the more challenging problems are indicated by highlighting the problem number in colour.

2.2.1   The other data which Todaro might have used to analyse the birth rate were:

Country	Birth rate	GNP	Growth	Income ratio
Bangladesh	47	140	0.3	2.3
Tanzania	47	280	1.9	3.2
Sierra Leone	46	320	0.4	3.3
Sudan	47	380	−1.3	3.9
Kenya	55	420	2.9	6.8
Indonesia	35	530	4.1	3.4
Panama	30	1910	3.1	8.6
Chile	25	2560	0.7	3.8
Venezuela	35	4220	2.4	5.2
Turkey	33	1540	3.5	4.9
Malaysia	31	1840	4.3	5.0
Nepal	44	150	0.0	4.7
Malawi	56	200	2.7	2.4
Argentina	20	2560	1.9	3.6

For *one* of the three possible explanatory variables (in class, different groups could examine each of the variables):

(a) Draw an *XY* chart of the data above and comment upon the result.

(b) Would you expect a line of best fit to have a positive or negative slope? Roughly, what would you expect the slope to be?

(c) What would you expect the correlation coefficient to be?

(d) Calculate the correlation coefficient, and comment.

(e) Test to see if the correlation coefficient is different from zero. Use the 95% confidence level.

(Analysis of this problem continues in Problem 2.2.5.)

2.2.2 The data below show alcohol expenditure and income (both in £s per week) for a sample of 17 families.

Family	Alcohol expenditure	Income	Family	Alcohol expenditure	Income
1	26.17	487	10	13.32	370
2	19.49	574	11	9.24	299
3	17.87	439	12	47.35	531
4	16.90	367	13	26.80	506
5	4.21	299	14	33.44	613
6	32.08	743	15	21.41	472
7	30.19	433	16	16.06	253
8	22.62	547	17	24.98	374

(a) Draw an *XY* plot of the data and comment.

(b) From the chart, would you expect the line of best fit to slope up or down? *In theory*, which way should it slope?

(c) What would you expect the correlation coefficient to be, approximately?

(d) Calculate the correlation coefficient between alcohol spending and income.

(e) Is the coefficient significantly different from zero? What is the implication of the result?

(The following totals will reduce the burden of calculation: $\Sigma Y = 137.990$; $\Sigma X = 7610$; $\Sigma Y^2 = 9\,918.455$; $\Sigma X^2 = 3\,680\,748$; $\Sigma XY = 181\,911.250$; Y is consumption, X is income. If you wish, you could calculate a logarithmic correlation. The relevant totals are: $\Sigma y = 50.192$; $\Sigma x = 103.079$; $\Sigma y^2 = 153.567$; $\Sigma x^2 = 626.414$; $\Sigma xy = 306.339$, where $y = \ln Y$ and $x = \ln X$.)

(Analysis of this problem continues in Problem 2.7.6.)

2.2.3 What would you expect to be the correlation coefficient between the following variables? Should the variables be measured contemporaneously or might there be a lag in the effect of one upon the other?

(a) Nominal consumption and nominal income.

(b) GDP and the imports/GDP ratio.

(c) Investment and the interest rate.

2.2.4 As Problem 2.7.3, for

(a) real consumption and real income;

(b) individuals' alcohol and cigarette consumption;

(c) UK and US interest rates.

2.2.5   Using the data from Problem 2.2.1, calculate the rank correlation coefficient between the variables and test its significance. How does it compare with the ordinary correlation coefficient?

2.2.6   (a) Calculate the rank correlation coefficient between income and quantity for the data in Problem 2.2. How does it compare to the ordinary correlation coefficient?

   (b) Is there significant evidence that the ranks are correlated?

2.2.7   (a) For the data in Problem 2.2.1, find the estimated regression line and calculate the R^2 statistic. Comment upon the result. How does it compare with Todaro's findings?

   (b) Calculate the standard error of the estimate and the standard errors of the coefficients. Is the slope coefficient significantly different from zero? Comment upon the result.

   (c) Test the overall significance of the regression equation and comment.

   (d) Taking your own results and Todaro's, how confident do you feel that you understand the determinants of the birth rate?

   (e) What do you think will be the result of estimating your equation using all 26 countries' data? Try it. What do you conclude?

2.2.8   (a) For the data given in Problem 2.2.2, estimate the sample regression line and calculate the R^2 statistic. Comment upon the results.

   (b) Calculate the standard error of the estimate and the standard errors of the coefficients. Is the slope coefficient significantly different from zero?

   (c) Test the overall significance of the regression and comment upon your result.

2.2.9   From your results for the birth rate model, predict the birth rate for a country with *either* (a) GNP equal to $3000, (b) a growth rate of 3% p.a., *or* (c) an income ratio of 7. How does your prediction compare with one using Todaro's results? Comment.

2.2.10 Predict alcohol consumption given an income of £700. Use the 99% confidence level for the interval estimate.

2.2.11 **(Project)** Update Todaro's study using more recent data.

2.2.12 Try to build a model of the determinants of infant mortality. You should use cross-section data for 20 countries or more and should include both developing and developed countries in the sample.
     Write up your findings in a report which includes the following sections: discussion of the problem; data gathering and transformations; estimation of the model; interpretation of results. Useful data may be found in the *Human Development Report* (use Google to find it online) or on the World Bank website.

2.3 Probability

Learning outcomes

By the end of this chapter you should be able to:

- understand the essential concept of the probability of an event occurring

- appreciate that the probability of a combination of events occurring can be calculated using simple arithmetic rules (the addition and multiplication rules)

- understand that the probability of an event occurring can depend upon the outcome of other events (conditional probability)

- know how to make use of probability theory to help make decisions in situations of uncertainty

→

Probability theory and statistical inference

In October 1985 Mrs Evelyn Adams of New Jersey, USA, won $3.9 million in the State lottery at odds of 1 in 3 200 000. In February 1986 she again won, although this time only (!) $1.4 million at odds of 1 in 5 200 000. The odds against both these wins were calculated at about 1 in 17 300 billion. Mrs Adams is quoted as saying 'They say good things come in threes, so . . .'.

The above story illustrates the principles of probability at work. The same principles underlie the theory of statistical inference, which is the task of drawing conclusions (inferences) about a population from a sample of data drawn from that population. For example, we might have a survey which shows that 30% of a sample of 100 families intend to take a holiday abroad next year. What can we conclude from this about *all* families? The techniques set out in this and subsequent chapters show how to accomplish this.

Why is knowledge of probability necessary for the study of statistical inference? In order to be able to draw inferences about a population from a sample, we must first understand how the sample was drawn from the population. The theory of probability helps with this and can tell us, for example, whether the sample is representative of the population or whether it might be biased in some way.

In many cases, the sample is a random one, i.e. the observations making up the sample are chosen at random from the population. If a second sample were selected, it would almost certainly be different from the first. Each member of the population has a particular probability of being in the sample (in simple random sampling the probability is the same for all members of the population). To understand sampling procedures, and the implications for statistical inference, we must therefore first examine the theory of probability.

As an illustration, consider estimating the wealth of a population from a sample, a subject covered in Chapter 1. As there is no annual wealth tax in the United Kingdom, there are no routine records of the wealth of all individuals, so estimates are based on tax records of wealth passed on by those who die in each year. This constitutes a random sample of all individuals but there is no guarantee it will be representative. Indeed, there are good reasons to believe it might not be, so various adjustments have to be made to obtain good estimates for the population as a whole. How to make these adjustments is partly based on probability considerations.

This chapter and the next therefore cover probability theory, dealing with the concepts and principles in a slightly abstract way before later chapters demonstrate how we then use these ideas to address more practical issues.

The definition of probability

The first task is to define precisely what is meant by probability. This is not as easy as one might imagine, and there are a number of different schools of thought on the subject. Consider the following questions:

● What is the probability of 'heads' occurring on the toss of a coin?
● What is the probability of a driver having an accident in a year of driving?

Now what is the probability of two boys? This can be seen in Figure 2.45(b). Half of all mothers have a boy first, and of these, 60% have another boy. Thus 30% (60% of 50%) of mothers have two boys. This is obtained from the rule:

$$\Pr(B1 \text{ and } B2) = \Pr(B1) \times \Pr(B2 \mid B1) \tag{3.13}$$
$$= 0.5 \times 0.6$$
$$= 0.3$$

The frequencies can be read directly from Figure 2.45(a) which might be more intuitive. On the first birth 500 mothers have a boy, and of these, 300 have a second boy (300 is 60% of 500). Hence, 30% of mothers have two boys.

Thus in general we have:

$$\Pr(A \text{ and } B) = \Pr(A) \times \Pr(B \mid A) \tag{3.14}$$

which simplifies to

$$\Pr(A \text{ and } B) = \Pr(A) \times \Pr(B) \tag{3.15}$$

if A and B are independent.

Independence may therefore be defined as follows: two events, A and B, are independent if the probability of one occurring is not influenced by the fact of the other having occurred. Formally, if A and B are independent, then

$$\Pr(B \mid A) = \Pr(B \mid \text{not } A) = \Pr(B) \tag{3.16}$$

and

$$\Pr(A \mid B) = \Pr(A \mid \text{not } B) = \Pr(A) \tag{3.17}$$

The concept of independence is an important one in statistics, as it usually simplifies problems considerably. If two variables are known to be independent, then we can analyse the behaviour of one without worrying about what is happening to the other variable. For example, sales of computers are independent of temperature, so if one is trying to predict sales next month, one does not need to worry about the weather. In contrast, ice cream sales do depend on the weather, so predicting sales accurately requires one to forecast the weather first.

Intuition does not always work with probabilities

Counter-intuitive results frequently arise in probability, which is why it is wise to use the rules to calculate probabilities in tricky situations, rather than rely on intuition. Take the following questions:

- What is the probability of obtaining two heads (HH) in two tosses of a coin?
- What is the probability of obtaining tails followed by heads (TH)?
- If a coin is tossed until either HH or TH occurs, what are the probabilities of each sequence occurring first?

The answers to the first two are easy: $\frac{1}{2} \times \frac{1}{2} = \frac{1}{4}$ in each case. You might therefore conclude that each sequence is equally likely to be the first observed, but you would be wrong.

Unless HH occurs on the first two tosses, then TH *must* occur first. HH is therefore the first sequence *only* if it occurs on the first two tosses, which has a probability of $\frac{1}{4}$. The probability that TH is first is therefore $\frac{3}{4}$. The probabilities are unequal, a strange result. Now try the same exercise but with HHH and THH and three tosses of a coin.

Combining the addition and multiplication rules

More complex problems can be solved by suitable combinations of the addition and multiplication formulae. For example, what is the probability of a mother having one child of each sex? This could occur in one of two ways: a girl followed by a boy or a boy followed by a girl. It is important to note that these are two different routes to the same outcome. Therefore, we have (assuming non-independence according to (3.12))

$$
\begin{aligned}
\Pr(1 \text{ girl}, 1 \text{ boy}) &= \Pr((G1 \text{ and } B2) \text{ or } (B1 \text{ and } G2)) \\
&= \Pr(G1) \times \Pr(B2 \,|\, G1) + \Pr(B1) \times \Pr(G2 \,|\, B1) \\
&= (0.5 \times 0.4) + (0.5 \times 0.4) \\
&= 0.4
\end{aligned}
$$

The answer can be checked if we remember (3.2) stating that probabilities must sum to 1. We have calculated the probability of two boys (0.3) and of a child of each sex (0.4). The only other possibility is of two girls. This probability must be 0.3, the same as two boys, since boys and girls are treated symmetrically in this problem (even with the non-independence assumption). The sum of the three possibilities (two boys, one of each or two girls) is therefore $0.3 + 0.4 + 0.3 = 1$, as it should be. This is often a useful check to make, especially if one is unsure that one's calculations are correct.

This answer can be seen in Figure 2.45(b). The two inner paths {Boy, Girl} and {Girl, Boy} are the relevant ones, combining to give a probability of 0.4. The same outcomes can also be seen in Figure 2.45(a) in terms of frequencies.

Note also that the problem would have been different if we had asked for the probability of the mother having one girl with a younger brother, rather than one girl and one boy.

Two further illustrations of conditional probability

Once again it may be helpful to illustrate our ideas using diagrams in order to gain a better understanding. First, we can use a Venn diagram, as in Figure 2.46. As we learned earlier, the (unconditional) probability of event B is given by area B relative to the whole of the sample space (the outer rectangle). But the probability of B *conditional on* A means that we can only consider outcomes in A, not in the whole of the sample space. Hence, the probability of B, conditional on A, is the intersection of the two sets (the hatched area), relative to A.

A second possibility is to draw up a cross-tabulation of the events, as in Figure 2.47. The four numbers in the interior of the table are those obtained in Figure 3.10(a), assuming a group of 1000 mothers. Thus we can see, for example, that there are 200 families with a girl followed by a boy (top right-hand cell). From this table we can work out the conditional probabilities. The probability of a boy

**Figure 2.46
Conditional probability**

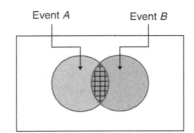

Event *A*   Event *B*

Figure 2.47
Conditional probability

		First child		
		Boy	Girl	Total
Second child	Boy	300	200	500
	Girl	200	300	500
	Total	500	500	1000

Figure 2.48
Conditional probability

		First child		
		Boy	Girl	Total
Second child	Boy	0.3	0.2	0.5
	Girl	0.2	0.3	0.5
	Total	0.5	0.5	1

on the second birth, conditional on a boy on the first is obtained from the first column of the table (outlined) which relates to only those 500 families with a boy born first. Here we can see that 300 of them went on to have another boy, so the conditional probability is $300/500 = 0.6$, as presented earlier.

The figures in the 'Total' row and column lead us to the unconditional probabilities (sometimes called the marginal probabilities because they are at the margins of the table) and we can see that they give a 50:50 chance of boy or girl on a single birth (ignoring what might have happened on the other birth), or $\Pr(\text{Boy}) = \Pr(\text{Girl}) = 0.5$.

Finally, the four interior numbers we initially looked at lead us to the joint probabilities. For example, the probability of a boy on the first birth followed by a girl on the second (upper right cell) is given by $200/1000 = 0.2$. One can also see this value in the tree diagram in Figure 2.45(a). We have presented Figure 2.47 in the form of frequencies but it is just as easy to present it in the form of probabilities – just divide all the numbers by 1000, as in Figure 2.48.

Exercise 2.17

(a) For the archer in Exercise 2.16(a) who has a 30% chance of hitting the bull's eye with a single arrow, what is the probability that she/he hits the bull's eye with one (and only one) of two attempts? Assume independence of the events. (You should write down the formula you use and evaluate it to get your answer, rather than just writing down the answer directly or the numbers in the calculation. It is worth developing this good practice as it aids your thinking and can easily be reviewed later on.)

(b) What is the probability that she hits the bull's eye with both arrows?

(c) Explain the importance of the assumption of independence for the answers to both parts (a) and (b) of this exercise.

(d) What is her probability of hitting the bull's eye with the first arrow and missing with the second? Compare your answer to that for part (a).

(e) If the archer becomes more confident after a successful shot (i.e. her probability of a successful shot rises to 50%) and less confident (probability falls to 20%) after a miss, how would this affect the answers to parts (a) and (b)? Again, take care to write down the probabilities using appropriate notation and make clear how you get your answer.

(f) Draw a tree diagram representing the case outlined in part (e). Confirm that it gives the same answers. What is the probability of the same outcome for both arrows (i.e. either both hit or both miss the bull's eye)? How does this compare to the case where independence is assumed?

Combinations and permutations

The methods described above are adequate for solving fairly simple probability puzzles but fall short when more complex questions are asked. For example, what is the probability of three girls and two boys in a family of five children? The tree diagram can obviously be extended to cover third and subsequent children, but the number of branches rapidly increases (in geometric progression). It takes time to draw the diagram (it has 32 end points), and identify the relevant paths and associated probabilities, and it is easy to make an error. If you do this correctly, you will find that there are 10 relevant paths through the diagram (e.g. GGGBB or GGBBG) and each individual path has a probability of 1/32 (½ raised to the power 5), so the answer is 10/32. Note that we are once again assuming independent events here, so the probability of having a boy or a girl is always 0.5.

Far better would be to use a formula in a complex case like this. To develop this, we introduce the ideas of **combinations** and **permutations**. The strategy for finding the probability of three girls and two boys in five children is two-fold:

(1) Work out the probability of three girls and two boys in one particular order (e.g. GGGBB). This is $0.5^5 = 1/32$.
(2) Use a formula to work out the number of different orderings, in this case 10.

It is this second point that we now focus on. How can we establish the number of ways of having three girls and two boys in a family of five children? One way would be to write down all the possible orderings:

GGGBB GGBGB GGBBG GBGGB GBGBG
GBBGG BGGGB BGGBG BGBGG BBGGG

This shows that there are 10 such orderings, so the probability of three girls and two boys in a family of five children is 10/32. In more complex problems, this soon becomes difficult or impossible. The record number of children born to a British mother is 39 (!) of whom 32 were girls. The appropriate tree diagram has over five thousand billion paths through it, and drawing one line (i.e. for one child) per second would imply 17 433 years to complete the task.

Rather than do this, we use the **combinatorial formula** to find the answer. Suppose there are n children, r of them girls, then the number of orderings, denoted nCr, is obtained from[2]

$$nCr = \frac{n!}{r!(n-r)!}$$

$$= \frac{n \times (n-1) \times \ldots \times 1}{\{r \times (r-1) \times \ldots \times 1\} \times \{(n-r) \times (n-r-1) \times \ldots \times 1\}} \quad (3.18)$$

In the above example $n = 5, r = 3$ so the number of orderings is

$$5C3 = \frac{5!}{3! \times 2!} = \frac{5 \times 4 \times 3 \times 2 \times 1}{\{3 \times 2 \times 1\} \times \{2 \times 1\}} = 10 \quad (3.19)$$

---

[2] $n!$ is read 'n factorial' and is defined as the product of all the integers up to and including n. Thus, for example, $3! = 3 \times 2 \times 1 = 6$.

If there were four girls out of five children, then the number of orderings or combinations would be

$$5C4 = \frac{5!}{4! \times 1!} = \frac{5 \times 4 \times 3 \times 2 \times 1}{\{4 \times 3 \times 2 \times 1\} \times 1} = 5 \qquad (3.20)$$

This gives five possible orderings, i.e. the single boy could be the first, second, third, fourth or fifth born.

Why does this formula work?

(If you are happy just to accept the combinatorial formula above, you can skip this section and go straight to the exercises below.) Consider five empty places to fill, corresponding to the five births in chronological order. Take the case of three girls (call them Amanda, Bridget and Caroline for convenience) who have to fill three of the five places. For Amanda there is a choice of five empty places. Having 'chosen' one, there remain four for Bridget, so there are $5 \times 4 = 20$ possibilities (i.e. ways in which these two could choose their places). Three remain for Caroline, so there are $60(=5 \times 4 \times 3)$ possible orderings in all (the two boys take the two remaining places). Sixty is the number of **permutations** of three *named* girls in five births. This is written as $5P3$ or, in general, nPr. Hence

$$5P3 = 5 \times 4 \times 3$$

or, in general,

$$nPr = n \times (n-1) \times \cdots \times (n-r+1) \qquad (3.21)$$

A simpler formula is obtained by multiplying and dividing by $(n-r)!$

$$nPr = \frac{n \times (n-1) \times \cdots \times (n-r+1) \times (n-r)!}{(n-r)!} = \frac{n!}{(n-r)!} \qquad (3.22)$$

What is the difference between nPr and nCr? The latter does not distinguish between the girls; the two cases Amanda, Bridget, Caroline, boy, boy and Bridget, Amanda, Caroline, boy, boy are effectively the same (three girls followed by two boys). So nPr is larger by a factor representing the number of ways of ordering the three girls. This factor is given by $r! = 3 \times 2 \times 1 = 6$ (any of the three girls could be first, either of the other two second, and then the final one). Thus to obtain nCr one must divide nPr by $r!$, giving (3.18).

Exercise 2.18

For this exercise we extend the analysis of Exercise 2.17 to a third shot by the archer.

(a) Extend the tree diagram (assuming independence, so $Pr(H) = 0.3, Pr(M) = 0.7$) to a third arrow. Use this to mark out the paths with two successful shots out of three. Calculate the probability of two hits out of three shots.

(b) Repeat part (a) for the case of non-independence. For this you may assume that a hit raises the problem of success with the next arrow to 50%. A miss lowers it to 20%.

Exercise 2.19

(a) Show how the answer to Exercise 2.18(a) may be arrived at using algebra, including the use of the combinatorial formula.

(b) Repeat part (a) for the non-independence case.

Bayes' theorem

Bayes' theorem is a factual statement about probabilities which in itself is uncontroversial. However, the use and interpretation of the result is at the heart of the difference between classical and Bayesian statistics. The theorem itself is easily derived from first principles. Equation (3.23) is similar to equation equation (3.14) covered earlier when discussing the multiplication rule:

$$\Pr(A \text{ and } B) = \Pr(A|B) \times \Pr(B) \tag{3.23}$$

hence,

$$\Pr(A|B) = \frac{\Pr(A \text{ and } B)}{\Pr(B)} \tag{3.24}$$

Expanding both top and bottom of the right-hand side,

$$\Pr(A|B) = \frac{\Pr(B|A) \times \Pr(A)}{\Pr(B|A) \times \Pr(A) + \Pr(B|\text{not } A) \times \Pr(\text{not } A)} \tag{3.25}$$

Equation (3.25) is known as Bayes' theorem and is a statement about the probability of the event A, conditional upon B having occurred. The following example demonstrates its use.

Two bags contain red and yellow balls. Bag A contains six red and four yellow balls, and bag B has three red and seven yellow balls. A ball is drawn at random from one bag and turns out to be red. What is the probability that it came from bag A? Since bag A has relatively more red balls to yellow balls than does bag B, it seems bag A ought to be favoured. The probability should be more than 0.5. We can check if this is correct.

Denoting:

$\Pr(A) = 0.5$ (the probability of choosing bag A at random) $= \Pr(B)$
$\Pr(R|A) = 0.6$ (the probability of selecting a red ball from bag A), etc.

we have

$$\Pr(A|R) = \frac{\Pr(R|A) \times \Pr(A)}{\Pr(R|A) \times \Pr(A) + \Pr(R|B) \times \Pr(B)} \tag{3.26}$$

using Bayes' theorem. Evaluating this gives

$$\Pr(A|R) = \frac{0.6 \times 0.5}{0.6 \times 0.5 + 0.3 \times 0.5} \tag{3.27}$$
$$= {}^{2}/_{3}$$

As expected, this result is greater than 0.5. (You can check that $\Pr(B|R) = 1/3$ so that the sum of the probabilities is 1.)

It may help us understand this if we draw another tree diagram, as Figure 2.49. Once again, this shows frequencies, 1000 trials of taking a ball from a bag. In 500 of the trials we would expect to select bag A, in the other 500 trials we select bag $B(\Pr(A) = \Pr(B) = 0.5)$. This is the first stage of the diagram. Of the 500 occasions we select bag A, 300 times we get a red ball $(\Pr(R|A) = 0.6)$ and 200 times we get yellow. From bag B we get 150 draws of a red ball $(\Pr(R|B) = 0.3)$ and 350 yellows.

Figure 2.49
Bayes' theorem

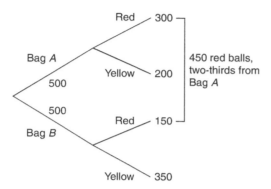

Red 300 ⌉
Bag A
500   Yellow 200   │ 450 red balls,
                          │ two-thirds from
500   │ Bag A
Red 150 ⌋
Bag B
Yellow 350

Hence, on 450 occasions we get a red ball. Two-thirds of those (300/450) came from bag A, which is $\Pr(A|R)$.

Bayes' theorem can be extended to cover more than two bags: if there are five bags, for example, labelled A to E, then

$$\Pr(A|R) = \frac{\Pr(R|A) \times \Pr(A)}{\Pr(R|A) \times \Pr(A) + \Pr(R|B) \times \Pr(B) + \cdots + \Pr(R|E) \times \Pr(E)} \quad (3.28)$$

In Bayesian language, $\Pr(A)$, $\Pr(B)$, etc., are known as the prior (to the drawing of the ball) probabilities, $\Pr(R|A)$, $\Pr(R|B)$, etc., are the likelihoods and $\Pr(A|R)$, $\Pr(B|R)$, etc., are the posterior probabilities. Bayes' theorem can alternatively be expressed as

$$\text{posterior probability} = \frac{\text{likelihood} \times \text{prior probability}}{\Sigma(\text{likelihood} \times \text{prior probability})} \quad (3.29)$$

This is illustrated below, by reworking the above example in a different format.

	Prior probabilities	Likelihoods	Prior × likelihood	Posterior probabilities
A	0.5	0.6	0.30	0.30/0.45 = 2/3
B	0.5	0.3	0.15	0.15/0.45 = 1/3
Total			0.45	

The general version of Bayes' theorem may be stated as follows. If there are n events labelled $E_1, \ldots, E_n$, then the probability of the event E_i occurring, given the sample evidence S, is

$$\Pr(E_i|S) = \frac{\Pr(S|E_i) \times \Pr(E_i)}{\Sigma(\Pr(S|E_i) \times \Pr(E_i))} \quad (3.30)$$

As stated earlier, debate arises over the interpretation of Bayes' theorem. In the above example, there is no difficulty because the probability statements can be interpreted as relative frequencies. If the experiment of selecting a bag at random and choosing a ball from it were repeated many times, then in two-thirds of those occasions when a red ball is selected, bag A will have been chosen. However, consider an alternative interpretation of the symbols:

A: a coin is fair
B: a coin is unfair
R: the result of a toss is a head

Then, given a toss (or series of tosses) of a coin, this evidence can be used to calculate the probability of the coin being fair. But this makes no sense according to the frequentist school: either the coin is fair or not; it is not a question of probability. The calculated value must be interpreted as a degree of belief and be given a subjective interpretation.

Exercise 2.20

(a) Repeat the 'balls in the bag' exercise from the text, but with bag A containing five red and three yellow balls, bag B containing one red and two yellow balls. The single ball drawn is red. Before doing the calculation, predict which bag is more likely to be the source of the drawn ball. Explain why. Then compare your prediction with the calculated answer.

(b) Bag A now contains 10 red and 6 yellow balls (i.e. twice as many as before, but in the same proportion). Does this alter the answer you obtained in part (a)?

(c) Set out your answer to part (b) in the form of prior probabilities and likelihoods, in order to obtain the posterior probability.

Decision analysis

The study of probability naturally leads to the analysis of decision-making where risk is involved. This is the realistic situation facing most firms, and the use of probability can help to illuminate the problem. To illustrate the topic, we use the example of a firm facing a choice of three different investment projects. The uncertainty which the firm faces concerns the interest rate at which to discount the future flows of income. If the interest/discount rate is high, then projects which have income far in the future become less attractive relative to projects with more immediate returns. A low rate reverses this conclusion. The question is: which project should the firm select? As we shall see, there is no unique, right answer to the question but, using probability theory, we can see why the answer might vary.

Table 2.22 provides the data required for the problem. The three projects are imaginatively labelled *A*, *B* and *C*. There are four possible states of the world, i.e. future scenarios, each with a different interest rate, as shown across the top of the table. This is the only source of uncertainty; otherwise the states of the world are identical. The figures in the body of the table show the present value of each income stream at the given discount rate.

Table 2.22 Data for decision analysis: present values of three investment projects at different interest rates (£000)

Project	Future interest rate			
	4%	5%	6%	7%
A	1475	1363	1200	1115
B	1500	1380	1148	1048
C	1650	1440	1200	810
Probability	0.1	0.4	0.4	0.1

Present value

The present value of future income is its value today and is obtained using the interest rate. For example, if the interest rate is 10%, the present value (i.e. today) of £110 received in one year's time is £100. In other words, one could invest £100 today at 10% and have £110 in one year's time. £100 today and £110 next year are equivalent.

The present value of £110 received in two years' time is smaller since one has to wait longer to receive it. It is calculated as £110/1.1^2 = 90.91. Again, £90.91 invested at 10% p.a. will yield £110 in two years' time. After one year it is worth £90.91 × 1.1 = 100 and after a second year that £100 becomes £110. Notice that, if the interest rate rises, the present value falls. For example, if the interest rate is 20%, £110 next year is worth only £110/1.2 = 91.67 today.

If we denote the interest rate by r, so $r = 0.1$ indicates an interest rate of 10%, the value now of £110 in two years' time is £110/(1 + r)^2 = £110/(1.1)^2 = 90.91, as above. In general, the present value of a sum X in t years' time is given by $X/(1 + r)^t$.

The present value of £110 in one year's time and another £110 in two years' time is £110/1.1 + £110/1.1^2 = £190.91. The present value of more complicated streams of income can be calculated by extension of this principle. In the example used in the text, you do not need to worry about how we arrive at the present value. Before reading on you may wish to do Exercise 2.20 to practise calculation of present value.

Thus, for example, if the interest rate turns out to be 4%, then project A has a present value of £1 475 000 while B's is £1 500 000. If the discount rate turns out to be 5%, the *PV* for A is £1 363 000 while for B it has changed to £1 380 000. Obviously, as the discount rate rises, the present value of the return falls. (Alternatively, we could assume that a higher interest rate increases the cost of borrowing to finance the project, which reduces its profitability.) We assume that each project requires a (certain) initial outlay of £1 100 000 with which the *PV* should be compared.

The final row of the table shows the probabilities which the firm attaches to each interest rate. These are obviously someone's subjective probabilities and are symmetric around a central value of 5.5%.

Exercise 2.21

(a) At an interest or discount rate of 10%, what is the present value of £1200 received in one year's time?

(b) If the interest rate rises to 15%, how is the present value altered? The interest rate has risen by 50% (from 10% to 15%): how has the present value changed?

(c) At an interest rate of 10% what is the present value of £1200 received in (i) two years' time and (ii) five years' time?

(d) An income of £500 is received at the end of years one, two and three (i.e. £1500 in total). What is its present value? Assume the interest rate is 10%.

(e) Project A provides an income of £300 after one year and another £600 after two years. Project B provides £400 and £488 at the same times. At a discount rate of 10%, which project has the higher present value? What happens if the discount rate rises to 20%?

Decision criteria: maximising the expected value

We need to decide how a decision is to be made on the basis of these data. The first criterion involves the **expected value** of each project. Because of the uncertainty about the interest rate, there is no certain present value for each project. We therefore

Table 2.23 **Expected values of the three projects**

Project	Expected value
A	1284.2
B	1266.0
C	1302.0

Note: 1284.2 is calculated as $1475 \times 0.1 + 1363 \times 0.4 + 1200 \times 0.4 + 1115 \times 0.1$. This is the weighted average of the four *PV* values. A similar calculation is performed for the other projects.

calculate the expected value, using the E operator which was introduced in Chapter 1. In other words, we find the expected present value of each project, by taking a weighted average of the *PV* figures, the weights being the probabilities. The project with the highest expected return is chosen.

The expected values are calculated in Table 2.23. The highest expected present value is £1 302 000, associated with project *C*. On this criterion, therefore, *C* is chosen. Is this a wise choice? If the business always uses this rule to evaluate many projects, then in the long run it will earn the maximum profits. However, you may notice that if the interest rate turns out to be 7%, then *C* would be the *worst* project to choose in this case and the firm would make a substantial loss in such circumstances. Project *C* is the most sensitive to the discount rate (it has the greatest *variance* of *PV* values of the three projects) and therefore the firm faces more risk by opting for *C*. There is a trade-off between risk and return. Perhaps some alternative criteria should be examined. These we look at next, in particular the maximin, maximax and minimax regret strategies.

Maximin, maximax and minimax regret

The maximin criterion looks at the worst-case scenario for each project and then selects the project which does best in these circumstances. It is inevitably a pessimistic or cautious view therefore. Table 2.24 illustrates the calculation. This time we observe that project *A* is preferred. In the worst case (which occurs when $r = 7\%$ for all projects), *A* does best, with a *PV* of £1 115 000 and therefore a slight profit. The maximin criterion may be a good one in business where managers tend towards over-optimism. Calculating the maximin may be a salutary exercise, even if it is not the ultimate deciding factor.

The opposite criterion is the optimistic one where the maximax criterion is used. In this case one looks at the *best* circumstances for each project and chooses the best-performing project. Each project does best when the interest rate is at its lowest level, 3%. Examining the first column of Table 2.22 shows that project $C(PV = 1650)$ performs best and is therefore chosen. Given the earlier warning about over-optimistic managers, this may not be suitable as the sole criterion for making investment decisions.

Table 2.24 **The maximin criterion**

Project	Minimum
A	1115
B	1048
C	810
Maximum	1115

Table 2.25 The costs of taking the wrong decision

Project	4%	5%	6%	7%	Maximum
A	175	77	0	0	175
B	150	60	52	67	150
C	0	0	0	305	305
Minimum					150

Note: The first figure in the 4% discount rate column indicates that Project A's payoff is 175(=1650 − 1475) worse than that of C, the best choice in this circumstance.

A final criterion is that of minimax regret. If project *B* were chosen but the interest rate turns out to be 7%, then we would regret not having chosen *A*, the best project under these circumstances. Our *regret* would be the extent of the difference between the two, a matter of 1115 − 1048 = 67. Similarly, the regret if we had chosen *C* would be 1115 − 810 = 305. We can calculate these regrets at the other interest rates too, always comparing the *PV* of a project with the best *PV* given that interest rate. This gives us Table 2.25.

The final column of the table shows the maximum regret for each project. The minimax regret criterion is to choose the minimum of these figures. This is given at the bottom of the final column; it is 150 which is associated with project *B*. A justification for using this criterion might be that you don't want to fall too far behind your competitors. If other firms are facing similar investment decisions, then the regret table shows the difference in *PV* (and hence profits) if they choose the best project while you do not. Choosing the minimax regret solution ensures that you won't fall too far behind. During the internet bubble of the 1990s it was important to gain market share and keep up with, or surpass, your competitors. The minimax regret strategy might be a useful tool during such times.

You will probably have noticed that we have managed to find a justification for choosing all three projects. No one project comes out best on all criteria. Nevertheless, the analysis might be of some help: if the investment project is one of many small, independent investments the firm is making, then this would justify use of the expected value criterion. On the other hand, if this is a big, one-off project which could possibly bankrupt the firm if it goes wrong, then the maximin criterion would be appropriate.

The expected value of perfect information

Often a firm can improve its knowledge about future possibilities via research, which costs money. This effectively means buying information about the future state of the world. The question arises: how much should a firm pay for such information? Perfect information would reveal the future state of the world with certainty – in this case, the future interest rate. In that case you could be sure of choosing the right project given each state of the world. If interest rates turn out to be 4%, the firm would invest in *C*, if 7% in *A*, and so on.

In such circumstances, the firm would expect to earn:

$$(0.1 \times 1650) + (0.4 \times 1440) + (0.4 \times 1200) + (0.1 \times 1115) = 1332.5$$

i.e. the probability of each state of the world is multiplied by the *PV* of the *best* project for that state. This gives a figure which is greater than the expected value calculated earlier, without perfect information, 1302. The expected value of perfect information is therefore the difference between these two, 30.5. This sets a *maximum* to the value of information, for it is unlikely in the real world that any information about the future is going to be perfect.

Exercise 2.22

(a) Evaluate the three projects detailed in the table below, using the criteria of expected value, maximin, maximax and minimax regret. The probability of a 4% interest rate is 0.3, of 6% 0.4 and of 8% 0.3.

Project	4%	6%	8%
A	100	80	70
B	90	85	75
C	120	60	40

(b) What would be the value of perfect information about the interest rate?

Summary

- The theory of probability forms the basis of statistical inference, the drawing of inferences on the basis of a random sample of data. The probability basis of random sampling is the reason for this.
- A convenient definition of the probability of an event is the number of times the event occurs divided by the number of trials (occasions when the event could occur).
- For more complex events, their probabilities can be calculated by combining probabilities, using the addition and multiplication rules.
- The probability of events A or B occurring is calculated according to the addition rule.
- The probability of A and B occurring is given by the multiplication rule.
- If A and B are not independent, then $\Pr(A \text{ and } B) = \Pr(A) \times \Pr(B|A)$, where $\Pr(B|A)$ is the probability of B occurring given that A has occurred (the conditional probability). With independence, the formula simplifies to $\Pr(A \text{ and } B) = \Pr(A) \times \Pr(B)$.
- Tree diagrams are a useful technique for enumerating all the possible paths in series of probability trials, but for large numbers of trials the huge number of possibilities makes the technique impractical.
- For experiments with a large number of trials (e.g. obtaining 20 heads in 50 tosses of a coin), the formulae for combinations and permutations can be used.
- The combinatorial formula *nCr* gives the number of ways of combining *r* similar objects among *n* objects, e.g. the number of orderings of three girls (and hence implicitly two boys also) in five children.
- The permutation formula *nPr* gives the number of orderings of *r* distinct objects among *n*, e.g. three named girls among five children.

- Bayes' theorem provides a formula for calculating a conditional probability, e.g. the probability of someone being a smoker, given they have been diagnosed with cancer. It forms the basis of Bayesian statistics, allowing us to calculate the probability of a hypothesis being true, based on the sample evidence and prior beliefs. Classical statistics disputes this approach.

- Probabilities can also be used as the basis for decision-making in conditions of uncertainty, using as decision criteria expected value maximisation, maximin, maximax or minimax regret.

Key terms and concepts

addition rule	maximax
axiomatic approach	maximin
Bayes' theorem	minimax
Bayesian statistics	minimax regret
classical statistics	multiplication rule
combinations	mutually exclusive
combinatorial formula	operator
complement	outcome or event
compound event	perfect information
conditional probability	permutations
degree of belief	posterior probabilities
event	prior belief
exhaustive	prior probabilities
expected value	probability
expected value of perfect information	proportion
experiment	sample space
frequentist view	states of the world
independent events	statistical inference
intersection	subjective view
joint probabilities	tree diagram
likelihoods	trial
marginal probabilities	union

Formulae used in this chapter

Formula	Description	Note
$nCr = \dfrac{n!}{r!(n-r)!}$	Combinatorial formula	$n! = n \times (n-1) \times \cdots \times 1$

Problems

Some of the more challenging problems are indicated by highlighting the problem number in colour.

2.3.1 Given a standard pack of cards, calculate the following probabilities:

(a) drawing an ace;

(b) drawing a court card (i.e. jack, queen or king);

(c) drawing a red card;

(d) drawing three aces without replacement;

(e) drawing three aces with replacement.

2.3.2 The following data give duration of unemployment by age.

Age	Duration of unemployment (weeks)				Total	Economically active
	≤8	8–26	26–52	>52	(000s)	(000s)
	(Percentage figures, rows sum to 100)					
16–19	27.2	29.8	24.0	19.0	273.4	1270
20–24	24.2	20.7	18.3	36.8	442.5	2000
25–34	14.8	18.8	17.2	49.2	531.4	3600
35–49	12.2	16.6	15.1	56.2	521.2	4900
50–59	8.9	14.4	15.6	61.2	388.1	2560
≥60	18.5	29.7	30.7	21.4	74.8	1110

The 'economically active' column gives the total of employed (not shown) plus unemployed in each age category.

(a) In what sense may these figures be regarded as probabilities? What does the figure 27.2 (top-left cell) mean following this interpretation?

(b) Assuming the validity of the probability interpretation, which of the following statements are true?

(i) The probability of an economically active adult aged 25–34, drawn at random, being unemployed is 531.4/3600.

(ii) If someone who has been unemployed for over one year is drawn at random, the probability that they are aged 16–19 is 19%.

(iii) For those aged 35–49 who became unemployed at least one year ago, the probability of their still being unemployed is 56.2%.

    (iv) If someone aged 50–59 is drawn at random from the economically active population, the probability of their being unemployed for eight weeks or less is 8.9%.

    (v) The probability of someone aged 35–49 drawn at random from the economically active population being unemployed for between 8 and 26 weeks is $0.166 \times 521.2/4900$.

(c) A person is drawn at random from the population and found to have been unemployed for over one year. What is the probability that they are aged between 16 and 19?

2.3.3 'Odds' in horserace betting are defined as follows: 3/1 (three-to-one against) means a horse is expected to win once for every three times it loses; 3/2 means two wins out of five races; 4/5 (five to four *on*) means five wins for every four defeats, etc.

(a) Translate the above odds into 'probabilities' of victory.

(b) In a three-horse race, the odds quoted are 2/1, 6/4 and 1/1. What makes the odds different from probabilities? Why are they different?

(c) Discuss how much the bookmaker would expect to win in the long run at such odds (in part (b)), assuming each horse is backed equally.

2.3.4 (a) Translate the following odds to 'probabilities': 13/8, 2/1 *on*, 100/30.

(b) In the 3.45 race at Plumpton the odds for the five runners were:

Philips Woody	1/1
Gallant Effort	5/2
Satin Noir	11/2
Victory Anthem	9/1
Common Rambler	16/1

Calculate the 'probabilities' and their sum.

(c) Should the bookmaker base his odds on the true probabilities of each horse winning, or adjust them depending upon the amount bet on each horse?

2.3.5 How might you estimate the probability of Peru defaulting on its debt repayments next year? What type of probability estimate is this?

2.3.6 How might you estimate the probability of a corporation reneging on its bond payments?

2.3.7 Judy is 33, unmarried and assertive. She is a graduate in political science, and involved in union activities and anti-discrimination movements. Which of the following statements do you think is more probable?

(a) Judy is a bank clerk.

(b) Judy is a bank clerk, active in the feminist movement.

2.3.8 A news item revealed that a London 'gender' clinic (which reportedly enables you to choose the sex of your child) had just set up in business. Of its first six births, two were of the 'wrong' sex. Assess this from a probability point of view.

2.3.9 A newspaper advertisement reads 'The sex of your child predicted, or your money back!' Discuss this advertisement from the point of view of (a) the advertiser and (b) the client.

2.3.10 'Roll six sixes to win a Mercedes!' is the announcement at a fair. You have to roll six dice. If you get six sixes you win the car, valued at £40 000. The entry ticket costs £1. What is your expected gain or loss on this game? If there are 400 people who try the game, what is the probability of the car being won? The organisers of the fair have to take out insurance against the car being won. This costs £400 for the day. Does this seem a fair premium? If not, why not?

2.3.11   At another stall, you have to toss a coin numerous times. If a head does not appear in 20 tosses you win £1 billion. The entry fee for the game is £100.

(a) What are your expected winnings?

(b) Would you play?

2.3.12   A four-engine plane can fly as long as at least two of its engines work. A two-engine plane flies as long as at least one engine works. The probability of an individual engine failure is 1 in 1000.

(a) Would you feel safer in a four- or two-engine plane, and why? Calculate the probabilities of an accident for each type.

(b) How much safer is one type than the other?

(c) What crucial assumption are you making in your calculation? Do you think it is valid?

2.3.13   Which of the following events are independent?

(a) Two flips of a fair coin.

(b) Two flips of a biased coin.

(c) Rainfall on two successive days.

(d) Rainfall on St Swithin's Day and rain one month later.

2.3.14   Which of the following events are independent?

(a) A student getting the first two questions correct in a multiple-choice exam.

(b) A driver having an accident in successive years.

(c) IBM and Dell earning positive profits next year.

(d) Arsenal Football Club winning on successive weekends.

How is the answer to (b) reflected in car insurance premiums?

2.3.15   Manchester United beat Liverpool 4–2 at soccer, but you do not know the order in which the goals were scored. Draw a tree diagram to display all the possibilities and use it to find (a) the probability that the goals were scored in the order L, MU, MU, MU, L, MU and (b) the probability that the score was 2–2 at some stage.

2.3.16   An important numerical calculation on a spacecraft is carried out independently by three computers. If all arrive at the same answer, it is deemed correct. If one disagrees, it is overruled. If there is no agreement, then a fourth computer does the calculation and, if its answer agrees with any of the others, it is deemed correct. The probability of an individual computer getting the answer right is 99%. Use a tree diagram to find:

(a) the probability that the first three computers get the right answer;

(b) the probability of getting the right answer;

(c) the probability of getting no answer;

(d) the probability of getting the wrong answer.

2.3.17   The French national lottery works as follows. Six numbers from the range 0 to 49 are chosen at random. If you have correctly guessed all six, you win the first prize. What are your chances of winning if you are allowed to choose only six numbers? A single entry like this costs one euro. For 210 euros you can choose 10 numbers, and you win if the 6 selected numbers are among them. Is this better value than the single entry?

2.3.18   The UK national lottery originally worked as follows. You choose six (different) numbers in the range 1 to 49. If all six come up in the draw (in any order), you win the first prize, generally valued at around £2m (which could be shared if someone else chooses the six winning numbers).

(a)   What is your chance of winning with a single ticket?

(b)   You win a second prize if you get five out of six right *and* your final chosen number matches the 'bonus' number in the draw (also in the range 1–49). What is the probability of winning a second prize?

(c)   Calculate the probabilities of winning a third, fourth or fifth prize, where a third prize is won by matching five out of the six numbers, a fourth prize by matching four out of six and a fifth prize by matching three out of six.

(d)   What is the probability of winning a prize?

(e)   The prizes are as follows:

Prize	Value	
First	£2 million	(expected, possibly shared)
Second	£100 000	(expected, for each winner)
Third	£1500	(expected, for each winner)
Fourth	£65	(expected, for each winner)
Fifth	£10	(guaranteed, for each winner)

Comment upon the distribution of the fund between first, second, etc., prizes.

(f)   Why is the fifth prize guaranteed whereas the others are not?

(g)   In the first week of the lottery, 49 million tickets were sold. There were 1 150 000 winners, of which 7 won (a share of) the jackpot, 39 won a second prize, 2139 won a third prize and 76 731 a fourth prize. Are you surprised by these results or are they as you would expect?

2.3.19   A coin is either fair or has two heads. You initially assign probabilities of 0.5 to each possibility. The coin is then tossed twice, with two heads appearing. Use Bayes' theorem to work out the posterior probabilities of each possible outcome.

2.3.20   A test for AIDS is 99% successful, i.e. if you are HIV+, it will be detected in 99% of all tests, and if you are not, it will again be right 99% of the time. Assume that about 1% of the population are HIV+. You take part in a random testing procedure, which gives a positive result. What is the probability that you are HIV+? What implications does your result have for AIDS testing?

2.3.21   (a)   Your initial belief is that a defendant in a court case is guilty with probability 0.5. A witness comes forward claiming he saw the defendant commit the crime. You know the witness is not totally reliable and tells the truth with probability p. Use Bayes' theorem to calculate the posterior probability that the defendant is guilty, based on the witness's evidence.

(b)   A second witness, equally unreliable, comes forward and claims she/he saw the defendant commit the crime. Assuming the witnesses are not colluding, what is your posterior probability of guilt?

(c)   If $p < 0.5$, compare the answers to (a) and (b). How do you account for this curious result?

2.3.22 A man is mugged and claims that the mugger had red hair. In police investigations of such cases, the victim was able correctly to identify the assailant's hair colour 80% of the time. Assuming that 10% of the population have red hair, what is the probability that the assailant in this case did, in fact, have red hair? Guess the answer first, and then find the right answer using Bayes' theorem. What are the implications of your results for juries' interpretation of evidence in court, particularly in relation to racial minorities?

2.3.23 A firm has a choice of three projects, with profits as indicated below, dependent upon the state of demand.

Project	Demand		
	Low	Middle	High
A	100	140	180
B	130	145	170
C	110	130	200
Probability	0.25	0.45	0.3

(a) Which project should be chosen on the expected value criterion?

(b) Which project should be chosen on the maximin and maximax criteria?

(c) Which project should be chosen on the minimax regret criterion?

(d) What is the expected value of perfect information to the firm?

2.3.24 A firm can build a small, medium or large factory, with anticipated profits from each dependent upon the state of demand, as in the table below.

Factory	Demand		
	Low	Middle	High
Small	300	320	330
Medium	270	400	420
Large	50	250	600
Probability	0.3	0.5	0.2

(a) Which project should be chosen on the expected value criterion?

(b) Which project should be chosen on the maximin and maximax criteria?

(c) Which project should be chosen on the minimax regret criterion?

(d) What is the expected value of perfect information to the firm?

2.3.25 There are 25 people at a party. What is the probability that there are at least two with a birthday in common? They do not need to have been born in the same year, just the same day and month of the year. Also, ignore leap year dates. (Hint: the *complement* is (much) easier to calculate.)

2.3.26 This problem is tricky, but amusing. Three gunmen, A, B and C, are shooting at each other. The probabilities that each will hit what they aim at are 1, 0.75 and 0.5, respectively. They take it in turns to shoot (in alphabetical order) and continue until only one is left alive. Calculate the probabilities of each winning the contest. (Assume they draw lots for the right to shoot first.)

Hint 1: Start with one-on-one gunfights, e.g. the probability of A beating B, or of B beating C. You need to solve this first, and *then* figure out the optimal strategies in the first stage when all three are alive.

Hint 2: You'll need the formula for the sum of an infinite series, given in Chapter 1.

Hint 3: To solve this, you need to realize that it might be in a gunman's best interest *not* to aim at one of his opponents . . .

Three special examples of the linear function $W = a + bX$ are important. The first example considers a constant function, $W = a$, for any constant a. In this situation the coefficient $b = 0$. In the second example $a = 0$, giving $W = bX$. The expected value and the variance for these functions are defined by Equations 4.11 and 4.12. The third example is significant in later chapters. The mean and variance of this special linear function are defined by Equations 4.13 and 4.14. Thus, subtracting its mean from a random variable and dividing by its standard deviation yields a random variable with mean 0 and standard deviation 1.

Summary Results for the Mean and Variance of Special Linear Functions

a. Let $b = 0$ in the linear function $W = a + bX$. Then let $W = a$ (for any constant a).

$$E[a] = a \quad \text{and} \quad Var(a) = 0 \tag{4.11}$$

If a random variable always takes the value a, it will have a mean a and a variance 0.

b. Let $a = 0$ in the linear function $W = a + bX$. Then let $W = bX$.

$$E[bX] = b\mu_X \quad \text{and} \quad Var(bX) = b^2\sigma_X^2 \tag{4.12}$$

c. To find the mean and variance of

$$Z = \frac{X - \mu_X}{\sigma_X}$$

let $a = -\mu_X/\sigma_X$ and $b = 1/\sigma_X$ in the linear function $Z = a + bX$. Then

$$Z = a + bX = \frac{X - \mu_X}{\sigma_X} = \frac{X}{\sigma_X} - \frac{\mu_X}{\sigma_X}$$

so that

$$E\left[\frac{X - \mu_X}{\sigma_X}\right] = \frac{\mu_X}{\sigma_X} - \frac{1}{\sigma_X}\mu_X = 0 \tag{4.13}$$

and

$$Var\left(\frac{X - \mu_X}{\sigma_X}\right) = \frac{1}{\sigma_X^2}\sigma_X^2 = 1 \tag{4.14}$$

EXERCISES

Basic Exercises

2.4.15 Consider the probability distribution function.

x	0	1
Probability	0.40	0.60

a. Graph the probability distribution function.
b. Calculate and graph the cumulative probability distribution.
c. Find the mean of the random variable X.
d. Find the variance of X.

2.4.16 Given the probability distribution function:

x	0	1	2
Probability	0.25	0.50	0.25

a. Graph the probability distribution function.
b. Calculate and graph the cumulative probability distribution.
c. Find the mean of the random variable X.
d. Find the variance of X.

2.4.17 Consider the probability distribution function

x	0	1
Probability	0.50	0.50

a. Graph the probability distribution function.
b. Calculate and graph the cumulative probability distribution.
c. Find the mean of the random variable X.
d. Find the variance of X.

2.4.18   An automobile dealer calculates the proportion of new cars sold that have been returned a various numbers of times for the correction of defects during the warranty period. The results are shown in the following table.

Number of returns	0	1	2	3	4
Proportion	0.28	0.36	0.23	0.09	0.04

a. Graph the probability distribution function.
b. Calculate and graph the cumulative probability distribution.
c. Find the mean of the number of returns of an automobile for corrections for defects during the warranty period.
d. Find the variance of the number of returns of an automobile for corrections for defects during the warranty period.

2.4.19   A company specializes in installing and servicing central-heating furnaces. In the prewinter period, service calls may result in an order for a new furnace. The following table shows estimated probabilities for the numbers of new furnace orders generated in this way in the last two weeks of September.

Number of orders	0	1	2	3	4	5
Probability	0.10	0.14	0.26	0.28	0.15	0.07

a. Graph the probability distribution function.
b. Calculate and graph the cumulative probability distribution.
c. Find the probability that at least 3 orders will be generated in this period.
d. Find the mean of the number of orders for new furnaces in this 2-week period.
e. Find the standard deviation of the number of orders for new furnaces in this 2-week period.

Application Exercises

2.4.20   Forest Green Brown, Inc., produces bags of cypress mulch. The weight in pounds per bag varies, as indicated in the accompanying table.

Weight in pounds	44	45	46	47	48	49	50
Proportion of bags	0.04	0.13	0.21	0.29	0.20	0.10	0.03

a. Graph the probability distribution.
b. Calculate and graph the cumulative probability distribution.
c. What is the probability that a randomly chosen bag will contain more than 45 and less than 49 pounds of mulch (inclusive)?
d. Two packages are chosen at random. What is the probability that at least one of them contains at least 47 pounds?
e. Compute—using a computer—the mean and standard deviation of the weight per bag.
f. The cost (in cents) of producing a bag of mulch is $75 + 2X$, where X is the number of pounds per bag. The revenue from selling the bag, regardless of weight, is $2.50. If profit is defined as the difference between revenue and cost, find the mean and standard deviation of profit per bag.

2.4.21   A municipal bus company has started operations in a new subdivision. Records were kept on the numbers of riders on one bus route during the early-morning weekday service. The accompanying table shows proportions over all weekdays.

Number of riders	20	21	22	23	24	25	26	27
Proportion	0.02	0.12	0.23	0.31	0.19	0.08	0.03	0.02

a. Graph the probability distribution.
b. Calculate and graph the cumulative probability distribution.
c. What is the probability that on a randomly chosen weekday there will be at least 24 riders from the subdivision on this service?
d. Two weekdays are chosen at random. What is the probability that on both of these days there will be fewer than 23 riders from the subdivision on this service?
e. Find the mean and standard deviation of the number of riders from this subdivision on this service on a weekday.
f. If the cost of a ride is $1.50, find the mean and standard deviation of the total payments of riders from this subdivision on this service on a weekday.

2.4.22   a. A very large shipment of parts contains 10% defectives. Two parts are chosen at random from the shipment and checked. Let the random variable X denote the number of defectives found. Find the probability distribution of this random variable.
   b. A shipment of 20 parts contains 2 defectives. Two parts are chosen at random from the shipment and checked. Let the random variable Y denote the number of defectives found. Find the probability distribution of this random variable. Explain why your answer is different from that for part (a).
   c. Find the mean and variance of the random variable X in part (a).
   d. Find the mean and variance of the random variable Y in part (b).

2.4.23   A student needs to know details of a class assignment that is due the next day and decides to call fellow class members for this information. She believes that for any particular call, the probability of obtaining the necessary information is 0.40. She decides to continue calling class members until the information is obtained. But her cell phone battery will not allow more than 8 calls. Let the random variable X denote the number of calls needed to obtain the information.

a. Find the probability distribution of X.
b. Find the cumulative probability distribution of X.
c. Find the probability that at least three calls are required.

2.4.24 Your school Ping-Pong team is not performing very well this season. After some rough calculations, you found out that your team's probability of winning a game is about 0.45. A fellow team member wants to know more and asked you also to determine the following.

    a. The probability of the team winning 2 games out of 5.
    b. The probability of winning 10 times out of 25.

2.4.25 A professor teaches a large class and has scheduled an examination for 7:00 p.m. in a different classroom. She estimates the probabilities in the table for the number of students who will call her at home in the hour before the examination asking where the exam will be held.

Number of calls	0	1	2	3	4	5
Probability	0.10	0.15	0.19	0.26	0.19	0.11

Find the mean and standard deviation of the number of calls.

2.4.26 Students in a large accounting class were asked to rate the course by assigning a score of 1, 2, 3, 4, or 5 to the course. A higher score indicates that the students received greater value from the course. The accompanying table shows proportions of students rating the course in each category.

Rating	1	2	3	4	5
Proportion	0.07	0.19	0.28	0.30	0.16

Find the mean and standard deviation of the ratings.

2.4.27 A store owner stocks an out-of-town newspaper that is sometimes requested by a small number of customers. Each copy of this newspaper costs her 70 cents, and she sells them for 90 cents each. Any copies left over at the end of the day have no value and are destroyed. Any requests for copies that cannot be met because stocks have been exhausted are considered by the store owner as a loss of 5 cents in goodwill. The probability distribution of the number of requests for the newspaper in a day is shown in the accompanying table. If the store owner defines total daily profit as total revenue from newspaper sales, less total cost of newspapers ordered, less goodwill loss from unsatisfied demand, what is the expected profit if four newspapers are order?

Number of requests	0	1	2	3	4	5
Probability	0.12	0.16	0.18	0.32	0.14	0.08

2.4.28 A factory manager is considering whether to replace a temperamental machine. A review of past records indicates the following probability distribution for the number of breakdowns of this machine in a week.

Number of breakdowns	0	1	2	3	4
Probability	0.10	0.26	0.42	0.16	0.06

    a. Find the mean and standard deviation of the number of weekly breakdowns.
    b. It is estimated that each breakdown costs the company $1,500 in lost output. Find the mean and standard deviation of the weekly cost to the company from breakdowns of this machine.

2.4.29 An investor is considering three strategies for a $1,000 investment. The probable returns are estimated as follows:

- *Strategy 1:* A profit of $10,000 with probability 0.15 and a loss of $1,000 with probability 0.85
- *Strategy 2:* A profit of $1,000 with probability 0.50, a profit of $500 with probability 0.30, and a loss of $500 with probability 0.20
- *Strategy 3:* A certain profit of $400

Which strategy has the highest expected profit? Explain why you would or would not advise the investor to adopt this strategy.

2.4.4 BINOMIAL DISTRIBUTION

We now develop the binomial probability distribution, which is used extensively in many applied business and economic problems. Our approach begins with the Bernoulli model, which is a building block for the binomial. Consider a random experiment that can give rise to just two possible mutually exclusive and collectively exhaustive outcomes, which for convenience we label "success" and "failure." Let P denote the probability of success, and, the probability of failure $(1 - P)$. Then, define the random variable X so that X takes the value 1 if the outcome of the experiment is success and 0 otherwise. The probability distribution of this random variable is then

$$P(0) = (1 - P) \quad \text{and} \quad P(1) = P$$

This distribution is known as the *Bernoulli distribution*. Its mean and variance can be found by direct application of the equations in Section 2.4.3.

Derivation of the Mean and Variance of a Bernoulli Random Variable

The **mean** is

$$\mu_X = E[X] = \sum_x xP(x) = (0)(1 - P) + (1)P = P \tag{4.15}$$

and the **variance** is

$$\sigma_X^2 = E[(X - \mu_X)^2] = \sum_x (x - \mu_X)^2 P(x)$$

$$= (0 - P)^2(1 - P) + (1 - P)^2 P = P(1 - P) \tag{4.16}$$

Example 2.4.6 Contract Sale (Compute Bernoulli Mean and Variance)

Shirley Ferguson, an insurance broker, believes that for a particular contact the probability of making a sale is 0.4. If the random variable X is defined to take the value 1 if a sale is made and 0 otherwise, then X has a Bernoulli distribution with probability of success P equal to 0.4. Find the mean and the variance of the distribution.

Solution The probability distribution of X is $P(0) = 0.6$ and $P(1) = 0.4$. The mean of the distribution is $P = 0.40$, and the variance is $\sigma^2 = P(1 - P) = (0.4)(0.6) = 0.24$.

Developing the Binomial Distribution

An important generalization of the Bernoulli distribution concerns the case where a random experiment with two possible outcomes is repeated several times and the repetitions are independent. We can determine these probabilities by using the binomial probability distribution. Suppose again that the probability of a success in a single trial is P and that n independent trials are carried out, so that the result of any one trial has no influence on the outcome of any other. The number of successes, X, resulting from these n trials could be any whole number from 0 to n, and we are interested in the probability of obtaining exactly $X = x$ successes in n trials.

Suppose that Shirley in Example 2.4.6 seeks a total of, $x = 3$ sales and to do this she contacts four $n = 4$ potential customers. She would like to know the probability of exactly 3 sales out of the 4 contacts. If we label a sale as (S) and a nonsale as (F), one possible sequence that results in 3 sales would be [S, S, S, F]. Given that each customer contact is independent, the probability of this particular event is as follows:

$$(0.40 \times 0.40 \times 0.40 \times 0.60) = 0.40^3 0.60^1 = 0.0384$$

The sequences of S and F can be arranged in combinations of 4 outcomes taken 3 at a time, and thus there are

$$C_3^4 = \frac{4!}{3!(4 - 3)!} = 4$$

possible ways that she can obtain 3 sales, and thus the probability of exactly 3 sales would be 4 times 0.0384, or 0.1536; expressed in equation form,

$$C_3^4 0.40^3 0.60^1 = 4 \times 0.0384 = 0.1536$$

Continuing from this specific example we develop the result in two stages. First, observe that the n trials will result in a sequence of n outcomes, each of which must be either success (S) or failure (F). One sequence with x successes and $(n - x)$ failures is as follows:

$$S, S, \ldots, S \qquad F, F, \ldots, F$$
$$(x \text{ times}) \qquad (n - x \text{ times})$$

In other words, the first x trials result in success, while the remainder result in failure. Now, the probability of success in a single trial is P, and the probability of failure is $(1 - P)$. Since the n trials are independent of one another, the probability of any particular sequence of outcomes is, by the multiplication rule of probabilities, equal to the product of the probabilities for the individual outcomes. Thus, the probability of observing the specific sequence of outcomes just described is as follows:

$$[P \times P \times \cdots \times P] \times [(1 - P) \times (1 - P) \times \cdots \times (1 - P)] = P^x (1 - P)^{(n-x)}$$
$$(x \text{ times}) \qquad\qquad (n - x \text{ times})$$

This line of argument establishes that the probability of observing *any specific sequence* involving x successes and $(n - x)$ failures is $P^x(1 - P)^{n-x}$. For example, suppose that there are 5 independent trials, each with probability of success $P = 0.60$, and the probability of exactly 3 successes is required. Using $+$ to designate a success and 0 to indicate a nonsuccess, the desired outcomes could be designated as follows:

$$+++00 \quad \text{or} \quad +0+0+$$

The probability of either of these specific outcomes is $(0.6)^3(0.4)^2 = 0.03456$.

The original problem concerned the determination not of the probability of occurrence of a particular sequence, but of the probability of precisely x successes, regardless of the order of the outcomes. There are several sequences in which x successes could be arranged among $(n - x)$ failures. In fact, the number of such possibilities is just the number of combinations of x objects chosen from n, since any x locations can be selected from a total of n in which to place the successes and the total number of successes can be computed using Equation 4.17. Returning to the example of three successes in five trials ($P = 0.60$), the number of different sequences with three successes would be as follows:

$$C_3^5 = \frac{5!}{3!(5 - 3)!} = 10$$

The probability of 3 successes in 5 independent Bernoulli trials is, therefore, 10 times the probability of each of the sequences that has 3 successes; thus,

$$P(X = 3) = (10)(0.03456) = 0.3456$$

Next, we generalize this result for any combination of n and x.

Number of Sequences with x Successes in n Trials
The number of sequences with x successes in n independent trials is

$$C_x^n = \frac{n!}{x!(n - x)!} \tag{4.17}$$

where $n! = n \times (n - 1) \times (n - 2) \times \cdots \times 1$ and $0! = 1$.

These C_x^n sequences are mutually exclusive, since no two of them can occur at the same time.

The event "x successes resulting from n trials" can occur in C_x^n mutually exclusive ways, each with probability $P^x(1 - P)^{n-x}$. Therefore, by the addition rule of probabilities the probability required is the sum of these C_x^n individual probabilities. The result is given by Equation 4.18.

The Binomial Distribution

Suppose that a random experiment can result in two possible mutually exclusive and collectively exhaustive outcomes, "success" and "failure," and that P is the probability of a success in a single trial. If n independent trials are carried out, the distribution of the number of resulting successes, x, is called the **binomial distribution**. Its probability distribution function for the binomial random variable $X = x$ is as follows:

$P(x \text{ successes in } n \text{ independent trials})$

$$= P(x) = \frac{n!}{x!(n-x)!} P^x (1-P)^{(n-x)} \text{ for } x = 0,1,2,\ldots,n \qquad (4.18)$$

The mean and variance are derived in the chapter appendix, and the results are given by Equations 4.19 and 4.20.

Mean and Variance of a Binomial Probability Distribution

Let X be the number of successes in n independent trials, each with probability of success P. Then X follows a binomial distribution with **mean**

$$\mu = E[X] = nP \qquad (4.19)$$

and **variance**

$$\sigma_X^2 = E[(X - \mu_X)^2] = nP(1-P) \qquad (4.20)$$

The binomial distribution is widely used in business and economic applications involving the probability of discrete occurrences. Before using the binomial, the specific situation must be analyzed to determine if the following occur:

1. The application involves several trials, each of which has only two outcomes: yes or no, on or off, success or failure.
2. The probability of the outcome is the same for each trial.
3. The probability of the outcome on one trial does not affect the probability on other trials.

In the following examples typical applications are provided.
Binomial distribution probabilities can be obtained using the following:

1. Equation 4.18 (good for small values of n); see Example 4.7
2. Tables in the appendix (good for selected values of n and P); see Example 4.8
3. Computer-generated probabilities (Example 2.4.9}

Example 2.4.7 Multiple Contract Sales

Suppose that a real estate agent, Jeanette Nelson, has 5 contacts, and she believes that for each contact the probability of making a sale is 0.40. Using Equation 4.18, do the following:

a. Find the probability that she makes at most 1 sale.
b. Find the probability that she makes between 2 and 4 sales (inclusive).
c. Graph the probability distribution function.

Solution

a. $P(\text{at most 1 sale}) = P(X \leq 1) = P(X = 0) + P(X = 1)$
$= 0.078 + 0.259 = 0.337$ since

$$P(0 \text{ sales}) = P(0) = \frac{5!}{0!5!}(0.4)^0(0.6)^5 = (0.6)^5 = 0.078$$

$$P(1 \text{ sale}) = P(1) = \frac{5!}{1!4!}(0.4)^1(0.6)^4 = 5(0.4)(0.6)^4 = 0.259$$

b. $P(2 \leq X \leq 4) = P(2) + P(3) + P(4) = 0.346 + 0.230 + 0.077 = 0.653$, since

$$P(2) = \frac{5!}{2!3!}(0.4)^2(0.6)^3 = 10(0.4)^2(0.6)^3 = 0.346$$

$$P(3) = \frac{5!}{3!2!}(0.4)^3(0.6)^2 = 10(0.4)^3(0.6)^2 = 0.230$$

$$P(4) = \frac{5!}{4!1!}(0.4)^4(0.6)^1 = 5(0.4)^4(0.6)^1 = 0.077$$

c. The probability distribution function is shown in Figure 2.52.

Figure 2.52 Graph of Binomial Probability Distribution for Example 2.4.7

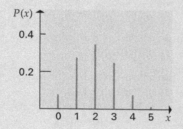

Comments

- This shape is typical for binomial probabilities when P is neither very large nor very small.
- At the extremes (0 or 5 sales), the probabilities are quite small.

Unless the number of trials n is very small, the calculation of binomial probabilities, using Equation 4.18, is likely to be extremely cumbersome. Therefore, binomial probabilities can also be obtained from tables in the appendix.

Example 2.4.8 College Admissions

Early in August an undergraduate college discovers that it can accommodate a few extra students. Enrolling those additional students would provide a substantial increase in revenue without increasing the operating costs of the college; that is, no new classes would have to be added. From past experience the college knows that the frequency of enrollment given admission for all students is 40%.

a. What is the probability that at most 6 students will enroll if the college offers admission to 10 more students?
b. What is the probability that more than 12 will actually enroll if admission is offered to 20 students?
c. If the frequency of enrollment given admission for all students was 70%, what is the probability that at least 12 out of 15 students will actually enroll?

Solution

a. We assume that the additional students admitted have the same probability of enrolling as the previously admitted students.

b. The probability can be obtained using the cumulative binomial probability distribution from Table 3 in the appendix. The probability of at most 6 students enrolling if $n = 10$ and $P = 0.40$ is as follows:

$$P(X \le 6 | n = 10, P = 0.40) = 0.945$$

c. $P(X > 12 | n = 20, P = 0.40) = 1 - P(X \le 12) = 1 - 0.979 = 0.021$

d. The probability that at least 12 out of 15 students enroll is the same as the probability that at most 3 out of 15 students do not enroll (the probability of a student not enrolling is $1 - 0.70 = 0.30$).

$$P(X \ge 12 | n = 15, P = 0.70) = P(X \le 3 | n = 15, P = 0.30) = 0.297$$

Most good computer packages can compute binomial and other probabilities for various probability distribution functions. Example 2.4.9 presents a probability table computed using Minitab, but other packages have similar capabilities.

Example 2.4.9 Sales of Airline Seats

Have you ever agreed to give up your airplane ticket in return for a free ticket? Have you ever searched for the cheapest flight so that you could visit a special friend? This example provides some of the analysis that leads to results such as overbooked flights and reduced fares on certain flights.

Suppose that you are in charge of marketing airline seats for a major carrier. Four days before the flight date you have 16 seats remaining on the plane. You know from past experience data that 80% of the people that purchase tickets in this time period will actually show up for the flight.

a. If you sell 20 extra tickets, what is the probability that you will overbook the flight or have at least 1 empty seat?

b. If you sell 18 extra tickets, what is the probability that you will overbook the flight or have at least 1 empty seat?

Solution

a. To find $P(X > 16)$, given $n = 20$ and $P = 0.80$, use the cumulative probability distribution in Table 2.30 that was computed using Minitab. You will find that all quality statistical packages have a capability to computer similar cumulative probability distributions.

Table 2.30 Cumulative Binomial Probabilities Obtained from Minitab for $n = 20, P = 0.80$.

x	$P(X \le x)$
10	0.0026
11	0.0100
12	0.0321
13	0.0867
14	0.1958
15	0.3704
16	0.5886
17	0.7939
18	0.9308
19	0.9885
20	1.0000

The probability of overbooking is

$$P(X > 16) = 1 - P(X \le 16) = 1 - 0.589 = 0.411$$

and we see that the probability of overbooking when 20 seats are sold is 41.1%. If 20 tickets are sold, this also means that the probability that 15 or fewer people will arrive is

$$P(X \le 15) = 0.37$$

so there is a 37% chance that selling 20 tickets results in at least one empty seat.

b. To find the chance that you overbook the flight by selling 18 tickets, compute the cumulative probability distribution using $n = 18$. The chance that you overbook the flight will be only 10%, but the probability of at least one empty seat will increase to 72.9%.

The airline management then must evaluate the cost of overbooking (providing free tickets) versus the cost of empty seats that generate no revenue. Airlines analyze data to determine the number of seats that should be sold at reduced rates to maximize the ticket revenue from each flight. This analysis is complex, but it has its starting point in analyses such as the example presented here.

EXERCISES

Basic Exercises

2.4.30 For a Bernoulli random variable with probability of success $P = 0.5$, compute the mean and variance.

2.4.31 For a binomial probability distribution with $P = 0.5$ and $n = 12$, find the probability that the number of successes is equal to 7 and the probability that the number of successes is fewer than 6.

2.4.32 For a binomial probability distribution with $P = 0.3$ and $n = 14$, find the probability that the number of successes is equal to 7 and the probability that the number of successes is fewer than 6.

2.4.33 For a binomial probability distribution with $P = 0.4$ and $n = 20$, find the probability that the number of successes is equal to 9 and the probability that the number of successes is fewer than 7.

2.4.34 For a binomial probability distribution with $P = 0.7$ and $n = 18$, find the probability that the number of successes is equal to 12 and the probability that the number of successes is fewer than 6.

Application Exercises

2.4.35 A production manager knows that 5% of components produced by a particular manufacturing process have some defect. Six of these components, whose characteristics can be assumed to be independent of each other, are examined.

a. What is the probability that none of these components has a defect?
b. What is the probability that one of these components has a defect?
c. What is the probability that at least two of these components have a defect?

2.4.36 A state senator believes that 25% of all senators on the Finance Committee will strongly support the tax proposal she wishes to advance. Suppose that this belief is correct and that 5 senators are approached at random.

a. What is the probability that at least 1 of the 5 will strongly support the proposal?
b. What is the probability that a majority of the 5 will strongly support the proposal?

2.4.37 A public interest group hires students to solicit donations by telephone. After a brief training period students make calls to potential donors and are paid on a commission basis. Experience indicates that early on, these students tend to have only modest success and that 70% of them give up their jobs in their first two weeks of employment. The group hires 6 students, which can be viewed as a random sample.

a. What is the probability that at least 2 of the 6 will give up in the first two weeks?
b. What is the probability that at least 2 of the 6 will not give up in the first two weeks?

2.4.38 In a Godiva shop, 40% of the cookies are plain truffles, 20% are black truffles, 10% are cherry cookies, and 30% are a mix of all the others. Suppose you pick one at random from a prepacked bag that reflects this composition.

a. What is the probability of picking a plain truffle?
b. What is the probability of picking truffle of any kind?
c. If you instead pick three cookies in a row, what is the probability that all three are black truffles?

2.4.39 A company installs new central-heating furnaces and has found that for 15% of all installations, a return visit is needed to make some modifications. Six installations were made in a particular week. Assume independence of outcomes for these installations.

a. What is the probability that a return visit will be needed in all these cases?
b. What is the probability that a return visit will be needed in none of these cases?
c. What is the probability that a return visit will be needed in more than 1 of these cases?

2.4.40 In a scuba-diving center in Sipadan (Malaysia), the dive master has tried calculating the probability of encountering some very rare fish underwater. The following are the probabilities of encountering several fish.

Leopard shark: 0.05
Barracuda: 0.41
Lemon shark: 0.04
Scorpion fish: 0.27
Mandarin fish: 0.07

Using these statistics, calculate each likelihood.

a. Of not encountering a shark
b. Of encountering a shark
c. Of not encountering a scorpion fish

2.4.41 A small commuter airline flies planes that can seat up to 8 passengers. The airline has determined that the probability that a ticketed passenger will not show up for a flight is 0.2. For each flight the airline sells tickets to the first 10 people placing orders. The probability distribution for the number of tickets sold per flight is shown in the accompanying table. For what proportion of the airline's flights does the number of ticketed passengers showing up exceed the number of available seats? (Assume independence between the number of tickets sold and the probability that a ticketed passenger will show up.)

Number of tickets	6	7	8	9	10
Probability	0.25	0.35	0.25	0.10	0.05

2.4.42 You are investigating the punctuality of the airlines in Asia. Your survey tells you that, out of 15 airlines, 80% of them are likely to be late at least once a month. Assume the punctuality random variable follows a binomial distribution. Determine the following.

a. Which assumptions do you need to make in order to be correct in considering a binomial distribution for your variable?
b. How many airlines will be late in one month?
c. What is the standard deviation of this random variable (i.e., the risk of being late)?
d. What is the probability that they all will be late?

2.4.43 A notebook computer dealer mounts a new promotional campaign. Purchasers of new computers may, if dissatisfied for any reason, return them within 2 days of purchase and receive a full refund. The cost to the dealer of such a refund is $100. The dealer estimates that 15% of all purchasers will, indeed, return computers and obtain refunds. Suppose that 50 computers are purchased during the campaign period.

a. Find the mean and standard deviation of the number of these computers that will be returned for refunds.
b. Find the mean and standard deviation of the total refund costs that will accrue as a result of these 50 purchases.

2.4.44 A family of mutual funds maintains a service that allows clients to switch money among accounts through a telephone call. It was estimated that 3.2% of callers either get a busy signal or are kept on hold so long that they may hang up. Fund management assesses any failure of this sort as a $10 goodwill loss. Suppose that 2,000 calls are attempted over a particular period.

a. Find the mean and standard deviation of the number of callers who will either get a busy signal or may hang up after being kept on hold.
b. Find the mean and standard deviation of the total goodwill loss to the mutual fund company from these 2,000 calls.

2.4.45 We have seen that, for a binomial distribution with n trials, each with probability of success P, the mean is as follows:

$$\mu_X = E[X] = nP$$

Verify this result for the data of Example 2.4.7 by calculating the mean directly from

$$\mu_X = \sum xP(x)$$

showing that for the binomial distribution, the two formulas produce the same answer.

2.4.46 A campus finance officer finds that, for all parking tickets issued, fines are paid for 78% of the tickets. The fine is $2. In the most recent week, 620 parking tickets have been issued.

a. Find the mean and standard deviation of the number of these tickets for which the fines will be paid.
b. Find the mean and standard deviation of the amount of money that will be obtained from the payment of these fines.

2.4.47 A company receives a very large shipment of components. A random sample of 16 of these components will be checked, and the shipment will be accepted if fewer than 2 of these components are defective. What is the probability of accepting a shipment containing each number of defectives?

a. 5%
b. 15%
c. 25%

2.4.48 The following two acceptance rules are being considered for determining whether to take delivery of a large shipment of components:

• A random sample of 10 components is checked, and the shipment is accepted only if none of them is defective.
• A random sample of 20 components is checked, and the shipment is accepted only if no more than 1 of them is defective.

Which of these acceptance rules has the smaller probability of accepting a shipment containing 20% defectives?

2.4.49 A company receives large shipments of parts from two sources. Seventy percent of the shipments come from a supplier whose shipments typically contain 10% defectives, while the remainder are from a supplier whose shipments typically contain 20% defectives. A manager receives a shipment but does not know the source. A random sample of 20 items from this shipment is tested, and 1 of the parts is found to be defective. What is the probability that this shipment came from the more reliable supplier? (*Hint:* Use Bayes' theorem.)

2.4.5 POISSON DISTRIBUTION

The **Poisson probability distribution** was first proposed by Simeon Poisson (1781–1840) in a book published in 1837. The number of applications began to increase early in the 20th century, and the availability of the computer has brought about further applications. The Poisson distribution is an important discrete probability distribution for a number of applications, including the following:

1. The number of failures in a large computer system during a given day
2. The number of replacement orders for a part received by a firm in a given month
3. The number of ships arriving at a loading facility during a 6-hour loading period
4. The number of delivery trucks to arrive at a central warehouse in an hour
5. The number of dents, scratches, or other defects in a large roll of sheet metal used to manufacture various component parts
6. The number of customers to arrive for flights during each 10-minute time interval from 3:00 p.m. to 6:00 p.m. on weekdays
7. The number of customers to arrive at a checkout aisle in your local grocery store during a particular time interval

We can use the Poisson distribution to determine the probability of each of these random variables, which are characterized as the number of occurrences or successes of a certain event in a given continuous interval (such as time, surface area, or length).

A Poisson distribution is modeled according to certain assumptions.

> ### Assumptions of the Poisson Distribution
> Assume that an interval is divided into a very large number of equal subintervals so that the probability of the occurrence of an event in any subinterval is very small. The assumptions of a Poisson distribution are as follows:
>
> 1. The probability of the occurrence of an event is constant for all subintervals.
> 2. There can be no more than one occurrence in each subinterval.
> 3. Occurrences are independent; that is, an occurrence in one interval does not influence the probability of an occurrence in another interval.

We can derive the equation for computing Poisson probabilities directly from the binomial probability distribution by taking the mathematical limits as $P \to 0$ and $n \to \infty$. With these limits, the parameter $\lambda = nP$ is a constant that specifies the average number of occurrences (successes) for a particular time and/or space. We can see intuitively that the Poisson is a special case of the binomial obtained by extending these limits. However, the mathematical derivation is beyond the scope of this book. The interested reader is referred to page 244 of Hogg and Craig (1995). The Poisson probability distribution function is given in Equation 4.21.

The Poisson Distribution Function, Mean, and Variance

The random variable X is said to follow the Poisson distribution if it has the probability distribution

$$P(x) = \frac{e^{-\lambda}\lambda^x}{x!}, \text{ for } x = 0, 1, 2, \ldots \qquad (4.21)$$

where

$P(x)$ = the probability of x successes over a given time or space, given λ

λ = the expected number of successes per time or space unit, $\lambda > 0$

$e \cong 2.71828$ (the base for natural logarithms)

The mean and variance of the Poisson distribution are

$$\mu_x = E[X] = \lambda \quad \text{and} \quad \sigma_x^2 = E[(X - \mu_x)^2] = \lambda$$

The sum of Poisson random variables is also a Poisson random variable. Thus, the sum of K Poisson random variables, each with mean λ, is a Poisson random variable with mean $K\lambda$.

Two important applications of the Poisson distribution in the modern global economy are the probability of failures in complex systems and the probability of defective products in large production runs of several hundred thousand to a million units. A large worldwide shipping company such as Federal Express has a complex and extensive pickup, classification, shipping, and delivery system for millions of packages each day. There is a very small probability of handling failure at each step for each of the millions of packages handled every day. The company is interested in the probability of various numbers of failed deliveries each day when the system is operating properly. If the number of actual failed deliveries observed on a particular day has a small probability of occurring, given proper targeted operations, then the management begins a systematic checking process to identify and correct the reason for excessive failures.

Example 2.4.10 System Component Failure (Poisson Probabilities)

Andrew Whittaker, computer center manager, reports that his computer system experienced three component failures during the past 100 days.

a. What is the probability of no failures in a given day?
b. What is the probability of one or more component failures in a given day?
c. What is the probability of at least two failures in a 3-day period?

Solution A modern computer system has a very large number of components, each of which could fail and thus result in a computer system failure. To compute the probability of failures using the Poisson distribution, assume that each of the millions of components has the same very small probability of failure. Also assume that the first failure does not affect the probability of a second failure (in some cases, these assumptions may not hold, and more complex distributions would be used). In particular, for this problem we assume that the past 100 days have been a good standard performance for the computer system and that this standard will continue into the future.

From past experience the expected number of failures per day is 3/100, or $\lambda = 0.03$.

a. $P(\text{no failures in a given day}) = P(X = 0 \mid \lambda = 0.03) = \dfrac{e^{-0.03}\lambda^0}{0!} = 0.970446$

b. The probability of at least one failure is the complement of the probability of 0 failures:

$$P(X \geq 1) = 1 - P(X = 0) = 1 - \left[\frac{e^{-\lambda}\lambda^x}{x!}\right] = 1 - \left[\frac{e^{-0.03}\lambda^0}{0!}\right]$$

$$= 1 - e^{-0.03} = 1 - 0.970446 = 0.029554$$

c. $P(\text{at least two failures in a 3-day period}) = P(X \geq 2 | \lambda = 0.09)$, where the average over a 3-day period is $\lambda = 3(0.03) = 0.09$:

$$P(X \geq 2 | \lambda = 0.09) = 1 - P(X \leq 1) = 1 - [P(X = 0) + P(X = 1)]$$

$$= 1 - [0.913931 + 0.082254]$$

and, thus,

$$P(X \geq 2 | \lambda = 0.09) = 1 - 0.996185 = 0.003815$$

The Poisson distribution has been found to be particularly useful in *waiting line*, or *queuing*, problems. These important applications include the probability of various numbers of customers waiting for a phone line or waiting to check out of a large retail store. These queuing problems are an important management issue for firms that draw customers from large populations. If the queue becomes too long, customers might quit the line or might not return for a future shopping visit. If a store has too many checkout lines, then there will be personnel idle waiting for customers, resulting in lower productivity. By knowing the probability of various numbers of customers in the line, management can balance the trade-off between long lines and idle customer service associates. In this way the firm can implement its strategy for the desired customer service level—shorter wait times imply higher customer-service levels but have a cost of more idle time for checkout workers.

Example 2.4.11 Customers at a Photocopying Machine (Poisson Probability)

Customers arrive at a photocopying machine at an average rate of 2 every five minutes. Assume that these arrivals are independent, with a constant arrival rate, and that this problem follows a Poisson model, with X denoting the number of arriving customers in a 5-minute period and mean $\lambda = 2$. Find the probability that more than two customers arrive in a 5-minute period.

Solution Since the mean number of arrivals in five minutes is 2, then $\lambda = 2$. To find the probability that more than 2 customers arrive, first compute the probability of at most 2 arrivals in a five-minute period, and then use the complement rule.

These probabilities can be found in Table 5 in the appendix or by using a computer:

$$P(X = 0) = \frac{e^{-2}2^0}{0!} = e^{-2} = 0.135335$$

$$P(X = 1) = \frac{e^{-2}2^1}{1!} = 2e^{-2} = 0.27067$$

$$P(X = 2) = \frac{e^{-2}2^2}{2!} = 2e^{-2} = 0.27067$$

Thus, the probability of more than 2 arrivals in a five-minute period is as follows:

$$P(X > 2) = 1 - P(X \leq 2) = 1 - [0.135335 + 0.27067 + 0.27067] = 0.323325$$

Example 2.4.12 Ship Arrivals at a Dock

The Canadian government has built a large grain-shipping port at Churchill, Manitoba, on the Hudson Bay. Grain grown in southern Manitoba is carried by rail to Churchill during the open-water shipping season. Unfortunately the port is open only 50 days per year during July and August. This leads to some critical crew staffing decisions by management. The port has the capacity to load up to 7 ships simultaneously, provided that each loading bay has an assigned crew. The remote location and short shipping season results in a very high labor cost for each crew assigned, and management would like to minimize the number of crews. Ships arrive in a random pattern that can be modeled using the Poisson probability model. If a ship arrives and all available loading bays are filled, the ship will be delayed, resulting in a large cost that must be paid to the owner of the ship. This penalty was negotiated to encourage ship owners to send their ships to Churchill.

Results of an initial analysis indicate that each ship requires six hours for loading by a single crew. The port can remain open only 50 days per year, and 500 ships must be loaded during this time. Each additional crew costs $180,000, and each boat delay costs $10,000. How many crews should be scheduled?

Solution The final decision is based on the probability of ship arrivals during a 6-hour period and the cost of additional crews versus the penalty cost for delayed ships. The first step is to compute the probabilities of various numbers of ships arriving during a 6-hour period and then the cost of ship delays. Then, we compute the cost of crews and the cost of ship delays for various levels of crew assignment.

Ship arrivals can be modeled by assuming that there are thousands of ships in the world and each has a small probability of arriving during a 6-hour loading period. An alternative model assumption is that during six hours there are a large number of small time intervals—say, 0.1 second—in this case, 216,000 such intervals. We also need to assume that ships do not travel in convoys. With 500 ships arriving over 50 days, we have a mean of 10 ships per day, or $\lambda = 2.5$ ship arrivals during a 6-hour period. The probability of x arrivals during a 6-hour period is computed using the following:

$$P(X = x \mid \lambda = 2.5) = \frac{e^{-2.5}2.5^x}{x!}$$

If four crews are scheduled, the probabilities of delaying ships are as follows:

$$P(\text{delay 1 ship}) = P(5 \text{ ships arrive}) = \frac{e^{-2.5}2.5^5}{5!} = 0.0668$$

$$P(\text{delay 2 ships}) = P(6 \text{ ships arrive}) = \frac{e^{-2.5}2.5^6}{6!} = 0.0278$$

$$P(\text{delay 3 ships}) = P(7 \text{ ships arrive}) = \frac{e^{-2.5}2.5^7}{7!} = 0.0099$$

The probabilities of idle crews are as follows:

$$P(1 \text{ crew idle}) = P(3 \text{ ships arrive}) = \frac{e^{-2.5}2.5^3}{3!} = 0.2138$$

$$P(2 \text{ crews idle}) = P(2 \text{ ships arrive}) = \frac{e^{-2.5}2.5^2}{2!} = 0.2565$$

$$P(3 \text{ crews idle}) = P(1 \text{ ship arrive}) = \frac{e^{-2.5}2.5^1}{1!} = 0.2052$$

$$P(4 \text{ crews idle}) = P(0 \text{ ship arrive}) = \frac{e^{-2.5}2.5^0}{0!} = 0.0821$$

With four crews scheduled, the expected number of boats delayed during a 6-hour period would be as follows:

$$(1 \times 0.0668 + 2 \times 0.0278 + 3 \times 0.0099) = 0.1521$$

With a 50-day shipping season there are 200 6-hour periods, and thus the delay cost is as follows:

$$(0.1521)(200)(10,000) = \$304,200$$

Following the same computational form, we would find that with 5 crews scheduled, the expected cost of delays would be $95,200 and, thus, the extra crew would save $209,000. Since the cost of an extra crew is $180,000 the scheduling of 5 crews would be the correct decision.

We note that scheduling an additional crew would also lead to increased crew idle time. However, the higher service level makes it economically sensible to have crews idle in order to reduce ship delays.

Poisson Approximation to the Binomial Distribution

Previously, we noted that the Poisson distribution is obtained by starting with the binomial probability distribution with P approaching 0 and n becoming very large. Thus, it follows that the Poisson distribution can be used to approximate the binomial probabilities when the number of trials, n, is large and at the same time the probability, P, is small (generally such that $\lambda = nP \leq 7$). Examples of situations that would satisfy these conditions include the following:

- An insurance company will hold a large number of life policies on individuals of any particular age, and the probability that a single policy will result in a claim during the year is very low. Here, we have a binomial distribution with large n and small P.
- A company may have a large number of machines working on a process simultaneously. If the probability that any one of them will break down in a single day is small, the distribution of the number of daily breakdowns is binomial with large n and small P.

Poisson Approximation to the Binomial Distribution
Let X be the number of successes resulting from n independent trials, each with probability of success P. The distribution of the number of successes, X, is binomial, with mean nP. If the number of trials, n, is large and nP is of only moderate size (preferably $nP \leq 7$), this distribution can be **approximated by the Poisson distribution** with $\lambda = Np$. The probability distribution of the approximating distribution is then

$$P(x) = \frac{e^{-nP}(nP)^x}{x!} \text{ for } x = 0, 1, 2, \ldots \tag{4.22}$$

Example 2.4.13 Probability of Bankruptcy (Poisson Probability)

An analyst predicted that 3.5% of all small corporations would file for bankruptcy in the coming year. For a random sample of 100 small corporations, estimate the probability that at least 3 will file for bankruptcy in the next year, assuming that the analyst's prediction is correct.

Solution The distribution of X, the number of filings for bankruptcy, is binomial with $n = 100$ and $P = 0.035$, so that the mean of the distribution is $\mu_x = nP = 3.5$.

Using the Poisson distribution to approximate the probability of at least 3 bankruptcies, we find the following:

$$P(X \geq 3) = 1 - P(X \leq 2)$$

$$P(0) = \frac{e^{-3.5}(3.5)^0}{0!} = e^{-3.5} = 0.030197$$

$$P(1) = \frac{e^{-3.5}(3.5)^1}{1!} = (3.5)(0.030197) = 0.1056895$$

$$P(2) = \frac{e^{-3.5}(3.5)^2}{2!} = (6.125)(0.030197) = 0.1849566$$

Thus,

$$P(X \leq 2) = P(0) + P(1) + P(2) = 0.030197 + 0.1056895 + 0.1849566 = 0.3208431$$

$$P(X \geq 3) = 1 - 0.3208431 = 0.6791569$$

Using the binomial distribution we compute the probability of $X \geq 3$ as:

$$P(X \geq 3) = 0.684093$$

Thus the Poisson probability is a close estimate of the actual binomial probability.

Comparison of the Poisson and Binomial Distributions

We should indicate at this point that confusion may exist about the choice of the binomial or the Poisson distribution for particular applications. The choice in many cases can be made easier by carefully reviewing the assumptions for the two distributions. For example, if the problem uses a small sample of observations, then it is not possible to find a limiting probability with n large, and, thus, the binomial is the correct probability distribution. Further, if we have a small sample and the probability of a success for a single trial is between 0.05 and 0.95, then there is further support for choosing the binomial. If we knew or could assume that each of 10 randomly selected customers in an automobile showroom had the same probability of purchase (assume $0.05 \leq P \leq 0.95$), then the number of purchases from this group would follow a binomial distribution. However, if the set of cases that could be affected is very large—say, several thousand—and the mean number of "successes" over that large set of cases is small—say, fewer than 30—then there is strong support for choosing the Poisson distribution. If we wanted to compute the probability of a certain number of defective parts in a set of 100,000 parts when the mean number of 15 defectives per 100,000 parts represented a typical production cycle, then we would use the Poisson distribution.

In the previous discussion we noted that, when P is less than 0.05 and n is large, we can approximate the binomial distribution by using the Poisson distribution. It can also be shown that when $n \geq 20, P \leq 0.05$, and the population mean is the same, we will find that both the binomial and the Poisson distributions generate approximately the same probability values. This result is shown in Exercise 2.4.63.

EXERCISES

Basic Exercises

2.4.50 Determine the probability of exactly four successes for a random variable with a Poisson distribution with parameter $\lambda = 2.4$.

2.4.51 Determine the probability of more than 7 successes for a random variable with a Poisson distribution with parameter $\lambda = 4.4$.

2.4.52 Determine the probability of fewer than 6 successes for a random variable with a Poisson distribution with parameter $\lambda = 3.4$.

2.4.53 Determine the probability of fewer than or equal to 9 successes for a random variable with a Poisson distribution with parameter $\lambda = 8.0$.

Application Exercises

2.4.54 Customers arrive at a busy checkout counter at an average rate of 3 per minute. If the distribution of arrivals is Poisson, find the probability that in any given minute there will be 2 or fewer arrivals.

2.4.55 The number of accidents in a production facility has a Poisson distribution with a mean of 2.6 per month.

    a. For a given month what is the probability there will be fewer than 2 accidents?

    b. For a given month what is the probability there will be more than 3 accidents?

2.4.56 A customer service center in India receives, on average, 4.2 telephone calls per minute. If the distribution of calls is Poisson, what is the probability of receiving at least 3 calls during a particular minute?

2.4.57 Records indicate that, on average, 3.2 breakdowns per day occur on an urban highway during the morning rush hour. Assume that the distribution is Poisson.

    a. Find the probability that on any given day there will be fewer than 2 breakdowns on this highway during the morning rush hour.

    b. Find the probability that on any given day there will be more than 4 breakdowns on this highway during the morning rush hour.

2.4.58 Blue Cross Health Insurance reported that 4.5% of claims forms submitted for payment after a complex surgical procedure contain errors. If 100 of these forms are chosen at random, what is the probability that fewer than 3 of them contain errors? Use the Poisson approximation to the binomial distribution.

2.4.59 A corporation has 250 personal computers. The probability that any 1 of them will require repair in a given week is 0.01. Find the probability that fewer than 4 of the personal computers will require repair in a particular week. Use the Poisson approximation to the binomial distribution.

2.4.60 An insurance company holds fraud insurance policies on 6,000 firms. In any given year the probability that any single policy will result in a claim is 0.001. Find the probability that at least 3 claims are made in a given year. Use the Poisson approximation to the binomial distribution.

2.4.61 A state has a law requiring motorists to carry insurance. It was estimated that, despite this law, 6.0% of all motorists in the state are uninsured. A random sample of 100 motorists was taken. Use the Poisson approximation to the binomial distribution to estimate the probability that at least 3 of the motorists in this sample are uninsured. Also indicate what calculations would be needed to find this probability exactly if the Poisson approximation was not used.

2.4.62 A new warehouse is being designed and a decision concerning the number of loading docks is required. There are two models based on truck-arrival assumptions for the use of this warehouse, given that loading a truck requires 1 hour. Using the first model, we assume that the warehouse could be serviced by one of the many thousands of independent truckers who arrive randomly to obtain a load for delivery. It is known that, on average, 1 of these trucks would arrive each hour. For the second model, assume that the company hires a fleet of 10 trucks that are assigned full time to shipments from this warehouse. Under that assumption the trucks would arrive randomly, but the probability of any truck arriving during a given hour is 0.1. Obtain the appropriate probability distribution for each of these assumptions and compare the results.

2.4.6 JOINTLY DISTRIBUTED DISCRETE RANDOM VARIABLES

Business and economic applications of statistics are often concerned about the relationships between variables. Products at different quality levels have different prices. Age groups have different preferences for clothing, for automobiles, and for music. The percent returns on two different stocks may tend to be related, and the returns for both may increase when the market is growing. Alternatively, when the return on one stock is growing, the return on the other might be decreasing. When we work with probability models for problems involving relationships between variables, it is important that the effect of these relationships is included in the probability model. For example, assume that a car dealer is selling the following automobiles: (1) a red two-door compact, (2) a blue minivan, and (3) a silver full-size sedan; the probability distribution for purchasing would not be the same for women in their 20s, 30s, and 50s. Thus, it is important that probability models reflect the joint effect of variables on probabilities.

Figure 2.54 Covariance Calculation Using Microsoft Excel

Joint Probability Distribution of X and Y						
			Y Return %			
X Return %	0	0.05	0.1	0.15	P(x)	E(X)
0	0.0625	0.0625	0.0625	0.0625	0.25	
0.05	0.0625	0.0625	0.0625	0.0625	0.25	
0.1	0.0625	0.0625	0.0625	0.0625	0.25	
0.15	0.0625	0.0625	0.0625	0.0625	0.25	
	0.25	0.25	0.25	0.25		0.075
E(Y)					0.075	
Calculation of Covariance						
	$xy\,P(x,y)$	$xy\,P(x,y)$	$xy\,P(x,y)$	$xy\,P(x,y)$		
$xy\,P(x,y)$	0	0	0	0		
$xy\,P(x,y)$	0	0.000156	0.000313	0.000469		
$xy\,P(x,y)$	0	0.000313	0.000625	0.000938		
$xy\,P(x,y)$	0	0.000469	0.000938	0.001406		
Sum $xy\,P(x,y)$	0	0.000938	0.001875	0.002813		0.005625
						Covariance
Sum $xy\,P(x,y) - E(X)E(Y)$			= 0.005625 − 0.005625			0

Covariance and Statistical Independence

If two random variables are **statistically independent**, the covariance between them is 0. However, the converse is not necessarily true.

The reason a covariance of 0 does not necessarily imply statistical independence is that covariance is designed to measure linear association, and it is possible that this quantity may not detect other types of dependency, as we see in the following illustration.

Suppose that the random variable X has probability distribution

$$P(-1) = 1/4 \quad P(0) = 1/2 \quad P(1) = 1/4$$

Let the random variable Y be defined as follows:

$$Y = X^2$$

Thus, knowledge of the value taken by X implies knowledge of the value taken by Y, and, therefore, these two random variables are certainly not independent. Whenever $X = 0$, then $Y = 0$, and if X is either -1 or 1, then $Y = 1$. The joint probability distribution of X and Y is

$$P(-1, 1) = 1/4 \quad P(0, 0) = 1/2 \quad P(1, 1) = 1/4$$

with the probability of any other combination of values being equal to 0. It is then straightforward to verify that

$$E[X] = 0 \quad E[Y] = 1/2 \quad E[XY] = 0$$

The covariance between X and Y is 0. Thus we see that random variables that are not independent can have a covariance equal to 0.

To conclude the discussion of joint distributions, consider the mean and variance of a random variable that can be written as the sum or difference of other random variables. These results are summarized below and can be derived using Equations 4.30, 4.31, and 4.32.

Summary Results for Linear Sums and Differences of Random Variables

Let X and Y be a pair of random variables with means μ_X and μ_Y and variances σ_X^2 and σ_Y^2. The following properties hold:

1. The **expected value of their sum** is the sum of their expected values:

$$E[X + Y] = \mu_X + \mu_Y \tag{4.35}$$

2. The **expected value of their difference** is the difference between their expected values:

$$E[X - Y] = \mu_X - \mu_Y \tag{4.36}$$

3. If the covariance between X and Y is 0, the **variance of their sum** is the sum of their variances:

$$Var(X + Y) = \sigma_X^2 + \sigma_Y^2 \tag{4.37}$$

But if the covariance is not 0, then

$$Var(X + Y) = \sigma_X^2 + \sigma_Y^2 + 2\,Cov(X, Y)$$

4. If the covariance between X and Y is 0, the **variance of their difference** is the *sum* of their variances:

$$Var(X - Y) = \sigma_X^2 + \sigma_Y^2 \tag{4.38}$$

But if the covariance is not 0, then

$$Var(X - Y) = \sigma_X^2 + \sigma_Y^2 - 2\,Cov(X, Y)$$

Let $X_1, X_2, \ldots, X_K$ be K random variables with means $\mu_1, \mu_2, \ldots, \mu_K$ and variances $\sigma_1^2, \sigma_2^2, \ldots, \sigma_K^2$. The following properties hold:

5. The expected value of their sum is as follows:

$$E[X_1 + X_2 + \cdots + X_K] = \mu_1 + \mu_2 + \cdots + \mu_K \tag{4.39}$$

6. If the covariance between every pair of these random variables is 0, the variance of their sum is as follows:

$$Var(X_1 + X_2 + \cdots + X_K) = \sigma_1^2 + \sigma_2^2 + \cdots + \sigma_K^2 \tag{4.40}$$

7. If the covariance between every pair of these random variables is not 0, the variance of their sum is as follows:

$$Var(X_1 + X_2 + \cdots + X_K) = \sum_{i=1}^{K} \sigma_i^2 + 2\sum_{i=1}^{K-1}\sum_{j>i}^{K} Cov(X_i, Y_j) \tag{4.41}$$

Example 2.4.17 Simple Investment Portfolio (Means and Variances, Functions of Random Variables)

An investor has $1,000 to invest and two investment opportunities, each requiring minimum of $500. The profit per $100 from the first can be represented by a random variable X, having the following probability distributions:

$$P(X = -5) = 0.4 \quad \text{and} \quad P(X = 20) = 0.6$$

The profit per $100 from the second is given by the random variable Y, whose probability distributions are as follows:

$$P(Y = 0) = 0.6 \quad \text{and} \quad P(Y = 25) = 0.4$$

Random variables X and Y are independent. The investor has the following possible strategies:

   a. $1,000 in the first investment
   b. $1,000 in the second investment
   c. $500 in each investment

Find the mean and variance of the profit from each strategy.

Solution Random variable X has mean

$$\mu_X = E[X] = \sum_x xP(x) = (-5)(0.4) + (20)(0.6) = \$10$$

and variance

$$\sigma_X^2 = E[(X - \mu_x)^2] = \sum_x (x - \mu_x)^2 P(x) = (-5 - 10)^2(0.4) + (20 - 10)^2(0.6) = 150$$

Random variable Y has mean

$$\mu_Y = E[Y] = \sum_y yP(y) = (0)(0.6) + (25)(0.4) = \$10$$

and variance

$$\sigma_Y^2 = E[(Y - \mu_Y)^2] = \sum_y (y - \mu_Y)^2 P(y) = (0 - 10)^2(0.6) + (25 - 10)^2(0.4) = 150$$

Strategy (a) has mean profit of $E[10X] = 10E[X] = \$100$ and variance of

$$Var(10X) = 100Var(X) = 15,000$$

Strategy (b) has mean profit $E[10Y] = 10E[Y] = \$100$ and variance of

$$Var(10Y) = 100Var(Y) = 15,000$$

Now consider strategy (c): $500 in each investment. The return from strategy (c) is $5X + 5Y$, which has mean

$$E[5X + 5Y] = E[5X] + E[5Y] = 5E[X] + 5E[Y] = \$100$$

Thus, all three strategies have the same expected profit. However, since X and Y are independent and the covariance is 0, the variance of the return from strategy (c) is as follows:

$$Var(5X + 5Y) = Var(5X) + Var(5Y) = 25Var(X) + 25Var(Y) = 7,500$$

   This is smaller than the variances of the other strategies, reflecting the decrease in risk that follows from diversification in an investment portfolio. Most investors would prefer strategy (c), since it yields the same expected return as the other two, but with lower risk.

Portfolio Analysis

Investment managers spend considerable effort developing investment portfolios that consist of a set of financial instruments that each have returns defined by a probability distribution. Portfolios are used to obtain a combined investment that has a given expected return and risk. Stock portfolios with a high risk can be constructed by combining several individual stocks whose values tend to increase or decrease together. With such a portfolio an investor will have either large gains or large losses. Stocks whose values move in opposite directions could be combined to create a portfolio with a more stable value, implying less risk. Decreases in one stock price would be balanced by increases in another stock price.

This process of **portfolio analysis** and construction is conducted using probability distributions. The mean value of the portfolio is the linear combination of the mean values of the stocks in the portfolio. The variance of the portfolio value is computed using the sum of the variances and the covariance of the joint distribution of the stock values. We will develop the method using an example with a portfolio consisting of two stocks.

Consider a portfolio that consists of a shares of stock A and b shares of stock B. We want to use the mean and variance for the market value, W, of a portfolio, where W is the linear function $W = aX + bY$. The mean and variance are derived in the chapter appendix.

The Mean and Variance for the Market Value of a Portfolio

The random variable X is the price for stock A, and the random variable Y is the price for stock B. The **portfolio market value**, W, is given by the linear function

$$W = aX + bY$$

where a is the number of shares of stock A, and b is the number of shares of stock B.

The **mean value for W** is as follows:

$$\mu_W = E[W] = E[aX + bY] = a\mu_X + b\mu_Y \tag{4.42}$$

The **variance for W** is

$$\sigma_W^2 = a^2\sigma_X^2 + b^2\sigma_Y^2 + 2ab\,Cov(X, Y) \tag{4.43}$$

or, using the correlation, is

$$\sigma_W^2 = a^2\sigma_X^2 + b^2\sigma_Y^2 + 2ab\,Corr(X, Y)\sigma_X\sigma_Y$$

The development here using discrete random variables is more intuitive compared to using continuous random variables. However, the results for means, variances, covariances, and linear combinations of random variables also apply directly to continuous random variables. Since portfolios involve prices that are continous randam variables.

Example 2.4.18 Analysis of Stock Portfolios (Means and Variances, Functions of Random Variables)

George Tiao has 5 shares of stock A and 10 shares of stock B, whose price variations are modeled by the probability distribution in Table 2.33. Find the mean and variance of the portfolio.

Table 2.33 Joint Probability Distribution for Stock A and Stock B Prices

STOCK A PRICE	STOCK B PRICE			
	$40	$50	$60	$70
$45	0.24	0.003333	0.003333	0.003333
$50	0.003333	0.24	0.003333	0.003333
$55	0.003333	0.003333	0.24	0.003333
$60	0.003333	0.003333	0.003333	0.24

Solution The value, W, of the portfolio can be represented by the linear combination

$$W = 5X + 10Y$$

Using the probability distribution in Table 2.33 we can compute the means, variances, and covariances for the two stock prices. The mean and variance for stock A are $53 and 31.3, respectively, while for stock B they are $55 and 125. The covariance is 59.17 and the correlation is 0.947.

The mean value for the portfolio is as follows:

$$\mu_W = E[W] = E[5X + 10Y] = 5(53) + (10)(55) = \$815$$

The variance for the portfolio value is as follows:

$$\sigma_W^2 = 5^2\sigma_X^2 + 10^2\sigma_Y^2 + 2 \times 5 \times 10 \times Cov(X, Y)$$
$$= 5^2 \times 31.3 + 10^2 \times 125 + 2 \times 5 \times 10 \times 59.17 = 19{,}199.5$$

George knows that high variance implies high risk. He believes that the risk for this portfolio is too high. Thus, he asks you to prepare a portfolio that has lower risk. After some investigation you discover a different pair of stocks whose prices follow the probability distribution in Table 2.34. By comparing Tables 2.33 and 2.34 we note that the stock prices tend to change directly with each other in Table 2.33, while they move in opposite directions in Table 2.34.

Table 2.34 Probability Distribution for New Portfolio of Stock C and Stock D

Stock C Price	Stock D Price			
	$40	$50	$60	$70
$45	0.003333	0.003333	0.003333	0.24
$50	0.003333	0.003333	0.24	0.003333
$55	0.003333	0.24	0.003333	0.003333
$60	0.24	0.003333	0.003333	0.003333

Using the probability distribution in Table 2.34 we computed the means, variances, and covariance for the new stock portfolio. The mean for stock C is $53, the same as for stock A. Similarly, the mean for stock D is $55, the same as for stock B. Thus, the mean value of the portfolio is not changed. The variance for each stock is also the same, but the covariance is now −59.17. Thus, the variance for the new portfolio includes a *negative covariance* term and is as follows:

$$\sigma_W^2 = 5^2\sigma_X^2 + 10^2\sigma_Y^2 + 2 \times 5 \times 10 \times Cov(X, Y)$$
$$= 5^2 \times 31.3 + 10^2 \times 125 + 2 \times 5 \times 10 \times (-59.17) = 7{,}365.5$$

We see that the effect of the negative covariance is to reduce the variance and, hence, to reduce the risk of the portfolio.

Figure 2.55 shows how portfolio variance—and, hence, risk—changes with different correlations between stock prices. Note that the portfolio variance is linearly related to the correlation. To help control risk, designers of stock portfolios select stocks based on the correlation between prices.

Figure 2.55 Portfolio Variance Versus Correlation of Stock Prices

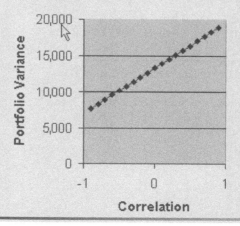

As we saw in Example 2.4.19, the correlation between stock prices, or between any two random variables, has important effects on the portfolio value random variable. A positive correlation indicates that both prices, X and Y, increase or decrease together. Thus, large or small values of the portfolio are magnified, resulting in greater range and variance compared to a zero correlation. Conversely, a negative correlation leads to price increases for X matched by price decreases for Y. As a result, the range and variance of the portfolio are decreased compared to a zero correlation. By selecting stocks with particular combinations of correlations, fund managers can control the variance and the risk for portfolios.

EXERCISES

Basic Exercises

2.4.61 A call center in Perth, Australia receives an average of 1.3 calls per minute. By looking at the date, a Poisson discrete distribution is assumed for this variable. Calculate each of the following.

a. The probability of receiving no calls in the first minute of its office hours.
b. The probability of receiving 1 call in the first minute.
c. The probability of receiving 3 calls in the first minute.

2.4.62 Consider the joint probability distribution:

		X	
		1	2
Y	0	0.25	0.25
	1	0.25	0.25

a. Compute the marginal probability distributions for X and Y.
b. Compute the covariance and correlation for X and Y.
c. Compute the mean and variance for the linear function $W = X + Y$.

2.4.63 Consider the joint probability distribution:

		X	
		1	2
Y	0	0.30	0.20
	1	0.25	0.25

a. Compute the marginal probability distributions for X and Y.
b. Compute the covariance and correlation for X and Y.
c. Compute the mean and variance for the linear function $W = 2X + Y$.

2.4.64 Consider the joint probability distribution:

		X	
		1	2
Y	0	0.70	0.0
	1	0.0	0.30

a. Compute the marginal probability distributions for X and Y.
b. Compute the covariance and correlation for X and Y.
c. Compute the mean and variance for the linear function $W = 3X + 4Y$.

2.4.65 Consider the joint probability distribution:

		X	
		1	2
Y	0	0.0	0.60
	1	0.40	0.0

a. Compute the marginal probability distributions for X and Y.
b. Compute the covariance and correlation for X and Y.
c. Compute the mean and variance for the linear function $W = 2X - 4Y$.

2.4.66 Consider the joint probability distribution:

		X	
		1	2
Y	0	0.70	0.0
	1	0.0	0.30

a. Compute the marginal probability distributions for X and Y.
b. Compute the covariance and correlation for X and Y.
c. Compute the mean and variance for the linear function $W = 10X - 8Y$.

Application Exercises

2.4.67 A researcher suspected that the number of between-meal snacks eaten by students in a day during final examinations might depend on the number of tests a student had to take on that day. The accompanying table shows joint probabilities, estimated from a survey.

Number of Snacks (Y)	Number of Tests (X)			
	0	1	2	3
0	0.07	0.09	0.06	0.01
1	0.07	0.06	0.07	0.01
2	0.06	0.07	0.14	0.03
3	0.02	0.04	0.16	0.04

a. Find the probability distribution of X and compute the mean number of tests taken by students on that day.
b. Find the probability distribution of Y and, hence, the mean number of snacks eaten by students on that day.
c. Find and interpret the conditional probability distribution of Y, given that X = 3.
d. Find the covariance between X and Y.
e. Are number of snacks and number of tests independent of each other?

2.4.68 A real estate agent is interested in the relationship between the number of lines in a newspaper advertisement for an apartment and the volume of inquiries from potential renters. Let volume of inquiries be denoted by the random variable X, with the value 0 for little interest, 1 for moderate interest, and 2 for strong interest. The real estate agent used historical records to compute the joint probability distribution shown in the accompanying table.

Number of Lines (Y)	Number of Inquiries (X)		
	0	1	2
3	0.09	0.14	0.07
4	0.07	0.23	0.16
5	0.03	0.10	0.11

a. Find the joint cumulative probability at X = 1, Y = 4, and interpret your result.
b. Find and interpret the conditional probability distribution for Y, given X = 0.
c. Find and interpret the conditional probability distribution for X, given Y = 4.
d. Find and interpret the covariance between X and Y.
e. Are number of lines in the advertisement and volume of inquiries independent of one another?

2.4.69 The accompanying table shows, for credit-card holders with one to three cards, the joint probabilities for number of cards owned (X) and number of credit purchases made in a week (Y).

Number of Cards (X)	Number of Purchases in Week (Y)				
	0	1	2	3	4
1	0.08	0.13	0.09	0.06	0.03
2	0.03	0.08	0.08	0.09	0.07
3	0.01	0.03	0.06	0.08	0.08

a. For a randomly chosen person from this group, what is the probability distribution for number of purchases made in a week?
b. For a person in this group who has three cards, what is the probability distribution for number of purchases made in a week?
c. Are number of cards owned and number of purchases made statistically independent?

2.4.70 A market researcher wants to determine whether a new model of a personal computer that had been advertised on a late-night talk show had achieved more brand-name recognition among people who watched the show regularly than among people who did not. After conducting a survey, it was found that 15% of

all people both watched the show regularly and could correctly identify the product. Also, 16% of all people regularly watched the show and 45% of all people could correctly identify the product. Define a pair of random variables as follows:

X = 1	if regularly watch the show	X = 0	otherwise
Y = 1	if product correctly identified	Y = 0	otherwise

a. Find the joint probability distribution of X and Y.
b. Find the conditional probability distribution of Y, given X = 1.
c. Find and interpret the covariance between X and Y.

2.4.71 A college bookseller makes calls at the offices of professors and forms the impression that professors are more likely to be away from their offices on Friday than any other working day. A review of the records of calls, 1/5 of which are on Fridays, indicates that for 16% of Friday calls, the professor is away from the office, while this occurs for only 12% of calls on every other working day. Define the random variables as follows:

X = 1	if call is made on a Friday	X = 0	otherwise
Y = 1	if professor is away from the office	Y = 0	otherwise

a. Find the joint probability distribution of X and Y.
b. Find the conditional probability distribution of Y, given X = 0.
c. Find the marginal probability distributions of X and Y.
d. Find and interpret the covariance between X and Y.

2.4.72 A restaurant manager receives occasional complaints about the quality of both the food and the service. The marginal probability distributions for the number of weekly complaints in each category are shown in the accompanying table. If complaints about food and service are independent of each other, find the joint probability distribution.

Number of Food Complaints	Probability	Number of Service Complaints	Probability
0	0.12	0	0.18
1	0.29	1	0.38
2	0.42	2	0.34
3	0.17	3	0.10

2.4.73 Refer to the information in the previous exercise. Find the mean and standard deviation of the total number of complaints received in a week. Having reached this point, you are concerned that the numbers of food and service complaints may not be independent of each other. However, you have no information about the nature of their dependence. What can you now say about the mean and standard deviation of the total number of complaints received in a week?

2.4.74 A company has 5 representatives covering large territories and 10 representatives covering smaller territories. The probability distributions for the numbers of orders received by each of these types of representatives in a day are shown in the accompanying table. Assuming that the number of orders received by any representative is independent of the number received by any other, find the mean and standard deviation of the total number of orders received by the company in a day.

Numbers of Orders (Large Territories)	Probability	Numbers of Orders (Smaller Territories)	Probability
0	0.08	0	0.18
1	0.16	1	0.26
2	0.28	2	0.36
3	0.32	3	0.13
4	0.10	4	0.07
5	0.06		

KEY WORDS

- Bernoulli random variable,
- binomial distribution,
- conditional probability distribution,
- continuous random variable,
- correlation,
- covariance,
- cumulative probability distribution,
- differences of random variable,
- discrete random variable,
- expected value,
- expected value of functions of random variables,
- hypergeometric distribution,
- independence of jointly distributed random variables,
- joint probability distribution,
- marginal probability distribution,
- mean,
- mean and variance of a binomial,
- Poisson approximation to the binomial distribution,
- Poisson probability distribution,
- portfolio analysis,
- portfolio market value,
- probability distribution function,
- properties of cumulative probability distributions,
- properties of joint probability distributions,
- random variable,
- relationship between probability distribution and cumulative probability distribution,
- variance of a discrete random variable,
- properties for linear functions of a random variable,

CHAPTER EXERCISES AND APPLICATIONS

2.4.75 As an investment advisor, you tell a client that an investment in a mutual fund has (over the next year) a higher expected return than an investment in the money market. The client then asks the following questions:

a. Does that imply that the mutual fund will certainly yield a higher return than the money market?
b. Does it follow that I should invest in the mutual fund rather than in the money market? How would you reply?

2.4.76 A contractor estimates the probabilities for the number of days required to complete a certain type of construction project as follows:

Time (days)	1	2	3	4	5
Probability	0.05	0.20	0.35	0.30	0.10

a. What is the probability that a randomly chosen project will take less than 3 days to complete?
b. Find the expected time to complete a project.
c. Find the standard deviation of time required to complete a project.
d. The contractor's project cost is made up of two parts—a fixed cost of $20,000, plus $2,000 for each day taken to complete the project. Find the mean and standard deviation of total project cost.
e. If three projects are undertaken, what is the probability that at least two of them will take at least 4 days to complete, assuming independence of individual project completion times?

2.4.77 A car salesperson estimates the following probabilities for the number of cars that she will sell in the next week:

Number of cars	0	1	2	3	4	5
Probability	0.10	0.20	0.35	0.16	0.12	0.07

a. Find the expected number of cars that will be sold in the week.
b. Find the standard deviation of the number of cars that will be sold in the week.
c. The salesperson receives a salary of $250 for the week, plus an additional $300 for each car sold. Find the mean and standard deviation of her total salary for the week.
d. What is the probability that the salesperson's salary for the week will be more than $1,000?

2.4.78 A multiple-choice test has nine questions. For each question there are four possible answers from which to select. One point is awarded for each correct answer, and points are not subtracted for incorrect answers. The instructor awards a bonus point if the students spell their name correctly. A student who has not studied for this test decides to choose an answer for each question at random.

a. Find the expected number of correct answers for the student on these nine questions.
b. Find the standard deviation of the number of correct answers for the student on these nine questions.
c. The student spells his name correctly:

i Find the expected total score on the test for this student.

ii Find the standard deviation of his total score on the test.

2.4.79 Develop realistic examples of pairs of random variables for which you would expect to find the following:

a. Positive covariance
b. Negative covariance
c. Zero covariance

2.4.80 A long-distance taxi service owns four vehicles. These are of different ages and have different repair records. The probabilities that, on any given day, each vehicle will be available for use are 0.95, 0.90, 0.90, and 0.80. Whether one vehicle is available is independent of whether any other vehicle is available.

a. Find the probability distribution for the number of vehicles available for use on a given day.
b. Find the expected number of vehicles available for use on a given day.
c. Find the standard deviation of the number of vehicles available for use on a given day.

2.4.81 Students in a college were classified according to years in school (X) and number of visits to a museum in the last year ($Y = 0$ for no visits, 1 for one visit, 2 for more than one visit). The joint probabilities in the accompanying table were estimated for these random variables.

| Number of | Years in School (X) | | | |
Visits (Y)	1	2	3	4
0	0.07	0.05	0.03	0.02
1	0.13	0.11	0.17	0.15
2	0.04	0.04	0.09	0.10

a. Find the probability that a randomly chosen student has not visited a museum in the last year.
b. Find the means of the random variables X and Y.
c. Find and interpret the covariance between the random variables X and Y.

2.4.82 A basketball team's star 3-point shooter takes six 3-point shots in a game. Historically, she makes 40% of all 3-point shots taken in a game. State at the outset what assumptions you have made.

a. Find the probability that she will make at least two shots.
b. Find the probability that she will make exactly three shots.
c. Find the mean and standard deviation of the number of shots she made.
d. Find the mean and standard deviation of the total number of points she scored as a result of these shots.

2.4.83 It is estimated that 55% of the freshmen entering a particular college will graduate from that college in four years.

a. For a random sample of 5 entering freshmen, what is the probability that exactly 3 will graduate in four years?

b. For a random sample of 5 entering freshmen, what is the probability that a majority will graduate in four years?
c. 80 entering freshmen are chosen at random. Find the mean and standard deviation of the proportion of these 80 that will graduate in four years.

2.4.84 The World Series of baseball is to be played by team A and team B. The first team to win four games wins the series. Suppose that team A is the better team, in the sense that the probability is 0.6 that team A will win any specific game. Assume also that the result of any game is independent of that of any other.

a. What is the probability that team A will win the series?
b. What is the probability that a seventh game will be needed to determine the winner?
c. Suppose that, in fact, each team wins two of the first four games.

i What is the probability that team A will win the series?

ii What is the probability that a seventh game will be needed to determine the winner?

2.4.85 Using detailed cash-flow information, a financial analyst claims to be able to spot companies that are likely candidates for bankruptcy. The analyst is presented with information on the past records of 15 companies and told that, in fact, 5 of these have failed. He selects as candidates for failure 5 companies from the group of 15. In fact, 3 of the 5 companies selected by the analyst were among those that failed. Evaluate the financial analyst's performance on this test of his ability to detect failed companies.

2.4.86 A team of 5 analysts is about to examine the earnings prospects of 20 corporations. Each of the 5 analysts will study 4 of the corporations. These analysts are not equally competent. In fact, one of them is a star, having an excellent record of anticipating changing trends. Ideally, management would like to allocate the 4 corporations whose earnings will deviate most from past trends to this analyst. However, lacking this information, management allocates corporations to analysts randomly. What is the probability that at least 2 of the 4 corporations whose earnings will deviate most from past trends are allocated to the star analyst?

2.4.87 A new brand of pizza is going to be sold in Park & Shop, and a market-research company in Admiralty (Hong Kong) has forecast that successful new brands normally obtain a 10% market share for the product in the first year. However, top management wants to achieve 12%. You may assume a normal distribution with a standard deviation of 3% (risk on the estimates). Determine each of the following.

a. The probability that the new pizza will actually achieve the target.
b. The probability of failure.
c. The probability of being even more successful, with 18% of market share in the first year.

2.4.88 A recent estimate suggested that, of all individuals and couples reporting income in excess of $200,000, 6.5% either paid no federal tax or paid tax at an effective rate of less than 15%. A random sample of 100 of those reporting income in excess of $200,000 was taken. What is the probability that more than 2 of the sample members either paid no federal tax or paid tax at an effective rate of less than 15%?

2.4.89 Your computer is in serious need of repair. You have estimated that the breakdowns occur on average 3.5 times per week. If you are right and the breakdown variable is a Poisson distribution, calculate the following.

    a. The probability that for an entire week your computer runs with no problems.
    b. The probability of getting only 1 shutdown.
    c. The probability of getting 5 shutdowns.

2.4.90 George Allen has asked you to analyze his stock portfolio, which contains 10 shares of stock D and 5 shares of stock C. The joint probability distribution of the stock prices is shown in Table 2.35. Compute the mean and variance for the total value of his stock portfolio.

Table 2.35 Joint Probability Distribution for Stock Prices

Stock C Price	Stock D Price			
	$40	$50	$60	$70
$45	0.00	0.00	0.05	0.20
$50	0.05	0.00	0.05	0.10
$55	0.10	0.05	0.00	0.05
$60	0.20	0.10	0.05	0.00

2.4.91 Consider a country that imports steel and exports automobiles. The value per unit of cars exported is measured in units of thousands of dollars per car by the random variable X. The value per unit of steel imported is measured in units of thousands of dollars per ton of steel by the random variable Y. Suppose that the country annually exports 10 cars and imports 5 tons of steel. Compute the mean and variance of the trade balance, where the trade balance is the total dollars received for all cars exported minus the total dollars spent for all steel imported. The joint probability distribution for the prices of cars and steel is shown in Table 2.36.

Table 2.36 Joint Distribution of Automobile and Steel Prices

Price of Steel (Y)	Price of Automobiles (X)		
	$3	$4	$5
$4	0.10	0.15	0.05
$6	0.10	0.20	0.10
$8	0.05	0.15	0.10

2.4.92 Delta International delivers approximately one million packages a day between East Asia and the United States. A random sample of the daily number of package delivery failures over the past six months provided the following results: 15, 10, 8, 16, 12, 11, 9, 8, 12, 9, 10, 8, 7, 16, 14, 12, 10, 9, 8, 11. There was nothing unusual about the operations during these days and, thus, the results can be considered typical. Using these data and your understanding of the delivery process answer the following:

    a. What probability model should be used and why?
    b. What is the probability of 10 or more failed deliveries on a typical future day?
    c. What is the probability of less than 6 failed deliveries?
    d. Find the number of failures such that the probability of exceeding this number is 10% or less.

2.4.93 Bright Star Financial Advisers receives a mean of 19 5 applications per week for a personal financial review. Each review requires one day of an analyst's time to prepare a review. Assume that requests received during any week are assigned to an analyst for completion during the following week. If the analysis is not completed during the second week the customer will cancel.

    a. How many analysts should be hired so that the company can claim that 90% of the reviews will be completed during the second week?
    b. What is the probability that two of the analysts hired for part a would have no clients for an entire week?
    c. Suppose that they decided to hire one less analyst than determined in part (a). What is the probability that customers would cancel given this staffing level?
    d. Given the number of analysts hired in part c, what is the probability that two analysts would be idle for an entire week?

2.4.94 Federated South Insurance Company has developed a new screening program for selecting new sales agents. Their past experience indicates that 20% of the new agents hired fail to produce the minimum sales in their first year and are dismissed. Their expectation is that this new screening program will reduce the percentage of failed new agents to 15% or less. If that occurs, they would save $1,000,000 in recruiting and training costs each year. At the end of the first year they want to develop an evaluation to determine if the new program is successful. The following questions are an important part of their research design.

    A total of 20 new agents were selected.

    a. If this group performs at the same level as past groups, what is the probability 17 or more successfully meet their minimum sales goals in the first year?

b. What is the probability 19 or more reach their minimum sales goals given performance at the same level?

c. If the program has actually increased the probability of success to 0.85 for each new agent, what is the probability that 17 or more meet their minimum sales goals?

d. Given the expected improvement, what is the probability that 19 or more reach their minimum sales goals?

2.4.95 Yoshida Toimi is a candidate for the mayor of a medium-sized Midwestern city. If he receives more than 50% of the votes, he will win the election. Prior to the election, his campaign staff is planning to ask 100 randomly selected voters if they support Yoshida.

a. How many positive responses from this sample of 100 is required so that the probability of 50% or more voters supporting him is 0.95 or more?

b. Carefully state the assumptions required for your answer in part (a).

c. Suppose the campaign is able to ask 400 randomly selected voters. Now what is your answer to the question in part (a)?

2.4.96 Faschip, Ltd., is a new African manufacturer of notebook computers. Their quality target is that 99.999% of the computers they produce will perform exactly as promised in the descriptive literature. In order to monitor their quality performance they include with each computer a large piece of paper that includes a direct—toll-free—phone number to the Senior Vice President of Manufacturing that can be used if the computer does not perform as promised. In the first year Faschip sells 1,000,000 computers.

a. If they are achieving their quality target, what is the probability that they will receive fewer than 5 calls? If this occurs what would be a reasonable conclusion about their quality program?

b. If they are achieving their quality target, what is the probability that they will receive more than 15 calls? If this occurs, what would be a reasonable conclusion about their quality program?

CHAPTER 2.5

Continuous Probability Distributions

CHAPTER OUTLINE

Introduction

In Chapter 4 we developed discrete random variables and probability distributions. Here, we extend the probability concepts to continuous random variables and probability distributions. The concepts and insights for discrete random variables also apply to continuous random variables, so we are building directly on the previous chapter. Many economic and business measures such as sales, investment, consumption, costs, and revenues can be represented by continuous random variables. In addition, measures of time, distance, temperature, and weight fit into this category. Probability statements for continuous random variables are specified over ranges. The probability that sales are between 140 and 190 or greater than 200 is a typical example.

Mathematical theory leads us to conclude that, in reality, random variables for all applied problems are discrete because measurements are rounded to some value. But, for us, the important idea is that continuous random variables and probability distributions provide good approximations for many applied problems. Thus, these models are very important and provide excellent tools for business and economic applications.

2.5.1 CONTINUOUS RANDOM VARIABLES

We define X as a random variable and x as a specific value of the random variable. Our first step is to define the *cumulative distribution function*. Then we will define the probability density function, which is analogous to the probability distribution function used for discrete random variables.

> ### Cumulative Distribution Function
> The **cumulative distribution function**, $F(x)$, for a continuous random variable X expresses the probability that X does not exceed the value of x, as a function of x:
>
> $$F(x) = P(X \leq x)$$
>
> (5.1)

The cumulative distribution function can be illustrated by using a simple probability structure. Consider a gasoline station that has a 1,000-gallon storage tank that is filled each morning at the start of the business day. Analysis of past history indicates that it is not possible to predict the amount of gasoline sold on any particular day, but the lower limit is 0 and the upper limit is, of course, 1,000 gallons, the size of the tank. In addition, past history indicates that any demand in the interval from 1 to 1,000 gallons is equally likely. The random variable X indicates the gasoline sales in gallons for a particular day. We are concerned with the probability of various levels of daily gasoline sales, where the probability of a specific number of gallons sold is the same over the range from 0 to 1,000 gallons. The distribution of X is said to follow a **uniform probability distribution**, and the cumulative distribution is as follows:

$$F(x) = \begin{cases} 0 & \text{if } x < 0 \\ 0.001x & \text{if } 0 \leq x \leq 1,000 \\ 1 & \text{if } x > 1,000 \end{cases}$$

This function is graphed as a straight line between 0 and 1,000, as shown in Figure 2.56. From this we see that the probability of sales between 0 and 400 gallons is as follows:

$$P(X \leq 400) = F(400) = (0.001)(400) = 0.40$$

Figure 2.56
Cumulative
Distribution Function
for a Random
Variable Over 0
to 1,000

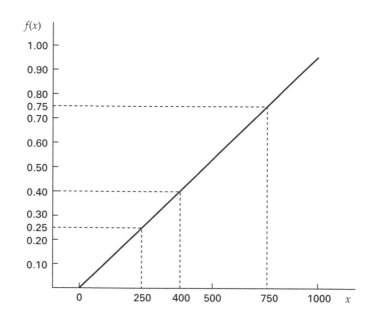

To obtain the probability that a continuous random variable X falls in a specified range, we find the difference between the cumulative probability at the upper end of the range and the cumulative probability at the lower end of the range.

> ## Probability of a Range Using a Cumulative Distribution Function
> Let X be a continuous random variable with a cumulative distribution function $F(x)$, and let a and b be two possible values of X, with $a < b$. The probability that X lies between a and b is as follows:
>
> $$P(a < X < b) = F(b) - F(a) \qquad (5.2)$$

For continuous random variables, it does not matter whether we write "less than" or "less than or equal to" because the probability that X is precisely equal to b is 0.

For the random variable that is distributed uniformly in the range 0 to 1,000, the cumulative distribution function in that range is $F(x) = 0.001x$. Therefore, if a and b are two numbers between 0 and 1,000 with $a < b$,

$$P(a < X < b) = F(b) - F(a) = 0.001(b - a)$$

For example, the probability of sales between 250 and 750 gallons is

$$P(250 < X < 750) = (0.001)(750) - (0.001)(250) = 0.75 - 0.25 = 0.50$$

as shown in Figure 2.56.

We have seen that the probability that a continuous random variable lies between any two values can be expressed in terms of its cumulative distribution function. This function, therefore, contains all the information about the probability structure of the random variable. However, for many purposes a different function is more useful. In Chapter 4 we discussed the probability distribution for discrete random variables, which expresses the probability that a discrete random variable takes any specific value. Since the probability of a specific value is 0 for continuous random variables, that concept is not directly relevant here. However, a related function, called the *probability density function*, can be constructed for continuous random variables, allowing for graphical interpretation of their probability structure.

> ## Probability Density Function
> Let X be a continuous random variable, and let x be any number lying in the range of values for the random variable. The **probability density function**, $f(x)$, of the random variable is a function with the following properties:
>
> 1. $f(x) > 0$ for all values of x.
> 2. The area under the probability density function, $f(x)$, over all values of the random variable, X *within its range*, is equal to 1.0.
> 3. Suppose that this density function is graphed. Let a and b be two possible values of random variable X, with $a < b$. Then, the probability that X lies between a and b is the area under the probability density function between these points.
>
> $$P(a \leq X \leq b) = \int_{a}^{b} f(x)\,dx$$

4. The cumulative distribution function, $F(x_0)$, is the area under the probability density function, $f(x)$, up to x_0,

$$F(x_0) = \int_{x_m}^{x_0} f(x)dx$$

where x_m is the minimum value of the random variable X.

The probability density function can be approximated by a discrete probability distribution with many discrete values close together, as seen in Figure 2.57.

Figure 2.57
Approximation of a
Probability Density
Function by a
Discrete Probability
Distribution

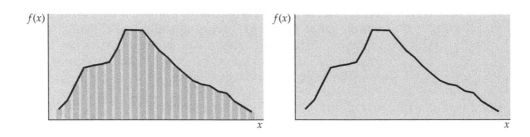

Figure 2.58 shows the plot of a probability density function for a continuous random variable. Two possible values, a and b, are shown, and the shaded area under the curve between these points is the probability that the random variable lies in the interval between them, as shown in the chapter appendix.

Figure 2.58
Shaded Area Is the
Probability That X is
Between a and b

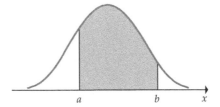

Areas Under Continuous Probability Density Functions
Let X be a continuous random variable with probability density function
$f(x)$ and cumulative distribution function $F(x)$. Then, consider the following
properties:

1. The total area under the curve $f(x)$ is 1.
2. The area under the curve $f(x)$ to the left of x_0 is $F(x_0)$, where x_0 is any
   value that the random variable can take.

These results are shown in Figure 2.59, with Figure 2.59(a) showing that the entire area under the probability density function is equal to 1 and Figure 2.59(b) indicating the area to the left of x_0.

Figure 2.59
Properties of the
Probability Density
Function

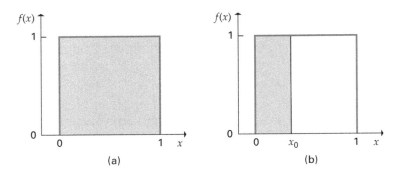

(a)   (b)

The Uniform Distribution

Now, we consider a probability density function that represents a probability distribution over the range of 0 to 1. Figure 2.60 is a graph of the uniform probability density function over the range from 0 to 1. The probability density function for the gasoline sales example is shown in Figure 2.61. Since the probability is the same for any interval of the sales range from 0 to 1,000, the probability density function is the uniform probability density function, which can be written as follows:

$$f(x) = \begin{cases} 0.001 & 0 \le x \le 1,000 \\ 0 & \text{otherwise} \end{cases}$$

Figure 2.60 Probability Density
Function for a Uniform 0 to 1
Random Variable

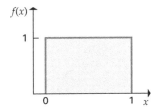

Figure 2.61 Density Function
Showing the Probability That X is
Between 250 and 750

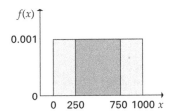

For any uniform random variable defined over the range from a to b, the probability density function is as follows:

$$f(x) = \begin{cases} \dfrac{1}{b - a} & a \le x \le b \\ 0 & \text{otherwise} \end{cases}$$

This probability density function can be used to find the probability that the random variable falls within a specific range. For example, the probability that sales are between 250 gallons and 750 gallons is shown in Figure 5.6. Since the height of the density function is $f(x) = 0.001$, the area under the curve between 250 and 750 is equal to 0.50, which is the required probability. Note that this is the same result obtained previously using the cumulative probability function.

We have seen that the probability that a random variable lies between a pair of values is the area under the probability density function between these two values. There are two important results worth noting. The area under the entire probability density function is 1, and the cumulative probability, $F(x_0)$, is the area under the density function to the left of x_0.

Example 2.5.1 Probability of Pipeline Failure (Cumulative Distribution Function)

A repair team is responsible for a stretch of oil pipeline 2 miles long. The distance (in miles) at which any fracture occurs can be represented by a uniformly distributed random variable, with probability density function

$$f(x) = 0.5$$

Find the cumulative distribution function and the probability that any given fracture occurs between 0.5 mile and 1.5 miles along this stretch of pipeline.

Solution Figure 2.62 shows a plot of the probability density function, with the shaded area indicating $F(x_0)$, the cumulative distribution function evaluated at x_0. Thus, we see that

$$F(x_0) = 0.5x_0 \quad \text{for } 0 < x_0 \leq 2$$

Figure 2.62 Probability Density Function for Example 2.5.1

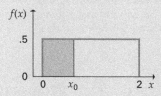

The probability that a fracture occurs between 0.5 mile and 1.5 miles along the pipe is as follows:

$$P(0.5 < X < 1.5) = F(1.5) - F(0.5) = (0.5)(1.5) - (0.5)(0.5) = 0.5$$

This is the area under the probability density function from $x = 0.5$ to $x = 1.5$.

EXERCISES

Basic Exercises

2.5.1 Using the uniform probability density function shown in Figure 2.62, find the probability that the random variable X is between 1.4 and 1.8.

2.5.2 Using the uniform probability density function shown in Figure 2.62, find the probability that the random variable X is between 1.0 and 1.9.

2.5.3 Using the uniform probability density function shown in Figure 2.62, find the probability that the random variable X is less than 1.4.

2.5.4 Using the uniform probability density function shown in Figure 2.62, find the probability that the random variable X is greater than 1.3.

Application Exercises

2.5.5 An analyst has available two forecasts, F_1 and F_2, of earnings per share of a corporation next year. He intends to form a compromise forecast as a weighted average of the two individual forecasts. In forming the compromise forecast, weight X will be given to the first forecast and weight $(1 - X)$, to the second,

so that the compromise forecast is $XF_1 + (1 - X)F_2$. The analyst wants to choose a value between 0 and 1 for the weight X, but he is quite uncertain of what will be the best choice. Suppose that what eventually emerges as the best possible choice of the weight X can be viewed as a random variable uniformly distributed between 0 and 1, having the probability density function

$$f(x) = \begin{cases} 1 & \text{for } 0 \leq x \leq 1 \\ 0 & \text{for all other } x \end{cases}$$

a. Graph the probability density function.
b. Find and graph the cumulative distribution function.
c. Find the probability that the best choice of the weight X is less than 0.25.
d. Find the probability that the best choice of the weight X is more than 0.75.
e. Find the probability that the best choice of the weight X is between 0.2 and 0.8.

2.5.6   The jurisdiction of a rescue team includes emergencies occurring on a stretch of river that is 4 miles long. Experience has shown that the distance along this stretch, measured in miles from its northernmost point, at which an emergency occurs can be represented by a uniformly distributed random variable over the range 0 to 4 miles. Then, if X denotes the distance (in miles) of an emergency from the northernmost point of this stretch of river, its probability density function is as follows:

$$f(x) = \begin{cases} 0.25 & \text{for } 0 < x < 4 \\ 0 & \text{for all other } x \end{cases}$$

a. Graph the probability density function.
b. Find and graph the cumulative distribution function.
c. Find the probability that a given emergency arises within 1 mile of the northernmost point of this stretch of river.
d. The rescue team's base is at the midpoint of this stretch of river. Find the probability that a given emergency arises more than 1.5 miles from this base.

2.5.7   The incomes of all families in a particular suburb can be represented by a continuous random variable. It is known that the median income for all families in this suburb is $60,000 and that 40% of all families in the suburb have incomes above $72,000.

a. For a randomly chosen family, what is the probability that its income will be between $60,000 and $72,000?
b. Given no further information, what can be said about the probability that a randomly chosen family has an income below $65,000?

2.5.8   At the beginning of winter, a homeowner estimates that the probability is 0.4 that his total heating bill for the three winter months will be less than $380. He also estimates that the probability is 0.6 that the total bill will be less than $460.

a. What is the probability that the total bill will be between $380 and $460?
b. Given no further information, what can be said about the probability that the total bill will be less than $400?

2.5.2 EXPECTATIONS FOR CONTINUOUS RANDOM VARIABLES

In Section 2.4.2 we presented the concepts of expected value of a discrete random variable and the expected value of a function of that random variable. Here, we extend those ideas to continuous random variables. Because the probability of any specific value is 0 for a continuous random variable, the expected values for continuous random variables are computed using integral calculus, as shown in Equation 5.3.

Rationale for Expectations of Continuous Random Variables

Suppose that a random experiment leads to an outcome that can be represented by a continuous random variable. If N independent replications of this experiment are carried out, then the **expected value** of the random variable is the average of the values taken as the number of replications becomes infinitely large. The expected value of a random variable is denoted by $E[X]$.

Similarly, if $g(X)$ is any function of the random variable X, then the expected value of this function is the average value taken by the function over repeated independent trials as the number of trials becomes infinitely large. This expectation is denoted $E[g(X)]$.

By using calculus we can define expected values for continuous random variables similar to those used for discrete random variables:

$$E[g(x)] = \int_x g(x)f(x)dx \qquad (5.3)$$

These concepts can be clearly presented if one understands integral calculus, as shown in the chapter appendix. Using Equation 5.3, we can obtain the mean and variance for continuous random variables. Equations 5.4 and 5.5 present the mean and variance for continuous random variables (Hogg & Craig, 1995). If you do not understand integral calculus, then merely extend your understanding from discrete random variables as developed in Chapter 4.

Mean, Variance, and Standard Deviation for Continuous Random Variables

Let X be a continuous random variable. There are two important expected values that are used routinely to define continuous probability distributions.

1. The **mean of X**, denoted by μ_X, is defined as the expected value of X:

$$\mu_X = E[X] \tag{5.4}$$

2. The **variance of X**, denoted by σ_X^2 is defined as the expectation of the squared deviation, $(X - \mu_X)^2$, of the random variable from its mean:

$$\sigma_X^2 = E[(X - \mu_X)^2] \tag{5.5}$$

An alternative expression can be derived:

$$\sigma_X^2 = E[X^2] - \mu_X^2 \tag{5.6}$$

The **standard deviation of X**, σ_X, is the square root of the variance.

The mean and variance provide two important pieces of summary information about a probability distribution. The mean provides a measure of the center of the distribution. Consider a physical interpretation as follows: Cut out the graph of a probability density function. The point along the x-axis at which the figure exactly balances on one's finger is the mean of the distribution. For example, in Figure 2.59 the uniform distribution will balance at $x = 0.5$, and, thus, $\mu_X = 0.5$ is the mean of the random variable.

The variance—or its square root, the standard deviation—provides a measure of the dispersion or spread of a distribution. Thus, if we compare two uniform distributions with the same mean, $\mu_X = 1$—one over the range 0.5 to 1.5 and the other over the range 0 to 2—we will find that the latter has a larger variance because it is spread over a greater range.

For a *uniform distribution* defined over the range from a to b, we have the following results:

$$f(x) = \frac{1}{b - a} \quad a \le X \le b$$

$$\mu_X = E[X] = \frac{a + b}{2}$$

$$\sigma_X^2 = E[(X - \mu_X)^2] = \frac{(b - a)^2}{12}$$

The mean and the variance are also called the first and second moments.

In Section 2.4.3 we showed how to obtain the means and variances for linear functions of discrete random variables. The results are the same for continuous random variables because the derivations make use of the expected value operator. The summary results from Chapter 4 are repeated here.

Linear Functions of Random Variables

Let X be a continuous random variable with mean μ_X and variance σ_X^2 and let a and b be any constant fixed numbers. Define the random variable W as follows:

$$W = a + bX$$

Then the mean and variance of W are

$$\mu_W = E[a + bX] = a + b\mu_X \tag{5.7}$$

and

$$\sigma_W^2 = Var[a + bX] = b^2\sigma_X^2 \tag{5.8}$$

and the standard deviation of W is

$$\sigma_W = |b|\sigma_X \tag{5.9}$$

An important special case of these results is the standardized random variable

$$Z = \frac{X - \mu_X}{\sigma_X} \tag{5.10}$$

which has mean 0 and variance 1.

Linear functions of random variables have many applications in business and economics. Suppose that the number of units sold during a week is a random variable and the selling price is fixed. Thus, the total revenue is a random variable that is a function of the random variable units sold. Quantity demanded is a linear function of price that can be a random variable. Thus, quantity demanded is a random variable. The total number of cars sold per month in a dealership is a linear function of the random variable number of cars sold per sales person multiplied by the number of sales persons. Thus, total sales is a random variable.

Example 2.5.2 Home Heating Costs (Mean and Standard Deviation)

A homeowner estimates that within the range of likely temperatures his January heating bill, Y, in dollars, will be

$$Y = 290 - 5T$$

where T is the average temperature for the month, in degrees Fahrenheit. If the average January temperature can be represented by a random variable with a mean of 24 and a standard deviation of 4, find the mean and standard deviation of this homeowner's January heating bill.

Solution The random variable T has mean $\mu_T = 24$ and standard deviation $\sigma_T = 4$. Therefore, the expected heating bill is

$$\mu_Y = 290 - 5\mu_T$$
$$= 290 - (5)(24) = \$170$$

and the standard deviation is

$$\sigma_Y = |-5|\,\sigma_T = (5)(4) = \$20$$

EXERCISES

Basic Exercises

2.5.9   The total cost for a production process is equal to $1,000 plus two times the number of units produced. The mean and variance for the number of units produced are 500 and 900, respectively. Find the mean and variance of the total cost.

2.5.10   The profit for a production process is equal to $1,000 minus two times the number of units produced. The mean and variance for the number of units produced are 50 and 90, respectively. Find the mean and variance of the profit.

2.5.11   The profit for a production process is equal to $2,000 minus two times the number of units produced. The mean and variance for the number of units produced are 500 and 900, respectively. Find the mean and variance of the profit.

2.5.12   The profit for a production process is equal to $6,000 minus three times the number of units produced. The mean and variance for the number of units produced are 1,000 and 900, respectively. Find the mean and variance of the profit.

Application Exercises

2.5.13   An author receives a contract from a publisher, according to which she is to be paid a fixed sum of $10,000 plus $1.50 for each copy of her book sold. Her uncertainty about total sales of the book can be represented by a random variable with a mean of 30,000 and a standard deviation of 8,000. Find the mean and standard deviation of the total payments she will receive.

2.5.14   A contractor submits a bid on a project for which more research and development work needs to be done. It is estimated that the total cost of satisfying the project specifications will be $20 million plus the cost of the further research and development work. The contractor views the cost of this additional work as a random variable with a mean of $4 million and a standard deviation of $1 million. The contractor wishes to submit a bid such that his expected profit will be 10% of his expected costs. What should be the bid? If this bid is accepted, what will be the standard deviation of the profit made by the project?

2.5.15   A charitable organization solicits donations by telephone. Employees are paid $60 plus 20% of the money their calls generate each week. The amount of money generated in a week can be viewed as a random variable with a mean of $700 and a standard deviation of $130. Find the mean and standard deviation of an employee's total pay in a week.

2.5.16   A salesperson receives an annual salary of $6,000 plus 8% of the value of the orders she takes. The annual value of these orders can be represented by a random variable with a mean of $600,000 and a standard deviation of $180,000. Find the mean and standard deviation of the salesperson's annual income.

2.5.3 THE NORMAL DISTRIBUTION

In this section we present the normal probability distribution, which is the continuous probability distribution used most often for economics and business applications. An example of the normal probability density function is shown in Figure 2.63.

Figure 2.63
Probability Density Function for a Normal Distribution

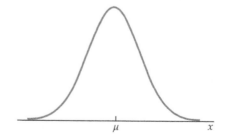

There are many reasons for its wide application.

1. The normal distribution closely approximates the probability distributions of a wide range of random variables. For example, the dimensions of parts and the weights of food packages often follow a normal distribution. This leads to quality-control applications. Total sales or production often follows a normal distribution, which leads us to a large family of applications in marketing and

in production management. The patterns of stock and bond prices are often modeled using the normal distribution in large computer-based financial trading models. Economic models use the normal distribution for a number of economic measures.

2. Distributions of sample means approach a normal distribution, given a "large" sample size.
3. Computation of probabilities is direct and elegant.
4. The most important reason is that the normal probability distribution has led to good business decisions for a number of applications.

A formal definition of the normal probability density function is given by Equation 5.11.

Probability Density Function of the Normal Distribution
The probability density function for a normally distributed random variable X is

$$f(x) = \frac{1}{\sqrt{2\pi\sigma^2}} e^{-(x-\mu)^2/2\sigma^2} \quad \text{for } -\infty < x < \infty \tag{5.11}$$

where μ and σ^2 are any numbers such that $-\infty < \mu < \infty$ and $0 < \sigma^2 < \infty$ and where e and π are physical constants, $e = 2.71828\ldots$, and $\pi = 3.14159\ldots.$

The normal probability distribution represents a large family of distributions, each with a unique specification for the parameters μ and σ^2. These parameters have a very convenient interpretation.

Properties of the Normal Distribution
Suppose that the random variable X follows a normal distribution with parameters μ and σ^2. Then, consider the following properties:

1. The mean of the random variable is μ:

$$E[X] = \mu$$

2. The variance of the random variable is σ^2:

$$Var(X) = E[(X - \mu)^2] = \sigma^2$$

3. The shape of the probability density function is a symmetric bell-shaped curve centered on the mean, μ, as shown in Figure 2.63.
4. If we know the mean and variance, we can define the normal distribution by using the following notation:

$$X \sim N(\mu, \sigma^2)$$

For our applied statistical analyses, the normal distribution has a number of important characteristics. It is symmetric. Central tendencies are indicated by μ. In contrast, σ^2 indicates the distribution width. By selecting values for μ and σ^2, we can define a large family of normal probability density functions.

The parameters μ and σ^2 have different effects on the probability density function of a normal random variable. Figure 2.64(a) shows probability density functions for two normal distributions with a common variance and different means. We see that increases in the mean shift the distribution without changing its shape. In Figure 2.64(b) the two density functions have the same mean but different variances. Each is symmetric about the common mean, but the larger variance results in a wider distribution.

Figure 2.64 Effects of μ and σ^2 on the Probability Density Function of a Normal Random Variable

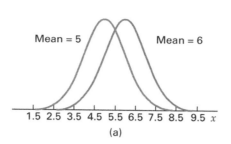

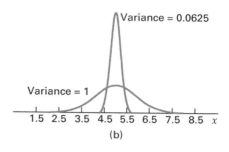

a. Two Normal Distributions with Same Variance but Different Means
b. Two Normal Distributions with Different Variances and Mean $= 5$

Our next task is to learn how to obtain probabilities for a specified normal distribution. First, we introduce the *cumulative distribution function*.

Cumulative Distribution Function of the Normal Distribution

Suppose that X is a normal random variable with mean μ and variance σ^2—that is, $X \sim N(\mu, \sigma^2)$. Then the **cumulative distribution function of the normal distribution** is as follows:

$$F(x_0) = P(X \le x_0)$$

This is the area under the normal probability density function to the left of x_0, as illustrated in Figure 2.65. As for any proper density function, the total area under the curve is 1—that is,

$$F(\infty) = 1$$

Figure 2.65 The Shaded Area Is the Probability That X Does Not Exceed x_0 for a Normal Random Variable

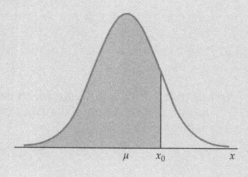

We do not have a simple algebraic expression for calculating the cumulative distribution function for a normally distributed random variable (see the chapter appendix). The general shape of the cumulative distribution function is shown in Figure 2.66.

Figure 2.66 Cumulative Distribution for a Normal Random Variable

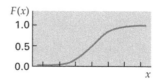

Range Probabilities for Normal Random Variables

Let X be a normal random variable with cumulative distribution function $F(x)$, and let a and b be two possible values of X, with $a < b$. Then,

$$P(a < X < b) = F(b) - F(a) \qquad (5.12)$$

The probability is the area under the corresponding probability density function between a and b, as shown in Figure 2.67.

Figure 2.67 Normal Density Function with the Shaded Area Indicating the Probability That X Is Between a and b

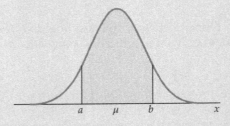

Any probability can be obtained from the cumulative distribution function. However, we do not have a convenient way to directly compute the probability for any normal distribution with a specific mean and variance. We could use numerical integration procedures with a computer, but that approach would be tedious and cumbersome. Fortunately, we can convert any normal distribution to a *standard normal distribution* with mean 0 and variance 1. Tables that indicate the probability for various intervals under the standard normal distribution have been computed and are shown inside the front cover and in Appendix Table 1.

The Standard Normal Distribution

Let Z be a normal random variable with mean 0 and variance 1—that is,

$$Z \sim N(0,1)$$

We say that Z follows the **standard normal distribution**.

Denote the cumulative distribution function as $F(x)$ and a and b as two possible values of Z with $a < b$; then,

$$P(a < Z < b) = F(b) - F(a) \qquad (5.13)$$

We can obtain probabilities for any normally distributed random variable by first converting the random variable to the standard normally distributed random variable, Z. There is always a direct relationship between any normally distributed random variable and Z. That relationship uses the transformation

$$Z = \frac{X - \mu}{\sigma}$$

where X is a normally distributed random variable:

$$X \sim N(\mu, \sigma^2)$$

This important result allows us to use the standard normal table to compute probabilities associated with any normally distributed random variable. Now let us see how probabilities can be computed for the standard normal Z.

The cumulative distribution function of the standard normal distribution is tabulated in Appendix Table 1 (also inside the front cover). This table gives values of

$$F(z) = P(Z \leq z)$$

for nonnegative values of z. For example, the cumulative probability for a Z value of 1.25 from Appendix Table 1 is as follows:

$$F(1.25) = 0.8944$$

This is the area, designated in Figure 2.68, for Z less than 1.25. Because of the symmetry of the normal distribution, the probability that $Z > -1.25$ is also equal to 0.8944. In general, values of the cumulative distribution function for negative values of Z can be inferred using the symmetry of the probability density function.

Figure 2.68
Standard Normal
Distribution with
Probability for
$Z < 1.25$

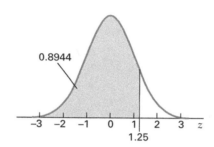

To find the cumulative probability for a negative Z (for example, $Z = -1.0$), defined as

$$F(-Z_0) = P(Z \leq -z_0) = F(-1.0)$$

we use the complement of the probability for $Z = +1$, as shown in Figure 2.69.

Figure 2.69
Standard Normal
Distribution for
Negative Z Equal
to −1

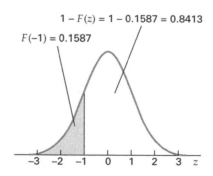

From the symmetry we can state that

$$F(-z) = 1 - P(Z \leq +z) = 1 - F(z)$$
$$F(-1) = 1 - P(Z \leq +1) = 1 - F(1)$$

Figure 2.70 indicates the symmetry for the corresponding positive values of Z.

Figure 2.70
Normal Distribution
for Positive

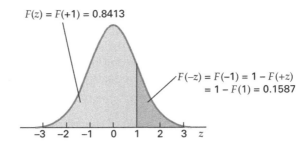

$F(z) = F(+1) = 0.8413$

$F(-z) = F(-1) = 1 - F(+z)$
$= 1 - F(1) = 0.1587$

In Figure 2.71 we can see that the area under the curve to the left of $Z = -1$ is equal to the area to the right of $Z = +1$ because of the symmetry of the normal distribution. The area substantially below $-Z$ is often called the lower tail, and the area substantially above $+Z$ is called the upper tail.

Figure 2.71
Normal Density
Function with Sym-
metric Upper and
Lower Values

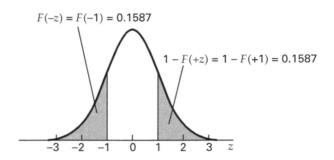

$F(-z) = F(-1) = 0.1587$

$1 - F(+z) = 1 - F(+1) = 0.1587$

We can also use normal tables that provide probabilities for just the upper-half, or positive Z, values from the normal distribution. An example of this type of table is shown inside the front cover of this textbook. This form of the normal table is used to find probabilities, the same as those previously shown. With positive Z values we add 0.50 to the values given in the table inside the front cover of the textbook. With negative values of Z we utilize the symmetry of the normal to obtain the desired probabilities.

Example 2.5.3 Investment Portfolio Value Probabilities (Normal Probabilities)

A client has an investment portfolio whose mean value is equal to $1,000,000 with a standard deviation of $30,000. He has asked you to determine the probability that the value of his portfolio is between $970,000 and $1,060,000.

Solution The problem is illustrated in Figure 2.72. To solve the problem, we must first determine the corresponding Z values for the portfolio limits. For $970,000 the corresponding Z value is as follows:

$$z_{970,000} = \frac{970,000 - 1,000,000}{30,000} = -1.0$$

And for the upper value, $1,060,000, the Z value is as follows:

$$z_{1,060,000} = \frac{1,060,000 - 1,000,000}{30,000} = +2.0$$

Figure 2.72 Normal Distribution for Example 2.5.3

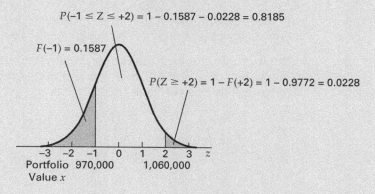

$P(-1 \leq Z \leq +2) = 1 - 0.1587 - 0.0228 = 0.8185$

$F(-1) = 0.1587$

$P(Z \geq +2) = 1 - F(+2) = 1 - 0.9772 = 0.0228$

As shown in Figure 2.72, the probability that the portfolio value, X, is between $970,000 and $1,060,000, is equal to the probability that Z is between −1 and +2. To obtain the probability, we first compute the probabilities for the lower and the upper tails and subtract these probabilities from 1. Algebraically, the result is as follows:

$$P(970,000 \leq X \leq 1,060,000) = P(-1 \leq Z \leq +2) = 1 - P(Z \leq -1) - P(Z \geq +2)$$
$$= 1 - 0.1587 - 0.0228 = 0.8185$$

The probability for the indicated range is, thus, 0.8185.

Recall from Chapter 2 that we presented the empirical rule, which states as a rough guide that $\mu \pm \sigma$ covers about 68% of the range, while $\mu \pm 2\sigma$ covers about 95% of the range. For all practical purposes, almost none of the range is outside $\mu \pm 3\sigma$. This useful approximation tool for interpretations based on descriptive statistics is based on the normal distribution.

Probabilities can also be computed by using Equation 5.14.

Finding Probabilities for Normally Distributed Random Variables

Let X be a normally distributed random variable with mean μ and variance σ^2. Then random variable $Z = (X - \mu)/\sigma$ has a standard normal distribution of $Z \sim N(0, 1)$.

It follows that, if a and b are any possible values of X with $a < b$, then,

$$P(a < X < b) = P\left(\frac{a - \mu}{\sigma} < Z < \frac{b - \mu}{\sigma}\right)$$

$$= F\left(\frac{b - \mu}{\sigma}\right) - F\left(\frac{a - \mu}{\sigma}\right) \tag{5.14}$$

where Z is the standard normal random variable and F denotes its cumulative distribution function.

Example 2.5.4 Analysis of Turkey Weights (Normal Probabilities)

Whole Life Organic, Inc., produces high-quality organic frozen turkeys for distribution in organic food markets in the upper Midwest. The company has developed a range feeding program with organic grain supplements to produce their product. The mean weight of its frozen turkeys is 15 pounds with a variance of 4. Historical experience indicates that weights can be approximated by the normal probability distribution. Market research indicates that sales for frozen turkeys over 18 pounds are limited. What percentage of the company's turkey units will be over 18 pounds?

Solution In this case the turkey weights can be represented by a random variable, X, and, thus, $X \sim N(15, 4)$, and we need to find the probability that X is larger than 18. This probability can be computed as follows:

$$
\begin{aligned}
P(X > 18) &= P\left(Z > \frac{18 - \mu}{\sigma}\right) \\
&= P\left(Z > \frac{18 - 15}{2}\right) \\
&= P(Z > 1.5) \\
&= 1 - P(Z < 1.5) \\
&= 1 - F(1.5)
\end{aligned}
$$

From Appendix Table 1, $F(1.5)$ is 0.9332, and, therefore,

$$
P(X > 18) = 1 - 0.9332 = 0.0668
$$

Thus, Whole Life can expect that 6.68% of its turkeys will weigh more than 18 pounds.

Example 2.5.5 Lightbulb Life (Normal Probabilities)

A company produces lightbulbs whose life follows a normal distribution, with a mean of 1,200 hours and a standard deviation of 250 hours. If we choose a lightbulb at random, what is the probability that its lifetime will be between 900 and 1,300 hours?

Solution Let X represent lifetime in hours. Then,

$$
\begin{aligned}
P(900 < X < 1{,}300) &= P\left(\frac{900 - 1{,}200}{250} < Z < \frac{1{,}300 - 1{,}200}{250}\right) \\
&= P(-1.2 < Z < 0.4) \\
&= F(0.4) - F(-1.2) \\
&= 0.6554 - (1 - 0.8849) = 0.5403
\end{aligned}
$$

Hence, the probability is approximately 0.54 that a lightbulb will last between 900 and 1,300 hours.

Example 2.5.6 Sales of Cell Phones (Normal Probabilities)

Silver Star, Inc., has a number of stores in major metropolitan shopping centers. The company's sales experience indicates that daily cell phone sales in its stores follow a normal distribution with a mean of 60 and a standard deviation of 15. The marketing department conducts a number of routine analyses of sales data to monitor sales performance. What proportion of store sales days will have sales between 85 and 95 given that sales are following the historical experience?

Solution Let X denote the daily cell phone sales. Then, the probability can be computed as follows:

$$P(85 < X < 95) = P\left(\frac{85-60}{15} < Z < \frac{95-60}{15}\right)$$
$$= P(1.67 < Z < 2.33)$$
$$= F(2.33) - F(1.67)$$
$$= 0.9901 - 0.9525 = 0.0376$$

That is, 3.76% of the daily sales will be in the range 85 to 95 based on historical sales patterns. Note that if actual reported sales in this range for a group of stores were above 10%, we would have evidence for higher than historical sales.

Example 2.5.7 Cutoff Points for Daily Cell Phone Sales (Normal Random Variables)

For the daily cell phone sales of Example 2.5.6, find the cutoff point for the top 10% of all daily sales.

Solution Define b as the cutoff point. To determine the numerical value of the cutoff point, we first note that the probability of exceeding b is 0.10, and, thus, the probability of being less than b is 0.90. The upper tail value of 0.10 is shown in Figure 2.73. We can now state the probability from the cumulative distribution as follows:

$$0.90 = P\left(Z < \frac{b-60}{15}\right)$$
$$= F\left(\frac{b-60}{15}\right)$$

Figure 2.73 Normal Distribution with Mean 60 and Standard Deviation 15 Showing Upper Tail Probability Equal to 0.10

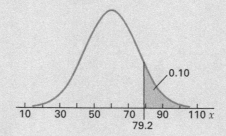

From Appendix Table 1, we find that $Z = 1.28$ when $F(Z) = 0.90$. Therefore, solving for b, we have the following:

$$\frac{b-60}{15} = 1.28$$
$$b = 79.2$$

Thus, we conclude that 10% of the daily cell phone sales will be above 79.2, as shown in Figure 2.73.

We note that daily sales, such as those in Examples 2.5.6 and 2.5.7, are typically given as integer values, and, thus, their distribution is discrete. However, because of the large number of possible outcomes, the normal distribution provides a very good approximation for the discrete distribution. In most applied business and economic problems, we are, in fact, using the normal distribution to approximate a discrete distribution that has many different outcomes.

Normal Probability Plots

The normal probability model is the most-used probability model for the reasons previously noted. In applied problems we would like to know if the data have come from a distribution that approximates a normal distribution closely enough to ensure a valid result. Thus, we are seeking evidence to support the assumption that the normal distribution is a close approximation to the actual unknown distribution that supplied the data we are analyzing. Normal probability plots provide a good way to test this assumption and determine if the normal model can be used. Usage is simple. If the data follow a normal distribution, the plot will be a straight line. More rigorous tests are also possible.

Figure 2.74 is a normal probability plot for a random sample of $n = 1,000$ observations from a normal distribution with $\mu = 100$ and $\sigma = 25$. The plot was generated using Minitab. The horizontal axis indicates the data points ranked in order from the smallest to the largest. The vertical axis indicates the cumulative normal probabilities of the ranked data values if the sample data were obtained from a population whose random variables follow a normal distribution. We see that the vertical axis has a transformed cumulative normal scale. The data plots in Figure 2.74 are close to a straight line even at the upper and lower limits, and that result provides solid evidence that the data have a normal distribution. The dotted lines provide an interval within which data points from a normally distributed random variable would occur in most cases. Thus, if the plotted points are within the boundaries established by the dotted lines, we can conclude that the data points represent a normally distributed random variable.

Figure 2.74
Normal Probability
Plot for a Normal
Distribution (Minitab
Output)

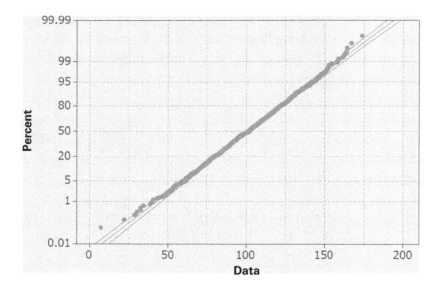

Next, consider a random sample of $n = 1,000$ observations drawn from a *uniform distribution* with limits 25 to 175. Figure 2.75 shows the normal probability plot. In this case the data plot has an S shape that clearly deviates from a straight line, and the sample data do not follow a normal distribution. Large deviations at the extreme high and low values are a major concern because statistical inference is often based on small probabilities of extreme values.

Figure 2.75
Normal Probability
Plot for a Uniform
Distribution (Minitab
Output)

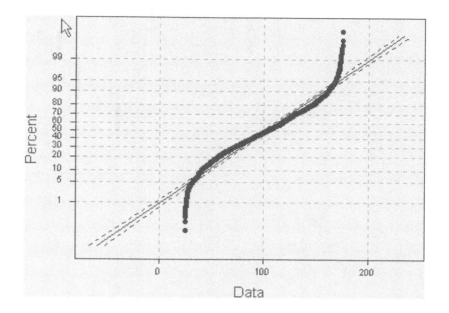

Next, let us consider a highly skewed discrete distribution, as shown in Figure 2.76. In Figure 2.77 we see the normal probability plot for this highly skewed distribution. Again, we see that the data plot is not a straight line but has considerable deviation at the extreme high and low values. This plot clearly indicates that the data do not come from a normal distribution.

Figure 2.76
Skewed Discrete
Probability Distribu-
tion Function

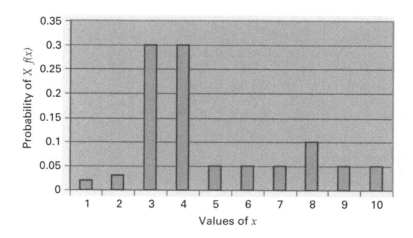

The previous examples provide us with an indication of possible results from a normal probability plot. If the plot from your problem is similar to Figure 2.74, then you are safe in assuming that the normal model is a good approximation. Note, however, that if your plot deviates from a straight line, as do those in Figures 2.75 and 2.77, then the sample data do not have a normal distribution.

Figure 2.77
Normal Probability Plot for a Highly Skewed Distribution (Minitab Output)

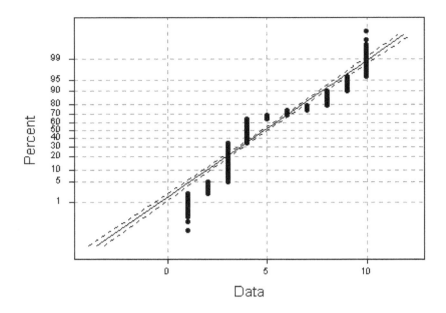

Exercises

Basic Exercises

2.5.17 Let the random variable Z follow a standard normal distribution.

a. Find $P(Z < 1.20)$.
b. Find $P(Z > 1.33)$.
c. Find $P(Z > -1.70)$.
d. Find $P(Z > -1.00)$.
e. Find $P(1.20 < Z < 1.33)$.
f. Find $P(-1.70 < Z < 1.20)$.
g. Find $P(-1.70 < Z < -1.00)$.

2.5.18 Let the random variable Z follow a standard normal distribution.

a. The probability is 0.70 that Z is less than what number?
b. The probability is 0.25 that Z is less than what number?
c. The probability is 0.2 that Z is greater than what number?
d. The probability is 0.6 that Z is greater than what number?

2.5.19 Let the random variable X follow a normal distribution with $\mu = 50$ and $\sigma^2 = 64$.

a. Find the probability that X is greater than 60.
b. Find the probability that X is greater than 35 and less than 62.
c. Find the probability that X is less than 55.
d. The probability is 0.2 that X is greater than what number?
e. The probability is 0.05 that X is in the symmetric interval about the mean between which two numbers?

2.5.20 Let the random variable X follow a normal distribution with $\mu = 80$ and $\sigma^2 = 100$.

a. Find the probability that X is greater than 60.
b. Find the probability that X is greater than 72 and less than 82.
c. Find the probability that X is less than 55.
d. The probability is 0.1 that X is greater than what number?
e. The probability is 0.6826 that X is in the symmetric interval about the mean between which two numbers?

2.5.21 Let the random variable X follow a normal distribution with $\mu = 0.2$ and $\sigma^2 = 0.0025$.

a. Find the probability that X is greater than 0.4.
b. Find the probability that X is greater than 0.15 and less than 0.28.
c. Find the probability that X is less than 0.10.
d. The probability is 0.2 that X is greater than what number?
e. The probability is 0.05 that X is in the symmetric interval about the mean between which two numbers?

Application Exercises

2.5.22 It is known that amounts of money spent on clothing in a year by students on a particular campus follow a normal distribution with a mean of $380 and a standard deviation of $50.

a. What is the probability that a randomly chosen student will spend less than $400 on clothing in a year?

b. What is the probability that a randomly chosen student will spend more than $360 on clothing in a year?

c. Draw a graph to illustrate why the answers to parts (a) and (b) are the same.

d. What is the probability that a randomly chosen student will spend between $300 and $400 on clothing in a year?

e. Compute a range of yearly clothing expenditures—measured in dollars—that includes 80% of all students on this campus? Explain why any number of such ranges could be found, and find the shortest one.

2.5.23 Anticipated consumer demand in a restaurant for free-range steaks next month can be modeled by a normal random variable with mean 1,200 pounds and standard deviation 100 pounds.

a. What is the probability that demand will exceed 1,000 pounds?

b. What is the probability that demand will be between 1,100 and 1,300 pounds?

c. The probability is 0.10 that demand will be more than how many pounds?

2.5.24 The tread life of Road Stone tires has a normal distribution with a mean of 35,000 miles and a standard deviation of 4,000 miles.

a. What proportion of these tires has a tread life of more than 38,000 miles?

b. What proportion of these tires has a tread life of less than 32,000 miles?

c. What proportion of these tires has a tread life of between 32,000 and 38,000 miles?

d. Draw a graph of the probability density function of tread lives, illustrating why the answers to parts (a) and (b) are the same and why the answers to parts (a), (b), and (c) sum to 1.

2.5.25 An investment portfolio contains stocks of a large number of corporations. Over the last year the rates of return on these corporate stocks followed a normal distribution with mean 12.2% and standard deviation 7.2%.

a. For what proportion of these corporations was the rate of return higher than 20%?

b. For what proportion of these corporations was the rate of return negative?

c. For what proportion of these corporations was the rate of return between 5% and 15%?

2.5.26 Southwest Co-op produces bags of fertilizer, and it is concerned about impurity content. It is believed that the weights of impurities per bag are normally distributed with a mean of 12.2 grams and a standard deviation of 2.8 grams. A bag is chosen at random.

a. What is the probability that it contains less than 10 grams of impurities?

b. What is the probability that it contains more than 15 grams of impurities?

c. What is the probability that it contains between 12 and 15 grams of impurities?

d. It is possible, without doing the detailed calculations, to deduce which of the answers to parts (a) and (b) will be the larger. How would you do this?

2.5.27 A contractor has concluded from his experience that the cost of building a luxury home is a normally distributed random variable with a mean of $500,000 and a standard deviation of $50,000.

a. What is the probability that the cost of building a home will be between $460,000 and $540,000?

b. The probability is 0.2 that the cost of building will be less than what amount?

c. Find the shortest range such that the probability is 0.95 that the cost of a luxury home will fall in this range.

2.5.28 Scores on an economics test follow a normal distribution. What is the probability that a randomly selected student will achieve a score that exceeds the mean score by more than 1.5 standard deviations?

2.5.29 A new television series is to be shown. A broadcasting executive feels that his uncertainty about the rating that the show will receive in its first month can be represented by a normal distribution with a mean of 18.2 and a standard deviation of 1.5. According to this executive, the probability is 0.1 that the rating will be less than what number?

2.5.30 A broadcasting executive is reviewing the prospects for a new television series. According to his judgment, the probability is 0.25 that the show will achieve a rating higher than 17.8, and the probability is 0.15 that it will achieve a rating higher than 19.2. If the executive's uncertainty about the rating can be represented by a normal distribution, what are the mean and variance of that distribution?

2.5.31 The number of hits per day on the Web site of Professional Tool, Inc., is normally distributed with a mean of 700 and a standard deviation of 120.

a. What proportion of days has more than 820 hits per day?

b. What proportion of days has between 730 and 820 hits?

c. Find the number of hits such that only 5% of the days will have the number of hits below this number.

2.5.32 I am considering two alternative investments. In both cases I am unsure about the percentage return but believe that my uncertainty can be represented by normal distributions with the means and standard deviations shown in the accompanying table. I want to make the investment that is more likely to produce a return of at least 10%. Which investment should I choose?

	Mean	Standard Deviation
Investment A	10.4	1.2
Investment B	11.0	4.0

2.5.33 Tata Motors, Ltd., purchases computer process chips from two suppliers, and the company is concerned about the percentage of defective chips. A review of the records for each supplier indicates that the percentage defectives in consignments of chips follow normal distributions with the means and standard deviations given in the following table. The company is particularly anxious that the percentage of defectives in a consignment not exceed 5% and wants to purchase from the supplier that's more likely to meet that specification. Which supplier should be chosen?

	Mean	Standard Deviation
Supplier A	4.4	0.4
Supplier B	4.2	0.6

2.5.34 A furniture manufacturer has found that the time spent by workers assembling a particular table follows a normal distribution with a mean of 150 minutes and a standard deviation of 40 minutes.

   a. The probability is 0.9 that a randomly chosen table requires more than how many minutes to assemble?
   b. The probability is 0.8 that a randomly chosen table can be assembled in fewer than how many minutes?
   c. Two tables are chosen at random. What is the probability that at least one of them requires at least 2 hours to assemble?

2.5.35 A company services copiers. A review of its records shows that the time taken for a service call can be represented by a normal random variable with a mean of 75 minutes and a standard deviation of 20 minutes.

   a. What proportion of service calls takes less than 1 hour?
   b. What proportion of service calls takes more than 90 minutes?
   c. Sketch a graph to show why the answers to parts (a) and (b) are the same.
   d. The probability is 0.1 that a service call takes more than how many minutes?

2.5.36 Scores on an achievement test are known to be normally distributed with a mean of 420 and a standard deviation of 80.

   a. For a randomly chosen person taking this test, what is the probability of a score between 400 and 480?
   b. What is the minimum test score needed in order to be in the top 10% of all people taking the test?
   c. For a randomly chosen individual, state, without doing the calculations, in which of the following ranges his score is most likely to be: 400–439, 440–479, 480–519, or 520–559.
   d. In which of the ranges listed in part (c) is the individual's score least likely to be?
   e. Two people taking the test are chosen at random. What is the probability that at least one of them scores more than 500 points?

2.5.37 It is estimated that the time that a well-known rock band, the Living Ingrates, spends on stage at its concerts follows a normal distribution with a mean of 200 minutes and a standard deviation of 20 minutes.

   a. What proportion of concerts played by this band lasts between 180 and 200 minutes?
   b. An audience member smuggles a tape recorder into a Living Ingrates concert. The reel-to-reel tapes have a capacity of 245 minutes. What is the probability that this capacity will be insufficient to record the entire concert?
   c. If the standard deviation of concert time was only 15 minutes, state, without doing the calculations, whether the probability that a concert would last more than 245 minutes would be larger than, smaller than, or the same as that found in part (b). Sketch a graph to illustrate your answer.
   d. The probability is 0.1 that a Living Ingrates concert will last less than how many minutes? (Assume, as originally, that the population standard deviation is 20 minutes.)

2.5.38 The amount of time necessary for a student of statistics to solve assignments is, on average, 15 minutes. This can be modeled as a random normal variable with a standard deviation of 2 minutes. Calculate the probability that an assignment is instead solved between 14 and 16 minutes.

2.5.4 NORMAL DISTRIBUTION APPROXIMATION FOR BINOMIAL DISTRIBUTION

In this section we show how the normal distribution can be used to approximate the discrete binomial and proportion random variables for larger sample sizes when tables are not readily available. The normal distribution approximation of the binomial distribution also provides a benefit for applied problem solving. We learn that procedures based on the normal distribution can also be applied in problems involving binomial and proportion random variables. Thus, you can reduce the number of different statistical procedures that you need to know to solve business problems.

Let us consider a problem with n independent trials, each with the probability of success $P = 4$. The binomial random variable X can be written as the sum of n independent Bernoulli random variables,

$$X = X_1 + X_2 + \cdots + X_n$$

where the random variable X_i takes the value 1 if the outcome of the ith trial is "success" and 0 otherwise, with respective probabilities P and $1 - P$. The number X of successes that result have a binomial distribution with a mean and variance:

$$E[X] = \mu = nP$$
$$Var(X) = \sigma^2 = nP(1 - P)$$

The plot of a binomial distribution with $P = 0.5$ and $n = 100$, in Figure 2.78, shows us that this binomial distribution has the same shape as the normal distribution. This visual evidence that the binomial can be approximated by a normal distribution with the same mean and variance is also established in work done by mathematical statisticians. This close approximation of the binomial distribution by the normal distribution is an example of the central limit theorem. A good rule for us is that the normal distribution provides a good approximation for the binomial distribution when $nP(1 - P) > 5$. If this value is less than 5, then use the binomial distribution to determine the probabilities.

Figure 2.78
Binomial Distribution
with $n = 100$ and
$P = 0.50$

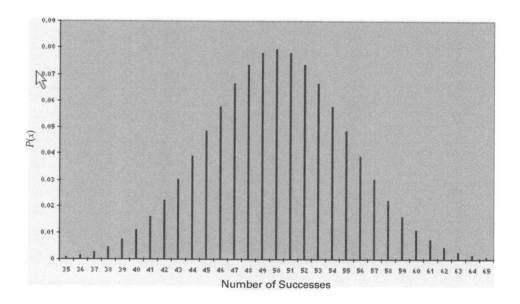

In order to better understand the normal distribution approximation for the binomial distribution, consider Figure 2.79(a) and (b). In both (a) and (b), we have shown points from a normal probability density function compared to the corresponding probabilities from a binomial distribution using graphs prepared using Minitab. In part (a) we note that the approximation rule value is

$$nP(1 - P) = 100(0.5)(1 - 0.5) = 25 > 5$$

and that the normal distribution provides a very close approximation to the binomial distribution. In contrast, the example in part (b) has an approximation rule value of

$$nP(1 - P) = 25(0.2)(1 - 0.2) = 4 < 5$$

Figure 2.79
Comparison of
Binomial and Normal
Approximation

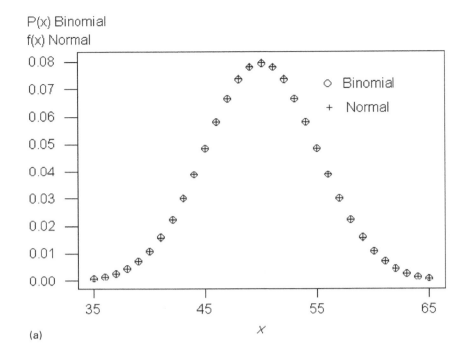

(a)

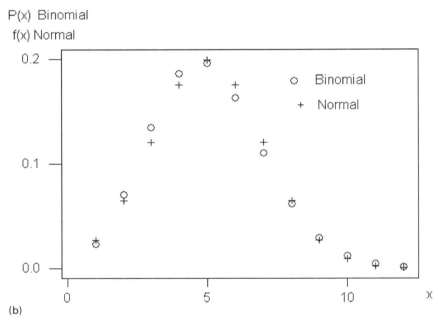

(b)

a. Binomial with $P = 0.50$ and $n = 100$, and Normal with $\mu = 50$ and $\sigma = 5$
b. Binomial with $P = 0.20$ and $n = 25$, and Normal with $\mu = 5$ and $\sigma = 2$

and the normal distribution does not provide a good approximation for the binomial distribution. Evidence such as that contained in Figure 2.79 has provided the rationale for widespread application of the normal approximation for the binomial. We will now proceed to develop the procedure for its application.

By using the mean and the variance from the binomial distribution, we find that, if the number of trials n is large—such that $nP(1 - P) > 5$—then the distribution of the random variable

$$Z = \frac{X - E[X]}{\sqrt{Var(X)}} = \frac{X - nP}{\sqrt{nP(1 - P)}}$$

is approximately a standard normal distribution.

This result is very important because it allows us to find, for large n, the probability that the number of successes lies in a given range. If we want to determine the probability that the number of successes will be between a and b, inclusive, we have

$$P(a \le X \le b) = P\left(\frac{a - nP}{\sqrt{nP(1 - P)}} \le \frac{X - nP}{\sqrt{nP(1 - P)}} \le \frac{b - nP}{\sqrt{nP(1 - P)}}\right)$$

$$= P\left(\frac{a - nP}{\sqrt{nP(1 - P)}} \le Z \le \frac{b - nP}{\sqrt{nP(1 - P)}}\right)$$

With n large, Z is well approximated by the standard normal, and we can find the probability using the methods from Section 2.5.3.

Example 2.5.8 Customer Visits Generated From Web Page Contacts (Normal Probabilities)

Mary David makes the initial telephone contact with customers who have responded to an advertisement on her company's Web page in an effort to assess whether a follow-up visit to their homes is likely to be worthwhile. Her experience suggests that 40% of the initial contacts lead to follow-up visits. If she has 100 Web page contacts, what is the probability that between 45 and 50 home visits will result?

Solution Let X be the number of follow-up visits. Then X has a binomial distribution with $n = 100$ and $P = 0.40$. Approximating the required probability gives the following:

$$P(45 \le X \le 50) \cong P\left(\frac{45 - (100)(0.4)}{\sqrt{(100)(0.4)(0.6)}} \le Z \le \frac{50 - (100)(0.4)}{\sqrt{(100)(0.4)(0.6)}}\right)$$

$$= P(1.02 \le Z \le 2.04)$$

$$= F(2.04) - F(1.02)$$

$$= 0.9793 - 0.8461 = 0.1332$$

This probability is shown as an area under the standard normal curve in Figure 2.80.

Figure 2.80 Probability of 45 to 50 Successes for a Binomial Distribution with $n = 100$ and $P = 0.4$

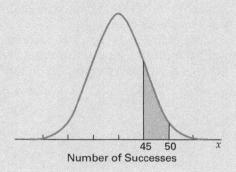

Number of Successes

Proportion Random Variable

In a number of applied problems we need to compute probabilities for proportion or percentage intervals. We can do this by using a direct extension of the normal distribution approximation for the binomial distribution. A proportion random variable, P, can be computed by dividing the number of successes, X, by the sample size, n:

$$P = \frac{X}{n}$$

Then, using the linear transformation of random variables, as shown in the chapter appendix, the mean and the variance of P can be computed as follows:

$$\mu = P$$
$$\sigma^2 = \frac{P(1 - P)}{n}$$

The resulting mean and variance can be used with the normal distribution to compute the desired probability.

Example 2.5.9 Election Forecasting (Proportion Probabilities)

We have often observed the success of television networks in forecasting elections. This is a good example of the successful use of probability methods in applied problems. Consider how elections can be predicted by using relatively small samples in a simplified example. An election forecaster has obtained a random sample of 900 voters, in which 500 indicate that they will vote for Susan Chung. Should Susan anticipate winning the election?

Solution In this problem we assume only two candidates, and, thus, if more than 50% of the population supports Susan, she will win the election. We compute the probability that 500 or more voters out of a sample of 900 support Susan under the assumption that exactly 50%, $P = 0.50$, of the entire population supports Susan.

$$P(X \geq 500) | n = 900, P = 0.50) \approx P(X \geq 500 | \mu = 450, \sigma^2 = 225)$$
$$= P\left(Z \geq \frac{500 - 450}{\sqrt{225}} \right)$$
$$= P(Z \geq 3.33)$$
$$= 0.0004$$

The probability of 500 successes out of 900 trials if $P = 0.50$ is very small, and, therefore, we conclude that P must be greater than 0.50. Hence, we predict that Susan Chung will win the election.

We could also compute the probability that more than 55.6% (500/900) of the sample indicates support for Susan if the population proportion is $P = 0.50$. Using the mean and variance for proportion random variables,

$$\mu = P = 0.50$$
$$\sigma^2 = \frac{P(1 - P)}{n} = \frac{0.50(1 - 0.50)}{900}$$
$$\sigma = 0.0167$$

$$P(P \geq 0.556 \mid n = 900, P = 0.50) \approx P(P \geq 0.556 \mid \mu = 0.50, \sigma = 0.0167)$$

$$= P\left(Z \geq \frac{0.556 - 0.50}{0.0167}\right)$$

$$= P(Z \geq 3.33)$$

$$= 0.0004$$

Note that the probability is exactly the same as that for the corresponding binomial random variable. This is always the case because each proportion or percentage value is directly related to a specific number of successes. Because percent is a more common term than proportion in business and economic language, we will tend to use percent more often than proportion in exercises and discussion in this textbook.

EXERCISES

Basic Exercises

2.5.39 Given a random sample size of $n = 900$ from a binomial probability distribution with $P = 0.50$ do the following:

a. Find the probability that the number of successes is greater than 500.
b. Find the probability that the number of successes is fewer than 430.
c. Find the probability that the number of successes is between 440 and 480.
d. With probability 0.10, the number of successes is fewer than how many?
e. With probability 0.08, the number of successes is greater than how many?

2.5.40 Given a random sample size of $n = 1,600$ from a binomial probability distribution with $P = 0.40$, do the following:

a. Find the probability that the number of successes is greater than 1,650.
b. Find the probability that the number of successes is fewer than 1,530.
c. Find the probability that the number of successes is between 1,550 and 1,650.
d. With probability 0.09, the number of successes is fewer than how many?
e. With probability 0.20, the number of successes is greater than how many?

2.5.41 Given a random sample size of $n = 900$ from a binomial probability distribution with $P = 0.10$ do the following:

a. Find the probability that the number of successes is greater than 110.
b. Find the probability that the number of successes is fewer than 53.
c. Find the probability that the number of successes is between 55 and 120.
d. With probability 0.10, the number of successes is fewer than how many?
e. With probability 0.08, the number of successes is greater than how many?

2.5.42 Given a random sample size of $n = 1,600$ from a binomial probability distribution with $P = 0.40$ do the following:

a. Find the probability that the percentage of successes is greater than 0.45.
b. Find the probability that the percentage of successes is less than 0.35.
c. Find the probability that the percentage of successes is between 0.37 and 0.44.
d. With probability 0.20, the percentage of successes is less than what percent?
e. With probability 0.09, the percentage of successes is greater than what percent?

2.5.43 Given a random sample size of $n = 400$ from a binomial probability distribution with $P = 0.20$ do the following:

a. Find the probability that the percentage of successes is greater than 0.25.
b. Find the probability that the percentage of successes is less than 0.15.
c. Find the probability that the percentage of successes is between 0.17 and 0.24.
d. With probability 0.15, the percentage of successes is less than what percent?
e. With probability 0.11, the percentage of successes is greater than what percent?

Application Exercises

2.5.44 A car-rental company has determined that the probability a car will need service work in any given month is 0.2. The company has 900 cars.

a. What is the probability that more than 200 cars will require service work in a particular month?
b. What is the probability that fewer than 175 cars will need service work in a given month?

2.5.45 It is known that 10% of all the items produced by a particular manufacturing process are defective. From the very large output of a single day, 400 items are selected at random.

a. What is the probability that at least 35 of the selected items are defective?

b. What is the probability that between 40 and 50 of the selected items are defective?

c. What is the probability that between 34 and 48 of the selected items are defective?

d. Without doing the calculations, state which of the following ranges of defectives has the highest probability: 38–39, 40–41, 42–43, 44–45, or 46–47.

2.5.46   A random sample of 100 blue-collar employees at a large corporation are surveyed to assess their attitudes toward a proposed new work schedule. If 60% of all blue-collar employees at this corporation favor the new schedule, what is the probability that fewer than 50 in the random sample will be in favor?

2.5.47   A hospital finds that 25% of its accounts are at least 1 month in arrears. A random sample of 450 accounts was taken.

a. What is the probability that fewer than 100 accounts in the sample were at least 1 month in arrears?

b. What is the probability that the number of accounts in the sample at least 1 month in arrears was between 120 and 150 (inclusive)?

2.5.48   The tread life of Stone Soup tires can be modeled by a normal distribution with a mean of 35,000 miles and a standard deviation of 4,000 miles. A sample of 100 of these tires is taken. What is the probability that more than 25 of them have tread lives of more than 38,000 miles?

2.5.49   Bags of a chemical produced by a company have impurity weights that can be represented by a normal distribution with a mean of 12.2 grams and a standard deviation of 2.8 grams. A random sample of 400 of these bags is taken. What is the probability that at least 100 of them contain fewer than 10 grams of impurities?

2.5.5 JOINTLY DISTRIBUTED CONTINUOUS RANDOM VARIABLES

In Section 2.4.6 we introduced jointly distributed discrete random variables. Here, we show that many of the concepts and results from discrete random variables also apply for continuous random variables. Many continuous random variables can be modeled using jointly distributed random variables. The market values of various stock prices are regularly modeled as joint random variables. Studies of the production and sales patterns for various companies and industries use jointly distributed continuous random variables. The number of units sold by a large retail store during a particular week and the price per unit can be modeled by joint random variables. Studies of import and export behavior for various countries regularly use joint random variables as part of the analysis.

After we have developed some basic concepts, we will present a number of application examples to show the importance of the procedures and how to analyze jointly distributed continuous random variables.

> **Joint Cumulative Distribution Function**
> Let $X_1, X_2, \ldots, X_K$ be continuous random variables.
>
> 1. Their **joint cumulative distribution**, $F(x_1, x_2, \ldots, x_K)$, defines the probability that simultaneously X_1 is less than x_1, X_2 is less than x_2, and so on—that is,
>
> $$F(x_1, x_2, \ldots, x_K) = P(X_1 < x_1 \cap X_2 < x_2 \cap \cdots \cap X_K < x_K) \qquad (5.17)$$
>
> 2. The cumulative distribution functions—$F(x_1), F(x_2), \ldots, F(x_K)$—of the individual random variables are called their **marginal distributions**. For any i, $F(x_i)$ is the probability that the random variable X_i does not exceed the specific value x_i.
>
> 3. The random variables are *independent* if and only if
>
> $$F(x_1, x_2, \ldots, x_K) = F(x_1)F(x_2) \cdots F(x_K) \qquad (5.18)$$

We note that the notion of independence here is precisely the same as in the discrete case. Independence of a set of random variables implies that the probability distribution of any one of them is unaffected by the values taken by the others. Thus, for example, the assertion that consecutive daily changes in the price of a share of common stock are independent of one another implies that information about the past price changes is of no value in assessing what is likely to happen tomorrow.

The notion of expectation extends to functions of jointly distributed continuous random variables. As in the case of discrete random variables, we have the concept of *covariance*, which is used in assessing linear relationships between pairs of random variables.

Covariance

Let X and Y be a pair of continuous random variables with respective means μ_X and μ_Y. The expected value of $(X - \mu_X)(Y - \mu_Y)$, is called the **covariance** (*Cov*), between X and Y,

$$Cov(X, Y) = E[(X - \mu_X)(Y - \mu_Y)] \tag{5.19}$$

An alternative, but equivalent, expression can be derived as

$$Cov(X, Y) = E[XY] - \mu_X \mu_Y \tag{5.20}$$

If the random variables X and Y are independent, then the covariance between them is 0. However, the converse is not necessarily true.

In Section 2.4.6 we also presented the *correlation* as a standardized measure of the relationship between two discrete random variables. The same results hold for continuous random variables.

Correlation

Let X and Y be jointly distributed random variables. The **correlation** (*Corr*) between X and Y is as follows:

$$\rho = Corr(X, Y) = \frac{Cov(X, Y)}{\sigma_X \sigma_Y} \tag{5.21}$$

In Section 2.4.6 we presented the means and variances for sums and differences of discrete random variables. The same results apply for continuous random variables because the results are established using expectations and, thus, are not affected by the condition of discrete or continuous random variables.

Sums of Random Variables

Let $X_1, X_2, \ldots, X_K$ be K random variables with means $\mu_1, \mu_2, \ldots, \mu_K$ and variances $\sigma_1^2, \sigma_2^2, \ldots, \sigma_K^2$. Consider the following properties:

1. The mean of their sum is the sum of their means—that is,

$$E[(X_1 + X_2 + \cdots + X_K)] = \mu_1 + \mu_2 + \cdots + \mu_K \tag{5.22}$$

a. What is the probability that the lowest of the other bids will be less than the consultant's cost estimate of $10,000?

b. If the consultant submits a bid of $12,000, what is the probability that he will secure the contract?

c. The consultant decides to submit a bid of $12,000. What is his expected profit from this strategy?

d. If the consultant wants to submit a bid so that his expected profit is as high as possible, discuss how he should go about making this choice.

2.5.67 The ages of a group of executives attending a convention are uniformly distributed between 35 and 65 years. If the random variable X denotes ages in years, the probability density function is as follows:

$$f(x) = \begin{cases} 1/30 & \text{for } 35 < x < 65 \\ 0 & \text{for all other values of } x \end{cases}$$

a. Graph the probability density function for X.

b. Find and graph the cumulative distribution function for X.

c. Find the probability that the age of a randomly chosen executive in this group is between 40 and 50 years.

d. Find the mean age of the executives in the group.

2.5.68 The random variable X has probability density function as follows:

$$f(x) = \begin{cases} x & \text{for } 0 < x < 1 \\ 2 - x & \text{for } 1 < x < 2 \\ 0 & \text{for all other values of } x \end{cases}$$

a. Graph the probability density function for X.

b. Show that the density has the properties of a proper probability density function.

c. Find the probability that X takes a value between 0.5 and 1.5.

2.5.69 An investor puts $2,000 into a deposit account with a fixed rate of return of 10% per year. A second sum of $1,000 is invested in a fund with an expected rate of return of 16% and a standard deviation of 8% per year.

a. Find the expected value of the total amount of money this investor will have after a year.

b. Find the standard deviation of the total amount after a year.

2.5.70 A hamburger stand sells hamburgers for $1.45 each. Daily sales have a distribution with a mean of 530 and a standard deviation of 69.

a. Find the mean daily total revenues from the sale of hamburgers.

b. Find the standard deviation of total revenues from the sale of hamburgers.

c. Daily costs (in dollars) are given by

$$C = 100 + 0.95X$$

where X is the number of hamburgers sold. Find the mean and standard deviation of daily profits from sales.

2.5.71 An analyst forecasts corporate earnings, and her record is evaluated by comparing actual earnings with predicted earnings. Define the following:

actual earnings = predicted earnings + forecast error

If the predicted earnings and forecast error are independent of each other, show that the variance of predicted earnings is less than the variance of actual earnings.

2.5.72 Let X_1 and X_2 be a pair of random variables. Show that the covariance between the random variables $Y_1 = (X_1 + X_2)$ and $Y_2 = (X_1 - X_2)$ is 0 if and only if X_1 and X_2 have the same variance.

2.5.73 Grade point averages of students on a large campus follow a normal distribution with a mean of 2.6 and a standard deviation of 0.5.

a. One student is chosen at random from this campus. What is the probability that this student has a grade point average higher than 3.0?

b. One student is chosen at random from this campus. What is the probability that this student has a grade point average between 2.25 and 2.75?

c. What is the minimum grade point average needed for a student's grade point average to be among the highest 10% on this campus?

d. A random sample of 400 students is chosen from this campus. What is the probability that at least 80 of these students have grade point averages higher than 3.0?

e. Two students are chosen at random from this campus. What is the probability that at least one of them has a grade point average higher than 3.0?

2.5.74 A company services home air conditioners. It is known that times for service calls follow a normal distribution with a mean of 60 minutes and a standard deviation of 10 minutes.

a. What is the probability that a single service call takes more than 65 minutes?

b. What is the probability that a single service call takes between 50 and 70 minutes?

c. The probability is 0.025 that a single service call takes more than how many minutes?

d. Find the shortest range of times that includes 50% of all service calls.

e. A random sample of four service calls is taken. What is the probability that exactly two of them take more than 65 minutes?

2.5.75 It has been found that times taken by people to complete a particular tax form follow a normal distribution with a mean of 100 minutes and a standard deviation of 30 minutes.

a. What is the probability that a randomly chosen person takes less than 85 minutes to complete this form?

b. What is the probability that a randomly chosen person takes between 70 and 130 minutes to complete this form?

c. Five percent of all people take more than how many minutes to complete this form?

d. Two people are chosen at random. What is the probability that at least one of them takes more than an hour to complete this form?

e. Four people are chosen at random. What is the probability that exactly two of them take longer than an hour to complete this form?

f. For a randomly chosen person, state in which of the following ranges (expressed in minutes) the time to complete the form is most likely to lie.

  70–89,   90–109,   100–129,   130–149

g. For a randomly chosen person, state in which of the following ranges (expressed in minutes) the time to complete the form is least likely to lie.

  70–89,   90–109,   110–129,   130–149

2.5.76 A pizza delivery service delivers to a campus dormitory. Delivery times follow a normal distribution with a mean of 20 minutes and a standard deviation of 4 minutes.

a. What is the probability that a delivery will take between 15 and 25 minutes?

b. The service does not charge for the pizza if delivery takes more than 30 minutes. What is the probability of getting a free pizza from a single order?

c. During final exams, a student plans to order pizza five consecutive evenings. Assume that these delivery times are independent of each other. What is the probability that the student will get at least one free pizza?

d. Find the shortest range of times that includes 40% of all deliveries from this service.

e. For a single delivery, state in which of the following ranges (expressed in minutes) the delivery time is most likely to lie.

  18–20,   19–21,   20–22,   21–23

f. For a single delivery, state in which of the following ranges (expressed in minutes) the delivery time is least likely to lie.

  18–20,   19–21,   20–22,   21–23

2.5.77 A video-rental chain estimates that annual expenditures of members on rentals follow a normal distribution with a mean of $100. It was also found that 10% of all members spend more than $130 in a year. What percentage of members spends more than $140 in a year?

2.5.78 It is estimated that amounts of money spent on gasoline by customers at a gas station follow a normal distribution with a standard deviation of $2.50. It is also found that 10% of all customers spent more than $25. What percentage of customers spent less than $20?

2.5.79 A market research organization has found that 40% of all supermarket shoppers refuse to cooperate when questioned by its pollsters. If 1,000 shoppers are approached, what is the probability that fewer than 500 will refuse to cooperate?

2.5.80 An organization that gives regular seminars on sales motivation methods determines that 60% of its clients have attended previous seminars. From a sample of 400 clients what is the probability that more than half have attended previous seminars?

2.5.81 An ambulance service receives an average of 15 calls per day during the time period 6 p.m. to 6 a.m. for assistance. For any given day what is the probability that fewer than 10 calls will be received during the 12-hour period? What is the probability that more than 17 calls during the 12-hour period will be received?

2.5.82 In a large department store a customer-complaints office handles an average of six complaints per hour about the quality of service. The distribution is Poisson.

a. What is the probability that in any hour exactly six complaints will be received?

b. What is the probability that more than 20 minutes will elapse between successive complaints?

c. What is the probability that fewer than 5 minutes will elapse between successive complaints?

d. The store manager observes the complaints office for a 30-minute period, during which no complaints are received. He concludes that a talk he gave to his staff on the theme "the customer is always right" has obviously had a beneficial effect. Suppose that, in fact, the talk had no effect. What is the probability of the manager observing the office for a period of 30 minutes or longer with no complaints?

2.5.83 A fish market in Hong Kong offers a large variety of fresh fish on its stands. You have found out that the average chunk of tuna sushi on sale has a weight of 3.2 grams, with a standard deviation of 0.8 gram. Assuming the weights of tuna sushi are normally distributed, what is the probability that a randomly selected piece of sushi will weigh more than 4.4 grams?

2.5.84 In a Godiva Chocolate Shop, there are different sizes and weights of boxes of truffles.

a. Find the probability that a box of truffles weighs between 283 and 285.4 grams. The mean weight of a box is 283 grams and the standard deviation is 1.6 grams.

b. After a more careful check, the standard deviation was found to be 2.2 grams. Find the new probability.

2.5.85 A management consultant found that the amount of time per day spent by executives performing tasks that could be done equally well by subordinates followed a normal distribution with a mean of 2.4 hours. It was also found that 10% of executives spent over 3.5 hours per day on tasks of this type. For a random sample of 400 executives, find the probability that more than 80 spend more than 3 hours per day on tasks of this type.

2.5.86 Financial Managers, Inc., buys and sells a large number of stocks routinely for the various accounts that it manages. Portfolio manager Andrea Colson has asked for your assistance in the analysis of the Johnson Fund. A portion of this portfolio consists of 10 shares of stock A and 8 shares of stock B. The price of A has a mean of 10 and a variance of 16, while the price of B has a mean of 12 and a variance of 9. The correlation between prices is 0.3.

a. What are the mean and variance of the portfolio value?

b. Andrea has been asked to reduce the variance (risk) of the portfolio. She offers to trade the 10 shares of stock A and receives two offers, from which she can select one: 10 shares of stock 1 with a mean price of 10, a variance of 25, and a correlation with the price of stock B equal to −0.2; or 10 shares of stock 2 with a mean price of 10, a variance of 9, and a correlation with the price of stock B equal to +0.5. Which offer should she select?

2.5.87 Financial Managers, Inc., buys and sells a large number of stocks routinely for the various accounts that it manages. Portfolio manager Sarah Bloom has asked for your assistance in the analysis of the Burde Fund. A portion of this portfolio consists of 10 shares of stock A and 8 shares of stock B. The price of A has a mean of 12 and a variance of 14, while the price of B has a mean of 10 and a variance of 12. The correlation between prices is 0.5.

a. What are the mean and variance of the portfolio value?

b. Sarah has been asked to reduce the variance (risk) of the portfolio. She offers to trade the 10 shares of stock A and receives two offers from which she can select one: 10 shares of stock 1 with a mean price of 12, a variance of 25, and a correlation with the price of stock B equal to −0.2; or 10 shares of stock 2 with a mean price of 10, a variance of 9, and a correlation with the price of stock B, equal to +0.5. Which offer should she select?

2.5.88 Big Nail Construction Inc. is building a large, new student center for a famous Midwestern liberal arts college. During the project Christine Buildumbig, the project manager, requests that a pile of sand weighing between 138,000 pounds and 141,000 pounds be placed on the newly constructed driveway. You have been asked to determine the probability that the delivered sand satisfies Christine's request. You have ordered that one big truck and one small truck be used to deliver the sand. Sand loads in the big truck are normally distributed with a mean of 80,000 and a variance of 1,000,000, and sand loads in the small truck are also normally distributed with a mean weight of 60,000 pounds and a variance of 810,000. From past experience with the sand-loading facility, you know that the weight of sand in the two trucks has a correlation of 0.40. What is the probability that the resulting pile of sand has a weight that is between 138,000 and 141,000 pounds?

2.5.89 An investment portfolio in Singapore specializes in airline stocks and contains two of them. One is Singapore Airlines (mean: 0.12; standard deviation: 0.02), and it accounts for 30% of the portfolio shares. The other airline present in the portfolio is AirAsia (mean: 0.25; standard deviation: 0.15), a higher-risk, higher-return investment.

a. What is the expected value and the standard deviation of the portfolio if the coefficient of correlation of the two stocks is 0.5?

b. What will they be if the correlation is 0.2 instead?

CHAPTER

2.6

Distributions of Sample Statistics

Introduction

The remainder of this book will develop various procedures for using statistical sample data to make inferences about statistical populations. This is the core of statistical analysis. Important questions include the following:

a. How can we use a sample of voters to predict election outcomes?
b. How can we use a sample of cereal box weights to estimate the mean weight of all cereal boxes produced in a particular week and the probability that a particular box weighs less than some minimum weight?
c. How can we use a sample of sales receivable for a company to estimate the mean dollar value of all sales receivables held by the company?
d. How can we use a sample of daily stock market prices to estimate the mean value and the risk for a stock over a 1-year interval?
e. How can we use a sample of selling prices for homes to estimate the mean selling price for all homes sold in a large city?

These examples indicate some of the vast array of important business and economic questions that can be studied using statistical procedures.

Statistical analysis requires that we obtain a proper sample from a population of items of interest that have measured characteristics. If we do not have a proper sample, then our statistical methods do not work correctly. Thus we must first learn how to obtain a proper sample. Sample observations can be shown to be random variables—if properly chosen. And, statistics such as the sample mean or proportion computed from sample observations are also random variables. Using our understanding of random variables from Chapters 4 and 5, we can make probability statements about the sample statistics computed from sample data and make inferences about the populations from which the samples were obtained. All this leads to some important and amazing results.

But first we need to have probability distributions for the sample statistics—for example, the sampling distribution of the sample mean. That is our task in this chapter, so let us get on with it!

2.6.1 Sampling from a Population

A population is generated by a process that can be modeled as a series of random experiment. Thus, consider a population of 500,000 cereal boxes, each having a specific weight—which can be treated as an infinite population in terms of our sampling procedures. The weight of each box is determined by the amount of cereal and the cereal density for each box filled. This weight results from a complex process that we will treat as the random experiment, and the weight of each box is treated as a random variable. Similarly, the diameter of engine pistons produced by a set of high production machines in a factory will have small variations. We can treat the production process as a random experiment and the piston diameters as random variables. Similarly, stock prices, daily store sales, and voting choices result from complex processes that can be treated as a random experiment, and the outcomes can be treated as randaom variables. Populations for various statistical studies are modeled as random variables whose probability distributions have a mean and variance, which are generally not known as we conduct our statistical sampling and analysis.

We will select a sample of observations—realizations of a random variable—from our population and compute sample statistics that will be used to obtain inferences about the population, such as the population mean and variance. To make inferences we need to know the sampling distribution of the observations and the computed sample statistics. The process of determining the sampling distribution uses observations that are obtained as a simple random sample.

Simple Random Sample
A **simple random sample** is chosen by a process that selects a sample of n objects from a population in such a way that each member of the population has the same probability of being selected, the selection of one member is independent of the selection of any other member, and every possible sample of a given size, n, has the same probability of selection. This method is so common that the adjective *simple* is generally dropped, and the resulting sample is called a **random sample**.

Random samples are the ideal. It is important that a sample represent the population as a whole. Random sampling is our insurance policy against allowing personal biases to influence the selection. In a number of real-world sampling studies, analysts develop alternative sampling procedures to lower the costs of sampling. But the basis for determining if these alternative sampling strategies are acceptable is how closely the results approximate those of a simple random sample.

In general, we achieve greater accuracy by carefully obtaining a random sample of the population instead of spending the resources to measure every item. There are three important reasons for this result. First, it is often very difficult to obtain and measure every item in a population, and, even if possible, the cost would be very high for a large population. For example, it is well known among statistical professionals that the census conducted every 10 years produces an undercount, in which certain groups are seriously underrepresented (Hogan 1992). Second, as we learn in this chapter, properly selected samples can be used to obtain measured estimates of population characteristics that are quite close to the actual population values. Third, by using the probability distribution of sample statistics we can determine the error associated with our estimates of population characteristics.

Random sampling can be implemented in many ways. To provide a reference metaphor for our thinking, we could consider placing N population items—for example, the numbered balls used in a bingo or lottery event—in a large barrel and mix them thoroughly. Then, from this well-mixed barrel, we select individual balls from different parts of the barrel. In practice, we often use random numbers to select objects that can be assigned some numerical value. For example, market-research groups may use random numbers to select telephone numbers to call and ask about preferences for a product. Various statistical computer packages and spreadsheets have routines for obtaining random numbers, and these are used for sampling studies. These computer-generated random numbers have the required properties to develop random samples. Organizations that require random samples from large human populations—for example, political candidates seeking to determine voter preference—will use professional sampling firms, which are organized to select and manage the sampling process. Sampling that accurately represents the population requires considerable work by experienced professionals and has a high cost.

We use sample information to make inferences about the parent population. The distribution of all values in this population can be represented by a random variable. It would be too ambitious to attempt to describe the entire population distribution based on a small random sample of observations. However, we can make quite firm inferences about important characteristics of the population distribution, such as the population mean and variance. For example, given a random sample of the fuel consumption for 25 cars of a particular model, we can use the sample mean and variance to make inferential statements about the population mean and variance of fuel consumption. This inference is based on the sample information. We can also ask and answer questions such as this: If the fuel consumption, in miles per gallon, of the population of all cars of a particular model has a mean of 30 and a standard deviation of 2, what is the probability that for a random sample of 25 such cars the sample mean fuel consumption will be less than 29 miles per gallon? We need to distinguish between the population attributes and the random sample attributes. The population mean μ, is a fixed (but unknown) number. We make inferences about this attribute by drawing a random sample from the population and computing the sample mean. For each sample we draw, there will be a different sample mean, and the sample mean can be regarded as a random variable with a probability distribution. The distribution of possible sample means provides a basis for inferential statements about the sample. In this chapter we examine the properties of *sampling distributions*.

Sampling Distributions

Consider a random sample selected from a population that is used to make an inference about some population characteristic, such as the population mean, μ, using a sample statistic, such as the sample mean, $\bar{x}$. We realize that every sample has different observed values and, hence, different sample means. The **sampling distribution** of the sample mean is the probability distribution of the sample means obtained from all possible samples of the same number of observations drawn from the population. Using the sampling distribution we can make an inference about the population mean.

Development of a Sampling Distribution

We illustrate—using a simple example—the concept of a sampling distribution by considering the position of a supervisor with six employees, whose years of experience are

2   4   6   6   7   8

The mean of the years of experience for this population of six employees is

$$\mu = \frac{2 + 4 + 6 + 6 + 7 + 8}{6} = 5.5$$

Two of these employees are to be chosen randomly for a particular work group. In this example we are sampling without replacement in a small population, and thus the first observation has a probability of 1/6 of being selected, while the second observation has a probability of 1/5 of being selected. For most applied problems, when sampling from large populations this is not an issue to worry about. If we were selecting from a population of several thousand or more employees, then the change in probability from the first to the second observation would be trivial and is ignored. Thus, we assume that we are sampling with replacement of the first observation in essentially all real-world sampling studies.

Now, let us consider the mean number of years of experience of the two employees chosen randomly from the population of six. Fifteen possible different random samples could be selected. Table 2.37 shows all the possible samples and associated sample means. Note that some samples (such as 2, 6) occur twice because there are two employees with 6 years of experience in the population.

Table 2.37 Samples and Sample Means from the Worker Population Sample Size $n = 2$

SAMPLE	SAMPLE MEAN	SAMPLE	SAMPLE MEAN
2, 4	3.0	4, 8	6.0
2, 6	4.0	6, 6	6.0
2, 6	4.0	6, 7	6.5
2, 7	4.5	6, 8	7.0
2, 8	5.0	6, 7	6.5
4, 6	5.0	6, 8	7.0
4, 6	5.0	7, 8	7.5
4, 7	5.5		

Each of the 15 samples in Table 2.37 has the same probability, 1/15, of being selected. Note that there are several occurrences of the same sample mean. For example, the sample mean 5.0 occurs three times, and, thus, the probability of obtaining a sample mean of 5.0 is 3/15. Table 2.38 presents the sampling distribution for the various sample means from the population, and the probability function is graphed in Figure 2.82.

Table 2.38 Sampling Distribution of the Sample Means from the Worker Population Sample Size $n = 2$

SAMPLE MEAN $\bar{x}$	PROBABILITY OF $\bar{x}$
3.0	1/15
4.0	2/15
4.5	1/15
5.0	3/15
5.5	1/15
6.0	2/15
6.5	2/15
7.0	2/15
7.5	1/15

Figure 2.82
Probability Function
for the Sampling
Distribution of
Sample Means:
Sample Size $n = 2$

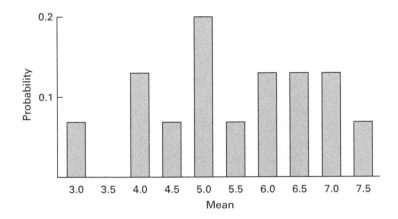

We see that, although the number of years of experience for the six workers ranges from 2 to 8, the possible values of the sample mean have a range from only 3.0 to 7.5. In addition, more of the values lie in the central portion of the range.

Table 2.39 presents similar results for a sample size of $n = 5$, and Figure 2.83 presents the graph for the sampling distribution. Notice that the means are concentrated over a narrower range. These sample means are all closer to the population mean, $\mu = 5.5$. We will always find this to be true—the sampling distribution becomes concentrated closer to the population mean as the sample size increases. This important result provides an important foundation for statistical inference. In the following sections and chapters, we build a set of rigorous analysis tools on this foundation.

Table 2.39 Sampling Distribution of the Sample Means from the Worker Population
Sample Size $n = 5$

SAMPLE	$\bar{x}$	PROBABILITY
2, 4, 6, 6, 7	5.0	1/6
2, 4, 6, 6, 8	5.2	1/6
2, 4, 6, 7, 8	5.4	1/3
2, 6, 6, 7, 8	5.8	1/6
4, 6, 6, 7, 8	6.2	1/6

Figure 2.83
Probability Function
for the Sampling
Distribution of
Sample Means:
Sample Size $n = 5$

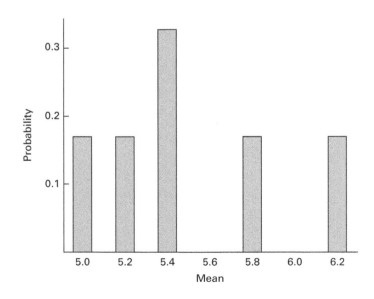

In this section we have developed the basic concept of sampling distributions. Here, the examples have come from a simple discrete distribution where it is possible to define all possible samples of a given sample size. From each possible sample, the sample mean was computed, and the probability distribution of all possible sample means was constructed. From this simple process we discovered that as the sample size increases, the distribution of the sample means—the sampling distribution—becomes more concentrated around the population mean. In most applied statistical work, the populations are very large, and it is not practical or rational to construct the distribution of all possible samples of a given sample size. But by using what we have learned about random variables, we can show that the sampling distributions for samples from all populations have characteristics similar to those shown for our simple discrete population. That result provides the basis for the many useful applications that will be developed in subsequent chapters.

EXERCISES

Basic Exercises

2.6.1 A five-a-side soccer club in Singapore buys a set of shirts numbered 1 to 5.

    a. What is the population distribution of shirt numbers?
    b. Determine the sampling distribution of the sample mean of the shirt numbers obtained by selecting two shirts.

2.6.2 Suppose that you have a fair coin and you label the head side as 1 and the tail side as 0.

    a. Now, you are asked to flip the coin 2 times and write down the numerical value that results from each toss. Without actually flipping the coin, write down the sampling distribution of the sample means.
    b. Repeat part (a) with the coin flipped 4 times.
    c. Repeat part (a) with the coin flipped 10 times.

Application Exercises

2.6.3 A population contains 6 million 0s and 4 million 1s. What is the approximate sampling distribution of the sample mean in each of the following cases?

    a. The sample size is $n = 5$
    b. The sample size is $n = 100$

    Note: There is a hard way and an easy way to answer this question. We recommend the latter.

2.6.4 Suppose that a mathematician said that it is impossible to obtain a simple random sample from a real-world population. Therefore, the whole basis for applying statistical procedures to real problems is useless. How would you respond?

2.6.2 SAMPLING DISTRIBUTIONS OF SAMPLE MEANS

We now develop important properties of the sampling distribution of the sample means. Our analysis begins with a random sample of n observations from a very large population with mean μ and variance σ^2; the sample observations are random variables X_1, $X_2, \ldots, X_n$. Before the sample is observed, there is uncertainty about the outcomes. This uncertainty is modeled by viewing the individual observations as random variables from a population with mean μ and variance σ^2. Our primary interest is in making inferences about the population mean μ. An obvious starting point is the *sample mean*.

> ### Sample Mean
> Let the random variables $X_1, X_2, \ldots, X_n$ denote a random sample from a population. The **sample mean** value of these random variables is defined as follows:
>
> $$\bar{X} = \frac{1}{n}\sum_{i=1}^{n} X_i$$

Consider the sampling distribution of the random variable $\bar{X}$. At this point we cannot determine the shape of the sampling distribution, but we can determine the mean and variance of the sampling distribution from basic definitions we learned in Chapters 4 and 5. First, determine the mean of the distribution. In Chapters 4 and 5 we saw that the expectation of a linear combination of random variables is the linear combination of the expectations:

$$E[\overline{X}] = E\left[\frac{1}{n}(X_1 + X_2 + \cdots + X_n)\right] = \frac{n\mu}{n} = \mu$$

Thus, the mean of **the sampling distribution of the sample means** is the population mean. If samples of n random and independent observations are repeatedly and independently drawn from a population, then as the number of samples becomes very large, the mean of the sample means approaches the true population mean. This is an important result of random sampling and indicates the protection that random samples provide against unrepresentative samples. A single sample mean could be larger or smaller than the population mean. However, on average, there is no reason for us to expect a sample mean that is either higher or lower than the population mean. Later in this section this result is demonstrated using computer-generated random samples.

Example 2.6.1 Expected Value of the Sample Mean (Expected Value)

Compute the expected value of the sample mean for the employee group example previously discussed.

Solution The sampling distribution of the sample means is shown in Table 2.38 and Figure 2.82. From this distribution we can compute the expected value of the sample mean as

$$E[\overline{X}] = \sum \overline{x}P(\overline{x}) = (3.0)\left(\frac{1}{15}\right) + (4.0)\left(\frac{2}{15}\right) + \cdots + (7.5)\left(\frac{1}{15}\right) = 5.5$$

which is the population mean, μ. A similar calculation can be made to obtain the same result using the sampling distribution in Table 2.39.

Now that we have established that the distribution of sample means is centered about the population mean, we wish to determine the variance of the distribution of sample means. Suppose that a random sample of 25 cars yields a mean fuel consumption of $\overline{x} = 31$ miles per gallon. But we also wish to know how good an approximation $\overline{x} = 31$ is of the population mean. We use the variance of the sampling distribution of the sample means to provide the answer.

If the population is very large compared to the sample size, then the distributions of the individual independent random sample observations are the same. In Chapters 4 and 5 we saw that the variance of a linear combination of independent random variables is the sum of the linear coefficients squared times the variance of the random variables. It follows that

$$Var(\overline{X}) = Var\left(\frac{1}{n}X_1 + \frac{1}{n}X_2 + \cdots + \frac{1}{n}X_n\right) = \sum_{i=1}^{n}\left(\frac{1}{n}\right)^2\sigma_i^2 = \frac{n\sigma^2}{n^2} = \frac{\sigma^2}{n}$$

The variance of the sampling distribution of $\overline{X}$ decreases as the sample size n increases. In effect, this says that larger sample sizes result in more concentrated sampling distributions. The simple example in the previous section demonstrated this result. Thus, larger samples result in greater certainty about our inference of the population mean. This is to be expected. The variance of the sample mean is denoted as $\sigma_{\overline{x}}^2$ and the corresponding standard deviation, called the standard error of $\overline{X}$, is given by the following:

$$\sigma_{\overline{x}} = \frac{\sigma}{\sqrt{n}}$$

If the sample size, n, is not a small fraction of the population size, N, then the individual sample members are not distributed independently of one another, as noted in

Section 2.6.1. Thus, the observations are not selected independently. It can be shown in this case that the variance of the sample mean is as follows:

$$Var(\overline{X}) = \frac{\sigma^2}{n} \cdot \frac{N-n}{N-1}$$

The term $(N-n)/(N-1)$ is often called a **finite population correction factor**. This result is included for completeness since almost all the real sampling studies use large populations. However, there are some examples in business applications, such as auditing, that involve finite populations. Careful evaluation of this expression would also dispel the notion that it is important that the sample be a substantial fraction of the population in order to provide useful information. It is the sample size—not the fraction of the population in the sample—that determines the precision—measured by the variance of the sample mean—of results from a random sample.

We have now developed expressions for the mean and variance of the sampling distribution of $\overline{X}$. For most applications the mean and variance define the sampling distribution. Fortunately, we will see that with some additional analysis these results can become very powerful for many practical applications. First, we examine these results under the assumption that the underlying population has a normal probability distribution. Next, we explore the sampling distributions of the sample mean when the underlying population does not have a normal distribution. This second case will provide some very powerful results for many practical applications in business and economics.

First, we consider the results if the parent population—from which the random sample is obtained—has a normal distribution. If the parent population has a normal distribution, then the sampling distribution of the sample means also has a normal distribution. This intuitive conclusion comes from the well-established result that linear functions of normally distributed random variables are also normally distributed. We saw applications of this in the portfolio problems in Chapter 5. With the sampling distribution as a normal probability distribution, we can compute the standard normal Z for the sample mean. In Chapter 5 we saw that we can use the standard normal Z to compute probabilities for any normally distributed random variable. That result also applies for the sample mean.

Standard Normal Distribution for the Sample Means
Whenever the sampling distribution of the sample means is a normal distribution, we can compute a **standardized normal random variable**, Z, that has a mean of 0 and a variance of 1:

$$Z = \frac{\overline{X} - \mu}{\sigma_{\overline{X}}} = \frac{\overline{X} - \mu}{\dfrac{\sigma}{\sqrt{n}}} \tag{6.1}$$

Finally, the results of this section are summarized in the following section.

Results for the Sampling Distribution of the Sample Means
Let $\overline{X}$ denote the sample mean of a random sample of n observations from a population with mean μ_X and variance σ^2.

   1. The sampling distribution of $\overline{X}$ has mean

$$E[\overline{X}] = \mu \tag{6.2}$$

2. The sampling distribution of $\overline{X}$ has standard deviation

$$\sigma_{\overline{X}} = \frac{\sigma}{\sqrt{n}} \qquad (6.3)$$

This is called the standard error of $\overline{X}$.

3. If the sample size, n, is not small compared to the population size, N, then the standard error of $\overline{X}$ is as follows:

$$\sigma_{\overline{X}} = \frac{\sigma}{\sqrt{n}} \cdot \sqrt{\frac{N-n}{N-1}} \qquad (6.4)$$

4. If the parent population distribution is normal and, thus, the sampling distribution of the sample means is normal, then the random variable

$$Z = \frac{X - \mu}{\sigma_{\overline{X}}} \qquad (6.5)$$

has a standard normal distribution with a mean of 0 and a variance of 1.

Figure 2.84 shows the sampling distribution of the sample means for sample sizes $n = 25$ and $n = 100$ from a normal distribution. Each distribution is centered on the mean, but as the sample size increases, the distribution becomes concentrated more closely around the population mean because the standard error of the sample mean decreases as the sample size increases. Thus, the probability that a sample mean is a fixed distance from the population mean decreases with increased sample size.

Figure 2.84
Probability Density
Functions for
Sample Means from
a Population with
$\mu = 100$ and $\sigma = 5$

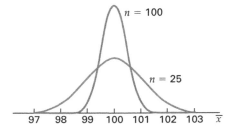

Example 2.6.2 Executive Salary Distributions (Normal Probability)

Suppose that, based on historical data, we believe that the annual percentage salary increases for the chief executive officers of all midsize corporations are normally distributed with a mean of 12.2% and a standard deviation of 3.6%. A random sample of nine observations is obtained from this population, and the sample mean is computed. What is the probability that the sample mean will be greater than 14.4%?

Solution We know that

$$\mu = 12.2 \quad \sigma = 3.6 \quad n = 9$$

Let $\overline{x}$ denote the sample mean, and compute the standard error of the sample mean:

$$\sigma_{\overline{x}} = \frac{\sigma}{\sqrt{n}} = \frac{3.6}{\sqrt{9}} = 1.2$$

Then we can compute

$$P(\overline{x} > 14.4) = P\left(\frac{\overline{x} - \mu}{\sigma_{\overline{x}}} > \frac{14.4 - 12.2}{1.2}\right) = P(z > 1.83) = 0.0336$$

where Z has a standard normal distribution and the resulting probability is obtained using the procedures developed in Chapter 5.

From this analysis we conclude that the probability that the sample mean will be greater than 14.4% is only 0.0336. If a sample mean greater than 14.4% actually occurred, we might begin to suspect that the population mean is greater than 12.2% or that we do not have a random sample that properly represents the population probability distribution.

Example 2.6.3 Spark Plug Life (Normal Probability)

A spark plug manufacturer claims that the lives of its plugs are normally distributed with a mean of 60,000 miles and a standard deviation of 4,000 miles. A random sample of 16 plugs had an average life of 58,500 miles. If the manufacturer's claim is correct, what is the probability of finding a sample mean of 58,500 or less?

Solution To compute the probability, we first need to obtain the standard error of the sample mean:

$$\sigma_{\bar{x}} = \frac{\sigma}{\sqrt{n}} = \frac{4,000}{\sqrt{16}} = 1,000$$

The desired probability is as follows:

$$P(\bar{x} < 58,500) = P\left(\frac{\bar{x} - \mu}{\sigma_{\bar{x}}} < \frac{58,500 - 60,000}{1,000}\right) = P(z < -1.50) = 0.0668$$

Figure 2.85(a) shows the probability density function of $\overline{X}$ with the shaded portion indicating the probability that the sample mean is less than 58,500. In Figure 2.85(b) we see the standard normal density function, and the shaded area indicates the probability that Z is less than -1.5. Note that in comparing these figures, we see that every value of $\overline{X}$ has a corresponding value of Z and that the comparable probability statements provide the same result.

Figure 2.85 (a) Probability That Sample Mean Is Less than 58,500 (b) Probability That a Standard Normal Random Variable Is Less than -1.5

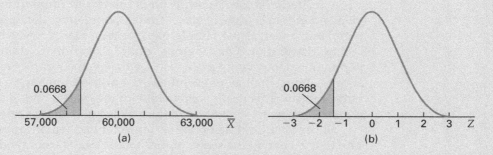

Using the standard normal Z, the normal probability values and the procedures from Chapter 5, we find that the probability that X is less than 58,500 is 0.0668. This probability suggests that if the manufacturer's claims— $\mu = 60,000$ and $\sigma = 4,000$—are true, then a sample mean of 58,500 or less has a small probability. As a result, if we obtained a sample mean less than 58,500 we would be skeptical about the manufacturer's claims. This important concept—using the probability of sample statistics to question the original assumption—is developed more fully in Chapter 9.

Central Limit Theorem

In the previous section we learned that the sample mean $\bar{x}$ for a random sample of size n drawn from a population with a normal distribution with mean μ and variance σ^2, is also normally distributed with mean μ and variance σ^2/n. In this section we present the *central limit theorem*, which shows that the mean of a random sample, drawn from a population with any probability distribution, will be approximately normally distributed with mean μ and variance σ^2/n, given a large-enough sample size. The central limit theorem shows that the sum of n random variables from any probability distribution will be approximately normally distributed if n is large, as noted in the chapter appendix. Since the mean is the sum divided by n, the mean is also approximately normally distributed and that is the result that is important for our statistical applications in business and economics.

This important result enables us to use the normal distribution to compute probabilities for sample means obtained from many different populations. In applied statistics the probability distribution for the population being sampled is often not known, and in particular there is no way to be certain that the underlying distribution is normal.

> ### Statement of the Central Limit Theorem
> Let $X_1, X_2, \ldots, X_n$ be a set of n independent random variables having identical distributions with mean μ, variance σ^2, and $\overline{X}$ as the mean of these random variables. As n becomes large, the **central limit theorem** states that the distribution of
>
> $$Z = \frac{\overline{X} - \mu_X}{\sigma_{\overline{X}}} \tag{6.6}$$
>
> approaches the standard normal distribution.

The central limit theorem provides the basis for considerable work in applied statistical analysis. Many random variables can be modeled as sums or means of independent random variables, and the normal distribution very often provides a good approximation of the true distribution. Thus, the standard normal distribution can be used to obtain probability values for many observed sample means.

The central limit theorem can be applied to both discrete and continuous random variables. In Section 2.6.3 we use this theorem with discrete random variables to develop probabilities for proportion random variables by treating proportions as a special case of sample means.

A related and important result is the **law of large numbers**, which concludes that given a random sample of size n from a population, the sample mean will approach the population mean as the sample size n becomes large, regardless of the underlying probability distribution. One obvious result is, of course, a sample that contains the entire population. However, we can also see that as the sample size n becomes large, the variance becomes small, until eventually the distribution approaches a constant, which is the sample mean. This result combined with the central limit theorem provides the basis for statistical inference about populations by using random samples.

The central limit theorem has a formal mathematical proof (Hogg and Craig 1995, 246) that is beyond the scope of this book. Results from random sample simulations can also be used to demonstrate the central limit theorem. In addition, there are homework problems that enable you to conduct further experimental analysis.

Monte Carlo Simulations: Central Limit Theorem

We now present some results using Monte Carlo sample simulations to obtain sampling distributions. To obtain each of these results, we selected 1,000 random samples of size n generated from computer simulations produced using Minitab 16 and displayed the sampling distributions of the sample means in histograms. This process constructs empirical sampling distributions of the sample means. Histograms showing the results of these simulations are shown in Figures 2.86, 2.87, and 2.88. The chapter appendix presents the pro-

Figure 2.86
Sampling
Distributions from a
Distribution of 100
Normally Distributed
Random Values with
Various Sample
Sizes: Demonstration
of Central Limit
Theorem

Distribution of Random Variable

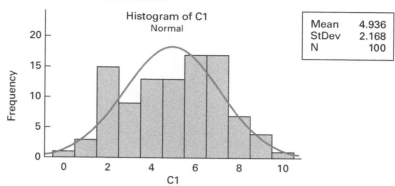

Sample Size $n = 10$

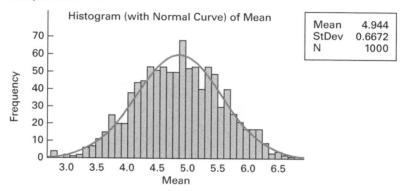

Sample Size $n = 25$

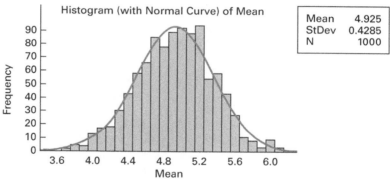

Sample Size $n = 50$

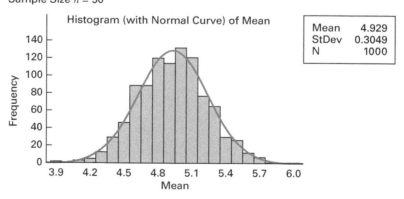

Figure 2.87
Sampling
Distributions from a
Uniform Distribution
with Various Sample
Sizes: Demonstration
of Central Limit
Theorem

Distribution of Random Variable

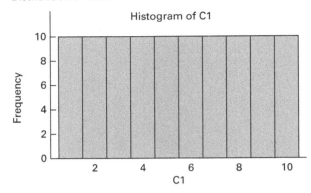

Sample Size $n = 10$

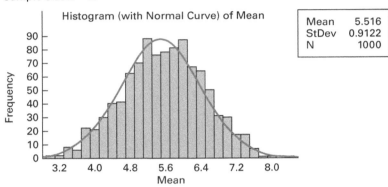

Mean	5.516
StDev	0.9122
N	1000

Sample Size $n = 25$

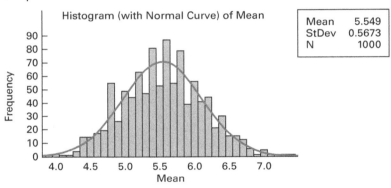

Mean	5.549
StDev	0.5673
N	1000

Sample Size $n = 50$

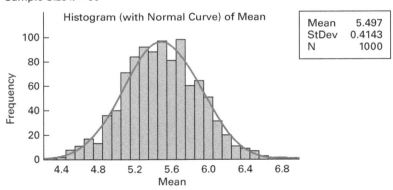

Mean	5.497
StDev	0.4143
N	1000

Figure 2.88
Sampling
Distributions from a
Skewed Distribution
with Various Sample
Sizes: Demonstration
of Central Limit
Theorem

Distribution of Random Variable

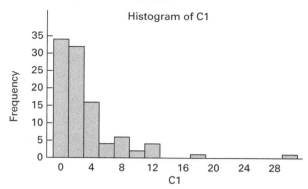

Distribution of Sample means with $n = 10$

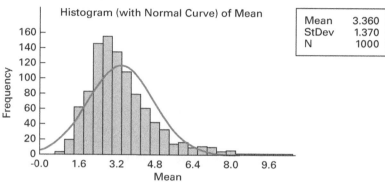

Distribution of Sample Means with $n = 25$

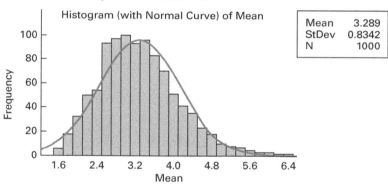

Distribution of Sample Means with $n = 50$

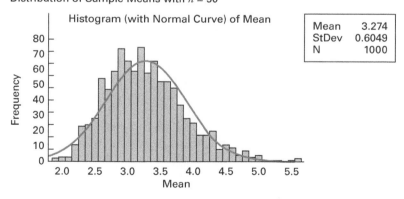

cedure for obtaining sampling distributions for the sample means from any probability distribution. In this appendix and in the data directory, we include a Minitab Computer Macro for you to use in easily obtaining your own sampling distributions.

First, for Figure 2.86 we constructed a population of 100 randomly selected values using the normal distribution. The actual histogram of the population used is shown. Next, we obtained 1,000 random samples—sampling with replacement—from this distribution using sample sizes $n = 10$, $n = 25$, and $n = 50$. In this example the histograms of the sample means for all three sample sizes follow a normal distribution, as shown by the normal curve drawn over the histogram. Note also that the distributions are narrower with increasing sample size because the standard deviation of the sample means becomes smaller with larger sample sizes. The normal distribution used to obtain the observations had a mean of 5 and a standard deviation of 2. Thus, about 95% of the observations for the histogram should be between 5 ± 2 standard deviations, or between 1 and 9. For the histogram with sample size 50, the interval for 95% of the sample means would be as follows:

$$5 \pm (1.96)\frac{2}{\sqrt{50}}$$

$$5 \pm 0.55$$

$$4.45 \rightarrow 5.55$$

When random samples of various sizes are obtained from a population with known mean and variance, we see that the ranges for various percentages of the sample means follow the results obtained using the normal distribution.

Next we considered a uniform probability distribution over the range 1 to 10. The probability distribution is shown in Figure 2.87. Clearly, the values of the random variable are not normally distributed, since the values are uniform over the range 1 to 10. The distributions of sample means for sample sizes 10, 25, and 50 are shown in Figure 2.87. A normal probability density function with the same mean and variance is sketched over each histogram to provide a comparison. Generally, the distribution of sample means from uniform or symmetric distributions can be closely approximated by the normal distribution, with samples of size 25 or more. The mean for the uniform distribution is 5.5, and the standard deviation is 2.886. From a normal distribution of sample means, with $n = 50$, we would expect to find 95% of the sample means in the following interval:

$$5.5 \pm (1.96)\frac{2.887}{\sqrt{50}}$$

$$5.5 \pm 0.80$$

$$4.70 \rightarrow 6.30$$

An examination of Figure 2.87 indicates that the normal interval applies here.

Next, let us consider a population with a probability distribution that is skewed to the right, as shown in Figure 2.88. Distributions of observations for many business and economic processes are skewed. For example, family incomes and housing prices in a city, state, or country are often skewed to the right. There is typically a small percentage of families with very high incomes, and these families tend to live in expensive houses. Consider the skewed probability distribution shown in Figure 2.88. This could be a distribution of family incomes for the United States of America. Suppose that you wanted to compare the mean income for the United States with the means for a larger set of countries with similar educational levels.

The sampling distributions of mean incomes are compared using random samples of size 10, 25, and 50 from the probability distribution. If you use a random sample of size $n = 10$ and assume that the sample mean is normally distributed, the chances for estimating incorrect probabilities are great. These mistakes in probability estimates are particularly large for sample means in the upper tail of the distribution. Note that the histogram is different from one that would be obtained from a normal distribution. But if you use a random sample of size $n = 25$, your results are much better. Note that the second histogram with $n = 25$ is much closer to a normal distribution. The results are even better when the sample size is 50. Thus, even when the distribution of individual observations is highly skewed, the sampling distribution of sample means closely approximates a normal distribution when $n \geq 50$. The mean and standard deviation for the skewed distribution are 3.3 and 4.247. Thus, the interval from the normal distribution for 95% of the sample means of size $n = 50$ is as follows:

$$3.3 \pm (1.96)\frac{4.247}{\sqrt{50}}$$

$$3.3 \pm 1.18$$

$$2.12 \rightarrow 4.48$$

The distribution of sample means for $n = 50$ appears to fit this interval.

From the random sampling studies in this chapter and our previous study of the binomial distribution, we have additional evidence to demonstrate the central limit theorem. Similar demonstrations have been produced numerous times by many statisticians. As a result, a large body of empirical evidence supports the application of the central limit theorem to realistic statistical applications, in addition to theoretical results. In Chapter 5 we learned that the binomial random variable has an approximate normal distribution as the sample size becomes large.

The question for applied analysis concerns the sample size required to ensure that sample means have a normal distribution. Based on considerable research and experience, we know that, if the distributions are symmetric, then the means from samples of $n = 20$ to 25 are well approximated by the normal distribution. For skewed distributions the required sample sizes are generally somewhat larger. But note that in the previous examples using a skewed distribution a sample size of $n = 50$ produced a sampling distribution of sample means that closely followed a normal distribution.

In this chapter we have begun our discussion of the important statistical problem of making inferences about a population based on results from a sample. The sample mean or sample proportion is often computed to make inferences about population means or proportions. By using the central limit theorem, we have a rationale for applying the techniques we develop in future chapters to a wide range of problems. The following examples show important applications of the central limit theorem.

Example 2.6.4 Marketing Study for Antelope Coffee (Normal Probability)

Antelope Coffee, Inc., is considering the possibility of opening a gourmet coffee shop in Big Rock, Montana. Previous research has indicated that its shops will be successful in cities of this size if the mean annual family income is above $70,000. It is also assumed that the standard deviation of income is $5,000 in Big Rock, Montana.

A random sample of 36 people was obtained, and the mean income was $72,300. Does this sample provide evidence to conclude that a shop should be opened?

Solution The distribution of incomes is known to be skewed, but the central limit theorem enables us to conclude that the sample mean is approximately normally distributed. To answer the question, we need to determine the probability of obtaining a sample mean of $\bar{x} = 72,300$ or larger if the population mean is $\mu = 70,000$.

First, compute the value for the standardized normal Z statistic:

$$z = \frac{\bar{x} - \mu}{\sigma/\sqrt{n}} = \frac{72,300 - 70,000}{5,000/\sqrt{36}} = 2.76$$

From the standard normal table we find that the probability of obtaining a Z value of 2.76 or larger is 0.0029. Because this probability is very small, we can conclude that it is likely that the population mean income is not $70,000 but is a larger value. This result provides strong evidence that the population mean income is higher than $70,000 and that the coffee shop is likely to be a success. In this example we can see the importance of sampling distributions and the central limit theorem for problem solving.

Acceptance Intervals

In many statistical applications we would like to determine the range within which sample means are likely to occur. Determining such ranges is a direct application of the sampling distribution concepts we have developed. An **acceptance interval** is an interval within which a sample mean has a high probability of occurring, given that we know the population mean and variance. If the sample mean is within that interval, then we can accept the conclusion that the random sample came from the population with the known population mean and variance. Thus acceptance intervals provide an operating rule for process-monitoring applications. The probability that the sample mean is within a particular interval can be computed if the sample means have a distribution that is close to normal. Acceptance intervals can also be computed for nonnormal probability distributions.

Acceptance intervals find wide application for monitoring manufacturing processes to determine if product standards continue to be achieved. For example, in a manufacturing process the manufacturing engineer carefully sets and tests a new process so that it will produce products that all meet the guaranteed specifications for size, weight, or other measured properties. Thus, the mean and standard deviation for the units produced are specified so that the desired product quality will be obtained. In addition, these intervals are also used for monitoring various business activities that involve customer service. Acceptance standards are established that meet stated marketing goals and customer service-level capability. These standards, in turn, are used to develop means, variances, and acceptance intervals to be used for process monitoring (Deming, 1986).

However, it is possible that the process could come out of adjustment and produce defective product items. Changes in either the mean or variance of the critical measurement result from a process that is out of adjustment. Therefore, the process is monitored regularly by obtaining random samples and measuring the important properties, such as the sample mean and variance. If the measured values are within the acceptance interval, then the process is allowed to continue. If the values are not, then the process is stopped and necessary adjustments are made.

Acceptance intervals based on the normal distribution are defined by the distribution mean and variance. From the central limit theorem we know that the sampling distribution of sample means is often approximately normal, and, thus, acceptance intervals based on the normal distribution have wide applications. Assuming that we know the population mean μ and variance σ^2, then we can construct a symmetric acceptance interval

$$\mu \pm z_{\alpha/2}\sigma_{\bar{x}}$$

provided that $\bar{x}$ has a normal distribution and $z_{\alpha/2}$ is the standard normal when the upper tail probability is $\alpha/2$. The probability that the sample mean $\bar{x}$ is included in the interval is $1 - \alpha$.

As noted, acceptance intervals are widely used for quality-control monitoring of various production and service processes. The interval

$$\mu \pm z_{\alpha/2}\sigma_{\bar{x}}$$

is plotted over time (the result is called an X-bar chart) and provides limits for the sample mean $\bar{x}$, given that the population mean is μ. Typically, α is very small ($\alpha < .01$), and standard practice in U.S. industries is to use $z = 3$. This is the source for the term *Six Sigma* used for various quality-assurance programs (Hiam, 1992). If the sample mean is outside the acceptance interval, then we suspect that the population mean is not μ. In a typical project engineers will take various steps to achieve a small variance for important product measurements that are directly related to product quality. Once the process has been adjusted so that the variance is small, an acceptance interval for a sample mean—called a *control interval*—is established in the form of a control chart (Montgomery, 1997). Then periodic random samples are obtained and compared to the control interval. If the sample mean is within the control interval, it is concluded that the process is operating properly and no action is taken. But if the sample mean is outside the control interval, it is concluded that the process is not operating properly and steps are taken to correct the process.

Example 2.6.5 Monitoring Health Insurance Claims (Acceptance Interval)

Charlotte King, vice president of financial underwriting for a large health insurance company, wishes to monitor daily insurance claim payments to determine if the average dollar value of subscriber claims is stable, increasing, or decreasing. The value of individual claims varies up and down from one day to the next, and it would be naive to draw conclusions or change operations based on these daily variations. But at some point the changes become substantial and should be noted. She has asked you to develop a procedure for monitoring the dollar value of individual claims.

Solution Your initial investigation indicates that health insurance claims are highly skewed, with a small number of very large claims for major medical procedures. To develop a monitoring process, you first need to determine the historical mean and variance for individual claims. After some investigation you also find that the mean for random samples of $n = 100$ claims is normally distributed. Based on past history the mean, μ, level for individual claims is \$6,000 with a standard deviation of $\sigma = 2,000$.

Using this information you proceed to develop a claims-monitoring system that obtains a random sample of 100 claims each day and computes the sample mean. The company has established a 95% acceptance interval for monitoring claims. An interval defined for the standard normal using $Z = \pm 1.96$ includes 95% of the values. From this you compute the 95% acceptance interval for insurance claims as follows:

$$6,000 \pm 1.96 \frac{2,000}{\sqrt{100}}$$

$$6,000 \pm 392$$

Each day the sample mean for 100 randomly selected claims is computed and compared to the acceptance interval. If the sample mean is inside the interval 5,608 to 6,392, Ms. King can conclude that claims are not deviating from the historical standard. You explain to her that if the claims are following the historical standard then 95% of the time the sample mean will be within the interval. The sample mean could be outside the interval even if the population mean is 6,000 with probability 0.05. In those cases Ms. King's conclusion that the mean claim level has changed from the historical standard would be wrong and this error would occur 5% of the time. Therefore if the sample mean is outside the interval there is strong evidence to conclude that the claims are no longer following the historical standard. To simplify the analysis, you instruct the analysts to plot the daily claims mean on a control chart, shown in Figure 2.89. Using this control chart Charlotte King and her staff can study the patterns of the sample means and determine if there are trends and if means are outside of the boundaries that indicate standard claims' behavior.

Figure 2.89 Ninety-Five Percent Acceptance Interval for Health Insurance Claims

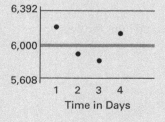

Example 2.6.6 Prairie View Cereal Package Weights (Acceptance Intervals)

Prairie View Cereals. Inc., is concerned about maintaining correct package weights at its cereal-packaging facility. The package label weight is 440 grams, and company officials are interested in monitoring the process to ensure that package weights are stable.

Solution A random sample of five packages is collected every 30 minutes, and each package is weighed electronically. The mean weight is then plotted on an X-bar control chart such as the one in Figure 2.90. When an X-bar chart is used for monitoring limits on product quality—this usage is practiced by numerous highly successful firms—the central limit theorem provides the rationale for using the normal distribution to establish limits for the small sample means. Thus, a fundamentally important statistical theory drives a key management process.

Figure 2.90 X-Bar Chart For Cereal-Package Weight

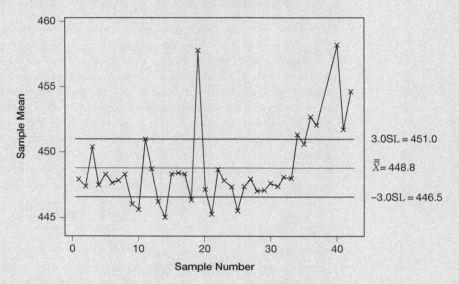

In this chart SL is the standard deviation for the sample mean. The upper and lower limits are set at $\pm 3\sigma_{\overline{X}}$ instead of $\pm 1.96\sigma_{\overline{X}}$, or 95%, the acceptance interval used in the previous example. The interval $\overline{X} \pm 3\sigma_{\overline{X}}$ (Minitab labels the mean for the entire population as $\overline{\overline{X}}$) includes almost all the sample means under the normal distribution, given a stable mean and variance. Thus, a sample mean outside the control limits indicates that something has changed and that adjustments should be made. Given the number of points outside the acceptance interval, we recommend that the process be stopped and adjusted.

EXERCISES

Basic Exercises

2.6.5 Given a population with a mean of $\mu = 100$ and a variance of $\sigma^2 = 81$, the central limit theorem applies when the sample size is $n \geq 25$. A random sample of size $n = 25$ is obtained.

   a. What are the mean and variance of the sampling distribution for the sample means?
   b. What is the probability that $\overline{x} > 102$?
   c. What is the probability that $98 \leq \overline{x} \leq 101$?
   d. What is the probability that $\overline{x} \leq 101.5$?

2.6.6 Given a population with a mean of $\mu = 100$ and a variance of $\sigma^2 = 900$, the central limit theorem applies when the sample size is $n \geq 25$. A random sample of size $n = 30$ is obtained.

   a. What are the mean and variance of the sampling distribution for the sample means?

b. What is the probability that $\bar{x} > 109$?

c. What is the probability that $96 \leq \bar{x} \leq 110$?

d. What is the probability that $\bar{x} \leq 107$?

2.6.7 Given a population with a mean of $\mu = 200$ and a variance of $\sigma^2 = 625$, the central limit theorem applies when the sample size $n \geq 25$. A random sample of size $n = 25$ is obtained.

a. What are the mean and variance of the sampling distribution for the sample mean?

b. What is the probability that $\bar{x} > 209$?

c. What is the probability that $198 \leq \bar{x} \leq 211$?

d. What is the probability that $\bar{x} \leq 202$?

2.6.8 Given a population with mean $\mu = 400$ and variance $\sigma^2 = 1,600$, the central limit theorem applies when the sample size is $n \geq 25$. A random sample of size $n = 35$ is obtained.

a. What are the mean and variance of the sampling distribution for the sample means?

b. What is the probability that $\bar{x} > 412$?

c. What is the probability that $393 \leq \bar{x} \leq 407$?

d. What is the probability that $\bar{x} \leq 389$?

2.6.9 When a production process is operating correctly, the number of units produced per hour has a normal distribution with a mean of 92.0 and a standard deviation of 3.6. A random sample of 4 different hours was taken.

a. Find the mean of the sampling distribution of the sample means.

b. Find the variance of the sampling distribution of the sample mean.

c. Find the standard error of the sampling distribution of the sample mean.

d. What is the probability that the sample mean exceeds 93.0 units?

Application Exercises

2.6.10 The lifetimes of lightbulbs produced by a particular manufacturer have a mean of 1,200 hours and a standard deviation of 400 hours. The population distribution is normal. Suppose that you purchase nine bulbs, which can be regarded as a random sample from the manufacturer's output.

a. What is the mean of the sample mean lifetime?

b. What is the variance of the sample mean?

c. What is the standard error of the sample mean?

d. What is the probability that, on average, those nine lightbulbs have lives of fewer than 1,050 hours?

2.6.11 The fuel consumption, in miles per gallon, of all cars of a particular model has a mean of 25 and a standard deviation of 2. The population distribution can be assumed to be normal. A random sample of these cars is taken.

a. Find the probability that sample mean fuel consumption will be fewer than 24 miles per gallon if

i. a sample of 1 observation is taken.

ii. a sample of 4 observations is taken.

iii. a sample of 16 observations is taken.

b. Explain why the three answers in part (a) differ in the way they do. Draw a graph to illustrate your reasoning.

2.6.12 The mean selling price of senior condominiums in Green Valley over a year was $215,000. The population standard deviation was $25,000. A random sample of 100 new unit sales was obtained.

a. What is the probability that the sample mean selling price was more than $210,000?

b. What is the probability that the sample mean selling price was between $213,000 and $217,000?

c. What is the probability that the sample mean selling price was between $214,000 and $216,000?

d. Without doing the calculations, state in which of the following ranges the sample mean selling price is most likely to lie:
$213,000 to $215,000; $214,000 to $216,000; $215,000 to $217,000; $216,000 to $218,000

e. Suppose that, after you had done these calculations, a friend asserted that the population distribution of selling prices of senior condominiums in Green Valley was almost certainly not normal. How would you respond?

2.6.13 Candidates for employment at a city fire department are required to take a written aptitude test. Scores on this test are normally distributed with a mean of 280 and a standard deviation of 60. A random sample of nine test scores was taken.

a. What is the standard error of the sample mean score?

b. What is the probability that the sample mean score is less than 270?

c. What is the probability that the sample mean score is more than 250?

d. Suppose that the population standard deviation is, in fact, 40, rather than 60. Without doing the calculations, state how this would change your answers to parts (a), (b), and (c). Illustrate your conclusions with the appropriate graphs.

2.6.14 A random sample of 16 junior managers in the offices of corporations in a large city center was taken to estimate average daily commuting time for all such managers. Suppose that the population times have a normal distribution with a mean of 87 minutes and a standard deviation of 22 minutes.

a. What is the standard error of the sample mean commuting time?

b. What is the probability that the sample mean is fewer than 100 minutes?

c. What is the probability that the sample mean is more than 80 minutes?

d. What is the probability that the sample mean is outside the range 85 to 95 minutes?

e. Suppose that a second (independent) random sample of 50 junior managers is taken. Without doing the calculations, state whether the probabilities in parts (b), (c), and (d) would be higher, lower, or the same for the second sample. Sketch graphs to illustrate your answers.

2.6.15 A company produces breakfast cereal. The true mean weight of the contents of its cereal packages is 20 ounces, and the standard deviation is 0.6 ounce. The population distribution of weights is normal. Suppose that you purchase four packages, which can be regarded as a random sample of all those produced.

a. What is the standard error of the sample mean weight?

b. What is the probability that, on average, the contents of these four packages will weigh fewer than 19.7 ounces?

c. What is the probability that, on average, the contents of these four packages will weigh more than 20.6 ounces?

d. What is the probability that, on average, the contents of these four packages will weigh between 19.5 and 20.5 ounces?

e. Two of the four boxes are chosen at random. What is the probability that the average contents of these two packages will weigh between 19.5 and 20.5 ounces?

2.6.16 Assume that the standard deviation of monthly rents paid by students in a particular town is $40. A random sample of 100 students was taken to estimate the mean monthly rent paid by the whole student population.

a. What is the standard error of the sample mean monthly rent?

b. What is the probability that the sample mean exceeds the population mean by more than $5?

c. What is the probability that the sample mean is more than $4 below the population mean?

d. What is the probability that the sample mean differs from the population mean by more than $3?

2.6.17 The times spent studying by students in the week before final exams follows a normal distribution with standard deviation 8 hours. A random sample of four students was taken in order to estimate the mean study time for the population of all students.

a. What is the probability that the sample mean exceeds the population mean by more than 2 hours?

b. What is the probability that the sample mean is more than 3 hours below the population mean?

c. What is the probability that the sample mean differs from the population mean by more than 4 hours?

d. Suppose that a second (independent) random sample of 10 students was taken. Without doing the calculations, state whether the probabilities in parts (a), (b), and (c) would be higher, lower, or the same for the second sample.

2.6.18 An industrial process produces batches of a chemical whose impurity levels follow a normal distribution with standard deviation 1.6 grams per 100 grams of chemical. A random sample of 100 batches is selected in order to estimate the population mean impurity level.

a. The probability is 0.05 that the sample mean impurity level exceeds the population mean by how much?

b. The probability is 0.10 that the sample mean impurity level is below the population mean by how much?

c. The probability is 0.15 that the sample mean impurity level differs from the population mean by how much?

2.6.19 The price-earnings ratios for all companies whose shares are traded on the New York Stock Exchange follow a normal distribution with a standard deviation of 3.8. A random sample of these companies is selected in order to estimate the population mean price-earnings ratio.

a. How large a sample is necessary in order to ensure that the probability that the sample mean differs from the population mean by more than 1.0 is less than 0.10?

b. Without doing the calculations, state whether a larger or smaller sample size compared to the sample size in part (a) would be required to guarantee that the probability of the sample mean differing from the population mean by more than 1.0 is less than 0.05.

c. Without doing the calculations, state whether a larger or smaller sample size compared to the sample size in part a would be required to guarantee that the probability of the sample mean differing from the population mean by more than 1.5 hours is less than 0.10.

2.6.20 The number of hours spent studying by students on a large campus in the week before final exams follows a normal distribution with a standard deviation of 8.4 hours. A random sample of these students is taken to estimate the population mean number of hours studying.

a. How large a sample is needed to ensure that the probability that the sample mean differs from the population mean by more than 2.0 hours is less than 0.05?

b. Without doing the calculations, state whether a larger or smaller sample size compared to the sample size in part (a) would be required to guarantee that the probability of the sample mean differing from the population mean by more than 2.0 hours is less than 0.10.

c. Without doing the calculations, state whether a larger or smaller sample size compared to the sample size in part (a) would be required to guarantee that the probability of the sample mean differing from the population mean by more than 1.5 hours is less than 0.05.

2.6.21 Greenstone Coffee is experiencing financial pressures due to increased competition for its numerous urban coffee shops. Total sales revenue has dropped by 15% and the company wishes to establish a sales monitoring process to identify shops that are underperforming. Historically, the daily mean sales for a shop have been $11,500 with a variance of 4,000,000. Their monitoring plan will take a random sample of 5 days' sales per month and use the sample mean sales to identify shops that are underperforming. Establish the lower limit sales such that only 5% of the shops would have a sample sales mean below this value.

2.6.22 In taking a sample of n observations from a population of N members, the variance of the sampling distribution of the sample means is as follows:

$$\sigma_{\bar{x}}^2 = \frac{\sigma_x^2}{n} \cdot \frac{N-n}{N-1}$$

The quantity $\dfrac{(N-n)}{(N-1)}$ is called the *finite population correction factor*.

a. To get some feeling for possible magnitudes of the finite population correction factor, calculate it for samples of $n = 20$ observations from populations of members: 20, 40, 100, 1,000, 10,000.
b. Explain why the result found in part a, is precisely what one should expect on intuitive grounds.
c. Given the results in part a, discuss the practical significance of using the finite-population correction factor for samples of 20 observations from populations of different sizes.

2.6.23 A town has 500 real estate agents. The mean value of the properties sold in a year by these agents is $800,000, and the standard deviation is $300,000. A random sample of 100 agents is selected, and the value of the properties they sold in a year is recorded.

a. What is the standard error of the sample mean?
b. What is the probability that the sample mean exceeds $825,000?
c. What is the probability that the sample mean exceeds $780,000?
d. What is the probability that the sample mean is between $790,000 and $820,000?

2.6.24 An English literature course was taken by 250 students. Each member of a random sample of 50 of these students was asked to estimate the amount of time he or she spent on the previous week's assignment. Suppose that the population standard deviation is 30 minutes.

a. What is the probability that the sample mean exceeds the population mean by more than 2.5 minutes?
b. What is the probability that the sample mean is more than 5 minutes below the population mean?
c. What is the probability that the sample mean differs from the population mean by more than 10 minutes?

2.6.25 For an audience of 600 people attending a concert, the average time on the journey to the concert was 32 minutes, and the standard deviation was 10 minutes. A random sample of 150 audience members was taken.

a. What is the probability that the sample mean journey time was more than 31 minutes?
b. What is the probability that the sample mean journey time was less than 33 minutes?
c. Construct a graph to illustrate why the answers to parts (a) and (b) are the same.
d. What is the probability that the sample mean journey time was not between 31 and 33 minutes?

2.6.3 SAMPLING DISTRIBUTIONS OF SAMPLE PROPORTIONS

In Section 2.4.4 we developed the binomial distribution as the sum of n independent Bernoulli random variables, each with probability of success P. To characterize the distribution, we need a value for P. Here, we indicate how we can use the sample proportion to obtain inferences about the population proportion. The proportion random variable has many applications, including percent market share, percent successful business investments, and outcomes of elections.

Sample Proportion

Let X be the number of successes in a binomial sample of n observations with the parameter P. The parameter is the proportion of the population members that have a characteristic of interest. We define the **sample proportion** as follows:

$$\hat{p} = \frac{X}{n} \qquad (6.7)$$

X is the sum of a set of n independent Bernoulli random variables, each with probability of success P. As a result, $\hat{p}$ is the mean of a set of independent random variables, and the results we developed in the previous sections for sample means apply. In addition, the central limit theorem can be used to argue that the probability distribution for $\hat{p}$ can be modeled as a normally distributed random variable.

There is also a variation of the law of large numbers that applies when sampling to determine the percent of successes in a large population that has a known proportion P of success. If random samples are obtained from the population and the success or failure is determined for each observation, then the sample proportion of success approaches P as the sample size increases. Thus, we can make inferences about the population proportion using the sample proportion and the sample proportion will get closer as our sample size increases. However, the difference between the expected number of sample successes—the sample size multiplied by P—and the number of successes in the sample might actually increase.

In Section 2.5.4 it was shown that the number of successes in a binomial distribution and the proportion of successes have a distribution that is closely approximated by a normal distribution (see Figures 2.78 and 2.79). This provides a very close approximation when $nP(1 - P) > 5$.

The mean and variance of the sampling distribution of the sample proportion $\hat{p}$ can be obtained from the mean and variance of the number of successes, X:

$$E[X] = nP \quad Var(X) = nP(1 - P)$$

Thus,

$$E[\hat{p}] = E\left[\frac{X}{n}\right] = \frac{1}{n}E[X] = P$$

We see that the mean of the distribution of $\hat{p}$ is the population proportion, P.

The variance of $\hat{p}$ is the variance of the population distribution of the Bernoulli random variables divided by n:

$$\sigma_{\hat{p}}^2 = Var\left(\frac{X}{n}\right) = \frac{1}{n^2}Var(X) = \frac{P(1 - P)}{n}$$

The standard deviation of $\hat{p}$, which is the square root of the variance, is called its standard error.

Since the distribution of the sample proportion is approximately normal for large sample sizes, we can obtain a standard normal random variable by subtracting P from $\hat{p}$ and dividing by the standard error.

Sampling Distribution of the Sample Proportion

Let $\hat{p}$ be the sample proportion of successes in a random sample from a population with proportion of success P. Then,

1. the sampling distribution of $\hat{p}$ has mean P:

$$E[\hat{p}] = P \tag{6.8}$$

2. the sampling distribution of $\hat{p}$ has standard deviation

$$\sigma_{\hat{p}} = \sqrt{\frac{P(1 - P)}{n}} \tag{6.9}$$

3. and, if the sample size is large, the random variable

$$Z = \frac{\hat{p} - P}{\sigma_{\hat{p}}} \tag{6.10}$$

is approximately distributed as a standard normal. This approximation is good if

$$nP(1 - P) > 5$$

Similar to the results from the previous section, we see that the standard error of the sample proportion, $\hat{p}$, decreases as the sample size increases and the distribution becomes more concentrated, as seen in Figure 2.91, using samples from a population with 80% success rate. This is expected because the sample proportion is a sample mean. With larger sample sizes our inferences about the population proportion improve. From the central limit theorem we know that the binomial distribution can be approximated by the normal distribution with corresponding mean and variance. We see this result in the following examples.

Figure 2.91
Probability Density Functions for the Sample Proportions with $P = 0.80$

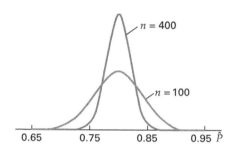

Example 2.6.7 Evaluation of Home Electric Wiring (Probability of Sample Proportion)

A random sample of 270 homes was taken from a large population of older homes to estimate the proportion of homes with unsafe wiring. If, in fact, 20% of the homes have unsafe wiring, what is the probability that the sample proportion will be between 16% and 24%?

Solution For this problem we have the following:

$$P = 0.20 \quad n = 270$$

We can compute the standard deviation of the sample proportion, $\hat{p}$, as follows:

$$\sigma_{\hat{p}} = \sqrt{\frac{P(1-P)}{n}} = \sqrt{\frac{0.20(1-0.20)}{270}} = 0.024$$

The required probability is

$$P(0.16 < \hat{p} < 0.24) = P\left(\frac{0.16 - P}{\sigma_{\hat{p}}} < \frac{\hat{p} - P}{\sigma_{\hat{p}}} < \frac{0.24 - P}{\sigma_{\hat{p}}}\right)$$

$$= P\left(\frac{0.16 - 0.20}{0.024} < Z < \frac{0.24 - 0.20}{0.024}\right)$$

$$= P(-1.67 < Z < 1.67)$$

$$= 0.9050$$

where the probability for the Z interval is obtained.

Thus, we see that the probability is 0.9050 that the sample proportion is within the interval 0.16 to 0.24, given $P = 0.20$, and a sample size of $n = 270$. This interval can be called a 90.50% acceptance interval. We can also note that if the sample proportion was actually outside this interval, we might begin to suspect that the population proportion, P, is not 0.20.

Example 2.6.8 Business Course Selection (Probability of Sample Proportion)

It has been estimated that 43% of business graduates believe that a course in business ethics is very important for imparting ethical values to students (David, Anderson, and Lawrimore 1990). Find the probability that more than one-half of a random sample of 80 business graduates have this belief.

Solution We are given that

$$P = 0.43 \quad n = 80$$

We first compute the standard deviation of the sample proportion:

$$\sigma_{\hat{p}} = \sqrt{\frac{P(1-P)}{n}} = \sqrt{\frac{0.43(1-0.43)}{80}} = 0.055$$

Then the required probability can be computed as follows:

$$P(\hat{p} > 0.50) = P\left(\frac{\hat{p} - P}{\sigma_{\hat{p}}} > \frac{0.50 - P}{\sigma_{\hat{p}}}\right)$$

$$= P\left(Z > \frac{0.50 - 0.43}{0.055}\right)$$

$$= P(Z > 1.27)$$

$$= 0.1020$$

The probability of having more than one-half of the sample believing in the value of business ethics courses is approximately 0.1.

Figure 2.92 The Probability that a Standard Normal Random Variable Exceeds 1.27

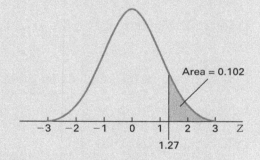

EXERCISES

Basic Exercises

2.6.26 Suppose that we have a population with proportion $P = 0.40$ and a random sample of size $n = 100$ drawn from the population.

   a. What is the probability that the sample proportion is greater than 0.45?

   b. What is the probability that the sample proportion is less than 0.29?

   c. What is the probability that the sample proportion is between 0.35 and 0.51?

2.6.27 Suppose that we have a population with proportion $P = 0.25$ and a random sample of size $n = 200$ drawn from the population.

   a. What is the probability that the sample proportion is greater than 0.31?

   b. What is the probability that the sample proportion is less than 0.14?

   c. What is the probability that the sample proportion is between 0.24 and 0.40?

2.6.28 Suppose that we have a population with proportion $P = 0.60$ and a random sample of size $n = 100$ drawn from the population.

    a. What is the probability that the sample proportion is more than 0.66?

    b. What is the probability that the sample proportion is less than 0.48?

    c. What is the probability that the sample proportion is between 0.52 and 0.66?

2.6.29 Suppose that we have a population with proportion $P = 0.50$ and a random sample of size $n = 900$ drawn from the population.

    a. What is the probability that the sample proportion is more than 0.52?

    b. What is the probability that the sample proportion is less than 0.46?

    c. What is the probability that the sample proportion is between 0.47 and 0.53?

Application Exercises

2.6.30 In 1992, Canadians voted in a referendum on a new constitution. In the province of Quebec, 42.4% of those who voted were in favor of the new constitution. A random sample of 100 voters from the province was taken.

    a. What is the mean of the distribution of the sample proportion in favor of a new constitution?

    b. What is the variance of the sample proportion?

    c. What is the standard error of the sample proportion?

    d. What is the probability that the sample proportion is more than 0.5?

2.6.31 According to the Internal Revenue Service, 75% of all tax returns lead to a refund. A random sample of 100 tax returns is taken.

    a. What is the mean of the distribution of the sample proportion of returns leading to refunds?

    b. What is the variance of the sample proportion?

    c. What is the standard error of the sample proportion?

    d. What is the probability that the sample proportion exceeds 0.8?

2.6.32 A record store owner finds that 20% of customers entering her store make a purchase. One morning 180 people, who can be regarded as a random sample of all customers, enter the store.

    a. What is the mean of the distribution of the sample proportion of customers making a purchase?

    b. What is the variance of the sample proportion?

    c. What is the standard error of the sample proportion?

    d. What is the probability that the sample proportion is less than 0.15?

2.6.33 An administrator for a large group of hospitals believes that of all patients 30% will generate bills that become at least 2 months overdue. A random sample of 200 patients is taken.

    a. What is the standard error of the sample proportion that will generate bills that become at least 2 months overdue?

    b. What is the probability that the sample proportion is less than 0.25?

    c. What is the probability that the sample proportion is more than 0.33?

    d. What is the probability that the sample proportion is between 0.27 and 0.33?

2.6.34 A corporation receives 120 applications for positions from recent college graduates in business. Assuming that these applicants can be viewed as a random sample of all such graduates, what is the probability that between 35% and 45% of them are women if 40% of all recent college graduates in business are women?

2.6.35 A charity has found that 42% of all donors from last year will donate again this year. A random sample of 300 donors from last year was taken.

    a. What is the standard error of the sample proportion who will donate again this year?

    b. What is the probability that more than half of these sample members will donate again this year?

    c. What is the probability that the sample proportion is between 0.40 and 0.45?

    d. Without doing the calculations, state in which of the following ranges the sample proportion is more likely to lie: 0.39 to 0.41, 0.41 to 0.43, 0.43 to 0.45, or 0.45 to 0.46.

2.6.36 A corporation is considering a new issue of convertible bonds. Management believes that the offer terms will be found attractive by 20% of all its current stockholders. Suppose that this belief is correct. A random sample of 130 current stockholders is taken.

    a. What is the standard error of the sample proportion who find this offer attractive?

    b. What is the probability that the sample proportion is more than 0.15?

    c. What is the probability that the sample proportion is between 0.18 and 0.22?

    d. Suppose that a sample of 500 current stockholders had been taken. Without doing the calculations, state whether the probabilities in parts (b) and (c) would have been higher, lower, or the same as those found.

2.6.37 A store has determined that 30% of all lawn mower purchasers will also purchase a service agreement. In 1 month 280 lawn mowers are sold to customers, who can be regarded as a random sample of all purchasers.

    a. What is the standard error of the sample proportion of those who will purchase a service agreement?

    b. What is the probability that the sample proportion will be less than 0.32?

    c. Without doing the calculations, state in which of the following ranges the sample proportion is most likely to be: 0.29 to 0.31, 0.30 to 0.32, 0.31 to 0.33, or 0.32 to 0.34.

2.6.38 A random sample of 100 voters is taken to estimate the proportion of a state's electorate in favor of increasing the gasoline tax to provide additional revenue for highway repairs. What is the largest value that the standard error of the sample proportion in favor of this measure can take?

2.6.39 In the previous exercise, suppose that it is decided that a sample of 100 voters is too small to provide a sufficiently reliable estimate of the population proportion. It is required instead that the probability that the sample proportion differs from the population proportion (whatever its value) by more than 0.03 should not exceed 0.05. How large a sample is needed to guarantee that this requirement is met?

2.6.40 A company wants to estimate the proportion of people who are likely to purchase electric shavers from those who watch the nationally telecast baseball playoffs. A random sample obtained information from 120 people who were identified as persons who watch baseball telecasts. Suppose that the proportion of those likely to purchase electric shavers in the population who watch the telecast is 0.25.

a. The probability is 0.10 that the sample proportion watching the telecast exceeds the population proportion by how much?

b. The probability is 0.05 that the sample proportion is lower than the population proportion by how much?

c. The probability is 0.30 that the sample proportion differs from the population proportion by how much?

2.6.41 Suppose that 44% of adult Australians believe that Australia should become a republic. Calculate the probability that more than 50% of a random sample of 100 adult Australians would believe this.

2.6.42 Suppose that 50% of adult Australians believe that Australia should apply to host the next rugby World Cup. Calculate the probability that more than 56% of a random sample of 150 adult Australians would believe this.

2.6.43 A journalist wanted to learn the views of the chief executive officers of the 500 largest U.S. corporations on program trading of stocks. In the time available, it was possible to contact only a random sample of 81 of these chief executive officers. If 55% of all the population members believe that program trading should be banned, what is the probability that less than half the sample members hold this view?

2.6.44 Forty percent of students at small colleges have brought their own personal computers to campus. A random sample of 120 entering freshmen was taken.

a. What is the standard error of the sample proportion bringing their own personal computers to campus?

b. What is the probability that the sample proportion is less than 0.33?

c. What is the probability that the sample proportion is between 0.38 and 0.46?

2.6.45 An employee survey conducted two years ago by Rice Motors, Inc., found that 53% of its employees were concerned about future health care benefits. A random sample of 80 of these employees were asked if they were now concerned about future health care benefits. Answer the following, assuming that there has been no change in the level of concern about health care benefits compared to the survey two years ago.

a. What is the standard error of the sample proportion who are concerned?

b. What is the probability that the sample proportion is less than 0.5?

c. What is the upper limit of the sample proportion such that only 3% of the time the sample proportion would exceed this value?

2.6.46 The annual percentage salary increases for the chief executive officers of all midsize corporations are normally distributed with mean 12.2% and standard deviation 3.6%. A random sample of 81 of these chief executive officers was taken. What is the probability that more than half the sample members had salary increases of less than 10%?

2.6.4 SAMPLING DISTRIBUTIONS OF SAMPLE VARIANCES

Now that sampling distributions for sample means and proportions have been developed, we consider sampling distributions of sample variances. As business and industry increase their emphasis on producing products that satisfy customer quality standards, there is an increased need to measure and reduce population variance. High variance for a process implies a wider range of possible values for important product characteristics. This wider range of outcomes will result in more individual products that perform below an acceptable standard. After all, a customer does not care if a product performs well "on average." She is concerned that the particular item that she purchased works. High-quality products can be obtained from a manufacturing process if the process has a low population variance, so that fewer units are below the desired quality standard. By understanding the sampling distribution of sample variances, we can make inferences about the population variance. Thus, processes that have high variance can be identified and improved. In addition, a smaller population variance improves our ability to make inferences about population means using sample means.

We begin by considering a random sample of n observations drawn from a population with unknown mean μ and unknown variance σ^2. Denote the sample members as x_1, $x_2, \ldots, x_n$. The population variance is the expectation

$$\sigma^2 = E[(X - \mu)^2]$$

which suggests that we consider the mean of $(x_i - \bar{x})^2$ over n observations. Since μ is unknown, we use the sample mean $\bar{x}$ to compute a sample variance.

Sample Variance

Let $x_1, x_2, \ldots, x_n$ be a random sample of observations from a population. The quantity

$$s^2 = \frac{1}{n-1}\sum_{i=1}^{n}(x_i - \bar{x})^2$$

is called the **sample variance**, and its square root, s, is called the *sample standard deviation*. Given a specific random sample, we could compute the sample variance, and the sample variance would be different for each random sample because of differences in sample observations.

We might be initially surprised by the use of $(n-1)$ as the divisor in the preceding definition. One simple explanation is that in a random sample of n observations, we have n different independent values or degrees of freedom. But after we know the computed sample mean, there are only $n-1$ different values that can be uniquely defined. In addition, it can be shown that the expected value of the sample variance computed in this way is the population variance. This result is established in the chapter appendix and holds when the actual sample size, n, is a small proportion of the population size N:

$$E[s^2] = \sigma^2$$

The conclusion that the expected value of the sample variance is the population variance is quite general. But for statistical inference we would like to know more about the sampling distribution. If we can assume that the underlying population distribution is normal, then it can be shown that the sample variance and the population variance are related through a probability distribution known as the *chi-square distribution*.

Chi-Square Distribution of Sample and Population Variances

Given a random sample of n observations from a normally distributed population whose population variance is σ^2 and whose resulting sample variance is s^2, it can be shown that

$$\chi^2_{(n-1)} = \frac{(n-1)s^2}{\sigma^2} = \frac{\sum_{i=1}^{n}(x_i - \bar{x})^2}{\sigma^2}$$

has a distribution known as the **chi-square (χ^2) distribution** with $n-1$ degrees of freedom.

The chi-square family of distributions is used in applied statistical analysis because it provides a link between the sample and the population variances. The chi-square distribution with $n-1$ degrees of freedom is the distribution of the sum of squares of $n-1$ independent standard normal random variables. The preceding chi-square distribution and the resulting computed probabilities for various values of s^2 require that the population distribution be normal. Thus, the assumption of an underlying normal distribution is more important for determining probabilities of sample variances than it is for determining probabilities of sample means.

Introduction

We now come to the heart of the subject of statistical inference. Up until now the following type of question has been examined: given the population parameters μ and σ^2, what is the probability of the sample mean $\bar{x}$, from a sample of size n, being greater than some specified value or within some range of values? The parameters μ and σ^2 are assumed to be known and the objective is to try to form some conclusions about possible values of $\bar{x}$. However, in practice it is usually the sample values $\bar{x}$ and s^2 that are known, while the population parameters μ and σ^2 are not. Thus a more interesting question to ask is: given the values of $\bar{x}$ and s^2 from a sample of size n, what can be said about μ and σ^2? For example, if a sample of 50 British families finds an average weekly expenditure on food ($\bar{x}$) of £37.50 with a standard deviation (s) of £6.00, what can be said about the average expenditure (μ) of *all* British families?

Schematically these issues can be shown as follows:

Sample information		Population parameters
$\bar{x}, s^2, n$	Probability statements about $\longleftarrow$	μ, σ^2
$\bar{x}, s^2, n$	Inferences about $\longrightarrow$	μ, σ^2

It is important to recognise the differences between making probability statements about sample statistics such as $\bar{x}$, and making inferences about unknown parameters such as μ. We will go into this in more detail in this chapter.

This chapter covers the estimation of population parameters such as μ and σ^2, while Chapter 8 describes testing hypotheses about these parameters. The two procedures are closely related, being two ways of drawing inferences about the parameters, but there are important differences between them.

Point and interval estimation

There are basically two ways in which an estimate of a parameter can be presented. The first of these is a point estimate, i.e. a single value which is in some sense the best estimate of the parameter of interest. The point estimate is the one which is most prevalent in everyday usage; for example, men spend an average of 43 minutes per day ogling women[1]. Although this is presented as a fact, it is actually an estimate, obtained from a survey. Since it is obtained from a sample, there must be some doubt about its accuracy – the sample will probably not exactly represent the whole population. For this reason, interval estimates are also used, giving a range of values which give an idea of the likely accuracy of the estimate. If the sample size is small, for example, then it is quite possible that the estimate is not very close to the

[1] *Daily Telegraph*, 4 August 2009. The survey was sponsored by an optician and was used to encourage people to get their eyesight checked. It also claimed that women spend an average of 20 minutes per day ogling men.

true value and this would be reflected in a wide interval estimate, for example, that the average man spends between 33 and 53 minutes ogling women per day[2]. A larger sample, or a better method of estimation, would allow a narrower interval to be derived and thus a more precise estimate of the parameter to be obtained, such as an average ogling time of between 40 and 46 minutes. Interval estimates are better for the consumer of the statistics, since they not only show the estimate of the parameter but also give an idea of the confidence which the researcher has in that estimate. The following sections describe how to construct both types of estimate.

Rules and criteria for finding estimates

In order to estimate a parameter such as the population mean, a rule (or set of rules) is required which describes how to derive the estimate of the parameter from the sample data. Such a rule is known as an estimator. An example of an estimator for the population mean is 'use the sample mean'. It is important to distinguish between an estimator, a rule, and an estimate, which is the value derived as a result of applying the rule to the data.

There are many possible estimators for any parameter, so it is important to be able to distinguish between good and bad estimators. The following examples provide some possible estimators of the population mean:

(1) the sample mean
(2) the smallest sample observation
(3) the first sample observation.

A set of criteria is needed for discriminating between good and bad estimators. Which of the above three estimators is 'best'? Two important criteria by which to judge estimators are bias and precision.

 Bias

It is impossible to know if a single estimate of a parameter, derived by applying a particular rule to the sample data, gives a correct estimate of the parameter or not. The estimate might be too low or too high and, since the parameter is unknown, it is impossible to check this. What *is* possible, however, is to say whether an estimator gives the correct answer *on average*. An estimator which gives the correct answer on average is said to be unbiased. Another way of expressing this is to say that an unbiased estimator does not *systematically* mislead the researcher away from the correct value of the parameter. It is important to remember, however, that even using an unbiased estimator does not guarantee that a single use of the estimator will yield a correct estimate of the parameter. Bias (or the lack of it) is a theoretical property.

Formally, an estimator is unbiased if its expected value is equal to the parameter being estimated. Consider trying to estimate the population mean using the

[2]The survey did not provide an interval estimate, so I have invented these figures to illustrate. The figure of 43 minutes did come from the survey, although its reliability must be suspect.

three estimators suggested above. Taking the sample mean first, we have already learned (see equation (3.15)) that its expected value is μ, i.e.

$$E(\bar{x}) = \mu$$

which immediately shows that the sample mean is an unbiased estimator.

The second estimator (the smallest observation in the sample) can easily be shown to be biased, using the result derived above. Since the smallest sample observation must be less than the sample mean, its expected value must be less than μ. Denote the smallest observation by x_s, then

$$E(x_s) < \mu$$

so this estimator is biased downwards. It underestimates the population mean. The size of the bias is simply the difference between the expected value of the estimator and the value of the parameter, so the bias in this case is

$$\text{Bias} = E(x_s) - \mu \tag{7.1}$$

For the sample mean $\bar{x}$ the bias is obviously zero.

Turning to the third rule (the first sample observation), this can be shown to be another unbiased estimator. Choosing the first observation from the sample is equivalent to taking a random sample of size one from the population in the first place. Thus, the single observation may be considered as the sample mean from a random sample of size one. Since it is a sample mean, it is unbiased, as demonstrated earlier.

Precision

Two of the estimators above were found to be unbiased, and, in fact, there are many unbiased estimators (the sample median is another, for example). Some way of choosing between the set of all unbiased estimators is therefore required, which is where the criterion of precision helps. Unlike bias, precision is a relative concept, comparing one estimator to another. Given two estimators A and B, A is more precise than B if the estimates A yields (from all possible samples) are less spread out than those of estimator B. A precise estimator will tend to give similar estimates for all possible samples.

Consider the two unbiased estimators found above: how do they compare on the criteria of precision? It turns out that the sample mean is the more precise of the two, and it is not difficult to understand why. Taking just a single sample observation means that it is quite likely to be unrepresentative of the population as a whole, and thus leads to a poor estimate of the population mean. The single observation might be an extreme value from the population, purely by chance. The sample mean, on the other hand, is based on all the sample observations, and it is unlikely that all of them are unrepresentative of the population. The sample mean is therefore a good estimator of the population mean, being more precise than the single observation estimator.

Just as bias was related to the expected value of the estimator, so precision can be defined in terms of the variance. One estimator is more precise than another if it has a smaller variance. Recall that the probability distribution of the sample mean is

$$\bar{x} \sim N(\mu, \sigma^2/n) \tag{7.2}$$

Figure 2.95
The sampling distributions
of two estimators

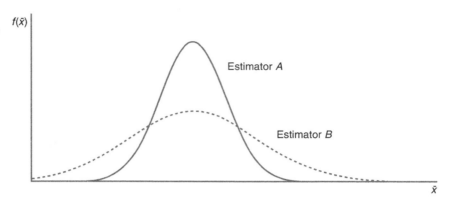

in large samples, so the variance of the sample mean is

$$V(\overline{x}) = \sigma^2/n$$

As the sample size n gets larger the variance of the sample mean becomes smaller, so the estimator becomes more precise. For this reason, large samples give better estimates than small samples, and so the sample mean is a better estimator than taking just one observation from the sample. The two estimators can be compared in a diagram (see Figure 2.95) which draws the probability distributions of the two estimators.

It is easily seen that Estimator A (the larger sample) yields estimates which are *on average* closer to the population mean.

Mean squared error

The two measures, bias and precision, can be combined in the **mean squared error** (MSE) of the estimate. This is defined, for an estimator θ, as

$$MSE = E((\hat{\theta} - \theta)^2)$$

where $\hat{\theta}$ is an estimate of θ. The larger the value of the MSE, the further the estimate is likely to be from the true value and hence the poorer the estimator. It can be shown the MSE is equal to the variance of the estimator plus the square of the bias:

$$MSE = variance + bias^2$$

The MSE therefore captures both variance and bias and estimators can be compared using this new concept. The estimator with the smaller MSE is considered superior.

Most of the estimators covered in this text turn out to be unbiased, so the MSE is then simply equal to the variance. A related concept using the variance is that of **efficiency**. The efficiency of one unbiased estimator, relative to another, is given by the ratio of their sampling variances[3]. Thus, the efficiency of the first observation estimator, relative to the sample mean, is given by

$$\text{Efficiency} = \frac{var(\overline{x})}{var(x_1)} = \frac{\sigma^2/n}{\sigma^2} = \frac{1}{n} \tag{7.3}$$

---

[3]For biased estimators we can take the ratio of their MSEs.

Thus the efficiency is determined by the relative sample sizes in this case. Other things being equal, a more efficient estimator is to be preferred.

Similarly, the variance of the median can be shown to be (for a Normal distribution) $\pi/2 \times \sigma^2/n$ in large samples. The efficiency of the median is therefore $2/\pi \approx 64\%$ (compared to using the sample mean) and so on this basis the sample mean is a preferred estimator.

The trade-off between bias and precision: the Bill Gates effect

It should be noted that just because an estimator is biased does not necessarily mean that it is imprecise. Sometimes there is a trade-off between an unbiased, but imprecise, estimator and a biased, but precise, one. Figure 2.96 illustrates this.

Although estimator A is biased (it is not centred around μ), it will nearly always yield an estimate which is fairly close to the true value; even though the estimate is expected to be wrong, it is not likely to be far wrong. Estimator B, although unbiased, can give estimates which are far away from the true value, so that A might be the preferred estimator.

As an example of this, suppose we are trying to estimate the average wealth of the US population. Consider the following two estimators:

(1) Use the mean wealth of a random sample of Americans.
(2) Use the mean wealth of a random sample of Americans but, if Bill Gates is in the sample, omit him from the calculation.

Bill Gates, the former Chairman of Microsoft, is one of the world's richest men. He is a dollar billionaire (about $50bn or more according to recent reports – it varies with the stock market). His presence in a sample of, say, 30 observations would swamp the sample and give a highly misleading result. Assuming Bill Gates has $50bn and the others each have $200 000 of wealth, the average wealth would be estimated at about $1.6bn, which is surely wrong.

The first rule could therefore give us a wildly incorrect answer, although the rule is unbiased. The second rule is clearly biased but does rule out the possibility of such an unlucky sample. We can work out the approximate bias. It is the difference between the average wealth of all Americans and the average wealth of all

Figure 2.96
The trade-off between bias and precision

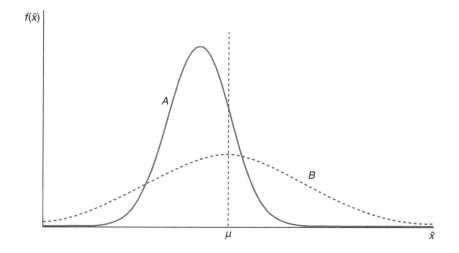

Americans except Bill Gates. If the true average of all 250 million Americans is $200000, then total wealth is $50000bn. Subtracting Bill's $50bn leaves $49 950bn shared amongst the rest, giving $199 800 each, a difference of 0.1%. This is what we would expect the bias to be.

It might seem worthwhile, therefore, to accept this degree of bias in order to improve the precision of the estimate. Furthermore, if we did use the biased rule, we could adjust the sample mean upwards by 0.1% or so to compensate (if only approximately).

Of course, this point applies to any exceptionally rich person, not just Bill Gates. It points to the need to ensure that the rich are not over- (nor under-) represented in the sample. In the rest of this text only unbiased estimators are considered, the most important being the sample mean.

Estimation with large samples

For the type of problem encountered in this chapter, the method of estimation differs according to the size of the sample. 'Large' samples, by which is meant sample sizes of 25 or more, are dealt with first, using the Normal distribution. Small samples are considered in a later section, where the t distribution is used instead of the Normal. The differences are relatively minor in practical terms and there is a close theoretical relationship between the t and Normal distributions.

With large samples there are three types of estimation problem we will consider.

(1) The estimation of a mean from a sample of data.
(2) The estimation of a proportion on the basis of sample evidence. This would consider a problem such as estimating the proportion of the population intending to buy an iPhone, based on a sample of individuals. Each person in the sample would simply indicate whether they have bought, or intend to buy, an iPhone. The principles of estimation are the same as in the first case but the formulae used for calculation are slightly different.
(3) The estimation of the difference of two means (or proportions), for example, a problem such as estimating the difference between men's and women's expenditure on clothes. Once again, the principles are the same, the formulae different.

Estimating a mean

To demonstrate the principles and practice of estimating the population mean, we shall take the example of estimating the average wealth of the UK population, the full data for which were given in Chapter 1. Suppose that we did not have this information but were required to estimate the average wealth from a sample of data. In particular, let us suppose that the sample size is $n = 100$, the sample mean is $\bar{x} = 180$ (in £000) and the sample variance is $s^2 = 75\,000$. Evidently, this sample has got fairly close to the true values (see Chapter 1), but we could not know that from the sample alone. What can we infer about the population mean μ from the sample data alone?

For the point estimate of μ the sample mean is a good candidate since it is unbiased, and it is generally more precise than other sample statistics such as the median. The point estimate of μ is simply £180 000, therefore.

The point estimate does not give an idea of the uncertainty associated with the estimate. We are not *absolutely* sure that the mean is £180 000 (in fact, it is not – it is £186 875). The interval estimate in contrast gives some idea of the uncertainty. It is centred on the sample mean, but gives a range of values to express the uncertainty.

To obtain the interval estimate we first require the probability distribution of $\bar{x}$

$$\bar{x} \sim N(\mu, \sigma^2/n) \tag{7.4}$$

From this, it was calculated that there is a 95% probability of the sample mean lying within 1.96 standard errors of μ[4], i.e.

$$\Pr(\mu - 1.96\sqrt{\sigma^2/n} \le \bar{x} \le \mu + 1.96\sqrt{\sigma^2/n}) = 0.95$$

We can manipulate each of the inequalities within the brackets to make μ the subject of the expression:

$$\mu - 1.96\sqrt{\sigma^2/n} \le \bar{x} \quad \text{implies} \quad \mu \le \bar{x} + 1.96\sqrt{\sigma^2/n}$$

Similarly

$$\bar{x} \le \mu + 1.96\sqrt{\sigma^2/n} \quad \text{implies} \quad \bar{x} - 1.96\sqrt{\sigma^2/n} \le \mu$$

Combining these two new expressions, we obtain

$$[\bar{x} - 1.96\sqrt{\sigma^2/n} \le \mu \le \bar{x} + 1.96\sqrt{\sigma^2/n}] \tag{7.5}$$

We have transformed the probability interval. Instead of saying $\bar{x}$ lies within 1.96 standard errors of μ, we now say μ lies within 1.96 standard errors of $\bar{x}$. Figure 2.97 illustrates this manipulation. Figure 2.97(a) shows μ at the centre of a probability interval for $\bar{x}$. Figure 2.97(b) shows a sample mean $\bar{x}$ at the centre of an interval relating to the possible positions of μ.

The interval shown in equation (7.5) is called the **95% confidence interval**, and this is the interval estimate for μ. In this formula the value of σ^2 is unknown, but in large ($n \ge 25$) samples it can be replaced by s^2 from the sample. s^2 is here used as an estimate of σ^2 which is unbiased and sufficiently precise in large ($n \ge 25$ or so) samples. The 95% confidence interval is therefore

$$[\bar{x} - 1.96\sqrt{s^2/n} \le \mu \le \bar{x} + 1.96\sqrt{s^2/n}] \tag{7.6}$$
$$= [180 - 1.96\sqrt{75\,000/100}, 180 + 1.96\sqrt{75\,000/100}]$$
$$= [126.3, 233.7]$$

Thus the 95% confidence interval estimate for the true average level of wealth ranges between £126 300 and £233 700. Note that £180 000 lies exactly at the centre of the interval[5] (because of the symmetry of the Normal distribution).

---

[4]Remember that ±1.96 is the z score which cuts off 2.5% in each tail of the Normal distribution.

[5]The two values are the lower and upper limits of the interval, separated by a comma. This is the standard way of writing a confidence interval.

Figure 2.97(a)
The 95% probability
interval for $\bar{x}$ around the
population mean μ

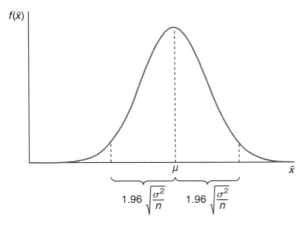

Figure 2.97(b)
The 95% confidence
interval for μ around the
sample mean $\bar{x}$

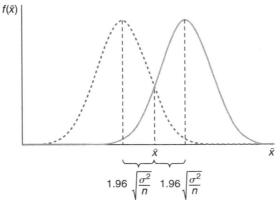

A more compact way of writing the confidence interval for μ, instead of equation (7.6), is

$$\bar{x} \pm 1.96\sqrt{s^2/n} \tag{7.6b}$$

which highlights the interval lying between the sample mean plus and minus 1.96 standard errors. This is easy to remember and can be used for different types of problem, as we show below.

By examining equation (7.6) or equation (7.6b), one can see that the confidence interval is wider

(1) the smaller the sample size,
(2) the greater the standard deviation of the sample.

The greater uncertainty which is associated with smaller sample sizes is manifested in a wider confidence interval estimate of the population mean. This occurs because a smaller sample has more chance of being unrepresentative (just because of an unlucky sample).

Greater variation in the sample data also leads to greater uncertainty about the population mean and a wider confidence interval. Greater sample variation suggests greater variation in the population so, again, a given sample could include observations which are a long way off the mean. Note that in this example there is great variation of wealth in the population and hence in the sample also. This means that a sample of 100 is not very informative (the confidence interval is quite wide). We would need a substantially larger sample to obtain a more precise estimate.

Note that the width of the confidence interval does *not* depend upon the population size – a sample of 100 observations reveals as much about a population of 10 000 as it does about a population of 10 000 000. In fact, this is not *quite* correct: if the sample were a large proportion of the population (of say 200 in this case), then the confidence interval should be narrower. However, in most cases this does not apply, and it is the sample size that really matters. This is a result that often surprises people, who generally believe that a larger sample is required if the population is larger.

Worked example 2.9

A sample of 50 school students found that they spent 45 minutes doing homework each evening, with a standard deviation of 15 minutes. Estimate the average time spent on homework by all students.

The sample data are $\bar{x} = 45$, $s = 15$ and $n = 50$. If we can assume the sample is representative, we may use $\bar{x}$ as an unbiased estimate of μ, the population mean. The point estimate is therefore 45 minutes.

The 95% confidence interval is given by equation (7.6b):

$$\bar{x} \pm 1.96\sqrt{s^2/n}$$
$$= 45 \pm 1.96\sqrt{15^2/50}$$
$$= 45 \pm 4.2 \text{ or } [40.8, 49.2]$$

The 95% confidence interval lies between 40.8 and 49.2 minutes. This might then be reasonably expressed as 'between 41 and 49 minutes'.

Exercise 2.23

(a) A sample of 100 is drawn from a population. The sample mean is 25 and the sample standard deviation is 50. Calculate the point and 95% confidence interval estimates for the population mean.

(b) If the sample size were 64, how would this alter the point and interval estimates?

Exercise 2.24

A sample of size 40 is drawn with sample mean 50 and standard deviation 30. Is it likely that the true population mean is 60?

Precisely what is a confidence interval?

There is often confusion over what a 95% confidence interval actually means. This is not really surprising since the obvious interpretation turns out to be wrong. It does *not* mean that there is a 95% chance that the true mean lies within the interval. We cannot make such a probability statement because of our definition of probability (based on the frequentist view of a probability). That view states that one can make a probability statement about a random variable (such as $\bar{x}$) but not about a parameter (such as μ). μ either lies within the interval or it does not – it cannot lie 95% within it. Unfortunately, we just do not know what the truth is.

It is for this reason that we use the term 'confidence interval' rather than 'probability interval'. Unfortunately, words are not as precise as numbers or algebra, and so most people fail to recognise the distinction. A precise explanation of the 95% confidence interval runs as follows. If we took many samples (all the same size) from a population with mean μ and calculated a confidence interval from each sample, we would find that μ lies within 95% of the calculated intervals. Of course, in practice we do not take many samples, usually just one. We do not know (and cannot know) if our one sample is one of the 95% or one of the 5% that miss the mean.

Figure 2.98 illustrates the point. It shows 95% confidence intervals calculated from 20 samples drawn from a population with a mean of 5. As expected, we see that 19 of these intervals contain the true mean, while the interval calculated from sample 9 does not contain the true value. This is the expected result, but is not guaranteed. You might obtain all 20 intervals containing the true mean, or fewer than 19. In the long run (with lots of estimates), we would expect 95% of the calculated intervals to contain the true mean.

A second question is, why use a probability (and hence a confidence level) of 95%? In fact, one can choose any confidence level, and thus confidence interval. The 90% confidence interval can be obtained by finding the z score which cuts off the outer 10% of the Normal distribution (5% in each tail). As $z = 1.64$, so the 90% confidence interval is given by the sample mean plus and minus 1.64 standard errors:

$$\bar{x} \pm 1.64\sqrt{s^2/n} \qquad (7.7)$$
$$= 180 \pm 1.64\sqrt{75\,000/100}$$
$$= 180 \pm 44.9 \text{ or } [135.1, 224.9]$$

Figure 2.98
Confidence intervals calculated from 20 samples

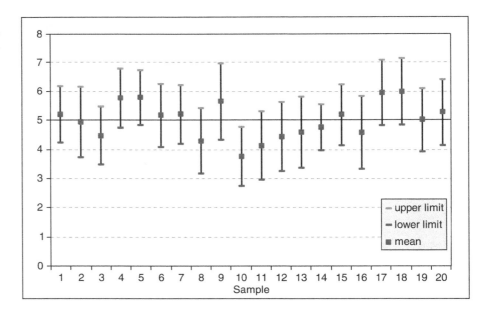

Notice that this is narrower than the 95% confidence level. The greater the degree of confidence desired, the wider the interval has to be. Any confidence level may be chosen, and by careful choice of this level the confidence interval can be made as wide or as narrow as wished. This would seem to undermine the purpose of calculating the confidence interval, which is to obtain some idea of the uncertainty attached to the estimate. This is not the case, however, because the reader of the results can interpret them appropriately, as long as the confidence level is made clear. To simplify matters, the 95% and 99% confidence levels are the most commonly used and serve as conventions. Beware of the researcher who calculates the 76% confidence interval – this may have been chosen in order to obtain the desired answer rather than in the spirit of scientific enquiry. The general formula for the $(100 - \alpha)\%$ confidence interval is

$$\bar{x} \pm z_\alpha \sqrt{s^2/n} \tag{7.8}$$

where z_α is the z score which cuts off the extreme $\alpha\%$ (in both tails, hence $\alpha/2$ in each tail) of the Normal distribution.

Exercise 2.25 will test your understanding of what a confidence interval really is.

Exercise 2.25

A study finds that the 95% confidence interval estimate for the mean of a population ranges from 0.1 to 0.4. Which of the following statements are true and which false?

(a) The probability that the true mean is greater than 0 is at least 95%.

(b) The probability that the true mean is 0 is less than 5%.

(c) The hypothesis that the true mean is 0 is unlikely to be correct.

(d) There is a 95% probability that the true mean lies between 0.1 and 0.4.

(e) We can be 95% confident that the true mean lies between 0.1 and 0.4.

(f) If we were to repeat the experiment many times, then 95% of the time the true mean lies between 0.1 and 0.4.

Estimating a proportion

It is often the case that we wish to estimate the proportion of the population that has a particular characteristic (e.g. is unemployed), rather than wanting an average. Given what we have already learned, this is fairly straightforward and is based on similar principles. Suppose that, following Chapter 1, we wish to estimate the proportion of educated people who are unemployed. We have a random sample of 200 individuals, of whom 15 are unemployed. What can we infer?

The sample data are:

$n = 200$, and
$p = 0.075 (= 15/200)$

where p is the (sample) proportion unemployed, 7.5% in this case. We denote the population proportion by the Greek letter π and it is this that we are trying to estimate using data from the sample.

The key to solving this problem is recognising p as a random variable just like the sample mean. This is because its value depends upon the sample drawn and will vary from sample to sample. Once the probability distribution of this random variable is established, the problem is quite easy to solve, using the same methods as were used for the mean. The sampling distribution of p is

$$p \sim N\left(\pi, \frac{\pi(1 - \pi)}{n}\right) \tag{7.9}$$

This tells us that the sample proportion is centred on the true value but will vary around it, varying from sample to sample. This variation is expressed by the variance of p, whose formula is $\pi(1 - \pi)/n$. Having derived the probability distribution of p, we can use the same methods of estimation as for the sample mean. Since the expected value of p is π, the sample proportion is an unbiased estimate of the population parameter. The point estimate of π is simply p, therefore. Thus, it is estimated that 7.5% of all educated people are unemployed.

Given the sampling distribution for p in equation (7.9), the formula for the 95% confidence interval for π can immediately be written down as:

$$p \pm 1.96\sqrt{\frac{\pi(1 - \pi)}{n}} \tag{7.10}$$

or alternatively

$$\left[p - 1.96\sqrt{\frac{\pi(1 - \pi)}{n}}, p + 1.96\sqrt{\frac{\pi(1 - \pi)}{n}}\right]$$

As usual, the 95% confidence interval limits are given by the point estimate plus and minus 1.96 standard errors.

Since the value of π is unknown, the confidence interval cannot yet be calculated, so the sample value of 0.075 has to be used instead of the unknown π. Like the substitution of s^2 for σ^2 in the case of the sample mean above, this is acceptable in large samples. Thus, the 95% confidence interval becomes

$$0.075 \pm 1.96\sqrt{\frac{0.075(1 - 0.075)}{200}} \tag{7.11}$$
$$= 0.075 \pm 0.037$$
$$= [0.038, 0.112]$$

We say that the 95% confidence interval estimate for the true proportion of unemployed people lies between 3.8% and 11.2%.

It can be seen that these two cases apply a common method. The 95% confidence interval is given by the point estimate plus or minus 1.96 standard errors. For a different confidence level, 1.96 would be replaced by the appropriate value from the standard Normal distribution.

With this knowledge, two further cases can be swiftly dealt with.

Worked example 2.10 Music down the phone

Do you get angry when you try to phone an organisation and you get an automated reply followed by music while you hang on? Well, you are not alone. Mintel (a consumer survey company) asked 1946 adults what they thought of music played to them while they were trying to get through on the phone; 36% reported feeling angered by the music played to them and more than one in four were annoyed by the automated voice response.

With these data we can calculate a confidence interval for the true proportion of people who dislike the music. First, we assume that the sample is a truly random one. This is probably not strictly true, so our calculated confidence interval will only be an approximate one. With $p = 0.36$ and $n = 1946$ we obtain the following 95% interval:

$$p \pm 1.96 \times \sqrt{\frac{p(1-p)}{n}} = 0.36 \pm 1.96 \times \sqrt{\frac{0.36(1-0.36)}{1946}}$$

$$= 0.36 \pm 0.021 = [0.339, 0.381]$$

Mintel further estimated that 2800 million calls were made by customers to call centres per year, so we can be (approximately) 95% confident that between 949 million and 1067 million of those calls have an unhappy customer on the line.

Source: *The Times*, 10 July 2000.

Estimating the difference between two means

We now move on to estimating differences. In this case we have two samples and want to know whether there is a difference between their respective populations. One sample might be of men, the other of women, or we could be comparing two different countries, etc. A point estimate of the difference is easy to obtain, but once again there is some uncertainty around this figure, because it is based on samples. Hence, we measure that uncertainty via a confidence interval. All we require are the appropriate formulae. Consider the following example.

Thirty-five pupils from school 1 scored an average mark of 70% in an exam, with a standard deviation of 12%; 60 pupils from school 2 scored an average of 62% with standard deviation 18%. Estimate the true difference between the two schools in the average mark obtained.

This is a more complicated problem than those previously treated since it involves two samples rather than one. An estimate has to be found for $\mu_1 - \mu_2$ (the true difference in the mean marks of the schools), in the form of both point and interval estimates. The pupils taking the exams may be thought of as samples of all pupils in the schools who could potentially take the exams.

Notice that this is a problem about sample means, not proportions, even though the question deals in percentages. The point is that each observation in the sample (i.e. each student's mark) can take a value between 0 and 100, and one can calculate the standard deviation of the marks. For this to be a problem of sample proportions, the mark for each pupil would each have to be of the pass/fail type, so that one could only calculate the proportion who passed.

One might think that the way to approach this problem is to derive one confidence interval for each sample (along the lines set out above), and then to somehow combine them; for example, the degree of overlap of the two confidence intervals could be assessed. This is not the best approach, however. It is sometimes a good strategy, when faced with an unfamiliar problem to solve, to translate it into a more familiar problem and then solve it using known methods. This procedure will be followed here. The essential point is to keep in mind the concept of a random variable and its probability distribution.

Problems involving a single random variable have already been dealt with above. The current problem deals with two samples and therefore there are two random variables to consider, i.e. the two sample means $\bar{x}_1$ and $\bar{x}_2$. Since the aim is to estimate $\mu_1 - \mu_2$, an obvious candidate for an estimator is the difference between the two sample means, $\bar{x}_1 - \bar{x}_2$. We can think of this as a single random variable (even though two means are involved) and use the methods we have already learned. We therefore need to establish the sampling distribution of $\bar{x}_1 - \bar{x}_2$.

$$\bar{x}_1 - \bar{x}_2 \sim N\left(\mu_1 - \mu_2, \frac{\sigma_1^2}{n_1} + \frac{\sigma_2^2}{n_2}\right) \tag{7.12}$$

This equation states that the difference in sample means will be centred on the difference in the two population means, with some variation around this as measured by the variance. One assumption behind the derivation of (7.12) is that the two samples are independently drawn. This is likely in this example; it is difficult to see how the samples from the two schools could be connected. However, one must always bear this possibility in mind when comparing samples. For example, if one were comparing men's and women's heights, it would be dangerous to take samples of men and their wives as they are unlikely to be independent. People tend to marry partners of a similar height to themselves, so this might bias the results.

The distribution of $\bar{x}_1 - \bar{x}_2$ is illustrated in Figure 2.99. Equation (7.12) shows that $\bar{x}_1 - \bar{x}_2$ is an unbiased estimator of $\mu_1 - \mu_2$. The difference between the sample means will therefore be used as the point estimate of $\mu_1 - \mu_2$. Thus, the point estimate of the true difference between the schools is

$$\bar{x}_1 - \bar{x}_2 = 70 - 62 = 8\%$$

The 95% confidence interval estimate is derived in the same manner as before, making use of the standard error of the random variable. The formula is[6]

$$(\bar{x}_1 - \bar{x}_2) \pm 1.96\sqrt{\frac{s_1^2}{n_1} + \frac{s_2^2}{n_2}} \tag{7.13}$$

Since the values of σ^2 are unknown, they have been replaced in equation (7.13) by their sample values. As in the single sample case, this is acceptable in large samples. The 95% confidence interval for $\mu_1 - \mu_2$ is therefore

$$(70 - 62) \pm 1.96\sqrt{\frac{12^2}{35} + \frac{18^2}{60}}$$
$$= [1.95, 14.05]$$

The estimate is that school 1's average mark is between 1.95 and 14.05 percentage points above that of school 2. Notice that the confidence interval does not include the value zero, which would imply possible equality of the two schools' marks. Equality of the two schools can thus be ruled out with 95% confidence.

---

[6]The term under the square root sign is the standard error for $\bar{x}_1 - \bar{x}_2$.

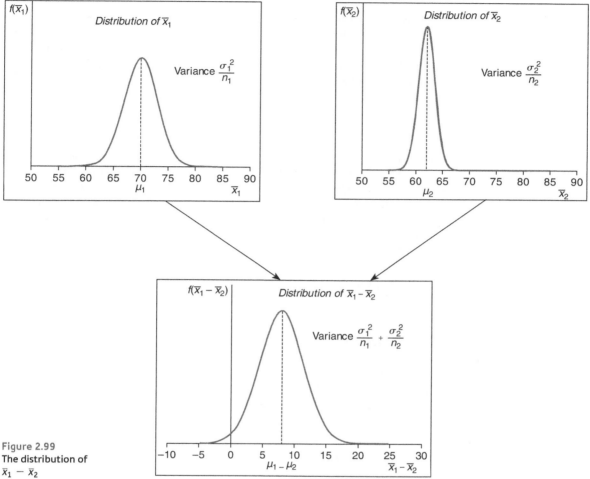

Figure 2.99
The distribution of
$\overline{x}_1 - \overline{x}_2$

Worked example 2.11

A survey of holidaymakers found that on average women spent 3 hours per day sunbathing, men spent 2 hours. The sample sizes were 36 in each case and the standard deviations were 1.1 and 1.2 hours, respectively. Estimate the true difference between men and women in sunbathing habits. Use the 99% confidence level.

The point estimate is simply one hour, the difference of sample means. For the confidence interval we have:

$$(\overline{x}_1 - \overline{x}_2) \pm 2.57 \sqrt{\frac{s_1^2}{n_1} + \frac{s_2^2}{n_2}}$$

$$= (3 - 2) \pm 2.57 \sqrt{\frac{1.1^2}{36} + \frac{1.2^2}{36}}$$

$$= 1 \pm 0.70 = [0.30, 1.70]$$

This evidence suggests women do spend more time sunbathing than men (zero is not in the confidence interval). Note that we might worry the samples might not be independent here – it could represent 36 couples. If so, the evidence is likely to underestimate the true difference, if anything, as couples are likely to spend time sunbathing together.

Estimating the difference between two proportions

We move again from means to proportions. We use a simple example to illustrate the analysis of this type of problem. Suppose we wish to compare the market share of Apple Mac computers in the United States and the United Kingdom. A survey of 1000 American computer users shows that 160 use Macs while a similar survey of 500 Britons shows 65 using Macs. What is our estimate of the true difference between the two countries?

Here the aim is to estimate $\pi_1 - \pi_2$, the difference between the two population proportions, so the probability distribution of $p_1 - p_2$ is needed, the difference of the sample proportions. The derivation of this follows similar lines to those set out above for the difference of two sample means, so is not repeated. The probability distribution is

$$p_1 - p_2 \sim N\left(\pi_1 - \pi_2, \frac{\pi_1(1 - \pi_1)}{n_1} + \frac{\pi_2(1 - \pi_2)}{n_2}\right) \tag{7.14}$$

Again, the two samples must be independently drawn for this to be correct.

Since the difference between the sample proportions is an unbiased estimate of the true difference, this will be used for the point estimate. The point estimate is therefore

$$p_1 - p_2 = 160/1000 - 65/500$$
$$= 0.16 - 0.13 = 0.03 \text{ or } 3\%.$$

Note that this means a three percentage point difference in market share, not that the US market is 3% bigger. The 95% confidence interval is given by

$$p_1 - p_2 \pm 1.96\sqrt{\frac{\pi_1(1 - \pi_1)}{n_1} + \frac{\pi_2(1 - \pi_2)}{n_2}} \tag{7.15}$$

π_1 and π_2 are unknown so have to be replaced by p_1 and p_2 for purposes of calculation, so the interval becomes

$$0.16 - 0.13 \pm 1.96\sqrt{\frac{0.16 \times 0.84}{1000} + \frac{0.13 \times 0.87}{500}} \tag{7.16}$$
$$= 0.03 \pm 0.0372$$
$$= [-0.0072, 0.0672]$$

The 95% confidence interval indicates that the US market share is between −0.7 and 6.7 percentage points larger than in the United Kingdom. Note that this interval includes the value of zero, so we cannot be 95% confident the US share is bigger.

These data are for the purpose of illustrating the methods and are not real. However, they are closely based on figures from StatCounter (http://gs.statcounter.com/)

and are collected automatically based on visitor statistics to 'more than three million web sites'. The market shares for December 2011 are reported as 16.5% and 13.3%. StatCounter does not give sample sizes, so what are we to make of these numbers?

The 'three million' might suggest a huge sample size and hence a much smaller confidence interval. (If there were one million in each country, then the width of the confidence interval would be ±0.0005.) However, there are likely to be many multiple visits by the same user, so the number of users (as opposed to visits) could be much smaller, we simply do not know. Furthermore, we should think whether there might be any kind of bias to the figures, for example if more US websites were dedicated to Apple customers.

Exercise 2.26

(a) Seven people out of a sample of 50 are left-handed. Estimate the true proportion of left-handed people in the population, finding both point and interval estimates.

(b) Repeat part (a) but find the 90% confidence interval. How does the 90% interval compare with the 95% interval?

(c) Calculate the 99% interval and compare to the others.

Exercise 2.27

Given the following data from two samples, estimate the true difference between the means. Use the 95% confidence level.

$$\bar{x}_1 = 25 \quad \bar{x}_2 = 30$$
$$s_1 = 18 \quad s_2 = 25$$
$$n_1 = 36 \quad n_2 = 49$$

Exercise 2.28

A survey of 50 16-year-old girls revealed that 40% had a boyfriend. A survey of 100 16-year-old boys revealed 20% with a girlfriend. Estimate the true difference in proportions between the sexes.

Estimation with small samples: the *t* distribution

So far only large samples (defined as sample sizes in excess of 25) have been dealt with, which means that (by the Central Limit Theorem) the sampling distribution of $\bar{x}$ follows a Normal distribution, whatever the distribution of the parent population. Remember that

- if the population follows a Normal distribution, $\bar{x}$ is also Normally distributed, and
- if the population is not Normally distributed, $\bar{x}$ is approximately Normally distributed in large samples ($n \geq 25$).

In both cases, confidence intervals can be constructed based on the fact that

$$\frac{\bar{x} - \mu}{\sqrt{\sigma^2/n}} \sim N(0, 1) \tag{7.17}$$

and so the standard Normal distribution is used to find the values which cut off the extreme 5% of the distribution ($z = \pm 1.96$). In practical examples, we had to replace σ by its estimate, s. Thus the confidence interval was based on the fact that

$$\frac{\bar{x} - \mu}{\sqrt{s^2/n}} \sim N(0, 1) \tag{7.18}$$

in large samples. For small sample sizes, equation (7.18) is no longer true. Instead, the relevant distribution is the t distribution, and we have[7]

$$\frac{\bar{x} - \mu}{\sqrt{s^2/n}} \sim t_{n-1} \tag{7.19}$$

The random variable defined in equation (7.19) has a t distribution with $n - 1$ degrees of freedom. As the sample size gets larger, the t distribution approaches the standard Normal, so the latter can be used for large samples.

The t distribution was derived by W.S. Gossett in 1908 while conducting tests on the average strength of Guinness beer (who says statistics has no impact on the real world?). He published his work under the pseudonym 'Student', since the company did not allow its employees to publish under their own names, so the distribution is sometimes also known as the Student distribution.

The t distribution is in many ways similar to the standard Normal, insofar as it is

- unimodal
- symmetric
- centred on zero
- bell-shaped
- extends from minus infinity to plus infinity.

The differences are that it is more spread out (has a larger variance) than the standard Normal distribution, and has only one parameter rather than two: the degrees of freedom, denoted by the Greek letter ν (pronounced 'nu'[8]). In problems involving the estimation of a sample mean, the degrees of freedom are given by the sample size minus one, i.e. $\nu = n - 1$.

The t distribution is drawn in Figure 2.100 for various values of the parameter ν. Note that the fewer the degrees of freedom (smaller sample size), the more dispersed is the distribution.

To summarise the argument so far, when

- the sample size is small, *and*
- the sample variance is used to estimate the population variance,

then the t distribution should be used for constructing confidence intervals, not the standard Normal. This results in a slightly wider interval than would be obtained using the standard Normal distribution, which reflects the slightly greater uncertainty involved when s^2 is used as an estimate of σ^2 when the sample size is small.

---

[7]We also require the assumption that the parent population is Normally distributed for (7.19) to be true.

[8]Once again, the Greeks pronounce this differently, as 'ni'. They also pronounce π 'pee' rather than 'pie' as in English. This makes statistics lectures in English hard for Greeks to understand.

Figure 2.100
The *t* distribution drawn
for different degrees of
freedom

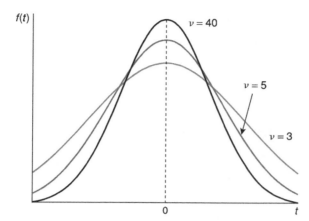

Apart from this, the methods are as before and are illustrated by the examples below. We look first at estimating a single mean, and then at estimating the difference of two means. The *t* distribution cannot be used for small sample proportions (explained below), so these cases are not considered.

Estimating a mean

The following example would seem to be appropriate. A sample of 15 bottles of beer showed an average specific gravity (a measure of alcohol content) of 1035.6, with standard deviation 2.7. Estimate the true specific gravity of the brew.
The sample information may be summarised as

$$\bar{x} = 1035.6$$
$$s = 2.7$$
$$n = 15$$

The sample mean is still an unbiased estimator of μ (this is true regardless of the distribution of the population) and serves as point estimate of μ. The point estimate of μ is therefore 1035.6.
Since σ is unknown, the sample size is small and it can be assumed that the specific gravity of all bottles of beer is Normally distributed (numerous small random factors affect the specific gravity), we should use the *t* distribution. Thus

$$\frac{\bar{x} - \mu}{\sqrt{s^2/n}} \sim t_{n-1} \tag{7.20}$$

The 95% confidence interval estimate is given by

$$\bar{x} \pm t_{n-1}\sqrt{s^2/n} \tag{7.21}$$

where t_{n-1} is the value of the *t* distribution which cuts off the extreme 5% (2.5% in each tail) of the *t* distribution with ν degrees of freedom.
The structure of the *t* distribution table is different from that of the standard Normal table. The first column of the table gives the degrees of freedom. In this example we want the row corresponding to $\nu = n - 1 = 14$. The appropriate

Table 2.40 Percentage points of the *t* distribution

ν	0.4	0.25	0.10	0.05	0.025	0.01	0.005
					Area in each tail		
1	0.325	1.000	3.078	6.314	12.706	31.821	63.656
2	0.289	0.816	1.886	2.920	4.303	6.965	9.925
⋮	⋮	⋮	⋮	⋮	⋮	⋮	⋮
13	0.259	0.694	1.350	1.771	2.160	2.650	3.012
14	0.258	0.692	1.345	1.761	2.145	2.624	2.977
15	0.258	0.691	1.341	1.753	2.131	2.602	2.947

Note: The appropriate *t* value for constructing the confidence interval is found at the intersection of the shaded row and column.

column of the table is the one headed '0.025' which indicates the area cut off in *each* tail. At the intersection of this row and column we find the appropriate value, $t_{14} = 2.145$. Therefore, the confidence interval is given by

$$1035.6 \pm 2.145\sqrt{2.7^2/15}$$
$$= 1035.6 \pm 1.5$$
$$= [1034.10, 1037.10]$$

We are 95% confident that the true specific gravity lies within this range. If the Normal distribution had (incorrectly) been used for this problem, then the *t* value of 2.145 would have been replaced by a *z* score of 1.96, giving a confidence interval of

$$[1034.23, 1036.97]$$

This underestimates the true confidence interval and gives the impression of a more precise estimate than is actually the case. Use of the Normal distribution leads to a confidence interval which is about 9% too narrow in this case.

Estimating the difference between two means

As in the case of a single mean, the *t* distribution needs to be used in small samples when the population variances are unknown. Again, both parent populations must be Normally distributed, and in addition it must be assumed that the population variances are equal, i.e. $\sigma_1^2 = \sigma_2^2$ (this is required in the mathematical derivation of the *t* distribution). This latter assumption was not required in the large-sample case using the Normal distribution. Consider the following example as an illustration of the method.

A sample of 20 Labour-controlled local authorities shows that they spend an average of £175 per taxpayer on administration with a standard deviation of £25. A similar survey of 15 Conservative-controlled authorities finds an average figure of £158 with standard deviation of £30. Estimate the true difference in expenditure between Labour and Conservative authorities.

The sample information available is

$$\bar{x}_1 = 175 \quad \bar{x}_2 = 158$$
$$s_1 = 25 \quad s_2 = 30$$
$$n_1 = 20 \quad n_2 = 15$$

We wish to estimate $\mu_1 - \mu_2$. The point estimate of this is $\bar{x}_1 - \bar{x}_2$ which is an unbiased estimate. This gives $175 - 158 = 17$ as the expected difference between the two sets of authorities.

For the confidence interval, the t distribution has to be used since the sample sizes are small and the population variances unknown. It is assumed that the populations are Normally distributed and that the samples have been independently drawn. We also assume that the population variances are equal, which seems justified since s_1 and s_2 do not differ by much. The confidence interval is given by the formula:

$$(\bar{x}_1 - \bar{x}_2) \pm t_\nu \sqrt{\frac{S^2}{n_1} + \frac{S^2}{n_2}} \tag{7.22}$$

where

$$S^2 = \frac{(n_1 - 1)s_1^2 + (n_2 - 1)s_2^2}{n_1 + n_2 - 2} \tag{7.23}$$

is known as the pooled variance and

$$\nu = n_1 + n_2 - 2$$

gives the degrees of freedom associated with the t distribution.

S^2 is an estimate of (common value of) the population variances. It would be inappropriate to have the differing values s_1^2 and s_2^2 in the formula for this t distribution, for this would be contrary to the assumption that $\sigma_1^2 = \sigma_2^2$, which is essential for the use of the t distribution. The estimate of the common population variance is just the weighted average of the sample variances, using degrees of freedom as weights. Each sample has $n - 1$ degrees of freedom, and the total number of degrees of freedom for the problem is the sum of the degrees of freedom in each sample. The degrees of freedom are thus $20 + 15 - 2 = 33$ and hence the value $t = 2.042$ cuts off the extreme 5% of the distribution. The t table in the appendix does not give the value for $\nu = 33$ so instead we used $\nu = 30$ which will give a close approximation.

To evaluate the 95% confidence interval, we first calculate S^2:

$$S^2 = \frac{(20 - 1) \times 25^2 + (15 - 1) \times 30^2}{20 + 15 - 2} = 741.6$$

Inserting this into equation (7.22) gives

$$17 \pm 2.042\sqrt{\frac{741.6}{20} + \frac{741.6}{15}} = [-1.99, 35.99]$$

Thus the true difference is quite uncertain and the evidence is even consistent with Conservative authorities spending more than Labour authorities. The large degree of uncertainty arises because of the small sample sizes and the quite wide variation within each sample.

One should be careful about the conclusions drawn from this test. The greater expenditure on administration could be either because of inefficiency or because of a higher level of services provided. To find out which is the case would require further investigation. The statistical test carried out here examines the levels of expenditure, but not whether they are productive or not.

 Estimating proportions

Estimating proportions when the sample size is small cannot be done with the t distribution. Recall that the distribution of the sample proportion p was derived from the distribution of r (the number of successes in n trials), which followed a Binomial distribution. In large samples the distribution of r is approximately Normal, thus giving a Normally distributed sample proportion. In small samples it is inappropriate to approximate the Binomial distribution with the t distribution, and indeed is unnecessary since the Binomial itself can be used. Small-sample methods for the sample proportion should be based on the Binomial distribution. These methods are not discussed further here, therefore.

Exercise 2.29

A sample of size $n = 16$ is drawn from a population which is known to be Normally distributed. The sample mean and variance are calculated as 74 and 121. Find the 99% confidence interval estimate for the true mean.

Exercise 2.30

Samples are drawn from two populations to see if they share a common mean. The sample data are:

$$\bar{x}_1 = 45 \quad \bar{x}_2 = 55$$
$$s_1 = 18 \quad s_2 = 21$$
$$n_1 = 15 \quad n_2 = 20$$

Find the 95% confidence interval estimate of the difference between the two population means.

Summary

- Estimation is the process of using sample information to make good estimates of the value of population parameters, e.g. using the sample mean to estimate the mean of a population.

- There are several criteria for finding a good estimate. Two important ones are the (lack of) bias and precision of the estimator. Sometimes there is a trade-off between these two criteria – one estimator might have a smaller bias but be less precise than another.

- An estimator is unbiased if it gives a correct estimate of the true value on average. Its expected value is equal to the true value.

- The precision of an estimator can be measured by its sampling variance (e.g. s^2/n for the mean of a sample).

- Estimates can be in the form of a single value (point estimate) or a range of values (confidence interval estimate). A confidence interval estimate gives some idea of how reliable the estimate is likely to be.

- For unbiased estimators, the value of the sample statistic (e.g. $\bar{x}$) is used as the point estimate.

- In large samples the 95% confidence interval is <u>given</u> by the point estimate plus or minus 1.96 standard errors (e.g. $\bar{x} \pm 1.96\sqrt{s^2/n}$ for the mean).
- For small samples the t distribution should be used instead of the Normal (i.e. replace 1.96 by the critical value of the t distribution) to construct confidence intervals of the mean.

Key terms and concepts

95% confidence interval	interval estimate
bias	mean squared error
confidence interval	point estimate
confidence level	pooled variance
degrees of freedom	precision
efficiency	proportion
estimation	testing hypothesis
estimator	unbiased
inference	

Formulae used in this chapter

Formula	Description	Notes
$\bar{x} \pm 1.96\sqrt{s^2/n}$	95% confidence interval for the mean	Large samples, using Normal distribution
$\bar{x} \pm t_\nu\sqrt{s^2/n}$	95% confidence interval for the mean	Small samples, using t distribution. t_ν is the critical value of the t distribution for $\nu = n - 1$ degrees of freedom
$p \pm 1.96\sqrt{\dfrac{p(1-p)}{n}}$	95% confidence interval for a proportion	Large samples only
$(\bar{x}_1 - \bar{x}_2) \pm 1.96\sqrt{\dfrac{s_1^2}{n_1} + \dfrac{s_2^2}{n_2}}$	95% confidence interval for the difference of two means	Large samples
$(\bar{x}_1 - \bar{x}_2) \pm t_\nu\sqrt{\dfrac{s^2}{n_1} + \dfrac{s^2}{n_2}}$	95% confidence interval for the difference of two means	Small samples. The pooled variance is given by $s^2 = \dfrac{((n_1-1)s_1^2 + (n_2-1)s_2^2)}{n_1 + n_2 - 2}, \nu = n_1 + n_2 - 2.$

Problems

Some of the more challenging problems are indicated by highlighting the problem number in colour.

2.7.1 (a) Why is an interval estimate better than a point estimate?

(b) What factors determine the width of a confidence interval?

2.7.2 Is the 95% confidence interval (a) twice as wide, (b) more than twice as wide and (c) less than twice as wide, as the 47.5% interval? Explain your reasoning.

2.7.3 Explain the difference between an estimate and an estimator. Is it true that a good estimator always leads to a good estimate?

2.7.4 Explain why an unbiased estimator is not always to be preferred to a biased one.

2.7.5 A random sample of two observations, x_1 and x_2, is drawn from a population. Prove that $w_1x_1 + w_2x_2$ gives an unbiased estimate of the population mean as long as $w_1 + w_2 = 1$. (Hint: Prove that $E(w_1x_1 + w_2x_2) = \mu$.)

2.7.6 Following the previous question, prove that the most precise unbiased estimate is obtained by setting $w_1 = w_2 = \frac{1}{2}$. (Hint: Minimise $V(w_1x_1 + w_2x_2)$ with respect to w_1 after substituting $w_2 = 1 - w_1$. You will need a knowledge of calculus to solve this.)

2.7.7 Given the sample data

$$\bar{x} = 40 \quad s = 10 \quad n = 36$$

calculate the 99% confidence interval estimate of the true mean. If the sample size were 20, how would the method of calculation and width of the interval be altered?

2.7.8　(a)　A random sample of 100 record shops found that the average weekly sale of a particular CD was 260 copies, with standard deviation of 96. Find the 95% confidence interval to estimate the true average sale for all shops.

(b)　To compile the CD chart it is necessary to know the correct average weekly sale to within 5% of its true value. How large a sample size is required?

2.7.9　Given the sample data $p = 0.4$, $n = 50$, calculate the 99% confidence interval estimate of the true proportion.

2.7.10　A political opinion poll questions 1000 people. Some 464 declare they will vote Conservative. Find the 95% confidence interval estimate for the Conservative share of the vote.

2.7.11　Given the sample data

$$\bar{x}_1 = 25 \quad \bar{x}_2 = 22$$
$$s_1 = 12 \quad s_2 = 18$$
$$n_1 = 80 \quad n_2 = 100$$

estimate the true difference between the means with 95% confidence.

2.7.12　(a)　A sample of 200 women from the labour force found an average wage of £26 000 p.a. with standard deviation £3500. A sample of 100 men found an average wage of £28 000 with standard deviation £2500. Estimate the true difference in wages between men and women.

(b)　A different survey, of men and women doing similar jobs, obtained the following results:

$$\bar{x}_W = £27\,200 \quad \bar{x}_M = £27\,600$$
$$s_W = £2225 \quad s_M = £1750$$
$$n_W = 75 \quad n_M = 50$$

Estimate the difference between male and female wages using these new data. What can be concluded from the results of the two surveys?

2.7.13　Sixty-seven percent out of 150 pupils from school A passed an exam; 62% of 120 pupils at school B passed. Estimate the 99% confidence interval for the true difference between the proportions passing the exam.

2.7.14　(a)　A sample of 954 adults in early 1987 found that 23% of them held shares. Given a UK adult population of 41 million and assuming a proper random sample was taken, find the 95% confidence interval estimate for the number of shareholders in the United Kingdom.

(b)　A 'similar' survey the previous year had found a total of 7 million shareholders. Assuming 'similar' means the same sample size, find the 95% confidence interval estimate of the increase in shareholders between the two years.

2.7.15　A sample of 16 observations from a Normally distributed population yields a sample mean of 30 with standard deviation 5. Find the 95% confidence interval estimate of the population mean.

2.7.16　A sample of 12 families in a town reveals an average income of £25 000 with standard deviation £6000. Why might you be hesitant about constructing a 95% confidence interval for the average income in the town?

2.7.17 Two samples were drawn, each from a Normally distributed population, with the following results:

$$\bar{x}_1 = 45 \quad s_1 = 8 \quad n_1 = 12$$
$$\bar{x}_2 = 52 \quad s_2 = 5 \quad n_2 = 18$$

Estimate the difference between the population means, using the 95% confidence level.

2.7.18 The heights of 10 men and 15 women were recorded, with the following results:

	Mean	Variance
Men	173.5	80
Women	162	65

Estimate the true difference between men's and women's heights. Use the 95% confidence level.

2.7.19 **(Project)** Estimate the average weekly expenditure upon alcohol by students. Ask a (reasonably) random sample of your fellow students for their weekly expenditure on alcohol. From this, calculate the 95% confidence interval estimate of such spending by all students.

2.8 Hypothesis testing

Learning outcomes

By the end of this chapter you should be able to:

● understand the philosophy and scientific principles underlying hypothesis testing

● appreciate that hypothesis testing is about deciding whether a hypothesis is true or false on the basis of a sample of data

● recognise the type of evidence which leads to a decision that the hypothesis is false

● carry out hypothesis tests for a variety of statistical problems

● recognise the relationship between hypothesis testing and a confidence interval

● recognise the shortcomings of hypothesis testing.

Introduction

This chapter deals with issues very similar to those of the previous chapter on estimation, but examines them in a different way. The estimation of population parameters and the testing of hypotheses about those parameters are similar techniques (indeed they are formally equivalent in a number of respects), but there are important differences in the interpretation of the results arising from each method. The process of estimation is appropriate when measurement is involved, such as measuring the true average expenditure on food; hypothesis testing is relevant when decision-making is involved, such as whether to accept that a supplier's products are up to a specified standard. Hypothesis testing is also used to make decisions about the truth or otherwise of different theories, such as whether rising prices are caused by rising wages; and it is here that the issues become contentious. It is sometimes difficult to interpret correctly the results of hypothesis tests in these circumstances. This is discussed further later in this chapter.

The concepts of hypothesis testing

In many ways hypothesis testing is analogous to a criminal trial. In a trial there is a defendant who is *initially presumed innocent*. The *evidence* against the defendant is then presented and, if the jury finds this convincing *beyond all reasonable doubt*, he or she is found guilty; the presumption of innocence is overturned. Of course, mistakes are sometimes made: an innocent person is convicted or a guilty person set free. Both of these errors involve costs (not only in the monetary sense), either to the defendant or to society in general, and the errors should be avoided if at all possible. The laws under which the trial is held may help avoid such errors. The rule that the jury must be convinced 'beyond all reasonable doubt' helps to avoid convicting the innocent, for instance.

The situation in hypothesis testing is similar. First, there is a maintained or null hypothesis which is initially *presumed* to be true. The empirical evidence, usually data from a random sample, is then gathered and assessed. If the evidence seems inconsistent with the null hypothesis, i.e. it has a low probability of occurring *if* the hypothesis were true, then the null hypothesis is *rejected* in favour of an alternative. Once again, there are two types of error one can make, either rejecting the null hypothesis when it is really true, or not rejecting it when in fact it is false. Ideally one would like to avoid both types of error.

An example helps to clarify the issues and the analogy. Suppose that you are thinking of taking over a small business franchise. The current owner claims the weekly turnover of each existing franchise averages £5000 and at this level you are willing to take on a franchise. You would be more cautious if the turnover is less than this figure. You examine the books of 26 franchises chosen at random and find that the average turnover was £4900 with standard deviation £280. What do you do?

The null hypothesis in this case is that average weekly turnover is £5000 (or more; that would be even more to your advantage). The alternative hypothesis is that turnover is strictly less than £5000 per week. We may write these more succinctly as follows:

$$H_0: \mu = 5000$$
$$H_1: \mu < 5000$$

H_0 is conventionally used to denote the null hypothesis, H_1 the alternative. Initially, H_0 is presumed to be true and this presumption will be tested using the sample evidence. Note that the sample evidence is *not* used in forming the null or alternative hypotheses.

You have to decide whether the owner's claim is correct (H_0) or not (H_1). The two types of error you could make are as follows:

● **Type I error** – reject H_0 when it is in fact true. This would mean missing a good business opportunity.
● **Type II error** – not rejecting H_0 when it is in fact false. You would go ahead and buy the business and then find out that it is not as attractive as claimed. You would have overpaid for the business.

The situation is set out in Figure 2.101.

Obviously a good decision rule would give a good chance of making a correct decision and rule out errors as far as possible. Unfortunately, it is impossible to completely eliminate the possibility of errors. As the decision rule is changed to reduce the probability of a Type I error, the probability of making a Type II error inevitably increases. The skill comes in balancing these two types of error.

Again a diagram is useful in illustrating this. Assuming that the null hypothesis is true, then the sample observations are drawn from a population with mean 5000 and some variance, which we shall assume is accurately measured by the sample variance. The distribution of $\bar{x}$ is then given by

$$\bar{x} \sim N(\mu, \sigma^2/n) \text{ or} \tag{8.1}$$
$$\bar{x} \sim N(5000, 280^2/26)$$

Under the alternative hypothesis the distribution of $\bar{x}$ would be the same except that it would be centred on a value less than 5000. These two situations are illustrated in Figure 2.102. The distribution of $\bar{x}$ under H_1 is shown by a dashed curve to signify that its exact position is unknown, only that it lies to the left of the distribution under H_0.

A **decision rule** amounts to choosing a point or dividing line on the horizontal axis in Figure 2.102. If the sample mean lies to the left of this point, then H_0 is rejected (the sample mean is too far away from H_0 for it to be credible) in favour of H_1 and you do not buy the franchise. If $\bar{x}$ lies above this decision point, then H_0 is not rejected and you go ahead with the purchase. Such a decision point is shown

Figure 2.101
The two different types of error

		True situation	
		H_0 true	H_0 false
Decision	Accept H_0	Correct decision	Type II error
	Reject H_0	Type I error	Correct decision

Figure 2.102
The sampling distributions
of $\bar{x}$ under H_0 and H_1

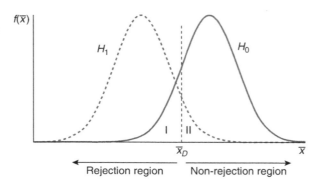

in Figure 2.102, denoted by $\bar{x}_D$. To the left of $\bar{x}_D$ lies the rejection (of H_0) region; to the right lies the non-rejection region.

Based on this point, we can see the probabilities of Type I and Type II errors. The area under the H_0 distribution to the left of $\bar{x}_D$, labelled I, shows the probability of rejecting H_0 given that it is in fact true: a Type I error. The area under the H_1 distribution to the right of $\bar{x}_D$, labelled II, shows the probability of a Type II error: not rejecting H_0 when it is in fact false (and H_1 is true).

Shifting the decision line to the right or left alters the balance of these probabilities. Moving the line to the right increases the probability of a Type I error but reduces the probability of a Type II error. Moving the line to the left has the opposite effect.

The Type I error probability can be calculated for any value of $\bar{x}_D$. Suppose we set $\bar{x}_D$ to a value of 4950. Using the distribution of $\bar{x}$ given in equation (8.1), the area under the distribution to the left of 4950 is obtained using the z score:

$$z = \frac{\bar{x}_D - \mu}{\sqrt{s^2/n}} = \frac{4950 - 5000}{\sqrt{280^2/26}} = -0.91 \tag{8.2}$$

From the tables of the standard Normal distribution we find that the probability of a Type I error is 18.1%. Unfortunately, the Type II error probability cannot be established because the exact position of the distribution under H_1 is unknown. Therefore, we cannot decide on the appropriate position of $\bar{x}_D$ by some balance of the two error probabilities.

The convention therefore is to set the position of $\bar{x}_D$ by using a Type I error probability of 5%, known as the significance level[1] of the test. In other words, we are prepared to accept a 5% probability of rejecting H_0 when it is, in fact, true. This allows us to establish the position of $\bar{x}_D$. We find that $z = -1.64$ cuts off the bottom 5% of the distribution, so the decision line should be 1.64 standard errors below 5000. The value -1.64 is known as the critical value of the test. We therefore obtain

$$\bar{x}_D = 5000 - 1.64\sqrt{280^2/26} = 4910 \tag{8.3}$$

Since the sample mean of 4900 lies below 4910, we reject H_0 *at the 5% significance level* or equivalently we reject *with 95% confidence*. The significance level is

---

[1]The term **size** of the test is also used, not to be confused with the sample size. We use the term 'significance level' in this text.

generally denoted by the symbol α and the complement of this, given by $1 - \alpha$, is known as the confidence level (as used in the confidence interval).

An equivalent procedure would be to calculate the z score associated with the sample mean, known as the **test statistic**, and then compare this to the critical value of the test. This allows the hypothesis testing procedure to be broken down into five neat steps:

(1) Write down the null and alternative hypotheses:

$$H_0: \mu = 5000$$
$$H_1: \mu < 5000$$

(2) Choose the significance level of the test, conventionally $\alpha = 0.05$ or 5%.
(3) Look up the critical value of the test from statistical tables, based on the chosen significance level. $z^* = 1.64$ is the critical value in this case.
(4) Calculate the test statistic:

$$z = \frac{\bar{x} - \mu}{\sqrt{s^2/n}} = \frac{-100}{\sqrt{280^2/26}} = -1.82 \tag{8.4}$$

(5) Decision rule. Compare the test statistic with the critical value: if $z < -z^*$ reject H_0 in favour of H_1. Since $-1.82 < -1.64$, H_0 is rejected with 95% confidence. Note that we use $-z^*$ here (rather than $+z^*$) because we are dealing with the left-hand tail of the distribution.

Worked example 2.12

A sample of 100 workers found the average overtime hours worked in the previous week was 7.8, with standard deviation 4.1 hours. Test the hypothesis that the average for all workers is 5 hours or less.

We can set out the five steps of the answer as follows:

(1) $H_0: \mu = 5$
$H_1: \mu > 5$
(2) Significance level, $\alpha = 5\%$.
(3) Critical value $z^* = 1.64$.
(4) Test statistic:

$$z = \frac{\bar{x} - \mu}{\sqrt{s^2 n}} = \frac{7.8 - 5}{\sqrt{4.1^2/100}} = 6.8$$

(5) Decision rule: $6.8 > 1.64$ so we reject H_0 in favour of H_1. Note that in this case we are dealing with the right-hand tail of the distribution (positive values of z and z^*). Only high values of $\bar{x}$ reject H_0.

One-tail and two-tail tests

In the above example the rejection region for the test consisted of one tail of the distribution of $\bar{x}$, since the buyer was only concerned about turnover being less than claimed. For this reason, it is known as a **one-tail test**. Suppose now that an accountant is engaged to sell the franchise and wants to check the claim about

Figure 2.103
A two-tail hypothesis test

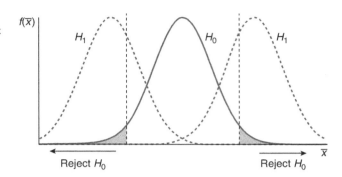

turnover before advertising the business for sale. In this case he or she would be concerned about turnover being either below *or* above 5000.

This would now become a **two-tail test** with the null and alternative hypotheses being

$$H_0: \mu = 5000$$
$$H_1: \mu \neq 5000$$

Now there are two rejection regions for the test. Either a very low sample mean *or* a very high one will serve to reject the null hypothesis. The situation is presented graphically in Figure 2.103.

The distribution of $\bar{x}$ under H_0 is the same as before, but under the alternative hypothesis the distribution could be *either* to the left *or* to the right, as depicted. If the significance level is still chosen to be 5%, then the complete rejection region consists of the *two* extremes of the distribution under H_0, containing 2.5% in each tail (hence 5% in total). This gives a Type I error probability of 5% as before. In other words, we would make a Type I error if the sample mean falls too far above or below the hypothesised value.

The critical value of the test therefore becomes $z^* = 1.96$, the values which cut off 2.5% in each tail of the standard Normal distribution. Only if the test statistic falls into one of the rejection regions beyond 1.96 standard errors from the mean is H_0 rejected.

Using data from the previous example, the test statistic remains $z = -1.82$ so that the null hypothesis cannot be rejected in this case, as -1.82 does not fall beyond -1.96. To recap, the five steps of the test are:

(1) $H_0: \mu = 5000$
  $H_1: \mu \neq 5000$
(2) Choose the significance level: $\alpha = 0.05$.
(3) Look up the critical value: $z^* = 1.96$.
(4) Evaluate the test statistic:

$$z = \frac{-100}{\sqrt{280^2/26}} = -1.82$$

(5) Compare test statistic and critical values: if $z < -z^*$ or $z > z^*$ reject H_0 in favour of H_1. In this case $-1.82 > -1.96$, so H_0 cannot be rejected with 95% confidence.

One- and two-tail tests therefore differ only at steps 1 and 3. Note that we have come to different conclusions according to whether a one- or two-tail test was used, with the same sample evidence. There is nothing wrong with this, however, for there are different interpretations of the two results. If the investor always uses his or her rule, he or she will miss out on 5% of good investment opportunities, when sales are (by chance) low. He or she will never miss out on a good opportunity because the investment appears too good (i.e. sales by chance are very high). For the accountant, 5% of the firms with sales averaging £5000 will not be advertised as such, *either* because sales appear too low *or* because they appear too high.

Another way of interpreting the difference between one- and two-tail tests is to say that the former includes some prior information, i.e. that the true value cannot lie above the hypothesised value (or that we are not interested in that region). Hence, although the sample evidence is the same, the overall evidence is not quite the same due to our prior knowledge. This additional knowledge allows us to sometimes reject a null via a one-tail test but not via a two-sided test.

It is tempting on occasion to use a one-tail test because of the sample evidence. For example, the accountant might look at the sample evidence above and decide that the franchise operation can only have true sales less than or equal to 5000. Therefore, she/he uses a one-tail test. This is a dangerous practice, since the sample evidence is being used to help formulate the hypothesis, which is then tested on that same evidence. This is going round in circles; the hypothesis should be chosen *independently* of the evidence which is then used to test it[2]. Presumably the accountant would also use a one-tail test (with $H_1: \mu > 5000$ as the alternative hypothesis) if she/he noticed that the sample mean was *above* the hypothesised value. Taking these possibilities together, she/he would in effect be using the 10% significance level, not the 5% level, since there would be 5% in each tail of the distribution. She/he would make a Type I error on 10% of all occasions rather than 5%.

It is acceptable to use a one-tail test when you have *independent* information about what the alternative hypothesis should be, or when you are not concerned about one side of the distribution (like the investor) and can effectively add that in to the null hypothesis. Otherwise, it is safer to use a two-tail test.

Exercise 2.31

(a) Two political parties are debating crime figures. One party says that crime has increased compared to the previous year. The other party says it has not. Write down the null and alternative hypotheses.

(b) Explain the two types of error that could be made in this example and the possible costs of each type of error.

Exercise 2.32

(a) We test the hypothesis $H_0: \mu = 100$ against $H_1: \mu > 100$ by rejecting H_0 if our sample mean is greater than 108. If in fact $\bar{x} \sim N(100, 900/25)$, what is the probability of making a Type I error?

(b) If we wanted a 5% Type I error probability, what decision rule (value of $\bar{x}$) should we adopt?

(c) If we knew that μ could only take on the values 100 (under H_0) or 112 (under H_1) what would be the Type II error probability using the decision rule in part (a)?

Exercise 2.33

Test the hypothesis $H_0: \mu = 500$ versus $H_1: \mu \neq 500$ using the evidence $\bar{x} = 530, s = 90$ from a sample of size $n = 30$.

──────

[2]Alternatively, we could say this is assuming the sample evidence provides the additional prior information that might justify a one-tail test. However, it is *not* additional evidence, and it would be wrong to use the sample evidence for two purposes in this way.

The choice of significance level

The explanation above put hypothesis testing into a framework of decision-making between hypotheses, balancing Type I and Type II errors. This was first developed by the statisticians Neyman and Pearson in the 1930s. It is fine for a situation where both null and alternative hypotheses are well defined (as, for example, in a court of law) but, as noted, is not helpful when the alternative hypothesis is only vaguely specified ('$H_1: \mu \neq 5000$', for instance) and we cannot calculate the Type II error probability.

In an ideal world we would have precisely specified null *and* alternative hypotheses (e.g. we would test $H_0: \mu = 5000$ against $H_1: \mu = 4500$, these being the only possibilities). Then we could calculate the probabilities of both Type I *and* Type II errors, for any given decision rule. We could then choose the optimal decision rule, which gives the best compromise between the two types of error. This is reflected in a court of law. In criminal cases, the jury must be convinced of the prosecution's case beyond reasonable doubt, because of the cost of committing a Type I error. In a civil case (libel, for example) the jury need only be convinced *on the balance of probabilities*. In a civil case, the costs of Type I and Type II error are more evenly balanced and so the burden of proof is lessened.

However, in statistics we usually do not have the luxury of two well-specified hypotheses. As in the earlier worked example, the null hypothesis is precisely specified (it has to be or the test could not be carried out) but the alternative hypothesis is imprecise (sometimes called a `composite hypothesis` because it encompasses a range of values). Statistical inference is often used not so much as an aid to decision-making but to provide evidence for or against a particular theory, to alter one's degree of belief in the truth of the theory. For example, a researcher might believe large firms are more profitable than small ones and wishes to test this. The null and alternative hypotheses would be:

H_0: large and small firms are equally profitable
H_1: large firms are more profitable

(Note that the null has to be 'equally profitable', since this is a precise statement. 'More profitable' is too vague to be the null hypothesis.). Data could be gathered to test this hypothesis, but it is not possible to calculate the Type II error probability (because 'more profitable' is too vague). Hence we cannot find the optimal balance of Type I and Type II errors in order to make our decision to accept or reject H_0. Another statistician, R.A. Fisher, proposed the use of the 5% significance level in this type of circumstance, arguing that a researcher could justifiably ignore any results that fail to reach this standard. Thus our procedures today are actually an uncomfortable mixture of two different approaches: Fisher did not agree with the decision-making framework; Neyman and Pearson did not propose a 5% convention for the Type I error probability.

The five sigma level of certainty

In particle physics the accepted level of certainty for the results of an experiment to be considered a valid discovery is five sigma (i.e. five standard deviations). A distance of five standard deviations cuts off approximately 0.00003% in one tail of the Normal distribution and represents an extremely low significance level. The reason for this is two-fold: (i) scientists are very reluctant to accept new hypotheses which may later turn out to be false, and (ii) there is a lot of random noise in the results of their experiments, so it would be easy to confuse noise with a valid finding unless a low significance level is chosen.

At the time of writing (February 2011), physicists are getting close to uncovering the existence of the Higgs boson but so far their results are only significant at about the three sigma level.

Update: The existence of the Higgs boson has been confirmed. More data (i.e. larger sample) allowed this conclusion to be reached.

The 5% significance level really does depend upon convention; therefore, it cannot be justified by reference to the relative costs of Type I and Type II errors. The 5% convention does impose some sort of discipline upon research; it sets some kind of standard which all theories (hypotheses) should be measured against. Beware the researcher who reports that a particular hypothesis is rejected at the 8% significance level; it is likely that the significance level was chosen so that the hypothesis could be rejected, which is what the researcher was hoping for in the first place. As we shall see later, however, this 'discipline upon research' is not a strong one.

The Prob-value approach

Fisher later changed his mind about the 5% significance level rule. He argued that this was too rigid to apply mechanically in all situations. Instead, one should present the Prob-value (also known as the P-value), which is the actual significance level of the test statistic. In this way one presents information (the likelihood of a false positive) rather than imposing a decision. The reader could then make their own judgement.

The Prob-value is calculated as follows. The test statistic calculated earlier for the investor problem was $z = -1.82$ and the associated Prob-value is obtained as 3.44%, i.e. -1.82 cuts off 3.44% in one tail of the standard Normal distribution. This means that the null hypothesis could be rejected at the 3.44% significance level or, alternatively expressed, with 96.56% confidence.

Thus for the accountant, using the two-tail test, the significance level is 6.88%, and this is the level at which the null hypothesis can be rejected. Alternatively, we could say we reject the null with 93.12% confidence. This does not meet the standard 5% criterion (for the significance level) which is most often used, so would result in non-rejection of the null. (Notice that, despite using P-values, we have slipped back into decision-making mode. It is difficult to avoid doing this.)

An advantage of using the Prob-value approach is that many statistical software programs routinely provide the Prob-value of a calculated test statistic[3]. If one understands the use of Prob-values, then one does not have to look up tables (this applies to any distribution, not just the Normal), which can save time.

---

[3]It is sometimes referred to as the 'P-value' in the statistical results. Excel uses this notation.

To summarise, one rejects the null hypothesis if either:

- (Method 1) the test statistic *is greater than* the critical value, i.e. $z > z^*$, or
- (Method 2) the Prob-value associated with the test statistic *is less than* the significance level, i.e. $P < 0.05$ (if the 5% significance level is used).

I have found that many students initially find this confusing, because of the opposing inequality in the two versions (greater than and less than). For example, a program might calculate a hypothesis test and report the result as '$z = 1.4$ (P-value $= 0.162$)'. The first point to note is that most software programs report the Prob-value for a two-tail test by default. Hence, assuming a 5% significance level, in this case we cannot reject H_0 because $z = 1.4 < 1.96$ or equivalently because $0.162 > 0.05$, against a two-tailed alternative (i.e. H_1 contains $\neq$).

If you wish to conduct a one-tailed test, you have to halve the reported Prob-value, becoming 0.081 in this example. This is again greater than 5%, so the hypothesis is still accepted, even against a one-sided alternative (H_1 contains $>$ or $<$). Equivalently, one could compare 1.4 with the one-tail critical value, 1.64, showing non-rejection of the null, but one has to look up the standard Normal table with this method. Computers cannot guess whether a one- or two-sided test is wanted, so take the conservative option and report the two-sided value. The correction for a one-sided test has to be done manually.

Exercise 2.34

This is a useful exercise to test your understanding of hypothesis tests. You carry out a one-tail hypothesis test and obtain the result $z = 2.3$, P-value $= 0.01$. Which of the following statements are true?

(a) You have disproved the null hypothesis.

(b) You have found the probability that the null hypothesis is true.

(c) You have proved the alternative hypothesis to be true.

(d) You can calculate the probability of the alternative hypothesis being true.

(e) If you reject the null, you know the probability of having made the wrong decision.

(f) If this experiment were repeated many times, a statistically significant result would be obtained in 99% of trials.

These questions are adapted from an original questionnaire in Oakes (1986).

Significance, effect size and power

Researchers usually look for 'significant' results; it is the way to get attention and to get published. Academic papers report that 'the results are significant' or that 'the coefficient is significantly different from zero at the 5% significance level'. It is vital to realise that the word 'significant' is used here in the *statistical* sense and not in its everyday sense of being *important*. Something can be statistically significant yet still unimportant.

Suppose that we have some more data about the business examined earlier. Data for 100 franchises have been uncovered, revealing an average weekly turnover of £4975 with standard deviation £143. Can we reject the hypothesis that the average weekly turnover is £5000? The test statistic is

$$z = \frac{4975 - 5000}{\sqrt{143^2/100}} = -1.75$$

Since this is below $-z^* = -1.64$, the null is rejected with 95% confidence. True average weekly turnover is less than £5000. However, the difference is only £25 per week, which is 0.5% of £5000. Common sense would suggest that the difference may be unimportant, even if it is significant in the statistical sense. One should not interpret statistical results in terms of significance alone, therefore; one should also look at the size of the difference (sometimes known as the **effect size**) and ask whether it is important or not. Even experienced researchers make this mistake; a review of articles in the prestigious *American Economic Review* reported that 82% of them confused statistical significance for economic significance in some way (McCloskey and Ziliak, 2004).

This problem with hypothesis testing paradoxically gets worse as the sample size increases. For example, if 250 observations reveal average sales of 4985 with standard deviation 143, the null would (just) be rejected at 5% significance. In fact, given a large enough sample size we can virtually guarantee to reject the null hypothesis even before we have gathered the data. This can be seen from equation (8.4) for the z score test statistic: as n gets larger, the test statistic also inevitably gets larger.

A good way to remember this point is to appreciate that it is the *evidence* which is significant, not the size of the effect or the results of your research. Strictly, it is better to say 'there is significant evidence of difference between . . .' than 'there is a significant difference between . . .'.

A related way of considering the effect of increasing sample size is via the concept of the **power** of a test. This is defined as

Power of a test $= 1 - \text{Pr}(\text{Type II error}) = 1 - \beta$ (8.5)

where β is the symbol conventionally used to indicate the probability of a Type II error. Since a Type II error is defined as not rejecting H_0 when false (equivalent to rejecting H_1 when true), power is the probability of rejecting H_0 when false (if H_0 is false, it must be *either* accepted *or* rejected; hence these probabilities sum to one). This is one of the correct decisions identified earlier, associated with the lower right-hand box in Figure 2.101, that of correctly rejecting a false null hypothesis. The power of a test is therefore given by the area under the H_1 distribution, to the left of the decision line, as illustrated (shaded) in Figure 2.104 (for a one-tail test).

Figure 2.104
The power of a test

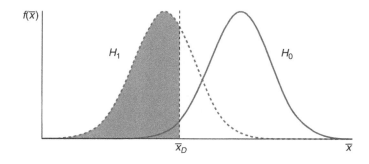

It is generally desirable to maximise the power of a test, as long as the probability of a Type I error is not raised in the process. There are essentially three ways of doing this:

- Avoid situations where the null and alternative hypotheses are very similar, i.e. the hypothesised means are not far apart (a small effect size).
- Use a large sample size. This reduces the sampling variance of $\bar{x}$ (under both H_0 and H_1) so the two distributions become more distinct.
- Use good sampling methods which have small sampling variances. This has a similar effect to increasing the sample size.

Worked example 2.13

This example shows how a larger sample size increases the power of a test. Suppose we wish to test the hypothesis $H_0: \mu = 500$ versus $H_0: \mu \leq 500$. We have a choice of two methods to test the hypothesis: (a) use a sample size of 100, or (b) use a sample size of 49. Which will give us a better test? Let us use the 5% significance level and assume. $\sigma = 200$ For test (a) we would then reject H_0 if $\bar{x} < 467.2$, and for test (b) we would reject if $\bar{x} < 453.1$. (You can check that these would lead to a z score of -1.64 in both cases, which cuts of the bottom 5% of the Normal distribution.)

Now what is the probability in each case of rejecting the null if it were false, i.e. what is the power of each test? Suppose the true mean were 470 (so H_0 above is false and should be rejected). For test (a) the probability of rejecting H_0 (i.e. $\bar{x} < 467.2$) given that the true mean is 470 is obtained by calculating the z score:

$$z = \frac{467.2 - 470}{200/\sqrt{100}} = -0.14$$

This cuts off 44% in the lower tail, so this is the power of the test. For test (b) the z score is -0.59 which cuts off only 28%, Hence test (a) is preferred having the greater power. Note that the same significance level is required for both tests.

Unfortunately, in economics and business the data (including sample size) are very often given in advance and there is little or no control possible over the sampling procedures. This leads to a neglect of consideration of power, unlike in psychology or biology, for example, where the experiment can often be designed by the researcher.

Exercise 2.35

If a researcher believes the cost of making a Type I error is much greater than the cost of a Type II error, should they prefer a 5% or 1% significance level? Explain why.

Exercise 2.36

(a) A researcher uses Excel to analyse data and test a hypothesis. The program reports a test statistic of $z = 1.77$ (P-value = 0.077). Would you reject the null hypothesis if carrying out (i) a one-tailed test (ii) a two-tailed test? Use the 5% significance level.

(b) Repeat part (a) using a 1% significance level.

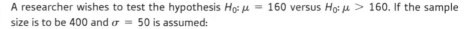

Exercise 2.37

A researcher wishes to test the hypothesis $H_0: \mu = 160$ versus $H_0: \mu > 160$. If the sample size is to be 400 and $\sigma = 50$ is assumed:

(a) What value of $\bar{x}$ should be used as the cutoff for rejecting H_0 at the 5% significance level?

(b) What is the power of the test if the true mean is (i) 163, (ii) 166?

Further hypothesis tests

We now consider a number of different types of hypothesis test, all involving the same principles but differing in details of their implementation. This is similar to the exposition in the last chapter covering, in turn, tests of a proportion, tests of the difference of two means and proportions, and finally problems involving small sample sizes.

Testing a proportion

A car manufacturer claims that no more than 10% of its cars should need repairs in the first three years of their life, the warranty period. A random sample of 50 three-year-old cars found that 8 had required attention. Does this contradict the maker's claim?

This problem can be handled very similarly to the methods used for a mean. The key, once again, is to recognise the sample proportion as a random variable with an associated probability distribution. The sampling distribution of the sample proportion in large samples is given by

$$p \sim N\left(\pi, \frac{\pi(1-\pi)}{n}\right) \tag{8.6}$$

In this case $\pi = 0.10$ (under the null hypothesis, the maker's claim). The sample data are

$$p = 8/50 = 0.16$$
$$n = 50$$

Thus 16% of the sample required attention within the warranty period. This is substantially higher than the claimed 10%, but is this just because of a non-representative sample or does it reflect the reality that the cars are badly built? The hypothesis test is set out along the same lines as for a sample mean:

(1) Set out the null and alternative hypotheses:
$$H_0: \pi = 0.10$$
$$H_1: \pi > 0.10$$

(The only concern is the manufacturer not matching its claim; hence a one-tail test is appropriate.)

(2) Significance level: $\alpha = 0.05$.

(3) The critical value of the one-tail test at the 5% significance level is $z^* = 1.64$, obtained from the standard Normal table.

(4) The test statistic is

$$z = \frac{p - \pi}{\sqrt{\dfrac{\pi(1-\pi)}{n}}} = \frac{0.16 - 0.10}{\sqrt{\dfrac{0.1 \times 0.9}{50}}} = 1.41$$

(5) Since the test statistic is less than the critical value, it falls into the non-rejection region. The null hypothesis is not rejected by the data. The manufacturer's claim is not unreasonable.

Note that for this problem, the rejection region lies in the *upper* tail of the distribution because of the 'greater than' inequality in the alternative hypothesis. The null hypothesis is therefore rejected in this case if $z > z*$.

Do children prefer branded goods only because of the name?

Researchers at Johns Hopkins Bloomberg School of Public Health in Maryland found young children were influenced by the packaging of foods. Sixty-three children were offered two identical meals, save that one was still in its original packaging (from McDonald's). Seventy-six per cent of the children preferred the branded French fries.

Is this evidence significant? The null hypothesis is $H_0: \pi = 0.5$ versus $H_1: \pi > 0.5$. The test statistic for this hypothesis test is

$$z = \frac{p - \pi}{\sqrt{\dfrac{\pi(1 - \pi)}{n}}} = \frac{0.76 - 0.50}{\sqrt{\dfrac{0.5 \times 0.5}{63}}} = 4.12$$

which is greater than the critical value of $z* = 1.64$. Hence we conclude children are influenced by the packaging or brand name.

Source: New Scientist, 11 August 2007.

 Testing the difference of two means

Suppose a car company wishes to compare the performance of its two factories producing an identical model of car. The factories are equipped with the same machinery but their outputs might differ due to managerial ability, labour relations, etc. Senior management wishes to know if there is any difference between the two factories. Output is monitored for 30 days, chosen at random, with the following results:

	Factory 1	Factory 2
Average daily output	420	408
Standard deviation of daily output	25	20

Does this produce sufficient evidence of a real difference between the factories, or does the difference between the samples simply reflect random differences such as minor breakdowns of machinery? The information at our disposal may be summarised as

$$\bar{x}_1 = 420 \quad \bar{x}_2 = 408$$
$$s_1 = 25 \quad s_2 = 20$$
$$n_1 = 30 \quad n_2 = 30$$

The hypothesis test to be conducted concerns the difference between the factories' outputs, so the appropriate random variable to examine is $\bar{x}_1 - \bar{x}_2$. This has the following distribution, in large samples:

$$\bar{x}_1 - \bar{x}_2 \sim N\left(\mu_1 - \mu_2, \frac{\sigma_1^2}{n_1} + \frac{\sigma_2^2}{n_2}\right) \tag{8.7}$$

The population variances, σ_1^2 and σ_2^2, may be replaced by their sample estimates, s_1^2 and s_2^2, if the former are unknown, as here. The hypothesis test is therefore as follows.

(1) $H_0: \mu_1 - \mu_2 = 0$
$H_1: \mu_1 - \mu_2 \neq 0$

The null hypothesis posits no real difference between the factories. This is a two-tail test since there is no *a priori* reason to believe one factory is better than the other, apart from the sample evidence.

(2) Significance level: $\alpha = 1\%$. This is chosen since the management does not want to interfere unless it is really confident of some difference between the factories. In order to favour the null hypothesis, a lower significance level than the conventional 5% is set.

(3) The critical value of the test is $z^* = 2.57$. This cuts off 0.5% in each tail of the standard Normal distribution.

(4) The test statistic is

$$z = \frac{(\bar{x}_1 - \bar{x}_2) - (\mu_1 - \mu_2)}{\sqrt{\dfrac{s_1^2}{n_1} + \dfrac{s_2^2}{n_2}}} = \frac{(420 - 408) - 0}{\sqrt{\dfrac{25^2}{30} + \dfrac{20^2}{30}}} = 2.05$$

Note that this is of the same form as in the single-sample cases. The hypothesised value of the difference (zero in this case) is subtracted from the sample difference and this is divided by the standard error of the random variable.

(5) Decision rule: $z < z^*$ so the test statistic falls into the non-rejection region. There does not appear to be a significant difference between the two factories (or, better expressed, there is not significant evidence of a difference between factories).

A number of remarks about this example should be made. First, it is not necessary for the two sample sizes to be equal (although they are in the example); 45 days' output from factory 1 and 35 days' from factory 2, for example, could have been sampled. Second, the values of s_1^2 and s_2^2 do not have to be equal. They are, respectively, estimates of σ_1^2 and σ_2^2, and although the null hypothesis asserts that $\mu_1 = \mu_2$ it does not assert that the variances are equal. Management wants to know if the *average* levels of output are the same; it is not concerned about daily fluctuations in output (although it might be).

The final point to consider is whether all the necessary conditions for the correct application of this test have been met. The example noted that the 30 days were chosen at random. If the 30 days sampled were consecutive, we might doubt whether the observations were truly independent. Low output on one day (due to a mechanical breakdown, for example) might influence the following day's output (if a special effort were made to catch up on lost production, for example).

Testing the difference of two proportions

The general method should by now be familiar, so we will proceed by example for this case. Suppose that, in a comparison of two holiday companies' customers, of the 75 who went with Happy Days Tours, 45 said they were satisfied, while 48 of the 90 who went with Fly by Night Holidays were satisfied. Is there a significant difference between the companies?

This problem can be handled by a hypothesis test on the difference of two sample proportions. The procedure is as follows. The sample evidence is

$$p_1 = 45/75 = 0.6 \qquad n_1 = 75$$
$$p_2 = 48/90 = 0.533 \qquad n_2 = 90$$

The hypothesis test is carried out as follows

(1) $H_0: \pi_1 - \pi_2 = 0$
    $H_1: \pi_1 - \pi_2 \neq 0$
(2) Significance level: $\alpha = 5\%$.
(3) Critical value: $z^* = 1.96$.
(4) Test statistic: The distribution of $p_1 - p_2$ is

$$p_1 - p_2 \sim N\left(\pi_1 - \pi_2, \frac{\pi_1(1 - \pi_1)}{n_1} + \frac{\pi_2(1 - \pi_2)}{n_2}\right)$$

so the test statistic is

$$z = \frac{(p_1 - p_2) - (\pi_1 - \pi_2)}{\sqrt{\dfrac{\pi_1(1 - \pi_1)}{n_1} + \dfrac{\pi_2(1 - \pi_2)}{n_2}}} \qquad (8.8)$$

However, π_1 and π_2 in the denominator of equation (8.8) have to be replaced by estimates from the samples. They cannot simply be replaced by p_1 and p_2 because these are unequal; to do so would contradict the null hypothesis that they *are* equal. Since the null hypothesis is assumed to be true (for the moment), it makes no sense to use a test statistic which explicitly supposes the null hypothesis to be false. Therefore, π_1 and π_2 are replaced by an estimate of their common value which is denoted $\hat{\pi}$ and whose formula is

$$\hat{\pi} = \frac{n_1 p_1 + n_2 p_2}{n_1 + n_2} \qquad (8.9)$$

i.e. a weighted average of the two sample proportions. This yields

$$\hat{\pi} = \frac{75 \times 0.6 + 90 \times 0.533}{75 + 90} = 0.564$$

This, in fact, is just the proportion of all customers who were satisfied, 93 out of 165. The test statistic therefore becomes

$$z = \frac{0.6 - 0.533 - 0}{\sqrt{\dfrac{0.564 \times (1 - 0.564)}{75} + \dfrac{0.564 \times (1 - 0.564)}{90}}} = 0.86$$

(5) The test statistic is less than the critical value so the null hypothesis cannot be rejected with 95% confidence. There is not sufficient evidence to demonstrate a difference between the two companies' performance.

Are women better at multi-tasking?

The conventional wisdom is 'yes'. However, the concept of multi-tasking originated in computing and, in that domain, it appears men are more likely to multi-task. Oxford Internet Surveys (http://www.oii.ox.ac.uk/microsites/oxis/) asked a sample of 1578 people if they multi-tasked while on-line (e.g. listening to music, using the phone); 69% of men said they did, 57% of women did. Is this difference statistically significant?

The published survey does not give precise numbers of men and women respondents for this question, so we will assume equal numbers (the answer is not very sensitive to this assumption). We therefore have the test statistic:

$$z = \frac{0.69 - 0.57 - 0}{\sqrt{\dfrac{0.63 \times (1 - 0.63)}{789} + \dfrac{0.63 \times (1 - 0.63)}{789}}} = 4.94$$

(0.63 is the overall proportion of multi-taskers). The evidence is significant and clearly suggests this is a genuine difference: men are the multi-taskers.

Exercise 2.38

A survey of 80 voters finds that 65% are in favour of a particular policy. Test the hypothesis that the true proportion is 50%, against the alternative that a majority is in favour.

Exercise 2.39

A survey of 50 teenage girls found that on average they spent 3.6 hours per week chatting with friends over the internet. The standard deviation was 1.2 hours. A similar survey of 90 teenage boys found an average of 3.9 hours, with standard deviation 2.1 hours. Test if there is any difference between boys' and girls' behaviour.

Exercise 2.40

One gambler on horse racing won on 23 of his 75 bets. Another won on 34 out of 95. Is the second person a better judge of horses, or just luckier?

Hypothesis tests with small samples

As with estimation, slightly different methods have to be employed when the sample size is small ($n < 25$) and the population variance is unknown. When both of these conditions are satisfied, the t distribution must be used rather than the Normal, so a t test is conducted rather than a z test. This means consulting tables of the t distribution to obtain the critical value of a test, but otherwise the methods are similar. These methods will be applied to hypotheses about sample means only, since they are inappropriate for tests of a sample proportion, as was the case in estimation.

 Testing the sample mean

A large chain of supermarkets sells 5000 packets of cereal in each of its stores each month. It decides to test-market a different brand of cereal in 15 of its stores. After a month the 15 stores have sold an average of 5200 packets each, with a standard deviation of 500 packets. Should all supermarkets switch to selling the new brand?

The sample information is

$$\bar{x} = 5200, s = 500, n = 15$$

The distribution of the sample mean from a small sample when the population variance is unknown is based upon

$$\frac{\bar{x} - \mu}{\sqrt{s^2/n}} \sim t_\nu \tag{8.10}$$

with $\nu = n - 1$ degrees of freedom. The hypothesis test is based on this formula and is conducted as follows:

(1) $H_0: \mu = 5000$
$H_1: \mu > 5000$
(Only an improvement in sales is relevant.)
(2) Significance level: $\alpha = 1\%$ (chosen because the cost of changing brands is high).
(3) The critical value of the t distribution for a one-tail test at the 1% significance level with $\nu = -1 = 14$ degrees of freedom is $t^* = 2.62$.
(4) The test statistic is

$$t = \frac{\bar{x} - \mu}{\sqrt{s^2/n}} = \frac{5200 - 5000}{\sqrt{500^2/15}} = 1.55$$

(5) The null hypothesis is not rejected since the test statistic, 1.55, is less than the critical value, 2.62. It would probably be unwise to switch over to the new brand of cereal.

Testing the difference of two means

A survey of 20 British companies found an average annual expenditure on research and development of £3.7m with a standard deviation of £0.6m. A survey of 15 similar German companies found an average expenditure on research and development of £4.2m with standard deviation £0.9m. Does this evidence lend support to the view often expressed that Britain does not invest enough in research and development?

This is a hypothesis about the difference of two means, based on small sample sizes. The test statistic is again based on the t distribution, i.e.

$$\frac{(\bar{x}_1 - \bar{x}_2) - (\mu_1 - \mu_2)}{\sqrt{\dfrac{S^2}{n_1} + \dfrac{S^2}{n_2}}} \sim t_\nu \tag{8.11}$$

where S^2 is the pooled variance (as given in equation (4.23)) and the degrees of freedom are given by $\nu = n_1 + n_2 - 2$.

The hypothesis test procedure is as follows:

(1) $H_0: \mu_1 - \mu_2 = 0$
$H_1: \mu_1 - \mu_2 < 0$
(a one-tail test because the concern is with Britain spending less than Germany.)
(2) Significance level: $\alpha = 5\%$.
(3) The critical value of the t distribution at the 5% significance level for a one-tail test with $\nu = n_1 + n_2 - 2 = 33$ degrees of freedom is approximately $t^* = 1.70$.
(4) The test statistic is based on equation (5.11):

$$t = \frac{(\bar{x}_1 - \bar{x}_2) - (\mu_1 - \mu_2)}{\sqrt{\dfrac{S^2}{n_1} + \dfrac{S^2}{n_2}}} = \frac{3.7 - 4.2 - 0}{\sqrt{\dfrac{0.55}{20} + \dfrac{0.55}{15}}} = -1.97$$

where S^2 is the pooled variance, calculated by

$$S^2 = \frac{(n_1 - 1)s_1^2 + (n_2 - 1)s_2^2}{n_1 + n_2 - 2} = \frac{19 \times 0.6^2 + 14 \times 0.9^2}{33} = 0.55$$

(5) The test statistic falls in the rejection region, $t < -t*$, so the null hypothesis is rejected. The data do support the view that Britain spends less on R&D than Germany.

Exercise 2.41

It is asserted that parents spend, on average, £540 p.a. on toys for each child. A survey of 24 parents finds expenditure of £490, with standard deviation £150. Does this evidence contradict the assertion?

Exercise 2.42

A sample of 15 final-year students were found to spend on average 15 hours per week in the university library, with standard deviation 3 hours. A sample of 20 freshers found they spend on average 9 hours per week in the library, with standard deviation 5 hours. Is this sufficient evidence to conclude that finalists spend more time in the library?

Are the test procedures valid?

A variety of assumptions underlie each of the tests which we have applied above, and it is worth considering in a little more detail whether these assumptions are justified. This will demonstrate that one should not rely upon the statistical tests alone; it is important to retain one's sense of judgement.

The first test concerned the weekly turnover of a series of franchise operations. To justify the use of the Normal distribution underlying the test, the sample observations must be independently drawn. If, for example, all the sample franchises were taken from vibrant and growing cities and avoided those in less fortunate parts of the country, then in some sense the observations would not be independent, and furthermore the sample would not be representative of the whole. The answer to this would be to ensure the sample was properly stratified, representing different parts of the country.

If one were using time-series data, as in the car factory comparison, similar issues arise. Do the 30 days represent independent observations or might there be an autocorrelation problem (e.g. if the sample days were close together in time)? Suppose that factory 2 suffered a breakdown of some kind which took three days to fix. Output would be reduced on three successive days and factory 2 would almost inevitably appear less efficient than factory 1. A look at the individual sample observations might be worthwhile, therefore, to see if there are any irregular patterns. It would have been altogether better if the samples had been collected on randomly chosen days over a longer time period to reduce the danger of this type of problem.

If the two factories both obtain their supplies from a common, but limited, source, then the output of one factory might not be independent of the output of the other. A high output of one factory would tend to be associated with a low output from the other, which has little to do with their relative efficiencies. This might leave the average difference in output unchanged but might increase the variance substantially (either a very high positive value of $\bar{x}_1 - \bar{x}_2$ or a very high negative value is obtained). This would lead to a low value of the test statistic and the conclusion of no difference in output. Any real difference in efficiency is masked by the common supplier problem. If the two samples are not independent, then the distribution of $\bar{x}_1 - \bar{x}_2$ may not be Normal.

Hypothesis tests and confidence intervals

Formally, two-tail hypothesis tests and confidence intervals are equivalent. Any value which lies within the 95% confidence interval around the sample mean cannot be rejected as the 'true' value using the 5% significance level in a hypothesis test using the same sample data. For example, our by now familiar accountant could construct a confidence interval for the firm's sales. This yields the 95% confidence interval

$$[4792, 5008] \qquad\qquad (8.12)$$

Notice that the hypothesised value of 5000 is within this interval and that this value was not rejected by the hypothesis test carried out earlier. As long as the same confidence level is used for both procedures, they are equivalent.

Having said this, their interpretation is different. The hypothesis test forces us into the reject/do not reject dichotomy, which is rather a stark choice. We have already seen how it becomes more likely that a null hypothesis is rejected as the sample size increases. This problem does not occur with estimation. As the sample size increases the confidence interval gets narrower (around the unbiased point estimate) which is entirely beneficial. The estimation approach also tends to emphasise importance over significance in most people's minds. With a hypothesis test one might know that turnover is significantly different from 5000 without knowing how far from 5000 it actually is.

On some occasions a confidence interval is inferior to a hypothesis test, however. Consider the following case. In the United Kingdom only 72 out of 564 judges are women (12.8%). The Equal Opportunities Commission had earlier commented that since the appointment system is so secretive, it is impossible to tell if there is discrimination or not. What can the statistician say about this? No discrimination (in its broadest sense) would mean half of all judges would be women. Thus, the hypotheses are

H_0: $\pi = 0.5$ (no discrimination)
H_1: $\pi < 0.5$ (discrimination against women)

The sample data are $p = 0.128$, $n = 564$. The z score is

$$z = \frac{p - \pi}{\sqrt{\dfrac{\pi(1 - \pi)}{n}}} = \frac{0.128 - 0.5}{\sqrt{\dfrac{0.5 \times 0.5}{564}}} = -17.7$$

This is clearly significant (*and* 12.8% is a long way from 50%) so the null hypothesis is rejected. There is some form of discrimination somewhere against women (unless women choose not to be judges). But a confidence interval estimate of the 'true' proportion of female judges would be meaningless. To what population is this 'true' proportion related?

The lesson from all this is that differences exist between confidence intervals and hypothesis tests, despite their formal similarity. Which technique is more appropriate is a matter of judgement for the researcher. With hypothesis testing, the rejection of the null hypothesis at some significance level might actually mean a small (and unimportant) deviation from the hypothesised value. It should be remembered that the rejection of the null hypothesis based on a large sample of data is also consistent with the true value possibly being quite close to the hypothesised value.

Independent and dependent samples

The following example illustrates the differences between independent samples (as encountered so far) and dependent samples (also known as matched or paired samples) where slightly different methods of analysis are required. The example also illustrates how a particular problem can often be analysed by a variety of statistical methods.

Dependent samples occur, for example, when the same individuals are sampled twice, at two points in time. Alternatively, the observations in a first sample might be matched to or related in some way with the observations in the second sample. To ignore these facts in our analysis would be to ignore some potentially valuable information and hence not obtain the optimum results from the data.

To proceed via an example, suppose a company introduces a training programme to raise the productivity of its clerical workers, which is measured by the number of invoices processed per day. The company wants to know if the training programme is effective. How should it evaluate the programme? There is a variety of ways of going about the task, as follows:

- Take two (random) samples of workers, one trained and one not trained, and compare their productivity. This would comprise two independent samples.
- Take a sample of workers and compare their productivity before and after training. This would be a paired sample.
- Take two samples of workers, one to be trained and the other not. Compare the improvement of the trained workers with any change in the other group's performance over the same time period. This would consist of two independent samples but we are controlling for any time effects that are unrelated to the training.

We shall go through each method in turn, pointing out any possible difficulties.

Two independent samples

Suppose a group of 10 workers is trained and compared to a group of 10 non-trained workers, with the following data being relevant:

$$\bar{x}_T = 25.5 \qquad \bar{x}_N = 21.00$$
$$s_T = 2.55 \qquad s_N = 2.91$$
$$n_T = 10 \qquad n_N = 10$$

Thus, trained workers process 25.5 invoices per day compared to only 21 by non-trained workers. The question is whether this is significant, given that the sample sizes are quite small.

The appropriate test here is a t test of the difference of two sample means, as follows:

$$H_0: \mu_T - \mu_N = 0$$
$$H_1: \mu_T - \mu_N > 0$$

$$t = \frac{25.5 - 21.0}{\sqrt{\dfrac{7.49}{10} + \dfrac{7.49}{10}}} = 3.68$$

(7.49 is S^2, the pooled variance). The t statistic leads to rejection of the null hypothesis; the training programme does seem to be effective.

One problem with this test is that the two samples might have other differences apart from the effect of the training programme. This could be due either to simple random variation or to some selection factor. Poor workers might have been reluctant to take part in training, departmental managers might have selected better workers for training as some kind of reward, or better workers may have volunteered. In a well-designed experiment this should not be allowed to happen, of course, but we do not rule out the possibility. Hence we should consider ways of conducting a fairer test.

Paired samples

If we compare the same workers before and after training, then we are controlling for the inherent quality of the workers. We hence rule out this form of random variation which might otherwise weaken our test. We should therefore obtain a better idea of the true effect of the training programme. This is an example of paired or matched samples, where we can match up and compare the individual observations to each other, rather than just the overall averages. Suppose the sample data are as follows:

Worker	1	2	3	4	5	6	7	8	9	10
Before	21	24	23	25	28	17	24	22	24	27
After	23	27	24	28	29	21	24	25	26	28

In this case, the observations in the two samples are paired, and this has implications for the method of analysis. One *could* proceed by assuming these are two independent samples and conduct a t test. The summary data and results of such a test are:

$$\bar{x}_B = 23.50 \quad \bar{x}_A = 25.5$$
$$s_B = 3.10 \quad s_A = 2.55$$
$$n_B = 10 \quad n_A = 10$$

The resulting test statistic is $t_{18} = 1.58$ which is not significant at the 5% level.

There are two problems with this test and its result. First, the two samples are not truly independent, since the before and after measurements refer to the same group of workers. Second, note that 9 out of 10 workers in the sample have shown an improvement, which is odd in view of the result found above, of no significant improvement. If the training programme really has no effect, then the probability of a single worker showing an improvement is $\frac{1}{2}$. The probability of nine or more workers showing an improvement is, by the Binomial method, $\left(\frac{1}{2}\right)^{10} \times 10C9 + \left(\frac{1}{2}\right)^{10}$, which is about one in a hundred. A very unlikely event seems to have occurred. Furthermore, the improvement is better measured as a proportion, which is 8.5% (25.5 versus 23.5), and any company would be pleased at such an improvement in productivity. Despite the lack of significance, it is worth investigating further.

The t test used above is inappropriate because it does not make full use of the information in the sample. It does not reflect the fact, for example, that the before and after scores, 21 and 23, relate to the same worker. The Binomial calculation above does reflect this matching. A re-ordering of the data would not affect the t test result, but would affect the Binomial, since a different number of workers would now show an improvement. Of course, the Binomial does not use all the sample information either – it dispenses with the actual productivity data for each worker and replaces it with 'improvement' or 'no improvement'. It disregards the amount of improvement for each worker.

Better use of the sample data comes by measuring the improvement for each worker, as follows (if a worker had deteriorated, this would be reflected by a negative number):

Worker	1	2	3	4	5	6	7	8	9	10
Improvement	2	3	1	3	1	4	0	3	2	1

These new data can be treated by single sample methods, and account is taken both of the actual data values and of the fact that the original samples were dependent (re-ordering of the data would produce different, and incorrect, improvement figures). The summary statistics of the new data are as follows:

$$\bar{x} = 2.00, s = 1.247, n = 10$$

The null hypothesis of no improvement can now be tested as follows:

$$H_0: \mu = 0$$
$$H_1: \mu > 0$$
$$t = \frac{2.0 - 0}{\sqrt{\dfrac{1.247^2}{10}}} = 5.07$$

This is significant at the 5% level, so the null hypothesis of no improvement is rejected. The correct analysis of the sample data has thus reversed the previous conclusion. It is perhaps surprising that treating the same data in different ways leads to such a difference in the results. It does illustrate the importance of using the appropriate method.

Matters do not end here, however. Although we have discovered an improvement, this might be due to other factors apart from the training programme. For example, if the before and after measurements were taken on different days of the week (that Monday morning feeling . . .), or if one of the days were sunnier, making people feel happier and therefore more productive, this might bias the results. These may seem trivial examples but these effects do exist, for example the 'Friday afternoon car', which has more faults than the average, constructed when workers are thinking ahead to the weekend.

The way to solve this problem is to use a control group, so called because extraneous factors are controlled for, in order to isolate the effects of the factor under investigation. In this case, the productivity of the control group would be measured (twice) at the same times as that of the training group, although no training would be given to them. Ideally, the control group would be matched on other factors (e.g. age) to the treatment group to avoid other factors influencing the results. Suppose that the average improvement of the control group were 0.5 invoices per day with standard deviation 1.0 (again for a group of 10). This can be compared with the improvement of the training group via the two-sample t test, giving

$$t = \frac{2.0 - 0.5}{\sqrt{\dfrac{1.13^2}{10} + \dfrac{1.13^2}{10}}} = 2.97$$

(1.13^2 is the pooled variance). This adds more support to the finding that the training programme is of value.

Exercise 2.43

A group of students' marks on two tests, before and after instruction, were as follows:

Student	1	2	3	4	5	6	7	8	9	10	11	12
Before	14	16	11	8	20	19	6	11	13	16	9	13
After	15	18	15	11	19	18	9	12	16	16	12	13

Test the hypothesis that the instruction had no effect, using both the independent sample and paired sample methods. Compare the two results.

Issues with hypothesis testing

The above exposition has served to illustrate how to carry out a hypothesis test and the rationale behind it. However, the methodology has been subject to criticisms, some of which we have already discussed:

- The decision-making paradigm is problematic since we are not sure what we are choosing between (the alternative hypothesis is vague).
- The 5% significance level is just a convention.
- The focus on 'significance' leads to a neglect of the effect size.
- The experimental (i.e. alternative) hypothesis is never itself tested. This is a pity as it is often the one favoured by the researcher.
- The process is easily and often misunderstood. People tend to confuse the probability of observing the sample data assuming that the null is true with the probability that the null is true given the data. More succinctly, $\Pr(\text{data} \mid H_0)$ is confused with $\Pr(H_0 \mid \text{data})$. The significance level (P-value) relates to the former, not the latter.

There are other problems too which we have not yet discussed. It is common in research to be looking at several hypothesis tests rather than just one. Suppose we are trying to improve teaching of statistics to a group of students. We try five alternative approaches: smaller class sizes, regular assignments, online tests, etc. We test each of these with a conventional hypothesis test at the 5% significance level. What is our chance of a Type I error, assuming none of these innovations truly works? The chance that all five come up with 'no effect' is $0.95^5 = 0.77$. Hence the overall Type I error probability is $1 - 0.77 = 0.23$. There is a 23% chance that we (erroneously) find something significant. This reveals the danger of looking for things in the data – there is a good chance you will find something, but it will likely be a false positive.

This problem is pervasive, and even the researcher himself herself might be unaware of doing it. He/she investigates whether workers are less productive on a Friday but finds no significant effect. So he/she wonders whether there is a Monday effect and tests that. Or (even worse) he/she notices in the data that productivity looks low on a Wednesday, so he/she tests that. The results of these tests are largely meaningless and the true significance level (P-value) may be much higher than 5%.

Why is it, therefore, that hypothesis testing is so frequently used? One attraction is that it provides clear guidance on what to do, which does not require too much thought to apply. Follow the procedures and you will obtain a result. Moreover, this method will be generally accepted by others and is needed if the researcher wishes to get published.

What can be done to avoid some of these pitfalls? Some suggestions are as follows.

- If doing a hypothesis test, plan it in detail *before* obtaining the data, i.e. the null hypothesis (or hypotheses) to test, the significance level, how to measure the variables appropriately (e.g. look at wage rates or total earnings?), sample size and so on. Stick to these choices, do not alter them in the light of what you might observe in the data.
- Do not be overawed by significance. Look at the effect size as well. In fact, look at the effect size first. Your significant result could be unimportant.
- Calculating a confidence interval might be a better way of analysing your data than a hypothesis test. It gives more focus to the effect size while also telling you about the reliability of your finding.
- Do not rely only on a hypothesis test, there are lots of ways of gaining insight into a problem. Look at the data using descriptive statistics and charts (and present these results to the reader). Perhaps your significant result occurs because of a few outliers in the data.

If possible, validate your findings on new data. If the effect you have found is genuine, it ought to occur in a new sample. If your original data suggest a new hypothesis to you, you must get new data to test it, you cannot use the same data to test the hypothesis suggested by those data.

| Exercise 2.44 | Generally, to be published in an academic journal, a study needs to reject the null hypothesis at the 5% significance level. Of all studies published in journals, what proportion of them are likely to be Type I errors, i.e. false positives? |

| Exercise 2.45 | Studies published in journals will usually have an effect size for the subject of study, e.g. smaller class sizes improve pupils' maths skills by 10% points. Would you expect a published effect size to be an underestimate, an accurate (unbiased) estimate, or an overestimate of the true effect size? Note that only 'significant' results get published. |

Summary

- Hypothesis testing is the set of procedures for deciding whether a hypothesis is true or false. When conducting the test, we presume the hypothesis, termed the null hypothesis, is true until it is proved false on the basis of some sample evidence.

- If the null is proved false, it is rejected in favour of the alternative hypothesis. The procedure is conceptually similar to a court case, where the defendant is presumed innocent until the evidence proves otherwise.

- Not all decisions turn out to be correct, and there are two types of error that can be made. A Type I error is to reject the null hypothesis when it is in fact true. A Type II error is not to reject the null when it is false.

- Choosing the appropriate decision rule (for rejecting the null hypothesis) is a question of trading off Type I and Type II errors. Because the alternative hypothesis is imprecisely specified, the probability of a Type II error usually cannot be specified.

- The rejection region for a test is therefore chosen to give a 5% probability of making a Type I error (sometimes a 1% probability is chosen). The critical value of the test statistic (sometimes referred to as the critical value of the test) is the value which separates the acceptance and rejection regions.

- The decision is based upon the value of a test statistic, which is calculated from the sample evidence and from information in the null hypothesis.

$$\left(e.g.\, z = \frac{\bar{x} - \mu}{s/\sqrt{n}} \right)$$

- The null hypothesis is rejected if the test statistic falls into the rejection region for the test (i.e. it exceeds the critical value).

- For a two-tail test there are two rejection regions, corresponding to very high and very low values of the test statistic.

- Instead of comparing the test statistic to the critical value, an equivalent procedure is to compare the Prob-value of the test statistic with the significance level. The null is rejected if the Prob-value is less than the significance level.

- The power of a test is the probability of a test correctly rejecting the null hypothesis. Some tests have low power (e.g. when the sample size is small) and therefore are not very useful.

Key terms and concepts

alternative hypothesis	one- and two-tail tests
composite hypothesis	paired samples
critical value	power
decision rule	prior information
dependent samples	Prob-value
effect size	rejection region
independent samples	significance level
matched samples	test statistic
non-rejection region	Type I and
null or maintained hypothesis	Type II errors

References

Michael Oakes, *Statistical Inference: A Commentary for the Social and Behavioural Sciences*, Wiley, 1986.

McCloskey, D., and S. Ziliak, Size Matters: the Standard Error of Regressions in the *American Economic Review*, *Journal of Socio-Economics*, 33, 527–46, 2004.

Formulae used in this chapter

Formula	Description	Notes
$z = \dfrac{\bar{x} - \mu}{\sqrt{s^2/n}}$	Test statistic for H_0: mean $= \mu$	Large samples. For small samples, distributed as t with $\nu = n - 1$ degrees of freedom
$z = \dfrac{p - \pi}{\sqrt{\dfrac{\pi(1 - \pi)}{n}}}$	Test statistic for H_0: true proportion $= \pi$	Large samples
$z = \dfrac{(\bar{x}_1 - \bar{x}_2) - (\mu_1 - \mu_2)}{\sqrt{\dfrac{s_1^2}{n_1} + \dfrac{s_2^2}{n_2}}}$	Test statistic for H_0: $\mu_1 - \mu_2 = 0$	Large samples
$t = \dfrac{(\bar{x}_1 - \bar{x}_2) - (\mu_1 - \mu_2)}{\sqrt{\dfrac{s^2}{n_1} + \dfrac{s^2}{n_2}}}$	Test statistic for H_0: $\mu_1 - \mu_2 = 0$	Small samples. $s^2 = \dfrac{(n_1 - 1)s_1^2 + (n_2 - 1)s_2^2}{n_1 + n_2 - 2}$ Degrees of freedom $\nu = n_1 + n_2 - 2$
$z = \dfrac{(p_1 - p_2) - (\pi_1 - \pi_2)}{\sqrt{\dfrac{\pi_1(1 - \pi_1)}{n_1} + \dfrac{\pi_2(1 - \pi_2)}{n_2}}}$	Test statistic for H_0: $\pi_1 - \pi_2 = 0$	Large samples $\pi = \dfrac{n_1 p_1 + n_2 p_2}{n_1 + n_2}$

Problems

Some of the more challenging problems are indicated by highlighting the problem number in colour.

2.8.1 Answer true or false, with reasons if necessary.

   (a) There is no way of reducing the probability of a Type I error without simultaneously increasing the probability of a Type II error.

   (b) The probability of a Type I error is associated with an area under the distribution of $\bar{x}$ assuming the null hypothesis to be true.

   (c) It is always desirable to minimise the probability of a Type I error.

   (d) A larger sample, *ceteris paribus*, will increase the power of a test.

   (e) The significance level is the probability of a Type II error.

   (f) The confidence level is the probability of a Type II error.

2.8.2 Consider the investor in the text, seeking out companies with weekly turnover of at least £5000. He or she applies a one-tail hypothesis test to each firm, using the 5% significance level. State whether each of the following statements is true or false (or not known) and explain why.

   (a) 5% of his or her investments are in companies with less than £5000 turnover.

   (b) 5% of the companies he *fails* to invest in have turnover greater than £5000 per week.

   (c) He invests in 95% of all companies with turnover of £5000 or over.

2.8.3 A coin which is either fair or has two heads is to be tossed twice. You decide on the following decision rule: if two heads occur you will conclude it is a two-headed coin, otherwise you will presume it is fair. Write down the null and alternative hypotheses and calculate the probabilities of Type I and Type II errors.

2.8.4 In comparing two medical treatments for a disease, the null hypothesis is that the two treatments are equally effective. Why does making a Type I error not matter? What significance level for the test should be set as a result?

2.8.5 A firm receives components from a supplier, which it uses in its own production. The components are delivered in batches of 2000. The supplier claims that there are only 1% defective components on average from its production. However, production occasionally gets out of control and a batch is produced with 10% defective components. The firm wishes to intercept these low-quality batches, so a sample of size 50 is taken from each batch and tested. If two or more defectives are found in the sample, then the batch is rejected.

(a) Describe the two types of error the firm might make in assessing batches of components.

(b) Calculate the probability of each type of error given the data above.

(c) If, instead, samples of size 30 were taken and the batch rejected if one or more rejects were found, how would the error probabilities be altered?

(d) The firm can alter the two error probabilities by choice of sample size and rejection criteria. How should it set the relative sizes of the error probabilities

  (i) if the product might affect consumer safety?

  (ii) if there are many competitive suppliers of components?

  (iii) if the costs of replacement under guarantee are high?

2.8.6 Computer diskettes (the precursor to USB drives) which do not meet the quality required for high-density diskettes are sold as low-density diskettes (storing less data) for 80 pence each. High-density diskettes are sold for £1.20 each. A firm samples 30 diskettes from each batch of 1000 and if any fail the quality test, the whole batch is sold as double-density diskettes. What are the types of error possible and what is the cost to the firm of a Type I error?

2.8.7 Testing the null hypothesis that $\mu = 10$ against $\mu > 10$, a researcher obtains a sample mean of 12 with standard deviation 6 from a sample of 30 observations. Calculate the z score and the associated Prob-value for this test.

2.8.8 Given the sample data $\bar{x} = 45$, $s = 16$, $n = 50$, at what level of confidence can you reject $H_0: \mu = 40$ against a two-sided alternative?

2.8.9 What is the power of the test carried out in Problem 2.8.3?

2.8.10 Given the two hypotheses

$$H_0: \mu = 400$$
$$H_1: \mu = 415$$

and $\sigma^2 = 1000$ (for both hypotheses):

(a) Draw the distribution of $\bar{x}$ under both hypotheses.

(b) If the decision rule is chosen to be: reject H_0 if $\bar{x} \geq 410$ from a sample of size 40, find the probability of a Type II error and the power of the test.

(c) What happens to these answers as the sample size is increased? Draw a diagram to illustrate.

2.8.11 Given the following sample data:

$$\bar{x} = 15 \qquad s^2 = 270 \qquad n = 30$$

test the null hypothesis that the true mean is equal to 12, against a two-sided alternative hypothesis. Draw the distribution of $\bar{x}$ under the null hypothesis and indicate the rejection regions for this test.

2.8.12 From experience it is known that a certain brand of tyre lasts, on average, 15 000 miles with standard deviation 1250. A new compound is tried and a sample of 120 tyres yields an average life of 15 150 miles, with the same standard deviation. Are the new tyres an improvement? Use the 5% significance level.

2.8.13 Test $H_0: \pi = 0.5$ against $H_0: \pi \neq 0.5$ using $p = 0.45$ from a sample of size $n = 35$.

2.8.14 Test the hypothesis that 10% of your class or lecture group are left-handed.

2.8.15 Given the following data from two independent samples:

$$\begin{aligned} \bar{x}_1 &= 115 & \bar{x}_2 &= 105 \\ s_1 &= 21 & s_2 &= 23 \\ n_1 &= 49 & n_2 &= 63 \end{aligned}$$

test the hypothesis of no difference between the population means against the alternative that the mean of population 1 is greater than the mean of population 2.

2.8.16 A transport company wants to compare the fuel efficiencies of the two types of lorry it operates. It obtains data from samples of the two types of lorry, with the following results:

Type	Average mpg	Std devn	Sample size
A	31.0	7.6	33
B	32.2	5.8	40

Test the hypothesis that there is no difference in fuel efficiency, using the 99% confidence level.

2.8.17 (a) A random sample of 180 men who took the driving test found that 103 passed. A similar sample of 225 women found that 105 passed. Test whether pass rates are the same for men and women.

(b) If you test whether the group of people who passed the driving test contained the same proportion of men as the group of people who failed, what result would you expect to find? Carry out the test to check.

(c) Is your finding in part (b) inevitable or one that just arises with these data? Try to support your response with a proof.

2.8.18 (a) A pharmaceutical company testing a new type of pain reliever administered the drug to 30 volunteers experiencing pain. Sixteen of them said that it eased their pain. Does this evidence support the claim that the drug is effective in combating pain?

(b) A second group of 40 volunteers were given a placebo instead of the drug. Thirteen of them reported a reduction in pain. Does this new evidence cast doubt upon your previous conclusion?

2.8.19 (a) A random sample of 20 observations yielded a mean of 40 and standard deviation 10. Test the hypothesis that $\mu = 45$ against the alternative that it is not. Use the 5% significance level.

(b) What assumption are you implicitly making in carrying out this test?

2.8.20   A photo processing company sets a quality standard of no more than 10 complaints per week on average. A random sample of 8 weeks showed an average of 13.6 complaints, with standard deviation 8.3. Is the firm achieving its quality objective?

2.8.21   Two samples are drawn. The first has a mean of 150, variance 50 and sample size 12. The second has mean 130, variance 30 and sample size 15. Test the hypothesis that they are drawn from populations with the same mean.

2.8.22   (a) A consumer organisation is testing two different brands of battery. A sample of 15 of brand *A* shows an average useful life of 410 hours with a standard deviation of 20 hours. For brand *B*, a sample of 20 gave an average useful life of 391 hours with standard deviation 26 hours. Test whether there is any significant difference in battery life.

(b) What assumptions are being made about the populations in carrying out this test?

2.8.23   The output of a group of 11 workers before and after an improvement in the lighting in their factory is as follows:

Before	52	60	58	58	53	51	52	59	60	53	55
After	56	62	63	50	55	56	55	59	61	58	56

Test whether there is a significant improvement in performance

(a) assuming these are independent samples,

(b) assuming they are dependent.

2.8.24   Another group of workers were tested at the same times as those in Problem 2.8.23, although their department *also* introduced rest breaks into the working day.

Before	51	59	51	53	58	58	52	55	61	54	55
After	54	63	55	57	63	63	58	60	66	57	59

Does the introduction of rest days alone appear to improve performance?

2.8.25   Discuss in general terms how you might 'test' the following:

(a) astrology

(b) extra-sensory perception

(c) the proposition that company takeovers increase profits.

2.8.26   **(Project)** Can your class tell the difference between tap water and bottled water? Set up an experiment as follows: fill *r* glasses with tap water and *n* − *r* glasses with bottled water. The subject has to guess which is which. If he or she gets more than *p* correct, you conclude he or she can tell the difference. Write up a report of the experiment including:

(a) a description of the experimental procedure

(b) your choice of *n*, *r* and *p*, with reasons

(c) the power of your test

(d) your conclusions.

2.8.27   **(Computer project)** Use the $= RAND()$ function in your spreadsheet to create 100 samples of size 25 (which are effectively all from the same population). Compute the mean and standard deviation of each sample. Calculate the z score for each sample, using a hypothesised mean of 0.5 (since the $= RAND()$ function chooses a random number in the range 0–1).

(a) How many of the z scores would you expect to exceed 1.96 in absolute value? Explain why.

(b) How many do exceed this? Is this in line with your prediction?

(c) Graph the sample means and comment upon the shape of the distribution. Shade in the area of the graph beyond $z = \pm 1.96$.

2.8.28   **(Project)** This is similar to Problem 2.8.26 but concerns digital music files. There is debate about whether listeners can tell the difference between high-quality WAV files and compressed MP3 files. Obtain the same song in both formats (most music players will convert a WAV file to MP3) and see if a listener can discern which is which. Some of your class colleagues might be better at this than others. You need to consider the same issues as in Problem 2.5.26.

The ABX comparison procedure would be interesting to follow (see http://wiki.hydrogenaudio. org/index.php?title=ABX) and you can download the WinABX program which automates much of the procedure (google 'WinABX' to find it).

Exercise 2.47

The following data show the observed and expected frequencies of an experiment with four possible outcomes, A–D.

Outcome	A	B	C	D
Observed	40	60	75	90
Expected	35	55	75	100

Test the hypothesis that the results are in line with expectations using the 5% significance level.

Exercise 2.48

(a) Verify the claim in worked example 2.15, that both χ^2 and z statistic methods give the same qualitative (accept or reject) result when the observed frequencies are 16, 55, 29 and when they are 14, 55, 31.

(b) In each case, look up or calculate (using Excel) the Prob-values for the χ^2 and z test statistics and compare.

Contingency tables

Data are often presented in the form of a two-way classification as shown in Table 2.48, known as a **contingency table**, and this is another situation where the χ^2 distribution is useful. It provides a test of whether or not there is an association between the two variables represented in the table.

The table shows the voting intentions of a sample of 200 voters, cross-classified by social class. The interesting question that arises from these data is whether there is any association between people's voting behaviour and their social class. Are manual workers (social class C in the table) more likely to vote for the Labour Party than for the Conservative Party? The table would appear to indicate some support for this view, but is this truly the case for the whole population or is the evidence insufficient to draw this conclusion?

This sort of problem is amenable to analysis by a χ^2 test. The data presented in the table represent the observed values, so expected values need to be calculated and then compared to them using a χ^2 test statistic. The first task is to formulate a null hypothesis, on which to base the calculation of the expected values, and an alternative hypothesis. These are

> H_0: there is no association between social class and voting behaviour
> H_1: there is some association between social class and voting behaviour

As always, the null hypothesis has to be precise, so that expected values can be calculated. In this case it is the precise statement that there is no association between the two variables, they are independent.

Table 2.48 **Data on voting intentions by social class**

Social class	Labour	Conservative	Liberal Democrat	Total
A	10	15	15	40
B	40	35	25	100
C	30	20	10	60
Totals	80	70	50	200

Constructing the expected values

If H_0 is true and there is no association, we would expect the proportions voting Labour, Conservative and Liberal Democrat to be the same in each social class. Further, the parties would be identical in the proportions of their support coming from social classes A, B and C. This means that, since the whole sample of 200 splits 80:70:50 for the Labour, Conservative and Liberal Democrat parties (see the bottom row of the Table 2.48), each social class should split the same way. Thus of the 40 people of class A, 80/200 of them should vote Labour, 70/200 Conservative and 50/200 Liberal Democrat. This yields:

Split of social class A:

Labour	$40 \times 80/200 = 16$
Conservative	$40 \times 70/200 = 14$
Liberal Democrat	$40 \times 50/200 = 10$

For class B:

Labour	$100 \times 80/200 = 40$
Conservative	$100 \times 70/200 = 35$
Liberal Democrat	$100 \times 50/200 = 25$

And for C the 60 votes are split Labour 24, Conservative 21 and Liberal Democrat 15.

Both observed and expected values are presented in Table 2.49 (expected values are in brackets). Notice that both the observed and expected values sum to the appropriate row and column totals. It can be seen that, compared with the 'no association' position, Labour gets too few votes from Class A and the Liberal Democrats too many. However, Labour gets disproportionately many class C votes, the Liberal Democrats too few. The Conservatives' observed and expected values are nearly identical, indicating that the propensities to vote Conservative are the same in all social classes.

A quick way to calculate the expected value in any cell is to multiply the appropriate row total by column total and divide through by the grand total (200). For example, to get the expected value for the class A/Labour cell:

$$expected\ value = \frac{row\ total \times column\ total}{grand\ total} = \frac{40 \times 80}{200} = 16$$

In carrying out the analysis care should again be taken to ensure that information is retained about the sample size, i.e. the numbers in the table should be actual numbers and not percentages or proportions. This can be checked by ensuring that the grand total is always the same as the sample size.

As was the case before, the χ^2 test is only valid if the expected value in each cell is not less than five. In the event of one of the expected values being less than five, some of the rows or columns have to be combined. How to do this is a matter of choice and depends upon the aims of the research. Suppose for example that the

Table 2.49 Observed and expected values (latter in brackets)

Social class	Labour	Conservative	Liberal Democrat	Total
A	10 (16)	15 (14)	15 (10)	40
B	40 (40)	35 (35)	25 (25)	100
C	30 (24)	20 (21)	10 (15)	60
Totals	80	70	50	200

expected number of class C voting Liberal Democrat were less than five. There are four options open:

(1) Combine the Liberal Democrat column with the Labour column.
(2) Combine the Liberal Democrat column with the Conservative column.
(3) Combine the class C row with the class A row.
(4) Combine the class C row with the class B row.

Whether rows or columns are combined depends upon whether interest centres more upon differences between parties or differences between classes. If the main interest is the difference between class A and the others, option 4 should be chosen. If it is felt that the Liberal Democrat and Conservative parties are similar, option 2 would be preferred, and so on. If there are several expected values less than five, rows and columns must be combined until all are eliminated.

The χ^2 test on a contingency table is similar to the one carried out before, the formula being the same:

$$\chi^2 = \Sigma \frac{(O - E)^2}{E} \tag{9.5}$$

with the number of degrees of freedom this time given by $v = (r - 1) \times (c - 1)$ where r is the number of rows in the table and c is the number of columns. In this case $r = 3$ and $c = 3$, so

$$v = (3 - 1) \times (3 - 1) = 4$$

The reason why there are only four degrees of freedom is that once any four interior cells of the contingency table have been filled, the other five are constrained by the row and column totals. The number of 'free' cells can always be calculated as the number of rows less one, times the number of columns less one, as given above.

Calculation of the test statistic

The evaluation of the test statistic then proceeds as follows, cell by cell:

$$\frac{(10 - 16)^2}{16} + \frac{(15 - 14)^2}{14} + \frac{(15 - 10)^2}{10}$$
$$+ \frac{(40 - 40)^2}{40} + \frac{(35 - 35)^2}{35} + \frac{(25 - 25)^2}{25}$$
$$+ \frac{(30 - 24)^2}{24} + \frac{(20 - 21)^2}{21} + \frac{(10 - 15)^2}{15}$$
$$= 2.25 + 0.07 + 2.50 + 0 + 0 + 0 + 1.5 + 0.05 + 1.67$$
$$= 8.04$$

This must be compared with the critical value from the χ^2 distribution with four degrees of freedom. At the 5% significance level this is 9.50 (from Table A3).

Since $8.04 < 9.50$ the test statistic is smaller than the critical value, so the null hypothesis cannot be rejected. The evidence is not strong enough to support an association between social class and voting intention. We cannot reject the null of the lack of any association with 95% confidence. Note, however, that the test statistic is fairly close to the critical value, so there is some weak evidence of an association, but not enough to satisfy conventional statistical criteria.

Oops!

A leading firm of chartered accountants produced a report for the UK government on education funding. One question it asked of schools was: Is the school budget sufficient to provide help to pupils with special needs? This produced the following table:

	Primary schools	Secondary schools
Yes	34%	45%
No	63%	50%
No response	3%	5%
Totals	100%	100%
$n =$	137	159

$\chi^2 = 3.50$ n.s.

Their analysis produces the conclusion that there is no significant difference between primary and secondary schools. But the χ^2 statistic is based on the percentage figures. Using frequencies (which can be calculated from the sample size figures) gives a correct χ^2 figure of 5.05. Fortunately for the accountants, this is still not significant.

Source: Adapted for *Local Management in School Report,1988* by Coopers and Lybrand for the UK government. Contains public sector information licensed under the Open Government Licence (OGL) v3.0. http://www. nationalarchives.gov.uk/doc/open-government-licence/open-government

Cohabitation

J. Ermisch and M. Francesconi examined the rise in cohabitation in the United Kingdom and asked whether it led on to marriage or not. One of their tables shows the relation between employment status and the outcome of living together. Their results, including the calculation of the χ^2 statistic for association between the variables, are shown in the figure.

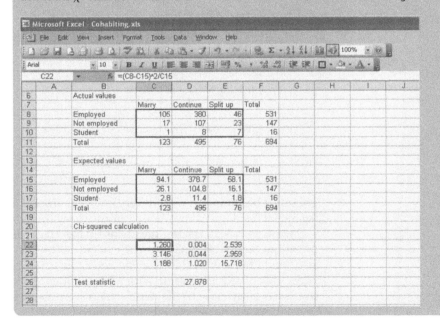

There were 694 cohabiting women in the sample. Of the 531 who were employed, 105 of them went on to marry their partner, 46 split up and 380 continued living together. Similar figures are shown for unemployed women and for students. The expected values for the contingency table then appear (based on the null hypothesis of no association), followed by the calculation of the χ^2 test statistic. You can see the formula for one of the elements of the calculation in the formula bar.

The test statistic is significant at the 5% level (critical value 9.49 for four degrees of freedom), so there is an association. The biggest contribution to the test statistic comes from the bottom right-hand cell, where the actual value is much higher than the expected. It appears that, unfortunately, those student romances often do not turn out to be permanent.

However, a reader of an earlier edition of this text pointed out that two of the expected values are less than five, so use of the χ^2 statistic is strictly inappropriate in this context.

Source: J. Ermisch and M. Francesconi, Cohabitation: not for long but here to stay, *J. Royal Statistical Society*, Series A, 163 (2), 2000.

Exercise 2.49

Suppose that the data on educational achievement and employment status in Chapter 1 were obtained from a sample of 999 people, as follows:

	Higher education	A-levels	Other qualification	No qualification	Total
In work	257	145	269	52	723
Unemployed	10	11	31	10	62
Inactive	33	38	87	56	214
Total	300	194	387	118	999

(These values reflect the proportions in the population data.) Test whether there is an association between education and employment status, using the 5% significance level for the test.

The F distribution

The second distribution we encounter in this chapter is the F distribution. It has a variety of uses in statistics; in this section we look at two of these: testing for the equality of two variances and conducting an **analysis of variance** (ANOVA) test. Both of these are variants on the hypothesis test procedures which should by now be familiar. The F distribution will also be encountered in later chapters on regression analysis.

The F family of distributions resembles the χ^2 distribution in shape: it is always non-negative and is skewed to the right. It has two sets of degrees of freedom (these are its parameters, labelled ν_1 and ν_2) and these determine its precise shape. Typical F distributions are shown in Figure 2.108. As usual, for a hypothesis test we define an area in one or both tails of the distribution to be the rejection region. If a test statistic falls into the rejection region, then the null hypothesis upon which the test statistic was based is rejected. Once again, examples will clarify the principles.

Testing the equality of two variances

Just as one can conduct a hypothesis test on a mean, so it is possible to test the variance. It is unusual to want to conduct a test of a specific value of a variance, since we usually have little intuitive idea of what the variance should be in most

Figure 2.108
The F distribution, for
different $\nu_1 (\nu_2 = 25)$

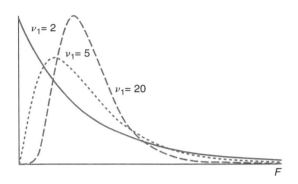

Figure 2.108
The F distribution, for
different $\nu_1 (\nu_2 = 25)$

circumstances. A more likely circumstance is a test of the equality of two variances (across two samples). In Chapter 8 two car factories were tested for the equality of average daily output *levels*. One can also test whether the *variance* of output differs or not. A more consistent output (lower variance) from a factory might be beneficial to the firm, e.g. dealers can be reassured that they are more likely to be able to obtain models when they require them. In the example in Chapter 8, one factory had a standard deviation of daily output of 25, the second of 20, both from samples of size 30 (i.e. 30 days' output was sampled at each factory). We can now test whether the difference between these figures is significant or not.

Such a test is set up as follows. It is known as a **variance ratio test** for reasons which will become apparent.

The null and alternative hypotheses are

$$H_0: \sigma_1^2 = \sigma_2^2$$
$$H_1: \sigma_1^2 \neq \sigma_2^2$$

or, equivalently

$$H_0: \sigma_1^2/\sigma_2^2 = 1 \tag{9.6}$$
$$H_1: \sigma_1^2/\sigma_2^2 \neq 1$$

It is appropriate to write the hypotheses in the form shown in (9.6) since the random variable and test statistic we shall use is in the form of the ratio of sample variances, s_1^2/s_2^2. This is a random variable which follows an F distribution with $\nu_1 = n_1 - 1$, $\nu_2 = n_2 - 1$ degrees of freedom. We require the assumption that the two samples are independent for the variance ratio to follow an F distribution. Thus we write:

$$\frac{s_1^2}{s_2^2} \sim F_{n_1-1, n_2-1} \tag{9.7}$$

The F distribution thus has two parameters, the two sets of degrees of freedom, one (ν_1) associated with the numerator, the other (ν_2) associated with the denominator of the formula. In each case, the degrees of freedom are given by the relevant sample size minus one.

Note that s_2^2/s_1^2 is also an F distribution (i.e. it doesn't matter which variance goes into the numerator) but with the degrees of freedom reversed, $\nu_1 = n_2 - 1$, $\nu_2 = n_1 - 1$.

The sample data are:

$$s_1 = 25, s_2 = 20$$
$$n_1 = 30, n_2 = 30$$

Table 2.50 Excerpt from the *F* distribution: upper 2.5% points

ν_1 / ν_2	1	2	3	...	20	24	30	40
1	647.7931	799.4822	864.1509	...	993.0809	997.2719	1001.4046	1005.5955
2	38.5062	39.0000	39.1656	...	39.4475	39.4566	39.4648	39.4730
3	17.4434	16.0442	15.4391	...	14.1674	14.1242	14.0806	14.0365
⋮	⋮	⋮	⋮	...	⋮	⋮	⋮	⋮
28	5.6096	4.2205	3.6264	...	2.2324	2.1735	2.1121	2.0477
29	5.5878	4.2006	3.6072	...	2.2131	2.1540	2.0923	2.0276
30	5.5675	4.1821	3.5893	...	2.1952	2.1359	2.0739	2.0089
40	5.4239	4.0510	3.4633	...	2.0677	2.0069	1.9429	1.8752

Note: The critical value lies at the intersection of the shaded row and column. Alternatively, use *Excel* or another computer package to give the answer. In *Excel* 2010 and later, the formula $= F.INV.RT(0.025, 29, 29)$ will give the answer 2.09, the upper 2.5% critical value of the *F* distribution with $\nu_1 = 29$, $\nu_2 = 29$ degrees of freedom.

The test statistic is simply the ratio of sample variances. In testing it is less confusing if the larger of the two variances is made the numerator of the test statistic (you will see why soon). Therefore, we have the following test statistic:

$$F = \frac{25^2}{20^2} = 1.5625 \tag{9.8}$$

This must be compared to the critical value of the *F* distribution with $\nu_1 = 29$, $\nu_2 = 29$ degrees of freedom.

The rejection regions for the test are the two tails of the distribution, cutting off 2.5% in each tail. Since we have placed the larger variance in the denominator, only large values of *F* reject the null hypothesis so we need only consult the upper critical value of the *F* distribution, i.e. that value which cuts off the top 2.5% of the distribution. (This is the advantage of putting the larger variance in the numerator of the test statistic.)

Table 2.50 shows an excerpt from the *F* distribution. The degrees of freedom for the test are given along the top row (ν_1) and down the first column (ν_2). The numbers in the table give the critical values cutting off the top 2.5% of the distribution. The critical value in this case is 2.09, at the intersection of the row corresponding to $\nu_2 = 29$ and the column corresponding to $\nu_1 = 30$ ($\nu_1 = 29$ is not given so 30 is used instead; this gives a very close approximation to the correct critical value). Since the test statistic 1.56 does not exceed the critical value of 2.09, the null hypothesis of equal variances cannot be rejected with 95% confidence.

Exercise 2.50

Samples of 3-volt batteries from two manufacturers yielded the following outputs, measured in volts:

Brand A	3.1	3.2	2.9	3.3	2.8	3.1	3.2
Brand B	3.0	3.0	3.2	3.4	2.7	2.8	

Test whether there is any difference in the variance of output voltage of batteries from the two companies. Why might the variance be an important consideration for the manufacturer or for customers?

Analysis of variance

In Chapter 8 we learned how to test the hypothesis that the means of two samples are the same, using a z or t test, depending upon the sample size. This type of hypothesis test can be generalised to more than two samples using a technique called analysis of variance (ANOVA), based on the F distribution. Although it is called analysis of variance, it actually tests differences in means. The reason for this will be explained below. Using this technique, we can test the hypothesis that the means of *all* the samples are equal, versus the alternative hypothesis that at least one of them is different from the others. To illustrate the technique, we shall extend the example in Chapter 8 where different car factories' outputs were compared.

The assumptions underlying the analysis of variance technique are essentially the same as those used in the t test when comparing two different means. We assume that the samples are randomly and independently drawn from Normally distributed populations which have equal variances.

Suppose there are three factories, whose outputs have been sampled, with the results shown in Table 2.51. We wish to answer the question whether this is evidence of different outputs from the three factories, or simply random variation around a (common) average output level. The null and alternative hypotheses are therefore:

H_0: $\mu_1 = \mu_2 = \mu_3$
H_1: at least one mean is different from the others

This is the simplest type of ANOVA, known as one-way analysis of variance. In this case there is only one factor which affects output – the factory. The factor which may affect output is also known as the independent variable. In more complex designs, there can be two or more factors which influence output. The output from the factories is the dependent or response variable in this case.

Figure 2.109 presents a chart of the output from the three factories, which shows the greatest apparent difference between factories 2 and 3. Their ranges scarcely overlap, which does suggest some genuine difference between them, but as yet we cannot be sure that this is not just due to sampling variation. Factory 1 appears to be mid-way between the other two and this must also be included in the analysis.

Table 2.51 Samples of output from three factories

Observation	Factory 1	Factory 2	Factory 3
1	415	385	408
2	430	410	415
3	395	409	418
4	399	403	440
5	408	405	425
6	418	400	
7		399	

Figure 2.109
Chart of factory output on sample days

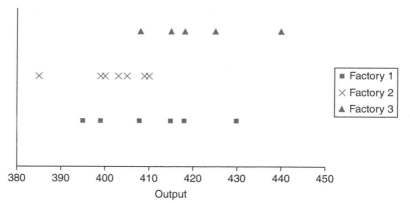

To decide whether or not to reject H_0, we compare the variance of output *within* factories to the variance of output *between* (the means of) the factories. Figure 2.110 provides an illustration. Where the variance between factories is large relative to the variance within each factory (Figure 2.110(a)), one is likely to reject H_0 and instead conclude there is a genuine difference. Alternatively, where the variance between factories is small relative to the within factory variance (Figure 2.110(b)), we are likely to accept H_0. The statistical test allows us to decide when the differences are large enough to warrant a particular conclusion and not just due to random variation.

Both *between* and *within* variance measures provide estimates of the overall true variance of output and, under the null hypothesis that factories make no difference, should provide similar estimates. The ratio of the variances should then be approximately unity. If the null is false however, the between-samples estimate will tend to be larger than the within-samples estimate and their ratio will exceed unity. This ratio has an F distribution and so if it is sufficiently large that it falls into the upper tail of the distribution, then H_0 is rejected.

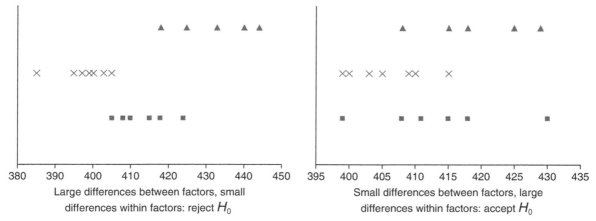

Figure 2.110
Illustration of when to reject H_0

To formally test the hypothesis, we break down the *total* variance of all the observations into

(1) the variance due to differences *between* factories, and
(2) the variance due to differences *within* factories (also known as the error variance).

Initially we work with sums of squares rather than variances. Recall from Chapter 1 that a sample variance is given by

$$s^2 = \frac{\sum(x - \bar{x})^2}{n - 1} \tag{9.9}$$

The numerator of the right-hand side of this expression, $\sum(x - \bar{x})^2$, gives the sum of squares, i.e. the sum of squared deviations from the mean.

Accordingly, we work with three sums of squares:

● The total sum of squares measures (squared) deviations from the overall or grand average using all the 18 observations. It ignores the existence of the different factors (factories).
● The between sum of squares measures how the three individual factor means vary around the grand average.
● The within sum of squares is based on squared deviations of observations from their own factor mean.

It can be shown that there is a relationship between these sums of squares, i.e.

$$\frac{\text{Time sum}}{\text{of squares}} = \frac{\text{Between sum}}{\text{of squares}} + \frac{\text{Within sum}}{\text{of squares}} \tag{9.10}$$

The larger is the between sum of squares relative to the within sum of squares, the more likely it is that the null is false.

Because we have to sum over factors and over observations within those factors, the formulae look somewhat complicated, involving double summation signs. It is therefore important to follow the example showing how the calculations are actually done.

The total sum of squares is given by the formula:

$$\text{Total sum of squares} = \sum_{j=1}^{n_i} \sum_{i=1}^{k} (x_{ij} - \bar{x})^2 \tag{9.11}$$

where x_{ij} is the output from factory i on day j and $\bar{x}$ is the grand average of all observations. The index i runs from 1 to 3 in this case (there are three classes or groups for this factor) and the index j (indexing the observations) goes from 1 to 6, 7, or 5 (for factories 1, 2 and 3, respectively). Note that we do not require the same number of observations from each factory.

Although this looks complex, it simply means that we calculate the sum of squared deviations from the overall mean. The overall mean of the 18 values is 410.11 and the total sum of squares may be calculated as:

$$\text{Total sum of squares} = (415 - 410.11)^2 + (430 - 410.11)^2$$
$$+ \cdots + (440 - 410.11)^2 + (425 - 410.11)^2 = 2977.778$$

An alternative formula for the total sum of squares is

$$\text{Total sum of squares} = \sum_{j=1}^{n_i} \sum_{i=1}^{k} x_{ij}^2 - n\bar{x}^2 \tag{9.12}$$

where n is the total number of observations. The sum of the squares of all the observations (Σx^2) is $415^2 + 430^2 + \cdots + 425^2 = 3\,030\,418$ and the total sum of squares is then given by

$$\sum_{j=1}^{n_i}\sum_{i=1}^{k} x_{ij}^2 - n\bar{x}^2 = 3\,030\,418 - 18 \times 410.11^2 = 2977.778 \tag{9.13}$$

as before.

The **between sum of squares** is calculated using the formula

$$\text{Between sum of squares} = \sum_j \sum_i (\bar{x}_i - \bar{x})^2 \tag{9.14}$$

where $\bar{x}_i$ denotes the mean output of factor i. This part of the calculation effectively ignores the differences that exist *within* factors and compares the differences *between* them. It does this by replacing the observations within each factor by the mean for that factor. Hence, all the factor 1 observations are replaced by 410.83, for factor 2 they are replaced by the mean 401.57 and for factor 3 by 421.2^3. We then calculate the sum of squared deviations of these values from the grand mean:

$$\text{Between sum of squares} = 6 \times (410.83 - 410.11)^2 + 7 \times (401.57 - 410.11)^2$$
$$+ 5 \times (421.2 - 410.11)^2 = 1128.43$$

Note that we take account of the number of observations within each factor in this calculation.

Once again there is an alternative formula which may be simpler for calculation purposes:

$$\text{Between sum of squares} = \sum_i n_i \bar{x}_i^2 - n\bar{x}^2 \tag{9.15}$$

Evaluating this results in the same answer as above:

$$\sum_i n_i \bar{x}_i^2 - n\bar{x}^2 = 6 \times 410.83^2 + 7 \times 401.57^2 + 5 \times 421.2^2 - 18 \times 410.10^2$$
$$= 1128.43 \tag{9.16}$$

We have arrived at the result that 37% ($= 1128.43/2977.78$) of the total variation (sum of squared deviations) is due to differences between factories and the remaining 63% is therefore due to variation (day to day) within factories. We can therefore immediately calculate the **within sum of squares** by straightforward subtraction as:

$$\text{Within sum of squares} = \text{Total sum of squares} - \text{Between sum of squares}$$
$$= 2977.778 - 1128.430 = 1849.348$$

For completeness, the formula for the within sum of squares is

$$\text{Within sum of squares} = \sum_j \sum_i (x_{ij} - \bar{x}_i)^2 \tag{9.17}$$

---

[3]Note that this is *not* the same as using the three factor means and calculating their variance.

The term $x_{ij} - \bar{x}_i$ measures the deviations of the observations from the factor mean and so the within sum of squares gives a measure of dispersion within the classes. Hence, it can be calculated as:

$$
\begin{aligned}
\text{Within sum of squares} = {} & (415 - 410.83)^2 + \cdots + (418 - 410.83)^2 \\
& + (385 - 401.57)^2 + \cdots + (399 - 401.57)^2 \\
& + (408 - 421.2)^2 + \cdots + (425 - 421.2)^2 \\
= {} & 1849.348
\end{aligned}
$$

This is the same value as obtained by subtraction.

The result of the hypothesis test

The F statistic is based upon comparing between and within sums of squares (*BSS* and *WSS*) but we must also take account of the degrees of freedom for the test. The degrees of freedom adjust for the number of observations and for the number of factors. Formally, the test statistic is

$$ F = \frac{BSS/(k - 1)}{WSS/(n - k)} $$

which has $k - 1$ and $n - k$ degrees of freedom. k is the number of factors, 3 in this case, and n the overall number of observations, 18. We thus have

$$ F = \frac{1128.43/(3 - 1)}{1849.348/(18 - 3)} = 4.576 $$

The critical value of F for 2 and 15 degrees of freedom at the 5% significance level is 3.682. As the test statistic exceeds the critical value, we reject the null hypothesis of no difference between factories.

The analysis of variance table

ANOVA calculations are conventionally summarised in an analysis of variance table. Figure 2.111 shows such a table, as produced by Excel. Excel can produce the

Figure 2.111
One-way analysis of
variance: Excel output

	A	B	C	D	E	F	G	H
13								
14								
15								
16	Anova: Single Factor							
17								
18	SUMMARY							
19	*Groups*	*Count*	*Sum*	*Average*	*Variance*			
20	Factory 1	6	2465	410.833	166.967			
21	Factory 2	7	2811	401.571	70.619			
22	Factory 3	5	2106	421.200	147.700			
23								
24								
25	ANOVA							
26	*Source of Variation*	*SS*	*df*	*MS*	*F*	*P-value*	*F crit*	
27	Between Groups	1128.430	2	564.215	4.576	0.028	3.682	
28	Within Groups	1849.348	15	123.290				
29								
30	Total	2977.778	17					
31								
32								

table automatically from data presented in the form shown in Table 2.51 and there is no need to do any of the calculations by hand. (In *Excel* you need to install the Analysis ToolPak in order to perform ANOVA. Other software packages, such as SPSS or Stata, also have routines to perform ANOVA.)

The first part of the table summarises the information for each factory, in the form of means and variances. Note that the means were used in the calculation of the *between sum of squares*. The ANOVA section of the output then follows, giving sums of squares and other information.

The column of the `ANOVA table` headed '*SS*' gives the sums of squares, which we calculated above. It can be seen that the between-group sum of squares makes up about 37% of the total, suggesting that the differences between factories (referred to as 'groups' by *Excel*) do make a substantial contribution to the total variation in output.

The '*df*' column gives the degrees of freedom associated with each sum of squares. These degrees of freedom are given by

Between sum of squares	$k - 1$
Within sum of squares	$n - k$
Total sum of squares	$n - 1$

The '*MS*' ('mean square') column divides the sums of squares by their degrees of freedom, and the *F* column gives the *F* statistic, which is the ratio of the two values in the *MS* column, i.e. $4.576 = 564.215/123.290$. This is the test statistic for the hypothesis test, which we calculated manually above. Excel helpfully gives the critical value of the test (at the 5% significance level) in the final column, 3.682. The P-value is given in the penultimate column and reveals that only 2.8% of the *F* distribution lies beyond the test statistic value of 4.576.

The test has found that the between sum of squares is 'large' relative to the within sum of squares, too large to be due simply to random variation, and this is why the null hypothesis of equal outputs is rejected. The rejection region for the test consists of the *upper* tail only of the *F* distribution; small values of the test statistic would indicate small differences between factories and hence non-rejection of H_0.

This simple example involves only three groups, but the extension to four or more follows the same principles, with different values of *k* in the formulae, and is fairly straightforward. Also, we have covered only the simplest type of ANOVA, with a one-way classification. More complex experimental designs are possible, with a two-way classification, for example, where there are two independent factors affecting the dependent variable.

Worked example 2.16

ANOVA calculations are quite complex and are most easily handled by software which calculates all the results directly from the initial data. However, this is a kind of 'black box' approach to learning, so this example shows all the calculations mechanically.

→

Suppose we have six observations on each of three factors, as follows:

A	B	C
44	41	48
35	36	37
60	58	61
28	32	37
43	40	44
55	59	61

(These might be, for example, scores of different groups of pupils in a test.) We wish to examine whether there is a significant difference between the different groups. We need to see how the differences *between* the groups compare to those *within* groups.

First, we calculate the total sum of squares by ignoring the groupings and treating all 18 observations together. The overall mean is 45.5 so the squared deviations are $(44 - 45.5)^2$, $(41 - 45.5)^2$, etc. Summing these gives 2020.5 as the TSS.

For the between sum of squares we first calculate the means of each factor. These are 44.17, 44.33 and 48. We compare these to the grand average. The squared deviations are therefore $(44.17 - 45.5)^2$, $(44.33 - 45.5)^2$ and $(48 - 45.5)^2$. Rather than sum these, we must take account of the number of observations in each group which in this case is 6. Hence we obtain

$$\text{Between sum of squares} = 6 \times (44.17 - 45.5)^2 + 6 \times (44.33 - 45.5)^2$$
$$+ 6 \times (48 - 45.5)^2 = 56.33$$

The within sum of squares can be explicitly calculated as follows. For group A, the squared deviations from the group mean are $(44 - 44.17)^2$, $(35 - 44.17)^2$, etc. Summing these for group A gives 714.8. Similar calculations give 653.3 and 596 for groups B and C. These sum to 1964.2, which is the within sum of squares. As a check, we note:

$$2020.5 = 56.3 + 1964.2$$

The degrees of freedom are $k - 1 = 3 - 1 = 2$ for the between sum of squares, $n - k = 18 - 3 = 15$ for the within sum of squares and $n - 1 = 18 - 1 = 17$. The test statistic is therefore

$$F = \frac{56.33/2}{1964.2/15} = 0.22$$

The critical value at the 5% significance level is 3.68, so we cannot reject the null of no difference between the factors.

Exercise 2.51

The reaction times of three groups of sportsmen were measured on a particular task, with the following results (time in milliseconds):

Racing drivers	31	28	39	42	36	30	
Tennis players	41	35	41	48	44	39	38
Boxers	44	47	35	38	51		

Test whether there is a difference in reaction times between the three groups.

Summary

- The χ^2 and F distributions play important roles in statistics, particularly in problems relating to the goodness of fit of the data to that predicted by a null hypothesis.

- A random variable based on the sample variance, $(n - 1)s^2/\sigma^2$, has a χ^2 distribution with $n - 1$ degrees of freedom. Based on this fact, the χ^2 distribution may be used to construct confidence interval estimates for the variance σ^2. Since the χ^2 is not a symmetric distribution, the confidence interval is not symmetric around the (unbiased) point estimate s^2.

- The χ^2 distribution may also be used to compare actual and expected values of a variable and hence to test the hypothesis upon which the expected values were constructed.

- A two-way classification of observations is known as a contingency table. The independence or otherwise of the two variables may be tested using the χ^2 distribution, by comparing observed values with those expected under the null hypothesis of independence.

- The F distribution is used to test a hypothesis of the equality of two variances. The test statistic is the ratio of two sample variances which, under the null hypothesis, has an F distribution with $n_1 - 1, n_2 - 1$ degrees of freedom.

- The F distribution may also be used in an analysis of variance, which tests for the equality of means across several samples. The results are set out in an analysis of variance table, which compares the variation of the observations *within* each sample to the variation *between* samples.

Key terms and concepts

actual and expected values	grand average
analysis of variance	independent variable
ANOVA table	one-way analysis of variance
between sum of squares	sums of squares
classes or groups	total sum of squares
contingency table	uniform distribution
dependent or response variable	variance ratio test
error variance	within sum of squares
factor	

Formulae used in this chapter

Formula	Description	Notes
$\left[\dfrac{(n-1)s^2}{U} \le \sigma^2 \le \dfrac{(n-1)s^2}{L}\right]$	Confidence interval for the variance	U and L are the upper and lower limits of the χ^2 distribution for the chosen confidence level, with $n-1$ degrees of freedom
$\chi^2 = \sum \dfrac{(O-E)^2}{E}$	Test statistic for independence in a contingency table	$\nu = (r-1) \times (c-1)$, where r is the number of rows, c the number of columns
$F = \dfrac{s_1^2}{s_2^2}$	Test statistic for $H_0: \sigma_1^2 = \sigma_2^2$	$\nu = n_1 - 1, n_2 - 1$. Place larger sample variance in the numerator to ensure rejection region is in right-hand tail of the F distribution
$\displaystyle\sum_{j=1}^{n_i}\sum_{i=1}^{k} x_{ij}^2 - n\bar{x}^2$	Total sum of squares (ANOVA)	n is the total number of observations, k is the number of groups
$\displaystyle\sum_i n_i \bar{x}_i^2 - n\bar{x}^2$	Between sum of squares (ANOVA)	A n_i represents the number of observations in group i and $\bar{x}_i$ is the mean of the group
$\displaystyle\sum_j \sum_i (x_{ij} - \bar{x}_i)^2$	Within sum of squares (ANOVA)	

Problems

Some of the more challenging problems are indicated by highlighting the problem number in colour.

2.9.1   A sample of 40 observations has a standard deviation of 20. Estimate the 95% confidence interval for the standard deviation of the population.

2.9.2   Using the data $n = 70$, $s = 15$, construct a 99% confidence interval for the true standard deviation.

2.9.3   Use the data in Table 2.38 to see if there is a significant difference between road casualties in quarters I and III on the one hand and quarters II and IV on the other.

2.9.4   A survey of 64 families with five children found the following gender distribution:

Number of boys	0	1	2	3	4	5
Number of families	1	8	28	19	4	4

Test whether the distribution can be adequately modelled by the Binomial distribution.

2.9.5   Four different holiday firms which all carried equal numbers of holidaymakers reported the following numbers who expressed satisfaction with their holiday:

Firm	A	B	C	D
Number satisfied	576	558	580	546

Is there any significant difference between the firms? If told that the four firms carried 600 holiday-makers each, would you modify your conclusion? What do you conclude about your first answer?

2.9.6 A company wishes to see whether there are any differences between its departments in staff turnover. Looking at their records for the past year, the company finds the following data:

Department	Personnel	Marketing	Admin.	Accounts
Number in post at start of year	23	16	108	57
Number leaving	3	4	20	13

Do the data provide evidence of a difference in staff turnover between the various departments?

2.9.7 A survey of 100 firms found the following evidence regarding profitability and market share:

Profitability	Market share		
	<15%	15–30%	>30%
Low	18	7	8
Medium	13	11	8
High	8	12	15

Is there evidence that market share and profitability are associated?

2.9.8 The following data show the percentages of firms using computers in different aspects of their business:

Firm size	Computers used in			Total numbers of firms
	Admin.	Design	Manufacture	
Small	60%	24%	20%	450
Medium	65%	30%	28%	140
Large	90%	44%	50%	45

Is there an association between the size of firm and its use of computers?

2.9.9 (a) Do the accountants' job properly for them (see the *Oops!* box in the text).

(b) It might be justifiable to omit the 'no responses' entirely from the calculation. What happens if you do this?

2.9.10 A roadside survey of the roadworthiness of vehicles obtained the following results:

	Roadworthy	Not roadworthy
Private cars	114	30
Company cars	84	24
Vans	36	12
Lorries	44	20
Buses	36	12

Is there any association between the type of vehicle and the likelihood of it being unfit for the road?

2.9.11 Given the following data on two sample variances, test whether there is any significant difference. Use the 1% significance level.

$$s_1^2 = 55 \quad s_2^2 = 48$$
$$n_1 = 25 \quad n_2 = 30$$

2.9.12 An example in Chapter 8 compared R&D expenditure in Britain and Germany. The sample data were:

$$\bar{x}_1 = 3.7 \quad \bar{x}_2 = 4.2$$
$$s_1 = 0.6 \quad s_2 = 0.9$$
$$n_1 = 20 \quad n_2 = 15$$

Is there evidence, at the 5% significance level, of difference in the variances of R&D expenditure between the two countries? What are the implications, if any, for the test carried out on the difference of the two means?

2.9.13 Groups of children from four different classes in a school were randomly selected and sat a test, with the following test scores:

Class	Pupil						
	1	2	3	4	5	6	7
A	42	63	73	55	66	48	59
B	39	47	47	61	44	50	52
C	71	65	33	49	61		
D	49	51	62	48	63	54	

(a) Test whether there is any difference between the classes, using the 95% confidence level for the test.

(b) How would you interpret a 'significant' result from such a test?

2.9.14 Lottery tickets are sold in different outlets: supermarkets, smaller shops and outdoor kiosks. Sales were sampled from several of each of these, with the following results:

Supermarkets	355	251	408	302
Small shops	288	257	225	299
Kiosks	155	352	240	

Does the evidence indicate a significant difference in sales? Use the 5% significance level.

2.9.15 **(Project)** Conduct a survey among fellow students to examine whether there is any association between:

(a) gender and political preference, or

(b) subject studied and political preference, or

(c) star sign and personality (introvert/extrovert – self-assessed: I am told that Aries, Cancer, Capricorn, Gemini, Leo and Scorpio are associated with an extrovert personality), or

(d) any other two categories of interest.

2.9.16 **(Computer project)** Use your spreadsheet or other computer program to generate 100 random integers in the range 0 to 9. Draw up a frequency table and use a χ^2 test to examine whether there is any bias towards any particular integer. Compare your results with those of others in your class.

Appendix	Use of χ^2 and F distribution tables

Tables of the χ^2 distribution

Table A3 presents critical values of the χ^2 distribution for a selection of significance levels and for different degrees of freedom. As an example, to find the critical value of the χ^2 distribution at the 5% significance level, for $\nu = 20$ degrees of freedom, the cell entry in the column labelled '0.05' and the row labelled '20' are consulted. The critical value is 31.4. A test statistic greater than this value implies rejection of the null hypothesis at the 5% significance level.

An Excel function can alternatively be used to find this value. The formula '=CHIISQ.INV.RT(0.05, 20)' will give the result 31.4.

Tables of the F distribution

Table A4 (see page 804) presents critical values of the F distribution. Since there are two sets of degrees of freedom to be taken into account, a separate table is required for each significance level. Four sets of tables are provided, giving critical values cutting off the top 5%, 2.5%, 1% and 0.5% of the distribution (Tables A5(a), A5(b), A5(c) and A5(d) respectively). These allow both one- and two-tail tests at the 5% and 1% significance levels to be conducted. Its use is illustrated by example.

Two-tail test

To find the critical values of the F distribution at the 5% significance level for degrees of freedom ν_1 (numerator) = 10, ν_2 = 20. The critical values in this case cut off the extreme 2.5% of the distribution in each tail, and are found in Table A5:

- Right-hand critical value: this is found from the cell of the table corresponding to the column ν_1 = 10 and row ν_2 = 20. Its value is 2.77.
- Left-hand critical value: this cannot be obtained directly from the tables, which only give right-hand values. However, it is obtained indirectly as follows:
  (a) Find the right-hand critical value for ν_1 = 20, ν_2 = 10 (note reversal of degrees of freedom). This gives 3.42.
  (b) Take the reciprocal to obtain the desired left-hand critical value. This gives $1/3.42 = 0.29$.

The rejection region thus consists of values of the test statistic less than 0.29 and greater than 2.77.

An Excel function can alternatively be used to find these values. The formula '=F.INV.RT(0.025, 10, 20)' will give the result 2.77. The formula '=F.INV.RT(0.975, 10, 20)' will give 0.29, the left hand value. Note that you do not need to reverse the degrees of freedom in the formula, Excel understands that the left-hand critical value is needed from the '0.975' figure.

One-tail test

To find the critical value at the 5% significance level for $\nu_1 = 15, \nu_2 = 25$. As long as the test statistic has been calculated with the larger variance in the numerator, the critical value is in the right-hand tail of the distribution and can be obtained directly from Table A4. For $\nu_1 = 15, \nu_2 = 25$ the value is 2.09. The null hypothesis is rejected, therefore, if the test statistic is greater than 2.09. Once again, in Excel Excel, '=F.INV.RT(0.05, 15, 25)' = 2.09.

Appendix Tables

APPENDIX TABLES

Table A1   Cumulative Distribution Function, $F(z)$, of the Standard Normal Distribution Table

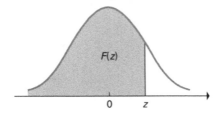

z	0	0.01	0.02	0.03	0.04	0.05	0.06	0.07	0.08	0.09
0.0	0.5000	0.5040	0.5080	0.5120	0.5160	0.5199	0.5239	0.5279	0.5319	0.5359
0.1	0.5398	0.5438	0.5478	0.5517	0.5557	0.5596	0.5636	0.5675	0.5714	0.5753
0.2	0.5793	0.5832	0.5871	0.5910	0.5948	0.5987	0.6026	0.6064	0.6103	0.6141
0.3	0.6179	0.6217	0.6255	0.6293	0.6331	0.6368	0.6406	0.6443	0.6480	0.6517
0.4	0.6554	0.6591	0.6628	0.6664	0.6700	0.6736	0.6772	0.6808	0.6844	0.6879
0.5	0.6915	0.6950	0.6985	0.7019	0.7054	0.7088	0.7123	0.7157	0.7190	0.7224
0.6	0.7257	0.7291	0.7324	0.7357	0.7389	0.7422	0.7454	0.7486	0.7517	0.7549
0.7	0.7580	0.7611	0.7642	0.7673	0.7704	0.7734	0.7764	0.7794	0.7823	0.7852
0.8	0.7881	0.7910	0.7939	0.7967	0.7995	0.8023	0.8051	0.8078	0.8106	0.8133
0.9	0.8159	0.8186	0.8212	0.8238	0.8264	0.8289	0.8315	0.8340	0.8365	0.8389
1.0	0.8413	0.8438	0.8461	0.8485	0.8508	0.8531	0.8554	0.8577	0.8599	0.8621
1.1	0.8643	0.8665	0.8686	0.8708	0.8729	0.8749	0.8770	0.8790	0.8810	0.8830
1.2	0.8849	0.8869	0.8888	0.8907	0.8925	0.8944	0.8962	0.8980	0.8997	0.9015
1.3	0.9032	0.9049	0.9066	0.9082	0.9099	0.9115	0.9131	0.9147	0.9162	0.9177
1.4	0.9192	0.9207	0.9222	0.9236	0.9251	0.9265	0.9279	0.9292	0.9306	0.9319
1.5	0.9332	0.9345	0.9357	0.9370	0.9382	0.9394	0.9406	0.9418	0.9429	0.9441
1.6	0.9452	0.9463	0.9474	0.9484	0.9495	0.9505	0.9515	0.9525	0.9535	0.9545
1.7	0.9554	0.9564	0.9573	0.9582	0.9591	0.9599	0.9608	0.9616	0.9625	0.9633
1.8	0.9641	0.9649	0.9656	0.9664	0.9671	0.9678	0.9686	0.9693	0.9699	0.9706
1.9	0.9713	0.9719	0.9726	0.9732	0.9738	0.9744	0.9750	0.9756	0.9761	0.9767
2.0	0.9772	0.9778	0.9783	0.9788	0.9793	0.9798	0.9803	0.9808	0.9812	0.9817
2.1	0.9821	0.9826	0.9830	0.9834	0.9838	0.9842	0.9846	0.9850	0.9854	0.9857
2.2	0.9861	0.9864	0.9868	0.9871	0.9875	0.9878	0.9881	0.9884	0.9887	0.9890
2.3	0.9893	0.9896	0.9898	0.9901	0.9904	0.9906	0.9909	0.9911	0.9913	0.9916
2.4	0.9918	0.9920	0.9922	0.9925	0.9927	0.9929	0.9931	0.9932	0.9934	0.9936
2.5	0.9938	0.9940	0.9941	0.9943	0.9945	0.9946	0.9948	0.9949	0.9951	0.9952
2.6	0.9953	0.9955	0.9956	0.9957	0.9959	0.9960	0.9961	0.9962	0.9963	0.9964
2.7	0.9965	0.9966	0.9967	0.9968	0.9969	0.9970	0.9971	0.9972	0.9973	0.9974
2.8	0.9974	0.9975	0.9976	0.9977	0.9977	0.9978	0.9979	0.9979	0.9980	0.9981
2.9	0.9981	0.9982	0.9982	0.9983	0.9984	0.9984	0.9985	0.9985	0.9986	0.9986
3.0	0.9987	0.9987	0.9987	0.9988	0.9988	0.9989	0.9989	0.9989	0.9990	0.9990
3.1	0.9990	0.9991	0.9991	0.9991	0.9992	0.9992	0.9992	0.9992	0.9993	0.9993
3.2	0.9993	0.9993	0.9994	0.9994	0.9994	0.9994	0.9994	0.9995	0.9995	0.9995
3.3	0.9995	0.9995	0.9995	0.9996	0.9996	0.9996	0.9996	0.9996	0.9996	0.9997

Dr. William L. Carlson, prepared using Minitab 16.